Irish Relatives and Friends

IRISH
RELATIVES AND FRIENDS

From "Information Wanted" Ads
in the *Irish-American*, 1850–1871

Compiled by

Laura Murphy DeGrazia, CG
& Diane Fitzpatrick Haberstroh, CGRS

Published by Genealogical Publishing Co., Inc.
1001 N. Calvert St., Baltimore, Md. 21202
Library of Congress Catalogue Card Number 2001-131268
International Standard Book Number 0-8063-1677-2
Made in the United States of America

Introduction

Background on the Newspaper and Advertisements

The *Irish-American* was a weekly newspaper published in New York City for the Irish immigrant population. It was started in August 1849 by Patrick Lynch and William Cole. The newspaper contained news items and political thought of interest to those of the Irish community. The paper also contained a popular classified section for people seeking information on relatives and friends. These ads, which ran in a column entitled "Information Wanted," are useful to researchers since they often state the Irish county, townland, or parish from which an immigrant came.

The advertisements that appear in this book were transcribed from microfilmed copies of the original newspapers available at the New York State Library and The New York Public Library.

Format of Transcriptions

The transcriptions are intended to be accurate reproductions of the original ads in terms of content and spelling, with the following exceptions:

1) To make it easier to locate proper names in the text, surnames have been changed to boldface type, place names are in all capital letters, and ships' names are italicized.

2) Names of countries, major cities, American states, Irish counties, and United States counties have been corrected to the commonly accepted spelling listed in the *Columbia-Lippincott Gazetteer*.

Only if the name of a large and fairly well known place was obviously misspelled, was a correction made. Irish towns, townlands, and parishes appear as they are spelled in the ad, as do names of smaller localities in the United States and elsewhere. This was done to insure that these smaller places would not be misinterpreted by the editors, especially since the names of many small localities in Ireland can be similar in spelling and sound. When certain letters or whole words could not be read due to poor print or faded areas in a particular issue, and there was a question as to the reading of a particular letter or word, a "best guess" was placed in square brackets.

Arrangements of Transcriptions

The transcribed personal advertisements are arranged chronologically. There are no ads for the year 1860, as no copies of the *Irish-American* could be found for that year. Usually the ads ran for three consecutive weeks (i.e., three consecutive issues), but they have been listed only once in the transcriptions.

The dates shown in the transcriptions refer to the issue of the newspaper in which the ad first appeared. If an ad was later revised, a note is included describing these later changes.

Indexes

The book contains five separate indexes: Personal Names, Irish Place Names, United States Place Names, Other Places, and New York City Streets. Since, as noted above, spellings of proper names was quite variable, it is recommended that a researcher try to check every possible spelling of any name for which he or she is searching.

Personal Names Index

The personal names index is arranged alphabetically first by surname, and then by given name. Names appear in the index spelled as they were in the ads. Most ads included first names of individuals but occasionally only a title is given, such as Mr. or Mrs. In these cases the titles are used in place of given names, since it would be useful to the researcher in determining the gender of an individual. Women whose maiden and married surnames could be determined from an ad have been indexed under both surnames, but without cross-references between them. Included in this category of individuals are those whose maiden surnames were deduced from information in the text of the ad. Some ads refer to people using only initials or a given name; these were not indexed. Names of officials at the Emigration Office have also not been indexed.

Ireland Place Names Index

Irish place names are arranged by county, with townlands, parishes, baronies, etc., mixed together within their county. In cases in which no county is directly mentioned in an ad, the locality referred to has been indexed under the county that the ad was listed under. The spelling of these Irish place names can be problematic, in that place names were not spelled consistently in the ads, and in many cases they were clearly misspelled, based upon all commonly accepted variations. Places of embarkation mentioned in ads were not indexed.

United States Place Names Index

United States places are organized by state, with counties, towns, and cities treated as localities of equal level. When the ads mention multiple equal-level localities (such as Patchogue and Suffolk Co. in the place "Patchogue, Suffolk Co., NY"), separate entries are included in the index for each of these place names, without cross-referencing. Ports of entry mentioned in ads were not indexed.

Other Places

Principal headings in this index are country names, such as Canada, England, etc., with all lower levels of jurisdictions treated equally as subentries. As in the Ireland Place Names Index, places of embarkation mentioned in ads were not indexed.

New York City Streets

A New York City Street index was included to help those who are interested in researching an address at which an ancestor resided or a limited area in its vicinity. Since the focus of the book is (old) New York City, only Manhattan streets are indexed, and not Brooklyn or other streets that might be mentioned in the ads. The named streets are arranged alphabetically and the numbered streets numerically.

Sample Entry

June 19, 1858

Of **Maria Collins**, a native of the Parish of KILMORE, Ireland, who came to America about four years ago, in the ship *Sheridan*; when last heard from was living in CANAL STREET, NEW YORK. Any information of her will be thankfully received by her distressed mother, **Mary Collins**, by writing her address, No. [5]08 GRENWICH STREET [Greenwich Street], NEW YORK. [Appeared under County TIPPERARY.]

Characteristics Illustrated:

The date in *italics* before a series of ads is the date they were first published.
Personal names are in **bold** print.
Place names and New York City street names are in CAPITAL letters.
Ship names are in *italics*.
Text in [square brackets] includes the following:
  – Questionable numbers, letters, or words
  – Suggested corrections, explanations, and comments
  – County under which the ad appeared if not mentioned in its text.

Advertisements

December 23, 1849

Of **Benjamin Maxwell**, Stone-Cutter by trade. Arrived in this port in September last, in the ship *Shannon*, from Liverpool Any information of his whereabouts will be thankfully received by his brother **John Maxwell**, No. 60 CHERRY-STREET.

January 20, 1850

Of **Mary Firnan**, now **Mrs. Carmondy**, who left Ireland three years ago, from the County LIMERICK, near NANTHAN, by her sister **Margaret Firnan**, who landed a few months ago, supposed to be in TROY, or DETROIT. Any information directed to her at No. 5 Little Street, BROOKLYN, will be thankfully received.

Of **David Ingham Fenner**, from County CAVAN, Ireland, who, with his sister **Maria**, lived last year at 86 WASHINGTON STREET, by his brother **Henry Fenner**. Please call, or address him at **Mr. P. Hatfield's**, 164 BROADWAY.

Of **John Mullany**, or his sister **Mary**, of BALLYROBE, County MAYO, Ireland, who came to NEW-YORK about three years since, by his brother, **James Mullany**, who came by the *Vandalia*, and is stopping at 26 MOORE STREET, East River.

January 27, 1850

Of **Margaret McCoy**, late of LIMERICK, now Mrs.—. She will please send her address to this office.

February 10, 1850

Of **Mary Ann Dermody**, who, when last seen by her uncle **Patrick**, was in May last, in GREENWICH STREET. Her father is in Bellevue Hospital at present, and any information of her by letter or verbally, will be thankfully received by **Colonel Mann**, of said place, for her father, **John McDermott**.

Of **Margaret Curr** who lived with **Richard Mason** in Plymouth Street, BROOKLYN, in the third house east of Hudson av.; from BALLYGARNEY in the County of ANTRIM, Ireland. Enquire of **James Linden**, 41 8th Av. N.Y.

March 17, 1850

Of **Patk. Fogarty**, County TIPPERARY, NENAGH, who left Ireland about 6 or 7 years ago in the ship *Primrose*, from Limerick. Is supposed to be at present in CINCINNATI. Should this meet his eye, he is requested to write to **Michael Quinn**, at the Irish American office N.Y., who has a message to him from his brother **Thomas**. Cincinnati papers please copy

April 7, 1850

Of **Denis Murphy**, native of the City of CORK. Sailed for Quebec, L. Canada in April, 1837. When last heard of was in ROCHESTER, N.Y. Any information of his whereabouts will be thankfully received by his nephew, **Patrick Creedon**, 31 WHITEHALL-STREET, N.Y. [Appeared April 21, 1850 with the following addition: Rochester papers please copy.]

June 2, 1850

Of **Patrick Fitzgerald**, late of FEDAMORE, LIMERICK, Ireland, who sailed for New York from Limerick on the 26th April, 1848, by his Mother and Sister (**Mrs. Batemen**) to whom he wrote from WOLCOTVILL, (CONNECTICUT) on the 16th July, 1849. They are now in great distress in NEW-YORK, not knowing where he is located. We entreat our exchanges to copy as the advertisers are in deep distress and much pained in mind. Address, **Mrs. Fitzgerald**, at this office.

June 16, 1850

Of **Anthony Hegarty**, from Co. MAYO, landed at New-Orleans about three years ago; after an attack of fever and ague, went to PORTUGAL. [?] N. YORK State. Sent home £18 last Christmas. Any information of his present whereabouts will be thankfully received by his mother and three sisters, **Catherine, Maria** and **Ann**. Please direct to the office of the Commissioners of Emigration in the Park, N.York City. Exchanges will please copy.

June 22, 1850

Of **Mary Coghlan**, of CLONDINA, County of CLARE. In QUEBEC two years since. When last heard from, about 8 months ago, was in BUFFALO N.Y. Any information respecting her present whereabouts will be thankfully received by her brother **William Coghlan**, at this office. Buffalo papers please copy.

July 6, 1850

Of **Mary Bowen**, of CHURCHTOWN, County CORK. Arrived in New York about 12 months since; last heard from about 3 months ago, when she was in NEW YORK. Any information of her present whereabouts, or her address, if in the City, will be thankfully received by her sister, **Bridget Bowen**, at **William Collins**, No. 3, YORK ST

July 27, 1850

Of **John Doran**, aged about 25 years, dark complexion; arrived here from Ireland some three weeks ago, and who left **Henry Mallon's** house, No. 87 WEST 18th STREET, N.YORK. If this should meet his eye, he will please call at the above place, where he will hear of something to his advantage.

August 10, 1850

Of **William Daulton**, who landed here about 15 years ago; a native of the Parish of KILL, County WESTMEATH, Ireland. Any information will be thankfully received by his first cousin, **Patrick Harrington**, 91 ELEVENTH STREET, NEW YORK.

September 7, 1850

Of **Johanna Donvan**, who left the Parish of CARNIVERSE, County CORK, Ireland, about seventeen years ago — is supposed to be in CUMBERLAND, MARYLAND. Information respecting her will be thankfully received by her daughter, **Mary Donovan**. Direct care of **Mr. Divanna**, 24, MADISON-STREET, NEW YORK. Maryland papers please copy.

September 28, 1850

Of **Michael Owens**, 18 years of age, who came to this City about the first week of last December, in the *Rappahannock*, from RIVERSDALE, GALWAY Ireland. He has not since been heard of by his sister, **Mary Owens**, who would be glad to hear from him immediately, as she has something of importance to communicate. Address 29, Morris Street, JERSEY CITY; or at the office of this paper.

October 5, 1850

Of **John Fowler**, of the Townland of LARRIGAN, Parish Of INNISMACSENT, FERMANAGH, Ireland, who came to this country two years ago, by his daughter **Ellen Johnson** arrived in the *Constellation*, 3rd October. The only account she can give of the whereabouts of this man is that the letter she received, was directed from GODERICH TOWN, and

NEWTOWN HAMILTON, (probably HAMILTON CANADA).— Application at the office of this paper. Canada papers please copy.

October 19, 1850

Of **Kitty Egan**, NENAGH, TIPPERARY, Ireland, who arrived in New York about the 15th July last. Apply at this office.

November 16, 1850

Of **Alicia** or **Alley Lannen**, who wrote to her sister, to KNONKACHOWN, DRANGAN, Parish of KILENALLE, TIPPERARY, Ireland, in 1847. She was then residing in BOSTON, MASS. Apply to Mr. Keatinge, Irish Emigrant Office, No. 1 Reade Street, N.Y., or at the office of this paper.

November 23, 1850

Of **Terence M'Intire, Thos. M'Intire**, and **Patrick M'Intire**, of BALLYSHANNON, County DONEGAL. When last heard from, were in SOUTH BRISTOL, within a few miles of the falls of NIAGARA. They are all carpenters by trade. Any information of them will be thankfully received by their sister, **Ellen M'Intire**, 208, CENTRE STREET, NEW YORK CITY.

November 30, 1850

Of **Maurice O'Connor, Denis O'Connor, Ellen O'Connor**, and **Mary O'Connor**, by **Margaret O'Connor**, daughter of the latter, who arrived in New York last April, from LONDON, where she had been the last fourteen years. When her brothers, sisters and mother were last heard from, they were living at POTTSVILLE, PA., and the letter was dated from CHERRYHILL.— Direct to Mr. Irwin, Office of Commissioners of Emigration, City Hall, N.Y.

December 14, 1850

Of **William Gorman**, a Plasterer by trade who left LIMERICK, Ireland, about 10 years ago, when last heard from was in MONTREAL, L.C., is supposed to have gone to the State of ILLINOIS. Any information of him will be thankfully received by his nephew, **John Hehir**, 42 TWENTY-EIGHTH STREET, NEW YORK, or at this office. Illinois papers will please copy.

December 28, 1850

Of **Daniel Ryan**, of HOLY-CROSS Co. TIPPERARY, Ireland. Landed in New York about a year ago, when last heard from was in the State of OHIO, is a laborer and about 27 years old. Any information respecting his present whereabouts, will be thankfully received by his sister **Catherine Ryan**. Direct to the office of this paper. Ohio papers will please copy.

Of **William Fetton**, of KILFINANE, County LIMERICK, Ireland, Shoemaker by trade, when last heard from was in BLOOMINGDALE, DU PAGE County, State of ILLINOIS. Any information of him will be thankfully received by his uncle **Daniel M'Carthy**. Direct to **Owen Guiry**, 56 CENTRE-STREET, NEW YORK, for Daniel M'Carthy. Illinois papers will please copy.

January 4, 1851

Of **Mary Harregidon** or **Hardiman** of WHITEHALL, in the State of NEW YORK, wrote to her sister **Bridget** to Ireland on the 28th of June last. Bridget and her Brother have arrived in New York and would wish to hear from their sister Mary immediately as they have no money to carry them to the country. Direct to the office of the Commissioners of Emigration. New York, 30th December, 1850.

January 11, 1851

Of **Patrick Cuddy**, by his Children and **Mary Naughten**, who arrived from Ireland, on the 1st January, 1851. They are from KILBEGGAN, County GALWAY. The last information of him was to write to **Daniel Keeffe**. Any tiding of his present whereabouts, will be thankfully received at 161, DUANE STREET

Of **Bridget Barry**, Wife of **Thomas Bulman**, of CASTLEBAR, County CORK, near BALLYHOOLY, Ireland. Arrived in New York, about 8th September last. Any information respecting her whereabouts will be thankfully received by her husband, Thomas Bulman, or **Johanna Quinlan**, 350 WATER STREET, having left his situation in the country for the purpose of ascertaining her present location.

January 18, 1851

Of **Bessy Flood** and **William Flood**, formerly of CASTLETOWN KILPATRICK, County of MEATH, Ireland. When Bessy Flood was last heard from, she lived with **Mr. Fisher**, GREENWICH STREET, NEW YORK. William Flood was at VERPOINTS PLANK, in the employment of **James Magnus** at the same time. Their Mother arrived in New York, on Tuesday, 7th January, and is anxious to hear from either, or both. Address, care of **John Fitzgerald**, 63 CHERRY STREET, NEW YORK, or at the office of this paper. Exchange Papers please copy.

January 25, 1851

Of **Patrick Murphy**, of the Parish of KNOCKLONG, County LIMERICK, Ireland, who sailed from Limerick, 3rd May, 1849, in the *Thorney Close*. When last heard of he was in MONTREAL, L.C. Any information of him will be thankfully received by his brother, **John Murphy**, 3 SIXTH STREET, or at this Office. Illinois papers please copy.

February 22, 1851

Of **Thomas Donohue**, formerly of HAWK HILL, near GORT, County GALWAY, Ireland. When last heard from was in HIGH PARK, RONDOUT, ULSTER County, State of NEW YORK. Any information of him will be thankfully received by his wife, **Catherine**, (who has lately arrived in this City,) at the Emigration office, 25 and 27 Canal Street.

March 1, 1851

*Of **John Mallowney**, who arrived in this City, from Limerick, about 18 months ago, formerly of the Parish of TULLA, Co. CLARE. When last heard from was in GOWANDA, CATTARAUGUS Co., NEW YORK. Any information of him will be thankfully received by his wife **Bridget**, (who has lately arrived in New York) at the Emigration Office, 25 and 27 Canal Street.

April 26, 1851

Of **Catherine Healy**, of Long Street, Town of DROMORE, WEST, SLIGO, Ireland; by her sister **Margaret**, 118 SPRING STREET, NEW YORK.

May 10, 1851

Of **Robert Hutchinson**, who left NEW YORK in the end of September, 1847 — said he was going to learn the tanning business, 10 miles from this City. When he left he was 17 years old, stout built, fair complexion, and auburn hair. Any information of him will be thankfully received by his disconsolate mother, **Mrs. Ryan**, 242 STANTON ST., NEW YORK.

May 24, 1851

Of **Dominick Kehoe**, late of Green St., KILKENNY, County KILKENNY, Ireland. It is supposed that he died within the last two years, either in the City of NEW YORK or PHILADELPHIA. Any information of him will be thankfully received by **Mr. Joseph Purcell**, 63, CATHARINE STREET, NEW YORK.

July 12, 1851

Of **Edmond Mooney**, late of DUNMORE, Co. GALWAY. Left Ireland some three years ago. When last heard from (about two months since) was in PRESTON, N.Y. Any information of him will be thankfully received by his brother, **Michael**, Emigrant office, 25 & 27 Canal St., or at this office.

July 19, 1851

Of **Winifred O'Neill**, of TUAM, County GALWAY, Ireland, who arrived in New York about the 17th of April last. When last heard of, was living at **Mr. Alexander's** 85 HESTER ST. Any information of her to be sent to her brother-in-law, **John Pell**, at the Emigration Office, Canal St., New York.

Of **Patrick Trainor**, PINES PASS, Co. DOWN, who left Ireland for Philadelphia, in October, 1849. When heard from in March, 1850, he was living with a person named **Joel McNutt**. Any information of him will be thankfully received by his sister, **Ann Fitzpatrick**, No. 100 MADISON STREET, NEW YORK.

August 2, 1851

Of **John** and **Patrick Moriarty**, brothers, from the Parish of LISELTON, County KERRY, Ireland, by their sister **Nancy Moriarty**. Patrick was in LOUISVILLE, KY. and John in GREAT BENDS or SUSQUEHANNA, N.Y., when last heard from. Should this meet them she requests they will write at once, and direct to **Maurice Murphy**, No. 175 FIRST AVENUE, NEW YORK.

Of **John Hogan** of the County FERMANAGH, when last heard from, was in QUEBEC, was at work on the Waterpolis. Any information of him will be thankfully received by his brother, **Bernard Hogan**, (lately from LONDON), 91 SHERRIFF-STREET, NEW YORK. [Appeared Aug. 9, 1851 with John Hogan Listed As **John Haggan**.]

August 23, 1851

Of **John Sullivan**, of GOOLEEN, Co. CORK, Ireland, who emigrated to this country five weeks before the Christmas of 1848. When last heard of, 5 months since, he was living at HOMESVILLE, STEUBEN Co., N.Y. Any information of him to be forwarded to his sister **Eliza**, at the Emigrant Office, 25 and 27 Canal Street, New York.

Of **Michael Stack**, of BELL HARBOUR, Parish of CLARE ABBEY, Co. CLARE, who sailed from Galway for New York, on the ninth of May last, in the Bark *Johnson*, of Wismer. He landed on the 11th June, was put in Quarantine Hospital, and left there on the 18th of July. His brother, **Thomas Stack**, of SOUTH NORWALK, CONN, would be glad to hear of or from him.

September 6, 1851

Of **James Dunn**, who arrived at New York 5 years ago, by his brother **Patrick** who resides in ALBANY. He is supposed to have gone, last time, to CINCINNATI. Cincinnati and New Orleans papers please copy.

September 13, 1851

Of the **Rev. Mark Healy**, from the Parish of CARRIGCASTLE, County of MAYO, by his second cousin **Anne Colman**, when last heard from was in KINGSTON, and TROY. — Should this meet him she expects he will favor her with a line, and let her know where he is at present. Please direct to **Michael Hart**, No. 175 FIRST AVENUE, NEW YORK, for Anne Colman.

Of **Maria Nangle**, from the Parish of KILTARD, County LEITRIM, Ireland, who emigrated to this country about 10 years ago. -Was in JAMAICA, L.I. about 2 weeks since, any information of her to be sent to **John Doherty**, RED HOOK, SOUTH BROOKLYN.

Of **Margaret O'Connor**, from KILKEEDY Parish, Co. CLARE, Ireland, who landed in February last, in New York, and lodged at **Michael Casey's**, (street not remembered) by her sisters **Eliza** and **Honora**, who board at present at **Mrs. Kane's,** 15 OAK STREET.

SITUATION WANTED, for a lad, from 12 to 14 years old, in a family Grocery or Liquor Store, in this City, BROOKLYN, or WILLIAMSBURGH. The amplest security will be given for his fidelity and capability. Apply to **Thomas O'Callaghan**, 48 ROSEVELT STREET [Roosevelt Street].

September 20, 1851

Of **John Carmody**, native of LISTOWEL, KERRY, Ireland, by his nephew **Patrick Scanlan**. When last heard from he resided in OSWEGO Co., NEW YORK. Any information of him will be thankfully received at 469 EAST 12th ST., NEW YORK.

September 27, 1851

Of **John, Thomas, & Con. Kearney**, Parish of FETHARD, Co. TIPPERARY, Ireland, who migrated to CANADA, ten years ago. When last heard from were in BUFFALO, N.Y. Any information respecting the above persons will be thankfully received by their brother **James Kearney**, 102 WASHINGTON ST. NEW YORK. Western papers, (please copy.)

October 18, 1851

John Clarke, late of "FREFFANS," TRIM, Ireland, is now in NEW YORK, and wishes to see or hear from his brother **Thos. Clarke**, who was last heard of at WORTHINGTON, FRANKLIN County, OHIO. A letter from him or information of his present residence will be thankfully received by **Thomas Taylor**, 35 MAIDEN LANE, NEW YORK. Ohio papers will please copy.

November 22, 1851

Of **Patrick Oats**, late of the Parish of CAULDRY, County SLIGO, arrived in New York in the *"Linden,"* in June 1849. Any information of his present whereabouts will be thankfully received by his brother **John**, at **Daniel Gallaher's**, 61, ALLEN STREET, N.Y.

Of **Mary Lawlor**, late of QUEEN'S County, Ireland, landed in New York or Boston, about February last. Any information of her present whereabouts will be thankfully received by her sister, **Bridget Lawlor**, 66, WASHINGTON STREET, NEW YORK, or at this office.

November 28, 1851

Of **Michael Malone**, a native of LIMERICK, 5 feet 6 in height, fresh complexion, age, 50 years, trade, ship-carpenter. Intelligence by letter, addressed to **James E. G. Barry**, WATERBURY, CONN. Something of vast importance to the benefit of the advertised will be made known.

December 13, 1851

Of **Daniel O'Neill**, who lived as a farm laborer at HILLSBORO, NEW JERSEY, with **Mr. Abraham Wickobb**, farmer. He left his place three months ago and has not been, since, heard of. D. O'Neill arrived in the *Manhattan*, on the 1ˢᵗ day of April, 1851. He is aged 18 years. Any information respecting him will be thankfully received by his father, **Michael O'Neill**, who resides at No. 6 LITTLE WATER STREET, or **John M'Carthy**, 55 GREENWICH STREET. Irish American papers please copy.

December 20, 1851

Of **William O'Tool**, Boot and Shoe maker, native of WESTPORT, Co. MAYO, Ireland, who arrived here (New-York), last fall. If this should meet his eye, he is requested to call for information at the office of this paper, or address a few lines to his brother **Patrick**, CLAYTON, SUFFOLK Co., NEW-YORK, letting him know his whereabouts.

February 14, 1852

Of **Patrick Flanagan**, of LOUGHILL, near SHANAGOLDEN, Co. LIMERICK, Ireland, or of **Ellen M'Namara**, of LIMERICK. Any information of either of those parties will be thankfully received by **Patrick Flanagan** (nephew to the former) at 295 AVENUE A, NEW YORK, or this office.

Of **Patrick Blake**, Carpenter, formerly of the Parish of RATHKENNY, CASTLETOWN, MEATH, Ireland, who has been in this country 7 or 8 years, and who wrote about 3 months ago to his brother-in-law, **Thomas Devlin**, (in which he mentioned that **Mary** and **John Price** were well) and gave as his address 64 YORK STREET, or some such name and number in NEW YORKor BROOKLYN, by **Anne M'Cabe**, (otherwise **Price**) lately of KNOCKCASTLETOWN KILPATRICK, MEATH, Ireland, arrived here by the *Great Western*. Apply at the office of this paper, or at the Emigrant's Home, Canal Street.

Of **James Scott**, a native of CLONMEL, County OF TIPPERARY, Ireland landed in New York, about 2½ years ago. If this meets his eye, or any of his acquaintances they will confer a favor by writing to his brother and sister **Patrick** and **Catherine Scott**, care of **William O'Dea**, No. 57 CHERRY STREET, NEW YORK.

Of **Thomas Spullen**, or his wife **Margaret Spullen**, from KING'S County Ireland, by her sister **Catherine Donahoe**, just landed from Ireland, and stopping at the Emigration office, 27 Canal Street, New York.

February 21, 1852

Of **Maurice King**, aged 15 years, formerly of CAHEVCIVEEN, County KERRY, Ireland. He landed in New York on March 27, 1851. When seen last it was in August, and he then said he worked with a farmer in or about JERSEY CITY. He promised to write to his father at WARD'S ISLAND. Any information respecting him will be thankfully received by his father, **Daniel King**, or **John Donegan**, GREENVILLE, NORWICH, CONN

Of **Bridget Dowling**, of the Parish of DRUM, County ROSCOMMON, Ireland, who arrived in this City 17ᵗʰ of last September, in the ship *Jersey*, from Liverpool. Any information respecting her will be thankfully received by her brother, **Edmond Dowling** care of **Wm. Carroll**, 149ᵗʰ STREET, NEW YORK.

Of **Mrs. Winefred Conroy**, son, and two daughters, **Thomas**, **Margaret**, and **Anne**, natives of the County GALWAY, Ireland; supposed to be in CINCINNATI. Any information of them will be thankfully received by her daughter, **Mary**, at **Mr. Hughes**, 476 PEARL STREET, NEW YORK. Cincinnati paper, please copy.

March 6, 1852

Of **Michael Egan**, of the Parish of ONAGH, County MAYO, Ireland, who came to this country in April, 1848. When last heard from was in BLACKSHIRES, FAIRMONT, MARION CO., VA. Any intelligence of him will be thankfully received by his wife **Honor**, who had arrived in this City, at **James Meehan**'s, 35 ORANGE STREET.

Of **Nicholas Tallan**, of KINGSTOWN, Co. DUBLIN, Ireland, who arrived in this City on the 1st of November last, in the *Rappahannock*, and went to TROY the 12th of December, to **Mr. P. Magrath**. Any information of him will be thankfully received by his wife **Jane**, corner of 47th ST., and 3rd AVENUE, NEW YORK.

Of **Richard Mullally**, of KILCOCK, Co KILDARE, Ireland, who came to this country last Fall two years; when last heard from he was in CINCINNATI, OHIO. Any information of him will be thankfully received by his sister, **Catherine Hynes**, 19 MARION ST, NEW YORK. Cincinnati papers please copy.

March 13, 1852

Of **Catherine Tiskey**, who arrived in New York per *Bryan Abbs* from LIMERICK, in February, 1849. Any information of her will be thankfully received by **James Supple**, of BUFFALO, N.Y., or Mr. Walsh, Emigration Office, New York City.

Of **John Henry Byrne**, of the City of DUBLIN, Ireland, who was formerly clerk in the Custom House there. By applying to Mr. Wash, Office of the Commissioners of Emigration, he will hear of something to his advantage.

If **John Shirley**, formerly of KILKENNY, Co. KILKENNY, Ireland, who left home in the August of 1848, will send his address to **William White**, 75 WEST STREET, NEW YORK, he will hear of something to his advantage. Ohio papers please copy.

March 20, 1852

Of **Patrick McConnell** who landed in New York in November last, in the ship *Martha*, from GLASCOW, in company with his father, mother and four children. He has been employed from the office of the commissioners of Emigration in Canal Street, on the 13th of November last, by a **Capt. Gilmartin** on a line boat bringing coal from PHILADELPHIA to NEW YORK. Any information of his whereabouts will be thankfully received by his parents, now at HAVRE-DE-GRACE, MARYLAND, or Mr. Irwin 25 and 27 Canal Street.

Of **Mr. Bernard O'Farrell** (formerly of LIMERICK City), Architect. His old friend **John Ryan** (Hatter), late of LIMERICK, now of NEWARK, NEW JERSEY, would be glad to hear from him. New Orleans papers please read.

Of **Michael Dwyer**, (FETHA) of BALLAGH, County TIPPERARY, Ireland, who left home on December, 26, 1849. Address **Mary Dwyer** (his wife) at **Mr. Sullivan**'s, 48 WEST 13TH STREET, NEW YORK.

Of **Michael M'Laughlin**, a native of ROSCOMMON, Ireland, who came to this country ten years ago; when last heard of was in NEW ORLEANS. Any information of him will be thankfully received by his nephew, **James Hoare**, No. 50 Mercer St., JERSEY CITY.

April 3, 1852

Of **Edmond Fitzgerald**, stone-mason formerly of NEWPORT, TIPPERARY, Ireland, who left home about 3 years ago, and is now supposed to be living in the city; or of his cousin, **Edmond Fitzgerald**, of KILMALLOCK, Co. LIMERICK. Any intelligence of either will be thankfully received by **John Fitzgerald** (brother to the former) at the Emigration office, 25 and 27 Canal Street.

Of **Mathew**, **Bridget**, and **Michael McIver** of OMAGH, TYRONE, Ireland; when last heard of, Bridget was in FULTON STREET, N.Y., and married to a **Mr. Watson**; Michael was in NEWARK, Plain St. Any intelligence of them will be thankfully received by their cousin, **Elizabeth McIver**, P.O., JERSEY CITY.

A light-colored leather TRUNK 2 ½ feet long, in which were the names of **Bridget Williamson** and **Thomas Fitzpatrick**, was taken by mistake, from the steam-boat *Worcester*, in New York, on the morning of the 16th of March; the owner can have it on application to **Clark M. Saunders**, WINCHESTER, VA. At the same time and place, Mr. Saunders' own trunk, of the same description and size as the former, was lost; any person sending information in relation to it, to his address as above, will be suitably rewarded.

April 10, 1852

Of **John M'Dermott**, a native of CARRICK-ON-SHANNON, LEITRIM, Ireland, who sailed for New Orleans, from Dublin, in 1817. His friends wish to ascertain if he is still living or not. Any person who can give the requisite intelligence of him, will be suitably rewarded by writing to **M. M'Dermott**, care of the American Consule, SOUTHAMPTON, ENGLAND. New Orleans papers please copy.

Of **Catherine Leonard**, of BANDON, County CORK, Ireland, who arrived here about two months since, in the ship *Guy Mannering*, from Liverpool. She left Bellview Hospital, 27th Street, on the 25th of February, and has not been heard of since. Any information of her will be thankfully received by her son, **Denis Leonard**, of PROVIDENCE, R.I., at the Commissioners' Office, 25 & 27 Canal Street. Exchange papers please copy.

April 17, 1852

Of **Mary Coleman**, or otherwise **Conran**, of the Parish of KILCORKY, Co. ROSCOMMON, Ireland, or of daughter, **Mary Coleman**, who arrived in this city in the *John Right*, on the 16th of April, 1847. Any person knowing anything of either will confer a great favor by addressing her husband, **Bernard Coleman**, 179 HUDSON ST., NEW YORK.

Of **Patrick Hoare**, 50 years old, a native of the Parish of ATHLEAGUE, ROSCOMMON, Ireland, who came to this country about 26 years ago. When last heard of he was in BALTIMORE, MD. Any intelligence of him will be thankfully received by his brother, **James Hoare**, 50 Mercer Street, JERSEY CITY.

Of **Mary McNamara**, from Parish of FEAKLE, County CLARE, Ireland, who arrived in New York, per ship *Sarah G. Hyde*, in November last. Apply to Gregory Dillon, President Irish Emigrant Society, 51 Chambers Street.

April 24, 1852

Of **James**, **William**, **Richard** and **Michael Walsh**, Millers, of CRAUGE, County TIPPERARY, Ireland, who left home in March, 1851, and have not since been heard of. Any intelligence of them will be thankfully received by their brother, **Nicholas Walsh**, CUDDEBACKVILLE, P.O., ORANGE COUNTY, NEW YORK. Boston papers please copy.

June 5, 1852

Of **Michael Clanchy**, from the Parish of ST. PATRICK'S LIMERICK, who came to this country about eleven years ago in the *Nerio* from that City; when last heard of he was living in LEXINGTON, MASS., where he is supposed to be still. Any information of him will be thankfully received by his brother, **Stephen**, care of **Michael M'Namara**, 6 OAK STREET, NEW YORK.

Of **Martin Heroughty** by his wife and family who have lately arrived in New York; he is a native of the Parish and County of MAYO, Ireland, and is supposed to be in the State of RHODE ISLAND. Any information respecting him shall be thankfully received by his brother, **Michael Heroughty**, 151 SOUTH STREET, NEW YORK. Rhode Island papers please copy.

June 12, 1852

Of **John**, **Ambrose** and **Ann Lavin** of SWINFORD, County MAYO, Ireland, who arrived in this country 4 years ago, when last heard from one of the two brothers worked in a tavern in PRINCETON, NEW JERSEY, in or about 2 years ago. Any information concerning any of them would be thankfully received by their sister **Rosanna Lavin**, who landed in New York, last July, care of **Mrs. Kent**, 74 ORANGE STREET, NEW YORK.

June 19, 1852

Should this meet the eye of **Peter Lynch**, from ALLEN, in the County of KILDARE, Ireland, a passenger in the *Guy Mannering* from Liverpool, or any person knowing him, will please let him know he will find a letter to his advantage from **Father Wier**, on application at 21 CHERRY ST, NEW YORK. This advertisement will not be repeated.

Of **Mary Lynch**, from BALLINAHINCH, Co. TIPPERARY Ireland, who was discharged from WARD'S ISLAND Hospital, on the 27th of last April, and has not since been heard of. Any person knowing anything that may lead to her recovery will confer a great favor by acquainting her mother, **Catherine Lynch**, at **Mr. Grant's**, corner of 27th STREET and 8th AVENUE.

Of **Margaret Lewis**, daughter of **George Lewis** of INABOY, Co. ANTRIM, Ireland, who resided about two years ago, with **Mr. Garey**, at YORKVILLE. Apply to Mr. Walsh, Office of Commissioners of Emigration.

Of **Patrick Connele**, of ATHY, Co. KILDARE, Ireland, who came here in 1842. He lived in FRIENDSVILLE, SUSQUEHANNA CO., PA., till last October when he left for the West; he is supposed to be somewhere in FOND DU LAC Co., WIS. Any intelligence of him will be thankfully received by his brother **Edward**, care of **Mary Keating**, Clark's buildings and dock, off Columbia Street, BROOKLYN, N.Y.

June 26, 1852

Of **Patrick** and **Thomas Currin**, natives of BALLINTOGHER, Co. SLIGO, Ireland, by their sister **Mary**, of BROOKLYN, who is anxious to hear from them, as their presence is required in New York without delay, on account of their brother **Timothy's** death. Direct to **Patk. Kearns**, No.101 GREENWICH ST., NEW YORK. Pennsylvania papers please to copy.

Of **Mathew Troy**, of the Parish of ST. KERNS, Ireland, when last heard from in December 1850, was in the State of MARYLAND. His wife whose maiden name was **Bridget Quinlin**, is anxious to know his address, and will feel thankful for any information. Address to **Mr. Reynolds**, Box 335, Post office, NEW YORK. Maryland papers please copy.

July 3, 1852

Of **Cornelius** and **Thomas Londrigan** of CLONMEL, County TIPPERARY, Ireland, who left New York about two years ago when last heard of were in GENEVA, N.Y. Any information respecting them will be thankfully received by their Sister **Johanna**, as she is most anxious to hear from them. Direct to the care of **William Dougherty**, corner of Court and Atlantic Street, BROOKLYN, N.Y.

Of **Mrs. Sullivan**, or **Honora** or **Norry Barrot**, (the latter being her maiden name,) of BALLYSHEDDY, in the Parish of DONOUGHMORE, County of LIMERICK, Ireland, who came to this country about a year and a half or two years ago, having with her, as is supposed, a child of 6 or 7 years named **Catherine Sullivan**, to join her husband, **Patrick Sullivan**, who preceded her to this country about two years. Since learning of her departure, her husband has been looking constantly, but in vain, for her arrival, any information respecting her, communicated to the Ohio State Journal or to Patrick Sullivan, at LANCASTER, OHIO, will be gratefully received by her husband and the father of her child.

July 10, 1852

Of **John O'Brien**, from the Townland of TUREEN, County LIMERICK, Ireland. He is supposed to be in some part of LOWER CANADA. His son was in NEW YORK, last May, and inquired from his cousin, **John O'Brien**, (son of his Uncle **James**,) who would be glad to her from him. Direct to 558 EIGHTH AVENUE, N.Y. Canada papers please copy.

July 17, 1852

Of **Mary Healy** (daughter of **Francis Healy** and **Margaret Burns**), who emigrated from Ireland to this country fifteen years ago. She landed in Quebec; went from there to TORONTO, where she lived in the family of **Dr. Baldwin**. After this she married, and now lives, it is thought, about seven miles from the Doctor's residence. Any information about her present place of Abode, directed to **Thomas Healy**, ARCHBALD (formerly of BLAKELY), LUZERNE Co., PA., will be most thankfully received by her mother and brothers, who are anxious to hear from her.

July 24, 1852

Of **Mary Murphy**, from the County CORK, Ireland, who landed in this City, on the 1st of May last, from the ship *Continent*. She went from the office of the Commissioners of Emigration, to live with **Mrs. Quinn**, of AIRYMONT, (supposed to be somewhere in WESTCHESTER CO.) Any information of her will be thankfully received by her brother in-law, **James Smith**, Box, 262, P.O., SYRACUSE, N.Y., or at the Commissioners Office, Canal Street, N.Y.

July 31, 1852

Of **William Keenan**, from the Parish of LOUGHLANISLAND Co. DOWN, Ireland. Who came to this country about, 20 or 22 years ago. If any person knowing whether he is alive or dead will direct a line to this office, stating such facts, they will confer an obligation.

Of **Patrick** and **George Jackson** from FLOWERHILL, Parish of LISMORE, Co. WATERFORD, Ireland: when last heard from they were in COLUMBIANA Co., OHIO. Any intelligence of their whereabouts, just now, directed to **Wm. O'Brien**, Esq., C.E., MOUNT VERNON, WESTCHESTER Co., N.Y., will be gratefully acknowledged by their brother, **Edward Jackson**.

Of **Biddy McCarran**, a native of the Townland of STRAWLANGFORD, Parish of CANVAY, in Ireland: when last heard of was in BROOKLYN. Any information respecting her will be thankfully received by her husband, **James McDermott**, No. 66, Bridge Street, BROOKLYN, care of Mr. **James Doherty**.

Of **James Cassidy**, aged 17 years, who arrived in this City, March 23rd, 1852, per ship *Manhattan*, he is from the Townland of DRUMGAVNEY, Parish of TULLOWSCORBEL, County MONAGHAN, Ireland. Also of **Catherine Lynch**, formerly **Catherine McCarthy**, who was married to **Denis Lynch** about nine years since at MILLSTREET, County CORK,

Ireland, she had recently resided in LONDON. Apply to Mr. Walsh, Office of the Commissioners of Emigration, Park, New York.

Of **Owen Kiernan** of TUBBERLINE, TEMPLEPORT, County CAVAN; when last heard of was in BROOKLYN. If this should reach his eye, his uncle, **Rev. Owen Kiernan** is most anxious to hear from him. Apply by letter or otherwise to **P. Taggart**, 54 North Second Street, WILLIAMSBURGH, N.Y.

August 7, 1852

Of **Maurice** and **David Walsh**, from CHARLEVILLE, Co. CORK, Ireland, who left home four years ago; they were living in GERMANTOWN, PRESTON Co., VA., last Christmas two years, since when they have not been heard from. Any person who may know anything of them will confer a great favor by directing such information to their brother, **Patrick Walsh**, care of **John Ryan**, 24 OAK STREET, NEW YORK. It is thought they are working somewhere on the Baltimore and Ohio Railroad.

If **Mary M'Cormick**, who lived about twelve months ago at 101 WILLIAM STREET, N.Y., will send her address to T.F., at this office, she will hear something to her advantage.

Of **Patt Brady**, from KILBLINE, County KILKENNY, Ireland, who left home about six years ago; when last heard of he was in CINCINNATI, OHIO. If this notice should meet his eye or any person knowing him, he will confer a great favor by writing to his sister-in-law, **Susan Haden**, at 217 WASHINGTON STREET, NEW YORK, for **Patt Carroll**. Ohio papers please copy.

August 14, 1852

Patrick M'Evoy, late of DERRYGILL, QUEEN'S County, Ireland, who left Dublin for New York in March, 1849, and is supposed to be in NEW YORK, is requested to communicate with his friend in DUBLIN, **W. Nolan**.

Of **Daniel Keleher**, from COURTBRACK, Co. CORK, Ireland, by his brother **Michael**, who has not heard of him since he worked in CONNECTICUT on the railroad under **Moore** and **Durham**. He would be extremely thankful for any information concerning him; he is supposed to be in ILLINOIS. Direct to **Cooper** and **Gilland**, Market Place, SAVANNAH, GA., or to **Jeremiah O'Neill**, 366 WATER ST., NEW YORK. Illinois papers please copy.

Of **Patrick Cox** or **Assle**, of BAGNALSTOWN, Co. CARLOW, Ireland, who came to this country four years ago, and also of **James Ryan**, from the same place, who came to this City from PHILADELPHIA, about two months ago. Any information respecting either will be thankfully received by **Eliza Ryan** (wife of the latter), care of **Mr. Apple**. 210 HESTER ST., NEW YORK.

Of **William Loughlan**, of GRAIGUE, near TULLAMORE, KING'S County; when last heard from was in GREENSBURG, WESTMORELAND County, PENNSYLVANIA. Any information will be thankfully received by his wife **Margaret** and daughter **Ellen**, at **Thomas Kelly's**, 73 HAMMERASLY STREET [Hamersley Street], NEW YORK. If **John** or **Wm. Daly** will make enquiry about him they would confer a great favor.

August 21, 1852

Of **Thomas** and **Patrick Lynch**, from the Parish of RATHFARNHAM, Co. WESTMEATH, Ireland, who emigrated to Canada, about eleven years ago, and have resided since that time near AYR VILLAGE (PLYMOUTH post-town) in UPPER CANADA. Their sister, **Catherine**, has landed in New York, and is anxious to hear from them. Any information of them directed to this office, will be gratefully received. She has two children with her and is destitute of funds to maintain herself here.

Of **Richard Harnett**, BALLYHOULIG, Parish of O'BRENNAN, Co. KERRY, Ireland, who came to this country about the 1st of December, 1850. When last heard from he was in MANLIUS CENTRE, ONONDAGA Co., N.Y. Any information respecting him will be thankfully received by his sister, **Mary Harrington**, care of **P. Hogan**, 14 WASHINGTON ST., NEW YORK.

August 28, 1852

Of **Patt Barrett**, from Parish of CROSSMOLINA, Co. MAYO, Ireland, by **Mary Barrett** and her two children, who arrived a few days ago; also of **Michael Brown**, from the same locality, who may give her any tidings of her sister, whose address she lost. Her maiden name was **Condon**. Direct to Mr. Walsh, Office of Commissioners of Emigration.

September 18, 1852

Of **Jane McAuliffe**, from the Parish of NEWMARKET, County CORK, Ireland. She landed in New York in December last, and was hired by a lady, for the country, with whom she left New York, on the 1st of March. Any intelligence of her whereabouts will be thankfully received by **Julia** and **Patrick McAuliffe**, (her sister and brother), 50, 30th STREET between Broadway and 6th Avenue, NEW YORK.

Of **Catherine Reiney**, by her brother **Francis**, of Hanberry Lane, DUBLIN, who is now in New York anxiously wishing to know of her whereabouts. Any information will be thankfully received at **Thomas Styles**, 495 12th STREET between Avenues B and C, or at **Mr. Talbot's** 53 MULBERRY STREET, NEW YORK.

Of **Peter Lynch**, of the County KILDARE, Ireland, who came a passenger by the ship *Guy Mannering*, from Liverpool, and landed in New York, in July last. If he will call or send his address, he will hear of something to his advantage. Any person giving information where he is will be suitably rewarded for their trouble. Application to be made to **Patrick Ryan**, 20 Columbia Street, near State Street, SOUTH BROOKLYN.

Of **Catherine Burke**, Adult; **Catherine Warren**, aged 9 years; **Richard Warren**, aged 5 years of RATHCORMACK, County CORK, Ireland, who sailed from Liverpool for New York in the packet ship *Saratoga*, and arrived in this City on 30th August last. According to instructions they called at the office of Messrs. Williams and Guion, Old Black Star Packet Office at which they were directed to proceed forthwith to WATERFORD, N Y; since then they have not been heard of. Any information concerning them will be thankfully received by the mother of the children, **Ellen Warren**, care of J Duffy, Agent for Messrs. Williams and Guion, at Waterford, or at the office of this paper.

September 25, 1852

Of **John Wallace**, and his sons **John, Stephen,** and **James**, from NEWCASTLE, Co. LIMERICK, Ireland. When last heard from (about two months ago) he and his sons John and James were in TINKER'S RUN, CUMBERLAND Co., PA., and Stephen was in CHICAGO, ILLINOIS. Any intelligence of them will be thankfully received by **William Wallace**, care of **Mrs. Nash**, 178 DIVISION ST., NEW YORK.

William Mullen, who arrived in this City from Liverpool, on or about the 12th September is requested to call at the Office of Dillon & O'Gorman, 39 William St., N.Y.

October 2, 1852

Of **Mary Shaughnessy**, who arrived in New York in February or March last. Money has been received for her from her sister in NEW ORLEANS. Enquire of Mr. Walsh, Office of the Commissioners of Emigration, in the Park.

Of **Michael** and **James Nugent**, from AUGHERMERRIGAN Parish of BADONEY, County TYRONE, Ireland. When last heard from in 1834, then were living in BALTIMORE, MD. Any intelligence of them will be thankfully received by their brother **Peter Nugent**, 640 WATER ST., NEW YORK.

October 9, 1852

Of **Denis Slater**, who arrived in this country in May 1851, per ship *John Henry*, from the port of London, by his wife **Catherine Slater**. He worked at the Union iron works, PATERSON, NEW JERSEY, in August 1851, and is supposed to be in the State of MASSACHUSETTS. By calling or writing to No. 54 HOWARD STREET, NEW YORK, he can get intelligence of his wife and children, who are anxious about him.

October 16, 1852

Of **John** and **Patrick Leo**, natives of the Parish of DONOUGHMORE, County of LIMERICK, Ireland. John left home on the 4th of May, 1845, in the ship, *China*, from Limerick, and Patrick left home in the summer of 1846; when last heard from, in December, 1849, was from ASBHURN post office, State of MASSACHUSETTS. Information wanted of them by their sister, **Margaret Leo** Enquire of Mr. Wash, Office of the Commissioners of Emigration.

Michael Fahy, from DANGAN, in the County GALWAY, Ireland, and about 18 months ago living at corner of Delhousie Street, GRIFFINSTOWN, MONTREAL, CANADA, is earnestly requested to write to his brother **Thomas** 146 GREENWICH STREET, NEW YORK. Montreal papers please copy.

Of **Bridget Murphy**, from near NEWCASTLE, County LIMERICK, Ireland, who arrived in this City on the 21st September, in the *E.C. Scranton*, in company with four children (a boy and three girls) her step-brother and step-sisters. Any intelligence of her whereabouts will be thankfully received by her step-mother, **Margaret Leahy**, care of Mr. Walsh, Office of the Commmissioners of Emigration, New York.

November 6, 1852

Of a girl named **Coghlan**, who left Liverpool for New York, in the ship *New York*, on or about the 3rd of August last. Address Dillion & O'Gorman, Attorneys &C, 39 William Street.

November 13, 1852

Of **William Reid**, who left New York on the 25th of April last, for RONDOUT, ULSTER County, N.Y., to seek employment. When he left he was 17 years old. Any information of his present whereabouts will be thankfully received by his uncle, **John Slattery**, at **Mr. O' Dea's**, 57 CHERRY ST., NEW YORK.

Of **Michael Murray**, of CLARA, KING'S County, Ireland and who resided at WOODLAWN. BLOOMINGDALE, N.Y., seven years since. His friends in Mo[ ]te are desirous of hearing from him. Direct the answer to this office.

November 27, 1852

Of **Laurence Byrne**, from Barrack Street CARLOW, Ireland, who came to this country about two years ago. When last heard from was in LOUISVILLE, KY. Any information of him will be thankfully received by his sister and brother (**Eliza** and **Denis Byrne**) care of **Mrs. Holohan**, 115 SHERIFF STREET, NEW YORK.

December 11, 1852

Of **John Minehan**, from LISMORE, Co. WATERFORD, Ireland. Something to his advantage, concerning his father, can be learned by calling at this Office.

December 25, 1852

Of **Denis Ryan**, from LIMERICK, Ireland. When last heard from, in October, 1848, he was living in NEW ORLEANS, LA., where he worked at his trade as a rigger. His sister **Catherine**, is anxious to hear from him as it has been reported that he was dead. Any information directed to her at 28 TRINITY PLACE, N.Y., or to this office, will be thankfully received. New Orleans papers please copy.

January 8, 1853

Of **Edward Raleigh**, plasterer, late of the City of LIMERICK, Ireland, who came to this country about nine months ago. Any information of him will be thankfully received by his wife **Bridget Raleigh**, and four sons at Mr. **Thomas Flynn's**, 319 FIRST AVENUE, NEW YORK. Cincinnati papers please copy.

Of **Andrew Byrnes** from DUBLIN, Ireland, who came to this country last September two years in the *John Henry*. When last heard from June, 1852, he was in PLANVEIN, MACOUPIN Co., ILL. Any information respecting him will be thankfully received by his wife **Margaret Byrnes**, care of **Peter Maher**, 167 ½ WASHINGTON ST., N.Y. Chicago papers please copy.

January 15, 1853

Of **Michael** and **Bridget** and **Ann Considine**, natives of the County TIPPERARY, Ireland who came to this country about two years ago. When last heard from they were at **Mrs. Bethen's** boarding house in NEWBURYPORT, MASSACHUSETTS. Direct to **Patrick Herbert**, 90 CROSBY STREET, N.Y. Boston papers please copy.

January 22, 1853

Of **James O'Brien**, who left the Parish of DROMING, County TIPPERARY, Ireland, in the month of April, about eight years since. When last heard of he was living in BOSTON, MASS. Any intelligence of him will be thankfully received by his sister, **Mary O'Brien**, 289 FRONT STREET, NEW YORK. Boston papers please copy.

Of **James Baker**, a native of the Parish of MOUGHAROUGH, County SLIGO, Ireland, who emigrated to America sometime ago. Should this meet his eye, or any person who knows him, they would oblige his sister, **Margaret Baker**, by addressing a letter to OYSTER BAY, QUEENS County, NEW YORK for **John Coughlen**.

January 29, 1853

Of **John Dunleavy**, who arrived in New York per ship *Albion* from Galway, in Sept last. Also of **Mary Farrelly**, arrived Per *Middlesex*, in December, native of CLONICKMARA, County CAVAN, Ireland. Also of **Edward B. Roughan**, arrived per *A Z*.in November, 1852. Apply to Gregory Dillon President Irish Emigration Society, 5 Chamber St., New York.

February 12, 1853

Of **Peter Hogan**, from BELMULLET, Co. MAYO, Ireland, who came to this country about 2 years and a half ago. He is supposed to be somewhere in OHIO. Any information respecting him will be thankfully received by **Miss Kerrigan** No. 5 Oxford St. BROOKLYN, N.Y.

February 26, 1853

Of **Thomas Collins**, from the Parish of KILKEELEY, Co. LIMERICK, Ireland, who came to this country last October twelve months, in the *Great Western*. Any information of him will be thankfully received by **William Murphy**, 24 ROSEVELT ST. [Roosevelt Street], NEW YORK, for his father, **Thos. Collins**.

Of **Hannah Connelly**, from DANGAN Co. GALWAY, Ireland who came to this country about five years ago. When last heard from was in this City. Any information of her whereabouts will be thankfully received by her cousin, **Hannah Healy**, of LISAVANNA, DANGAN, Co. GALWAY, Ireland. Direct to the Care of **Mrs. Hannan**, 231 ELEVENTH ST. near Tompkins' Square, NY, or to the office of this paper.

Of **John Carroll**, a native of the Parish of BURRIS County TIPPERARY, Ireland, who landed in November 1852. When heard of last was in New York, on his way to ALBANY. Any information respecting him will thankfully received by **Thomas Nugent**, No. 102 CHERRY ST., NEW YORK.

Of **Mary Conway**, from the Parish of BALLYCROY, County MAYO, Ireland, who left home three months ago for the purpose of coming to America, and has not been since heard from. Any information respecting her, directed to **Mr. P. Kerrigan**, 504 WASHINGTON STREET, or to the office of this paper, will be thankfully received.

March 5, 1853

Of **Thomas Murray**, a native of KILMACTHOMAS, County WATERFORD, Ireland, who arrived in this country about 4 years ago: he left his brother in BROOKLYN, NY, about 3 years, and went to NEW ORLEANS; he is now suppose to be in ST LOUIS, MO., working in a paint shop. Any information will be thankfully received by his brother **Patrick Murray**, No 152 York Street, BROOKLYN. If **Mr. Edward Mulligan**, of ST. LOUIS, will enquire for him he will much oblige. St Louis papers copy

Of **Mary Kelly**, by her brother **Matthew Kelly**. Said Mary Kelly is a native of DUNANEY, County KILDARE Ireland. When last heard from she was in CINCINNATI, OHIO. Any information from her will be thankfully received by addressing **P. Master**, MANHATTANVILLE, N Y

March 12, 1853

Of **James M'Loughlin**, from BRAY, County DUBLIN, Ireland, who came to this country in April 1850. He was in EAGLE RIVER, MICH., working in the Lake Superior Copper Mines, in November of that year, since when he has not been heard from. Any intelligence of him will be thankfully received by his father, **Thomas M'Loughlin**, care of **John Macky** 115, 20th STREET between 6th and 7th Avenues, NEW YORK

March 19, 1853

Of **Michael M'Dermott**, from ROSCOMMON County, Parish of KILLGLASH, Ireland. When last heard from he was in ALBANY, NEW YORK. Any information of his whereabouts will be thankfully received by his father, **Thomas M'Dermott**, No 297 FIRST AVENUE, corner of Eighteen Street, NEW YORK

Of **Bernard Reilly**, and his Uncle, **Hugh Reilly**, from the Parish of DRUMLANE, Co. CAVAN, Ireland, who came to this country, about three years ago. When last in this City, about two years ago, he was about to go to PENNSYLVANIA, when he has not been heard from. Any intelligence respecting him will be thankfully received by his sisters **Margaret** and **Mary**, 236 FOURTH AVENUE, NEW YORK. Pennsylvania papers please copy three years ago.

March 26, 1853

Of **Margaret M'Govern**, from the Parish of KELDANNAN, Co. CAVAN, Ireland, who called at the Office of the Commissioners of Emigration, on the 10th of this month. If this should reach her notice she will hear from her husband by calling on Mr. Irwin at the office of the commissioners in Canal St. Where a sum of $5 has been left for her use.

April 9, 1853

Of **Richard**, **Patrick**, and **Mary Mullally**, from KILCOCK, Co KILDARE, Ireland. When last heard from (about five months ago), Richard and Patrick were in CLEVELAND, and Mary in CINCINNATI, OHIO. Any intelligence of them will be thankfully received by their sister, **Catherine Hynes**, care of **Daniel Hynes**, 11 MARION STREET, NEW YORK.

Of **Charles O'Donnell**, aged 19, from the Parish of URNEY, County DONEGAL, Ireland, who arrived in this country in May 1852, and left for NEW ORLEANS on the 29th of September last. His brother, **George O'Donnell**, having heard that a person answering his description has died lately at a place called BOY'S BRIDGE, is anxious to hear any intelligence of him, for which he will be thankful. Direct to No. 1 FERRY STREET, NEW YORK. New Orleans papers please copy.

Of **Daniel Hartneady**, of BALLYCOGRAN, Parish of KILLALOE, County CLARE, Ireland. Any information of him will be thankfully received by **Patrick Molony**, 345 GREENWICH STREET, NEW YORK. New Orleans papers please copy.

Of **James McGlinn**, a native of MONASTEREVAN, County KILDARE, will hear something to his advantage by leaving his address at 10 VANDEWATER STREET.

Of **Charles McDonnell**, a native of LISNAGARRAN, Co ANTRIM, Ireland. He was discharged by expiration of service, from Company I, 1st Regiment U.S. Infantry, at FORT COLUMBIA, N.Y., on the 19th of August, 1848, since which time nothing has been heard of him. Any information concerning him will be thankfully received by **Gregory Dillon**, office Irish Emigrant Society, 51 Chambers Street, New York

April 16, 1853

Of **Patrick Halloran**, of BALLINRUAN, near CRUSHEEN, Co.CLARE, Ireland; when last heard from was in BRIDGEPORT, CONNECTICUT, but supposed to be at present living in BROOKLYN CITY or vicinity. Any information respecting him will be thankfully received by his brother **Michael**, who is at present in the village of DUNKIRK, CHAUTAUQUA Co., N.Y.

Of **John Deignan**, of the Parish of DUNBOYNE in the County of MEATH, married to **Mary Ann King**, and who went to America, in the year 1847; was afterwards with the United States Army, in MEXICO, in February 1848, and was last heard of in 1848, in the City of BOSTON, will hear of something to his advantage by communication with the subscribers. If dead any one who will furnish proof of his death, will be rewarded for their trouble. He is fair-haired, pale complexion, tall, and slight. He as then aged about 25 years, and would now, if alive, be 40 years old. **George McBride, Jr.**, and Co. 14 BROADWAY, NEW YORK.

Of **Natey Comey**, from the Parish of KILLINCAHIR, GRANNAFARNA Townland. County CAVAN, Ireland; or of his sister-in-law, **Catherine McCabe**. When last heard from they were living in NEW YORK. Any information regarding them will be thankfully received by **Anne McCabe**, who arrived here about six weeks since. Care of **James Tierney**, 52 CHERRY STREET, NEW YORK.

Of **Mary** and **Eliza Barnacke**, of GALWAY, Ireland, supposed to be at present in BOSTON. Their mother, at present in NEW YORK, will feel grateful to any person who may let her know their present address, by writing to her in care of **William Quinn**, 28 SPRUCE STREET, N Y.

April 23, 1853

Of **James Brady**, of the Parish of KILLOW County LONGFORD, Ireland, who came to New York by way of QUEBEC, between five and six years ago. In the latter place his wife (**Mary Duffy**) was taken sick and left in hospital, through which means they are lost to each other. Any information of him will be thankfully received by his wife, who is at present in NEW YORK, care of **Thomas McGuire**, 12 BROAD STREET, NEW YORK, or Cole Street, JERSEY CITY. Boston and New Orleans papers please copy

Of **Peter Brown** from the County ROSCOMMON, Ireland. When last heard from, about 6 years ago, he was in PENNSYLVANIA. Also of his brothers **Patrick** and **Michael**, who arrived in last April. Any information of them will be thankfully received by their sister, **Ellen Brown**, care of **Richard M'Govern**, 91 25th STREET, between 6th and 7th Avenues NEW YORK. Pennsylvania papers please copy.

April 30, 1853

Of **Catharine Eagan**, from the Parish of CLONRUSH, Co. GALWAY, Ireland, who came in this City on the 11th of April from the ship *Manhattan*. She called at the office of the Commissioners of Emigration on the 12 of April, and has not been heard from since. She is supposed to be in service somewhere in this city o[r] vicinity. Any information of her will be thankfully received by her sister **Mary Redington**, care of **Wm. W. Murray**, MIDDLETOWN, MONMOUTH Co, NJ. If she should see this advertisement, her sister wishes her to write at once.

Of **Terence Sullivan**, or of his brothers **Timothy**, **Daniel** and **Dennis**, who left CANNOWEE, Co. CORK, Ireland, ten years ago. When last heard from were in PENNSYLVANIA. Any information respecting them will be thankfully received by **Mrs. Honora Sullivan**, wife of **Terence**, at **Mr. Costello's**, No 7 Water Street, BROOKLYN. Pennsylvania papers please copy.

May 14, 1853

Of **Thomas Shannon**, grandson of **Tobias Burke**, of LISDEEN, Co. CLARE, Ireland, who arrived at Quebec, in the ship *Limerick*, about four years ago. When last heard of was in TROY, N.Y., or BURLINGTON, VT. Any information of him will be thankfully received by his mother **Bridget Burke Shannon**, No. 19 Columbia Street, Tenth BROOKLYN, N.Y. or by **James O'Loghlen**, of the same place.

Of **Bridget Molony**; from the Parish of TULLA, Co. CLARE Ireland, who arrived in this country about the middle of December, She lived it is supposed, for some time after her arrival at **Mrs. Wolf's**, 81 MOTT STREET, in this City, who moved away from there, and thus all trace of her has been lost. Any intelligence of her will be thankfully received by a friend of hers care of P. & J. Hogan, No. 12 West Street, New York.

May 21, 1853

If **Mathew Butler Baker**, and **Patrick O'Keefe**, both of the City of CORK, Ireland and residing about 25 years in this city, sons of **Mary Healy** (that being her maiden name) will apply at 64 PRINCE STREET, they will hear of something to their satisfaction.

If **Cornelius Foley**, son of **John Foley** deceased, farmer, of GLASHEN, near the City of CORK, and about 20 years in this city, supposed to be a stoker or engineer on board a steamer plying between NEW YORK and NEW ORLEANS, will apply at 64 PRINCE STREET, he will hear something to his satisfaction

Of the **Widow Heslan**, her maiden name was **Jane Connaughton**, supposed to be in NEW YORK. Any information concerning her will be thankfully received by her brother **James Connaughton**, corner of Gabriel and George Streets, MONTREAL, CANADA.

Of **Patrick**, **Edmund**, **Daniel**, and **Terence Carmody**, sons of the late **Terence Carmody**, of ASHFORTH, Co. LIMERICK, Ireland. When last heard from, in 1851, Patrick, Daniel, and Terrene were stopping at **John McGown's**, No. 3 McClusky's Court, 6th

Street, between Lombard and South Sts., PHILADELPHIA – should any of them see this advertisement, they are requested to write immediately, or any person knowing anything about them will confer a great favor by writing to their mother, **Mrs. Bridget Carmody**, care of **William Dundon**, BARNAKYLE, PATRICK'SWELL, Co. LIMERICK, Ireland. Pennsylvania papers please copy.

Of **Matthew Keough**, who emigrated from the City of LIMERICK, about 3 years ago. Left in or about the month of November – His daughter, **Mary Keogh**, wishes to hear from him, should this meet his eye or any person, acquainted with his whereabouts- a letter, will be thankfully received by **Thomas Taylor**, 255 GREENWICH STREET, NEW YORK.

Of **Mary Ryan**, otherwise **King**, wife of **John Ryan**, resident of WAKEHILL, YORKSHIRE, ENGLAND. Her husband came to this country last August, and has written several letters to her since then (one containing money), but has received no answer. He is anxious to hear from her and would feel obligated by any person who may know anything about her, directing such intelligence to the office of the Irish American, 47 Ann St., New York. Manchester Guardian and Examiner please copy.

Of **Margaret** or **Peggy Carmody** otherwise **Malone**, from GLANDREE, Co. CLARE, Ireland, or of her husband **Michael Carmody** of MANUS, in the same County, When last heard from about 2 years ago, they were in or near LOUISVILLE, KENTUCKY. Any intelligence of them, directed to the office of this paper, will be thankfully received by **Mary Russell**, mother of the former, who is anxious to hear about them.

May 28, 1853

Of **Michael Kinnealy**, from the County LIMERICK Ireland, and lately from LIVERPOOL, ENGLAND, who came to this country in November, 1851, in the ship *Sydney*, When last heard from last August, he was working in a quarry at SLOATSBURG, ROCKLAND Co., N.Y. Any intelligence of him will be thankfully received by his friend **James Taohy**, or **Thomas Fitzgibbon**, 37 State St., BROOKLYN, N.Y.

Of **John Gilchrist**, a native of the Parish of KILLOUGTURK, and County of LEITRIM, who left Ireland in the year 1846: the last account received from him he was in the employ of **Mr. Andrew Bigam**, Railroad Contractor, SARATOGA, State of NEW YORK. Any information of him will be thankfully received, by addressing English neighborhood post-office, BERGEN County, BULL'S FERRY, NEW JERSEY, to his brother **James Gilchrist**.

June 11, 1853

Of **John Coghlan**, boot and shoemaker, from KILKEE, Co. CLARE, Ireland. He is residing somewhere in this city. Any information of his residence, directed to **John Cullen**, 40 WHITEHALL STREET, will be thankfully received by **Ellen Moore**, from the same place.

June 18, 1853

Of **Jeremiah Driscoll**, Painter, who left NORWALK, CONNECTICUT March 28th, '53. When last heard from in April, he was in BUFFALO. Any information of him will be thankfully received by his wife, **Mary Anne Driscoll**, NORWALK, FAIRFIELD Co, CONNECTICUT.

Of **Patrick Flynn**, by his wife, **Bridget Flynn**, native of ATHENRY, Co. GALWAY, Ireland, landed about six weeks. Address **Joel Elsas**. No. 12, ORANGE STREET

June 25, 1853

Of **Mrs. Maria Fisher**, native of TUAM, Co. GALWAY, Ireland, when last heard of was in PHILADELPHIA. Any information respecting her will be thankfully received by her daughter **Catherine**. Address **Joseph Wilmot**, Shoemaker, 205 EIGHTH STREET. Philadelphia papers please copy.

July 2, 1853

Of **Andrew Mulligan**, once of COBBS, Parish of CLOON, County of LEITRIM, Ireland, who arrived in New York about 13 or 14 years ago; when last heard of was living between the 2nd and 3rd Avenues, New York. He is supposed to be living in NEW YORK or its vicinity. Also his brother **Michael Mulligan**, who arrived in New York from Liverpool. He is supposed to be still living in the City of NEW YORK or its vicinity. Also **James Mulligan**, and **John Mulligan**, who deserted from the British army, on the 27th of April, 1852, and came to the United States; he is supposed to be with his brothers in the City of NEW YORK or its vicinity. Those four men are sons of **James Mulligan**, and **Judith Colrevy**, GOBBS, Parish of CLOON, County LEITRIM, Ireland. Any intelligence of them will be thankfully received by their brother **Patrick Mulligan**, who arrived in New York in the ship *Shannon*, on the 9th of March last. He and his comrade, **William Reilly**, late of ST. HELENS, ENGLAND, are working on a railroad in VIRGINIA. If any of those men should see this advertisement, please to write immediately to CLARKSVILLE Post-Office, MECKLENBURG County, VIRGINIA.

Of **Patrick O'Toole**, of BROWNSTOWN, Parish of SUNCRAFT, County KILDARE, Ireland, six years since last heard from, was at that time on a railroad in SULLIVAN County, NEW YORK. – Any information of him will be thankfully received by his brother, **Maurice O'Toole**, who landed here in April last. Direct by letter to **John Conway**, KINGSTON, ULSTER County, N.Y.

July 16, 1853

Of **Edward Fitzgerald**, aged sixteen, son of **John Fitzgerald**, of TAUNTON, MASS. Who left his home on the 14th of June, in company with two other boys, and came on to NEW YORK. Any intelligence of him will be thankfully received by his afflicted parents at Davenport & Mason's office, 74 Broadway. His father has paid his passage back, and if he will return all will be forgiven. His mother has been unwell since his departure.

Of **David O'Connell**, a native of the Parish of ABINGTON, County LIMERICK, Ireland, who landed in this country about 30 years ago. When last heard from he was in SOUTH BOSTON, MASS. Direct to **J. O'Connell**, MIANUS, FAIRFIELD Co, CONN., or to the office of this paper. Boston papers please copy.

Of **Michael Mitchell**, from BALLYFORAN, Ireland, who arrived in this country last May and stopped at **Richard Murray's**, CEDAR ST. He is supposed to be working on the Pennsylvania Railroad. Any intelligence of him will be thankfully received by his cousins **Hugh** and **Michael Mitchell**, corner of 28th STREET and 2nd AVENUE.

Of **Anne McMahon**, who lived or formerly in the Parish of AUGHNAMULLIN, County MONAGHAN, Ireland, who landed here about the latter part of December last. Her aunt, **Alice McSally** would be thankful for any intelligence of her. Direct to 117 20th STREET, NEW YORK, care of **Michael McEntire**.

Of **John** and **Catherine Hallinan**, natives of PETER'S WELL, Parish of KILTHOMAS, County GALWAY, Ireland, who landed in New York in May last. Any information of them will be thankfully received by their sister, **Sebina Hallinan**, 181 MADISON ST., NEW YORK

If **Jas. Welsh**, from CASTLEBLANEY, County MONAGHAN, Ireland, who arrived in the *J Z.* from Liverpool, will call at 94 MAIDEN LANE, he will hear of his father.

July 23, 1853

Of **Mary McCarthy**, from LEITER, near CLONAKILTY, County CORK, Ireland, who came to this country about two years ago; when last heard from, about two months since, she was living in CHARLESTOWN, MASS,. where she used to visit at **James Sweeney's**. Any intelligence of her will be thankfully received by her sister, **Margaret**, care of **Cornelius Collins**, 64 GOVERNEUR ST [Gouverneur Street]., corner of Cherry St., N.Y.

July 30, 1853

Of **Edward Clancy**, lately come out from Ireland, who will hear of something immensely to his advantage, and receive something, by applying to **Edward Robinson**. 35 CEDAR STREET.

Of **William Donlon**, from CELBRIDGE, County KILDARE, Ireland, who arrived in this country about eighteen months ago. When last heard from he was in RUTH, MONTGOMERY NEW YORK. Also his brother **Joseph Donlan**, who arrived her last November. He is supposed to [b]e in NEW YORK or its vicinity. Any information of them will be thankfully received by their brother, **John Donlan**, at 161 LEONARD STREET, NEW YORK. He has been in this country for the last four months.

Of **Michael Keary** or **Cary**, of CLONCOLEMAN, CLARE, Ireland, by his wife **Bridget**, who landed six weeks since. Michael arrived in New Orleans about 4 years and a half since. When last heard from (February 6th, 1853) he was in CIRCLEVILLE, OHIO. Any information respecting him will be thankfully received by **Michael Clancey**, 483 WASHINGTON STREET, N.Y.

Of **Michael Halloran**, from BALLIRUAN, County CLARE, Ireland, who advertised in this paper for his brother **Patrick** in April last; he was then in CHAUTAUQUA County, N.Y. His brother resides in HYDE PARK, DUTCHESS County, where a letter will find him.

Of **James Dunne**, from the Townland of GLABE, Parish of REARY, QUEEN'S County, Ireland. When last heard from he was in DETROIT, MICHIGAN, in 1850. Any information of him will be thankfully received by his brother **Denis Dunne**, No. 287 17th STREET, between 9th and 10th Aves., NEW YORK. Michigan papers please copy.

August 6, 1853

Of **Patrick Foley**, aged 14 years, who arrived here in the ship *Balmoral* from Liverpool, July 17th, and strayed away on the 20th of the same month. Any information respecting him will be thankfully received by **Mrs. McCarty** No. 34 ROSEVELT STREET [Roosevelt Street], N.Y.

If **James** and **Micheal** [sic] **Kelly** two brothers, one aged about 18 years, the other about 20 years – who arrived here in the ship *John & Lucy*, 25h of May, 1853, will call at 95 and 97 FRONT STREET and enquire for **Asa S. Porter**, they will get information of their father and sister.

August 13, 1853

Of **Patrick Connors**, from CASTLETOWN-CONYERS, Co. LIMERICK, Ireland, who landed in this country with his wife about four years ago, and has lived in RED HOOK POINT, BROOKLYN, since. He left home on Sunday, July 10th, for the purpose of going to a funeral, since when his wife has not heard of him. Any information of him, directed to **Ellen Connors**, care of **William Collins**, No. 7 CONOVER STREET, will be thankfully received.

Of **Jeremiah Healy**, from the Parish of DURUS, Co. CORK, Ireland, who arrived in this country six years ago. When last heard from about five years ago, he was living at COXSACKIE, in this State. Any information will be thankfully received by his **Honora Daly**, care of **Mr. John Radley**, WESTFIELD, ESSEX County, NEW JERSEY. She has been in this country since the 26th of July.

August 20, 1853

Of **Mary Lynch**, who arrived July 20th, per *Bark Rosa*, from Limerick. Apply to Gregory Dillon, President of the Irish Emigrant Society, 51 Chambers Street.

August 27, 1853

Of **Christopher Flanigan**, from the MOUNTAIN Parish, County WESTMEATH, Ireland. When last heard from was in AUBURN ALABAMA. Any information will be thankfully received by his father, **Nicholas Flanigan**, at 147 EAST 11th STREET, NEW YORK, care of **Thomas McCormick**. Alabama papers please copy.

Of **Mary Cowan**, from the Parish of DRUMINAGHER, Co. ARMAGH, Ireland, who arrived here in the *Centurion*, last June. Any information respecting her will be thankfully received by her husband, **George Cowan**, care of **John Bermingham**, 61 WASHINGTON STREET, N.Y.

Of **Mary Nally**, from the Parish of CROSSBOYNE, County MAYO, Ireland, who arrived in this City on the 9th of August. Her cousin, **John Hennelly**, has deposited a sum of money for her with Mr. Irwin, at the Office of the Commissioners of Emigration, where she will hear from her friends by applying immediately.

Of **Mary Kearney**, from KELLS, County MEATH, Ireland, who landed in this City on the 11th of August, from the ship *New World*. She stopped till the following Monday at **Mrs. Murray's** No. 33 WASHINGTON STREET, since when she has not been heard of. Any person knowing anything of her will confer a great favor by sending such intelligence to her sister, **Bridget**, care of **P. W. Van Este**, BOUND BROOK, NJ

September 17, 1853

Mr. Patrick Byrne of **James Brown**, Tailors are requested to call for a letter, at the General Post Office, CINCINNATI, or send their address forthwith to **Patrick Brown**. 48 FORSYTH STREET, NEW YORK, and they will hear of something to their advantage. Cincinnati papers please copy.

Mary Madden, from County TIPPERARY, who came out in the ship *Colonel Cutt*, from Liverpool, wishes to find her daughter, **Eliza Madden**, being in great desolation and trouble. Please direct to **Andrew Brosnahan**, No. 281 WATER STREET, or to the Commissioners of Emigration, 25 & 27 Canal Street.

September 24, 1853

Of **Margaret Flaherty**, thirteen years of age, from the County GALWAY, Ireland. She arrived in August last in the ship *Andrew Foster*, from Liverpool. Any knowledge of her will be thankfully received by Mr. Walsh, Chief Clerk at the Office of the Commissioners of Emigration.

October 1, 1853

Of **Michael O'Keeffe**, Cabinetmaker or carver, native of CORK, Ireland, who left his wife and children in BALTIMORE, in May, 1853. He had $10 with him. He was seen two or three weeks after he left his home, in the streets of Baltimore. His wife fears he has met with some accident, as she can get no account of him. If this should meet his eye she requests him to do something for his children, as she has no means to support them, or to write to his brother-in-law, **Patrick Sullivan**, CORK, Ireland. [London, Ireland, Texas, New Mexico, California, and Australia papers please copy] **Kate O'Keeffe**, No. 58 Sharp St., BALTIMORE, MD.

Of **Patrick Walsh**, supposed to be from OLD COURT, CORK, Ireland. His wife died on board the ship *Niagara*, leaving 2 children who are now on WARD'S ISLAND. The wife's name is believed to have been **Margaret Walsh** or **Cronin** – Any knowledge of him will be thankfully received at the Office of the Commissioners of Emigration, by M. Walsh, Chief Clerk.

Of **Patrick Fields**, from the Parish of DEZENRATH, Co. MEATH, Ireland, who came to this country in April last. Any information of him will be thankfully received by his wife, **Margaret** and 3 children at **John O'Leary's**, 152 LEONARD STREET, N.Y., who landed here a week since.

Of **Francis Bohen**, by his brother **John**, of the Co. LEITRIM, Parish Town of MOHILL, Ireland; if this should meet his eye, he will hear of is brother, by directing a line to No. 118 WASHINGTON ST., NEW YORK, care of **Patrick Molony**. Had seen him last at SHEFFIELD, ENGLAND.

Of **Bridget** and **Nancy Cooney**, from the Parish of FEAKLE, Co. CLARE, Ireland, who arrived in Quebec, on the 26th of June last, from the ship *Huron*. Any information of them will be thankfully received by their sister **Mary Cooney**, 310 Atlantic S., BROOKLYN, N.Y.

Of **William Tyrrel**, from CLONMEL, Co. TIPPERARY, Ireland. House-painter, by his brother **Thomas**, at **Thomas Bergin's**, 28 ROSEVELT ST. [Roosevelt Street], NEW YORK. He is supposed to be in NEW ORLEANS. New Orleans papers please copy.

October 8, 1853

Of **Catherine** (now **Mrs. Meany**) **Mary** and **Sarah Connelly**, of KINLAUGH, County LEITRIM, Catherine came to this country some 7 years ago; Mary about 4 years ago; and Sarah some 9 months ago. Any information of their present whereabouts will be thankfully received by their sister **Ellen Connelly**, at **Mr. Jeremiah Horrigan's**, SOUTH DANVERS, MASS. Sarah Connelly, was living at No. 8 SULLIVAN ST., NEW YORK, when last heard from.

Of **William Cusack Crowe**, from LIMERICK, Ireland, who left NEW YORK in November' 49 [f]or MOBILE, ALABAMA. He wrote to his sister last winter, directed to PEARL STREET to **Maurice O'Neill**, printer; he kept the letter and she heard he got letters and money for her – she was then dangerously ill – he was sailing then from MOBILE. Five years ago he was a clerk in a grocery store; he used to be in a pleasure boat of **Judge Cutbert's** down the bay five years ago; he now goes to sea. Information will be thankfully received by an only sister, at the Hat Store, 386 1-2 Grand Street, MOBILE. Savannah, New Orleans papers please copy.

Of **Thomas Buckley**, from the Parish of FRATKIN, near CARRIGALINE, County CORK, Ireland, who arrived in New York in April, 1851, and was in RICHMOND, VA., in June, '53, and came north in search of his brother. His wife and six children arrived in the *Secret*, from Newport, five weeks ago; they are now on WARD'S ISLAND. The brother's name is **Daniel Buckley** and he is in America nine years. Please address to M. Walsh Chief Clerk, Office Commissioners of Emigration.

October 15, 1853

Of **Pat Lannan**, a Carpenter, by **Mr. Croson**, 77 WEST 19th STREET, between 6th and 7th Avenues.

Of **Norah Keleher**, (otherwise **Warren**) from the Parish of GLANFISK, County KERRY, Ireland, who came to America by way of QUEBEC, about three years ago. When last heard from, in April last, she was in CHICAGO, ILLINOIS. Any intelligence of her will be thankfully received by her son and daughter, **Ellen** and **Denis Warren**, who have arrived in this City. Direct to **Mrs. Batt**, 17 WALL ST., NEW YORK. Western Tablet please copy.

Of **Margaret Connelly**, daughter of **Patrick Connelly**, of the Parish of TEMPLEORUM, Townland of RAHENE, Co. of KILKENNY, who left home for the United States last September twelve months. Any information of her whereabouts will be thankfully received by her sister **Catherine O'Donnell**, NYACK, ROCKLAND Co., N.Y.

October 22, 1853

Of **Michael Sheehy**, from BALLINGARRY, Co. LIMERICK, Ireland, who came to this country in June, three years ago. When last heard of he was in YAZOO CITY, MISSISSIPPI. Any intelligence of him will be thankfully received by his wife (**Mary Sheehy**,) and child, who have arrived in New York. Direct to care of **John Sheehy**, 445 WASHINGTON STREET.

Mr. Albert Anderson, of KILKENNY, Ireland, who arrived in this City in July last, is requested to communicated with **Michael Phelan**, 21 LUDLOW STREET, NEW YORK. M.P. was out of town at the time he called and has but now heard of his arrival.

October 29, 1853

Of **Jane Connelly**, of TUAM, County of GALWAY, Ireland, who lived with **Mr. Shannon**, of BIRKENHEAD, ENGLAND, for a short time. She sailed, in the ship *Jamestown* for New York, where it is supposed she landed about the month of September 1849. Any information respecting her present place of residence will be thankfully received by **Michael J. Connelly**, WATERTOWN, JEFFERSON County, N.Y.

Denis Whelan, from LISMORE, Co. WATERFORD, who is at present in CALIFORNIA (supposed somewhere in the mines) is informed that the letter he sent to his parents in NEW YORK was not delivered, and they are very anxious for his return home, and to hear from him immediately, Direct to **Patrick Whelan**, 43rd STREET, NEW YORK, between 3rd and 4th Avenues.

Of **Margaret Cahill** a native of the County KILKENNY, who left Ireland in March 1851; and arrived in New York the following month. Any information of her will be thankfully received by her sister, **Ann**, at 63 DUANE STREET, NEW YORK.

Of **Patrick Kennedy**, a native of DUBLIN, Ireland, who came to this country about four years ago. He had lived in the County of GALWAY for some years in the capacity of coachman, with **Mr. Bernard Brown**, and others – the last situation he lived in was with **Captain Peyton**, in the County of LEITRIM. Any humane or honorable person, by sending any intelligence of his whereabouts or death, will greatly oblige his anxious son, Martin. Please address **Martin Kennedy**, 57 GREAT JONES' [GREAT JONES ST.], care of **Mr. Kavanagh**. Boston papers please copy.

November 5, 1853

Of **Ann Gleeson**, had a letter, from her in the beginning of the winter '52. She lived with a Boot and Shoe Maker in BANKSVILLE, CONNECTICUT Any person knowing her and seeing this advertisement, will please let her know that her Father **Mathew Gleeson** will be glad to hear from her and desires she would come to him as soon as possible as she will derive something to her advantage by doing so. Address Mathew Gleeson, CHATHAM, COLUMBIA CO. NEW YORK. Connecticut papers please copy.

November 12, 1853

Of **John Starr**, Mason, native of Ireland; when last heard from he was in the Daniel O'Connell Hotel, CINCINNATI, OHIO; any information will be thankfully received by his brother **Edward Starr**, at 171 EAST 16th STREET, N.Y.

Of **John Morgan**, who left Ireland about 15 years ago; when last heard from he was in LONG ISLAND; he is a native of the Parish of LUSK, County DUBLIN. Any intelligence of him will be thankfully received by **Thos. Urell**, 128 Market Street, NEWARK, N.J.

Of **Marg't. Griffen**, from the County of WATERFORD, Ireland, who arrived in this City August 17th, 1853, per ship *George Washington*, from Liverpool, address M. Walsh; Chief Clerk, Office Commissioners of Emigration.

Of **Ann Prior**, a native of BALLINAMORE, County LEITRIM, Ireland, who came in the packet ship *Australia*, which landed on Monday last, supposed to be in the city. If this should meet her eye, or any honorable person, she would do an act of Justice by communication personally, or by letter addressed to **Michael Carrigan**, No. 359 WEST 26th STREET, close to the 11th Avenue. Providence papers please copy.

November 19, 1853

Of **Mary Keane**, of KILMORE, Co. CLARE, Ireland, who sailed from Kilrush in a ship of **Mr. Blair's** and landed in Quebec about 2 years ago – when last heard from, she was in GREENBUSH, TROY, N.Y. Any intelligence will be thankfully received by **Honora Keane**, care of **P. Molony**, 345 GREENWICH STREET, NEW YORK (rear building.)

Of **Charles O'Donnell**, son of the late **Patrick O'Donnell**, of PHILADELPHIA. The last information received of him was in 1835. If this should meet his eye or the eye of **Mr. John Whitcraft**, of NEW LONDON, CROSS ROADS, they would confer a favor by directing a few lines to his brother **John O'Donnell**, corner of Marshal Street, & Hudson Avenue, BROOKLYN. NEW YORK, Philadelphia and Delaware papers please copy.

November 26, 1853

Of **Cornelius McCarthy**, of INNISKEAN, Parish of KINNEAGH, Co. CORK, Ireland.- When last heard from about 2 years ago, was living in BLOOMSBURY, NEW JERSEY. Any information concerning him will be thankfully received by his sister **Julia McCarthy**, care of **Timothy Donaovan**, Ferry Street, SPRINGFIELD, MASS.

Of **Mary Carroll**, from LAMBSTOWN, Co. WEXFORD, Ireland. Who left home about 2 years ago. When last heard from, about 12 months since, she was stopping at No. 11 PEARL ST., in this City. Any intelligence of her present where abouts will be thankfully received by **Patrick Carroll**, care of **J. F. Clew**, HYDE PARK, DUTCHESS County, N.Y.

Of **Mary Woods**, from CROSSMAGLEN, Co. ARMAGH, Ireland, who arrived here in the *Sarah G. Hyde*, 18 months ago. She is supposed to be living in this City, uptown. Any intelligence of her will be thankfully received by her brother **James Woods**, care of **James Conroy**, 114 MULBERRY STREET, N.Y.

December 17, 1853

Of **Thomas** and **Michael Slattery**, natives of the County TIPPERARY, Ireland. Thomas sailed from Limerick 5 years ago, and Michael two years last April, from Limerick, in the *Jane Slack*. When last heard of they were in LIMA, LIVINGSTON Co., NEW YORK. Any information of them will be thankfully received by their nephew, **John Powell**, No. 55 CROSBY STREET, NEW YORK.

Of **Jeremiah Hegarty**, Tailor, of MIDDLETOWN, Co. CORK, who left CORK, Ireland, about August, 1850. Any information concerning him will be very thankfully received by his last employer of the BRICKFIELDS, CORK, (Wm.F.) who now follows business in NORTH ORANGE, ESSEX Co., NEW JERSEY, who would wish to see him as soon as possible.

December 24, 1853

Of **Thomas Walsh**, a native of the County ARMAGH, Parish of LOWER CREEGAN, Ireland. When last heard of (five years ago) he was driving a carriage in NEW ORLEANS. Any information concerning him will be thankfully received by his brother **Patrick**, at the Novelty Iron Works, NEW YORK.

Of **Terence Priory**, from WHITE QUARRY, County MEATH, Ireland, who came to this country two years ago last May. He was seen about twelve months since in JERSEY CITY, and is supposed to be somewhere in LONG ISLAND at present. Any intelligence of him will be thankfully received by his brother **Michael**, TRENTON, NJ

Of **William Kerns** shoemaker, from LIMERICK, Ireland. Who went to QUEBEC about two years ago. When last heard from he was in MONTREAL, UPPER CANADA. Any intelligence of him will be thankfully received by his sister **Bridget Kerns**. Direct to the Office of this Paper.

Of **Thomas** and **Michael Neagle**, from CAPPEWHITE, County TIPPERARY, Ireland, who left NEW YORK on the 16th of last November, to work on the Central Railroad, ILLINOIS. Any intelligence of them will be thankfully received by their mother and brother (**Mary** and **Edward Neagle**), who landed on the 27th [?] Direct to the care of **William Ryan**, 43 BEEKMAN STREET, NEW YORK. Western Tablet please copy.

If this notice should meet the eye of **Martin Keenan**, (supposed to be in BOSTON) or any relative of **John Keenan**, of POMFRET, CT., (lately deceased,) they will hear something to their advantage by addressing a letter to **Charles Burton**, POMFRET, WINDHAM County, CT.

Of **Morty Lynch**, from REHA WEST, County CLARE, Ireland, who came to this country about two years since in company with his daughters, **Mary** and **Bridget**; when last heard from, in August last, he was stopping at **John Lynch's**, in G Street, WASHINGTON, D.C. Any intelligence of his present whereabouts will be thankfully received by his wife, **Honora**, and his son, who are in the City, Direct to the Commissioners of Emigration, Canal-street, New York.

Of **John Brown**, a native of HOSPITAL, County LIMERICK, Ireland, who came to this country three years since. Any information of him will be thankfully received by his brother-in law and sister, **Phillip** and **Ellen Maher**, residing at 75, MOTT STREET, NEW YORK.

January 14, 1854

Of **Mrs. White**, formerly resident of MOTT HAVEN, WESTCHESTER County, N.Y. Her husband died last summer. If this should meet the eye of **Mr. Michael Ryan**, who worked at MORRISANIA, and was a constant visitor at Mrs. White's, and also reader of the "Irish American", he will confer a favor by sending Mrs. White's present address to this Office.

Of **John Donovan**, of PALLASKENRY, County LIMERICK, Ireland, who sailed from Limerick, about 17 years ago, in the ship *Agnes* to America, When last heard from, about seven years ago was in the State of ILLINOIS, GRUNDY County, GREEDON Post Office. Any information of him will be thankfully received at the Irish American Office, 47 Ann Street, New York, or by **John Lynch**, 323 MONROE ST, NEW YORK, Illinois papers please copy.

Of **Michael Eagan**, from BALLYVANNAN, Parish of TOMGRAINY, County of CLARE, Ireland. When last heard from was in GENESSEE Co., N.Y. Any intelligence of him will be thankfully received by his sister **Julia**, and mother (late of Ireland). Address, 44 Union Street, BROOKLYN, N.Y.

Of **Charles Daly**, aged 15, who left his home, 69 JAMES STREET, N.Y., last May or June and has not been since heard of. Any intelligence of him will be thankfully received by his father, **Peter Daly**, 241 FIRST AVENUE, NEW YORK. Rondout papers please copy.

Of **Alice Quaid**, (otherwise **Renehan**,) from DOHERA, Parish of CROOME, County LIMERICK, Ireland, who left Ireland about three years since. She is supposed to be in this City or BROOKLYN. Any intelligence of her will be thankfully received by her daughter, **Catherine Quaid**, who has arrived in this City. Direct to the care of **Widow Hayes**, 73 DUANE STREET.

Of **Bridget Connor**, native of the Parish of ANNA, Co. CAVAN, who arrived in this country in May, 1847. When last heard of, about one year ago, she was in GREENWICH, CONN. Any information of her will be thankfully received by her father **Thos. Connor**, RANDOLPH, MA.

Of **William Gallagher**, native of BALLYFATTAN, Co. TYRONE, who shipped for this country about the first of August last. Information of him will be thankfully received by his brother **Michael Galleher**, NO. EASTON, MS.

Of **Michael Roe**, from Co. KILKENNY, Parish of WINAGAH; sailed from Liverpool in July, 1855. – When last heard from was in PHILADELPHIA. Any information will be thankfully received by his cousin **James Tobin**, TERRE HAUTE, INDIANA, to the care of **Michael Leahy**.

Of **Mary McGrath**, a native of Co. FERMANAGH, Parish of KINAULTY; who landed in New York in April, 1847; when last heard of in March, '51, was in WASHINGTON; he is now supposed to be in CHICAGO, ILL. Information respecting him will be thankfully received by his brother **Patrick McGrath**, 250 7th AVENUE, NEW YORK, or **Thomas McGrath**, 29 Fair Street, NEWARK, NEW JERSEY. [Appeared Jan. 21, 1854, with **Mary McGrath** changed to **John McGrath**.]

of **Patrick & Timothy Molin**, the former a saddler and Harness Maker, and the latter a laborer, who sailed from Cork about 7 years ago; their place of residence being CORROGANE, Parish of MITCHELSTOWN, County CORK. Direct to **John Moylan**, CENTON, BRADFORD Co., PA.

January 21, 1854

Of **William**, **Robert**, or **Alexander Moore**, who when last heard from, resided at STEEL CREEK, NORTH CAROLINA. By applying to the undersigned they may hear of something to their advantage. **Geo. M'Bride**, & Co., 14 BROADWAY, N.YORK.

Of **John McGuire**, from the Townland of ARTOGHER, Parish of KILLINEAGH, Co. CAVAN who landed in New York, June 1851. When last heard from (Nov 1, '53) was at work in LA SALLE, ILL. Information of him will be thankfully received by his wife, **Bridget McGuire**. Address **James Earley**, Glendon Rolling Mills, EAST BOSTON

January 28, 1854

Of **John M'Creath**, of BALLYPOREEN, Co. TIPPERARY, Ireland, who sailed from Liverpool about three years ago. When last heard from he was in EAST TROY, State of NEW YORK. Any information of his present whereabouts will be thankfully received by his sisters, **Margaret** and **Mary M'Creath**, No. 100 Fiftieth Street, CARMENSVILLE.

February 4, 1854

Of **Johanna Buckly**, from the Parish of DUBLIN, County CORK, Ireland, who arrived at New York per *American Congress*, Dec 13, 1853, with her children, namely, **John**, **William**, **Pat**, and **Maryanne**. She is supposed to be 10 miles outside the City. Her son Pat, who is in charge of the Commissioners of Emigration, WARD'S ISLAND, is anxious to hear from her; address, care of Mr. Walsh, Chief Clerk, office of the Commissioners of Emigration. Friends supposed to be in CHERRY STREET.

Of **Mrs. Fitzpatrick**, from KILRUSH, County CLARE, Ireland, who landed in New York, per *Antarctic*, Nov. 18, 1853, and supposed now to be in some part of PENNSYLVANIA. Her son, **John Fitzpatrick**, who is now in care of the Commissioners of Emigration, on WARD'S ISLAND, is anxious to hear of her whereabouts. Address, care of Mr. Walsh, Chief Clerk, Office of the Commissioners of Emigration.

Of **William** and **Edward Finn**, from the Parish of CASHEL, County TIPPERARY, Ireland, who came to this country seven years since. When last heard from they were in **Nashville, Tenn.**, Dec. 28, 1852. Any information of them will be thankfully received by their mother and sister **Elisabeth**. Address, **Mrs. Finn**, No. 10 FIFTH ST. (in the rear), NEW YORK.

Of **Florence Duggan**, Parish of NEWTOWN, Townland of BALLYHOWRA, County CORK, Ireland, who landed in New York, about eight years ago. Any information of him will be kindly received by his sister **Mary Duggan**, or his niece, **Mary Bevin**, at 35 THOMPSON STREET, NEW YORK.

Of **James Barry**, of KILBENNY, County OF LIMERICK, Ireland, aged 16 years; also of **Roger Kiely**, of KILBENNY, who sailed for Quebec about 17 years ago. When last heard from was in ILLINOIS. Any information of them will be thankfully received by his brother, **James Kiely**, No. 262 EAST THIRTEENTH STREET, NEW YORK. Charleston, South Carolina, papers please copy.

Of **John Hegarty**, a native of the County ROSCOMMON, Ireland. When last heard from he was in ALTONA. Any intelligence of him will be thankfully received by his wife, **Catherine Hegarty**, care of **Bernard Conniff**, 446 FOURTH STREET, NEW YORK.

February 11, 1854

Of **Mary Hart**, from the Parish of KILBARRY, County MEATH, Ireland, who arrived here on the 2nd of last December, and was hired on the 6th by **J. C. Carpenter**, of MIDDLETOWN, ORANGE County, N.Y. Any intelligence of her will be thankfully received by her brother, **Matthew Hart**, GREENPOINT, P.O., Long Island.

Of **Marcus Bush**. When last heard from was at SPRINGFIELD, CLARK County, OHIO. Also of **George Tate** and his wife, **Honora Magner**; last heard of at GRAND RAPIDS, KENT County, MICHIGAN; all from DONERAILE, Co. CORK, Ireland. Please address **Jeremiah Bush**, 136 ORANGE STREET, NEW YORK.

Of **John** and **James Quinn**, of CASHEL, County TIPPERARY, Ireland: when last heard of were in the State of NEW YORK. Any information of them will be thankfully received by their brother **Timothy F. Quinn**, late of CALIFORNIA. Address, by letter, to **William Quinn Perrymansville**, HARTFORD County, MARYLAND.

February 18, 1854

Of **Michael** and **Bartholomew Sullivan**, natives of TAHALLA, County KERRY, Ireland. When last heard from, one was in ST. LOUIS and the other within 300 miles of that City.

Any information will be thankfully received by their brother, **Cornelius Sullivan**, at No. 12 WASHINGTON STREET, NEW YORK.

February 24, 1854

Of **Ellen Vaughan**, daughter of the late **Edward Vaughan,** M.D., of INNISCARRA, County CORK, Ireland. If she has arrived in PHILADELPHIA, she will please to write to her sister, **Mrs. Walsh**, 329 First Street, WILLIAMSBURGH, L.I. Philadelphia papers please copy.

Of **James Burns**, a native of BALLINGLEN, County WICKLOW, Ireland. Left NEW YORK about two years ago. When last heard from, about 18 months since, he was in MADISON County, ALABAMA, and is now supposed to be working on the railroad Any information of him will be thankfully received by his sister, **Susan McKeon**, 128 EAST 22nd STREET, between 2nd and 3rd Avenues. Alabama papers please copy.

Of **John Furey**, of FRENCH PARK, ROSCOMMON County, Ireland. Arrived in this country about three years ago. When last heard from was in the City of NEW YORK, about six months ago. Any information of him will be thankfully received by his brother, **Thomas Furey**, 868 Hicks, corner o[f] State St., SOUTH BROOKLYN.

Of **Francis Kenny**, a native of BIRR, KING'S County, Ireland. When last heard from, was at NEW BRITAIN, CONN. Any information respecting him will be thankfully received by his sister, **Jane Kenny**, care of **John Donnelly**, corner of Pacific and Willard Streets, SOUTH BROOKLYN.

March 4, 1854

Of **Richard Barrett**, of MALLOW, Co. CORK, Ireland, When last heard of was in VIRGINIA. Any information of him will be thankfully received by his daughter, **Julia**, 376 MADISON STREET, who wishes to see him on particular business.

Of **Michael Treacy**, a native of the Town of TEMPLEMORE, Co. TIPPERARY, Ireland, a laborer, is in this country about 5 years. Any intelligence of him will be thankfully received by **John Connor** at **John Fitzgerald's** 61 JAMES STREET in the rear.

Of **John Moriarty**, of ACRES, BALLYBRACK, Parish of AGLISH, County KERRY, Ireland, who left home in February 1849, to go to his cousin, **Edmond Scott**. Any information of him will be kindly received by his daughter **Elizabeth Moriarty**, at STONINGTON, CONN. New Orleans papers please copy.

March 11, 1854

Of **Thomas** and **Patrick Burk**, of the Parish of FETHARD, County TIPPERARY. Thomas when last heard from, was in MONTREAL. Any information respecting the above will be thankfully received by their brother **Michael**. Address to **Thomas Neville**, 16 ROSEVELT STREET [Roosevelt Street], NEW YORK. Canada and Western papers please copy.

Of **Bartholomew Lynch,** Baker, son of **Patrick Lynch**, ARDLOW, Parish of MULLAGH, County CAVAN, Ireland. When last heard of about four years ago, was in SAN JOSE, UPPER CALIFORNIA. Any information of him will be most thankfully received by his mother, **Mrs. Lynch**, 484 GREENWICH STREET; or by his brothers, **John** and **Thomas Lynch**, provision dealers, 65 CLINTON MARKET, NEW YORK. California papers please copy.

March 18, 1854

Of **Thomas Mangan**, who left his home, WATERFORD SARATOGA County, NEW YORK, and has not since been heard from. He is 18 years of age, and was formerly from the County of LIMERICK, Parish of RATHKEALE, Ireland and is a cooper by trade. He went from home on the 7th of July last. Any information respecting him will be thankfully received by his father, **Wm. Mangan**.

March 28, 1854

Of **Daniel Foley**, who left PLATTSBURG, June 29, 1853, bound for MARQUETTE, LAKE SUPERIOR, MICHIGAN, and since then has not been heard of. Any information of him will be thankfully received by his father, **A. P. Foley**, CADYVILLE, CLINTON County, N.Y. "Citizen" please copy.

April 1, 1854

Of **Owen** and **Philip Smith**, from the Parish of KILLALA, County MEATH, Ireland. Any information of them will be thankfully received by their brother, **William Smith**, who has been in AUSTRALIA. Call or address to No. 18 READE ST., NEW YORK.

Of **Martin Cady**, who came to this country seven years since. When last heard of was near BOSTON Also of **Thomas Foland**, three years in this country, and **Stephen Sloan**, eight years in this country, all from County GALWAY, Ireland. Address **Julia Carr**, at **Mrs. Roe's**, MONROEVILLE, ORANGE Co., N.Y. : or M. Walsh, Office of Commissioners of Emigration, N.Y.

April 8, 1854

Of **David Donnelly**, from the Parish of RATHMOLYNE, County MEATH, Ireland, who came to this country five years ago. He is supposed to be somewhere in the State of NEW YORK. Any intelligence of him will be thankfully received by **Peter Connolly**, HARLEM, P.O., N.Y.

Of **Patrick Kinney**, of the Parish of BALLISADERY, County MAYO, Ireland, who left BOSTON for NEW YORK on the 17th of October last, to sail for Ireland, and has not been heard from since. Any information concerning him will be gladly received by his sister, **Mary Kinney**, EAST STOUGHTON, MASS.

Of **Michael Murray**, of TALLOW, County WATERFORD, Ireland. When last heard from he was living in WATERLOO, N.Y.; supposed now to be in the west part of NEW YORK or PENNSYLVANIA. Any information concerning him will be thankfully received by his brother, **Denis Murray**, NEWTON, CONN. Rochester papers please copy.

April 15, 1854

Of **William** and **Patrick Furlong**, of the Parish of KILLEDY, County LIMERICK, Ireland. William came to this country five years ago last Christmas; his brother Patrick sailed from Limerick two years ago last August. When last heard from they were in MILFORD DEPOT, CAROLINE County, VIRGINIA. Any intelligence of them will be thankfully received by their sister, **Betty Furlong** or their aunt, **Ellen Galvin**, at 136 29th STREET, between 2nd and 3rd Avenues, NEW YORK. Virginia papers please copy.

Of **Michael Delany**, from the Parish of URLINGFORD, County KILKENNY, Ireland, who sailed from Liverpool about 5 or 6 years ago. He is about 22 years of age. Should this meet his eye, or any person who knows of his whereabouts, they would confer a favor on his afflicted mother, **Mary Delany**, by dropping a line in the Post Office, to the care of **John Collins**, 107 Atlantic St., BROOKLYN.

Of **Thomas Quincannon**, laborer, of the County ROSCOMMON, Ireland, who landed in New York about three years ago. Any information respecting him will be thankfully received by **Patk. Tiernan**, care of **Michael Walsh**, No. 3 CATHERINE SLIP, NEW YORK.

Of **Michael** and **Patrick McKeon**, from the Parish of KILGEEVAR, County MAYO, Ireland, who came to this country about sixteen years ago. When last heard from they were in CHICAGO, ILL. Any intelligence of them will be thankfully received by their sister, **Honora McKeon**, 29 ORANGE STREET, NEW YORK.

Of **Johanna Keenan**, aged 20 years, who arrived in New York per ship *Anglo Saxon* from Liverpool, Jan, 9th, 1854. Her mother, who is in TORONTO, CANADA, is anxious to hear from her. Address M. Walsh Chief Clerk's Office, Commissioners of Emigration.

April 22, 1854

Of **Terence McEntee**; when last heard from, about three and a half years ago, he was taking care of **Mr. Jessy's** stables. Bull's Head, 24th STREET, N.Y. If this should meet the eyes of him, or of **James McEntee**, Who lives on the corner of Avenue C, in ELEVENTH STREET, or any other of his friends, they would confer a great favor on his friend, **John McEntee**, who resides in MOUNT SAVAGE, by writing him a letter and letting him know the whereabouts of said Terence McEntee. Direct, John McEntee, Carpenter, MOUNT SAVAGE, ALLEGANY County, MARYLAND.

April 29, 1854

Of **Anne Bryan**, from CARRIGFIN, Co. WESTMEATH, who came to this country seven or eight years ago. When last heard of she was in ROXBURY, MASS. Any intelligence of her will be thankfully received by her nephew **Edward Bryan**, care of **John Reilly**, 300 Hicks St., BROOKLYN, N.Y. Boston papers please copy.

Of **John Hanley**, from the City of LIMERICK, Ireland, who came to this country about three years ago. When last heard from he was working in a factory at SOUTH GLASTONBURY, CONN. Any intelligence of him will be thankfully received by his nephew, **James Ryan**, at Florence's Hotel, 400 BROADWAY,N.Y.

Of **Patrick** and **Judith Brady**, Parish of TULLYALLEN, County LOUTH, Ireland, who arrived in New York about two years ago. Supposed to be some place in the State of NEW YORK. Any information of them will be thankfully received by their son, **Bartholomew Brady**.

May 6, 1854

Of **Anthony Shortall**, or his sister **Catherine**, from BALLYLARKIN, Parish of FRESHFORD, Co. KILKENNY, Ireland. They are supposed to be in JERSEY CITY. Any person knowing anything of them will confer a favor by sending their address to **Bridget Dowling**, care of **Wm. Welsh**, No. 11 Stephen's Court, NEWARK, N.J.

May 13, 1854

Of **Thomas Moran**, or his sister **Eliza Moran**, from the Parish of JARMONBARRY, County ROSCOMMON, Ireland. Any information of them will be thankfully received by their cousin, **Thomas Hanly**, at 123 WEST 33rd STREET, or corner of 61st STREET and 9th AVENUE, NEW YORK, as there is a letter from their brother, **Edward Moran**, of the 55th Regiment, now stationed at GIBRALTAR.

Of **Jeremiah Linehan**, a native of MALLOW, Co. CORK, Ireland. He left NEW YORK CITY for VIRGINIA last January. Any information of him will be thankfully received by his wife, **Mary Linehan**, lately arrived with her children from LONDON. His brother from CALIFORNIA is also in the City. Address, **Mary Linehan**, 23 BATAVIA STREET, N.Y. Virginia papers please copy.

Of **Honora O'Neil**, of DERIMEHIN, near CASTLETOWN, BEREHAVEN, County CORK, Ireland, who landed in New York about the 24th of June, 1853, in ship *"Connecticut."* Information of her will be thankfully received by her sister, **Catharine O'Neil**, in care of **Dennis Sullivan**, No. 87 Bedford Street, FALL RIVER, MASS.

Of **Catharine** and **Edmond Murphy**, from GANAVANE, Parish of DOON, Co. LIMERICK, Ireland, who landed in Quebec five years ago. When last heard of, Catherine was in PLATTSBURG, VERMONT, and married to a man named **John Johnson**. Edmond left UPPER CANADA last June, to go to LEWISTON, near NIAGARA, N.Y. Any intelligence of them will be thankfully received by their father, **Daniel Murphy**, NEW DURHAM P.O., HUDSON County, N.J. Vermont and Buffalo papers please copy.

May 20, 1854

Of **Bridget** and **Margaret Conlan**, sisters to **William Conlan**, flagger, from the Town of SLIGO, Ireland. They landed in Quebec some six or seven years ago. Any intelligence of them will be thankfully received by their brother, **Wm. Conlan**, RONDOUT, ULSTER County, N.Y. Canada papers please copy.

If **Michael St. Clair**, House Painter, a native of CORK, Ireland, will send his address to **Michael Foley**, No. 23 FIRST AVENUE, NEW YORK, he may hear of a friend.

Of **Mary Steal**, a native of the County DOWN, Ireland. Sailed from Liverpool twelve months ago for this port. When last heard from she lived with **Patrick Rurke** in this city. If she calls at Cornelison & McKay's, No. 3 Division Street, New York, she will find her mother.

May 27, 1854

Ann Carney, of BALLINA, Co. MAYO, Ireland, who left 249 18th STREET, NEW YORK on the 27th of December last and has not been heard of since. Any information of her will be thankfully received by **John Boyle**, Prescott House, BROADWAY, NEW YORK.

June 3, 1854

Of **John Smyth**, Plasterer, and father, of the City of DUBLIN, Ireland. John landed in New Orleans about six years ago, and his father, John Smyth, landed in New York about five months afterwards. Their whereabouts will be thankfully received by **Timothy Quigley**, 18 READE STREET, N.Y., who shall inform them of something to their advantage.

Of **Patrick McElroy** and **Bridget Grogan**, from the Parish of CLOGHER, Co. TYRONE, who arrived in New York on the 18th May, in the ship *Jacob A. Westervelt*. Any intelligence of them will be thankfully received by **John McElroy**, or **John Grogan**, care of **Lawrence Farrell**, News Agent, PROVIDENCE, R.I.

Of **Michael Lyons**, Teacher, from CROOM, Co. LIMERICK, Ireland, who arrived in this country about twelve years ago. When last heard from (three years ago,) he was in NASHVVILLE, TENN. Any intelligence of him will be thankfully received by his brother, **John Lyons**, No. 7, HESTER ST., N.Y. Ohio and Tennessee papers please copy.

June 10, 1854

Of **Patrick Hayes**, boot-maker, his wife and three children, from LIMERICK, Ireland. When last heard from, in November, 1853, he was about to sail from Liverpool for New Orleans, La., in the ship *Warable Capt. Westcott*. Any intelligence of him will be thankfully received by his brothers, **Jeremiah** and **William Hayes**, No. 9 Rose Street, NEW HAVEN, CONN. New Orleans papers please copy.

Of **John Harris**, of COOKSTOWN, Co. TYRONE, Ireland, left there, for AUSTRALIA about 5 years ago. Any intelligence of him will be thankfully received by his brothers, **Patrick** and **James Harris**, care of **Mr. Gaw**, 8 AMITY STREET, NEW YORK. Melbourne Argus please copy.

If **Mr. Samuel Davis**, a native of DUBLIN, Ireland, now in America, and residing in KENTUCKY, when last heard of, will apply personally, or by letter, to **Mr. Patrick Lynch**, 195 EAST 7th STREET, NEW YORK, he will learn something eminently to his advantage.

June 17, 1854

Of **Bridget Keenan**, from BOYLE, Co ROSCOMMON, Ireland, who came to NEW ORLEANS about six years ago; or of her brother-in-law, **John Fineran**. They were to have left New Orleans on or about the 1st of May last, for ST. LOUIS or some place up the Mississippi. Any one knowing anything of them will confer a great favor by writing to **Anne Keenan** (mother of Bridget), who has arrived in New York with her daughter **Ellen**. Direct to the care of **James Byrnes**, 59 MULBERRY STREET, N.Y.

Of **Margaret O'Connor**, native of the Parish of LOUGHILL, County ANTRIM, Ireland. When last heard of by her brother **Hugh**, was living in NEW YORK, and married to a man supposed to be named **Simpson**. – Any information concerning her will be thankfully received by her brother. Address **Hugh O'Connor**, DIAMOND SPRINGS, EL DORADO Co., CALIFORNIA.

Of **Mrs. Honor Ward**, from the Co. SLIGO (three miles from the Town of SLIGO); is eighteen months in America, and supposed to be in some part of VIRGINIA. Her daughter, **Ellen Ward**, nine months in this country, is anxious to hear from her. Address, M. Walsh, Chief Clerk, office of Commissioners of Emigration, New York.

Of **John Hurley**, Shoemaker, from CARRICK-ON-SUIR, Co. TIPPERARY, Ireland, who came to this country about three years ago. Any intelligence of him will be thankfully received by his wife, **Eliza Hurley**, at 6 ½ RECTOR ST., NEW YORK.

Of **Margaret Jackson**, from the City of LIMERICK, Ireland, who sailed from Liverpool on the 2nd of May last, and landed here on Friday last in the ship called the *Isaac Webb*. Any information of her will be thankfully received by her cousin, **Ellen Riordan**, at 285 WEST 27th st., between the 9th and 10th Aves.

Of **Mrs. John Hyland**, (her maiden name is **Julia Cahill**), born at KILLWORTH, County CORK, Ireland, also of **Mrs. Phillip Carline**, her maiden name is **Mary Cahill**, born at the above place. Sailed from England in the ship *Mediator*, for New York, June 1853, by her sister **Margaret Birdseye**, 91 South Fourth Street, PHILADELPHIA. Cincinnati and New Orleans papers please copy.

June 24, 1854

Of **Matthew Connor**, his wife, and six children, from the Parish of CORRELSTOWN, County WESTMEATH, Ireland, who left home over three months ago to come to NEW YORK. If this should meet their eye, or anyone knowing their whereabouts, they would confer a favor by writing to **John Coyne**, 67 10th AVE, N.Y.

Of **Ellen McGrath**, aged 16 years – from the Town of CARLOW, Ireland, who came to this City about the middle of last September, with her mother and sister. She left the Boarding house, where they were stopping (137 WASHINGTON STREET) on the 22nd of September, to look for employment, and has not been since heard of. – Any information of her will be thankfully received by her mother, **Rosa McGrath**, care of the Post Master, WASHINGTON, N.J.

Of **Michael Coffey**, who had a brother, named **Patrick**, who lived with **John Barry**, in LYONS, N.Y., will learn something to his advantage by sending his address to **Michael Scanlan**, Blacksmith, SAVANNAH, GA. His brother died in the hospital of Savannah, and has left a letter for him in the hands of Mich'l Scanlan.

Of **James Rowane**, of NEWTONCORMICK Co. MAYO, Ireland. He left BROOKLYN two years and three months ago. When last heard of he was in NEW ORLEANS. Any information respecting him will be thankfully received by his mother, **Ellen Rowane**, 250 Columbia St., SOUTH BROOKLYN, N.Y. New Orleans papers please copy.

Of **John Mulholland**, from the Parish of BALLYMONEA, near BANDON, Co. CORK, Ireland. He was in MEMPHIS, TENN., last winter. Any intelligence of him will be thankfully received by his sister, **Catherine Mulholland**, care of **Mr. Cornelius Daly**, Memphis, Tenn.

July 1, 1854

Of **Timothy Sullivan**, native of County KERRY, Ireland, who landed in America, about five years ago, and is supposed to be in some part of MASSACHUSETTS. His sister **Johanna**, who landed here a few days ago, would be anxious to hear from him. Address care of Mr. Walsh, Office of Commissioners of Emigration.

Of **Daniel** and **Cornelius Cane**, natives of the Parish of CAHARAGH, County CORK, Ireland. Daniel landed in New York, twelve months ago, Cornelius three years ago. When last heard of they worked on a railroad in the State of PENNSYLVANIA. Any information respecting them will be thankfully received by their sister **Margaret**, lately landed, in care of **Michael O'Neill**, No. 40 ORANGE STREET, NEW YORK, (is the rear, second floor, room No. 3) Philadelphia papers please copy.

Of **Patrick Martin**, who left ARCHBALD, LUZERNE County, PA., on the 14th of April. He is supposed to be in the State of OHIO. Any information of him will be thankfully received by his father. Ohio papers please copy.

Of **James Dwyer**, Carpenter, from the Black Boy Pike, City of LIMERICK, Ireland. When last heard of he was in the State of OHIO. Any information of him will be thankfully received by **Michael Quin**, at No. 494 GREENWICH STREET, NEW YORK. Ohio and Montreal papers please copy.

July 8, 1854

Of **Michael Malone**, from GLANDREE Parish of FEAKLE, County CLARE, Ireland. He is supposed to have arrived in this City, from England, a few weeks ago, and to be still in NEW YORK. He will hear of his sister **Mary** by calling at the office of this paper.

July 15, 1854

Of **Mary McCabe**, from the Parish of DOWNS, County MONAGHAN, Ireland, who came to this country five years since. Any intelligence of her will be thankfully received by her sister **Catherine McCabe**, care of **Mrs. Gilmore**, 157 MULBERRY ST., NEW YORK.

Of **Michael Herrick**, formerly of BALLINURE, Parish of KILLENAULE, County TIPPERARY, Ireland. He emigrated to this country about thirteen years ago. When last heard from he was in DUNKIRK, NEW YORK, and is supposed to have crossed the lake. Any information of him will be thankfully received by his brother, **Edward Herrick**, HYDE PARK, DUTCHESS County, State of NEW YORK.

Of **John**, **Patrick**, **Owen**, **Catharine**, and **Alice O'Brien** from the Parish of KILLINCAHIR, County CAVAN, Ireland. They are supposed to be somewhere in NEW YORK. Any intelligence of them will be thankfully received by their brother, **Terence O'Brien**, GREENWICH STREET, NEW YORK.

July 22, 1854

Of **John McHale**, a native of the Parish of BALLISHEKEW, Co. MAYO, Ireland. When last he was with his sister in HAMILTON, three years ago, he said that he was living with a farmer within five miles of ROCHESTER. Any intelligence of him will be thankfully received by his sisters **Margaret** and **Catharine McHale**, care of **John Malone**, DUNMORE, LUZERNE County, PA.

Of **John Harrington**, who left here last November, and when last heard of was in the State of DELAWARE, near ST. GEORGE'S Post Office. Is a native of BOLOMORE, Parish of DRUMLARIFFE County CORK, Ireland. Any information of him will be thankfully received by his sister, **Honora Harrington**, at 228 MOTT STREET, NEW YORK.

Of **Dominick Casey**, of COOTEHALL, Co. ROSCOMMON, Ireland, who emigrated to this country in 1848. When last heard of he was in the State of ILLINOIS, west of CHICAGO. He is supposed to have bought land there. Any information respecting him will be thankfully received by **Patrick Martin**, MOUNT SAVAGE Iron works, ALLEGANY County, MARYLAND. Illinois papers please copy.

Of **Mathew Greene**, **Mary Greene**, or of **Bridget (Greene) Simms**, of the Parish of BALLYMAQUAD, County GALWAY, Mathew Greene, when last heard of, was living in BROOKLYN; Bridget was living with her husband, **Wm. Simms**, some place near the City Hall, NEW YORK. Any information of them will be thankfully received by their sister, **Margaret Greene**, who was lately sick in WARD'S ISLAND, and is now to be found at the Emigrant Office, No 2 Canal Street.

July 29, 1854

Of **Mary Quilty**, from CASTLETOWNCONYERS, Co. LIMERICK, Ireland, who was taken out of WARD'S ISLAND in March, 1851, by **Wm. Gessner**, barber, of NEWARK, N.J. She was afterwards sent to a friend of Gessner's across the river. Any intelligence of her will be thankfully received by her father, **James Quilty**, No. 22 JAMES STREET, NEW YORK.

Of **Michael Cournane**, a native of CAPPATIGUE, Co. KERRY, Ireland, by his daughter lately come out, and now staying with her uncle **John**, 309, AVENUE A, second floor. He was in DELAWARE, DELAWARE County, OHIO, on 1st Nov., 1853.

Of **Michael Hanley**, from CROOM, Co. LIMERICK, Ireland, who came to this country about 18 years ago. He is supposed to be somewhere in the vicinity of MILWAUKEE, WISCONSIN. Any intelligence of him will be thankfully received by his brother-in-law, **Rody Barden**, care of **Gould Hoyt**, Esq., 45 WEST 17th STREET, New York.

August 5, 1854

Of **Daniel Lalor**, who had been in ST. LOUIS last fall. He can find his brother **Michael R. Lawlor**, by addressing or calling on **R. H. Harty**, ST. LOUIS, MO. Any information concerning him will be thankfully received by his brother Michael, late of CALIFORNIA.

Of **Michael**, **Mary**, and **Margaret Purcell**, from the Parish of UPPER CHURCH, Co. TIPPERARY, Ireland, who were living in ST. LOUIS when last heard from, about a year and four months ago. Any intelligence of them will be thankfully received by their sister, **Bridget Purcell**, care of **Michael Keleher**, 57 HUDSON STREET, NEW YORK.

Of **John Kennedy**, of BALLINEETY, County LIMERICK, Ireland, who sailed from Liverpool in the *Harvest* of 1852. When last heard from by his friends he was working in a brickyard in some part of OSWEGO County, N.Y. Any information of him will be thankfully received by his sister, **Margaret**, who landed in this City on the 7th of July, and is now living at 131 AVENUE C, corner of Eighth Street.

August 12, 1854

Of **John Rowan**, a native of the Parish of BUNNECONLIN, County MAYO, Ireland, who landed in May or June last, from the ship *Kossuth*. It is supposed that he is in hospital or in FALL RIVER, MASS. Any information respecting him will be thankfully received by his sister, **Bridget**, or **Mrs. Jordan**, Direct to **Wm. Jordan**, DUNMORE Post Office, LUZERNE County, PA.

Of **James** and **Timothy Long**, natives of the City of CORK, Ireland. James came to America about sixteen years ago, and his brother Timothy met him in BOSTON the day he landed, about five years ago. –They came to this country from South Wales, England. When last heard of they were in the State of PENNSYLVANIA. Any information respecting them will be thankfully received by their brother and sisters **John, Julia, Ann**, and **Ellen Long**, who lately landed in New York. Address to the care of **Kieran Kelly**, 167 WEST 13th STREET, between 7th and 8th Avenues. Boston papers please copy.

Of **Martin Burke**, from RATHMOY, Parish of BORRISOLEIGH, Co. TIPPERARY, Ireland, who landed in New York about the 24th ult. Any information respecting him will be thankfully received by his brother, **James Burke**, at WEST CHESHIRE, NEW HAVEN Co., CONN.

Of **Susan Finnegan**, from the County CAVAN, Ireland, who sailed from Liverpool, May 30th, 1854. If this should happen to find any one knowing her, they will confer a favor on her brother, **Peter Finnegan**, by sending her address to the care of **J. Lynch**, No. 34 CHRISTIE [CHRYSTIE]ST., N.Y.

August 19, 1854

Of **Jane Hodgins**, a native of ARDBRACHEN, County MEATH, Ireland, who landed in New York on the 24th September. Any intelligence of her will be thankfully received by her brother, **Thomas Hodgins**. Direct to JOHNSTOWN P.O., CAMBRIA Co., PA.

Of **Maurice Bowler**, from ARTNACONNA, Parish of FERRITER, County KERRY, Ireland, who landed in Montreal in the Spring of 1847. When last heard from he was in the State of VIRGINIA. Any information concerning him will be thankfully received by his wife, **Bridget Bowler**, otherwise **Kavanagh**, care of **Mr. C. Cook** THOMPSON, CONNECTICUT. Virginia papers please copy.

Of **James Leddy**, son of **Matthew Leddy**, of MACROOM, Co. CORK, Ireland, who came to this country three years ago from England, and sailed the 16th of June, two years since, in the ship *Defiance* to CALIFORNIA. Any information of him will be thankfully received by his sister **Ellen**, at 42 HENRY ST., Room 13. Savannah, California, and Australian papers please copy.

Of **Patrick Cummins**, aged 28, from INNISCARRA, County CORK, Ireland, who left NEW YORK for PANAMA, last November. He is said to have escaped at SENNETTAor CAIRE, and nothing has been heard of him since. Any intelligence of him will be thankfully received by his brother, **John Cummins**, at **Mr. Higgins**, Carpet Factory, 43rd ST., near 11th Ave., New York.

August 26, 1854

Of **Denis O'Brien**, from the Parish of LISGOOLD, County CORK, Ireland, who left CHICAGO a year ago last Spring and went to MINNESOTA TERRITORY. When last heard of he was in ST. PAUL'S. Any intelligence of him directed to this office will be thankfully received by his sister **Mary**.

Of **Michael Hannivan**, from CALLENAFERSY, County KERRY, Ireland who landed in Quebec about five years ago. When last heard from he was in GENESEO Court House, LIVINGSTON County, NEW YORK. – Any information of him will be thankfully received by his wife **Betsy** and child, who are now in NEW YORK in the Alms House.

Of **Bridget** and **Elizabeth Tyrell** from the County KILDARE, Ireland. Any information of them will be thankfully received by their sister **Jane Tyrell**, No. 70 JAMES ST., between Hudson St. and 8th Avenue, NEW YORK.

September 2, 1854

Of **Simeon Kennedy**, from the Parish of KILLENAULE, Co. TIPPERARY, Ireland, who came to this country street about four years ago. He left EAST NEWARK on the 3rd of last April, and went to CHICAGO, from whence he wrote about the end of May. He was then stopping at No. 18 Clark Street in that City. Any intelligence of him will be thankfully received by his sisters, **Mary** and **Margaret**, in care of **Mr. John Quinn**, No. 6 Mulberry Street, NEWARK, N.J.

Of **Dennis Murphy**, Mason, from RATHCORMACK, Co. CORK, Ireland, who left NEW YORK on the 2nd of March, 1853, and went to ST. LOUIS, MO. The last time he was heard from was about ten months since. Any intelligence of him will be thankfully received by his wife, **Ellen Murphy**, at 365 PEARL STREET, in this City.

Of **Richard** and **John Lynch**, County WESTMEATH, Ireland, who left this city three years past. When last heard of they were in SAVANNAH. Any intelligence of them will be thankfully received by their sister **Anne Lynch**, 64 PRINCE STREET, as she is going to LONDON.

September 9, 1854

Of **Arthur Hollowood**, blacksmith, from RAHEENEY, County DUBLIN, Ireland, who came to this country eighteen years ago. When last heard from (seventeen years ago last February) he was in NEW JERSEY. Any intelligence of him will be thankfully received by his sister, **Mary Hollowood**, care of **Mrs. Gray**, 76 MULBERRY ST., N.Y.

Of **Daniel, Florence, Michael**, and **Honora McCarthy**, from the Parish of MEELICK, Co. CORK, Ireland. When last heard from (17th March last) they were in TIFFLIN, SENECA County, OHIO. Any intelligence of them will be thankfully received by their brother **James**, who landed three weeks since in the ship *Washington*. – Direct to the care of **Mr. Brady**, STATEN ISLAND, N.Y. or to the office of this paper.

September 16, 1854

Of **James Duffey**, from the Parish of KILLECAVEN, County ROSCOMMON, Ireland, who came to this country about 12 years ago. When last heard from (about five years ago) he was in the City of WASHINGTON. – Any intelligence of him will be thankfully received by his wife, **Mary Duffy**. Address, care of **Mr. Patrick Byrne**, 34 Hill Street, NEW HAVEN, CONNECTICUT. Washington papers please copy.

Of **Michael Conners**, native of the Parish of KILLACONTY, County GALWAY, Ireland. When last heard from he was in MADISON, INDIANA, and is supposed to be there or on the Ohio River. Any person knowing of his whereabouts would be thankfully rewarded by his brother, **John Conners**, by writing to him to STONINGTON, CONNECTICUT.

September 23, 1854

Of **Eliza Drake**, nine years old, who came per ship *Empire State*, from Liverpool, July 19, '54, and was admitted to the Marine hospital, from which she was discharged on the 25th of last August, and was hired from the Emigrant Labor Exchange by **Mrs. McKenny**, 53 FRANKFORT STREET, by her father, **Pat Drake**, at the office of the Commissioners of Emigration, No 76 Franklin Street.

September 30, 1854

Of **Dominick Joyce**, of KILLUNADEERNA, County GALWAY, Ireland. He landed in New York six years ago. When last heard from he was in POTTSVILLE, PENNSYLVANIA. Any information concerning him will be thankfully received by his mother, **Bridget Joyce**, MERIDEN, CONNECTICUT. Pottsville papers please copy.

October 7, 1854

Of **James T. Campbell**, late of LIMERICK, Ireland, by his son, **Joseph Campbell**. Please address, Joseph Campbell, in care of Taws, Russell & Co., Printers, 24 Spruce Street, New York. N.B, - if he see this, he will do well to write, as he will hear of something of importance.

October 14, 1854

Of **Patt McLaughlin**, a native of Ireland. When last heard from he was in CINCINNATI, OHIO. Any information concerning him will be thankfully received by his sisters **Mary** and **Margaret**. Please address, **Mrs. Ann Kenny**, 79 Degraw Street, BROOKLYN. Ohio papers please copy.

Of **Mary Butler**, from INCH, Co. TIPPERARY, Ireland, who arrived in the ship *Albion* from Liverpool on the 29th of June last. Her name appears in the ship's manifest as "Mary Dwyer, aged 17 years." Any intelligence of her will be thankfully received by her cousin, **James Dwyer**, care of M. O'Flaherty, Office of the Commissioners of Emigration, City Hall, N.Y.

Of **Michael Dalton**, from the Parish of BALLYHAIGUE or KILLURIG, Co. KERRY, Ireland, who came to this country about three years ago. When last heard from (about twelve months since) he was in DAYTON, OHIO. Any intelligence of him will be thankfully received by his brother, **John Dalton**, mason, care of **Eugene Parker**, 115 ORANGE STREET, NEW YORK.

Of **James Nunan**, from RATHKEALE, Co. LIMERICK, Ireland, who came to this country about three years ago. When last heard from (in July, 1853,) he was living with **Jeremiah Donnelly**, in GENEVA, ROME County, ILLINOIS. Any intelligence of him will be thankfully received by his sister, **Eliza Nunan**, care of **Henry Ranihan**, 21 CHERRY STREET, NEW YORK. Illinois papers please copy.

Of **Nancy** and **Catharine Buckley**, from the City of CORK, Ireland. Came to this country – Catharine three years, and Nancy nine years since. When last heard from, Nancy was in CANADA, and Catharine in BOSTON. Any information will thankfully received by their sister, **Hannah Buckley**, 420 8th AVENUE.

Of **William Duggan**, of the Parish of WATERGRASSHILL, Co. CORK, Ireland. Any information of him will be thankfully received by his brother, **Matthew Duggan**, 221 SEVENTH STREET, NEW YORK CITY. Ohio papers please copy.

Of **Joseph Dunne**, a native of DUBLIN, Ireland, and a blacksmith by trade. He is supposed to be in this country between five and six years. Any information of him will be thankfully received by his sister **Maryanne**, at 16 ROSE STREET, or **Michael Keane**, 215 FULTON STREET, N.Y.

Of **Jeremiah** and **John Sheehan**, from LARANTH, Co. KERRY, Ireland. When last heard from (about three years since) they were in WARREN, N.H. – John is supposed to be in LOWELL, MASS., and Jeremiah somewhere in the vicinity of BOSTON. Any intelligence of them will be thankfully received by their brother, **Mathew Sheehan**, No. 10, FULTON STREET, N.Y.

October 21, 1854

Of **Catherine, Mary,** and **Ellen** and **Anne Tuohill,** who came from Greenock, Scotland, and arrived in New York. Mary in the Spring of 1851, and the others in 1852. The four sisters are grown women; their ages average from 23 to 30. Their native place in the Parish of KILLFINE, within four miles of KILALLA, County MAYO, Ireland. Any account of their present residence, or any information concerning them, will be thankfully received by their father, **Michael Tuohill,** and their mother **Mary Tuohill,** by addressing them at this office, or to the care of **Cornelius Drew.** 11 MULBERRY STREET, NEW YORK. The last time they were heard from was from CINCINNATI. When they remitted £16 in a letter bearing date the 5th of March of this year, to their parents in Ireland, their answer to be directed to **Andrew McGoran,** P.O., Cincinnati.

Of **Timothy Farrell,** aged 18 years, a native of the City of CORK, Ireland. When last seen (on the 28th of May last) he was in GREEN POINT, L.I. He is supposed to be in RICHMOND, VA. Any intelligence of him will be thankfully received by his father, **John Farrell,** care of **John Moriarty,** at the Shades, GREEN POINT, L. I.

By **Honora** and **James O'Brien,** 13 and 5 years old. From Co. CLARE, Ireland. Who landed in New York, on the 3rd inst., in the ship *Elizabeth Taylor,* from Limerick, of their Father and Mother, who they suppose, are somewhere in the State of NEW YORK. Apply at the office of the Commissioners of Emigration in the Park.

Of **Alexander McGuire,** who recently arrived in New York from the old country. Any intelligence of him will be kindly received at No. 40 THIRTY SECOND STREET, by his loving and affectionate wife, **Mary Jane McGuire.**

Of **John Murphy** and his brother **Jeremiah** and his cousin, **Jeremiah Ready,** natives of TRALEE and CASTLE ISLAND, Co. KERRY, Ireland.-When last heard of, resided in CLEVELAND, State of OHIO. Any information will be thankfully received by their sister, **Hannah Murphy,** at No. 12 PEARL ST., N.Y

October 28, 1854

Of **Charles O'Neill,** painter, from the City of LIMERICK, Ireland. When last heard from (last Spring) he was in WILLIAMSTOWN, ME., and was then thinking of going to ST. ANDREWS, on the CANADA side. Any information of his whereabouts will be thankfully received by his father, **Charles O'Neill,** at 194 14th STREET, 1st AVENUE, NEW YORK.

Of **William Cavanagh,** of the Parish of BALLYFIN, QUEEN'S County, Ireland. When last seen (about five weeks ago) he was in NEW YORK, and is supposed to be gone to ALBANY. Any information of his whereabouts will be thankfully received by his wife **Bridget,** at **Martin Delany's** 33 CROSS STREET, N.Y.

November 5, 1854

Of **Sarah Judge,** or **Sarah Jecks,** of the Parish of O'CONROE, Co. SLIGO, Ireland, has been in America for the last twenty years. When last heard of she was in ILLINOIS. Any information concerning her will be thankfully received by her brother's daughter, **Catharine Judge,** PEMBERTON, post office, NEW JERSEY.

Of **Patrick Lee,** from DRUMALEE, near CAVAN, Ireland. When last heard from (on the 19th of last June) he was living in PORT JERVIS, ORANGE County, N.Y. Any intelligence of him will be thankfully received by his brother, **Michael Lee,** painter, care of **John Dureen,** Eagle Factory, PATERSON, N.J.

November 11, 1854

Of **Anne** and **Margaret Madden**, of DULEEK, Co. MEATH, Ireland, who arrived in Boston about the 1st of April, 1853. Any information respecting them will be thankfully received by **Michael Egan**, REYNOLDSVILLE, HARRISON County, VA. Boston papers please copy.

Of **Luke O'Donnell**, from LISMORE, Co WATERFORD, Ireland, by his sister, **Mary O'Donnell**. About 12 months ago he worked on a railroad in SUSSEX County NEW JERSEY, since which time he has not been heard from. Any person hearing of his whereabouts will confer a great favor on her by addressing a few lines to that effect. 92 Ferry St., NEWARK, N.J.

Of **Jeremiah Meehan**, from INNISCLARE, Co. CLARE, Ireland, who landed in Quebec about 4 months ago. He is supposed to be at present either in NEW YORK or BOSTON. Any intelligence of him will be thankfully received by his wife, **Margaret Meehan**, care of **John Touhy**, 61 FRANKFORT ST., N.Y. Boston papers please copy.

November 18, 1854

Of **Mrs. Driscoll**, widow, five children, who arrived in this City 7 years ago, from the Parish of NEW GLANMIRE, County CORK, Ireland. Any information of them will be thankfully received by her cousin, **Margaret Cashman**, at 284 6th Av., N.Y.

November 25, 1854

Of **Michael O'Donnell**, from the Co. LIMERICK, Ireland, Parish of CROOM. When last heard from, about seven months ago, he boarded with **Patrick Lynch** in CHICAGO, COOK County, State of ILLINOIS. Any information regarding him will be thankfully received by his mother, **Jane O'Donnell**, MILFORD, MASS.

Of **John McCudden**, of the County ANTRIM, laborer, who left home about three years ago. When last heard of was in the City of NEW YORK. Information will be thankfully received by his brother, **Arthur McCudden**, residing at **Mr. Teigh's**, 113 WASHINGTON ST., N.Y.

Of **Patrick O'Dea**, from ADARE, County LIMERICK, Ireland, who came to this country about five years ago. When last heard from (about two years since) he was in NORTHFIELD County, VERMONT. Any intelligence of him will be thankfully received by **Michael O'Dea**, care of **James O'Grady**, FACTORYVILLE, STATEN ISLAND.

December 2, 1854

Of **John Cody** from CLOMANTO, County KILKENNY, Ireland. He left his home, 39 MADISON STREET, NEW YORK, on the 5th of December, 1849; got slight account of his being in LITTLE VALLEY, outside ALBANY. Any information relating to him will be thankfully received by his wife, **Catherine Cody**, 373 BROADWAY. Albany papers please copy.

Of **Barney M'Cluskey**, Stonecutter, native of DUNGIVEN, near LONDONDERRY, Ireland. Has been in this country 24 years; was married in St. Joseph's Church, New York, eight years ago; afterwards moved to TUCKAHOE, WESTCHESTER Co., N.Y.; resided there about six years; moved to NEW YORK CITY, where he lived eighteen months, and acted as Treasurer to the Stonecutter's Association. He left New York about twelve months ago, since which he has not been heard of. Any information of him will be thankfully received by his injured wife, **Mary M'Cluskey**. Address **James Deeny**, Flower St. No. 5, Reid's Avenue, PHILADELPHIA. Georgia and Chicago papers please copy.

Of **Michael Donovan**, from the Parish of AFFADOWN, County CORK, Ireland. He arrived in New York about twelve months since and proceeded to ILLINOIS, to his brother

James. When last heard from, about three months ago, he was in LEE Co. Any intelligence of him will be thankfully received by his children, **Mary** and **Daniel Donovan**, who arrived from Ireland about six weeks since, and are stopping with **James Sullivan**, STATEN ISLAND, N.Y.

December 9, 1854

Of **Patt Brennan**, from KILKEE, County CLARE, Ireland, who landed here last May twelve months, and who sent to Ireland for his brother and sister, **Thomas** and **Bridget Brennan**, who landed here on the 15th of October, and wrote several letters to their brother at LAMIRA post-office, BELMONT County, OHIO and have not been heard from him since. Any information of him will be thankfully received by his brother and sister, who are at present with **Andrew Curtin** No. 297 FULTON STREET, N.Y.

December 16, 1854

Of **Mrs. Lane**, a native of the Parish of MITCHELSTOWN, Co. CORK, Ireland. She left NEW YORK for KANKAKEE, ILLINOIS, last June. Any information respecting her will be thankfully received by her daughter, **Mrs. Corbit**. Address No. 15 6th ST., NEW YORK, care of **Owen Kenny**, for **Margaret Corbit**.

December 23, 1854

Of **Pat. McLAUGHLIN**, a native of Co. MAYO, Ireland. When last heard from was in CINCINNATI, OHIO. Any information concerning him will be thankfully received by his sisters **Mary** and **Margaret**. Address **Mrs. Ann Kenny**, 179 Degraw Street, BROOKLYN. Ohio papers please copy.

Of **Mary, Bridget, Nancy**, and **Margaret Hearn**, and **Johanna O'Donnell**, of ONING, County KILKENNY, Ireland. Who have lately arrived, by their nephew, **Terence O'Donnell**, corner of North 5th and 5th Streets, WILLIAMSBURGH, N.Y. **John Shelly**.

December 30, 1854

Of **Owen Devery**, and **Mary**, his wife, whose maiden name was **Tracy**, and sister of **Denis, Peter**, and **Bridget Tracy**, children of **Patrick** and **Catherine Tracy**, of the Parish of BALAGH, County ROSCOMMON, Ireland. Information was received by their brother, **Peter Tracy**, from **Mr. Cornelius Banahan**, Ireland, that Owen and Mary, his wife, were in NEW YORK when last heard of. Any information of them will be thankfully received by their brother, Peter Tracy, who left Ireland about eighteen years ago, and who was thought long since dead. Address Peter Tracy, 67 Union St., NEWARK, N.J.

Of **Thomas, John**, and **James Russell**, three brothers, from the Parish of LUSMAGH KING'S County, Ireland. Thomas came to this country some four years ago; when last heard from, Stated he was going to the State of PENNSYLVANIA. John is some six years in this country; when last heard from was in the City of NEW YORK. James, who is some two years here, is supposed to be at present in the City of NEW YORK. Any information regarding them will be most gratefully received by their sister, **Teresa**, who landed here by the *North America*, a month ago, and now resides at 22 CATHARINE STREET.

Of **Michael Murray**, of COUPLE CARIGAHOLT, Parish of MIART, County CLARE, Ireland. Apply to **Phillip Carrol**, 250 10th AVENUE and you will find your brother, **Daniel Murray**, there.

Of **Elizabeth Kerley**, from Parish of LOWTH, Ireland, late of JERSEY CITY, by her sister, **Ann Branigan**. Please direct 18 Cottage Place, Columbia St., near Sackett St., BROOKLYN. Pennsylvania papers please copy.

January 6, 1855

Of **Mrs. Goggin**, of the County WESTMEATH, Ireland. Her maiden name was **Mary Fagan**. Any information of her will be thankfully received by her husband, **William Goggin**, South easterly corner of 43rd STREET and 9th Avenue, NEW YORK CITY. Albany and Troy papers please copy.

January 13, 1855

Of **John Finegan**, native of Co. CAVAN, Ireland. When last heard from was in CAMBRIA County PENNSYLVANIA. Any information respecting him will be thankfully received by his brother, **James Finegan**, 39 WILLETT ST., N.Y. Pennsylvania papers please copy.

Of **James O'Donnell**, a native of KNUCKBRACK, ABBEYFEALE, County LIMERICK, Ireland, who left MICHIGAN CITY, INDIANA, for ST. LOUIS, about a year ago. He is a single man, about 30 years of age and of fair complexion. Any intelligence of him will be thankfully received by his sister, **Ellen O'Donnell**, PIERMONT, N.Y.

Of **James Clare**, formerly of CLOHANES, near BIRCHFIELD, County CLARE, Ireland, who left this country some few years since. He was unmarried and a laborer. His age about 40. He resided for sometime in the State of OHIO. He has not written home for the last two years, and his friends wish to know whether he is dead or alive. Any information relative here to will be thankfully acknowledged by his friends or by Messrs. Geo. McBride, Jr. & Co., 14 Broadway, New York.

Of **Edward Morin**, son of **Hugh Morin** and **Mary King**, of the County LEITRIM, Ireland. He is a Tailor, and some years ago kept a shop in NEW YORK CITY. Any information respecting him will be thankfully received by his brother, **Michael Morin**. Address, Michael Morin MOMENCE, KANKAKEE County, ILLINOIS.

I wish to inform all persons that **Capt. Jas. Ewart**, of DONAGHADES, Co. DOWN, Ireland, is a married man since the year, 1846. It has been reported that he was married, on the 15th of April, 1853, to **Charles Hurst's** daughter, of DONAGHADEE. The party knows his wife for the last three years; she has seen her often at his mother's house, and she noticed the lady by letter and by speaking not to keep her husband's company in her absence. The only cause for this treatment to his wife and children is that she is a Roman Catholic and he is a Presbyterian. He has told her if she would not join his church he would leave her, and live with someone who would do so. He had command of the Bark *Kiza* of Belfast, Ireland, belonging to Messrs. Hayne & Co. This is his wife's Statement, **Mrs. Ellen J. Ewart**, NEW YORK. Friends of the woman to whom he was married in 1853, are the cause of his wife's being unable to correspond with him. European and West Indian papers please copy.

$10 Reward – For such information as may lead to the discovery of **John McGovern**: height, 5 feet 9 inches: hair, dark brown; eyes, blue; Complexion, fresh; age, about 23 years; native of County MONAGHAN, Ireland. The above reward, with many thanks, may be had by addressing a note to his brother **Jas. McGovern**, WATERBURY, CT.

January 20, 1855

Of **James Campbell**, by his son, **Joseph Campbell**. – I wish you would write to me immediately, as I am very much in need of your assistance. Do not delay, or it may be to[o] late. When I write to you I shall let you know all the particulars about "it is done." Direct your letter to Joseph Campbell, care of **Margaret Lynch**, 41 MULBERRY ST., NEW YORK.

Of **John Sullivan**, Townland of KNOC, Parish of KILMEEN, County CORK, Ireland. Was in WALES for three years, and left there three years last April, in the Ship *Emily*, for

Boston. When last heard from, six months ago was working in the tunnel in BLUE RIDGE, AUGUSTA County, State of VIRGINIA. Any person knowing his whereabouts will confer a great favor on his sister, **Mrs. O'Driscoll**, No. 107 WASHINGTON ST., N. YORK.

Of **Hugh Gallaher**, formerly of LONDONDERRY, Ireland, who came to this country about six years ago-supposed to be in NEW ORLEANS. He has not been heard from by an anxious friend since March, 1849. A letter from himself, or any one acquainted with him, will be thankfully received by C.L. P.O. PHILADELPHIA.

Of **Patrick** and **Anne Egan**. of BORRISOKANE, County TIPPERARY, Ireland. Who resided in SHEFFIELD, ENGLAND, which place he left for NEW YORK in Feb., 1852. Any information of him will be thankfully received by Patrick's wife **Mary Egan**, 16 ½ HAMILTON STREET, who landed here fourteen months since.

Of **Michael Eagan**, who emigrated, about three years ago, from the Parish of ATHENRY, County GALWAY, Ireland. When last heard from he was in ILLINOIS. Any information of him will be thankfully received by his wife, **Mary Eagan**, at No. 5 HESTER ST. Illinois Papers please copy.

January 27, 1855

Thomas and **Martin Rooney**, of CRANAGH, County MAYO, Ireland. The former is a blacksmith and the latter a shoemaker. When last heard from they were at MOUNT SAVAGE, ALLEGANY County, MARYLAND. Any information of them will be thankfully received by their nephew, **Brian Rooney**, 313 WATER ST., N.Y.

Of **Thomas Kervan**, of the Parish of KILBIM, County CORK, Ireland, who came to this country some twelve years ago. When last heard of, he was living in CINCINNATI. Any information will be thankfully received by his brother James. Address **James Kervan**, care of Manhattan Gas Company, NEW YORK. St. Louis papers please copy.

Of **John Cronin**, Mason, from the Parish of BALLYVOURNA, near MACROOM, County CORK, Ireland, who left Cork to come to America three years ago last October. When last heard from (last July two years) he was in NEW YORK. He is supposed to be somewhere out West. Any intelligence of him will be thankfully received by his wife, **Margaret Cronin**, care of **Michael Reardon**, 305 FIRST AVENUE, NEW YORK. Western papers please copy.

Of **Ellen** and **Mary Anne Sweeney**, (sisters) from Anne Street, City of CORK, Ireland. Ellen left home in 1847, and Mary Anne in 1848, and arrived in New York; went from thence to MOUNT MORRIS, LIVINGSTON County, State of NEW YORK; when last heard from was in BOSTON. Any information respecting them will be thankfully received by their sister, **Margaret Sweeney**, care of **Thomas Kelly** 212 WEST 25th ST., NEW YORK. Boston papers please copy.

February 3, 1855

Of **Michael McLaughlin**, He removed from NORTH EAST STATION, DUTCHESS County, N.Y., to some place in ILLINOIS. His brother, **Laurence McLaughlin** resides in or near BUFFALO; should either of them see this notice, they will confer a great favor by writing to **Mary M'Cue**, care of **J. Sutherland**, 103 NASSAU STREET, NEW YORK.

February 10, 1855

Of **Michael Walsh**, of YOUGHAL, and his wife, **Catharine Clooney**, of WATERFORD, Ireland, by **Johanna Clooney**, her sister, and **Ellen Clooney**, her niece. When last heard from was in BUFFALO, but is supposed to be now in CANADA. Address Johanna Clooney, in care of **Michael Comber**, 20th Street, between Walnut and Georges Sts., PHILADELPHIA.

Of **Patrick Keegan**, of TINNACROSS, KING'S County. When last heard of he was in NEW ORLEANS in May last. Any information will be thankfully received by his brother **Edward**, 19 Morgan St., ST. LOUIS care of **Widow Burke**. Also his brother **Michael**, who came to New York about twelve or fourteen years ago and when last heard from (about five years ago,) he was in NEW YORK.

February 24, 1855

Of **John Huffinan**, of BALLYMACARIGATE, County KERRY. When last heard from November four years ago, he was in PHILADELPHIA, and he is now supposed to be somewhere in the State of INDIANA. Any information of him will be thankfully received by his mother, **Catherine Huffinan**, care of **Sherman P. Fitch**, WILTON Post Office, FAIRFIELD County, CONNECTICUT. Indiana papers please copy.

March 10, 1855

Of **Michael O'Donnell**, Parish of BEHE, County GALWAY, Ireland, who emigrated to this country in 1848. When last heard from was in KENTUCKY. Any information of him will be thankfully received by his brother and sister, **Thomas** and **Bridget O'Donnell**. Address **Patrick Costello**, LANCASTER, PENNSYLVANIA.

Of **John** and **Patrick Head**, CARREW, Parish of TYNAUGH, County GALWAY. John left home in June, 1847, and landed in Boston May 7th, 1848; when last heard of they worked in CHATEAUGAY, FRANKLIN County, N.Y., on the Champlain and Ogdensburg Railroad. Information will be received by their brother **James Head**, STERLING, MASS.

Of **Laurence Costello**, a native of the Parish of TYNAGH, County GALWAY, who sailed from there with wife and child in the fall of 1847, supposed to have gone to HALIFAX, N.S. and proceeded from thence to BOSTON. Information of him will be received by his mother, sisters, and brother. Address **John M'Keon**, WOODSTOOD, CARLETON County, NEW BRUNSWICK.

Of **Michael Stare**, of PALICE, Parish of YOUGHAL, County TIPPERARY, who emigrated to this country from Liverpool in November, 1853; when last heard from was in ST.LOUIS, MO. If this should meet his eye, or any person knowing him, will please address his uncle, **Patrick Stare**, for his sister **Mary**, HYDEVILLE post office, RUTLAND County, VT.

Of **Martin** and **Stephen Currin**, Parish RAHON, County GALWAY. Information of them will be received by their brother **Patrick**. Address **Patrick Daly**, No. 338 Fourth Street, TROY, N.Y.

Of **Mary Barrett**, native of MORAHAN, Parish of KILMORE ERIS, County MAYO, sister of **William** and **Catherine**; when last heard of about 4 years ago, by **John Car**, was in RYFIELD, STANLY TOWNSHIP, U.C. she landed in Canada eight years ago. Information will be received by her brother **William**, SUMMIT HILL, CARBON County, PA.

Of **Charles O'Donnell**, from CROSSREENONUCH, Parish of KILMORE, County MAYO, who sailed from Liverpool for New York in March, 1853. When last heard from he was in RICHMOND, VA. His sister **Margaret** wishes to hear from him. Address her, in care of **Mr. Thomas Cannon**, COLUMBUS, O

Of **John** and **Philip Crowley**, natives of the Parish of TEMPELMARTIN, Townland of GRANNE, County CORK, when last heard of John was in the State of OHIO. Philip was in BOSTON 20 years ago. Their brother **James** i[s] anxious to hear of them. Direct to **Michael Leahy**, TERRE HAUTE, IND.

Of **John Morrisey**, school teacher, formerly of MITCHELSTOWN, County CORK, who sailed from Cork, about six years ago, it is supposed, for Boston. Since which time he has not been heard from. His parents and friends are in great distress about him. Any person knowing where he is, if alive, will confer a favor on them by addressing his aunt **Mary Connor**, 92 Ferry Street, NEWARK, N.J.

March 17, 1855

Of **William McLane**, of BAWN BRACK, Parish of GOLDEN, County TIPPERARY, who was in CHICAGO, ILL., 8 years ago. Information of him will be received by his brother-in-law. **Edward Birmingham**, WILLIAMSTOWN P.O., OSWEGO County, N.Y.

Of **Mary Hogan**, from the Parish of BOHER, Townland of GLINACRE, County TIPPERARY. When last heard from, 3 years ago, she was in the Island of CUBA. Information of her will be received by her brother **Denis** LA PORTE post office, LA PORTE County, IA.

Of **Owen Bennet**, of NEWRY, County DOWN, who landed in New York last winter, and is supposed to have enlisted in the U.S.A. He was living after his arrival in WILLIAMSBURGH, N.Y., with a man named **John Kerr**. Please address his brother, **Henry Bennett**, care of **John Nichol**, MILWAUKEE, WIS.

Of **John Kelly**, Parish of BALLYADAMS, QUEEN'S County. When last heard of was in TAZEWELL County, ILL. Please address his sister **Ellen**, care of P. J. Fallon Catholic Bookseller, 3rd St., below Market, ST. LOUIS, MO.

Of **Michael Sparrow**, Parish of CLOUGHLIN, QUEEN'S County, who emigrated from Ireland, 7 years ago. Information will be received by his brother **James**, GENEVA, ONTARIO County, N.Y.

Of **Thos. J. Fitzsimmons**, of LIMERICK City, who landed in New Orleans in 1846; soon after went to MEXICO, and became attached to a military company. Information will be received by his cousin, **Wm. Fitzsimmons**, moulder, at Hart & Brown's Foundry, MASSILLON, OHIO.

Of **Charles McCarthy**, of Parish of EFFIN, County LIMERICK, who sailed from Liverpool in 1851, and landed in New Orleans in company with **John Casey**, and when last heard of was near ST. CLOUD, LA., and is supposed to be in MOBILE. Information will be received by his brother **Denis**, PLEASANT VALLEY, P.O., FAIRFAX County, VA.

Of **Michael Welsh** and sisters, **Bridget** and **Ann**, Parish of BALLYRAGGAT, County KILKENNY, who came to this country in 1847, and landed in New York. Michael left there for CANADA, and Bridget lived in No. 18 Pearl St., BROOKLYN, N.Y., 2 years ago. Her husband is **James Coragan**. Ann lived in NEW YORK CITY. Their sister **Margaret** wants to know of their whereabouts. Address **John Delaney**, WAVERLY, TIOGA County, N.Y.

Of **William Gorman**, of CORRAMORE, Parish of TEMPELARAM, County KILKENNY, who came to NEW YORK about 4 years and 6 months ago. When last heard of he was in DOVER, MASS. Information will be received by his cousin **William Skully**, WALNUT GROVE, KNOX County, ILL.

Of **Philip Moran**, of BALLINAFAD, Parish of LYSANUFY, County ROSCOMMON, who came to America about 5 years ago, and when last heard from he was in MEMPHIS, TENN., one year ago last June. Direct to his brother **Patrick**, or **James Moran**, HARTFORD, CONN.

Of **Thomas Blake**, native of the County MEATH. When last heard from in June last, he was in GALENA, ILL. Information of him will be received by his brother **James**, PHOENIXVILLE, CHESTER County, PA.

Of **Mary Keneda**, daughter of **Patrick Keneda**, of Parish of HARRAN, County MEATH, who came to America about 10 years ago. Information will be received by her sister

Catherine Keneda Lyman, wife of **John Lyman**. Address John Lyman, care of **Joseph Wykoff**, ROMULUS, SENECA County, N.Y.

Of **Mary Brady**, (maiden name,) and **Margaret Tierney**, both of CARGABAWN, Parish of AGHNAMULLEN, County MONAGHAN, who came to America 11 years ago, and when last heard from were in SECKONK, MASS. Information will be received by **Hugh McDonald**, BLOOMINGTON, MCLEAN County, ILL.

Of **Patrick O'Donnel, Mary O'Donnell**, and **Michael Welsh**, of Parish of BRODFORD, County CLARE, who were in SUSQUEHANNA County 2 years ago. Information of them will be received by **Mr. Lewis Bane** and wife (their sister **Margaret**,) 26 Almond St., PHILADELPHIA, PA.

Of **Patrick** and **Margaret Savage**, of CLOHERBREENA, Parish of TRALEE, County KERRY. Margaret lived in JERSEY CITY about three years ago, also **Mary Sullivan**, GREENLANE, DINGLE, same County, who married **Michael Garvey**. Information of them will be received by **Mrs. John Savage**, care of **Daniel Lyons**, KNOXVILLE, KNOX County, EAST TENNESSEE.

Of **Patrick McVerney**, of County CAVAN, who was four years ago in POUGHKEEPSIE, N.Y. Information will be received by his brother **John**, care of **Mr. P. Leo**, CARBONDALE, PA.

Of **Patrick Lynch**, Parish of KILAND, County CAVAN, who came to this country several years ago with his brother **Thomas**. When last heard of was farming in MADISON County, MO. Information of himself or his children will be received at Mr. O'Brien's office, 46 Chestnut Street, ST. LOUIS, MO., in care of **A. D. O'Brien**, at the above place.

Of **Timothy Cassin**, of Grafton Street, DUBLIN, who sailed from Liverpool in the ship *Elizabeth Hamilton*, and landed in New York. When last heard of, 3 years ago, he was in WATER STREET, NEW YORK. Information of him will be received by his father **Patrick Cassin**, CHILLICOTHE, ROSS County, O.

Of **John Cluncy**, who left RUSK, County DUBLIN, for NEW ORLEANS, in 1847. When last heard of was in CINCINNATI. Any person who can give information of him will please address his sister **Ellen**, NEWARK, LICKING County, O.

Of **Thomas Clancy**, stone-cutter, of DUBLIN, who left there in April, 1847 or '48. When last heard of was in the West. Information of him will be received by his cousin, **Patrick Gill**, DUBUQUE, IOWA.

Of **Daniel Harrison**, Parish of KILLIBEGS, County DONEGAL, who came to this country 8 years ago. When last heard of he worked in LOCKPORT, PA. Should this meet the notice of any person knowing him they will confer a favor on his wife and child by directing to **James Hagan**, No. 222 Bedford St., PHILADELPHIA, PA.

Of **Bridget Narey**, of GARR, KING'S County, who is supposed to be in BROOKLYN City. Also **James** and **Michael Narey**, her brothers. Information respecting them will be received by their brother **Thomas**, at **Pat'k Magee's** of the Run, TUSCARORA, SCHUYLKILL County, PA.

Of **John Haden**, from the barony of ST. MULLINS Parish of TENNABINCH, County CARLOW. When last heard from last St. Patrick's Day he was in ALTONA, PA. His brother **Patrick** was killed in POTTAFIELD. Information of him will be received by his wife **Catherine** and his two children, **Maria** and **Patrick**, at No. 118 Lydius St., ALBANY, N.Y.

Of **Joseph Lynch**, TULLAHAN, Parish of ROSSINVER, County LEITRIM, aged 19 years, who left PHILADELPHIA in August. He intended going to work near HARRISBURG, PA., under a boss by the name of **Healy**, and has not been heard of since. Information of him will be received by his brother **Terence**, 266 South & 4th St., PHILADELPHIA, PA.

Of **William Seery**, Carpenter, a native of MULLINGAR, County WESTMEATH, Ireland. When last heard from he was in LOWER ALTON, ILLINOIS. Any information of him will be thankfully received by his brother **Thomas**, direct to JERSEY CITY P.O., N.J. Illinois and St. Louis papers please copy.

Of **George Cue**, a native of the Parish of CAHARAGH, County CORK, Ireland, who landed in New York, six years ago. When last heard of, he was in MONTREAL, CANADA, two years ago. Any information respecting him will be thankfully received by his brother, **John Cue**, care of **Mich Neill**, No. 40 BAXTER STREET, (in the rear) NEW YORK. Montreal papers please copy.

Of **Michael Burns**, and his wife **Sarah**, who emigrated to CANADA, from WATERFORD, about the year 1841. When last heard of, 3 years ago, they were in ALBANY, N.Y. Any information would be thankfully received by Sarah Burns' brother, **William Jones**, No. 7 Sullivan Place, Federal St., BOSTON, MASS.

March 24, 1855

Of **Michael Eagan**, (son of **Roger Eagan**, deceased,) from BALLYVANNAN, Parish of TOMGRAINY, County CLARE, Ireland; when last heard of he was near NEWBURGH, CUYAHOGA County, OHIO. Any information of him will be most thankfully received by his sister **Julia** and his mother. Address Julia Eagan, 67 WEST 28th ST., NEW YORK. If **Mary Coghlan**, his cousin, should see this she will please write, or call at the above address.

Of **Michael** and **Peter M'Aneny**, from CARRICKMACROSS, County MONAGHAN, Ireland, who left there about 17 or 18 years ago. When last heard from about 5 years since, they were in the City of BALTIMORE, MD. Any intelligence of them will be thankfully received by their brother and sister **Andrew** and **Rose M'Aneny**, care of **Patrick Keenan**, 233 EAST ELEVENTH STREET, NEW YORK. Baltimore papers please copy.

March 31, 1855

Of **Michael** and **Daniel M'Namara**, late of County CLARE, Ireland. When last heard from they were residing in CINCINNATI, OHIO. Any person knowing the exact residence of the above parties will confer a favor by leaving the same with Mr. Walsh, Emigration Office, 81 Anthony Street, New York.

Of **Patrick M'Carty**, from GRANASICK, five miles from KINSALE, County CORK, Ireland. He lived in ENGLAND for nine or ten years, married two years before coming here, arrived here in the ship *Ocean Queen* three years ago, left his wife in NEW YORK two years and a half ago, and was never heard of since. He has two sisters living in BOSTON, one in WALES, and two brothers in ENGLAND. He also goes by the name of **Patrick Minough**. Any information respecting him will be thankfully received by his wife, **Eleanor M'Carty**, care of **Mrs. Flynn**, 38 ½ BOWERY, NEW YORK. Boston papers please copy.

Of **Andrew** (or **Alphonsus**) **A. Crawford**, from FINNEA, County MEATH, Ireland. He resided about two years ago in LODI, BERGEN County, N.J. at which time he was a subscriber to this paper. By writing or sending his address to this office he will learn something of importance to him.

Of **Catherine M'Niff**, from ENNISKILLEN, County FERMANAGH, Ireland. When last heard from, 24 years ago, she was living in NEW YORK. Also of **Francis** and **Susan Gallagher**, brother and sister to the late **Sergt. James Gallagher**, 96th Regt., British

Army. Any information respecting them will be thankfully received by her brother, **Thomas M'Niff**, and brother-in-law to the late Sergeant J. Gallagher, at 302 WEST 31st STREET, (top floor). NEW YORK.

April 7, 1855

Of **John** and **Mary Walsh**, late of PRESCOTT, in ENGLAND, and arrived in New York, about a year ago or more, by their daughter, **Mary Walsh**, at the office of the Commissioners of Emigration.

Of **Rory Conaghty**, of CROVER, Parish of BALLY MCHUGH, County CAVAN, Ireland, who came to this country in the summer of 1854, by his sister **Mary Fahy**, living at No. 131 AVENUE C, NEW YORK.

April 14, 1855

Of **Michael Foley**, formerly of BOSTON; supposed to be in some pickling establishment in PHILADELPHIA, and going by the name of **Michael O'Connor**. Information of him will be kindly received by his wife and children at **Martin Caughlin's**, CHILICOTHE, OHIO; or **John Coleman**, Washington Square, Fort Hill, BOSTON.

Of **Jerome** and **John Madden**, natives of CLONAKILTY. When last heard of, Jerome was inspector on Barry & Sons' Railroad Works. Also of **John Madden**, blacksmith, from ROSS CARBERRY; supposed to be on JAMES RIVER, VIRGINIA. Any information respecting them will be thankfully received by **Timothy Madden**, or **Patrick Blake**, No. 141 EAST 11th ST., NEW YORK. [Appeared under County CORK].

Of **Margaret Sweeny**, FREEMOUNT, County CORK, Ireland, who sailed from Cork six years since. When last heard of was in Water Street, CHICAGO, ILL. Any information of her will be thankfully received by her brother. **Edmonde Sweeny**,141 EAST 24th ST., NEW YORK. Chicago papers please copy.

Of **Jeremiah** and **Joseph Bourke O'Shaughnessy**, County LIMERICK, when last heard from they were in Scott & Wells' employment, ELMIRA, N.Y. Any information of them will be thankfully received by their niece, **Mrs. Maguire**, (her maiden name was **Mary Ryan**) No. 682 HOUSTON STREET, NEW YORK.

Of **William Bourke**, of NENAGH, County TIPPERARY. When last heard from was in the State of OHIO, but was about starting for CALIFORNIA. Any information of him will be thankfully received by his sister, **Ellen Hartigan**, 20 Washington Square, BOSTON.

April 21, 1855

Of **James Hanrahan**, from the Parish of RATHKEALE, Co. LIMERICK, Ireland. When last heard from (about two months since) he wrote from SCHENECTADY, in this State. Any information of him directed to this office will be thankfully received by his sister, **Ellen Hanrahan**.

Of **Martin Clifford**, from the Parish of FEDAMORE, Co. LIMERICK, Ireland. When last heard from he was in WILLIAMSBURGH. Any information of him will be thankfully received by addressing a note to No. 6 Vanbrunt Street, near William Street, BROOKLYN, for **Ellen Ryan**.

Of **Maria Coleman**, who landed in New York, in June 1854, with **Bridget Murphy**, from the Bazzar, City CORK, Ireland, by her sister **Margaret**. Enquire of **John F. Pinson**, 307 MADISON STREET, N.Y.

Of **John Lynan**, son of **Thomas Lynan**, Parish of KIMALY, County FERMANAGH. Arrived in this country about 11 years ago. When last heard from about three years since, was in County State, FILBRET, GEORGIA. Any information of him will be thankfully received by his brother, **Philip Lynan**, care of **Ann Cassidy**, 175 WEST 24th STREET, NEW YORK CITY.

Of **Thomas Newell**, of HEADFORD, County GALWAY, Ireland. When last heard from he was in PITTSBURGH, PENNSYLVANIA. Any information respecting him will be thankfully by his daughter, **Catharine Newell**. Who is lately landed in New York. Address to **John Wolfe**, 62 CHERRY STREET, NEW YORK.

Of **Michael Meagher**, who embarked for this country about the year 1848, and subsequently sent letters to Ireland dated from CLEVELAND, OHIO. The place of his nativity is KNOCKANORAN, CASTLE DURROW, QUEEN'S County; and also the **ROBERT's** from BURNCHURCH, Co. KILKENNY. Should this come under the notice of any person that may know anything to lead to his or their address, the informant will confer a desirable favor by communication it to his brother **Denis Meagher**, North 10th Street, next to 1st St., WILLIAMSBURGH, N.Y. Ohio and Illinois papers please copy.

May 5, 1855

Of **Daniel Sheehan**, from KENMARE, Co. KERRY, Ireland, who came to this country the 17th of March 1851. When last heard of about seven months ago, he was on a steamboat on LAKE SUPERIOR. Any intelligence of him will be thankfully received by his mother, **Jane Sheehan**, 146 ANTHONY STREET, N.Y. Chicago papers please copy.

Of **Catherine Mahony** and child **Mary**, from MITCHELSTOWN, County CORK, Ireland, who landed in New York on the 28th of August last, per packet ship *Cynosure*. She went to the Marine Hospital in a few days after, and was discharged on the second of October. She was at some boarding house near the EAST RIVER before going to Hospital. Any information respecting her or the child left at the office of Williams & Guion, 40 Fulton Street, where there is commands for her since November, will be gratefully acknowledged by her distressed husband, **Jeremiah Mahony**, ST. LOUIS.

May 12, 1855

Of **James M'Devitt**, who left No. 127 CHERRY STREET about six weeks ago, since which nothing has been heard from him. Any information of him will be thankfully received by his son-in-law, **James M'Ardle**, 127 Cherry Street.

Of **William Branegan**, late of DUBLIN, who landed in New York in August, 1850, and when last heard from was in PERTH AMBOY, N.J. Any intelligence of his whereabouts will be most thankfully received by his wife, **Elizabeth Branegan**, 124 Atlantic Street, BROOKLYN.

Of **Lancelot Tierney**, from the Parish of CANNANDROCK, County TYRONE, Ireland, who left his home in YORKVILLE, about three weeks ago, and has not been heard from since. Any information concerning him will be thankfully received and liberally rewarded by his disconsolate wife, **Elizabeth Tierney**, corner 80th Street and 3rd Avenue, YORKVILLE, N.Y

May 26, 1855

Of **Mary Moren**, who left the Town of DINGLE, County KERRY, Ireland and expected to be in BOSTON. Do not know how long she is out. Address to her sister, **Ellen Moren**, No. 224 WEST SIXTEENTH STREET, N.Y. Boston papers please copy.

Of **Edmond Cotter** and Wife, also of her sister, **Nancy**, whose maiden names are **Harding** – all from NEWTOWN, Parish of SHANDRUM, County CORK, Ireland, who landed here sixteen years ago, in the packetship *Clifton*. When last heard from they resided in SPRINGFIELD, MASS. Any information respecting them will be thankfully received by their brother, **Thomas Harding**, at 160 WILLIAM STREET, N.Y.

Of **John** and **James Walsh**, of the City of CORK, Ireland. John has been in this country four years, and James seven years. When last heard from they were in CUMBERLAND, OHIO. Any information of their present whereabouts will be thankfully received by their brother, **Patrick Walsh**. Direct, care of **Maurice Meara**, No. 16 THAMES STREET, N.Y.

June 2, 1855

Of **James Cloyne**, late of the Parish of CASHEL, County LONGFORD, Ireland; left there nearly four years ago; when last heard of was said to be in WAUKEGAN, ILL. Any intelligence of him will be thankfully received by his sister's daughter, **Maria Donnelan**, 217 MOTT STREET, NEW YORK

Of **Peter Oxbury**, or Wife, who left LIVERPOOL in 1851, and subsequently sent letters to his mother, dated from NEW ORLEANS, LA. Should this come under the notice of any person that may know anything to lead to their address, they will confer a great favor by communicating it to their brother, **John Oxbury**, LYNN, MASS; or **Mr. John Kennedy**, RANDOLPH, MASS. New Orleans papers please copy.

Of **Daniel Flavin**, of the County CORK, Parish of YOUGHAL, near KILLEAGH, or of **Johanna**, his wife, who is about fourteen or fifteen years in this country; supposed to be in NEW ORLEANS; when last heard from about twelve years ago were in New Orleans. Any information from them will be thankfully received by their son, **Dan Flavin**, who arrived in this country a few weeks ago, and wishes to hear from his parents. A line can be addressed to **Thomas Egan**, WATERFORD, SARATOGA County, NEW YORK.

June 9, 1855

Of **James**, **Timothy**, and **John Hartnett**: When last heard of they were in BINGHAMTON, BROOME County, N.Y. Any intelligence of them will be thankfully received by their sister, **Mary Hartnett**, 682 HOUSTON STREET, N.Y., care of **James Maguire**. [Appeared under LIMERICK]

Of **William Crocon**, from STROKESTOWN, Co. ROSCOMMON, Ireland, who landed in New York, in December last. Any information of him will be thankfully received by his sister, **Ellen Crocon**, 66 Portland Street, BALTIMORE, MARYLAND.

June 16, 1855

Will **John H. Fox**, Tailor and Cutter, please send his address to the undersigned so that he may write to him. **John Kelly** at the Office of the Irish American.

Of **Catherine Dowdall**, of SHANCOBANE, Parish o[f]' INNISKEEN, County MONAGHAN, who arrived in the bark *Perseverance* from Dublin, on the 25th of December 1851. When last heard of was in STEUBIN [Steuben] County Hospital, N.Y., in 1853. Any information of her will be thankfully received by her sisters **Anne** and **Margaret Dowdall**, also by her brother in law and sister, **Peter** and **Mary McKenna**, 179 South 1st Street, WILLIAMSBURGH, L.I. Steuben Co. papers please copy.

Of **James**, **Thomas** and **Richard Kenna**, of the RACE COURSE, Parish of THURLES. Richard came to this country about ten years ago. Thomas married to **Peggy Hayes**, came to this country eleven years ago; and James, married to **Peggy Mars**, came out five years ago. Any information of them will be gratefully received by their brother **Patrick Kenna**, lately landed, and residing at No. 224 42nd STREET, NEW YORK CITY.

June 23, 1855

Of **Margaret Daly**, about 13 years of age, was hired about 2 months ago from Manning's office, Bowery, by a lady calling herself **Mrs. Ferris**, of HOPPUSTOWN NEW JERSEY. It is feared she has been enticed away. Any information of her will be handsomely rewarded, and would confer a lasting favor on her disconsolate mother, **Ellen Daly**, Metropolitan Hotel, NEW YORK.

Of **Catherine** and **Eliza Hagarty**, the first from the Parish of BALLYMACORMICK, and the second TEARLICKING, County LOUTH. Catharine is eight and Eliza five years in this country, and are supposed to be living in NEW YORK or BROOKLYN. Information of them will be thankfully received by their brother, **James Hagarty**, SUMMITVILLE, CAMBRIA Co., PA., care of **John Fox**. [P.]M., CRESSON STATION.

June 30, 1855

Of **Margaret Collins**, of the City of GLASGOW, SCOTLAND, who landed in New York, on the 17th instant from the City of MOBILE. Any information of her will be thankfully received by her father, **John Collins** at **Mr. Peter White's**, 43 PECK SLIP, NEW YORK.

Of **John** and **Thomas Gleeson**, formerly of CAHER, County TIPPERARY, Ireland. Thomas arrived in New York in the *Manhattan* about 16 months ago. When last heard of were in WARREN Co., State of OHIO. Any information of them will be thankfully received by their brother **Patrick Gleeson**, FLUSHING Post Office, L.I.

Of **Daniel Sheehan**, from KENMARE, Co. KERRY, Ireland who came to this country the 17th of March 1851, and left NEW YORK three years since. When last heard from, was on the Missouri River, and is now supposed to be in TEXAS. Any intelligence of him will be thankfully received by his mother, **Jane Sheehan**, 146 ANTHONY STREET, N.Y. Missouri and Texas papers please copy.

July 7, 1855

Of **Francis Grimes**, tailor by trade of BELFAST who sailed from Liverpool for New York by the *Lucy Thausan* in the month of August 1853. Information of him will be thankfully received by his wife **Bridget Grimes**, 133 WEST 40th STREET, between 7th and 8th Avenues. California papers please copy.

Of **Thomas Moran**, of BALLYNOE, near NEWCASTLE WEST, County LIMERICK. When last heard of lived in 101 8th Street, between Broadway and Canal, CINCINNATI: any information of him will be thankfully received by his brother **Michael** (late of London,) at 138 29th ST., between 2nd and 3rd Avenues NEW YORK. Cincinnati papers please copy.

Will **William Nealon** painter, of BOHERBUOY, LIMERICK please to send his address to the undersigned, so that he may write to him and settle an old score. **D. Flanery**. BATON ROUGE LOUISIANA.

July 14, 1855

Of **Julia** and **Ann Byrnes**, from the COMMONS OF CASHEL, County TIPPERARY, Ireland. When last heard from were some place in BOSTON. Any information of them will be thankfully received by their sister **Margaret Byrnes**. Address 90 CATHARINE STREET, NEW YORK, Care of **John Dwyer**. Boston papers please copy.

Of **Margaret Riley**, wife of **Mathew Riley** of KILDALIAR, County CAVAN, Ireland. When last heard from was in BALTIMORE – some four years ago. Any information respecting her will be thankfully received by **John** and **Catherine Gilhooley**. Address to PENATAQUIT Post Office, Long Island, N.Y.

Of **Patrick Goss**, KILKENNY, Ireland. Landed in America, about six years ago. Any information respecting him will be thankfully received by his brother **William Goss**, at No. 526 PEARL STREET, NEW YORK.

Of **Patrick York**, a native of LONGFORD. When last heard from he was in this city. Any intelligence of him will be thankfully received by his sister, **Eliza York**, at No. 71 DUANE STREET.

Of **Daniel Ryan**, of GLASHA; **Patrick Murphy**, TALLOW BRIDGE; **Bridget Browne**, RUSSELSTOWN. Information of all, or either of the above, will be thankfully received by **John Browne**, 20 JAY ST., NEW YORK. [Appeared under WATERFORD]

July 21, 1855

Of **Joseph Hodgens**, of the City of DUBLIN, who arrived in New York about two years ago. When last heard of was living with **Dr. Cook**, of HOLMSDELL, MONMOUTH County, NEW JERSEY. Should this come under the notice of any person that may know anything that might lead to his address they will confer a great favor by communicating it to his brother, **Augustine Hodges**, at **Hugh M'Cabe's**, 156 WEST 32^d STREET, NEW YORK, in the rere [sic]. New Orleans papers please copy.

Of **Mr. Marin**, Boot and Shoemaker, and his wife **Alicia**, of MALAHIDE, County DUBLIN. A friend of his who would be of service to him is anxiously waiting to see him at 101 DELANCEY STREET; a few doors below Ludlow Street, in the rere [sic].

Of **Patrick** or **(John) Ahern**: When last heard from was in CALAIS, State of MAINE, but is now supposed to be in BANGOR. Any information of him will be thankfully received by his wife, **Mary Ahern**, at **Patrick Drury's**, 32 MADISON STREET, NEW YORK. Maine papers please copy.

Of **Honora Buckley**, from the Parish of AGLISH, County CORK, Ireland, who came to this country with her cousin, **Ellen Connell**, in the ship *Onward*. When last heard from she was in NEW YORK, and is now supposed to be in BOSTON. Any information of her will be thankfully received by her cousin, Ellen Connell, at 345 FRANKLIN SQUARE, NEW YORK. Boston papers please copy.

Of **Patt Shanahan**, Parish of BALLYMACODY, County CORK, Ireland. Address **Thomas Carroll**, Orderly of Ward 28, WARD'S ISLAND, N.Y.

Of **William Scott**, of Parish and County MONAGHAN, Ireland, who sailed in ship *Lucy Thompson* from Liverpool in May, 1854. Any information that may lead to his address, will be thankfully received by **James M'Culloch**, 436 GRAND STREET, N.Y.

August 4, 1855

Of **James Croghan**, a native of the Co. ROSCOMMON and Parish of THELBRIDE, Ireland. When last heard from he was in CLAY County, ILLINOIS. Any information respecting him will be thankfully received by his wife **Ellen Croghan**, at No. 520 WASHINGTON ST., NEW YORK.

August 11, 1855

Of **Michael Murray**, of CARBERRY, Co. KILDARE, who left this city in the early part of 1853, deserting his wife to whom he was only three weeks married. He is supposed to be in HARTFORD, CT., where his brother **James** resides. Any information of him will be thankfully received by his wife **Ann Murray**, 64 Warren Street, between Henry and Clinton Streets, BROOKLYN, N.Y.

Of **Catherine Maloney**, native of WEXFORD, Ireland, who landed in New York in the ship *Universe* from Liverpool about the middle of the present year. If any of the passengers that came in the vessel at the time can give any information of her it will be thankfully received by **Richard Maloney**, 54 Park Street, BALTIMORE, M.D.; or **George Donaldson**, sadler, 203 BOWERY, NEW YORK.

Of **John Hartnett**, Parish of BALLYBAHILL, County LIMERICK, who landed in America in the beginning of the present year. Is supposed to be in NEW ORLEANS. Any information of him will be thankfully received by **Michael** or **Mary Enright**, his brother and sister, 19 State Street, BROOKLYN, N.Y.

August 18, 1855

Of **Deaglan Kane**, of ARDMORE, County WATERFORD, Ireland, who arrived in the America about one and a half years since. When last heard of was in CHICAGO, ILL. Any information of him will be thankfully received by his brother **Patrick Kane**, who arrived in New York four months since. Address **James O'Neill**, cor. 39th STREET and 11th AVENUE.

Of **Michael Anthony**, formerly of MAYNOOTH, County KILDARE, Ireland. Is supposed to be in BOSTON. Any information of him will be thankfully received by his sister, **Catherine Anthony**, 210 GREENWICH STREET, NEW YORK.

Of **Hugh Pathen**, son of **James Pathen**, of the Town of FRENCH, County DERRY, Ireland, who is now in this country. Any one knowing the party will please address **Mrs. Kelly**, 174 Endicot Street, BOSTON, MASS.

August 25, 1855

Of **Richard Healy**, formerly of MOUNTMELLERAY, Co. WATERFORD, Ireland, and of his brother, **Michael Healy**, of same place, who landed in this country about seven years since. Any account of her children will be thankfully received by their aged mother, at **Mr. Owen Connery's**, 189 GREEN STREET [GREENE ST.], NEW YORK. Philadelphia papers please copy.

Of **Susanna Cunning**, who left County DOWN Ireland, about 25 years ago. If this should find her, or any of her friends, they will hear of something to her advantage by applying to **Mr. E. Wilson**, No. 135 South Front Street, PHILADELPHIA, or **Mr. James Ferguson**, BALLYMAGREECHNAN, Ireland.

Of **Thomas Hoy**, who arrived at the port of New York, 18th of April, 1852, from WEESTOWN, one mile from ASHBORDEN, County DUBLIN, Ireland. Is supposed to have gone to INDIANA. When last heard from was on the railroad, any information of his whereabouts, dead or alive, will be thankfully received by his anxious sister, **Martha Handlen**, HOBOKEN, N.J. Indiana papers please copy.

Of **John Conlon**, of SHINRONE, GURK GREEN, KING'S County, Ireland. When last heard from was in WOMELSDORPH, BERKS County, PA., employed on the Lebanon Valley Railroad. Any account of him will be thankfully received by his afflicted mother, **Margaret Conlon**, No. 5 VANDEWATER ST., N.Y. Philadelphia papers please copy.

If this advertisement should meet the eye of **James Lawler**, or **Lawless**, of CASTLE DERMOTT, County KILDARE, Ireland, please send your address to the Office of this paper, to M.A.L. Sydney and Hobart Town papers please copy.

Of **John** and **Patrick Hanly**, of BALLINACARRGA, Barony of KENRY, County LIMERICK, Ireland. John came to America about eight years since, and Patrick came about five years since. When last heard from was in PLEASANT VALLEY, KENTUCKY. Any information of them will be thankfully received by **John Lynch**, 36 ½ SCAMYLL STREET [Scammel Street], or at the Irish American Office.

September 1, 1855

Of **Michael Walsh**, of AHALUSKY, Parish of KILMALOODA, County CORK, Ireland, whose mother's name is **Betty Ryan**. When last heard from the 14th of last January, he worked on the Iron Mountain Railroad, WASHINGTON Co., MO. **Richard Whelan**, of the County TIPPERARY, was his butty [sic]. Any information of him will be thankfully received by his brother, **Patrick**, Hopewell Cottonworks, CHESTER Co. PA, or his uncle **Humphry Hennessey**, 82 SHERIFF ST., NEW YORK.

September 8, 1855

John O'Brien, aged ten years, who arrived in this City on the 20th of July last in the ship *Aurora*, from Liverpool, is anxious to see or hear from his uncle **William Fahey**, who lately resided at No. 100 ANTHONY STREET. Apply or address Commissioners of Emigration, 81 Anthony Street.

Of **Michael Murphy**, from CARAHANE, Parish of ARDFERT, County KERRY, Ireland, who emigrated to the State of TENNESSEE, from NEW YORK about twelve months ago. Any information respecting him will be, thankfully received by his sister **Margret**, addressed to this Office.

Of **Edward Mohan** who came from BALBRIGGAN, County DUBLIN, Ireland. Any intelligence of him will be thankfully received by his wife, No. 264 Main Street, CHARLESTOWN, MASS.

Of **Joseph Doyle**, laborer, who left DUNDRUM, DUBLIN, Ireland, for America, in or about the month of February, 1852, since when no account has been heard of him. His age is about twenty-seven years, of stout make; he is 5 feet 6 inches high. Any intelligence of him will be thankfully received by his brother **Laurence Doyle**, No. 23 Canal Street, ALBANY, N.Y.

Of **John Corcoran** who left SALEM, MASS., in June, 1854, for NEW YORK. The said John Corcoran came from CHARLEVILLE, County CORK, Ireland. Any intelligence respecting him will be thankfully received by his sister, No. 264 Main Street, CHARLESTOWN, MASS.

September 15, 1855

Of **John Osborne** and **Jane Blake** from the Parish of MULLIN, County CAVAN, Ireland. When last heard from was about 3 months ago. Jane Blake is probably in OHIO. Any intelligence of them will be thankfully received by **Mary Smith**, niece of Jane Blake, care of **Michael Dawson**, 76 Amity St., BROOKLYN, N.Y.

September 22, 1855

Of **Patrick Begly**, of PRESCOTT, LANCASHIRE, ENGLAND, who left Liverpool on the 28th September, 1852, and landed in New York. When last heard from he was at **John Bourke's** Main and Morgan Streets, ST. LOUIS, MO. Any information of him will be thankfully received by his wife **Catherine Begly**, 105 MADISON STREET, N.Y., care of **Michael Coughlan**.

September 29, 1855

Of **Denis Keary**, of KILLISLAND MILLS, near LOUGHREA, Co. GALWAY, Ireland, who landed in New York in August, 1848. Should this meet his eye or any person knowing his whereabouts, they will confer a favor by communicating with his brother, **Darby Keary**, at TARRYTOWN, WESTCHESTER County, N.Y. Cincinnati papers please copy.

Of **Lawrence McCarthy** of LISQUINLAN, Parish of LADY'S BRIDGE, Co. CORK, Ireland. When last heard of he was in ST. LOUIS. Any information of him will be thankfully received by his sister, **Betty McCarthy**, 450 CHERRY STREET, NEW YORK.

October 6, 1855

Of **Launcelot Tierney**, by his brother and sister, **Patrick** and **Margaret Tierney**. By calling at, or writing to **Mr. Weeks**, No. 4 HALL PLACE, he will see them.

Of **John Caisey** and family of BALLYPORTRY, Parish of LOUGHGILL, County ANTRIM, Ireland, who landed in New York about three years ago in the ship *George Washington*. When last heard from he resided in CHATHAM, COLUMBIA County, State of NEW YORK. Any information of him or his whereabouts will be thankfully received by his wife's sister, **Margaret M'Coay**, at No. 129 Court Street, BROOKLYN, Long Island, near New York, or if this should meet his eye I wish he would answer this advertisement. Albany papers please copy.

If this Advertisement should meet the eye of **Patrick Carroll** or his brother **James**, of KINSKELLA, County MAYO, Ireland, one of them will please call at or write to **John McE[ ]ly**, 95 WEST 19th STREET, NEW YORK, and they will hear from their sister **Bridget**, who is in AUSTRALIA.

Of **John Ronan**, for the Parish of CLAREABBEY, Co. CLARE, Ireland. When last heard from was in GALENA, ILLINOIS. Any information about him will be thankfully received by **H. Klison**, 324 Atlantic Street, BROOKLYN.

October 13, 1855

Of **Peter Calden**, Bricklayer, who left NEW YORK about 14 months ago, 23 years of age, and is supposed to be in the State of PENNSYLVANIA. Any information concerning him will be thankfully received by his wife or mother. Direct to **Maria Calder**, 340 SEVENTH AVENUE, N.Y.

Of **John Corless**, from the Parish of KILCOLEMAN, Co.: MAYO, Ireland, stone mason and stonecutter by trade. Left NEW YORK 4th of January, 1852, and went to the New York and Erie Canal. The last heard from him was in LOUISVILLE, KY. Direct to his brother, **James Corless**, 78 NORFOLK ST., N.Y.

If **Margaret O'Mara**, who left her parents in BRIDGEWATER, MASS, in January, 1853 will call at **James Spellman's** 248 WEST STREET, NEW YORK she will meet her father and mother who are anxious to embrace her for any person knowing her present address will confer a great favor by sending it to the same place.

Of **Kyran Fitzpatrick**, Engineer and land Surveyor, also his sister **Anne Fitzpatrick**, natives of CASTLE DURROW, QUEEN'S County, Ireland. Any information concerning them will be thankfully received by **Mrs. Purcell** 125 24th STREET, between 6th and 7th Avenues. Other papers please copy.

October 20, 1855

Of **David Fleming**. When last heard of was in LOWDEN County, VIRGINIA. His mother and sisters are expected to land here every [sic] day. **Julia O'Connell**, NEW YORK CITY.

Of **Philip Dunn**, who came to this country about four years ago, from DUBLIN. When last heard from was with **James Madden**, New York, from where he wrote to his father, who is employed by W. & E. Ryan. No. 1 Merchants Quoy, Dublin. If this should meet his eye or that of any one that knows him, they will confer a favor by addressing **James Madden**, Bookseller and News Depot, Tompkins Market, THIRD AVENUE, N.Y., or his troubled father **Patk. Dunn**, care of W. and E. Ryan, No. 1 Merchants Quay, DUBLIN. San Francisco papers please copy.

Of **Michael Hughes**, a native of BALLINAGARE, Co. ROSCOMMON, Ireland, who landed in this country about the year 1851, and in July, 1851 sent letters to SPRING GARDENS, NEW

JERSEY, dated from BRIDGEPORT Post-office, HARRISON County, VIRGINIA. Should any person notice this advertisement, that may knew anything to lead to his address, they would aliay the anxiety of his despondent sister, **Mary Hughes**, by addressing her at No. 4 Division Avenue, WILLIAMSBURGH, N.Y. Virginia papers please copy.

Of **William Fitzgibbons**, of MITCHELSTOWN, County CORK, Ireland who arrived in this County three years ago last July. When heard from last April was in MAU[ ]NA CENTRE, PORTAGE County, OHIO. Any information of him will be thankfully received by his sister, **Alice Fitzgibbons**, at **Mr. Fenton's** 43 ½ CHERRY STREET, NEW YORK.

Of **Finton Delaney**, a laborer, a native of QUEEN'S County, Ireland. Left PATERSON, N.J. about 18 months ago, and is supposed to be now in or about NEW YORK CITY. Any information concerning him will be thankfully received by his wife, **Julia Delany**. Address in care of **Coddington**, Esq., Paterson, N.J.

October 27, 1855

Of **Ralph Mason**, from the Parish of BALLY M'ELLIGOT, County KERRY, Ireland, who came to this country in the barque *Toronto*, in May 1851. When last heard from he was in NEW HAMDEN, NEW JERSEY. Any information of him will be thankfully received by his three children who arrived in New York about a month since. Direct to **Mr. Decourcey**, 20 PEARL STREET, NEW YORK.

Of **Daniel Armstrong**, a Bricklayer, from MALLOW, Co. CORK, Ireland; has been in the Mexican War; was seen in NEW YORK about three years ago. – Any information of him will be thankfully received by his sister **Honora Armstrong**, No. 23 NINTH AVENUE, N.Y., care of **Mr. John Clancy**.

November 3, 1855

Of **John Mackel**, of MAGHERAFELT, Co. LONDONDERRY, Ireland, who arrived in New York between seven and eight years since. When last heard from, about six months since, was in DELAWARE, OHIO, with **Mr. Thos. Tighe**. Any information of him will be thankfully received by his sister **Sarah Mackel**, care of **Mr. Hewy**, No. 1 BOWERY.

Of **Michael Kenny**, of LONGFORD, Ireland, who arrived in New York about fourteen or fifteen years since. He is supposed to be residing in BOSTON, where he was keeping a boarding house some few years since. – Any information of him will be thankfully received by his sister **Fanny Kenny**, No. 5 WASHINGTON STREET, NEW YORK.

Of **Daniel Hoarhen** and **Thomas Conway**, Parish of TOMGREANY, Co. CLARE, Ireland. When heard from last April, Daniel Hoarhen was in CINCINNATI, corner of Fifth and Butler Sts. Information also of **Catherine Conway** of same place; when last heard of was in ALBANY, N.Y. Any information of them will be thankfully received by **Mary Hoarhen**, wife of Daniel Hoarhen, and sister of Thomas and Catherine Conway. Address Emigrant Intelligence Office, Canal St., N.Y.

November 10, 1855

By **Patrick** and **Garrett Murphy**, of their brother, **John Murphy**, of NEWTOWN, County CARLOW, Ireland. He enlisted in the 19th Regiment of foot about seven years ago, and deserted from the same about five years ago in MONTREAL, CANADA, and came to the United States. If this should meet his eye he would do well by sending a few lines to the care of **Mr. N. Stetson**, ORANGE, N.J. for Patrick Murphy, where it will meet prompt attention.

Of **Philip Reilly**, a native of the Parish of BALLINTEMPLE, Co. CAVAN, Ireland, aged 15 years. When last heard of, two years ago, he was with his mother in NEW HAVEN, CONN. He then went to NEW YORK, and lived a few months with a cabinetmaker there, but has not been since heard of. Any information of him will be thankfully received by his afflicted mother. Address care of **Alfred Walker**, Esq., 52 Wall Street, NEW HAVEN, CONN., for **Widow Catherine Reilly**.

November 24, 1855

Of **Margaret Byrne**, of CASHEL, County TIPPERARY, Ireland, wishes to inform her sister **Julia**, residing in MARLBORO, MASS., that she has received all her letters, in one of which was money, and has answered them. If she will write, directing her letter to **John Dwyer**, 90 CATHARINE STREET, N.Y., stating with whom she is living, she will write to her.

Of **Catherine Walsh**, from near LIGHTFORD, MAYO, Ireland, by her Uncle, **Martin Henaghon**, at the Wyoming House, 41 Walnut Street, PHILADELPHIA, PA.

December 1, 1855

Of **John Manning**, When last heard from was in NEW ORLEANS. Any news of him will be thankfully received by his wife, **Anne Manning**. Direct CARMANSVILLE, FORT WASHINGTON Post-office, State of NEW YORK. New Orleans papers please copy.

Of **Richard Fennessy**, of the Parish of GLANVERT, County CORK, Ireland, by his mother **Mary Fennessy**, who arrived here a few weeks ago. Any information of him will be thankfully received by his cousin **Michael Pigott**, 59th STREET and 2nd AVENUE.

December 8, 1855

Of **Maria Doyle** and sister **Bridget**, from the County KILDARE, Ireland. When last heard from they were in NEW YORK. They can have information of their deceased sister **Catharine Doyle**, by addressing **Michael McLoughlin**, JACKSON, MISS.

Of **Susan M'Cabe**, from the Parish of BALLYHAISE, Townland of KILNACREEVA, County CAVAN, Ireland, aged 18 years, who landed about two years ago, and is supposed to be in NEW YORK with her aunt. Any information of her will be thankfully received by her aunt **Susan M'Cabe**, at No. 13 HESTER ST., N.Y.

December 15, 1855

Of **Richard Cleary**, late of WEST FARMS, N.Y. When last heard of was in WISCONSIN, WALWORTH Co., near EAST TROY. Address **John Cleary**, 53 Water St., NEWBURGH, N.Y.

Of **Christopher Hand**, of DEAN HILL, Co MEATH, Ireland. He left NEW YORK about 18 months ago, and has not been heard of since. Any information of him will be thankfully received by his anxious mother, **Jane Hand**, addressed to the care of her son, **Geo. Hand**, No. 57 42nd STREET, between 5th and 6th Avenues, NEW YORK.

Of **James Sullivan**, of the Co. MEATH, Ireland, who arrived here three years since. When heard of five months since, was in SAUTE STE MARIE, MICH. Any information of him will be thankfully received by his sister **Mary**, who arrived here two months since. Address, Mary Sullivan, care of **Mrs. Lynch**, 46 HAMMERELY STREET [Hamersley Street], N.Y.

Of **Thomas Blanchfield**, formerly of LISHEEN, CASHEL, Co. TIPPERARY, Ireland, who emigrated to this country in the year 1836. Is supposed to be in Toloum[n]e co]., CAL, at present. Any information of him will be thankfully received by his sister, **Catharine Blanchfield**, 36 WEST THIRTY THIRD STREET, N.Y.

Of **Patrick Murphy**, a native of BALLISODARE, County SLIGO, Ireland. When last heard from was stopping at **Michael White's**, ROME, N.Y.; is suppose to be now in OHIO. Any information about him will be thankfully received by his sister **Catharine**: care of **Thomas Plunkett**, 13 MOTT STREET, N.Y. Ohio papers please copy.

December 22, 1855

Of **Michael Hogan**, by his step-daughter, **Mary Kelly**, of LIMERICK, Ireland. He was in OHIO, when last heard from, six months ago. Please direct your letter to **Thomas Doody**, 139 CHERRY STREET, N.Y.

January 5, 1856

Of **Pat Mulron**, a native of BIRMINGHAM in ENGLAND, who has been in some part of VIRGINIA for upwards of two years, or of his wife **Ann Mulron** otherwise **Hyland**. Any information of their whereabouts send to the office of the Commissioners of Emigration, New York, will be thankfully received by **Catherine Hyland**, the daughter of the latter.

Of **Timothy Mahony**, Printer, who left FREDERICKSON, NEW BRUNSWICK, in July, 1854, is supposed to be in NEW YORK. Please address his brother, **John Mahony**, No. 3 Stillman Place, BOSTON.

The Subscribe[r] will be thankful for any information in regard to her brother, **John Moloney**. When last heard from in 1853, he was living in NEWCASTLE, in HENRY Co., INDIANA. Any communication respecting him, addressed to **Mr. Heman Mead**, MORRISTOWN, NEW JERSEY, will be gratefully received by her anxious sister **Catherine Bergen**.

January 12, 1856

Of **Peter** and **Thomas Mathews**, from NEWGRANGE, Co. MEATH, Ireland. Peter left home about 9 years ago, and Thomas about 5 years. When last heard of Thomas was in a brick-yard at PLANKS POINT, N.Y., which he left for the White House Railroad, since when he has not been heard of. Any intelligence of them will be thankfully received by their brother **James** or their sister **Anne**, care of **John Devlin**, 33 PRINCE ST., N.Y.

Of **William Doherty**, for the Parish of KOLLMAIN, Co. CLARE, Ireland, who came to this country about twelve years ago. Any information respecting him will be thankfully received by his brother **Michael Doherty**.

January 26, 1856

Of **Bridget Bradley**, from the City of LONDONDERRY, Ireland, who came to this country about 8 years ago. She got married to a man named **John Bogan**. About two years ago she was in PHILADELPHIA on a visit to her sister. Any intelligence of her present address will be thankfully received by her sister, who is now in this city. Address, **Mrs. Douglass**, No. 8 Furman Street, BROOKLYN.

Of **James Prendergast**, who left NEWARK, N.J., on the 29th of August, 1855; is supposed to be on some public works in the State of NEW YORK. Any information of him will be thankfully received by his wife **Bridget** and brother **Patrick Prendergast**, at 38 Prospect Street, Newark, N.J. Exchange papers please copy.

February 2, 1856

Of **Catharine Lysten**, from BALLYDWAN, Parish of MUNGRET, Co. LIMERICK, Ireland. Took shipping on the 3[ ]th of August, 1855, in the packet *Australia*, and landed in New York on the 19th of October, 1855 – Any information respecting her will be thankfully received by her brother, **John Lysten**, at WEST TROY, ALBANY County, N.Y.

Of **David Fleming**, from KILLARNEY, Co. KERRY, Ireland, by his mother and sisters, who arrived here some time since. Any information respecting his whereabouts will be thankfully received by addressing **Jos. Rice**, 273 PEARL STREET, N.Y.

Of **Patrick** and **James Lacy**, for THOMASTOWN, Parish of GOLD[ ]N, Co. TIPPERARY, Ireland. – When last heard of was in ILLINOIS. Any information of them will be thankfully received by their brother, **John Lacy**, No. 60 MULBERRY STREET, N.Y. Illinois papers please copy.

February 16, 1856

Of **James O'Brien**, Stone-cutter, a native of WILMINGTON, DEL., where he served his apprenticeship to **Mr. Nelson Cleveland**. He did some stone cutting on the church of MOUNT HOLLY, N.J. Any intelligence of him will be thankfully received by his sister **Catharine**. Direct to the care of **Hugh O'Brien**, 110 Walnut Street, Wilmington, Del.

Of **Michael Finan**, a native of SLIGO, Ireland, who left his wife in LOUISVILLE, KY., on the 17th of December, 1854, for the purpose of getting work, intending to be absent only a short time, since when he was not been heard of. He had the initials of his name in blue letters on his left arm. Any intelligence of him, whether living or dead, will be thankfully received by his wife **Bridget Finan**, at 485 WASHINGTON STREET, NEW YORK. Cincinnati, St. Louis, and New Orleans papers, will confer a favor on his afflicted wife by copying the above.

Of **Thomas Connolly**, a native of the Co. MONAGHAN, Ireland, who emigrated from COOTEHILL, Co. CAVAN, about 4 years since, and landed in New York. – Any information of him will be thankfully received on behalf of his friends in Ireland, by **Mr. George Bennett**, corner of HENRY and CATHARINE STREETS, N.Y.

Of **Peter McGivney**, a native of the Parish of KILLINKERE, Co. CAVAN, Ireland. He was residing in the City of NEW YORK in June last (1855), since when he has not been heard of by any of his relations or friends. He is supposed to have gone to the country. – Any information respecting him will be thankfully received by his sister **Ann McGivney**. Address **Mr. John G. Butler**, No. 330 8th AVENUE, between 27th and 28th Streets, N.Y.

February 23, 1856

William Forney, your aged parents and friends are most anxious to hear from you at 93 BEDFORD STREET, NEW YORK. Western papers please copy. [Appeared March 1, 1856 with the surname **Forney** changed to **Torney**. Appeared September 27, 1856, with some additional information.]

March 1, 1856

Of **Edmond** and **John Powers**, natives of the Parish of KILL, Co. WATERFORD, Ireland. The former is about twenty years in the country, and when last heard from was in BROOKLYN; and the latter landed in New York about the year 1850. Any information concerning them will be thankfully received by their nephew, **James R Powers**, SAULT STE., MARIE, MICH.

Richard Farrell, a native of WATERFORD, Ireland. He left NEW YORK about six years ago; when last heard from he was in MOBILE, ALA. Any person who knows of his whereabouts will confer a favor by letting his parents know. Address **John Farrell**, corner of FORTIETH ST. and SECOND AVENUE, N.Y. Cincinnati, S. Louis, and New Orleans papers please copy.

Of **Mary Brady**, daughter of **Charles Brady** of CROSSERLOGH, Co. CAVAN, Ireland, who left her father about three years ago. Any information respecting will be thankfully received by **John Gaffney**, TIONET MILLS, MASSACHUSETTS.

March 8, 1856

Patrick Murphy, of TALLOW BRIDGE, Co. WATERFORD who replied to an advertisement in the "Irish American" in September last, will find several letters in the BLACKROCK (ERIE County, N.Y.) Post Office, from **R. Browne**, 170 EIGHTH AVENUE, N.Y.

Of **John Kelly**, a native of the Parish of CLASHMORE MON[S]TER, Co. WATERFORD, Ireland, who left home about 28 years ago. He had four brothers, **Edmond, Thomas, James**, and **Darby**. When last heard from he was in HALIFAX. Any intelligence of him will be thankfully received by his nephew, **John Kelly** (son of Edmond), care of Edmond O'Neill, MIANUS, FAIRFIELD County, CT. Halifax papers please copy.

Of **James Fegan**, of DONARD, Co. WICKLOW, Ireland, who left Liverpool in March, 1848. When last heard from was in NEW ORLEANS. Any information of him will be thankfully received by his cousin, **Patrick Doody**, at Tapicott & Coles office, [86] SOUTH STREET, NEW YORK. New Orleans and St. Louis papers please copy.

March 15, 1856

Of **Mary Downs**, daughter of **Francis Downs**, a native of KILRUSH, County CLARE, Ireland. – When last heard from, in 184[ ], was in NEW ORLEANS, married to a man of the name of **William P. Kennedy**, a County LIMERICK man. She is supposed to be in New Orleans. Any information of her will be thankfully received at this office, or by her brother, **John Downs**, SCHAGHTICOKE, RENSSELAER County, N.Y. New Orleans Catholic Standard please copy.

Of **Owen Conlon**, Stonemason, a native of the Parish of KILLANY, County MONAGHAN, Ireland, who emigrated to New York about nine years ago. When last heard from he was in PATERSON, NEW JERSEY. Any information respecting him will be thankfully received by his brother, **Patrick Conlon**, directed to CHELSEA Post Office, MASS.

Boy Lost. Left BEDFORD, WESTCHESTER County, N.Y., on the 9th of August last, a boy named **Edmond Tuomy**, a native of the Town of TIPPERARY, Ireland, 15 years old, with fair hair and round features; is rather thickset. Any person knowing anything of such a boy, will relieve his anxious mother's heart by dropping a line to **Mr. O'Brien**, 58 HAMMOND STREET, N.Y. (in the rear) Sing Sing and Pennsylvania papers please copy.

March 22, 1856

Of **Henry Kelly**, who left Bergen Iron Works about twelve months ago, and the last that was heard of him, he was working at BORDENTOWN, in a Rolling Mill, in company with **James Crothers**. Any information of his whereabouts, or anything concerning him whether dead or alive, will be thankfully received by his brother, **James Kelly**, Bergen Iron Works, N.J.: also anything of the whereabouts of James Crothers. Bordentown and Trenton papers please copy.

Of **John O'Brien**, Carpenter, who left CARRICK-ON-SHANNON, Co. LEITRIM, Ireland, in May, 1842, in company with **Terence** and **Margaret Boland**, for ST. JOHN, N.B. Where John last worked was in Carrick-on-Shannon, with his brother **Michael**, at the Poorhouse. Should he notice this, or any person who can give information of him, they would confer a favor on his brother, **Augustine O'Brien**, by writing a few lines to him. Direct to Augustine O'Brien, in care of **Mr. Andrew Coakly**, 27th STREET and 8th AVENUE, NEW YORK. Lowell papers please copy.

March 29, 1856

Of **Thomas T. Farrell**, who left MANCHESTER, N.H. on business to BOSTON, July 2nd, 1851, and has not returned since. When last heard from Oct, 1851, he was in

RICHMOND, VA. Any information of him, dead or living, will be thankfully received by his affectionate wife and child. **Elizabeth Farrell**, [STONEHAM] MASS.

Of **James W. McNamara**, from BALLINNEW, CASTLEBAR County MAYO, Ireland. He left BOSTON, MASS., on the 12th of January last, and has not been heard from since; supposed to be gone to ST. LOUIS, where his brother **Thomas McNamara** and family reside. Should this meet the eye of his brother, or any person acquainted with his whereabouts, they would confer a favor on his wife and family, by addressing a line to **Mrs. McNamara**, No. 7 Bunker-hill Street, CHARLESTOWN, BOSTON, MASS. St. Louis and Canada papers please copy.

Of **John Colman**, from BALLYSHEE, Parish of KILCHRIST. He sailed from Galway six years ago and landed in New York. Any information respecting him will be thankfully received by his sister **Bridget**. Direct to the care of **Patrick Moran**, Wallace St., NEW HAVEN, CONN. Western papers please copy.

April 5, 1856

Of **Peter McCormack**, Carpenter, from TUS[L]K, County ROSCOMMON, Ireland, who left his residence in NEW BRIGHTON, STATEN ISLAND, in August last, since which time he has not been heard of. Any intelligence of him, dead or alive, will be thankfully received by his sister **Bridget McCormack**, No.3 McCou[r]ter St., NEWARK, N.J.

Of **William Byrne**, of the Town of LONGFORD, Ireland. He is supposed to have sailed from Liverpool on the 28[th] of last January. Any information of him will be thankfully received by his brother **Michael Byrne**, corner of Concord and Lombard Streets, BALTIMORE, MARYLAND.

Of **Mary Raverty**, a native of GORTNAGARN, PLIMEROY, County TYRONE, Ireland. Came to this country about twelve years since; when last heard from she was in NEW YORK CITY. Her sister **Martha** is very anxious to see or hear from her. Any person given any information of her whereabouts will be liberally rewarded by her sister by calling on or addressing **B. Wood**, 225 NINTH AVENUE, near 25th ST., Philadelphia Ledger please copy.

Of **William Fitzgerald**, a native of CARLOW, Ireland. He landed in New Orleans about five years and a half ago. Any information of him will be meet thankfully received by his sister **Isabela Fitzgerald**. Direct, General Post Office, NEW YORK. St. Louis papers please copy.

April 12, 1856

Of **Anne** and **Bridget Garvey**, of CARRICKMAC[ROS]S, County MONAGHAN, Ireland. When last heard from, about five years ago, were living in CLEVELAND, OHIO. If this should meet the eye of anyone who can give the detailed information. They will please direct to **Mary Garvey**, 161 WEST 36th STREET, N.Y. Cleveland papers please copy.

Of **Martin** and **Mary Murphy**, from COOLMANNA, Parish of HACKETSTOWN, County CARLOW, Ireland. When last heard from they were in JACKSONVILLE, ILLINOIS. Any information of them will be thankfully received by their sister **Julia**. Address to the care of **John Kelly**, 87 EAST 32nd STREET, NEW YORK. Illinois papers please copy.

April 19, 1856

Of **Catharine Callaghan** otherwise **Mrs. Riordan**, formerly of the County CORK, Ireland. When last heard from she kept a large boarding house in the State of CONNECTICUT. Any information of her present whereabouts will be thankfully received by her present whereabouts will be thankfully received by her cousin, **Denis Duggan**, care of **Michael Shields**, No. 10 FRANKLIN STREET, NEW YORK.

Of **Thomas Ha[s]lep** or his son **James** from the Parish of MULAHORAN, County CAVAN, Ireland. When last heard from was in BUFFALO. Any information of him will be thankfully received by **Miss Ellen Dawson**. Address 242 EAST 14[th] STREET, NEW YORK, in care of **Richard Bergen**. Buffalo papers please copy.

May 3, 1856

Of **James Darcy** from the City of WATERFORD, Ireland. Any information of him will be thankfully received by his brother, **Joseph Darcy**. Direct to House's Telegraph Office, 31 State Street, BOSTON.

May 10, 1856

Of **Henry Murray** and **Margaret** his wife (before her marriage **Margaret Donegan**), natives of Ireland. They can hear of something greatly to their advantage on addressing (post paid) **Alexander Garesche**, ST. LOUIS, MO.

Of **John Gill** who left NEW YORK about two years ago, and has not been heard of since. Any information of him will be thankfully received by his sister at 166 EAST NINTH STREET, N.Y.

Of **John Noonan**, from LOUGHREA, Ireland, who left ST. JOHN'S, NEW BRUNSWICK, two years ago, for the State of OHIO. Any information respecting him will be thankfully received by his brothers **Timothy** and **Stephen Noonan**, or the **Rev. Father Kelly**, JERSEY CITY Post Office. Boston papers please copy. [Appeared under County GALWAY].

Of **Patrick H. Caffrey**, a native of the County CAVAN, Ireland, but for many years a resident in this country. When last heard from (in1848) he was residing in HANOVER County, VA. His intention then was to move South. Any information respecting will be thankfully received by his uncle, **J. P. Gilroy**, DONCASTER, CHARLES County, MD.

May 24, 1856

Of **James Gibney**, of OLD CASTLE, County MEATH, Ireland, who landed in New York about two years ago. Any person known of his present residence would confer a great favor by informing him or this advertisement, or by writing to his cousin, **Bryan Gibney**, care of **J. M. Crawford**, ST. LOUIS, MO.

Of **Hugh Smith**, of the Townland of TULLYDONNALD, Parish of CREGAN County ARMAGH, Ireland. Who came to this country about eleven years since. When last heard of he was living convenient to NIAGARA FALLS. Any information respecting him will be thankfully received by his sister **Margaret**. Direct to the care of **Hugh Byrnes**, No. 313 TWELFTH STREET, NEW YORK, between Avenues B and C.

Of **Patrick** and **James Lacey**, of THOMASTOWN, Parish of GOLDEN, County TIPPERARY, Ireland. When last heard from they were in COOK County, ILLINOIS. Any information of their whereabouts will be thankfully received by their brother, **John Lacey**, No. 60 MULBERRY STREET, NEW YORK. Illinois, St. Louis and New Orleans papers please copy.

Of **Richard Michael**, and **James Healy**, of MOUNT MELLARY, County WATERFORD, Ireland. When last heard of they were said to be living in the State of TENNESSEE, and to be working on a steamboat on the Mississippi River. Any intelligence of them will be thankfully received by their mother, **Widow Healy**, at **Edmond Connolly's**, 229 WEST 29th ST., N.Y.

Of **Mary McKernan**, a native of the Co. CAVAN, Ireland. Any information of her will be thankfully received by her brother **Thomas McKernan**, of No. 149 READE STREET, NEW YORK. Eastern and Western papers please copy.

May 31, 1856

Of **Timothy Mara**, from the Parish of LISTRY, County KERRY, Ireland, who left home in June, 1853. When last heard from was in ST. LOUIS. Any information respecting him will be thankfully received by his sister **Mary Mara**, by directing to **Michael Fitzgerald**, 9 VANDEWATER STREET, NEW YORK. St. Louis papers please copy.

Of **Mary O'Connor** a native of CAUSEWAY, County KERRY, Ireland. When last heard from she was living with **Mrs. Doyle**, 18 CANAL STREET. By calling at 26 VANDEWATER STREET or 41 FRANKFORT STREET, she will hear of her brother.

Of **Patrick Kearney**, from MOUNTMELLICK, QUEEN'S County, Ireland. When heard from last February, he was in some part of CONNECTICUT. He is married and has one child. His aunt, **Catharine Carroll**, would be glad to hear from him. Address to **Patrick Donnelly**, WEST MERIDEN, CONN.

Of **Michael Byrne** of MONEYSTOWN, Parish of ANNEMOE, County WICKLOW, Ireland. When last heard from was in PHILADELPHIA. Any information of him will be thankfully received by addressing **Andrew Byrne**, No. 10 STATE STREET, NEW YORK, where he will hear of something to his advantage.

June 14, 1856

Strayed from her home, No. 145 EAST 28th STREET, N.Y., **Anne Grey**, age 12 years. Any person that knows anything of her would confer a great favor by sending word to her mother at the above address. The child was thin and delicate looking, with light hair and dark blue eyes.

Of **Michael McDermott** and his wife **Mary McDermott**, natives of the Parish of MEELICK, Co. MAYO, Ireland, who left Liverpool in March, 1852, and landed in New York in May following. Also **Martin Gollagher**, **[James]Gollagher**, and **Peter Gollagher**, their uncle. Any information of any of them will be thankfully received by their sister, **Alice Gollagher**, at 154 WEST 16th STREET, NEW YORK. Illinois and Ohio papers please copy.

June 21, 1856

Of **Peter Farrell**, who arrived in New York from Liverpool last April twelve months, in the ship *[Westpoint]*. When last heard from he was in NEW YORK. Any information of him will be thankfully received by **Denis Mullin**, FORT WASHINGTON, 165th STREET, N.Y.

Of **Patrick O'Brien** a native of CASTLETOWNROACH, County CORK, Ireland. Is supposed to be in ORANGE County, N.Y. He will hear from his sister **Elizabeth** and her husband **David Mahoney**, who landed in New York on the 3rd of May, by addressing a few lines to **Hugh Torpy**, No. 37 FRANKFORT ST., N.Y.

Of **Jeremiah** and **Daniel Mahoney**, from the Parish of MONLUBISH, Co. CORK, Ireland, by their sister **Johanna**. Address to **John Larkin**, 349 SECOND AVENUE, NEW YORK. Troy Papers please copy.

Of **James** and **Thomas Moynihan**, two brothers, from the Parish of BALLYSTEEN, County LIMERICK, Ireland. James sailed from Liverpool in the ship *Underwriter* for New York, in 1851. Thomas sailed from Limerick in the ship *Wave* for Quebec in 1850. When last heard from James was in NEW JERSEY and Thomas was attending a Captain on some steamboat which sails from NEW YORK. Any information of them will be thankfully received by their sister, **Catharine Lynch**, No. 21 ALBANY STREET, NEW YORK CITY.

Of **Patrick Bergin**, who left CASTLECOMER, County KILKENNY, Ireland, in 1848, and landed in Quebec, Canada. When last heard from he was in VIRGENES, State of VERMONT, occupied as a contractor under Chamberian & Walker, on the railroads. Any information of him will be thankfully received by his brother, **Michael Bergen**, last of the British army, at No. 211 Myrtle Avenue, BROOKLYN, or at the Office of the Irish-American. Vermont papers please copy.

June 28, 1856

If **Miss Anna McMahon** who arrived in New York in the year 1847, and when last heard of was with a **Mrs. Young** PEARL STREET, N.Y., will communicate her address to **Mr. Charles Prior** at the office of this paper, she will hear of something greatly to her advantage. Any information of her will be thankfully received by letter to the above address. Philadelphia papers please copy.

Of **Bernard**, **Patrick**, **Thomas** and **Peter Kelley**, natives of the Co. MONAGHAN, Ireland. They emigrated to this country from Dublin in the ship *Princess*, and landed the 1st day 1831. When last heard from, Bernard, Patrick and Thomas were in the State of OHIO and Peter in NEWBURGH, State of NEW YORK. Any information of them will be thankfully received by their sister, **Anne Kelley**, in care of **John Hoey**, NEW BRUNSWICK, N.J. Western papers please copy

July 5, 1856

Of **Walter Burke**, of MILTON MILLS, County DUBLIN. He left Ireland, in 1832-3, and when last heard from, was in the State of WISCONSIN. Any information respecting him will be thankfully received by his cousin **Catherine O'Donnell**, of LEWISTON, ME.

Of **John Molony**, of O'BRIEN'S BRIDGE, Co. CLARE, Ireland, Engineer by trade. Left JERSEY CITY in October 1854, bound for CLEVELAND, OHIO. Any information of him will be thankfully received by his sister **Mary Molony**, No. 7 HARRISON STREET, N.Y. Cleveland, Cincinnati and Savannah papers please copy.

July 19, 1856

Of **Nicholas Mangan**; when last heard of lived in EAST 23rd ST., near Second Avenue, NEW YORK. Any information concerning him will be thankfully received by Sergeant **James Fagan**, Company I, Second Infantry, FORT PIERRE, NEBRASKA TERRITORY.

Of **John Landers** alias **John Callahan**, from the Parish of DUNGARRAN, County WATERFORD, Ireland. When last heard from he was between CLINTON and the WHITEHOUSE, in the State of NEW JERSEY, working on the railroad. Any information of his whereabouts will be thankfully received by his wife **Ellen Landers**, No. 214 EAST TWENTY FIRST ST., N.Y.

Of **Edward Emberson Power**, a native of BALLYNACARAGY, County WESTMEATH, Ireland, who left Dublin in December 1852. Any information respecting him will be thankfully received by addressing R.H. at the office of this papers.

Of **Thomas** and **Catherine Leonard**, from BLUE BALL, near TULLAMORE, KING'S County, Ireland. Any information respecting them will be thankfully received by their sister **Mary**, at 59 GREENWICH STREET, N.Y.

Of **Ellen Corcoran**, wife of **Patrick Corcoran**, late of STROKESTOWN, County ROSCOMMON, Ireland. Who arrived in New York in the ship *Robert Kelly*, in April last. Address **Patrick Igo**, SAVANNAH, GA., or AT.C., at the office of this paper. Fort Wayne, Indiana papers please to copy.

Of **William Trainor**, from the Parish of TULLYCORBET, County MONAGHAN, Ireland, who left NEWARK in 1853. When last heard from was in NEW ORLEANS, LOUISIANA; heard since he went to BLACK RIVER. Any information of him will be thankfully received by his brother and sister, **John** and **Anne Trainor**, 58 MULBERRY STREET, N.Y. New Orleans papers please copy.

Of **Anne** and **Eliza Good**, natives of CARBUE, County CORK, Ireland, who left Cork about 15 months ago, in the ship *Middlesex* for New York. Any information of their whereabouts will be thankfully received by **Timothy Quigley**, Globe Hotel, corner of FRANKFORT and WILLIAM STREETS, NEW YORK CITY, who will inform them of something to their advantage.

July 26, 1856

Of **Mathew Brady**, shoemaker, from BALBRIGGAN, Co. DUBLIN, Ireland, who came to this country from the North of England, in February last. When last heard from he was boarding with a person named **John Smith**, at 80 COLUMBIA STREET. Any intelligence of his whereabouts will be thankfully received by his sister **Elizabeth**, who arrived in the ship *Calhoun* on the 14th inst., at 51 Butler-street, BROOKLYN or at the office of this paper.

Of **Bridget Gilespie**, from the Townland of ARAGLE, Parish of KILCAR, County DONEGAL, Ireland, who arrived in New York in June, 1855, and got a situation in some part of the State of NEW YORK. Any person knowing anything of her would confer a great favor by addressing a few lines to her brother, **Peter Gillespie**, at **Mr. Geatings**, 134 ½ LUDLOW-STREET, NEW YORK.

Of **John Farrell** and his sister **Ann**, natives of the Parish of ANAMO, County WICKLOW, Ireland. When last heard from (about a year ago,) they were in NEW YORK CITY. Please address their cousin, **Isabella Russell**, at **E. Carroll's**, 72 6th AVENUE, NEW YORK.

Of **Mary Moore**, whose maiden name was **Hurley**, (and her two children, **John** and **Ellen Moore**, natives of the County GALWAY,) who left Ireland about 14 years ago. Any intelligence of her will be thankfully received by her husband, **William Moore**, care of **William Hallinan**, No. 25 MARION STREET, NEW YORK.

August 2, 1856

Of **Michael** and **Edwin Sheehy**, natives of the County LIMERICK, Ireland. Michael sailed from Limerick about 13 years ago. When last heard of he was working at his trade (blacksmith) at DUNKIRK, N.Y. Any information of them will be thankfully received by their brother **Patrick Sheehy**, GLIN Co. LIMERICK, Ireland. Please address **John Maguire**, SLOATSBURG, ROCKLAND County, N.Y.

Of **James** and **Patrick Whelan**, who left the Parish of STRADBALLY, QUEEN'S County, Ireland in 1852. When last heard from they were in the State of NEW YORK. Any information of them will be thankfully received by their brother **John Whelan**, NORTH ORANGE, N.J.

Of **Arthur O'Neil**, of NEWTOWNHAMILTON, County ARMAGH, Ireland, by his sister **Mary O'Neil**, as she is about going home. When last heard from he was in COLD SPRING, N.Y. Address No. 84 OLIVER STREET or 50 CHERRY STREET, NEW YORK CITY, for Mary O'Neil.

August 9, 1856

Of **Patrick O'Donovan**, of BANTRY, County CORK, Ireland. When last heard from he was living in ORANGE County. Any information of him will be thankfully received by his sister **Mary**, at 146 CHRISTOPHER ST., N.Y. Orange County papers please copy.

Of **Jeremiah Lynch**, from BANTRY, County CORK, Ireland. He left Ireland June 3, 1852, and when last heard from he was in MONTREAL, CANADA. Any information respecting him will be thankfully received by his mother **Catherine Lynch**, 173 EAST ELEVENTH STREET, between Avenues A and B.

Of **Ellen Whelan**, from BALLYBACON, Co. TIPPERARY, Ireland. When last heard from she was in WINNEBAGO County, ILLINOIS. Any information concerning her will be thankfully received by her sisters **Honora** and **Margaret** by addressing **Thomas Ward**, No. 109 Columbia St., BROOKLYN. N.Y.

Of **James Ward**, of BOLEIGH, QUEEN's County, Ireland. Any information respecting him will be thankfully received by his sister **Catherine**, No. 39 London Terrace, WEST TWENTY THIRD ST., N.Y. When last heard from he was in CHICAGO, ILL. Chicago and New Orleans papers please copy.

Of **William McGuinness**, a native of BALLINASLOE, County GALWAY, Ireland. Any information respecting him will be thankfully received by his sister **Bridget**, No.39 London Terrace, WEST TWENTY-THIRD ST., NEW YORK. When last heard from he was in TORONTO, UPPER CANADA. Canada papers please copy.

August 16, 1856

Thomas Kinsule and two sisters, **Bridget** and **Anne**, natives of WEXFORD, Ireland. Anne sailed from Dublin on the 19th of March, 1853, and arrived in New York. Thomas and Bridget are supposed to be in NEW YORK CITY. Any information of them will be thankfully received by their brother **James Kinsule**, at No. 63 MULBERRY STREET, N.Y.

Of **Thomas Murphy**, son of **Michael Murphy**, of ACLARE, SUTTON's Parish, County WEXFORD, Ireland. -When last heard of was in BYTOWN, CANADA WEST, engaged in the lumbering business. Any information of his present whereabouts will be thankfully received by his sisters, **Mrs. Mary Nolan** and **Mrs. Anestatia Quinn**, GEORGETOWN, PRINCE EDWARD ISLAND.

Of **Rose McCoughy**, a native of the Townland of MAG[B]AREA, Parish of KILKERLY, Co. LOUTH, Ireland. She sailed from Liverpool in 1850, and is supposed to be still in this city. Please apply to John Manning, Vice-President Irish Emigrant Society, 51 Chamber Street, N.Y.

Of **John Mullara**, Parish of KILLGLASS, Co ROSCOMMON, Ireland. When last heard from, January 19th, 1856, was in SHEEHANINGO, MOLICE County State of NEW YORK. Any information of him will be kindly received by his brother-in-law, **Peter Douly**, formerly of DERRYCARRIE, DROMOD. Direct to 48 Academy Street, NEWARK. N.J.

Of **John Sherlock**, a native of JOHNSTOWN, County MEATH, Ireland. When last heard of he was in MONTREAL, CANADA, and then left for BUFFALO, N.Y. Any information concerning him will be thankfully received by his sister Margaret at the Bancroft House, No. 916 BROADWAY. New York City and Buffalo papers please copy.

Of **Patrick O'Donovan**, of BANTRY, County CORK, Ireland. When last heard from he was living in ORANGE County. Any information of him will be thankfully received by his sister **Mary**, at 145 CHRISTOPHER ST., N.Y. Orange County papers please copy.

Of **Thomas Hayde**, or **Lant Beary**, of CASHEL, County TIPPERARY, Ireland. Thomas lived in NEW YORK two years ago, and **Lant Beary** in NEWARK, N.J. Any of their friends seeing this advertisement will please write to **Patrick Hayde** (Bricklayer), who served his time to Higgins & Thurston, N.Y., to KEOKUK, IOWA.

August 23, 1856

Of **Eliza Bourke**, native of CLOUGHJORDAN, County TIPPERARY, Ireland. When last Heard of was in PITTSBURGH, PA. Address her mother, **Mary Bourke**, 46 PEARL STREET, NEW YORK.

Of **Martin Byrne**, a native of JOHN'S-WELL, County KILKENNY, Ireland. When last heard from he was in the vicinity of SAVANNAH, GA. Any information concerning him will be most thankfully received by his brother **Garrett J. Byrne**, MARYSVILLE, CALIFORNIA, or **James H. Fay**, Post Office, NEW YORK.

August 30, 1856

Of **James** and **Edward McDonnell** by their sister, **Alice McDonnell**. Any information of them will be thankfully received at 51 Second place, BROOKLYN, or at 386 CHERRY STREET, NEW YORK. Brother James is supposed to be drowned.

Of the relatives of **Edward Scanlan**, a native of Co. TIPPERARY, Ireland, who was accidentally drowned on the 14th of August, inst. He had when found letters in his possession dated from LEBANON, and NORTHFORTH, from his brother, and MONTREAL from his sister. All information concerning his burial and other matters can be obtained by addressing a few lines or applying personally to **Mr. Rodger Hogan**, Morgan Iron Works, 9th STREET, EAST RIVER, NEW YORK

September 6, 1856

Of **John Manning**, a native of the County GALWAY, Ireland. When last heard from was in NEW ORLEANS. Should he notice this, or any person who can give intelligence of him, they would confer a favor by writing to his wife, **Anne Manning**, CARMANSVILLE, WASHINGTON HEIGHTS, NEW YORK.

Of **Patrick Bowes**, of MOCKLER'S HILL, CASHEL, County TIPPERARY, Ireland. When last heard from he was working with a man named **Archer**, about fourteen miles from MEMPHIS, TENN. Address, **John Coyne**, care of **Mr. P. Morrissey**, Grand Street, NEW HAVEN, or to the Editor of the Irish-American, 116 Nassau Street, New York.

Of **James Ash**, son of **Patrick** and **Mary Ash**, from TRALEE, County KERRY, Ireland. He left Ireland in 1852, for LONDON, and worked there 3 years, and left London in 1855 for America. When last heard from he was living in the State of CONNECTICUT. Any intelligence of him will be thankfully received by his brother **John Ash**, No. 32 VANDEWATER ST., N.Y.

Of **Charles** or **Constantine O'Donnell** sons of the late **Daniel O'Donnell**, of AUGHAWELL, Parish of DESERTAGENY, Co. DONEGAL, Ireland. They emigrated to this country in the year '98, or shortly after it. When last heard of they resided in the State of OHIO. If this should meet their eye, or any persons knowing their whereabouts, they would confer a favor on their brother **Patrick's** son, **John O'Donnell**, who is anxious to gain intelligence of them. Direct to John O'Donnell, 22 Marshall Street, corner of Hudison Avenue, BROOKLYN, N.Y. Exchange papers please copy.

Of **Denis Mooney**, from the Parish of LEIGHLIN, County CARLOW, Ireland, who left BROOKLYN, N.Y., last September. When last heard from he was supposed to be working in a coal mine near PHILADELPHIA, PENN. Any information concerning him will be thankfully received by his wife, by addressing **Johanna Mooney**, No. 4 CLIFF ST., N.Y.

Of **Patrick Rahily**, from the Parish of MILFORD, County CORK, Ireland. When last heard from, in 1851, was in FRANKLIN County, State of KENTUCKY. Any information of him will be thankfully received by is sister **Mary Rahily**, No. 141 5th AVENUE, N.Y. Kentucky papers please copy.

September 13, 1856

Of **Catherine Magrath**, daughter of **Daniel** and **Anne Magrath**, of ARDOUGH County LIMERICK, Ireland. She is married to **John Manging**, from SHANAGOLDEN, County LIMERICK, and when last heard from was in RUSH, N.Y. Any person knowing anything about her will confer a great favor on her mother by writing to Anne Magrath, ROCK ISLAND.

September 20, 1856

Of **Mrs. Anne McCarthy** and two sons, one named **Richard** and the other **Laurence**, natives of the Town of SWORDS, County DUBLIN, Ireland, who arrived in America from Liverpool, England, in 1852. _ Any information of them would be thankfully received by addressing her son, **Patk T. McCarthy**, No. 12 South Main Street, PROVIDENCE, R.I., or the office of the Irish-American.

Of **Christopher** or **Andrew Quin**, from the City of DUBLIN, Ireland, who left NEW YORK CITY in February, 1855, for PENNSYLVANIA. Any information of them will be of great consolation to their afflicted mother. Address, **Hugh Quin**, No. 1 CHAMBERS STREET, NEW YORK.

September 27, 1856

If this should meet the eye of **Margaret** or **Mary Plunkett**, who sailed in the ship *Arctic* from Dublin in May 1853, and when last heard of was in NEWARK, NEW JERSEY. They will confer a favor by addressing **James Callans**, 148 Pine Street, PHILADELPHIA, below 5th. Newark paper please copy.

Any information of **William Torney**, a native of County DOWN, Ireland, will be kindly received by his parents, at No. 93 BEDFORD STREET, NEW YORK CITY. [Appeared February 23, 1856 with less information.]

Of **John Loyd O'Grady**, of BALLINGARRY, County LIMERICK, Ireland. The last heard of him, he was in BALTIMORE. Any person knowing his whereabouts will confer a favor by directing a note to the Brickhouse, Third Avenue, 14th St., Gowanus, SOUTH BROOKLYN, L.I., to **Mrs. Bott**.

October 4, 1856

If **Patrick Spillane**, who formerly worked with O'Connor & Scott at 290 WATER STREET, in this City, calls at this office he will find a letter of importance. – any information of him will be thankfully received.

Of **Susan C. Henry**, a native of the City of DUBLIN, Ireland. When last heard of was living in Hoyte Street, BROOKLYN. Any information respecting her will be thankfully received by her sister. Address, M.A.R., Union Square Post Office, N.Y.

Of **Andre Gilless**, from the County CAVAN, Ireland. When last heard from was residing between the Second and Third Avenues, NEW YORK. Any information of him will be thankfully received by his sister **Mary Gilless**, MEMPHIS, TENN.

Of **Catherine** and **Margaret Griffin**, of KINCULUE, Parish of KILMACTIGUE, Co. SLIGO, Ireland. Who left home about nine years ago; were the first three or four years in BOSTON, and afterwards went to NEW YORK, where Catherine got married. Any information respecting them will be thankfully received by their sister **Nabby**. Please **Martin Haran**, ROXBURY, MASS. Exchange papers please copy.

Of **Mr. John Glynn**, o[f] GORT, Co. GALWAY, Ireland. He left home about five years ago, and is supposed to be in the United States. He is son of **Mr. Patrick Glynn**, hotel and shopkeeper, Gort. Any intelligence of him will be thankfully received by **Patrick**

Moran, PLANTSVILLE, HARTFORD County, CONN. New Orleans and Western papers please copy.

October 11, 1856

Of **Roger Gilroy**, by his brother **Thomas**. When last heard from worked on the Union Canal, near MEYERSVILLE, PENNSYLVANIA. Pennsylvania papers please copy.

Of **James Kelly**, from ANNAGH, County TIPPERARY, Parish of LOROUGH, Ireland. He landed in New York, 25th day of April, 1853, in the ship *Gangus*. When last heard of he was in ST. LOUIS. Any information of him would be thankfully received by his sister **Bridget**, No. 66 SIXTH AVENUE, corner 14th Street, NEW YORK CITY. St. Louis papers please copy.

October 18, 1856

Of **Daniel Hallesy**, lately of SOUTH WALES, GREAT BRITAIN, who landed here a year ago. When last heard of he worked on the Canastota Railroad, N.Y. – Any person knowing him or his whereabouts. Will oblige his son **William** by addressing a few lines to **Mrs. Kelly**, 591 GREENWICH ST., N.Y.

If **Mrs. Bridget Hanhard**, formerly **Bridget Matthews** (from DUBLIN), who resided in Anne Street. Will call on **P.M. Haverty**, 110 FULTON STREET, NEW YORK, she will received money from her relatives.

Of **John Garah**, a native of the Parish of GLYNN, COLUMKILL, County DONEGAL, Ireland. Landed in New York June, 1854. When last heard from he was in MICHIGAN. Any information of him will be thankfully received by his sisters, **Ann** and **Mary Garah**. – Direct care of **James C. Matheson**, YELLOW HOOK, KINGS County, Long Island, N.Y. Western papers please copy.

Of **James** and **Michael Carroll**, Laborers, natives of CREA, KING'S County, Ireland. When last heard from were in VIRGINIA. Any information will be thankfully received by their brother, **John Carroll**, at 113 ½ THIRD AVENUE, NEW YORK. Virginia papers please copy.

Of **John** and **Ellen McKenna**, who landed in New York in the year 1847. Any information of them will be thankfully received by their mother **Alice McKenna**, by addressing a note to her at the post-office. MOUNT VEAL, PALMERSTOWN, CONN. They are natives of the County ARMAGH, Ireland. Their father, **Daniel McKenna**, died in Bellevue hospital.

October 25, 1856

Of **Charles Kirk**, a native of GLENMACOFFEE, Parish of LOWER [B]ADONEY, County TYRONE, Ireland, who sailed from Liverpool on the 8th of April, 1856, in the ship *"Ontario"*. Any information of him will be thankfully received by his brother **Felix Kirk**, COMORN post office, LAKE TOWNSHIP, COOK County ILL.

November 1, 1856

Of **Denis Clancy** and **Bridget** his wife, formerly of SHEAHAN'S CROSS, County of LIMERICK, Ireland. Who emigrated to SYDNEY, NEW SOUTH WALES, the former in 1837, and the latter in 1840. Also of **Mrs. Mary O'Connor** and daughter, formerly of BRUFF, County of LIMERICK, who emigrated [to] Sydney in 1842. Any information concerning them, or any of them, would be thankfully received by addressing a letter to **James O'Donnell**, 100 Columbia St., BROOKLYN, KINGS Co., N.Y. Editors of Sydney papers would confer a great favor by copying of the above.

Of **Patrick Adams**, a native of the Parish of BALLINAKILL, near CLIFDEN, Co. GALWAY, Ireland. When last heard from was in PITTSBURGH, PA. If this should meet his eye or any person who knows him a letter addressed WILLIAMSBURGH, N.Y., would ease very much the mind of his mother, **Mary Adams**, who had lately arrived here. Pittsburgh papers please copy.

November 8, 1856

Of **Maryanne Nerny**, of MOYANA, Parish of STRADBALLY, QUEEN'S County, who came out here about 12 years ago; was married to one **Francis Galway** in the City of NEW YORK. When last heard of she was a widow in New York. Any information will be kindly received by her brother **Frederick** or **Thomas Nerny**, SPUYTEN DUYVIL Post office, N.Y.

Of **Julia Fahy**, a native of the Parish of TYNAGH, County GALWAY, Ireland, who arrived in New York in December 1851, with her sister **Mary**. Julia was about 30 years of age, low sized, with dark hair, and florid complexion. She parted with her sister Mary last July two years. Any information of her will be thankfully received by addressing a note to **Ned Kelly** No. 42 HAMMERSLY STREET [Hamersley Street], NEW YORK.

Of **James Kelly**, from BROADFARD, Co. CLARE, Ireland, who arrived in this City a few weeks since in the ship *"Emerald Isle."* from Liverpool. There is a letter from him, from his friends in ILLINOIS, at the office of this paper.

November 15, 1856

Of **James Ford**, late a resident of WOLVERHAMPTON, ENGLAND. Who came to this country October, 1855, supposed to be at work in some Rolling mill, east of the Alleghanies. A line addressed to his brother, **John Ford**, at PITTSBURGH, PA., will be attended in.

By **Sarah Scott**, of her brother and sister, **John** and **Martha Scott**, who sailed from Derry, Ireland, six years ago. Please direct to the care of **Mrs. Paskett**, 18 Cottage Place, Columbia Street, SOUTH BROOKLYN.

Of **William O'Shea**, bookbinder, who left the City of LIMERICK, Ireland, about 5 ½ years ago. If this should meet his eye, he will hear of something to his advantage by addressing **M. O'Brien**, 177 Adams st, BROOKLYN. Any person knowing his whereabouts will confer a favor by sending a note as above.

Of **Kiernan Mannion**, son of **Patrick Mannion**, CLONADERIG, Parish of SEVEN CHURCHES, KING'S County. Any information of him will be thankfully received by his sister **Mary Mannion**, 67 Joreloman Street, BROOKLYN, N.Y. New Orleans and Western papers please copy.

Of **Thomas McGrath**, from the Parish of CASTLETOWN, County TIPPERARY, Ireland. If this should meet his eye or any one knowing his present address, they will oblige by sending a letter addressed as usual to **Michael McGrath**, 12 ½ WEST STREET, NEW YORK CITY. Canada papers please.

Of **Patrick, James** or **John Hamilton**, natives of the Parish of COOLSTUFF, County WEXFORD, Ireland. Patrick left his place in ALBANY, N.Y., the latter part of July last, and has not since been heard from. - Any information of them will be thankfully received by addressing **John Gorman**, No. 275, AVENUE A, NEW YORK CITY.

November 22, 1856

Of **Jeremiah Toomey**, from the Parish of GIRNOUGH, County CORK, Ireland, who arrived in New York about four years ago. When heard from last on May, 1856, he was at SPRING VALLEY, and is supposed he left to see his sister who resides at MONROE County, N.Y. Any information of him will be thankfully received by addressing his brother **James** at **John Crowley's**, No. 146 CHERRY STREET, N.Y.

Of **Daniel, Patrick, David** and **Catherine Leahy**, from the Parish of BALLYREGAN, NEWCASTLE WEST, County LIMERICK, Ireland. When last heard from (about three years since) they were in MADRID ST. LAWRENCE County, N.Y. David was teaching school in that place. Any intelligence of them will be thankfully received by their brother **Cornelius Leahy**, care of **James Riordon**, 242 CHERRY STREET, N.Y. Western exchange papers please copy.

Of **Bridget Morgan**, a native of the Parish of DERRYNOOSE, County ARMAGH, Ireland, who arrived in New York in April, 1855, and stopped for some time in the Convent of the Sisters of Mercy, HOUSTON ST., NEW YORK. If this should meet the eye of any person who knows anything about her, they would confer a great favor by writing to her brother Thomas, as he is going to LIVERPOOL. Address **Thomas Morgan**, Lovejoy's Hotel, NEW YORK CITY.

Of **Henry Kearns** and wife who left Ireland seven years ago, and is supposed to be in the State of OHIO. He will hear of something to his advantage by addressing **P. T. Noonan**, CONTENTON, MISSISSIPPI, or his nephew, **Henry Kearns**, LEXINGTON, KY. P.S. – He is a native of DROMONA, Parish of PARTEEN, Co. CLARE, Ireland.

Of **Edward Murphy**, a native of KILLHARD, County WEXFORD, Ireland, who came to America about six years ago, and worked at CANANDAIGUA, ONTARIO County, N.Y. When last heard of he was working on some part of LONG ISLAND. Any information of him will be thankfully received by addressing his brother, **Thomas Murphy**, ROCKLAND, SULLIVAN Co., N.Y.

November 29, 1856

Of **Dan Honan**, of DUNSFORD, County DOWN, Ireland, by a friend that wishes to communicate with him; when last heard of was in the State of IOWA. If this should meet his eye, he will please address C.S., 169 WEST 23rd STREET, NEW YORK CITY. Western papers please copy. [Appeared Dec. 6, 1856 with the surname **Honan** changed to **Monan**.]

Of **Cornelius Hickey**, a native of KANTURK, County CORK, Ireland, who landed in New York in 1849 or 1850; aged about 21 years. When last heard from he was at the JUNCTION, PAULDING County, OHIO; that was in June 1855. Any information concerning him will be kindly received by his cousin **Richard Gregg**, TROY, NEW YORK. California and Ohio papers please copy.

Of **Margaret Dehey** and **Bridget Sheehy** (daughter of **John Sheehy**), of CASTLEMAINE, County KERRY, Ireland. They came to this country about four years ago. Should this meet their eye, or that of any person who knows where they are, they will oblige their brother **William** by sending a line to **Alexander Patton**, SHARON SPRINGS, SCHOHARIE County, N.Y.

Of **James Kelaher**, of ROOSKEY, County ROSCOMMON, Ireland. When last heard from was working in RICHMOND, VIRGINIA. He is a painter by trade. Any information of him will be thankfully received by his brother, **Michael Kelaher**, 43 SPRING STREET, NEW YORK. Charleston papers please copy.

Of **Joseph McDonald**, from the Parish of DRUMGOON, Co. CAVAN, Ireland, who arrived in the City in May last in the ship "*James R. Keeler*," from Liverpool. Address Irish Emigrant Society, 51 Chambers Street, New York City.

December 6, 1856

Of **Michael Burke**, who left LEAN'S COVE, ROCKPORT, MASS., with **Thomas Kirby**. They sailed from New York on the 20th March, 1855, for CALIFORNIA. When last heard from he was working in the mines, and was boarding with one **Denis Keeffe**, in GRASS VALLEY, NEVADA County, CALIFORNIA. Any person knowing anything of him will confer a favor on his sister **Bridget Burke**, by addressing a few lines to her, care of **Henry Russell**, Esq., No. 18 Brown Street, SALEM, MASS., or to the office of the Irish American. California papers please copy.

Of **Michael Garland**, painter by trade, and a native of CARRICKMACROSS, County MONAGHAN, Ireland. Who left BOSTON, MASS., one year ago, and is supposed he came to NEW YORK, but since has not been heard of; it is thought he is now in CALIFORNIA. Any person knowing anything about him would confer a great favor on his brother **Mathew**, of ORANGEBURGH VILLAGE, SOUTH CAROLINA, by addressing a few lines to him, or to **Patrick McKeon**, No. 189 EAST 47th STREET, NEW YORK CITY. New Orleans and California papers please copy.

Of **Dorothea Curran**; born at SCRIPPLESTOWN, County DUBLIN; left NEW YORK for NANTUCKET in January, 1852; supposed to be living in EDGARTON. Any information of her will be thankfully received by her brother **James Curran**, 66 WASHINGTON STREET, NEW YORK. Exchange papers please copy.

Of **Honoria O'Brien**, a native of KILFINAN, County LIMERICK, Ireland, who arrived in New York in September, 1853, and lived last in COLUMBIA STREET, NEW YORK CITY. The last seen of her was on the last day of October, when she parted with her mother to go to hire to a new place; since that time nothing has been heard of her. Any person knowing of her whereabouts would confer a great favor on her mother by addressing a note to **Margaret O'Brien**, No. 12 MULBERRY STREET, NEW YORK CITY.

December 13, 1856

Of **John Penderguest**, of BALLINDERRY, Parish of KILBRIDE, County ROSCOMMON, Ireland, by his brother, **Peter Penderguest**; when last heard of he was in MANCHESTER. Direct to **James Farrell**, 110 EAST 29th STREET, NEW YORK CITY. Manchester papers please copy.

Of **Patrick Conly**, a native of DUBLIN, Ireland, who served his time to the Billard marking, at No. 5 Lower Abbey Street, in the City of DUBLIN. He went to AUSTRALIA about 13 years ago and returned. - Any person knowing anything about him, living or dead, would confer a great favor on his sister by addressing a note to the care of **Mrs. T. Dunn**, No. 81 EAST 11th STREET, NEW YORK CITY. Dublin papers please copy.

Of **Daniel Shea**, of CASTLE BEREHAVEN, County CORK, who left Ireland about 18 years ago. When last heard from (some 4 years ago) he was employed as overseer on a railroad in the State of PENNSYLVANIA. – Any information respecting him will be thankfully received by his nephew, **Denis Shea**, No. 10 Borden Street, FALL RIVER, MASS.

Of **Peter Murphy**, a native of BALLIVALLEN, County WEXFORD, Ireland. When last heard from he was in LEVELIN, State of PENNSYLVANIA. Any person knowing anything of him would confer a great favor on his father by addressing a few lines to **George Murphy**, No. 65 LAUREN STREET [Laurens Street], NEW YORK CITY.

December 20, 1856

Of **James**, **John** and **Charles Bartley**. – when last heard from, James was in the City of NEW YORK. Also of their sisters, **Mrs. Eliza Chandler** and **Mrs. Mary Pollock**. Any intelligence of them will be thankfully received by their sister **Bridget Bartley**, MEMPHIS, TENN.

Of **Thomas Ratician**, a native of Ireland, County ROSCOMMON, Parish of CLUNINSCUT; he landed February, 1856. Any information concerning him will be thankfully received by his sister **Bridget**, at No. 81 WEST 28th STREET, between 6th and 7th Avenues, NEW YORK.

Of **John Roach**, an axe-maker by trade, a native of the Parish of SOL[I]HEAD County TIPPERARY, Ireland who arrived in Quebec about fourteen years ago; when heard from last June twelve months, he was in ROCHESTER, State of NEW YORK. Any information of him will be thankfully received by addressing a few lines to his sister **Margaret**, at No. 139 Mulberry Street, NEWARK, State of NEW JERSEY.

December 27, 1856

If this should meet the eye of **Mr. Neal McMahon**, of CARRICKMACROSS, County MONAGHAN, Ireland, by calling at 250 SEVENTH AVENUE, he will hear of something to his advantage.

Of **Jane Higgins**, a native of the Parish of FUERTY, County ROSCOMMON, Ireland, who arrived in New York in July, 1844. When last heard from she was living at **Mr. Montlau's** in LAFAYETTE PLACE, NEW YORK CITY, in May, 1848; since that time nothing has been heard of her. Any information concerning her will be thankfully received by addressing a few lines to the Irish-American office, for her brother **John Higgins**.

Of **Thomas Meehan**, of the Parish of MARYBOROUGH, QUEEN'S County, Ireland he left home in January, 1847, and is supposed to have gone West. Any information of him will be thankfully received by his sisters **Maria** and **Margaret**, by addressing a few lines to the care of **William Brophy**, No. 127 EAST 31st STREET, NEW YORK CITY.

January 3, 1857

Of **James Dacy**, of the Parish of KILMOON, County CORK, Ireland. When last heard from (last May twelve months) he was living in QUEBEC. If this should meet his eye or any one knowing his address they will confer a favor by writing to **Patrick Dacy**, care of **Martin M'Gowan**, 72 ½ MULBERRY STREET, NEW YORK.

Of **Peter** and **Denis Bolger**, natives of the Parish of ARKLOW, County WEXFORD, Ireland. If this should meet their eye, or any one knowing anything of them, they will confer a great favor by addressing a letter to their sisters **Catherine** and **Eliza Bolger**, at the office of this paper. Wisconsin and New Orleans papers please copy.

January 17, 1857

Of **Michael Casey**; left BROOKLYN about 18 months ago, for PHILADELPHIA; is a native of Ireland, 24 years old, about 5ft. 8in., light hair; lived in MANCHESTER ENGLAND. Any information addressed to his mother will be thankfully received. **Catherine Casey**, No. 9, Chapel Street, BROOKLYN.

Of **Stephen** or **Mark Carney**, natives of the County SLIGO, Ireland. They are in America for the last thirteen or fourteen years. When last heard from were in VIRGINIA. Any information respecting them will be thankfully received by their sister **Ann Carney**, at **Mrs. Cane's** 262 EAST 13th STREET, N.Y. Virginia papers please copy.

Of **Andrew Smith**, of the Parish of LANEY, County CAVAN. When last heard from was boating on PHILADELPHIA and PITTSBURGH canal. Any information of him sent to 502 6th AVENUE, will be thankfully received by his brothers and sister. Philadelphia Ledger please copy.

Of **Mary Hannegan**, of FOXFORD, wife of **Patrick Nary** of BALLINA, County MAYO, Ireland, who came to this country twelve years ago. When last heard from, about six years ago, was in MADISON, State of INDIANA. Any information respecting her will be thankfully received by her mother. Please address **Mr. Thomas Caveney**, No. 489 PEARL STREET, NEW YORK, for **Margaret Hannegan**. Indiana papers please copy. [Appeared under County MAYO]

Of **Mat Curry**, **Dennis Caisy**, and **John Dwyre**, all of the Parish of KILTEELY, County LIMERICK.-Direct to **J. Quaid**, cor. 9th and Smith Streets, BROOKLYN, for **Ellen Curry**.

Of **Patrick M'Namara**, from the City of LIMERICK, ST. PATRICK Parish. Left Limerick about four years ago. When last heard from was in Quakers Street, BUCKS County, PHILADELPHIA, PA. Any person knowing his whereabouts will confer a favor by directing a letter to Roche, Bros & Coffey, 68 SOUTH STREET, or to **Wm. Clancy**, 29 WASHINGTON STREET, NEW YORK. Pennsylvania papers please copy.

Of **William**, **Richard**, and **Thomas Smith**, County CORK, Ireland, Parish of LADYSBRIDGE. When last heard from William and Richard lived in BOSTON, MASS., and Thomas lived in SPRINGFIELD, MASS. Any information respecting them will be thankfully received by their brother, **James Smith**, who lately landed in New York in 26th STREET, between the 10th and 11th Avenues, No. 337. Direct to **Maurice Mead** of said place.

Of **Corneluis Keleher**, a native of RUSHEEN, County CORK, Ireland, who died last September, in the Sisters' Hospital, in ST. LOUIS, MO. Any person knowing any thing about his death would confer a favor on his brother, **Daniel Keleher**, by addressing a few lines [to] his address, HASTINGS UPON HUDSON, N.Y.

Of **John Holland** or **Houlahan**, a tailor by trade, a native of CASTLEGREGORY, County KERRY, Ireland, who left LONDON 4 years last November, and arrived in New York. When last heard from he was living at LAFAYETTE, INDIANA. Any information concerning him will be thankfully received by his wife, **Mary Holland**, by directing a few lines to No. 16 WASHINGTON STREET, NEW YORK CITY.

January 24, 1857

A Reward of ten Dollars will be paid for information of **John**, son of **Bernard** and **Mary Cunningham**, of MERTHYE TYDVILLE, WALES, who sailed from Cardiff in 1851, in the ship *Brandywine*. He landed in BALTIMORE, and left that City in the same year for NEW YORK. Any one knowing his whereabouts will received the above reward, and will confer a favor on the disconsolate wife and mother of the above John Cunningham, by writing to the Irish-American office, or to **Simon Donovan**, No. 2 Mullikin Street, BALTIMORE, MD. California papers please copy.

Of **Denis Mullins**, whose family resides at present in CHARLEHURST, KENT County, ENGLAND. He came to this city about three years ago from England. –Address C., Box 3050, NEW YORK Post-Office.

Of **John Molloy**. He left his employer on the 16th or 17th of September last; he was driving a horse on the MORRIS CANAL when last heard of. Any information of him will be thankfully received by his mother **Catherine Molloy**, at No. 2 MONTGOMERY STREET, NEW YORK CITY. [Appeared March 21, 1857 with additional information.]

Of **Thomas Doyle**, son of **Patrick Doyle**, of TANKARDSTOWN, near TULLOW, County CARLOW, Ireland, who emigrated to this country about eight years ago. –Any information regarding him will be received at No. 300 South 5th Street, WILLIAMSBURGH, N.Y.

Of **Myles Gillooly**, of the County of LEITRIM, Ireland, by **Myles McNiff**. When last seen, the said Myles Gillooly was in the house of **Mr. Thomas McGrath**, ST. LOUIS, MO. Any person Knowing anything of his whereabouts will do a great favor by communicating the same to **Mr. John Joyce**, No. 111 Front Row, MEMPHIS, TENN.

Of **Catherine McAlister**, of LISBURN, County ANTRIM, Ireland. When last heard of was residing in 38th STREET in this City. Address C., Box 3050, NEW YORK CITY.

Five dollars will be given for the present address of **Elizabeth Moran**, late of SLIGO, Ireland, who will hear of something to her advantage by writing to H.S., care of the **Rev. N. Walsh**, St. Charles' Seminary, PHILADELPHIA.

Of **James Stanley** of CARRIGBUIE, BANDON, Ireland. When last heard of was teaching school in this City. Address C., Box 3050, NEW YORK CITY.

Of **Patrick Adams**, of BALLINAKILL, County GALWAY, Ireland; when last heard from was in PITTSBURGH, PENNSYLVANIA. Any information of him will be thankfully received by his mother **Mary Adams**, alias **Cosgrave**, at the house of her son-in-law, **Thomas Hanlon**, in North 1st Street, between 10th and Union Ave., WILLIAMSBURGH. Exchange papers please copy.

January 31, 1857

Of **Martin Finlan**, a native of the Parish of ROAR, County KILKENNY, Ireland. He left New Ross on the 29th of May last, in the ship *Woodstock*, for Quebec. When last seen (by **Robert Lanigan**,) he left MONTREAL for HAMILTON, CANADA WEST. Any information of him will be thankfully received by his brother **Thomas Finlan**, 514 High Street, NEWARK, N.J.

Of **Owen Kelly**, a native of TIPPERARY, Ireland, who came to NEW YORK five years ago. If this should meet his eye, or any one knowing his whereabouts, they will confer a favor by addressing a note to his nephew, **Christopher Gannon**, WOODBRIDGE, N.J., who arrived here on the 15th of last July.

Of **Ellen Keane**, alias **Boyce**, a native of the Parish of MULTIFARHAM, County WESTMEATH, Ireland, who arrived in America about 25 years ago. When last heard from, about 10 years ago, she was living at POTTSVILLE, ASHFORD TOWN, PENNSYLVANIA. Any information concerning her will be thankfully received by addressing a few lines to **Christopher Connolly**, 574 SECOND AVENUE, NEW YORK CITY, where she will hear of something to her advantage.

February 7, 1857

Of **James** and **Michael Mulloick**' or **Merrick**, (who came to this country about seventeen years ago,) by their sister, **Abbey Merrick**, at 311 EAST 12th STREET, NEW YORK. If this should meet the eye of their Uncles, **Edward** and **William Lynch**, they will please answer it. County Cork and British American papers please copy.

Of **Joseph Farrell**. He sailed from Liverpool in the *William Tapscot*, in August, 1855, for New York; has not since been heard of; is a butcher by trade. Any information concerning him will be thankfully received by his cousin, **Daniel Bergin**, 35 Remsen Street, WILLIAMSBURGH. Southern papers please copy. [Appeared under DUBLIN]

Of **Michael**, **Thomas**, and **Martin Hanioughon**, or **Bird**, of the Parish of BALLA, County MAYO, Ireland. Any information of them will be thankfully received by **Denis Ryan**, 444 GREENWICH STREET, NEW YORK, or their brother **William Hanioughon**, SAN ANDRESS [San Andreas], CALAVAREZ County [Calavaras County], CALIFORNIA. Boston papers please copy.

Of **Johanna Denehy**, daughter **Owen Denehy**, of CASTLEBLA, BALLYHOOLY, County CORK, Ireland, whose first husband' name was **William Hennesey**. – When last heard from she was living in some part of VERMONT. Any information respecting her will be thankfully received by her brother and sister. Address **Owen** and **Margaret Denehy**, 146 Plymouth Street, BROOKLYN, N.Y.

Of **Mathew Williams**, of SLIGO, Ireland; when last heard from was in ONONDAGA County, NEW YORK. Any information of him will be thankfully received by his brother **John Williams**, 187 HESTER STREET, NEW YORK.

February 14, 1857

Of **Jeremiah Cashman**. When last heard from he was in the State of ILLINOIS. Any information of him will be thankfully received by **George Cashman**, N.W. corner of 32nd STREET and FIRST AVENUE NEW YORK. Western papers please copy.

Of **Thomas McLaughlin**, a native of OLD CONNAUGHT, County DUBLIN, Ireland. When last heard from was in NEW YORK. Any information of him will be received by his daughter, **Elizabeth Keely**, 137 Queen Street, Southwark, PHILADELPHIA. Southern and Western papers, please copy.

Of **Martin Dunne**, from CLONAD, Parish of RAHEEN, QUEEN'S County, Ireland, by his brother **William**. When last heard from in Sept., 1856, was in ST. LOUIS, MO. Address care of Andrew Carrigan, Esq., Commissioner of Emigration, New York.

Of **James Higgins**, a native of DUNDALK, County LOUTH, Ireland. Who left NEW YORK in October, 1854. When last heard from he was in some place near HALIFAX, NOVA SCOTIA. Any information of him will be thankfully received by addressing a few lines to his sisters, **Catherine** or **Elizabeth** 272½ WEST 28th STREET, NEW YORK.

Of **Thomas** and **Patt Egan**, last LOUGHREA, County of GALWAY, Ireland, by Thomas's afflicted wife, **Anne Egan**, who is in NEW YORK since Christmas last. Any information of him will be thankfully received by his friend, **Denis Haverty**, butcher, 45 ELM STREET, NEW YORK. New Jersey papers please copy.

Of **Jeremiah Murphy**, a native of DINGLE STRAND, County KERRY, Ireland. He went to SYDNEY, NEW SOUTH WALES, about six or seven years ago. When last heard from he was at Macquarice River. If those few lines will meet him, he can write to his sister and brother, **Patt Murphy**, 430 WATER STREET, NEW YORK, America; care of **James Downes**, same place. Sydney papers please copy.

Of **Michael Clancy**, of County LEITRIM, Ireland. When last heard of was in HARTFORD, CONNECTICUT. Any information of him will be thankfully received by his sister, **Mary Clancy**, 196 WEST 27th STREET, NEW YORK. Hartford papers please copy.

February 21, 1857

Of **John Regan**, native of the Parish ROSSCARBERRY, County CORK, Ireland, who came to this country about twenty years ago. when last heard from he was in ROXBURY, near BOSTON. Any information of him will be thankfully received by addressing his brother **Michael's** wife and family, at No. 162 CHERRY STREET, NEW YORK.

Of **James Kellay**, of FINISGLEN, Parish of KILLTROST, County LEITRIM, Ireland, by his sister **Catherine**. When last heard from he was in OHIO County, VIRGINIA. Any communications, either personally or by letter, will be kindly received at 222 EAST 23rd ST., N.Y. Care of **Edward Mellon**. Virginia papers please copy.

February 28, 1857

Of **William Troy**, late of OLNEYVILLE, R.I., aged 14 years. He is dark complexioned, slightly freckled, and stout built. He left his home on September 10th, and is supposed to have gone to NEW BEDFORD to go on a whaling voyage. Any information concerning him will be thankfully received by his father **James Troy**, OLNEYVILLE Post Office, R.I., or by his cousin, **Denis Quinlan**, 91 WEST 41st STREET, NEW YORK. Boston and New Bedford papers please copy.

Of **Thomas Tucker**, a native of the Parish of KILTEELY, County LIMERICK, Ireland, by his wife, **Catherine Tucker**, who came to this country about five months ago. When last heard from he was in WISCONSIN. Any information respecting him will be thankfully received by his wife, Catherine Tucker, now living in GREEN POINT, Long Island, State of NEW YORK. Western papers please copy.

Of **Denis** and **Richard Whalen**, natives of GLENOGRA, Parish of BRUFF, County of LIMERICK, Ireland. Denis was seen in TROY, in this State, about four years ago, and Richard is supposed to be in the U.S. Army. Any information of them will be thankfully received by their brother, **John Whelan**, who is most anxious to hear from them. Please direct to the Irish-American office, or **Mr. Mathew Hartigan**, 197 WEST STREET, NEW YORK.

Of **Daniel King**, of SALT ROCK, County GALWAY, Ireland. He landed in New Orleans five or six years ago. Any information of him will be thankfully received by his sister-in-law, **Catherine Hiland**. When heard from last he was on board a steamboat from NEW ORLEANS to some city in OHIO. Direct to the care of **John Coughlan**, 261 TENTH AVENUE, cor. 21st Street, NEW YORK.

Of **Hannah Walsh**, a native of CORK, who left BRADFORD, ENGLAND, lately. Any information of her will be thankfully received by her niece, **Ellen Walsh**, 29 Wood Street, between Second and Third Streets, PHILADELPHIA, PA.

Of **Patrick Carney**, a native of SHINRONE, KING'S County, Ireland, who arrived in New York about two years ago. When last heard from he was going to some part of the country. Any information of him will be thankfully received by his brother, **Michael Carney**, by addressing a few lines to the Irish American office, 116 Nassau Street, New York.

March 7, 1857

Of **James** and **John Mahony** (brothers), natives of MILLTOWN, County KERRY, Ireland, who left NEW YORK some four or five years ago. When last heard from, John, the younger, was in INDIANA and the other in ILLINOIS, working on a railroad, but they have both left those places since. Any intelligence of them will be thankfully received by their afflicted mother, **Mary Mahony**, care of **Mrs. Courcey**, 72 CHERRY STREET, NEW YORK.

Of **William** and **Ellen King**, natives of the Parish of FILEMORE GLEESK, County of KERRY, Ireland, who came to MONTREAL in 1853. Any information of them will be thankfully received by their sister, **Mary King**, at 252 MOTT STREET, NEW YORK. Montreal papers please copy.

Of **Joseph Cullen** or **Quillen**, boot and shoemaker, who came to this country about 29 years, and has lived in NEW YORK CITY until about three years ago. He went out a short distance in the country to live with a man who keeps a tannery. He is a native of County CAVAN, Parish of MULAH, Townland of ANNAHARNATY. Any information of him will be thankfully received by his brother **Mathew's** son, by letter addressed **James Cullen**, No.56 Valley Street, LAWRENCE, MASS.

Of **Michael**, **John**, Joseph, **James** and **Dan Daly**, brothers; also of **Elizabeth**, **Bridget** and **Mary Daly**, sisters, who sailed from Liverpool about ten years ago for ILLINOIS. Their sister **Julia Daly** wishes to hear from them. Direct to 156 Grand-street, PATERSON, NEW JERSEY. Illinois papers please copy. [Appeared under QUEEN'S County].

If **Patrick Hallegan**, carpenter, of the Town of KILDARE, Ireland, will call or write to **John Murphy**, carpenter, UNION PLACE, LONG ISLAND, he will hear of something to his advantage. When last heard of he was in the State of KENTUCKY. Kentucky papers please copy.

Of **Felix Kirk**, a native of MINADUFF, Parish of LOWER BADONEY, County TYRONE, Ireland. When last heard from his address was a[t] COMORN Post Office, LAKE TOWNSHIP, COOK County, ILLINOIS. Any information of him will be thankfully received by addressing a few lines to his brother, **Charles Kirk**, 216 Grand St., WILLIAMSBURGH, L.I., State of NEW YORK, who arrived in the ship *Ontario* on the 24th May, 1856, and who wrote to his brother Felix to the above address several times and got no answer.

Of **Michael Ford**, a native of the Parish of ENNISMAGRATH, County LEITRIM, Ireland. When last heard of (about five years ago,) he was in WISCONSIN. He wrote a letter to his brother-in-law, **Dan O'Connell**, to the effect that he was about leaving there and going among the Indians. Any intelligence of him will be thankfully received by his sister, **Mrs. Sarah O'Connell**. Who is anxious to hear from him. Direct to 186 DIVISION STREET, NEW YORK. California and New Orleans papers please copy.

March 21, 1857

Of **Stephen Sullivan**, a native of GLASHEEN, Parish of ST. FINBAR, City of CORK, Ireland, who landed in New York about four years ago; after that he was working with his brother **Jeremiah** at the Blue Ridge Railroad in VIRGINIA, and left him there working. When last heard of he was in NEW BOSTON, MERCER County, ILLINOIS. Any information concerning him would be thankfully received by his brother, Jeremiah Sullivan, 72 CHERRY STREET, NEW YORK. Western papers please copy.

Of **John** and **James McDonnell**, natives of the City of CORK, Ireland, who emigrated to Australia in the year 1838. They resided for some time in SYDNEY, and when last heard from were in WOLONGONG. Any information of them will be thankfully received by addressing a few lines to **Mr. Patrick Finney** 198 First Street, WILLIAMSBURGH, NEW YORK, U. S. Sydney Freeman's Journal please copy.

Of **John Keily** and his wife **Mary**, from the Parish of KILLIHENY, County KERRY, Ireland, who arrived in New York about eleven years ago. When last heard from they were in some part of the State of INDIANA. Any information of them will be thankfully received by addressing a few lines to **Sarah Carmody**, 2 STATE STREET, NEW YORK, where she is stopping with **Michael McMahon**, a grandson of John Keily's. She wrote several times and got no answer, and is most anxious to hear from them.

Of **Bartholemew Doyle**, a native of the Parish of CLASHMORE, in the County of WATERFORD, Ireland. He left NEW YORK in April 1855, and is supposed to be in UPPER CANADA. Any information of him will be thankfully received by his sister, **Catherine Doyle**, 219 MADISON STREET, NEW YORK.

Of **Jeremiah** and **John Sheehan**, from NEWCASTLE WEST, County LIMERICK. Jeremiah left in 1853. When last heard from he was in MADEVILLE, CRAWFORD County, State of PENNSYLVANIA. John left about eight years ago. When last heard of he was in CINCINNATI, OHIO. Any information of them will be thankfully received by their brother, **Timothy Sheehan**, care of **Thomas Ambrose**, 27 MARION STREET, NEW YORK. Western papers please copy.

Missed, a boy of thirteen years of age, since last September, named **John Molloy**, a native of CLONASLEE, QUEEN'S County, Ireland. When last heard from he was driving on the MORRIS CANAL, in the employ of **Michael Courtney**. Any information of him will be rewarded and thankfully received by his distressed mother, **Catherine Molloy**, 2 MONTGOMERY STREET, NEW YORK. [Appeared Jan. 24, 1857 with less information.]

March 28, 1857

Keefe.—**Dora Keefe**, of KILKENNY, Ireland is requested to call on **Mrs. Dr. G---**(with whom she lived 3 years ago), at 118 EAST 14th STREET, cor. 3rd Avenue.

Of **Thomas Heffernan**, a native of the City of KILKENNY, Ireland, who arrived in New York about 2 years ago. When last heard from he was at ALEXANDRA, VA. Any information of him will be thankfully received by his brother **John Heffernan**, at **Patrick Fleming's**, 496 PEARL STREET, NEW YORK CITY.

Of **Rose Connaughty**, a native of the Parish of KILLESHANDRA, County CAVAN, Ireland, who arrived in New York in 1852. When last heard from she was living at **Mr. Henry Van Buren's**, builder, SING SING, NEW YORK. Any information of her will be thankfully received by her cousin **John Leddy**. Please direct letter to **Cornelius O'Reilly**, No. 132 EAST 29th STREET, NEW YORK CITY. Sing Sing papers please copy.

Of **John Dillon**, brother of the late **Patt Dillon**, of ROSS, near MARYBORO', QUEEN'S County; was living in this city about 10 years ago. From which place it is said he went to reside in RICHMOND, STATEN ISLAND. Any person knowing anything about him, dead or alive, will confer a favor by addressing a line to **John Fitzpatrick**, 154 8th AVENUE, NEW YORK CITY.

April 4, 1857

Andrew (or **Alphonsus**) **A. Crawford**, of FINNEA, Co. MEATH, Ireland. Who formerly resided at LODI, N.J., will please call or send his address to this office before Saturday next (4th inst). His brother **J. M. Crawford**, of ST. LOUIS, is in the City and wishes to see him.

Of **John Londrigan**, a native of TEMPLETOOHY, Co. TIPPERARY, Ireland. When last heard from about three years ago, he was in ST. LOUIS, MO. Any information of his whereabouts will be thankfully received by his father **James Londrigan**, at No. 652 WATER ST. NEW YORK. St. Louis papers please copy.

Of **James Rowane**, of NEWTOWN-CORMICK, ERRIS, Co. MAYO, Ireland. Left BROOKLYN, five years since. Any information concerning him will be thankfully received by his mother **Ellen Rowane**, No. 643 WASHINGTON ST. NEW YORK. New Orleans, Havana, Illinois and Ohio papers please copy.

Of **Michael Dougherty**, a native of the Co. MAYO, Ireland. Who left home in 1853 and is supposed to have landed in New York. Any intelligence of him will be thankfully received by his sister **Mary Dougherty**. Address to the care of **James Daly**, LOWER REDHOOK, DUTCHESS CO., N.Y.

Of **Joseph Kelly**, son of the late **Denis Kelly**, Esq., of MELTRANE, Parish of KILTULLA, County ROSCOMMON, Ireland. He came to America about the year 1852, and remained in NEW YORK or its vicinity for some time. It is reported that he was on board the steamship *San Francisco*, which was lost on the voyage to CALIFORNIA a few years since. She had on board at the time 600 passengers, 200 of whom were rescued by an English vessel and carried to Liverpool, 200 more were saved by an American ship, and the remainder found a watery grave. It has been reported that the said Joseph Kelly was among those who were carried to LIVERPOOL, and that he died there after arriving; but his friends cannot find any clue to the fact. If still alive he would be about 23 years of age, about 5 feet 8 inches high, fair-haired, with smooth, fair complexion. Any person having any knowledge of him alive or dead, will please communicate it to **Patrick Kearney**, 263 WEST 35th STREET, NEW YORK, who will acquaint his friends in Ireland. Herald and Sun please copy.

April 11, 1857

Of **Thomas Mulvey**, a native of RATHCOOL, County DUBLIN, Ireland; left home in May, 1856. Any information of him will be thankfully received by his sister **Margaret**, at No. 26 WEST 24th STREET, NEW YORK.

April 18, 1857

Of **Catherine Singleton**, a native of BANTEER, County CORK, Ireland, who arrived in NEW ORLEANS eight years ago this spring. When last heard from was still living there. Any information of her will be thankfully received by her brother, **Timothy Singleton**, by addressing a few lines to him, care of **Mr. John Halloran**, CANTERBURY, ORANGE County, NEW YORK.

Of **Mary Leahy**, native of the County CORK, Parish of KILLGAY, Town of ASHGROVE, Ireland, who arrived in New York about eight years ago, in company with her father and family. Any information of her will be thankfully received by her father, **Michael Leahy**, APPLETON Post-office, OUTAGANIA County, WISCONSIN; or by **Mrs. Rieves**, 20 WEST 15th STREET, NEW YORK.

Of **John** and **Joseph Keyes** (shoemakers), natives of MALANYBENEY, Parish of CLOGHER, County TYRONE, Ireland. When last heard of they were in UPPER CANADA. Any information of them will be thankfully received by **William** and **James Fettresch**, builders 491 SECOND AVENUE, NEW YORK CITY.

April 25, 1857

Of **Jeremiah Cashman**. When last heard from in 1853, he was a contractor for sections 22, 23, and 24 of the Illinois Central Railroad; his address then was in care of **Judge P. Corcoran**, CAIR, ILLINOIS. If this should meet his eye, or any person knowing his whereabouts, they will confer a great favor by writing a few lines to **George Cashman**, N. W. cor. of 32nd STREET, and 1st AVE., NEW YORK.

Of **Peter Hanly**, or **Mary**, his sister, by their brother **Hugh**. Also, of **Patrick** and **Hugh Clarke**, by their brother **Edward**. By calling at 26 WEST 19th STREET, they can get full information of them by a friend from LEIXLIP.

Of **William Reffter**, a native of Meath Street, DUBLIN, who left his home in 1846, with his father, and arrived in NEW ORLEANS, at which place his father died. Any information of him will be thankfully received by his sister **Anna**, at 17 South Second Street, WILLIAMSBURGH, N.Y. New Orleans papers please copy.

Of **Richard Power**, a native of GARDENMORRIS, County WATERFORD, Ireland. When the writer of this left Ireland, Richard was living with his uncle, **John Power**, of GURTEEN, but is supposed to be in NEW YORK State at present. Any information respecting him will be thankfully received by his brother, **Thomas R. Power**, of MANATEE, FLORIDA.

Of **Eliza Byrne**, a native of the County CARLOW, Ireland. When last heard from was in LOUISVILLE, KENTUCKY; but it is thought she is gone to NEW ORLEANS. Any information of her will be thankfully received by addressing a few lines to **Mr. James Shepherd**, 452 GRAND STREET, NEW YORK CITY, where she will hear of something to her advantage. New Orleans and Kentucky papers please copy.

Of **Edmond** and **Daniel McCarthy**, naives of the Parish of DRISHANE, County CORK, Ireland. When Last heard from they were working for some time in FITCHBURG, MASSACHUSETTS. Any information of them will be thankfully received by their brother, **John McCarthy**, by addressing a few lines to him, to the care of **Cornelius Keleher**, No. 428 WATER STREET, NEW YORK CITY. Boston papers please copy.

May 2, 1857

Of **Thomas Treanor**, a native of Ireland. Any account of him will be thankfully received by his sister, **Catherine Treanor**, 32 DOMINICK ST.

Of **Hugh McGerver**, a lad of about 16 years, who arrived in the ship *Harvest Queen*. Any information concerning his whereabouts will be thankfully received by his father, at the store of T. H. & E. H. Brown & Co., 44 VESEY STREET, N.Y.

Of **Rose McArdle**, a native of DUBLIN, Ireland. Who emigrated to America in the summer of 1854, in the ship *Trimountain*. She can get a silver medal and important information by either calling or sending her address to the office of the Irish-American. Also of **John Nolan**, who came passenger in the same ship. He can get a sum of money by calling as above. Boston, Brooklyn, and New Jersey papers please copy.

Of **Bridget Butler**, daughter of **Thomas Butler** and **Ellen Nugent**, aged 20 years, a native of the Parish of MOTHEL, County WATERFORD, Ireland. Who arrived at New York in the ship *Robert Kelly*, on the 19th of April, and stopped at Castle Garden for one or two days. She is supposed to have hired from there, and is living at present in some part of NEW YORK CITY. Any information concerning her will be thankfully received by her uncle **Michael Butler**, MECHANICSVILLE, SARATOGA Co., N.Y.

Of **Daniel**, **Charles**, **Jeremiah**, **Denis** and **Florence O'Sullivan**, from the Townland of INCH, Parish of PONLABUSH, County CORK. Information received by their nephews, **Daniel** and **John O'Neill**. Address Daniel O'Neill, FARRANDSVILLE Post Office, CLINTON Co., PA.

Of **Edmond Ryan**, son of the late **Patrick Ryan**, provision merchant, Roche's St. LIMERICK, Ireland. When last heard of was in CATSKILL, GREEN Co., NEW YORK State. Any information of him will be gratefully received by his brother, **Thomas Ryan**, box 1068, Post-office, ST. LOUIS, MO.

Of **Denis O'Connell** and **Michael M'Namara**, natives of BALLYSIMON, County LIMERICK, Ireland, who arrived in New York last March three years, in the ship *New York*. When last heard from they were working on some railway in the State of MICHIGAN. Any information of them will be thankfully received by addressing a few lines to **Catherine O'Connor**, care of **Owen M'Carthy**, corner of Harrison and Columbia sts., BROOKLYN, N.Y. Who is a sister of Denis O'Connell's and niece of Michael M'Namara. She is most anxious to hear from them.

Of **John Loran**, who sailed from Limerick in the ship *Primrose* for New York, on the 11th of April, 1855. He is 25 years of age, about 5 feet 7 inches in height, thin features, dark complexion-a native of LIMERICK. There is rumor of his death. His wife, **Catherine**, is anxious to hear from him. Address her, in care of **Patrick Pillman**, 154 Longworth Street, CINCINNATI.

Of **John Finnegan**, who left Ireland, County LOUTH, about 5 years ago, and came to the United States. When last heard from was in the State of TENNESSEE. Any information will be thankfully received by his mother, **Betty Finnegan**, or his sister, **Anne Finnegan**, corner of MAIDEN LANE and CHAPEL ST., or Betty Finnegan, 62 Nucella St., ALBANY, N.Y.

Of **Patrick, John** and **James Gilleran**, natives of NEWCASTLE, some of whom lived in BOSTON, and may be thereabouts yet. It is supposed that one of them is heir to the estate of their uncle, **Thomas Dillon**, whose widow is anxious that some relative of his would take charge of the property. It is situated 1 ½ miles from the village of SMITHS FALLS, CANADA WEST. There is also some money in bank, which no person can draw but the heir-at-law. [Appeared under County MEATH]

Of **Patrick Lauler**, from the Parish of ROSE GARDEN, who left OSWEGO, July 4th, 1856, and is supposed to be in TORONTO, C.W. He is about 17 years old. Information respecting him received by **Rev. Father Kelly**, OSWEGO, N.Y.

Of **Thomas Brogan**, a native of Co. MAYO, Ireland. Came to this country about ten years ago. The last heard from him he was in CLEVELAND, OHIO. Any information will be thankfully received by his brother, **John Brogan**, corner of Water and Columbia sts., ALBANY.

Of **James Donaghue**, who left STRADONE, Co. CAVAN, in Nov., 1854, and was in BOSTON in October, 1856, and has not since been heard from. Information received by his sister, **Ellen**, MEREDITH BRIDGE, N. H.

Of **Michael Blake**, son of **Patrick Blake** and **Mary Eustace**, a native of GARRANATOGHA, Parish of KNOCKERRA; when last heard from was in NEW ORLEANS, working in a marble yard, and boarding with **Patrick Kelly**, Poydress Street. Information received by **Thomas Donovan**, CLEVELAND, OHIO. [Appeared under County CLARE]

Of **Patrick Sheren**, of NEWTOWN, Parish of KILLEMADE; when last heard from, 7 years ago last Christmas, he was in the ALLEGHANY MOUNTAINS. Any person knowing his whereabouts will confer a great favor by writing to his sister **Hannah**, SILVER SPRING, LANCASTER County, PA. [Appeared under County DONEGAL]

Of **Patrick Bourke**, and his sister, **Eliza McCrate**, from Parish of KNOCKARAFIN, County TIPPERARY, Ireland; when last heard from four years ago, was in BYTOWN, UPPER CANADA and was going to ILLINOIS. Information received by **John Moroney**, LANSVILLE CENTRE, SUSQUEHANNA Co. PA.

Of **Edward McElligott**, of BALLYSHEEN, Parish of ODORNEY. Also of **Timothy Sheahan**, and his sons, **Timothy, John, Daniel** and **Michael**, and his daughters, **Jane, Mary** and **Ellen**; when last heard from they were in TOMPKINS County, N.Y. Please address their uncle, **John McElligott**, CRAWFORDSVILLE, MONTGOMERY County, IND. [Appeared under County KERRY]

Of **Peter McCook**, Parish of KILBEACOUNTY, near GORT, County GALWAY, who came to this country 10 or 12 years ago; when last heard from he was in VIRGINIA. Information received by his brother, **Patrick**, MILTON, MASS.

May 9, 1857

If this should meet the eyes of **Bridget Leahy** of EAST BALLYRYAN, County TIPPERARY, who married a **Mr. Brady**, she will learn something to her advantage by calling on or addressing her sister, **Johanna Leahy**, 133 13th STREET, between 6th and 7th Avenues, NEW YORK.

May 16, 1857

Of **John Gallagher**, a mason by trade, a native of the Town of SLIGO. When last heard of was in NEW YORK. Send information to his brother **Patrick Gallagher**, at **Michael Corcoran's**, 42 PRINCE STREET, NEW YORK.

Of **Patrick McMahon**, a native of the Parish of KELEVIN, County MONAGHAN, Ireland, who left his home in SALEM, MASS, on the 2nd of June, 1855. Since that time nothing has been heard from him. He was married about five years ago at St. James's Church, NEW YORK, and worked for some time in a distillery in Franklin Avenue, EAST BROOKLYN, Long Island, and removed to MASSACHUSETTS on the 2nd of May 1855. Any information concerning him will be thankfully received by his afflicted wife, **Ann McMahon**, No. 166 Federal Street, SALEM, MASS.

Of **John Condon**, from MITCHELSTOWN, Co. CORK, Ireland, who came to this country five years ago [1st]March. When last heard from (four years ago) he was living in PLEASANT HILL, KY. Any intelligence of him will be thankfully received by his sister, **Mary Condon**, 233 ELIZABETH STREET, NEW YORK.

May 23, 1857

Of **Thomas Culligan**, a native of the Parish of ST. PATRICK, City of LIMERICK, Ireland. When last heard from he was serving his apprenticeship to the copper and tinsmith business, at CLEVELAND, OHIO. Any information of him will be thankfully received by his brother, **James Culligan**, by addressing a few lines to him, care of **Mr. James Simms**, No. 89 WASHINGTON ST., NEW YORK CITY.

Of **Patrick** and **Thomas Downes**, natives of BALLYSEEDA, Parish of DONOUGHMORE, County of LIMERICK, Ireland. Thomas came here in 1850, and Patrick in 1853. When last heard from was in COLUMBIANA County, State of OHIO; is supposed since to be gone to ARKANSAS. Any information of them, dead or alive, will be thankfully received by their cousin, **James Considine**, by addressing a note to **Mr. Denis Toomey**, No. 17 CITY HALL PLACE, NEW YORK CITY. Ohio and Arkansas papers please copy.

Of **James McInteggert**, from the County LOUTH, Ireland, who is supposed to be in MASSACHUSETTS. Any information of him will be thankfully received by his sister **Ellen**, who lives at 213 TENTH STREET, NEW YORK, between First and Second Avenues.

Of **Miley Leary**, a native of the County WEXFORD, Parish of OILLVIEW, who emigrated to CANADA in the spring of 1852. When last heard from he was working on a railroad in OHIO. Any information will be thankfully received by writing to his brothers, **Patt** and **John**, 284 4th STREET, NEW YORK CITY, or by addressing his mother, **Bridget Leary**, COOLAMAIN, County WEXFORD, Ireland. Ohio and Savannah papers please copy.

Of **Timothy** or **Stephen Noonan**, from the Parish of BULLAWN, near LOUGHREA, County GALWAY, Ireland. Any information respecting them will be thankfully received by their brother, **John Noonan**, or **J. M. Jones**, shipbuilder, MILWAUKEE, WISCONSIN.

Of **Bridget Potter**, a native of the Parish of MOYLOUGH, County GALWAY, Ireland, who arrived in ST. JOHN's in 1847. When last heard from she was living with a **Mr. Burke** of that place, and mentioned that she purposed leaving and coming into the States. From that period up to the present there has been no account received from her. Any information of her will be thankfully received by Lynch & Cole, 32 Beekman Street, who will transmit all such information to her brother, **Patrick Potter**, DUNMORE, TUAM, County GALWAY, Ireland.

May 30, 1857

Of **Eugene Madden**, of BALLYCONNERY, Parish of LISELTON, who was learning the carriage-making trade in PARIS, KENTUCKY, about 3 years ago. Information received by his brother, **Edward Madden**, KEOKUK, IOWA. [Appeared under County KERRY]

Of **Felix McGinnis**, a native of DRUMHULLI[GAN], who came to this country in 1845. When last heard of he was in PENNSYLVANIA. Information received by his daughter, **Catherine**, VALLEY FALL, R. I. [Appeared under County LEITRIM]

Of **Patrick Keegan**, a native of the City of DUBLIN, Ireland. When last heard from was in ST. LOUIS, MO. Any information of him will be thankfully received by addressing a few lines to his son, **John Keegan**. Weather Street, near Graham Avenue, WILLIAMSBURGH, Long Island, N.Y.

Of **Patrick Costelloe**, a native of the County TIPPERARY, Ireland. When last heard from he was living outside BOSTON. If this should meet his eye, or any person knowing him, please direct a note to his sister-in-law, **Ellen Costelloe**, No. 81 LEWIS STREET, N.Y. Boston papers please copy.

Of **Eliza Tracy**, Parish of LOUGHMORE, Townland of WHITEFIELD, County TIPPERARY, who left home on October last, and landed in New York, and is suppose to have gone to UPPER CANADA. She will hear of her sister, **Johanna**, by writing to **John Tyrrel**, No.33 New Church st, BALTIMORE, MD.

Of **John Daly**, her step-father, by **Mary Donohoe**, also of **Winfred Daly**, her mother, **Patrick** and **John Daly**, her step-brothers, **Ellen** and **Anne Daly**, her step-sisters, **Margaret** and **Bridget Donohoe**, her full sisters, all from the Parish of KILLEE, Townland of GURTEEN, KING'S County, Ireland. They all came to America about ten years ago and landed in New Orleans, and from there went to CINCINNATI, State of OHIO. Any information concerning them will be thankfully received by addressing a few lines to Mary Donohoe, No. 156 SULLIVAN STREET, (rear building) NEW YORK.

Of **Ellen Delaney**, from the Parish of BARNA, who arrived in New Orleans in 1852. Any information of her will be thankfully received by her cousin, **A. Larkin**, 1107 WASHINGTON STREET, NEW YORK. New Orleans papers please copy. [Appeared under KING'S County]

Of **Mary** and **Julia Lynch**, daughters of the widow **Ellen Lynch**, natives of the City of CORK, Ireland. Who left BOSTON on the 10th of April, 1854, and are supposed to have come to NEW YORK. Since that time nothing has been heard of them. By sending their address to the **Rev. Thomas Lynch**, ROXBURY, MASS., they will receive a sum of money and news of importance to them.

June 6, 1857

Of **Michael Hanlon**, from the Parish of CLONTUBRET, County MONAGHAN. When last seen he was in NEW YORK in the U. S. Service recruiting. If this should meet his eye, or any person knowing his whereabouts they would confer a great favor on his brother and sister, **Francis** and **Mary Hanlon**, by addressing a few lines to them in the care of **John Agnew**, No. 19 Paul Street, PHILADELPHIA, PA.

Of **James Flynn**, a native of BANTEER, County CORK, Ireland. When last seen by his uncle **Thomas** he was in PHILADELPHIA. Any information of him will be thankfully received by sending a few lines to his sister **Margaret**, No. 12 MACDOUGAL STREET, NEW YORK.

Of **Timothy Lyons**, a native of the City of CORK, Ireland. Who landed in Quebec in June, 1844, and then came to NEW YORK. When last heard from he was supposed to be in MULBERRY STREET, in the latter City. Any information of him will be thankfully received by his step-brother, **Richard Murphy**, JEFFERSON CITY, MO.

William McCready, who worked on the PANAMA Railroad, in the Spring and Summer of 1853, on Juan Grande Station, will hear of something to his advantage by sending his address to **Bernard Conway**, No. 56 ELM STREET, NEW YORK. Harrisburgh and Lancaster, Pa., papers please copy.

Of **Thomas Garmly**, who left his home in 28th STREET, on the 17th of March, and has not been heard from since. Any information of him will be thankfully received by his cousin, **Edward Garmly**, on board the steamer Hendric Hudson. Albany and Connecticut papers please copy.

Of **Timothy O'Neil**, a native of the Parish of IRLES, BEREHAVEN, County CORK, Ireland, aged 23, who left home in June 1851. When last heard from, two years ago, was in ELMIRA, CHEMUNG County, NEW YORK. Any information of him will be thankfully received by his brother **Denis**, who landed in this country three weeks ago. Address to him at SOMERSET, MASSACHUSETTS.

June 13, 1857

Of **Eugene O'Shea**, who was formerly in the employment of Messrs Pell, Nevers and O'Sullivan, Pearl Street, NEW YORK. Any intelligence of him will be thankfully received by his brother **James E. O'Shea**, JEFFERSON CITY, MO., or at the office of this paper.

Of **James** and **Michael Kenna**, from GREEN LANE, Co. CARLOW, Ireland. When last heard from about three years ago, they were in LOUISVILLE, KY. Since that time they wrote two letters to their sister, but she did not receive either of them. Any intelligence of them will be thankfully received by their sister **Mary Ann Kenna**, care of **Patrick O'Donohue**, 115 BAXTER ST., NEW YORK, or NEWBURGH Post Office, N.Y.

Of **Thomas Shanahan**, a native of the County WATERFORD, Ireland. When last heard from he was in NEW YORK CITY, and then left for some part unknown. Any information of him will be thankfully received by **Patrick Flemming**, No. 496 PEARL ST., NEW YORK.

Of **Misses Rosanna** and **Margaret McCarron**, who left the north of Ireland some years since. Also of **Mrs. O'Driscoll**, **Mrs. Moony** or **Mrs. Power** OF CASTLETOWN, BEARHAVEN, CORK Co. Also of **Mr. James Shea**, who left BANTRY, CORK Co. in the end of 1848 or sometime in 1849. Any information as to where a letter would reach any of the above, would much oblige. Address A. B. care of **P. M. Haverty**, 110 FULTON ST., N.Y.

Of **Martin** and **Thomas Walsh**, natives of the Parish of LADY'S BRIDGES, Co. CORK, Ireland. Martin supposed to be in this country about 26 years; Thomas about 29. Any information given of them will be kindly received by their brother **Patrick's** wife **(Mary Walsh)** and children, at 163 AVENUE A, NEW YORK.

Of **Daniel J. Kenny**, of LIMERICK, Ireland. Any information of him will be gratefully received by **M. H. Corbett**, late of Limerick. Address by letter NEW YORK Post Office.

Of **James Didgen**, a native of the County DONEGAL, Ireland; when last heard from, about four months ago, he was living in CANAL STREET, NEW YORK CITY. Any information of him will be thankfully received by his cousin, **James Kirscodden**, by addressing a few lines to the Irish-American office, 32 Beekman St., New York.

Of **Catherine Martin**, a native of the Parish of PORTUMNA, village of DROMSCAR, County GALWAY, Ireland, who came to America about eleven years ago. When last heard from she was living at GREAT FALLS, State of NEW HAMPSHIRE. Any information of her will be thankfully received by her brother, **Patrick Martin**, by addressing a few lines to him, care of **John Dowd**, No. 79 WASHINGTON STREET, NEW YORK.

June 20, 1857

John Heath, a native of the Parish of COOLRY, County WESTMEATH, Ireland, who left NEW YORK about ten years ago, and is supposed to have gone to PENNSYLVANIA, or on the York and Erie Railroad. Any information of him will be thankfully received by **William Heath**, No. 31 Tallman Street, BROOKLYN, State of NEW YORK. Southern papers please copy.

Of **Dan Moloney**, a native of MOUNTRATH, QUEEN'S County, Ireland. When last heard from he lived in TORONTO, CANADA WEST, behind the soldiers' barracks, Black Bull. Any information of him will be thankfully received by **John Delaney**, 30 Bridge Street, NEWARK, NEW JERSEY. Toronto papers please copy.

Of **Patrick Whelan** and **Edmond Reeves** of the Parish of FEDAMORE, County of LIMERICK, Ireland. When last heard of were in the State of ILLINOIS. Any information of them will be thankfully received by his brother **William Whelan**, now residing in TEMPLETON, County of WORCESTER, MASS.

June 27, 1857

Of **Michael Grant**, from near CASHEL, County TIPPERARY, Ireland, who came to this country a few years ago. Should this meet his eye or any person who knows his present residence and address, they will confer a favor by writing or sending to his brother, **John**, 83 Gold Street, between Plymouth and Water Street, BROOKLYN, N.Y.

M. H. Corbett, late of LIMERICK, Ireland, will find a letter from **D. J. Kenny** (now of BALTIMORE.)by calling at the General Post Office, NEW YORK.

July 18, 1857

Of **Michael Monaghan**, aged about 48 years. A native of CROSSAKEIL, who came to this country about 7 years ago, and is supposed to be in NEW YORK. Please address **Miss Hogan**, care of **T. O'Donnell**, Esq., NEW ORLEANS, LA. [Appeared under County MEATH]

Of **Margaret Daly**, of MUNALOUR, Parish of CAPPOQUIN: when last heard from 2 years ago, was in NASHUA, NEW HAMPSHIRE. Please address her sister **Bridget**, care of **John O'Donnell**, TERRE HAUTE, IND. [Appeared under County MEATH]

Of **Edward Daly**, a native of KILMESSON, County MEATH, Ireland; when last heard from he was working in a towel factory in COLUMBUS, OHIO. Any information of him, dead or alive, will be thankfully received by sending a few lines to his sister, **Rose Gerlity**, ASTORIA, Long Island, QUEENS County, NEW YORK.

Of **Edward Walsh**, of the Town of CLONMEL; when last heard from was in MERIN County, OHIO. Information will be thankfully received by his sister **Margaret**, care of **John Nalon**, LOCKHAVEN, CLINTON County, PENNSYLVANIA. [Appeared under County TIPPERARY]

Of **Patrick** and **Thomas Burke**, aged from 20 to 22 years, natives of the Parish of MOYNE and TEMPLETOUHY. Patrick worked in LA SALLE four years ago for a railroad company, and Thomas worked at the same time in NEW YORK. They will find something to their advantage by addressing their uncle, **Nicholas Burke**, LA SALLE, ILLINOIS. [Appeared under County TIPPERARY]

Of **Patrick, William** and **John Reygans**, who lived near GREENFIELD, OHIO, about 4 years ago. Any information will be thankfully received by **Timothy Tracy**, DUNLEITH, JO DAVIESS County, ILLINOIS. [Appeared under County TIPPERARY]

Of **Patt**, **John**, **William**, or **Thomas Marten**, from NEWCASTLE, County CARLOW. If this should meet the eye of any person knowing them, they will confer a great favor by writing to their cousin, **Anne Dawson**, from MOUNTMELLICK, QUEEN'S County. Direct to ASHUELOT, NEW HAMPSHIRE.

Of **Patrick**, **Peter**, **Bridget** and **Ellen Tierny**, natives of LETTERMULLIN, Parish of KILCUMMIN; when last heard from, December, 1854, Patrick, Bridget and Ellen lived in NEW YORK CITY, and Peter on LONG ISLAND, with **Thomas McKeon**. Information will be thankfully received by their sister, **Honor**. Address her husband, **John Joyce**, PARKERSBURG, VA. [APPEARED under County CARLOW]

Of **James Lynch**, of BALLINACODA, Parish of BALLINACODA; when last heard from was at work on a railroad near BOSTON, MASS, about 3 years ago. Information will be thankfully received by his sister **Catherine**, in care of **Wm. Collins**, LEWISTON, MASS. [Appeared under County CORK]

Of **Maurice Glassett**, a native of BALLYHAY, near CHARLEVILLE, who came to this country about 2 years ago, and left BOSTON last December. Please address his sister **Mary**, at MEDFORD, MASS. [Appeared under County CORK]

Of **Catherine O'Grady**, a native of Ireland, Parish of MURROE, County LIMERICK; left Ireland May 6. Any information will be gladly received by her sister **Eliza**. Address Post-office, YONKERS.

Of **Denis Murphy**, of CLOODAH, County CORK, Ireland; when last heard from was in GENESEE County, MICH. Any information will be thankfully received by his sister **Margaret Desmond**, or brother, **John Murphy**, No. 128 Butler Street, BROOKLYN, N.Y.

Of **Patrick Keough**, a native of CELBRIDGE, County KILDARE, Ireland; when last heard from he was in ST. LOUIS, MO. Any information of him will be thankfully received by his brother, **Peter Keough**, by addressing a few lines to him at No. 25 Mulberry St., FALL RIVER, MASS.

Of **James** and **Mary Cosgrove**, who came from GLENCARTLE Parish, County MAYO, to NEW YORK CITY, about nine years ago; supposed to have gone to a sister **Bridget**, some twenty miles from the City, and has not been heard of since. Their sister **Sarah** is very anxious to find their whereabouts, and may be heard from by inquiring at No. 3 WEST WASHINGTON PLACE, NEW YORK.

Of **Thomas Curran**, a native of BALLINA, who came to this country about 7 years ago; when last heard from was in LOCKPORT, N.Y., 4 years ago. Information will be thankfully received by his brother **Patrick**, SCRANTON, LUZERNE County, PA. [Appeared under County MAYO]

Of **Patrick** and **Thomas Gavan**, of ROSE-HILL, Parish of KILMENA; when last heard from was in VIRGINIA. Information will be thankfully received by their brother, **John Gavan**, DUNMORE, LUZERNE County, PA. [Appeared under County MAYO]

Of **Peter** and **Hanna Naughton**, natives of the Parish of ADRAGOOL, DERRAFADA, who came to this country about 4 years ago. When last heard of were in NEW YORK. Information will be thankfully received by their brother **James**, CAIRO, VA. [Appeared under County MAYO]

Of **Denis**, **Edward** and **William Byrnes**, natives of STRATFORD-ON-SLANEY, Parish of BALTINGLASS, County WICKLOW, Ireland, who came to this country 9 years ago. Denis is supposed to be keeping a dairy near NEW YORK: Edward and William when last heard of were in NEW YORK. Any information as to the whereabouts of the above-named brothers will be thankfully received by addressing **Thomas Byrne**, 257 WEST 33rd STREET, 9th AVENUE.

Of **Phil Mornahan** and **Edward Gaynor**, from County CAVAN. Their sister and brother-in-law have just arrived, and wish to find them. Address **Patrick Fitzpatrick**, NEW YORK.

Of **John McAvoy**, a native of the County CAVAN; when last heard of was in ILLINOIS. Information will be thankfully received by his nephew, **Michael McCann**, JEANESVILLE, LUZERNE County, PA.

Of **Ellen Murphy**, of BALLYREADY, Parish of TOLOGHER, County KILKENNY, who landed in New York June, 1854. Should this meet her eye, or any one knowing her whereabouts, will confer a favor by addressing her brother, **James Murphy**, PEORIA, ILL.

Of **Thomas McClelland**, of the Townland of FIDDOWN, Parish of TEMPLORAM, County KILKENNY, who came to this country about 3 or 4 years ago, and landed in New York with his mother and sister, and stopped with **Nicholas Dunn**, his brother-in-law, and has not been heard from since. Information will be thankfully received by his brother, **William McClelland**, CHILLICOTHE, PEORIA County, ILL.

Of **John Doherty**, carpenter by trade, who left DUNGLOE, County DONEGAL, Ireland, about 3 years ago; when last heard of he was in MILWAUKEE. Any information of him will be kindly received by his brother, **Joseph Doherty**, at Dr. Dillon's Drug Store, No. 421 PEARL, corner of Rose Street, NEW YORK. Western papers please copy.

Of **John O'Brien**, from BUNDORAN, County DONEGAL; when last heard from he was in HAVRE in FRANCE. Any one knowing anything concerning his present whereabouts will please address his brothers, **James K.** or **Francis O'Brien**, Greenmount Avenue, BALTIMORE, MD.

Of **John Myres**, of the Parish of KILDYSART, who landed in New York about 10 years ago; when last heard from was in ERIE, PENNSYLVANIA, in September, 1856. Please address his brother, **Thomas Myres**, BUFFALO, NEW YORK. [Appeared under County CLARE]

Of **John Gallaher**, of the Parish of O'GONOLOE; when last heard from was in LOOKOUT, MISSOURI. Information will be thankfully received by his brother **Thomas**, COOPERSTOWN, MANITOWOC Co., WIS. [Appeared under County CLARE]

Of **Michael McMahon**, of KILKEREN, Parish of KILLIFIN, County CLARE, who landed in Quebec two years ago last September; when last heard from was with his sister **Honora**, in PARIS, CANADA WEST, in Nov., 1855. Please address his cousin, **Timothy McMahon**, DYERSVILLE, DUBUQUE County IOWA.

Of **Bridget Hanlon**, a native of MUCKERSTAFF, County LONGFORD; when last heard of she lived in GOSHEN, ORANGE County, N.Y., with **Mrs. Gardner**. About 3 years ago her brother received a letter from her, wherein she Stated that she was going to live in BOSTON. Should she or any person acquainted with her see this, they would confer a favor by addressing **Michael Hanlon**, FROSTBURG, ALLEGANY County, MD.

Of **Miles Dougherty**, of the Parish of INNIS, County LEITRIM, who left ST. LOUIS, MO., for CALIFORNIA, on the 10th of April, 1855; and also of his cousin, **Miles McNiff**, who left ST. LOUIS in the summer of 1855. Please address their sister and cousin, **Ann Dougherty**, care of **William Hughes**, corner of Tenth and Christy Avenue, St. Louis, Mo.

July 25, 1857

Of **Patrick Cox**, a native of the Parish of CLONETUSKARD, County ROSCOMMON, Ireland; when last heard from he was in HUMMELSTOWN, DAUPHIN County, PENNSYLVANIA. Any information of him will be thankfully received by his wife, **Mary Cox**, who is most anxious to her from him, by addressing a few lines to her at No. 390 CHERRY STREET, NEW YORK.

Of **James Clark**, a native of DOON, Parish of MULAUGH, County of CAVAN, Ireland, who emigrated to America from Liverpool in January '53; when last heard from he was living with a farmer at SPRINGFIELD, OHIO, in '54. Any account of him will be thankfully received by his brother, **Andrew Clark**, by addressing a few lines to UTICA, ILLINOIS.

Of **Philip Monaghan** and **Edward Gainor**, natives of GLENCURRAN, Parish of KILMORE, County CAVAN, Ireland; who arrived in America about five years ago. When last heard from they were at OXFORD, BUTLER Co., State of OHIO. Any information will be thankfully received by **Patrick Fitzpatrick** at the office of this paper.

August 1, 1857

Of **James Moran**, a native of the Co. ROSCOMMON, Ireland, who came to this country from MANCHESTER, ENGLAND. When Last heard of was at No. 18 OAK STREET, NEW YORK. His wife and child landed in May and resides at No. 16 Washington Street, FALL RIVER, MASS., and are anxious to find him. Any information of him will be thankfully received.

Of **John Stone**, a native of CALLAN, County KILKENNY, Ireland, shoemaker. When last heard from was in NORTH BENNINGTON, VERMONT. Any information respecting him, will be thankfully received by his sister, **Mrs. Johanna Carew**, NORWALK, CONNECTICUT.

August 8, 1857

Of **James Cashman**, a native of ARDDOE, Parish of ARDMORE, County WATERFORD, Ireland, who left home in July, 1848. When last heard from, about seven years ago, he was living at YONKERS, N.Y. Any Information of him will be thankfully received by his brother and sister by addressing a few lines to the care of **John Herse**, No. 188 EAST TWELFTH STREET, NEW YORK.

Of **Denis O'Neill**, a native of CASTLETOWN-BEAREHAVEN, County CORK, Ireland, who left FALL RIVER, MASS., two years ago. When last heard from, six months ago, he was in KENTUCKY. Any information of him will be thankfully received by his wife, **Honora O'Neill**, by directing a letter for her, care of **Patrick D. Sullivan**, 10 Spring Street, FALL RIVER, MASS. New Orleans papers please copy.

Of **Catherine Watson**, from the Parish of MILFORD, County CORK, Ireland. Who arrived in New York on the 22nd June 1857, in the ship *Empire State*, from Liverpool. If she will call at the Commissioners of Emigration office, she will hear of something to her advantage.

Of **Patrick** and **Daniel McMahon**, from the Parish of KILLEEDY, County LIMERICK, Ireland. Patrick came to this country in 1849 and Daniel in '51. When last heard of, about twelve months since they were in KEOKUK, IOWA. Any information of them will be thankfully received by their brother **Denis M'Mahon**, care of **John Leary**, 295 13th STREET, between Ave. A & B, NEW YORK. Iowa papers please copy.

Of **Michael Murphy**, a native of the Parish of BALLENSTENE, County LIMERICK, Ireland. When last heard from he was in PENNSYLVANIA, working on a railroad. Any account of him will be thankfully received by his sister **Mrs. Ellen Murry**, at corner of Partition and Conover Streets, SOUTH BROOKLYN, L. I., State of NEW YORK.

Of **Margaret Rielly**, and **Patt Connor**, from the County of GALWAY, Parish of ROUNDSTONE, who came to New York, in the ship *Benjamin Adams*, in May 1856, and left New York for PHILADELPHIA. Any information of them will be thankfully received by Margaret's sister or Patt's niece **Honora Rielly** in care of **Mrs. McCrosson**, 114 WEST 19th STREET, between 6th and 7th Avenues, NEW YORK. Philadelphia papers please copy.

Of **Patrick Murphy**, from the Parish of MOORE, west of DINGLE, County of KERRY, Ireland. He came to this country about a year and six months ago. When last heard from he was working in PALATINE BRIDGE, MONTGOMERY County. His boss's name is **Christopher Snell**. If this will meet his eye let him write to **Thomas Scanlon**, 430 WATER STREET, NEW YORK, care of **James Downes**.

August 15, 1857

Of **Patrick Kenny**, a native of the Parish of CLANARD, village of CLINAGARD, County WESTMEATH, Ireland, who arrived in New York in the ship *"West Point"* on the 6th of May last, and went to work to **Mr. Wyant's** brickyard, in some part of NEW JERSEY. Any information of him will be thankfully received by his wife, **Julia Kenny**, by directing a letter to her address, 60 SIXTH STREET, between 1st and 2nd Avenues, NEW YORK. New Jersey papers please copy.

Of **John Neylon**, a native of CARRIGAHOLT, County CLARE, Ireland. When last heard from he was living in SOMERSET, State of ILLINOIS. Any information of him will be thankfully received by **John Mangan**, 126 CEDAR STREET, NEW YORK. Illinois papers please copy.

Of **Mary McAvaddy**, who emigrated to CANADA about twenty-seven years ago, a native of the Parish of MOCHOLA; also of **Mary** and **Bridget McAvaddy**, of the Parish of MEELICK, who emigrated about seven years ago to the United States; also of **Mark McDonald**, who sailed in the *"Excelslor"* in the year 1851, a native of the Parish of KILLDAN, who left NEW YORK for SYRACUSE; of **Thomas McAvaddy**, of the Parish of MOCHOLA, who emigrated in the year 1851, and landed in New Orleans; all of them natives of the County MAYO, Ireland. Any information of them will be thankfully received by **John McAvaddy**, Thomas's brother, 154 WEST 16th STREET, NEW YORK. United States and Canada papers please copy.

Of **James** and **Peter McNulty**, Parish of CRAGIN, Town of CRIVEKRIN. When last heard from, in October 1855, Peter was working on the Memphis and Charleston Railroad, TENNESSEE. Please address their brother **John**, SAND PATCH, SOMERSET County, PENNSYLVANIA. [Appeared under County ARMAGH]

Of **Mrs. Kitty Walsh**, a native of the County MONAGHAN, and son **James**. Her husband left her fourteen years ago; her brother, **Peter Curran**, lived in PRINCE EDWARD ISLAND. Please address her husband, **Richard Walsh**, WARWICK, County of LAMBTON, C. W., of **Mary A. Walsh**, TWO RIVERS, MANITOWOC, WISCONSIN.

Of **Edward**, **Francis**, **Henry** and **Michael Donoughy**, natives of MACNAUGH, three miles from MAHARA, County DERRY. When last heard from were supposed to be farming in OHIO. Information received by their nephew, **Henry McLaughlin**, AMBOY, LEE County, ILLINOIS.

Of **Hugh Winters**, of MINNANNOUREGHY, Parish of LONGFIELD, who sailed for Quebec about 30 years ago. His wife (maiden name **Catherine McGin**) and two children perished in the *"lady of the Lake,"* on their way from Derry to Quebec. Please address his nephew, **Thomas Winters**, in care of **Henry Crilly**, N. W. corner of Thompson and Germantown Road, PHILADELPHIA, PA. [Appeared under County TYRONE]

Of **Ellen Close**, a native of BANBRIDGE, Parish of SEAPATRICK. When last heard from, in 1855, was in NEW YORK. Please address her brother, **W. T. Close**, Royal Artillery, ST. JOHN, N.B. [Appeared under County DOWN]

August 22, 1857

Of **Mary Boyle**, aged seventeen years, a native of the County of LEITRIM, Ireland, who emigrated from Liverpool about seven weeks ago in the ship *William Stetson*, and landed in New York July 31st, was bound for NEW HAVEN, CONN., where her friends are; but having missed her way in New York, she has not yet reached her friends nor has she been since heard from. Any information of her will be gratefully received by **Patrick Lee**, 30 Hill Street, NEW HAVEN, CONN., or **Mr. Patrick Reynolds**, 54 PRINCE STREET, NEW YORK.

Of **Miles Mathews**, a native of the Parish of CARNORRAS, KELLS, County MEATH, Ireland. He left NEW YORK in November, 1851. Since that time nothing has been heard from him, in company with a man by the name **Leahy**, bound for ST. LOUIS or NEW ORLEANS. Any information of him will be thankfully received by his father, **Owen Mathews**, or his brother, **Stephen Mathews**, porter at the St. Nicholas Hotel, New York. St. Louis and New Orleans papers please copy.

Of **Tim McCarty**, from TELLARBY, Parish of ALACKY, County LIMERICK, Ireland, by his niece **Mary Sullivan**, 43 OAK STREET, NEW YORK. Boston and New York papers please copy.

Of **Martin Cannon**, who came to this country twenty years ago. When last heard from (eight years since) he was in NEW ORLEANS. Also of his brothers **John** and **Thomas Cannon**, who came to this country, the former nine years and the latter eight years ago. The above three brothers were born in the Townland of HEATHLAWN, Parish of KILLIMOR, County GALWAY, Ireland. Should this meet their eye, or any one who knows anything of their whereabouts, they will confer a favor on their sister, **Catherine Cannon**, by sending her a few lines in care of **Mr. James Joyce**, 490 BROADWAY, NEW YORK. New Orleans papers please copy.

Of **Michael Dooley**, Parish of KILMAIN, County ROSCOMMON, Ireland. When last heard from (about two years ago) was in KENTUCKY. Any information of him will be thankfully received by his brother, **Patrick Dooley**, by addressing a few lines to **Bridget Casey**, 197 WEST 23rd STREET, NEW YORK and his brother will receive them. Kentucky papers please copy.

Of **Bat Rourke**, a native of CASTLE ISLAND, County KERRY, Ireland. When last heard from he was serving his time to the coach-making business in some part of NEW JERSEY. Any information of him will be thankfully received by his sisters, **Kate** and **Mary Rourke**, at the office of this paper.

Of **Michael**, **Bridget**, **John** and **Ellen Grandeson**, natives of the Parish of BLACK DITCHES, Ireland, who arrived in St. John, New Brunswick, about eighteen years ago. Any information of them will be thankfully received by their brothers **John** and **Thomas**, by directing a letter to John, to RYE, WESTCHESTER County, NEW YORK, or at the office of this paper. [Appeared under County WICKLOW]

August 29, 1857

Of **Bridget Hendley**, who came from LONDON, about four years ago, and is supposed to be living some place near BOSTON. Any information of her will be thankfully received by her sister, **Mary Hendley**, at No. 41 VESEY STREET, NEW YORK.

Of **John Cantwell**, a shoemaker by trade, and a native of the City KILKENNY, Ireland. When last heard of he was in NEW YORK, and supposed to have left for NEW ORLEANS or some of the Western States. Any information of him will be thankfully received by his wife and children, at **John Murphy's**, 56 MULBERRY STREET, NEW YORK.

Of **Michael Ward**, thirteen years of age, a native of CARLOW, Ireland. When last heard of he was in NEW HAVEN, CONN. Any information of him will be thankfully received by his father **Timothy Ward**, 284 EAST SEVENTEENTH STREET, NEW YORK.

Of **James Brady**, of DRUMCRAVE, Co. CAVAN, Ireland, who left NEW YORK last January, two years ago, and when last heard of was near PHILADELPHIA. Any information of him will be thankfully received by his sister **Rose**, at the Tremont House, corner of 40th STREET and 6th AVENUE, NEW YORK. Philadelphia papers please copy.

Of **Patrick** and **Michael Lawlor**, natives of the Parish of ST. PATRICK'S, City of LIMERICK, Ireland. When last heard from they were in COVINGTON, KY. Any information of them will be thankfully received by their brothers and sister, **James**, **Malachy** and **Honora Lawlor**, by directing a letter for them to **John Doyle**, 33 WASHINGTON STREET, or James Lawlor, 18 OAK STREET, NEW YORK.

September 5, 1857

Luke and **Patrick Logan**, natives of the City of DUBLIN, (the former supposed to be in ILLINOIS, the latter in INDIANA,) would hear of something to their advantage by addressing a note to **Thomas Kearns**, 81st STREET, between 1st and 2nd Avenues, NEW YORK.

Of **Patrick Mannix**, of the Parish of BOHER, County TIPPERARY, Ireland; when last heard from was discharged from the U. S. Army, in BATON ROUGE, LOUISIANA. Any information respecting him will be thankfully received by addressing his brother, **John Mannix**, 406 WATER STREET, NEW YORK. Southern and Western papers please copy.

Of the whereabouts of **Thomas** and **Bridget Madden**, who emigrated to this country from the Townland of TOUR, County TIPPERARY, Ireland; when last heard from they were in some part of VIRGINIA. Any information left at **Mr. Mead's**, corner of 59th STREET and 2nd AVENUE, NEW YORK, will be thankfully received by his brother **James**.

September 12, 1857

Of **Mary Clinton**, aged about 23 years, a daughter of **Patrick Clinton** and **Catherine Kearney**, from EDGESTOWN, County LONGFORD, Ireland. By calling at **Bernard Lynch's**, No. 214 WAVERLY PLACE, NEW YORK, she will hear of something to her advantage. Boston papers please copy.

Of **John Quinn**, a native of TICKNEVIN, County KILDARE, Ireland, who sailed from Liverpool in the month of June, 1853, in the ship *Salem*, bound for Canada, but is supposed to be in the States at present. Any information of him will be kindly received by his cousin, **John Quinn**, Lunatic Asylum, NASHVILLE, TENN.

Of **Michael Grant**, of the Parish of KILMACOW, County WATERFORD, Ireland, by his sister **Margaret Doyle**, at 392 EIGHTH STREET, corner of Avenue D, NEW YORK.

Of **Andrew Byrne**, a native of BALLYMACFADDEN, or the Town of MACFADDEN, Parish of KILLKAR, County DONEGAL, Ireland, who came to this country about 40 years ago; when last heard from he left NEW YORK for a place named MOUNT SERENE, BARBOUR County, ALABAMA. He was married in this country. Any information of him will be thankfully received by his sister, **Mary Byrne**, alias **Alice Shevlin**, at 179 LUDLOW ST., or **Charles Shevlin**, 26 SPRUCE STREET, NEW YORK. Exchange papers please.

Of **William Byrnes**, a native of the County CARLOW, Ireland; when last heard from, two years ago, he was in SUMMIT County, OHIO. Any information of him will be thankfully received by his sister, **Sarah Byrnes**, by directing a letter for her to No. 22 RIVINGTON STREET, NEW YORK.

Of **James** and **Francis Gulch**, from RICE HILL, Parish of KILMORE, County CAVAN, Ireland, by their brothers, **Patrick**, **Terence** and **Bernard Gulch**, at 132 ELIZABETH STREET, NEW YORK.

Of **John Vaughey**, a native of GRANGE, Parish of GRANGEGAETH, County MEATH, Ireland, who emigrated from Liverpool in April, 1850, for New York; he was last seen in NEW ORLEANS by a friend, in May 1854, and is supposed to be in some of the Western States, or above ST. LOUIS. He is about 28 years of age, has sandy hair, and is about 5 feet 8 inches in height. Any information of him will be thankfully received at the Irish News office, 100 Nassau Street, New York.

Of **John McDonald**, a sawyer by trade, from the City of CORK, Ireland; when last heard of, about two years since, was working at a saw mill, in WISCONSIN. Any information will be thankfully received by his sister **Mary**, by directing to **John Kirk**, 184 AVENUE A, NEW YORK. Wisconsin papers please copy.

Of **John Dore**, from the County LIMERICK, Ireland, who came to this country about 12 years since, and was in NEW YORK two years ago. His mother received a letter from him in BINGHAMTON, 3 years since, in which he desired her to direct her answer to "Virginia P.O" (probably in CASS Co., ILL) she has not heard from him since. Any information of him she will thankfully receive. Direct to **Ellen Dore**, 201 EAST 12th STREET, NEW YORK.

September 19, 1857

Of **James** and **John Galvin**, who came to this country about nine years ago, from the Parish of MAROUGH, County CORK, Ireland. Any information respecting them will be thankfully received by their sister **Mary**, at 79 LEONARD STREET, NEW YORK. Boston papers please copy.

Of **Laurence Twomey**, a native of the Parish of MAGOURNEY, County CORK, Ireland, who arrived in New York six years ago, and left for VIRGINIA, remained there for one week, and then left for the West, in company with a man by the name of **John Lynch**. Any information of him will be thankfully received by his brother, **Cornelius Twomey**, by directing a letter to him care of **James Looney**, PIERMONT, ROCKLAND Co., NEW YORK.

September 28, 1857

Of **James**, **Bridget** and **Ann Lynch**, children of the late **Denis Lynch**, of QUIN, County CLARE, Ireland. If this should catch their attention they will please write and send their address to their sister **Catherine**, who has arrived in this City. Direct to the care of Patrick J. Meehan, Irish-American office.

Of **Garrett Nagle**, or his aunts **Honora** and **Margaret Walsh**, (the latter married to **Jeremiah Walsh**.) from the City of CORK, Ireland, who came to this country about six years ago, and are living in or near NEW HAVEN, CONN. If this should meet their eyes (or any one who knows their address) they will please write immediately to **Barbara Nagle**, sister of Garrett, who arrived in this City by the ship *Cynosure*. Direct to the office of the Irish-American, or to the care of R. Casserly, Esq., Secretary to the Commissioners of Emigration, New York.

Of **Johanna Sullivan**, by her niece **Johanna Sullivan**, who arrived in this country, Sept, 3rd, from SHANNAGOLDEN, County LIMERICK, Ireland. Please call at 357 BOWERY, in the Saloon.

Of **Annie Hanly**, now married, and goes by the name of **Annie Ears**, or **Sears**, a native of the Parish of KILMORE, County ROSCOMMON, Ireland; when last heard from she sent a letter home to the old country from CHICAGO, ILL., without giving the name of the street or number. Any information of her will be thankfully received by her sister and brother, **Catherine** and **Michael Hanly**, at **Thomas McDonald's**, 23 State Street, BROOKLYN. Chicago papers please copy.

October 3, 1857

Of **Edward Doherty**, a cooper by trade, born in BARHEAD, SCOTLAND, who shipped for NEW ORLEANS, in October, 1854, from BROOKLYN. Any information concerning him will be thankfully received by his mother, **Jane Doherty**, in care of **John Roddy**, No. 10 Furman Street, BROOKLYN.

Of **John Hovenden**, who left Ireland for this City, last spring, will call on the undersigned, he will receive a sum of money which is due to him. O'Gorman & Wilson, 24 William St., New York.

Mrs. Munay, SOMERVILLE, CONN., wishes information of her sister, **Jane Allen**, (maiden name **Sands**,) who arrived here from Liverpool in 1845 or '46. Her children's names are **John**, **Francis** and **Alexander**. Her last known residence was in 7th AVENUE, in this City. Information of her whereabouts will be thankfully received by addressing a note to the above address, or No. 176 AVENUE B, corner of 11th Street, N.Y.

Of **Marcella Keena**, a native of the Parish of LANEY, County WESTMEATH, Ireland, who arrived in New York on the fourth of July, in the ship *Great Western*, and has not been heard of since. Any information of her, will be thankfully received by her sister, **Bridget Keena**, by directing a letter for her, care of **Patrick Kilbride**, 112 Navy St., cor. Fulton Avenue, BROOKLYN, N.Y.

Of **Andrew** and **George Phalon**, natives, of KYLDELLEG, Parish of AHAVO, QUEEN'S County, Ireland. When last heard from, Andrew, was living with a farmer near COLUMBUS, OHIO. George, was living at PORT JERVIS, in this State, and came to NEW YORK CITY, and then left for some place unknown. Any information of them will be thankfully received by their sister, **Mary Phalon**, by directing a letter for her care of **Michael Murphy**, 414 CHERRY STREET, NEW YORK, or **James Corby**, WILLIAMSBURGH, L.I.

Of **Bryan Conaghen**, a native of LARGY, Parish of KILLIBEGS, Co. DONEGAL, Ireland. Left Ireland, for America in October last. When last heard from was in SPRINGFIELD, NEW JERSEY, working in a paper mill. Any information of him will be kindly received by his brother, **John Conaghen**, in care of **Mr. James Mourne**, ST. LOUIS Post Office, MISSOURI.

Of **John Barron**, a native of the City of KILKENNY, Ireland, who arrived in New York about five years ago. When last heard from he was at HAVERSTRAW, State of NEW YORK. Any information of him will be thankfully received by his brother, **James Barron**, 56 SPRING STREET, NEW YORK.

Of **Johanna Seney**, or **Sooney**, by her niece, **Johanna Sullivan**, who arrived in this country, Sept. 3rd, from SHANNAGOLDEN, County LIMERICK, Ireland. Please call at 357 BOWERY, in the Saloon.

Of **Maurice Prendiville**, from TRALEE, County KERRY, Ireland, who sailed from Liverpool in March 1854, to New York; when last heard from was in PHILADELPHIA. Any information of him will be thankfully received by his nephew, **Maurice Prendiville**, at **P. C. Slattey's** 96 GREENE STREET, NEW YORK.

October 10, 1857

Of **Edward McDonnell**, by his wife **Sarah McDonnell**, who has arrived from ASHTON-UNDER-LYNE, ENGLAND. When last heard of he worked for **Mr. Wright**, at ATTLEBORO, MASS. Direct letter to 202 EAST 17th STREET, NEW YORK.

Of **Martin Kean**, a native of MINOLA, County MAYO, Ireland, who arrived in New York in 1847, and left for CARBONDALE, State of PENNSYLVANIA, at which place he was when last heard from; but it is supposed he has removed to SYRACUSE. Any information of him will be thankfully received by his nephew, **Anthony Kelly**, by addressing a few lines to him at 190 MERCER STREET, NEW YORK.

October 17, 1857

Of **William Dunne**, of CAREHEN, and of **Thomas Scanlan**, of POWERSTOWN. Any information of them will be thankfully received by their cousin, **Catherine Phelan**, formerly of CRINCOR County WATERFORD, Ireland. Direct letter to care of Pine & Carber, No. 1228 Mifflin Street, between 12th and 13th Streets, PHILADELPHIA, PA. Virginia and New Orleans papers please copy. [Appeared under County WATERFORD]

Of **John Aylward**, baker by trade, native of KNOCATOPHER, County KILKENNY, Ireland. When last heard of was in Georgetown Brick Works, WASHINGTON. Any information of him will be thankfully received by his sister, **Mrs. Julia Pendergast** alias **Aylward**. If this should meet the eye of any person knowing anything of him, they will please address No. 73 MAIDEN LANE, NEW YORK, care of **Mr. E. Cleare**.

Of **William Byrne**, a native of the Parish of HACKETTSTOWN, County CARLOW, Ireland; a baker by trade; when last heard from two years ago, he was in SUMMIT County, OHIO. Any information of him will be thankfully received by his sister, **Sarah Bryne**, by directing a letter for her to No. 122 RIVINGTON STREET, NEW YORK.

October 24, 1857

Of the Parents of **Patrick Fitzgerald**, aged about 8 years, a native of KILLYNAGH, near ABBEYFEALE, County LIMERICK, Ireland, who arrived on the 16th inst. per ship *Emerald*, from Liverpool. They were, when last heard from, in BALTIMORE, MD. Address John Manning, V.P., Irish Emigrant's Society, 61 Chambers St., New York.

Of **John McGrath**, who landed in New York about eight years ago; when last heard from he was in the State of PENNSYLVANIA, working on a railroad. Any information of him will be thankfully received by his sister, **Julia McGrath**. Direct your letter to MECHANICSVILLE, N.Y. [Appeared under County WATERFORD]

Of **Luke**, **James**, **Margaret** and **Mary Greehy**, from FORGE LANE, County WATERFORD, Ireland, by their sister, **Catherine Greehy**, who landed in New York five months ago, in the ship *Australia*, from Liverpool. Will be seen at the Passiac County Hotel, 121 CEDAR ST., NEW YORK.

Of **Michael**, **John** and **Patrick Moore**, natives of the Parish of CASTLERAGHAN, County CAVAN, Ireland. Any information of them will be thankfully received by their sister **Mary**, or their brother-in-law, **Michael McCabe**, by addressing a letter to either of them to OCEAN SOUND, LEITH Post Office, CANADA WEST.

Of **Michael Sweeney**, a native of the Parish of MALLABUSH, County CORK, Ireland, who left WORCESTER County, N.Y., three years ago last November; when last heard from he was in INDIANA, two years ago last December. Any information of him will be thankfully received by his brother **Terry**. Address **William Smith**, SOMERSET, MASS. Western papers please copy.

Of **John Madden**, of LIME HILL, Parish of DUNERY, County GALWAY, Ireland; when last heard from was in MILWAUKEE, WIS. Any information of him will be thankfully received by **Catherine Quirk**, who arrived in New York last July, by addressing a few lines to her at the office of the Irish-American, 32 Beekman Street, New York.

October 31, 1857

Of **Eliza Kelly**, by her brother **William**. When last heard from she was in NEW YORK. Direct to MULVILLE, GRANT Co., WIS.

Of **James Coussens**, a native of COMJAMES, in the Parish of SECOMSHL, County WEXFORD, Ireland; when last heard from, eighteen months ago, he was living some place near NEW YORK CITY. Any information of him will be thankfully received by his sister, **Ellen Coussens**, by addressing a few lines to her, care of **Mrs. Fox**, 121 CEDAR STREET, NEW YORK.

Of **Owen Grimes**, **Patrick Gilfeather**, and **Patrick Fox**, natives of ATHFARNA, County DONEGAL, Ireland; supposed to be in NEW YORK CITY. Any person knowing their address will please send it to **Ann Grimes**, 231 WEST 17th STREET, NEW YORK.

Of **James Kelly**, from BALLYSHANNON, County DONEGAL, Ireland, who left NEW YORK for California about the 5th of June, 1855. When last heard from, in April 1856, he was living with **F. A. Coffee**, in either Front or South Street, SAN FRANCISCO. Any intelligence of him will be thankfully received by his sister **Catherine Kelly**, care of **Mr. Uriah Henry**, 163 BLEECKER ST., NEW YORK.

Of **Luke Gray**, a native of the City of DUBLIN, Ireland. When last heard from he was in DRUMSILL, County ARMAGH. Any information of him will be thankfully received by his Sister, **Catherine McCaffrey**, YONKERS, WESTCHESTER County, State of NEW YORK. Dublin Nation and Telegraph please copy.

November 7, 1857

Of **Charles Rodgers**, a native of the County TYRONE, in the Parish of UPPER BERDONEY, Townland of L[I]GONS, Ireland. Any information of him will be thankfully received by his sister **Bridget Rodgers**, by addressing a few lines to her in care of **Patrick Rodgers**, No. 777 Swanson St., PHILADELPHIA.

November 14, 1857

Of the relatives or friends of **Michael Dunn**, who died on board ship *Lucy Thompson*, on her last voyage from Liverpool to New York. They are requested to make themselves known to **C. B. Pendleton**, 275 PEARL STREET, or 19 RUTGERS PLACE, NEW YORK.

Of **James & William Timmins**, sons of the late **James Timmins**, of SOUTH BROOKLYN, and for some time scholars at the Catholic Orphan Asylum, in Clinton Street, BROOKLYN. By applying to the undersigned, they may learn something to their advantage. **H. Hawley**, 360 Carlton Avenue, BROOKLYN.

Of **Mary** and **Catherine Flynn**, natives of AUGHAMORE, Parish of GRANARD, County LONGFORD, Ireland. They came to this country about twenty years ago. When last heard from they were in NEW ORLEANS; Mary married to a man named **Mathew Gainor**, a native of DUBLIN. Any information of them will be thankfully received by their brother, **John Flynn**, RONDOUT, ULSTER County, NEW YORK. New Orleans papers please copy.

Of **Richard Cahill**, a native of SPA HILL, near JOHNSTOWN, County KILKENNY, Ireland. He had lived for the last three years in SALINA, near SYRACUSE, State of NEW YORK, until about six weeks ago, when he left that place, assuring his wife that he intended to settle down in ANNIDA, N.Y. He was seen a few days afterwards in ALBANY, and sent word to his wife and child that he was on his way to NEW HAVEN, CONN., where they are in a very destitute condition, and no account of him. Any information of him will be gratefully received by his afflicted wife, **Julia Cahill**, care of **Mr. Michael Corcoran**, Wallace Street, New Haven, Conn.

Jane MacNeal, just arrived from DUNDALK, Ireland, wants to know where her brother, **Archy O'Neal**, lives in NEW YORK. She is staying at the Emigrant Depot, Castle Garden. [Appeared under County LOUTH]

November 21, 1857

Of **Simon Reilly**, Carpenter, from SEARESTOWN, Co. MEATH, Ireland, who worked for **Mr. Peter O'Reilly**, of BAL[LIN]LOUGH, when at home, and who arrived in this City by the ship *Lucy Thompson*, on the 26th ult., will call or send his address to **John Gurin**, No. 160 EAST 27th STREET, he will hear of something to his advantage.

Of **Margaret Ryan**, daughter of **Michael Ryan** and **Mary Connors**, native of Parish OGONNELEY, aged about 25 years, who sailed from Cork for New York, and has not been heard of but once since. She is supposed to be somewhere near NEW YORK still. Information received by her brothers, **John, Stephen** and **Daniel** - address John Ryan, CAIRO, ILLINOIS. [Appeared under County CLARE]

Of **Charles Carney** and his wife **Mary**, (maiden name **Bradley**) daughter of **Hugh** and **Hannah Bradley**, of the Parish of RAPHOE, who were married in PHILADELPHIA, February, 1852, and went from there to POTTSVILLE. Please address their sister **Catherine Bradley**, PHOENIXVILLE, CHESTER County, PA. [Appeared under County DONEGAL].

November 28, 1857

A large reward. Information wanted of **Margaret Hughes** or **Mary Donnelly**, who lived at service at 461 BROOME STREET, in 1855 and 56. If any person knows of a Margaret Hughes or a Mary Donnelly and will leave word at the Globe Hotel, 202 WILLIAM STREET, by note or otherwise, they may chance to give information of the right persons, and get a large reward. They are wanted as witnesses.

Of **John Foley**, brother of **Patrick Foley**, of the Co. WATERFORD, Parish of CAPPEQUIN, who emigrated to this country, about seven years ago. When last heard from was in COPAICK Iron Works, COLUMBIA County State of NEW YORK. Any information respecting his whereabouts will confer a favor on his brother Patrick and family. Address **Mr. John Lee**, liquor Merchant, cor. 1st AVENUE and 3rd STREET, NEW YORK, for Patrick Foley.

December 5, 1857

Of **John** and **Anthony Kennedy**, late of the Parish of DONARD, County WICKLOW, Ireland. Any information concerning them will be thankfully received by their sister, **Hannah Kennedy**, at No. 162 HESTER STREET, NEW YORK.

Mary Daly, who sailed from Tralee, Ireland, in the ship *Lady Russell*, on the 18th of September last, and landed in Castle Garden on the 21st of October last. Any information of her will be thankfully received by her brother, **John Daly**, corner of 3rd Street and Mass. Avenue, WASHINGTON, D. C. [Appeared under County KERRY]

Of **Michael**, and **William Ryan**, natives of the Parish of DRUME, County TIPPERARY, Ireland. When last heard from they were in NEWBURGH, State of NEW YORK. Any information of them will be thankfully received by their sister, **Ann Ryan**, by directing a letter for her to the Irish-American office, 32 Beekman Street, New York.

Ten Dollars Reward will be given to any person who will give true information of **Patrick Lunny**, a native of the Townland of CURROWKEEL, Parish of DROMARD, County SLIGO, Ireland; when last heard from, about three years since, was between ST. LOUIS and ROCK ISLAND, ILLINOIS. Any information will be thankfully received by his father and mother, or his brother and sister, **James** and **Mary Lunny**, when the above reward will be paid by them. Please address **Mr. David Henry**, No. 104 EAST 23rd STREET, NEW YORK, for James Lunny.

December 12, 1857

Of **William Kery**, a native of LONDON, ST. JAMES Parish: he landed in New York on the 14th of April, 1857. When last heard from was in PERTH AMBOY with his father, **Patrick Kery**. Any information of him will be thankfully received by his father and mother, by directing a few lines to 35 MONROE ST., NEW YORK.

Of **Michael McCool**, a native of NEW YORK. A plasterer by trade: when last heard from was in DUBUQUE, State of IOWA, and is supposed to have left for NEW ORLEANS. Any information of him will be thankfully received by his father, **John McCool** by directing a letter to him to No. 548 GREENWICH STREET, NEW YORK.

Of **Mary O'Callaghan**, aged 19 years, a native of THOMOUDGATE, ST. MUNCHIN'S Parish, LIMERICK, Ireland. She left her native place about the 5th of June, 1854. Address P. J. C., office of the Irish American.

Of **Catherine Gately**, (maiden name **Farrell**) a native of ATHLONE, Co. WESTMEATH, Ireland. She came to NEW YORK, in the *Ashburton* about the 26th of last August. Address P. J. C., office of the Irish American.

Of **Timothy Moynihan**, of the Parish of CHURCHTOWN, County of CORK, Ireland, who emigrated to this country about seven years ago. He is about 25 years old, about six feet high, and stout accordingly. When last heard from he was in FALL RIVER, and was supposed to work on a steamboat from NEW YORK to FALL RIVER, MASS. Any information respecting will be thankfully received by **Michael Murphy**, No. 116 EAST 42nd STREET, NEW YORK.

Of **Thomas Cooper**, a native of Co. WICKLOW, Ireland, who sailed from Dublin, January, 1847 and is supposed to be settled down in WISCONSIN or ILLINOIS. Any information of him will be thankfully received by his cousin **Thomas Kavanagh** at No. 270 FIRST AVENUE, NEW YORK.

Of **Joshua Moore**, son of **William Moore**, of BALLENATREW, Co. WATERFORD, Ireland. Address P. J. C., office of the Irish American.

Of **John Toole**, aged about 17 years, a native of WATERFORD, Ireland, which City he left about eighteen months since, and it is supposed proceeded to NEW YORK immediately, where he is believed to be now residing. Any information of him, or his whereabouts, will be thankfully received by his father, **John Toole**, master of the brig Downes, Waterford, or at the News office, Waterford, Ireland. If this should meet his eye he is requested to write, as his friends are anxious to know if he is doing well.

Of **James** and **Bridget Murphy**, of the Townland of BALLINREADY, Parish of TULLAHAR, County KILKENNY, Ireland. When last heard from was in PEORIA County, State of ILLINOIS. Any information of them would be thankfully received by their sister **Ellen**, care of **Mr. Morley**, 282 HENRY ST., NEW YORK CITY. Illinois papers please copy.

December 19, 1857

Of **John Power**, who left DUBLIN City in 1849, son of **William** and **Bridget Power**, of 16 Upper Liffey Street. When last heard of was in the service of **Mr. McMenomy**, 156 BOWERY. Any information respecting him will be thankfully received by his brother, **Lawrence Power**, No. 110 MULBERRY STREET, NEW YORK.

Of **Martin McCue** and his wife **Catherine**, natives of the Parish of KILCOMMON, Ireland. When last heard from they were in ST. CLAIR, State of PENNSYLVANIA. Any information of them will be thankfully received by their son, **Patt McCue**, by addressing a few lines to him at HASTINGS, State of NEW YORK, or by **Thomas Farrington**, No. 9 MULBERRY STREET, NEW YORK.

Of **John Melady** from the Parish of LEITRIM, County GALWAY, Ireland. When last heard from in March last, he was in the City of NEW YORK. Any information of his present whereabouts will be thankfully received by his sisters **Mary** and **Bridget Melady**, NORTHCASTLE, WESTCHESTER County, N.Y.

Of **Martin** and **Francis Ryan**, of RATHMOY, County TIPPERARY; supposed to be in ILLINOIS. Also, **Michael Ryan** and **James Poor**; supposed to be in CINCINNATI, OHIO; and **Thomas** and **Mary Quinlan**, children of **John Quinlan**, near COLLEGE HILL, Parish of KI[LI]EA, County TIPPERARY, Ireland. Any information of them will be thankfully received by their uncle, **James Ryan**, care of **Patrick Ryan**, grocer, 240 Columbia Street, near State, BROOKLYN, N.Y.

December 26, 1857

Of **Jerry Garvey**, by his brother, **Patrick Garvey**. He left WASHINGTON, PA., four years ago, and went to MEMPHIS, TENN.; when last heard of was in the Parish of TILAS, LA., care of **Richard R. Coin**. Any information will be thankfully received at No. 421 Pine Street, PHILADELPHIA.

Of **Mary Murray**, who arrived per ship *Ellen Austin* in November last; also of **Mary Cronan**, who arrived November 10th. Apply to John Manning, Vice President, Irish Emigrant Society, 61 Chambers Street, New York.

Of **William Dwyer** and **John Roe**, natives of DUBLIN, Ireland. Any information respecting them addressed to their brother, **Thomas N. Dwyer**, at 42 MAIDEN LANE, or 94 READE STREET, will be thankfully received by him. Galway and Dublin papers please copy.

Of **Timothy Tynan**, a native of TULLAMORE, KING'S County, Ireland, who left NEW ORLEANS, three years ago, last June, for CALIFORNIA. Any information of him will be thankfully received by his brother, **Wm. Tynan**, by addressing a letter for him, care of **Mr. John Keegan**, Flushing Avenue (near Dean Street), BROOKLYN, NEW YORK. California and New Orleans papers, please copy.

Of **Richard** and **Patrick Mullally**, also of **Mary** and **John Davis**, from KILCOCK, County KILDARE, Ireland. When last heard from they were in CINCINNATI, OHIO. Any information of them will be thankfully received by her sister, **Mrs. Catherine Hynes**, by addressing a few lines to her at No. 15 MARION STREET, NEW YORK. Cincinnati and Illinois papers please copy.

Of **John Keogh**, of LAUGHDAVAN, County CAVAN, Ireland. He left NEW YORK, about 12 years ago for ALBANY and worked in a place called GREENBUSH; he left for CANADA, and is supposed to be in the State of WISCONSIN. Any information of him will be thankfully received by his brother, **Edward Keogh**, No. 38 36th STREET, NEW YORK CITY. Western papers copy.

Of **Patrick, Thomas** and **Margaret Kinnan**, formerly of the Parish of KILLDYCART, County CLARE, Ireland, but now supposed to be residing in NEW YORK. Any communication respecting them, addressed to their sister, **Mary Kinnan**, care of the True Witness office, MONTREAL, C. E., will be thankfully received.

Of **Patrick Commons**, by his sister-in-law, **Bridget Purtill**, a native of FETHARD, County TIPPERARY, Ireland. Any information of him will be thankfully received by calling or addressing at No. 12 UNION COURT, University Place, NEW YORK.

January 16, 1858

Of **Moses Murphy** from NEWTONBARRY, Co. WEXFORD, Ireland; when last heard from he was in MEDINA, ORLEANS Co., N.Y. Any intelligence of him will be thankfully received by his father, **Michael Murphy**, who has lately arrived in this country. Direct to the care of **John Cleer**, No. 9 WASHINGTON STREET, NEW YORK.

Of **Mary Smith**, native of CORYRORK, Parish of MULLAGH, County of CAVAN, Ireland. When last heard from in 1851, she lived in JERSEY CITY. Any information of her will be thankfully received by her brother and sister, **Bryan** and **Bridget Smith**. Address in care of **John Osborne**, 320 Market Street, NEWARK, N. J. Boston papers please copy.

Of **Catherine, Anna, Mary, Margaret** and **James Galager**, who emigrated some years ago from DONEGAL, Ireland, to SCOTLAND, and from thence to NEW YORK, where it is believed some or all of them reside at the present time, by their brother, **John Galager**, late of Donegal, Ireland, now in PHILADELPHIA, care of Merchant's Advertising Agency, 241 Dock Street.

Of **Margaret Sullivan**, a native of CAPPINICASH, KILLMARE, County of KERRY, Ireland, who arrived in this country about a year since, wishes to find out her brother **Cornelius**, who is in the United States about five years ago, and her sister **Honora**, who is about three years ago. When last heard from Cornelius was in VIRGINIA, and Honora in PHILADELPHIA. Any information concerning them will be thankfully received by addressing a line to **Margaret Sullivan**, 118 RIVINGTON STREET, NEW YORK CITY. Virginia and Philadelphia papers please copy.

January 23, 1858

Of **Hannah McClain**, when last heard from she was with **Mr. George Halman**, NEW YORK. Any information of her will be thankfully received by her sister, **Bridget McClain**, No. 15 North Caroline Street, BALTIMORE, MD.

January 30, 1858

Of **Daniel O'Reilly**, who left DUBLIN thirteen years ago in the ship *James Fagan*. He was employed as a waiter in the Globe Hotel, in NEW YORK, and afterwards as a steward on a steamboat on the Hudson River. Any information concerning him will be thankfully received. Address P. I. C., Irish American Office.

Of **John Shannon**, who resided during the year of 1854 in 21st STREET, between 8th and 9th Avenues, NEW YORK. Any information of him will be thankfully received. Address P. I. C., Irish American Office.

Of **Daniel Dunovan**, native of the County of WATERFORD, Parish of STRAYVILLA, Ireland, who came to this country in November, 1853. If this should meet the eye of any one acquainted with him, or who knows his whereabouts, they will confer a favor by addresssing a note to his sister **Mary**, at the Clarendon Hotel, cor. of 18th STREET and 4th AVENUE, NEW YORK.

Of **John Wafer**, of GOREY, County of WEXFORD, Ireland. When last heard from was in CINCINNATI, OHIO. He followed the sea for a living. Any information of his present whereabouts will be thankfully received by his wife **Sarah**, in care of **Mrs. Mary Neill**, at No. 267 WEST 29th STREET, between 9th and 10th Avenues, NEW YORK CITY.

February 6, 1858

Of **John Mannix** and **David Dodd**, natives of CROOM, County LIMERICK. When last heard of was in WASHINGTON, NEW JERSEY. Any information respecting them will be thankfully received by his brother, **Thomas Mannix**, lately landed, at 351 GREENWICH STREET, NEW YORK.

Of **John O'Brien**, carpenter, a native of the County GALWAY, Ireland. Who left CARRICK-ON-SHANNON, County LEITRIM, with **Terence** and **Margaret Boland**, and sailed on 11th May, 1842, from Sligo, in ship *Argo*, for St. John's British Province; after his friends heard he had sailed in LOWELL, MASS. John's father was a carpenter, and died in BOYLE; also his two brothers are same trade, **Michael** and **Augustine**. Should he notice this, or any person who can give information of him, they would confer a favor by writing a few lines to his brother, Augustine O'Brien, 287 WEST 33rd STREET NEW YORK CITY. Boston and Lowell papers please copy. [Appeared under County GALWAY]

Of **David Quirk**, from the County of TIPPERARY, Ireland. When last heard from he was in POINT WASHINGTON, WASHINGTON County, MISS. He left WASHINGTON, D. C., about one month ago. Any information of him will be thankfully received by his brother, **Edward Quirk**, No. 451 Pennsylvania Avenue, WASHINGTON, D. C.

Of **William**, **Michael** and **Catherine Perkinson**, of the County TIPPERARY, ROSCREA, Ireland. Any information of them will be thankfully received by their brother, **John Perkinson**, 345 RIVINGTON STREET, NEW YORK.

Of **Mrs. Johanna Lucy Barry** and her children, **William, Garrett, Michael, John, Catherine, Ellen** and **Johanna Barry**, natives of the County CORK, Parish of [E]AVELEARY, Ireland. Any information concerning them will be thankfully received by their cousin, **Ellen Barry**, who lately arrived in this country, at No. 108 Smith Street, BROOKLYN, between Pacific and Dean Streets.

Of **Michael Mahoney** and family, natives of the OLD PARK, BANDON, County CORK, Ireland. They came to this country about fifteen years ago. Any information of them would be thankfully received by their cousin, **Michael Foley**, No. 105 FIRST AVENUE, NEW YORK. Canada papers please copy.

Of **Paul Donovan**, a native of ROSSCARBERRY, County CORK, Ireland; when last heard from he was at FALMOUTH, KENTUCKY. Any information of him will be thankfully received by his sisters, **Julia** and **Ellen**, by directing a letter for them to the care of Messrs. Lynch & Cole, Irish-American Office, 32 Beekman Street, N.Y.

February 13, 1858

Of **Patrick Halloran**, a native of CREEVA, Parish of QUIN, County CLARE, Ireland. When last heard from he was in WASHINGTON County, NEW YORK. Any information of him will be thankfully received by his sister, **Mary Halloran**, by addressing a letter for her, to the care of **John McNamara**, Rail Road Office, 43rd STREET, 6th AVENUE, NEW YORK.

February 20, 1858

Of **Mary Camfield**, from MOATE, County WESTMEATH, Ireland, who was married to **John Malony**, a native of the County LIMERICK at TROY, NEW YORK, about nine years ago. They are supposed to be somewhere in ILLINOIS; also, of her stepmother, **Mary Camfield**, and her daughter **Bridget**, who are supposed to be in NEW YORK. Any information of them will be thankfully received by **Ellen Camfield**, SPRINGFIELD, MASSACHUSETTS.

Of **John Noonan**, from CAHERMURPHY, Parish of FEAKLE, County CLARE, Ireland. When last heard from he was in LEECHBURG, ARMSTRONG County, PENNSYLVANIA. He was the son of **Denis Noonan**, agent of **Patrick Molony**, of CRAGG, near TULLA. Any information of him will be thankfully received by his brother **Patrick** and sister **Mary**, at the office of this paper. Pittsburgh papers please copy.

Of **Michael Morony**, a native of TIERMACLANE, County CLARE, Ireland. When last heard from he was in CHICAGO, and is supposed to be working on the Central Illinois Railroad. Any information of him will be thankfully received by his brother, **Robert Morony**, No. 9 East Capitol St. (Capitol Hill), WASHINGTON, D. C.

Of **John Sullivan**, a native of the County CORK, Parish of CLONMEEN, Ireland, who landed in New York last November, six years ago, and went in May following to BROOME County; when last heard from he was in BUFFALO. Any information of him will be thankfully received by his sister, **Johanna Sullivan**, at **Thos. McAulige's**, No. 104 ½ THIRD AVENUE, between 13th and 14th Streets, NEW YORK. Southern papers please copy.

March 6, 1858

Of **Mary Jones**, a native of CORGLASS, County CAVAN, Ireland; when last heard from, about thirteen years ago, she was living at THOROLD, UPPER CANADA. Any information of her will be thankfully received by her brother and sister, **Sylvester** and **Bridget Jones**, by directing a letter for them to No. 197 AVENUE A, NEW YORK CITY. Canada papers please copy.

Of **Ellen Hefferan**, from the County TIPPERARY, Ireland. Any information of her will be thankfully received by her sister, **Catherine Kelly**, at No. 39 Water Street, BROOKLYN, L. I.

Of **Thomas Lenaghan**, a native of NEWRY, County DOWN, Ireland. When last heard from he was living about eighty miles from NEW YORK CITY. Any information of him will be thankfully received by his nephew, **Owen Lenaghan**, by directing a letter to him, to No. 5 BARCLAY STREET, or 88 CATHARINE STREET, NEW YORK.

Of **John Clarke**, a native of DUBLIN, Ireland, who sailed from Liverpool for New York, on board the ship *William Tapscott*, in the latter part of June or the beginning of July, 1854. Should he observe this notice, or any person knowing his whereabouts, and address a line to **E. Cahill**, of NEWBURGH, N.Y., intelligence of great importance will be communicated to him in answer.

Of **William Waugh**, who came from BANDON, County CORK, Ireland, some ten to twelve years ago; when last heard from he was in READING, State of PENNSYLVANIA. Any information will be thankfully received by his sister, **Agnes Tobin** 4[ ]7 FOURTH STREET, NEW YORK CITY.

Of **Peter Hill**, by his brother **Benjamin**, a native of the Parish of ROSCARBERRY, County CORK, Ireland; when last heard from about two years since, he was in the State of MISSOURI. Direct letter to **James Leary**, 161 AVENUE A, NEW YORK CITY.

March 13 1858

Of **James Riordan**, a native of KILFINAN, Co. LIMERICK, Ireland; when last heard of he was in NEW YORK. Any information respecting him will be thankfully received by his cousins, **Michael**, **Patt** and **Ellen Meade**. Address to the care of **George Meade**, No 2048 Hamilton Street, PHILADELPHIA, for **Patrick Meade**.

Of **John O'Connor** and his sister **Mary**, natives of the QUEEN'S County, Ireland, Parish of MOUNTRATH. John sailed for America about twenty three years ago, and is supposed to be in PHILADELPHIA. His sister went to England about six years ago, and lived with her sister **Bridget**, in BOLTON; from there she came to America, about three years ago. Any information of them will be thankfully received by their niece, **Mary O'Connor**, daughter of **Barney O'Connor**, 76 CHRISTIE STREET [Chrystie St.], NEW YORK. Philadelphia papers please copy.

Of **Nano Hickey**, a native of LISMORE, Co. WATERFORD, Ireland. If she will call or address 245 WATER STREET, she will hear of something to her advantage. When last heard from (about two months since) she resided with a family in YONKERS, N.Y. Any information of her will be thankfully received as above, or 360 EAST 10th STREET. **Maurice Walsh.**

March 20 1858

Of **Patrick Kavanagh**, from KILBEGGAN, County WESTMEATH, Ireland. When last heard from, about nineteen months since, he was in DUNMORE, NEW YORK (or LUZERNE Co., PENNSYLVANIA). Any intelligence of him will be thankfully received by his sister, **Mary Kavanagh**, 17 EAST 24th STREET, NEW YORK.

Of **Mary** and **Ellen Noonan**, of the County GALWAY, Parish of BEAGH. When last heard from they were in PROVIDENCE, R. I. Any information of them will be thankfully received by their brother, **John Noonan**, by addressing a letter to him at the Washington Gas Works, WASHINGTON, D. C.

March 27, 1858

Of **John Brady**, of CARRIGARREN, Parish of KILMORE, County CAVAN, Ireland. When last heard from (about five years ago) he was working in the Sinsinnana lead mines, FAIRPLAY, WISCONSIN, and is supposed to have gone South. Any information of him will be thankfully received by his brother, **James Brady**, No. 138 EAST 36th STREET, NEW YORK. Wisconsin papers please copy.

Of **Samuel Kingston**, who left DROUMGAR [ ]RIFF, Parish of CLONAKILTY, County CORK, Ireland. Any information of him will be thankfully received by his cousin, **James Kingston**, by directing a letter for him to the care of **John Leary**, No. 227 CHERRY STREET, NEW YORK. It is supposed that he is in BOSTON, and a resident there for twelve years. Boston papers please copy.

Of **Ellen**, **John** and **James Dawson**, natives of BRUFF, County LIMERICK, Ireland. Sailed from Limerick in the *British Queen* about six years ago. When last heard from they were in UPPER CANADA. Any information of them will be thankfully received by their sister **Catherine**, late of ENGLAND, by directing a letter to No. 51 CHERRY STREET, NEW YORK, in care of **Mr. Burke**. Canada papers please copy.

Of **William Tracy**, or any of his descendants, who left KILBEGGAN, County WESTMEATH about 35 years ago. When last heard of (about 25 years since) he was living on LONG

ISLAND. Any information of him will be thankfully received by his relative, **Joseph Tracy**, 182 DIVISION STREET, NEW YORK. Long Island papers please copy.

Of **John Joyce**, a native of the Parish of LETTERMORE, County GALWAY, Ireland, who emigrated to this country about eight years ago. Any information of him will be thankfully received by his sister **Mary Joyce**, by addressing a letter to NORTH HEMPSTEAD, QUEENS County, Long Island, N.Y., for **Mary Joyce**.

Of **Thomas, Stephen, Richard** and **Mary Mitchel**, from TWO MILE HOUSE, County KILDARE, Ireland, who left Dublin about eight years ago. When last heard from was in BOSTON. Any information of them will be thankfully received by **Mrs. Elizabeth John Mitchel**, No. 78 42nd STREET, corner of 6th Avenue, NEW YORK. Boston papers please copy.

April 3, 1858

Of **Hugh Morris**, a native of the County ROSCOMMON, Ireland. When last heard of was working in EASTPORT, MASS. Any information of him will be thankfully received by his daughter, **Anne Kenney**. Address **Patrick Kenney**, 142 HOUSTON STREET, NEW YORK. Western papers please copy.

Of **Catherine Doherty**, a native of the Parish of GALBA[L]LY, County LIMERICK, Ireland; when last heard of she lived up town with a dressmaker. Any information of her will be thankfully received by her aunt **Mrs. Dunne**, who lives in BRIDGEPORT, CONNECTICUT.

Of **Edward Rabbit**, of the County WESTMEATH, Parish of RAHARNEY. When last heard from was with his uncle, **Thomas Swords**, in LEXINGTON, RICHLAND County, State of OHIO. Any information of him or his whereabouts will be thankfully received by his brother, **Michael Rabbit**, at 204 HESTER STREET, NEW YORK. Ohio papers please copy.

April 10, 1858

Of **John** and **Mary Donleavy**, who left Ireland for Australia about 13 years ago, from DRUMLANE, Parish of LARHA, County CAVAN. When last heard from (about five years since) were in PORT SYDNEY. Any information of them will be thankfully received by their daughter **Alice**, by addressing a letter to 67 RIDGE STREET, NEW YORK. Sydney Freeman's Journal please copy.

April 17, 1858

Of **Bartholomew Roony**, of the County of SLIGO, Parish of AHAMLISH, Ireland. When last heard of was in the State of MAINE. Any information of him will be thankfullly received by his sister, **Mary**. Address **Hugh Clancy**, No. 16 FRANKLIN STREET, NEW YORK.

April 24, 1858

Of **Martin Dixon**, a native of NEW YORK, who was a steward on board the *Sultan*, a steamer which plied between ST. LOUIS and NEW ORLEANS, and was burned about two weeks ago, and he was among the missing. Any information of him will be thankfully received by his wife, **Ellen Dixon**, by writing to her at No. 386 WATER STREET, NEW YORK. St. Louis papers please copy.

Of **John Halvey**, from CALLAN, County, KILKENNY, Ireland. When last heard from about six years ago, was in BATON ROUGE, LOUISIANA. Any information of him will be most thankfully received by his sister, **Eliza McGovern**. Address **Michael McGovern**, 63 PEARL STREET, NEW YORK. Southern papers please copy.

Of **Edward Shannon**, from the County KILDARE, Ireland, who arrived at New York in the packet ship *Jacob A. Westervelt*, on March 24th, and stopped at Castle Garden until

March 26th; since that time nothing has been heard of him. Any information of him will be thankfully received by his brother, **Christopher Byrnes**, by directing a letter for him to CHATHAM CENTRE, COLUMBIA County, N.Y.

Of **Michael** and **Bridget Glasgow** (maiden name **Donovan**) of FETHARD, County TIPPERARY, Ireland. They lived in TROY, N. Y, 12 years ago, and went to CANADA, near Terra Haute Railroad. Any one knowing them or their sons, **Thomas**, **John** and **Edward**, will confer a favor by writing to **James** or **John Donovan**, 103 BAYARD STREET, NEW YORK CITY.

May 1, 1858

Of **Felix Duffy**, hatter, a native of BELATRAINE, County MONAGHAN, Ireland, who left NEW YORK, three years ago, last October; when last heard from he was in PETERSBURGH, VIRGINIA. Should this meet his eye or any of his acquaintances, they will confer a great favor by writing to his family, at No. 19 MARION STREET, NEW YORK. California and Virginia papers please copy.

May 8, 1858

Of **Ann Samon**, maiden name **Ann O'Brien**, a native of MIDDLESBURGH, ENGLAND; who married **John Samon**, a native of CARRICKMACROSS, County MONAGHAN, Ireland, who left England about thirteen years ago for PHILADELPHIA, and is supposed they are in some part of the West. Any information of them will be thankfully received by either her brothers, **John** or **James O'Brien**, 147 Prospect Street, BROOKLYN, N.Y. Western papers please copy.

Of **James O'Conner**, a native of the County LIMERICK, Ireland, who left his home in TROY, N.Y., in August, 1854, for STONINGTON, CT., to see his sisters and when last heard from was at 35 Friendship Street, PROVIDENCE, R. I. Any information of him will be thankfully received by his sister, **Ellen O'Conner**, at No. 257 Chestnut Street, ST. LOUIS, MO.

Of **John Scanlan**, a native of the City of LIMERICK, Ireland; when last heard from he was in ST. LOUIS, MO. Any information of him will be thankfully received by his sister, **Ellen Scanlan**, who has just arrived in New York. Address in care of **John Tuomey**, No. 17 CITY HALL PLACE, NEW YORK.

Of **John Neyland**, or any of his sons, **Michael**, **William**, or **John**. Natives of the Town of FOXFORD, County MAYO, Ireland. Michael is supposed to be living in MILWAUKEE, and John in or about MADISON CITY, WISCONSIN. Any information of them will be thankfully received by addressing a letter to **Patrick Brown**, 15 FORSYTH STREET, NEW YORK.

Of **Thomas Hayes**, from the County of TIPPERARY, Ireland. When last heard from he was residing at 15 BRIDGE STREET, NEW YORK. Any information of him will be thankfully received by his sister, **Mrs. Mary Handley**, KEOKUK, IOWA.

Of **Martin Byrne**, a native of JOHNSWELL, County KILKENNY, Ireland, by his brother **Garrett**. Any information concerning his whereabouts will be thankfully received by **Garrett J. Byrne**, MARYSVILLE CAL., or **J. H. Fay**, Post-office, N.Y. City.

May 15, 1858

Of **William Hooley, Michael Hooley, Andrew Hooley**, and their mother, **Catherine Hooley**, from the Parish of KILCOE, County CORK, Ireland. When last heard from (about three years ago) they were in OHIO and then left for CALEDONIA, MINNESOTA TERRITORY. Any information of them will be thankfully received by their brother-in-law, **Daniel Sullivan**, corner Columbia and Nelson Streets, BROOKLYN, N.Y.

May 22, 1858

Of **Catherine Carney**, formerly of MILTOWN, MALBAY, County CLARE, Ireland, who came to NEW YORK about two years ago from BAMBER BRIDGE, NEW PRESTON, LANC[ASHIRE], ENGLAND. When last heard from was living at Taylor's Saloon, BROADWAY, NEW YORK. Any information respecting her will be thankfully received by **Col. M. Doheny**, at his office, No. 15 CENTRE STREET, N.Y.; or at the office of the Irish American.

May 29, 1858

Of **Mary Woods**, of SUNDERLAND, ENGLAND. Any information of her will be thankfully received by her husband **Michael Woods**, by writing to him, to the care of Messrs. Lynch & Cole, Irish American Office, 32 Beekman Street, New York.

Of **Michael Nolan**, (shoemaker by trade,) who lives somewhere in the State of NEW YORK, native of the County CARLOW, Parish of BURRIS, will please write to his old mother, who is in a destitute condition, his brother **John** being dead. Direct in care of **Edward Monaghan**, Bank Street, between Lombard and South Schuyikill, PHILADELPHIA, PA.

Of **David Lillis**, a native of the Parish of TRACTON, County CORK, Ireland. When last heard from he was living in one of the BRITISH PROVINCES OF NORTH AMERICA. Any information of him will be thankfully received by his brother, **John Lillis**, by directing a letter for him to the care of **Luke Carrigan**, 291 FRONT STREET, NEW YORK.

June 5, 1858

Of **John Murphy**, a native of COOLATOHER, County KILKENNY, Ireland. When last heard from he was at the Niagara House, OSWEGO, State of NEW YORK. Any information of him will be thankfully received by his brother **Thomas Murphy**, by writing to him at No. 524 SECOND AVENUE, NEW YORK.

Of **Patrick Unlack**, a native of CLONMEL, County TIPPERARY, Ireland, who sailed from Cork about ten years ago, destined for the United States; when last heard from was living in OSWEGO. His whereabouts will be thankfully received by **Timothy Quigley**, No. 14 EAST 11th STREET, NEW YORK, who will inform him of something to his advantage.

Of **Michael Frawley**, a native of the County CLARE, Parish of NEWMARKET-ON-FERGUS. When last heard from, over two years since, he was in the employ of Grey & Kennedy, TUSCUMBIA, FRANKLIN Co., ALABAMA. Any information of him will be gratefully received by his sister, **Mary Frawley**. Direct to Box 3317, General Post Office, N.Y. CITY.

June 12, 1858

Of **Susan** and **Bridget Martin**, natives of the Parish of DRUNG, County CAVAN, Ireland; when last heard from they were living in FOURTH AVENUE, NEW YORK, about three years since. Any information of them will be thankfully received by **Margaret Martin**, MILTON, MASS. Western papers please copy.

Of **Patrick Foley**, a native of LISMORE, Co. WATERFORD, Ireland; when last heard from two years since, was in the State of ILLINOIS. Address **Maurice Foley**, HASTINGS ON THE HUDSON, WESTCHESTER County, NEW YORK.

Of **John** and **Charles Read**, from the Parish of KILMORE, County MAYO, Ireland. They live somewhere in BOSTON, where John keeps a dry goods store, and Charles a liquor store. Any one knowing their address will please communicate it to their cousin, **John Rooney**, at the office of the Irish American, New York.

June 19, 1858

Of **Maria Collins**, a native of the Parish of KILMORE, County TIPPERARY, Ireland, who came to America about four years ago, in the ship *Sheridan*; when last heard from was living in CANAL STREET, NEW YORK. Any information of her will be thankfully received by her distressed mother, **Mary Collins**, by writing her address, No. [5]08 GREENWICH STREET, NEW YORK.

Of **Mary Hill**, a native of NENAGH, County TIPPERARY, Ireland; when last heard from she left Galway, Ireland for America. Any information of her will be thankfully received by her distressed mother, **Bridget Hill**, by writing to her address, No. 308 GREENWICH STREET, NEW YORK.

Of **Mrs. Michael Reilly**, by her brother-in-law, **John Reilly**, son of **Bernard Reilly** and **Rosana Lee**, of LISGREY, Parish of LURGAN, County CAVAN, Ireland; when last heard from was in SAN FRANCISCO, CALIFORNIA. Any information of her will be thankfully received by writing to **John Reilly**, No. 100 WEST 17th STREET, NEW YORK.

Of **Martin Casey** and wife, **Anne Dooley**, natives of the Parish of KNOCKANY, PATRICKSWELL, County LIMERICK, Ireland; when last heard from, over two years since, they were in PITTSBURG, KINGSTON MILL UPPER CANADA. Any information of them will be thankfully received by Anne's mother, **Mrs. Dooley**. Direct to the care of **James O'Connor**, 263 MONROE STREET, NEW YORK.

Of **Patrick** and **Michael Lawlor**, natives of the City of LIMERICK, Ireland; when last heard from Patrick was in DAVIS County, ILLINOIS, and was about going to NEW ORLEANS. Any information of them will be thankfully received by their brothers or sister, **Malachy**, **James**, and **Honora**, by writing to any of them, to the care of **Christopher Farrell**, No. 23 OAK STREET, or James Lawlor, 29 OAK STREET, NEW YORK. New Orleans and Illinois papers please copy.

June 26, 1858

Of **Charles Kirk**, a native of GLENMACOPA, County TYRONE, Ireland. Who left Liverpool on the 8th of April, 1856, in the ship *Ontario*. Any information of him will be thankfully received by his brother, **Felix Kirk**, PORTLAND, DALLAS County, ALABAMA.

Of **Catherine Hayes**, a native of the County LIMERICK, but late of CHARLEVILLE, County CORK. It is supposed she is in NEW YORK. Any information of her will be thankfully received by her sisters, **Johanna** and **Margaret Hayes**, by writing to them to ULLIN, PULASKI Co., State of ILLINOIS.

July 3, 1858

Of **Edmond Coady** and his son, **Patrick Coady**, and **Ellen Meagher**, natives of the Parish of MULLINAHONE, County TIPPERARY, Ireland. When last heard of they were in NEW JERSEY; **Ellen Coady**, daughter of Edmond is anxious to hear from them. Any one who knows of their whereabouts will please write to **Rev. Father V[a]rden**, Catholic College, ST. LOUIS, MO.

Of **Christopher Murphy**, a native of the Parish of KINEGAD, County WESTMEATH, Ireland; when last heard from he was at BENTON'S PORT, VAN BUREN Co., State of IOWA. Any information of him will be thankfully received by **Peter Hughes**. No. 158 WEST 28th STREET, NEW YORK, when he will hear something to his advantage.

Of **Peter Talty**, a native of CARRADOTA, County CLARE, Ireland. When last heard from he was at BARRYVILLE, SULLIVAN County, State of NEW YORK. Any information of him will be thankfully received by his sister, **Mary Talty**, No. 32 ½ EAST 24th STREET, NEW YORK

July 24, 1858

Of **Johannah Haley**, of WATERFORD, Ireland, aged 58 years, who came to America in 1852; and of **Thomas Haley**, stone-cutter, aged 22 years, who left Ireland in 1854.

Of **Thomas Stephenson**, late of the City of DUBLIN who disappeared from his boarding house, No. 28 Fulton Street, BROOKLYN, during the first week in November 1857. He is about 24 years of age, 5 feet eight inches in height, sandy complexion, rather slight. Any information concerning him will be thankfully received at the office of this paper.

Of **Matthew Williams**, from the Town of SLIGO, Ireland. When last heard from was in CHICAGO, ILL., and is supposed to have gone to the State of IOWA. Any information of him will be thankfully received by his brother, **John Williams**, No. 187 HESTER STREET, NEW YORK. Iowa papers please copy.

July 31, 1858

Of **Thaddeus** and **Jeremiah Cronin**, natives of CASTLE McCAULIFF, Parish of CLONFERT, NEW MARKET, County of CORK, Ireland. Thaddeus came to this country 21 or 22 years ago; formerly he was a writer for the press in EDINBURGH, SCOTLAND. He has not been heard of since 1850. Some years before then he was practicing law in SOUTH CAROLINA. He is supposed to be in WASHINGTON, D. C. Jeremiah, when last heard from, in 1848, was living in the City of CHICAGO, ILL. Any information of them will be thankfully received by their brother **John Cronin**, NEW BRIGHTON, RICHMOND County, N.Y.

Of **Anthony Convery**, a native of GARVAGH, County DERRY, Ireland, who was an assistant to **James Wallace**, in the post office and Woolen drapery business. Any information of him will be thankfully received by his brother, **Patrick Convery**, by writing to him to WENONA, MARSHALL County, ILL.

August 7, 1858

Of **Jonathan Mason**, Copper and tin smith, formerly of LIMERICK. When last heard from, he and his family removed from ROCK ISLAND, ILL., to St. LOUIS, MO. By his communication with **William Penrose**, Irish-American Office, he will hear of something to his advantage. Rock Island, St.Louis, and New Orleans papers please copy.

Of **Patrick McGuinness**, a native of ARDEE, County LOUTH, Ireland, a blacksmith by trade; when last heard from was in PHILADELPHIA, August 1857. Any information respecting him will be thankfully received by his brother **Thomas**, 160 Wallace Street, NEW HAVEN, CONNECTICUT. Pennsylvania papers please copy.

August 14, 1858

Of **John** and **Michael Lochry**, from GORT, County GALWAY, Ireland. When last heard from, John was in Sheffield Street, NEW ORLEANS: he is supposed to have removed to LOUISVILLE or some other place in KENTUCKY. Michael went to him last May, and has not been heard from since. Any intelligence of them will be thankfully received by their brother **Wm. Lochry**, 179 GREENWICH STREET, NEW YORK.

Of **Andrew Gillice**, a native of the County CAVAN, Ireland; when last heard from, he was leaving NEW ORLEANS, for NEW YORK; since that time nothing has been heard of him. Any information of him will be thankfully received by his brother-in-law, **Edward McGlinn** by writing to him to No. 65 WEST THIRTIETH STREET, NEW YORK.

Of **Thomas O'Connor**, a native of the Parish of BANTEER, County CORK, Ireland; when last seen by his relatives and sister **Mary**, he was starting from WHEELING, VA., to ST. LOUIS, or some part of KENTUCKY. Any one who knows of his whereabouts will please write to his brother, **John O'Connor**, 450 WATER STREET, NEW YORK.

August 21, 1858

Of **James Caulfield**, from PROSPECT, SCARIFF, County CLARE, Ireland. Any intelligence of him will be thankfully received by **Denis Flannery**, corner of Kent and Flushing Avenues, EAST BROOKLYN, N.Y.

Of **John** and **Catherine O'Shaughnessy**, natives of the County of LIMERICK, Ireland, who emigrated to Canada in June, 1848. John was in RUTLAND County, State of VERMONT, in '49, and Catherine was in ST. CATHERINE'S, CANADA; since then there has been no account from them. Any information regarding them would be thankfully received by their brother, **Peter O'Shaughnessy**, 78 HUDSON STREET, NEW YORK. Western papers please copy.

September 4, 1858

Of **Honora Mahan**, aged about twelve years. She landed in New York 26th July last, per ship *James Foster*. She came with a woman named **Catherine Flanagan**. Address **Bridget Cooney**, care of **J. McDonough**, UTICA, N.Y.

Of **George**, **Margaret**, and **Bridget Connay**, natives of the Parish of KILLDRESS, County TYRONE, Ireland. When last heard from Margaret was living in some part of RHODE ISLAND, and married to a man by the name of **James Mitchell**: Catherine and Bridget are supposed to be living in NEW YORK. Any information of them will be thankfully received by their sister, **Alice Connay**, by directing a letter for her to the care of **John A. Kennedy**, Esq., Castle Garden, New York, where she arrived last week from Glasgow.

Of **Joseph Hurly**, a native of FERMOY, County CORK, Ireland. He has been seen in WILLIAMSBURGH. He is a baker. His sister, **Catherine Kehoe**, is anxious to hear from him. Any communication sent to **Mrs. Burke**, 447 GRAND STREET, NEW YORK or to **Mr. William Summers**, BRIDGEPORT, CONN., will be received by his sister.

September 11, 1858

Of **Daniel Delahunty** and brothers **Thomas** and **John**, and sisters **Mary**, **Margaret**, **Catherine** and **Bridget**, natives of LISANURE, Parish of TEMPLETOOHEY, Co. TIPPERARY, Ireland by their brother **James**. When last heard of Thomas was in SYRACUSE. Address **John Fitzpatrick**, 326 WEST 29th STREET. Other papers please copy.

Of **Patrick Siney**, a native of the Parish of MOUNTMELLICK, QUEEN'S County, Ireland. Who arrived in New York in 1850, and lived with **Dr. E. Chrisbell**, at HURLEY WOODS, State of NEW YORK, and left for ILLINOIS; since that time nothing has been heard of him. Any information of him will be thankfully received by his brother, **John Siney**, by directing a letter for him to the care of **Michael Bergan**, RONDOUT, ULSTER County, N.Y.

September 18, 1858

Of **David** or **Maurice Walsh**, natives of CHARLEVILLE, County CORK, Ireland; when last heard from, they were in BLAIRSVILLE, PA. Any information of them will be thankfully received by their brother, **Patrick Walsh**, by writing to him, in care of **John Ryan**, 76 JAMES STREET, NEW YORK.

September 25, 1858

Of **Sarah Burke Cormac**, who left SLIGO, Ireland, about nine or ten years ago. When last heard from she was married, and lived in or near CINCINNATI. Any information concerning her will be thankfully received by her sister **Bedelia** at the industrial school, FORTY SECOND STREET, between Eighth and Ninth Avenues, NEW YORK.

Of **James** and **Thomas Minahen**, natives of the Parish of BALLYSTEEN, County LIMERICK, Ireland. When last heard from James was in NEW BRUNSWICK, SOMERSET CO., N. J.; Thomas was attending a Captain on some of the steamers coming to NEW YORK. Any information of them will be thankfully received by their mother and sister, **Bridget Minahen** and **Catherine Lynch**, by directing a letter to them to No. 111 BROADWAY, Trinity Building, NEW YORK. New Jersey papers please copy.

October 8, 1858

Of **Hugh O'Mealy** and wife, maiden name, **Lewel Hopkins**; when last heard from, in the year 1853, they were living in NEW YORK CITY. **Mrs. Hopkins** sailed that year in the ship *Eliza Gillis*, to St. Johns. Any intelligence of them will be thankfully received by their daughter, **Eliza O'Mealy**, in care of **P. Penny**, No. 22 [?] Street, PORTLAND, ME.

Of **John McCarthy**, aged 26 years, a native of the Parish of TUOSIST, County KERRY, Ireland, who left NEW YORK four years ago, and has not since been heard of by his wife, except that he worked in OHIO, and went by the name of **John Sullivan**. Any account of him will be thankfully received by his wife, **Mrs. McCarthy**, 31 BAXTER STREET, NEW YORK; in care of **Timothy O'Shea**. Ohio and Michigan papers please copy.

Of **John Murphy**, a native of BALLINAKILL, County WEXFORD, Ireland, who came to this country about twenty years ago. When last heard of he was in UPPER CANADA. Any information of him will be thankfully received by his brother **Michael Murphy**. Direct to **John Clear**, No. 9 WASHINGTON STREET, NEW YORK.

Of **Timothy Kennedy**, about fifty years of age, from Parish and County ROSCOMMON. When last heard of he was in the Town of HOPE, [?], State of NEW YORK. Any information of him will be thankfully received by his friend, **Lawrence Glennan**, 20[ ] East 13th STREET, NEW YORK.

October 16, 1858

Of **Thomas Smith**, son of the widow **Mary Smith**, a native of RAKANE, near COOTEHILL, County CAVAN, Ireland. When last heard from he was in some of the Western States. Any information of him will be thankfully received by his mother, by directing a letter for her to the care of **Dr. M. E. Foy**, No. 106 WEST 25th STREET, NEW YORK.

Of **Patrick McCormack**, of BALLINAMORE, County LEITRIM, Ireland. When last heard from he was night-watch in a tan-yard in NEW YORK, and he had some land in the country. His son, **John McCormack** would be happy to hear from him at 389 NINTH AVENUE, NEW YORK. Direct to **Thomas Brennan**.

Of **Charles Walsh**, son of **Patrick Walsh** and **Margaret Devlin**, of the Parish of BALLYCLOG, County TYRONE, Ireland. When last heard of he was in a place called WALDRON or CHINA, near NEW YORK. His sister **Mary** and her husband **John O'Neill** came out with him about twenty years ago. Any information concerning him will be thankfully acknowledged by his sister's husband, **Arthur McEvin**, LONG ISLAND [D]OCKS, Post-Office, RIDEAU CANAL, CANADA WEST.

Of **Thomas Fitzgerald**, a native of GOWLANE, Parish of MOLAHIFFE, County KERRY, who left Tralee with his uncle **Garret** eight years since. When last heard from he was in BUFFALO. Any information of him will be thankfully received by his mother and sister, at No. 8 BIRMINGHAM STREET, NEW YORK. Boston papers please copy.

October 23, 1858

Of **Peter**, **Ellen** and **Ann McMahon**, from near LISNASKEA, County FERMANAGH, Ireland. Ellen arrived in New York in 1854, Ann in 1855, and Peter in 1856, from Belfast, and resided in BROOKLYN for some time. Any information of them will be thankfully received by sending their address to, or calling at this office.

Of **Terence**, **Honora** and **Bridget Tiernan**, from CARABAN, Parish of BALLINTUBBER, County ROSCOMMON, Ireland, by their sister **Mary**, who landed here two months ago. When last heard from they were in TRENTON, N. J. Any communication respecting them, addressed to **J. Daly**, Box 1085, Post-office, NEW YORK, will reach their sister.

Of **John Flynn**, a native of AUGHAMORE, Parish of GRANARD, County LONGFORD, Ireland. It is thought he came to this country some years past, and is supposed to be living in or about the City of NEW YORK. He will hear of something to his advantage by addressing a note to **Thomas Gaynor**, NEW ORLEANS Custom House, as there is a share of real estate property left him by his deceased sister, **Mary Flynn**, late widow **Mary Gaynor**, as no other person can claim but the heir at law. New York papers please copy.

Of **William Daniel** and wife, natives of TWO MILE BRIDGE, County TIPPERARY, Ireland. When last seen, they were in ST. LOUIS, MISSOURI. Any information of them will be thankfully received by **Henry Jones**, Company G, 2nd Calvalry, FORT CHADBOURNE, TEXAS.

October 30, 1858

Of **Ann Vaughan**, maiden name **McGrath**. When last heard of she was living in NEW YORK. If this should meet her eye, she will hear of something to her advantage by applying or addressing a few lines to the care of **John McGrath**, for G. V,. 237 MADISON STREET, NEW YORK; or to **Patrick Collins**, 15 State Street, TROY, N.Y., for G. V.

Of **John** and **William Brennan**, natives of ARMAGH, Ireland. John arrived in New York about thirteen years ago, and is supposed to be living in LAKE County, MICH. William arrived in Philadelphia about 4 years ago. When last heard from was in LISBON, LINN County, IOWA. Any information of them will be thankfully received by their mother, **Rosana Brennan**; or brother, **Thomas Brennan**, by writing them to 412 THIRD AVENUE, NEW YORK.

Of **James Daly** and wife, son of **Patrick Daly**, formerly of the Parish of ORANMORE, BALINAMONA, County GALWAY, Ireland. He last lived with **Sir Thos. N. Redington**. He came to this country some time ago, and has not been heard of since. Any information concerning him will be thankfully received by his friend, **Michael McCormick**, 131 NINTH ST, cor. Broadway, NEW YORK. Eastern and Western papers please copy.

Of **John Melody** from the Parish of LATRIM, County GALWAY, Ireland, who arrived in New York two years ago last September; he has been living on STATEN ISLAND, left there a year ago, and is supposed to have gone to SAVANNAH. Any information of him will be thankfully received by his sisters, **Mary**, **Bridget** and **Catherine Melody**, by writing to them in care of **Rev. J. D. Vermula**, Arnmonk [Armonk], WESTCHESTER Co., NEW YORK. Southern and Western papers please copy.

Of **John Holland**, tailor, who arrived in this City about six years ago, in the ship *Christiana*, from London. He was in LAFAYETTE, IND, when last heard from. If his nephews, **Thomas** and **Michael Moriarty** of OHIO, or any other person know where he is, or anything about him, they will confer a great favor by writing to his wife, **Mary Holland**, care of **Wm. Sweeney**, 61 GREENWICH STREET, NEW YORK. Ohio papers please copy. [Appeared under County GALWAY]

November 13, 1858

Of **Solomon Frost**, a native of the City of LIMERICK, Ireland, who arrived in New York in 1852. When last seen was, about eighteen months ago, in this city. Any information concerning him will be thankfully received by his brothers, **James**, and **Robert Frost**, No. 19 BRIDGE STREET, NEW YORK. Cincinnati Examiner please copy.

Of **Michael Doyle** of BALLYPRECUS, County WEXFORD, Ireland, who came to this country in May, 1844. Any information of him will be thankfully received by his brother, **John Doyle**, of EAST WINFIELD, HERKIMER County, N.Y.

November 20, 1858

If this should meet the eye of **Edmund Power**, who arrived here in the ship *New World* about six years ago, he would oblige his brother **Patrick** by calling to see him, on the U. S, Receiving ship *North Carolina*, Navy Yard, BROOKLYN. P.S.-Enquire for **Wm. Walsh**, Seaman.

Of **James Conners**, who left Ireland in February, 1857, and landed in New York, April 21st, 1857. Any information of him will be thankfully received by his wife, **Mary Conners**, by writing to her to PHILADELPHIA Post Office, PENNSYLVANIA.

Of **John Murphy**, a native of GRAIGUENAMANA, County KILKENNY, Ireland. When last heard from, was at HORNELLESVILLE, STEUBEN County, N.Y. Any information of him will be thankfully received by his wife, **Anne Murphy**, who arrived in the ship *Cultivator*, from Liverpool on the 5th instant, by writing to her, in care of **Philip Whalon**, No. 10 WASHINGTON STREET, NEW YORK.

Of **Michael Gerraghty**, a native of CASTLETOWN, Parish of DRUMCLIFF, County SLIGO, Ireland. Who came to America about the year 1853. When last heard from, he was in ELIZABETHTOWN, State of NEW JERSEY. Any information concerning him will be thankfully received by his brother, **James Gerraghty**. Address **James Gi[ll]in**, No. 49 BAXTER STREET, N.Y.

Of **Daniel**, **Timothy**, **James**, and **Patrick Sullivan**, natives of CASTLETOWN, County CORK, Ireland. When last heard from they were all working together on some Railroad in Southern VIRGINIA. Any information of them will be thankfully received by their brother, **John Sullivan**, SOUTH DEDHAM, MASS.; or their cousin **Jeremiah Sullivan**, 119 MOTT ST., N.Y. Virginia papers please copy.

Of **John** and **Bernard Fitzpatrick**, natives of the Parish of KILMORE, County CAVAN, Ireland. When last heard from were in ALTOONA, BLAIR County, PA. Any information of them will be thankfully received by their sisters **Margaret** and **Mary**, by directing a letter to Margaret's husband, **Mr. Thomas Sanders**, No. 172 LEWIS STREET, NEW YORK. Pennsylvania papers please copy.

December 4, 1858

Of **Patrick Boyle**, or his wife, **Mary Dugan**, from the ISLAND of ARANMORE, County DONEGAL, Ireland. When last heard from they were in ALBANY. Any information of them will be thankfully received by writing to their sister, **Bridget Dugan**, No. 43 Tenth Street, WILLIAMSBURGH, Long Island, N.Y.

Of **Patrick Walsh**, a native of ATHENRY, County GALWAY, Ireland, who landed in New York in August 1849. Any information of him will be thankfully received by his brother, **Luke Walsh**, 188 EAST ELEVENTH STREET, NEW YORK.

Of **John Falin**, who left Ireland in the year 1856, and came from the County KILKENNY, Parish of GALLMOY. When last heard from he was in EAST MERRYLAND, CHAMPLAIN County, ILL., in May, 1858. Any information respecting him will be thankfully received by his brother, **James Falin** (Phalon), No. 39 Cross Street, PATERSON, N. J., or to **B. O'Neill**, Bookseller, No. 81 Congress Street, PATERSON, N. J. [Appeared Dec. 11, 1858 with the surname **Falin** changed to **Phalon**.]

December 11, 1858

Of **John Hyland** and wife; also of his two daughters, **Catherine** and **Julia**, who left QUEBEC in 1834. When last heard from were living in NEW YORK CITY. Any information of them will be thankfully received by **Mrs. Ellen Condon**, No. 233 NINTH AVENUE, NEW YORK.

December 18, 1858

Of **Michael Langton**, gun maker, a native of LUSK, County DUBLIN, Ireland. When last heard from was leaving LOUISVILLE, KY., for PHILADELPHIA. Any information of him will be thankfully received by his brother, **Laurence Langton**, by writing to him to No. 235 RIVINGTON STREET, NEW YORK.

Of **Joseph** and **John Cleary**, of RATHNEW, County WICKLOW, Ireland, who left Dublin in February, 1849, and when last heard from were in NEW YORK. Any information of them will be thankfully received by their cousins, **Sylvester** and **Mary**, 1024 Locust Street, PHILADELPHIA, PA.; or **Joseph Loughlin**, 233 Union St., PHILADELPHIA. Eastern papers please copy. [Appeared Jan. 1, 1859 without mentioning Mary Cleary.]

Of **James Carraher**, a native of the Townland of DRUMGHOST, County MONAGHAN, Ireland. When last heard from he was living either UPPER or LOWER CANADA. Any information of him will be thankfully received by his brother, **Patrick Carraher**; by writing to him care of **Francis M. Toal**, NEWBURGH, N.Y.

Of **Mary** and **Ellen Brennan**, who emigrated to this country in the ship *Primson* from Galway bound for Quebec, on the 6th of September, 1853. The last information received from them they were in TORONTO, UPPER CANADA. Any information of them will be thankfully received by their brother, **Martin Brennan**, ELIZABETHPORT Post Office, NEW JERSEY. Toronto papers please copy. [Appeared under County GALWAY]

Of **Bernard** and **Michael Boylan**, of CULLOW, Parish of CROSSERLOUGH, County CAVAN, Ireland. When last heard from they were in some of the manufactoring towns of CONNECTICUT or MASSACHUSETTS. By addressing **J. B. Tully**, No. 40. Hall of Records, NEW YORK. They will hear something to their advantage.

December 25, 1858

Of **Patrick** and **James Flynn**, natives of BANTRY, County CORK, Ireland. Patrick came to this country thirteen years since. Any information of them will be thankfully received by their mother and brother at No. 182 MOTT STREET, N.Y. Wisconsin papers please copy.

January 1, 1859

Henry Hewitt, late of SNUGBOROUGH, County CLARE, who came to this country about ten years ago, and was last heard of either in VERMONT, or DETROIT, MICH. Will hear of something to his advantage by sending his address to the office of this paper. Or any one knowing his whereabouts will confer a favor by writing us.

January 8, 1859

Of **Bernard Burns**, from the Parish of BELNASCREEN, County DERRY, Ireland, who left MORRISTOWN MONTGOMERY County, PA., last June, in search of employment. When last heard from about four months ago, he was leaving SAN JOSE for ST. LOUIS, MISSOURI. Any information of him will be most thankfully received by his afflicted wife, **Bridget Burns**, Morristown, Pa., or at the office of the Irish-American.

Of **Patrick** and **Anne Monaghan**, from the Parish of LAVY, County CAVAN, Ireland. They came to this country about seven years ago. When last heard from Patrick was living in NEW YORK CITY, and Anne was in SAVANNAH, Ga. Any information of them will be thankfully received by their sister **Mary Monaghan**, by writing in care of **Michael Vaughan**, GEORGETOWN, FAIRFIELD County, CONN.

January 15, 1859

Of **Thomas Enright**, a native of BALLYLONGFORD, County KERRY, Ireland. When last heard from he was working at ALBION, ERIE County, PA. Any information of him will be thankfully received by his sister, **Johanna Enright**, by directing a letter for her in the care of **Timothy Carr**, 22 THAMES STREET, NEW YORK.

January 22, 1859

Of **Eugene Cunningham**, native of INCHIGEELA, County CORK, Ireland. When last heard of he was in WISCONSIN. Any information concerning him will be thankfully received by directing a letter to the **Widow Cunningham**, OSHAWA, CANADA WEST.

Of **Margaret Ryan**, a native of CLANMORE, Parish of MUNROW, Co. TIPPERARY; also of **Timothy Stapleton**, a native of COOGA, Parish of UPPER CHURCH, County TIPPERARY, Ireland, Margaret Ryan left Ireland seven or eight years ago, and when last heard of she was in or about BUFFALO; Timothy left at the same time and date. Any information of them will be thankfully received by their cousin, **Timothy Stapleton**, HOOSICK FALLS, RENSSELAER County, NEW YORK.

Of **Michael** and **Patrick King**, of the Town of NEWPORT, County MAYO, Ireland, who arrived in this country about ten years ago. When last heard from through **Mr. Dominick M'Laughlin**, of No. 2 Biddle Water Street, St. Louis, they were in the City of ST. LOUIS, MO. Any information of them will be thankfully received by their brother, **Dominick King**, care of **Wm. Patterson**, No. 59 WASHINGTON STREET, NEW YORK.

Of **Thomas King** and wife, natives of the Parish of KILLAND, County CAVAN, Ireland. When last heard from they were in MILWAUKEE, WIS. Any information of them will be thankfully received by **Thomas McCaul**, No. 213 MOTT STREET, NEW YORK.

January 29, 1859

Of **Thomas Mooney**, a native of PHOENIX PARK, County DUBLIN, Ireland, who left NEW YORK on the 30th of June, 1858, for CLEVELAND, Ohio. Some property has been left him by the death of his aunt, **Catherine Butler**, and a power-of-attorney from him to **Thomas M'Kenze**, the Executor, is needed to administer to it. Should this meet his eye, or that of any one knowing his whereabouts, they will please write to Mr. Thomas M'Kenzie, 81 SIXTH AVENUE, NEW YORK; or to **John Mooney**, 56 River Street, NEWARK, N. J.

Of **Bernard Lynam**, a native of the Parish of CILLAIR, County WESTMEATH, Ireland. He left NEW YORK two years ago. When last heard from he was in NEW ORLEANS, about six months ago. Any information of him will be thankfully received by his afflicted mother, brothers and sisters, at No. 514 SECOND AVENUE, N.Y., for **Mrs. R. Lynam**, cor. of 32nd ST. New Orleans papers please copy.

Of **Patrick Lannen**, a native of CAMROOS, Parish of KILGARVIN, County WEXFORD, Ireland. When last seen was working near the Town of COLUMBIA, in the State Of INDIANA. Any person knowing of his whereabouts would confer a favor on an aged father by addressing a line to **Mr. John Lannen**, KENOSHA, WISCONSIN

February 5, 1859

Of **William A. Flynn**. When last heard from he was living at PERRYSBURGH, WOOD County, OHIO. Any information of him will be thankfully received by **Miss O'Malley**, corner of Thomas and George's Streets, LIMERICK, Ireland.

Of **Michael** and **James Nolan**, natives of CROWSGAP, Parish of KILMAIN, County ROSCOMMON, Ireland. When last heard from was living in PITTSBURGH, State of PENNSYLVANIA. Any information of them will be thankfully received by their niece, **Bridget Nolan**, by directing a letter to her to No. 9 WEST 24th STREET, NEW YORK.

Of **Patrick Griffin Murray**, of GALWAY, Ireland, who left NEW YORK on July 14th, 1858. He is a brother-in-law to **Hugh Cooney**, of UPTON, MASS; also of **John Monahan**, of TAUNTON, MASS. Any information of him will be thankfully received by his distressed wife and child, at 127 AVENUE D, corner 9th Street, NEW YORK, by Maria Murray. Boston papers please copy.

Of **James Coleman**, aged about 27 years, a native of FERMOY, Co. CORK, Ireland. When last heard from he was in the State of VIRGINIA, near the IRON MOUNTAIN Post Office. Any information of him will be thankfully received by his sister **Mary Coleman**, care of **Richard Condon**, 143 Wallace Street, NEW HAVEN, CT.

February 12, 1859

Of **Michael Condon**, aged about 30 years, from NERNEY, County KILDARE, Ireland. When last heard from one year ago, he was in DICKSON, LEE County, ILLINOIS. Any information of him will be thankfully received by sister **Marcella** or **Margaret Condon**. Address care of **Right Rev. James F. Wood**, PHILADELPHIA, PENN.

Of **John Hogan**, boot and shoe-maker by trade, a native of the Parish of MONALEEN, County of LIMERICK, Ireland; left TROY three years ago. When last heard from he was in PHILADELPHIA, working at his trade. Any information of him will be thankfully received by his cousins, **Michael** and **William Cahill**, by writing to them in care of **Mr. James Garner**, 242 Fourth Street, EAST TROY, N.Y.

February 19, 1859

Of **John Rynne** and sister, natives of the Parish of CRUGOYNE, County TIPPERARY, Ireland, who came to America about twelve years ago. When last heard from they were in OHIO. Any information of them will be thankfully received by their sister's children, **Ellen** and **Catherine**, by writing to them to No. 24 JAMES STREET, (rear building) NEW YORK. [Appears March 5, 1859 with additional information.]

Of **Lawrence Navan**, son of **John Navan**, from the Parish of TYNAGH, County GALWAY, Ireland, who with his parents, emigrated to America fifteen years ago. Should this meet his eye, or any person knowing him, they will confer a favor by writing his aunt, **Bridget Navan**, 296 WEST 27th STREET, NEW YORK.

February 26, 1859

If **Mr. James Bowden** will call at 365 BROOME STREET, NEW YORK, he will hear of his mother. [Appeared under County KILKENNY]

Of **Thomas** and **Margaret Daily**, children of **Bernard Daily**, formerly of MOUNT TALBOT, Parish of TERSAHER, County ROSCOMMON, Ireland. When last heard from they were living in BALLINASLOE, County GALWAY, Ireland. Any information of them will be thankfully received by their cousins, **Thomas Stanton** and **Tully McDonnell**, by writing to them, care of **Michael Begg**, No. 71 MULBERRY ST., or at the office of the Irish-American. Ballinsloe and Roscommon papers please copy.

Of **Mary Melvin**, of GALWAY, Ireland. When last heard of was living in NEW YORK. Any information of her will be thankfully received by her sisters, **Margaret** and **Bridget**, 137 READE STREET; or to **Martin Gorman**, 38 MADISON STREET, NEW YORK. Boston papers please copy.

March 5, 1859

Of **William Munroe**, a native of DUBLIN, Ireland, who left PROVIDENCE, R. I., in the year 1849, for NEW YORK, and has not been heard from since. Any information about him will be thankfully received by his sister, **Anna Munroe**, care of **J. P. Richardson**, Esq., CAMBRIDGEPORT, MASS.

Of **Daniel Hoy**, a native of TULLY, Parish of CLUNGUSH, County LONGFORD, Ireland, who arrived in New York, in March, 1848. When last heard from, about six years ago, he was in NEW YORK, and is supposed to have gone to ILLINOIS. Any information of him will be thankfully received by **Edward Dillon**, cor. of Smith and Wykoff Streets, BROOKLYN, N. Y.

Of **William Bergin**, ship-carpenter, from NENAGH, County TIPPERARY, Ireland, who went to SAVANNAH, about twelve months ago. Any person knowing his present whereabouts will confer a great favor, by writing to his cousin, **James Dalton**, No. 90 North 6th Street, WILLIAMSBURGH, L.I., as he is particulary wanted with regard to his property in Nenagh.

Of **Hannah Cavanagh**, of BALLINGLINN, County WEXFORD, Ireland, married to **Michael Barrett**, of KELLS, MEATH County. When last heard of, was in JASPER County, SAINTE MARIE, ILL. Any information of her will be thankfully received by her sister **Sarah** by directing a letter to RAHWAY, N. J., in care of **Ralph Marsh**. Illinois papers please copy.

Of **John Ryan** and sister, natives of the Parish of CRAGRYAN, County TIPPERARY, Ireland, who came to America about twelve years ago. When last heard from they were in OHIO. Any information of them will be thankfully received by their sister's children, **Ellen** and **Catherine Shinners**, by writing to them to No. 24 JAMES STREET, (rear building) NEW YORK. [Appeared under County LIMERICK].

Of **John Barry**, from the Parish of KILDORRERY, County CORK, Ireland, who emigrated to this country four years ago. When last heard from (in May '58), he was in ST. LOUIS, MO. Any intelligence of him will be thankfully received by his brother **Thomas Barry**. Direct to WASHINGTON HEIGHTS Post-office, NEW YORK.

March 12, 1859

Of **John Hannan**, of FERMOY, County CORK, Ireland. When last heard from was in ASHLAND, HANOVER County, VIRGINIA. Any information concerning him will be thankfully received by his brother, **Mr. George Hannan**, butcher's stall, No. 110 and 112 Centre Market, BALTIMORE, MD. Virginia papers please copy.

March 19, 1859

If any of the children or grand-children of the late **James Selden Young**, of NEW ORLEANS, are alive, they will please send their address to their cousin **Henrietta**, care of Mr. W. L. Cole, 32 Beekman Street, New York City. New Orleans papers please copy.

Of **Michael Tully**, a native of the Townland of HEADFORD, County GALWAY, Ireland. When last heard from, (about two years ago,) he was in the Parish of ST. JAMES, LOUISIANA. Any information of him will be thankfully received by his father and brothers. Address **Mathew Tully**, 144 CHERRY STREET, NEW YORK. Louisiana papers please copy.

Of **James Long**, a native of the Parish of KILTEELY, County LIMERICK, Ireland, who worked with **Matthew Guerin** in Kilteely. When last heard from he was working in the Brooklyn Water Works. It is now supposed he is in LAFAYETTE, IND. Any information of him will be thankfully received by his brother **Matthew Long**, by writing to him to the care of **Denis Hassett**, Bergen Street, between Washington and Grand Avenues, BROOKLYN, N. Y.; or at the office of the Irish-American. Lafayette papers please copy.

March 26, 1859

Of **Ellen Tierney**, eleven years old, who arrived in New York in May, 1858, in the ship *Yorkshire*, from Liverpool. Her father, **Michael Tierney**, is anxious to find her. Apply at the Office of the Commissioners of Emigration, No. 81 Worth Street.

Of **Martin Finan**. When last heard from was in WATERTOWN, WISCONSIN. Any information of him will be thankfully received by his sister, **Jane Smith**, 307 MOTT STREET, NEW YORK.

Of **John Cullen**, formerly of the Town of WICKLOW. When last heard from was in AUBURN, SCHUYLKILL County, PA. Any information concerning him will be thankfully received by his sisters, **Mary** and **Anne Cullen**. Address care of **Patrick Fortune**, 1024 Locust Street, PHILADELPHIA.

Of **Mr. Albert Irvin McDonogh**, by his sister **Jane**. When last heard from was at Trinity College, DUBLIN in 1850. Address care of **Mrs. Bond**, No. 215 MULBERRY STREET, NEW YORK. Dublin papers please copy.

Of **Catherine Gilmore**, and **Mulvey** by marriage, a native of the Parish of KILLTUBRITT, County LEITRIM, Ireland, who emigrated to this country four years ago next August. When last heard from she resided in ORANGE County, NEW YORK. Any information of her will be thankfully received by her brother, **Edward Gilmore**, by writing to him to ELIZABETH PORT, NEW JERSEY.

Of **Eliza McKim**, daughter of **Susan** and **Thos. McKim** of COLLOONEY, County OF SLIGO, Ireland, who left Sligo in August, 1849, for Quebec. Any information of her will be gratefully received by her mother Susan McKim, 535 THIRD AVENUE, NEW YORK.

Of **Hobart** or **Robert Synott**, a native of DROMORE WEST, County of SLIGO, Ireland, who left NEW YORK in May, 1854, with the intention of going to ILLINOIS, since which time nothing has been heard of him. Any information concerning him will be most gratefully received by his afflicted sisters, by addressing **James Sanford**, 73 KING STREET, NEW YORK.

Of **Owen McCaffrey**, a native of the County CAVAN, Parish of DRUMBLANE, Ireland; when last heard from, about five years ago, he was living in NEW YORK. Any information respecting him will be thankfully received by his brother, **John McCaffrey**, MERIDEN, CONNECTICUT.

Of **Timothy Doheney**, a native of GORTNAHO, County TIPPERARY, Ireland, son of **Widow Doheney** is in America sixteen years. When last heard of he was in BOSTON and worked on a farm. Any persons knowing of his whereabouts will confer a favor on his sisters, **Johana** and **Maria Doheney**, by sending a line to Maria Doheney, in care of **Mr. Gillis**, No. 146 EAST 45th STREET, NEW YORK.

Of **John Rogers**, a native of CONHA, Parish FETHARD, County WEXFORD, Ireland, who sailed from Waterford to New York, about a year and ten months ago, and is supposed to be in LONG ISLAND. Any person knowing of his whereabouts would, oblige **Henry Drummond**, by telling him to call to his place of residence, 123 FIRST AVENUE, near Eighth Street, NEW YORK.

April 2, 1859

Of **Denis Guinan**, a native of WEST MELLICK, QUEEN'S County, Ireland, who came to this country in 1853 and left NEW YORK in January, 1854, to go to KENTUCKY with a **Mr. Lynch**. When last heard from (three years ago) he was in ROCK ISLAND, ILL. Any person knowing anything of his whereabouts will confer a great favor on his sister by sending a few lines to 312 Portland Avenue, BROOKLYN, N. Y., for **Mary Guinan**. Western papers please copy. [Appeared April 16, 1859 with WEST MELLICK changed to MOUNTMELLICK]

Of **Dan Daly**, a native of LIMERICK, Ireland, who left home in 1849. When last heard of was in PITTSBURGH. Any information of him will be thankfully received by his sister **Catherine**, by addressing a few lines to **Patrick Callaghan**, 446 CHERRY STREET, NEW YORK.

April 9, 1859

Of **Eliza M'Manus**, from the County LEITRIM, who sailed from Liverpool in the ship *John Bright*, and arrived at Castle Garden, New York. She left to go to her aunt in CONNECTICUT on the 25th of January last. Any information of her will be thankfully received by her afflicted mother, **Bridget M'Manus**, by writing to her to 1009 Wallace Street, NEW HAVEN, CT.

Of **George Hines**, a native of the County CAVAN, Ireland, who came to this country nearly six years ago; was in the Constabulary some time, stationed at ATHENRY, Co. GALWAY. When last heard of was in PHILADELPHIA, where he is still supposed to be. Any information respecting him will be thankfully received by his brother and sister, **Walter** and **Jane Hines**, at the office of this paper. Philadelphia Ledger please copy.

Of **Timothy Baldwin**, of the County TIPPERARY, Ireland, who was married to **Nancy Corcoran**, in the year 1844, in the Parish of BORRISOLEIGH, by **Rev. W. Morris**; emigrated to America in the year 1848, leaving his wife and two children in Ireland. Any information respecting him may be directed to **Pierce Bergan**, 45 Day Street, NEW HAVEN, CONN; or **Rev. E. J. O'Brien**, Pastor St. Mary's Church.

Of **Eliza Delaney**, a native of BALLYANLON, County CORK, Ireland. It is supposed she is married and living in BROOKLYN. When last seen, was living in Water, near Jay Street.

Any information of her will be thankfully received by her brother, **Francis Delaney**, by writing to him to No. 35 FERRY STREET, NEW YORK. Country papers please copy.

April 16, 1859

Of **Ann** and **John Ginnis** and **Rose Daly**, natives of the County LEITRIM, Ireland. If any of the above persons will call or write to **T. Smith**, 250 7th AVENUE, NEW YORK, near 26th Street, they will hear of something to their advantage. Country and Canada papers please copy.

April 23, 1859

Sarah Jane Hall, may hear of something to her advantage by addressing K. T,. 37 LISPENARD STREET, NEW YORK. Any information which will lead to discovering her whereabouts will be thankfully received and rewarded. Direct as above. When last heard of she was in FLATBUSH, L.I.; is about twenty years of age.

Of **Stephen Murphy**, a native of Ireland, who sailed from Glasgow, Scotland, in 1852. When last heard from (last June,) he was working at PORT DEPOSIT, MARYLAND. Any information concerning him will be thankfully received by his cousin, **Neal McBride**, 611 South Fourth Street, PHILADELPHIA, PA. Baltimore papers please copy.

Of **Thomas Leech**, who left SPROSON, near MIDDLEWICH, CHESHIRE, ENGLAND, in 1843. If he will please write to his sister, **Mrs. Ann Sadler**, of LITTLE LINDON, near WIMSHAW, CHESHIRE; or to **Thomas McNamara**, PATERSON, N. J., he will hear of some property left him in England. Country papers please copy.

Of **James Bowden**. When last heard of (last summer,) was in NEW YORK. Any person knowing of his whereabouts would oblige his mother by calling at 365 BROOME STREET, NEW YORK. [Appeared under County KILKENNY]

Of **Bryan Connors**, of GOREY, County WEXFORD, Ireland. When last heard from was in PARADISE, COLES County, ILLINOIS. Any information of him will be thankfully received by his sister, **Sarah Connors**, No. 192 Jay Street, BROOKLYN, N. Y. Illinois papers please copy.

April 30, 1859

Of **Patrick** and **William Loftus**, from the County MAYO, Parish of KILMOORE, Town AU[J]OCEN, Ireland, who came to this country twelve or thirteen years since. The former married **Catherine Burk**. of the same place. Address their sister, **Catherine Loftus**, care of **John Scott**, No. 900 Fitzwater Street, PHILADELPHIA, PA.

Of **Peter Naughten** and **Anne Loftus**, from the Parish of CROSSMOLINA, County MAYO, Ireland; also of **Cornelius Griffin**. When last heard from they were living in KINGSTON. Any information of them will be thankfully received by **Mary Murphy**, by writing to her to No. 10 Barbareen St., BROOKLYN, N. Y.

Of **Daniel Harrington**, a native of the Parish of KILGAVEN, County KERRY, Ireland. When last heard from he was living at ELGIN, ILLINOIS. Any information of him will be thankfully received by his mother **Ellen Harrington**, by writing to her to the care of **Mr. Perkins**, SOUTH SIDE, PRINCESS BAY, STATEN ISLAND, N. Y.

Of **Thomas** and **James Duane**, natives of GRAYFORT, near BORRISOKANE, County TIPPERARY, Ireland. When last heard from about three years since, Thomas was living in BUFFALO, N. Y. Any intelligence of them will be thankfully received by their brother, **Daniel Duane**, care of **Michael O'Connor**, FORT HILL, YONKERS, WESTCHESTER Co., N.Y. Buffalo papers please copy.

May 7, 1859

Of **Michael Price**, a native of BALLYWILLIAMROW, Co. CARLOW, Ireland, who came to this country some thirty years ago; when last heard of, he was in PHILADELPHIA. Any information of him will be thankfully received by his sister **Ellen**. Address **Mrs. O'Grady**, 14 WEST 17th STREET, N.Y. Philadelphia papers please copy.

May 21, 1859

Of **John Gallaghan**, a native of the City of LIMERICK, Ireland, who arrived in New York in March 1857. When last heard from he was living in CHICAGO, ILLINOIS. Any information of him will be thankfully received by his son, **Michael Gallaghan**, by writing to him, in care of **Daniel Collins**, No. 15 ROSEVELT [Roosevelt Street] STREET, NEW YORK.

Of **Thomas** and **Catherine Butler**, natives of the Town of THURLES, County TIPPERARY, Ireland, who arrived in New York about five years ago. When last heard from they were living in some part of the State of NEW YORK. Any information of them will be thankfully received by their brother, **Patrick Butler**, by writing to him to the office of this paper.

May 28, 1859

Of **John Robinson**, of AUGHAMORE, Barony of COSTELLOE, County MAYO, Ireland, who left DUNKIRK, about twelve months ago, in the freight cattle train for NEW YORK. His sister **Delia**, is most anxious to hear of his whereabouts, fearful some accident had occurred to him on the train. The last time he was seen was in HORNESVILLE, from which place he could not be traced any further. Any information respecting him will be gratefully received by his aunt and sister, at **Mr. James G. Smith's** 121 Degraw Street, SOUTH BROOKLYN, N.Y.

June 11, 1859

Of **Martin Crodock**, a native of KINLOUGH, Parish of SHRUEL, County MAYO, Ireland; arrived here 11 years ago. And also **Mary Walsh**, Native of KILMAIN; came to NEW YORK about 4 years ago. Any information of the parties will be thankfully received by **Robert** and **Julia Crodock**. Address Robert Crodock, GREENPOINT, Long Island, NEW YORK.

June 18, 1859

Of **Peter Duffy**, a native of GREENMOUNT, County LOUTH, Ireland. When last heard of (in March last) he was in NEW YORK. Any information of him will be thankfully received by his brother **Charles Duffy**, at 169 HESTER STREET, NEW YORK.

Of **Edward** and **Miles Burke**, sons of **Miles Burke**, Carpenter, ULAGH, County TIPPERARY. When last heard from they were in PHILADELPHIA. Any information of their whereabouts will be thankfully received by their aunt, **Bridget Downey**, FORDHAM, WESTCHESTER County, N.Y.

June 25, 1859

Of **John Thompson**, who left CARDIFF, in WALES, in 1853, and landed in New York in May of the same year. Went from NEW YORK to SALEM, MASS.; left Salem in 1854; and the last heard of him was that he worked in the North Brick-yard about sixteen miles from the City of NEW YORK. Any information of him will be thankfully received by his wife and three children, at No. 4 ELM STREET, N.Y.

Of **Mary** and **Ellen Brennan**, natives of the Parish of KILLIAN, County GALWAY, Ireland, who landed in Quebec in 1855, and moved from that place to TORONTO. Any information of them will be thankfully received by their brother, **Martin Brennan**, ELIZABETHPORT, NEW JERSEY. Canada papers please copy.

Of **Michael** and **William Sullivan**, from the County WATERFORD, Ireland; have been five years in this country. When last heard from, their address was DOVER Post-office, MORRIS County, N.J. Their sister **Bridget Sullivan**, would like to hear from them at **James Sullivan's** No.5 87th STREET, YORKVILLE, between 3rd and 4th Avenues, NEW YORK.

Of **Mary McGrath**, of the Parish of CUMMARAGH, Townland of GLENDALLIGAN, County WATERFORD, Ireland. When last heard from was living with **Thomas O'Brien**, WATER STREET, N.Y. Any person knowing of her whereabouts will please address a note, or call to **Mrs. Corcoran**. No 359 SECOND AVENUE, between Twenty -Second and Twenty - Third Streets, where her sister **Catherine** resides.

Of **Honora Heaveran**, a native of the Parish of KILMORE, County MAYO, Ireland. When last heard from, was living in PORTAGEVILLE, WYOMING County, NEW YORK. Any information of her will be thankfully received by her brother, **Laurence Heaveran**, by writing to him to SOUTH RIVER, State of NEW JERSEY.

Of **Thomas Mulhern**, a native of the Parish of SCREEN, County SLIGO, Ireland. When last heard from, he was living in the State of VIRGINIA. Any information of him will be thankfully received by his sister, **Mary Mulhern**, by writing to her to No. 311 WEST 21st STREET, N.Y.

July 2, 1859

Of **John Hart**, who left COATBRIDGE, SCOTLAND, and emigrated to this country in the year 1857. When last heard from was leaving for PIKE'S PEAK, KANSAS. Any information of him will be thankfully received by his brother, **Patrick Hart**, 551 GRAND ST., NEW YORK. Ohio papers, please copy.

Of **Edward McGlinn**, native of CLARA, KING'S County, Ireland, who landed in New York about 7 years ago; supposed to have gone to his brother, **James McGlinn**, who was for some years settled in MILWAUKEE, State of WISCONSIN. If this should meet either of their notice they will confer a favor by communicating to their married sister, **Honora Coffee**, No. 335 EAST 8th STREET, NEW YORK, between Avenues B and C. Milwaukee papers please copy.

Of **Ellen Laughnan**, daughter of **John Laughnan**, a naive of MINOSH, Parish of KILLARNEY, County KERRY, Ireland. When last heard from, she was living in NEW YORK, two years ago. Any information of her will be thankfully received by her brother, **Thomas Laughnan**, SOUTH DANVERS, MASS.

July 9, 1859

Of **Daniel** and **Thomas Doody**, natives of FERMOY, County CORK. When last heard from, in February, 1858, they were in VIRGINIA. Any information of them will be most thankfully received by their sister, **Margaret Doody**, (who arrived in this country in May, 1859) at her residence, No. 11 Woodhull St., BROOKLYN, care of **Mr. Thos. Brennan**.

Of **James Grennan**, a native of the County CARLOW, Ireland, who arrived in the packet ship, *Monarch of the Sea*, in company with **Dudley Kavanagh**, of GLEEM, County CARLOW. Any information of him will be thankfully received by his brother **Matthew Grennan**, by writing to him in care of **John Miller**, HOOSICK FOUR CORNERS, State of NEW YORK; or, to **P. Rourke**, 265 GREENWICH ST., NEW YORK.

Of **Owen Gartland**, a native of the County MONAGHAN, Ireland. When last seen, was at YONKERS, State of NEW YORK. If still alive any information in reference to his whereabouts will be thankfully received by his brother, **Patrick Gartland**, at No. 2[6]2[8] Filbert Street, PHILADELPHIA.

Of **Michael Guary**, a native of the County of GALWAY, Ireland, who left the City of NEW YORK in 1854 for HARTFORD, ILLINOIS. Any information respecting him will be thankfully received by his niece, **Mary O'Flattery**, 286 WEST 23rd STREET, NEW YORK.

July 16, 1859

Of **John** and **Michael Brennen**, who left TROY, N.Y., about one year ago; when last heard from John was in CAIRO, ILLINOIS, and Michael in CLEVELAND, OHIO. Any information of them will be thankfully received by addressing **Maria Brennen**, wife of John. Box 517, Troy P.O., N.Y., who is most anxious to hear from them. Western papers please copy.

Of **Thomas Power**, a cooper by trade, who left QUEBEC last November for UPPER CANADA; when last heard from he was living in ALBANY, N.Y., and then left for CINCINNATI, OHIO. Any information of him will be thankfully received by Lynch & Cole, 32 Beekman Street, New York.

July 23, 1859

Of **Michael Green**, a native of COLLON, Co. LOUTH, Ireland; when last heard from he was in TRENTON, NEW JERSEY; it is said he has left there to go West some 18 months ago. Any information of him will be thankfully received by his wife, **Mary Green**, who has landed here a few months ago, in care of **Thomas McGoveran**, 70 HAMERSLEY STREET, NEW YORK.

July 30, 1859

Of **Michael Conarty**, who left NEWARK, October, 1853, and of **Michael Moran** who left HAVERSTRAW, October, 185[3], and when last heard from they were in the State of ILLINOIS, and Michael Conarty got his letters in SYCKEMORE Post Office. Any information of them would be thankfully received by their brothers, **James Conarty** and **Moran**, No. 27 Lock Street, NEWARK, NEW JERSEY. Western papers please copy.

Of **John Russell**, of QUILLAW, Parish of RUSNAREE, County MEATH, Ireland. When last heard from he was living in PHILADELPHIA. Any information of him will be thankfully received by his brother **James**, at the Mansion House, Hicks Street, BROOKLYN. Philadelphia and California papers please copy.

Of **John Sheedy McNamara**, a native of the Parish of CARRIGARA, in the County of CLARE, Ireland. Who arrived in this country in or about ten years ago. Any information respecting him will be thankfully received by his brother, **Thomas**, at No. 12 WEST STREET, NEW YORK. Western papers please copy.

August 6, 1859

Of **Timothy Molloy**, a native of the Parish of WOOLA, County TIPPERARY, Ireland. When last heard from he was in NEW YORK CITY. Any information of him will be thankfully received by his brother, **Denis Molloy**, by writing to him in care of John A. Kennedy, Esq., Castle Garden, New York.

August 13, 1859

Of **Cornelius Mahoney**, who left NEW YORK in March, 1848. When last heard from was in MILWAUKEE. He left there for TORONTO in CANADA. He is about 25 years of age, five feet eleven inches in height, fair complexion, long yellow hair, and a ship-carpenter by trade. Any information concerning him will be thankfully received by his distressed mother, corner of Columbia and Luqueer Streets, SOUTH BROOKLYN. Canada papers please copy.

If **Mary Reilly**, daughter of the late **Edward Reilly** hotel keeper, STONEYBATTER, DUBLIN, will apply to **Thomas Russell**, 209 FULTON STREET, NEW YORK, or to **John McGauran**, 32 Westland Row, DUBLIN, she will hear of something to her advantage. Her mother's name is **Margaret McDermott**.

Of **Charles Daly**, son of **John Daly**, carpenter, CORK, Ireland, as there is some property left at his disposal. When last heard from he was in BUFFALO. Any person knowing of his whereabout will confer a favor by communication with **J. Reardon**, 24 EAST 17th STREET, NEW YORK.

Of **Annie Doyle**, a native of HARRISTOWN, Co. CARLOW, Parish of ST. MULLINS, Ireland. Any person hearing of her would confer a great favor by writing to her mother to the care of **Henry Curran**, 119th STREET, HARLEM, NEW YORK. Western papers please copy.

Of **Susan Nangle**, of SLIGO, Ireland. When last heard from, some sixteen years ago, was in the Military Asylum, QUEBEC. Any information of her present whereabouts will be thankfully received by her sister, **Ann Nangle**, BURKELEW, SOUTH AMBOY, N.J. Canada papers please copy.

August 20, 1859

Of **Patrick Sullivan Dorohy**, who left County KERRY, in 1851. He proceeded to MONTREAL, with his mother and sister and came to NEW YORK the same year. In 1857 he was in NEW YORK, and is supposed to be there yet. A letter addressed, as to his whereabouts to **Miss McCudden**, No. 44 Queen St., TORONTO, CANADA WEST, would meet the prompt attention of his cousin, **Mary Green**.

Of **John** and **Bridget Ryan**, natives of the Parish of CRAIG RYAN, County TIPPERARY, Ireland. When last heard from was in OHIO, about four years ago. Any information of them will be gladly received by their sister's children, **Catherine** and **Ellen Shinners**, No. 24 JAMES STREET, rear building, room 5.

Of **John Hickey**, native of the Parish DONOHILL, County TIPPERARY, Ireland. When last heard from, five years ago, was in WATERTOWN, NEW YORK State, any information respecting him will be thankfully received by his sister, **Catherine Hickey**, Tremont House, CHICAGO, ILL.

August 27, 1859

Of **Miss Eliza Hayes**, also of **Mary Rollins**, natives of the Town of KANA, County LONGFORD, Ireland; when last heard from they were in NEW YORK. Any information of them will be thankfully received by **Ellen Armstrong**, by writing to her in care of **Mr. Abraham Van Nostrand**, 373 PEARL STREET, NEW YORK. Miss Hayes will hear something to her advantage from her sister **Miss Frances**, by writing or calling the above address.

Of **Laurence** and **Martin Devany**, natives of County GALWAY, Ireland; when last heard from they were in PITTSBURGH, PA. Any information of them will be thankfully received by their sister **Bridget Devany**, otherwise **Mrs. Bannon**; by writing to her to No. 4[0] HAMILTON ST., NEW YORK CITY, they will hear something to their advantage.

Thomas Ward, of CRUSHSHOOHA, Parish of KINVARA, County GALWAY, Ireland who left home about the 20th of April, 1859, for Quebec, from Galway. Any information of his whereabouts will be gratefully received by his uncle **Thomas Linnane**, 450 corner of

Degraw and Columbia Streets, SOUTH BROOKLYN, or his brother **Patrick Ward**, RONDOUT, P.O., N.Y.

Of **Sally Love**, a native of WHITE PARK, Parish of GLACK, County FERMANAGH, Ireland; when last heard from she was in NEW YORK, on her way from NEW HAVEN, CT., to the West to purchase land; her husband's name is **Christy Carroll**, from KILDARE. Any information of her will be thankfully received by her sister **Mary Love**, by addressing a note to **Thomas D. Norris**, No. 25 COENTICS SLIP, NEW YORK. Western papers please copy.

Of **William Ryan**, a native of the Parish of DAVISTOWN, County WEXFORD, Ireland. When last heard from about nine years ago. he was living at PERTH, UPPER CANADA, and is supposed he resides there now. Any information of him will be thankfully received by his brother, **Michael Ryan**, by writing to him to No. 363 WEST 29th STREET, NEW YORK.

Of **Bridget Daly**, a native of the Parish of OGLE, County ROSCOMMON. When last heard from she lived in MOTT STREET, NEW YORK. Any intelligence respecting her will be thankfully received if addressed to **Mary Daly**, care of the Sisters of Charity, St. Vincent's Hospital, 11th STREET, near 7th Avenue, NEW YORK.

September 3, 1859

Of **Henry Hurel**, a native of BALLYMONA, County ANTRIM, Ireland. When last heard from he was in NEW ORLEANS. Any information of him will be thankfully received by his sister, **Teresa Hurel**, by writing to her to No. 100 ELEVENTH STREET, between 1st and 2nd Avenues, NEW YORK.

Of **Mary Menoton**, County GALWAY, Ireland. When last heard from was in the State of MICHIGAN. Information thankfully received by **Thomas McC----**, DIAMOND SPRINGS, EL DORADO County, CALIFORNIA.

Of **Hanorah Murphy**, native of the Parish of EVELEARY, County CORK, Ireland, who came to this country in the year 1856, and landed in New York, and received no account since. Any one knowing of her whereabouts would confer a favor by writing to **Dennis Lency**, her brother, or to her uncle, **Timothy Lency**, of HOOSICK FALLS, N. Y.

Of **Richard Farrent**, from BALLYCLOUGH, County CORK, Ireland. When last heard from was in NEW YORK. Any information respecting him will be thankfully received by his sister, **Ellen Farrent**, No. 288 WEST 16th STREET, NEW YORK. [Appeared Sept. 10, 1859 with the surname **Farrent** changed to **Tarrent**]

September 10, 1859

Of **Denis Casey**, who emigrated with his father and family from CAHIRCIVEEN, County KERRY, Ireland, about nine years ago, and arrived in New York. Any information of any of the family will be thankfully received by **James McCarron**, Hyland Hotel, NEWBURGH, N.Y.

September 17, 1859

Of **Michael Campbell**, of the County MEATH, Ireland who left NEW YORK in May 1858 for INDIANA. When last heard from he was on his way to NEW ORLEANS. Any information of him will be thankfully received by his aunt, **Ann Boyle**, 181 VARICK STREET, NEW YORK. Southern and Western papers please copy.

Of **Thomas Reidy**, of CASTLE ISLAND, County KERRY who left CHARLESTON, SOUTH CAROLINA, over two years ago. Any information of him will be gratefully acknowledged by his uncle, who has something of advantage to communicate to him. Address **John Reidy**, cor. Third and F Street, WASHINGTON, D.C.

Of **William Sullivan**, a native of LISTOWELL, County KERRY, Ireland. When last heard from he was in GALENA, ILLINOIS. Any information of him will be thankfully received by his sister **Catherine Connors** by writing to her to No. 496 WATER STREET, N.Y., in care of **Dan Daly**. Illinois papers please copy.

September 24, 1859

Of **Patrick McCann**, a carpenter by trade, and is supposed to be in NEW YORK. Any information of him will be thankfully received by T.D. at the office of this paper.

Of **Peter Doherty**, a painter by trade, a native of the City of DUBLIN, Ireland. When last heard from he was in CINCINNATI, OHIO. Any information of him will be thankfully received by his brother **William L. Doherty**, Sexton of St. Mary's R.C. Church, Erie Street, JERSEY CITY, N.J.

Of **Michael Walsh**, a native of LIMERICK, Ireland and who kept a leather store in the Town of ENNIS, County CLARE. It is supposed he resides in the EIGHTH AVENUE, NEW YORK. If he will call the office of the Irish American he will hear of something to his advantage.

Of **James Dolan** a native of the Parish of TEMPLEPORT, County CAVAN, Ireland, who arrived in New York in May 1844. Any information of him will be thankfully received by his brother, **Charles Dolan**, by writing to him in care of Lynch & Cole, Irish American Office, 32 Beekman Street, New York. Canada papers please copy.

If this should meet the eye of **Henry Bateman**, Cabinet maker, native of the Town of KILKENNY, Ireland he will hear of something to his advantage by calling on **Mr. Donnellan**, 84 HAMERSLEY STREET, NEW YORK. Chicago and St. Louis papers please copy.

Of **Catherine** and **William Dollan**, natives of County FERMANAGH, Ireland. When last heard of were in LOCKPORT, CONNECTICUT. Any information will be thankfully received by **John McDermott**, No. 96 WEST 19th STREET, N.Y.

October 1, 1859

Of **John** and **Mary Freeman**. Any information of them will be received by their daughter **Annie**, by writing or calling at **Mr. Doty's**, 273 Union Street, BROOKLYN.

Of **James O'Grady**, a native of the City of LIMERICK, Ireland. When last heard from he was in JACKSON, MISSISSIPPI. Any information of his whereabouts will be thankfully received by his brother, **Patrick O'Grady**, No. 68 South 9th Street, WILLIAMSBURGH, Long Island. Jackson and St. Louis papers please copy.

Of **Thomas Smith**, a native of GLENAGONE, Parish of CLOHER, County TYRONE, Ireland, who left Ireland about eight years ago. When last heard from (about four years ago) he was in PHILADELPHIA. Any information concerning him will be thankfully received by his brother, **Charles Smith**, by directing a letter to him to MERIDEN Post Office, CONNECTICUT, in the care of **Mr. Albert Bacon**, WESTFIELD.

Of **Eugene Doody**, of KILLVOOLY, County KERRY, Ireland. He came to NEW YORK about ten years ago, lived in NORWALK, CONN., a short time and when last heard from was in BUFFALO, N.Y. Any information of him may be sent to **Mary Doody** in care of **L. Meeker**, STAMFORD, CONN.

Of **Daniel Collins**, a native of KNOCKGORRUM, Parish of CAHARAGH, County CORK, Ireland, aged 23 years. He sailed from London in May, 1857, in company of his uncle,

Patrick Sullivan and family on the *Devonshire*; landed in New York in June following, remained with said uncle a short time in NEW YORK, and is supposed to have gone to some one of the Western States. Any information respecting his whereabouts (whether dead or alive) will be thankfully received by his friend **Michael O'Neill**, No. 128 LEONARD STREET, NEW YORK. Western papers please copy.

October 8, 1859

Of **Denis McIvers**, a native of CLAREMORRIS, County MAYO, Ireland, who left BROOKLYN for NEW ORLEANS on the 15th of November 1858. Any information of him will be thankfully received by his cousin **Peter Delany**, who lives in 181 LUDLOW STREET, NEW YORK. New Orleans papers please copy.

Of **Bernard McDonough**, of the Town of LONGFORD, Ireland by his distressed mother, **Mrs. Snowden**, at 154 FIRST AVENUE, NEW YORK. Chicago, St. Louis, and New Orleans papers please copy.

Of **Henry Burns**, of TURLOGH, Parish of RAHARA, County ROSCOMMON, Ireland. When last heard from he was in BALTIMORE, MD. Any information of him will be thankfully received by his nephew, **Thomas Connor**, by writing to No. 500 WEST STREET, NEW YORK.

Of **Patrick Quinn**, musician, native of the City of DUBLIN, Ireland, formerly of the 79th Highland Regiment in the British Army, who went as a musician to the U.S. Army in May, 1855 and left in July, 1857, for FORT DALLES, OREGON. Any information will be thankfully received by his widowed sister, **Margaret Fondan**, at 204 Jay Street, BROOKLYN, L.I., State of NEW YORK. Oregon and California papers please copy. [Appeared Oct. 15, 1859 with the surname **Fondan** changed to **Jordan**.]

Of **James Scallan**, a native of FEDDENS, County FERMANAGH, Ireland, who left NEW YORK in 1849 for the West. Any information of him will be thankfully received by his sister, **Susan Scallan**, by writing to her to CARMANSVILLE, Post Office, NEW YORK. Western papers please copy.

October 15, 1859

Of **Robert Shay**, boiler maker, who left home in 1857 for WISCONSIN. Any information of him will be thankfully received by his wife, **Mary Shay**, residing at 335 WEST 26th STREET, NEW YORK. Western papers please copy.

Of **Richard** and **Alice Hern**, natives of URLINGFORD, County KILKENNY, Ireland. Any information concerning them will be thankfully received by their brother, **Edmond**, at **Michael McBride's**, No. 13 FORSYTH STREET, NEW YORK. Cincinnati papers please copy.

Of **Julia** and **Margaret Balf**, natives of the Parish of OLD CASTLE, County MEATH, Ireland. Julia arrived in New York about 30 years ago, and when last heard from was in MICHIGAN. Margaret arrived about 14 years ago and when last heard from was living in BOSTON. Any information of them will be thankfully received by their brother, **Michael Balf**, by writing to him in care of **Mr. Noonan**, No. 145 South 1st Street, WILLIAMSBURGH, L.I.

October 22, 1859

Of **Thomas** and **John Farrell**, natives of BALLYNOLAN, Parish of WHITE FORGE, County LIMERICK, Ireland. When last heard from they were in NEW YORK. Any information of them will be thankfully received by addressing **John Farrell**, INDIANAPOLIS, INDIANA.

October 29, 1859

Of **John Doyle**, a native of the Parish of KILCORNEY, County CORK, Ireland. When last heard from he was in MILLTOWN, NORTHUMBERLAND County, PENNSYLVANIA. It is supposed he now resides in some of the Western States. Any information of him will be thankfully received by his brother, **David Doyle**, or his cousin, **Mike Sullivan**, by writing to them to 251 WEST 30th ST., NEW YORK.

November 5, 1859

Of **Patrick Lyons**, who left MONTREAL for NEW YORK, about nine years ago, and has not since been heard of. Any information of his whereabouts will be thankfully received by his sister, **Eliza Lyons**, at this office.

Of **Peter Luddy**, 15 years of age, a native of the Parish of BALLYLANDERS, County LIMERICK, Ireland, who arrived in New York last April, in the steamer *Pacific*, from Galway. Any information of him will be thankfully received by his father, **Peter Luddy**, SAVANNAH, GA.

Of **Michael** and **William Murphy**, butchers, brothers of **James Murphy**, THOMASTOWN, County KILKENNY, Ireland. Any information of him will be thankfully received by **Patrick Barrett**, 37 FRANKFORT STREET, NEW YORK. Philadelphia and country papers please copy.

November 12, 1859

Of **Ellen Ryan**, who embarked from the County CLARE, and landed in New York on the 24th of last August. She came out in the ship *Dreadnought*. Any information respecting her will be gladly received by her sister **Mary Ryan** at **Miss Alice McCudden's**, 54 Queen Street, TORONTO, CANADA.

Of **Thomas Molony**, a native of the Parish of CARABANE, County of CLARE, Ireland, who landed in this country in December 1854. Any information respecting him will be thankfully received by his brother **Daniel**, No. 74 WEST STREET, NEW YORK CITY.

Of **Michael Tucker**, of SLIGO, who left NEW YORK in June, 1857 for CHICAGO, ILL. Any information of him will be thankfully received by his brother **James Tucker**, who is now in NEW YORK. Address in care of **John Tucker** & Bro., 22 ANN STREET, NEW YORK. Country papers please copy.

Of **John Doyle**, a native of MOHILL, County of LEITRIM, Ireland. Any information of him will be thankfully received by his sister **Mary**, at 161 Clinton Street, BROOKLYN, L.I.

Of **John Riley**, who left BELFAST, Ireland, in May 1851, in the ship *Hercules*. When last heard from was in BALTIMORE bound to the painting and glazing trade. Information of him will be thankfully received by his mother **Ann Riley**, 55 ½ MULBERRY STREET, NEW YORK. Baltimore papers please copy. [Appeared under County ANTRIM]

November 19, 1859

Of **Johana Delehanty**, from the Parish of KILMURRY, KING'S County, Ireland, who left NEW YORK in 1853 for CINCINNATI, and is supposed to be in KEOKUK, IOWA. Any information concerning her will be thankfully received by her sister, **Maria Craven**, by addressing a note to her, at NORTH SHORE, STATEN ISLAND, NEW YORK. Keokuk and country papers please copy.

Of **Thomas Harris**, shoemaker, a native of the Parish of EDENDERRY, KING'S County, Ireland. Who emigrated to this country about twenty years ago. When last heard from was living either in BROOKLYN or NEW YORK. Any information of him will be thankfully received by **James McCauley**, by writing or calling at No. 118 ½ AMITY STREET, NEW YORK.

Of **Michael McPartlen**, from the Parish of INNIS MCGRATH, County LEITRIM, Ireland. It is supposed he resides in some part of VIRGINIA. Any information of him will be thankfully received by his brother **Miles McPartlen**, by writing to him to No. 47 Willow Street, BROOKLYN, NEW YORK.

Of **Michael Green**, a native of the Parish of CRAUGHWELL, County GALWAY, Ireland. When last heard from he was in NEW YORK CITY. Any information of him will be thankfully received by his brother, **Denis Green**, by writing to him, in care of **Henry Shelton**, Esq., BRIDGEPORT, CONN.

Of **John** and **Michael Galligan**, from LIMERICK, Ireland. Michael when last heard from, was in VIRGINIA, in Dec., 1858; John is supposed to be in ST. LOUIS, MO. Any information of them will be thankfully received by their wife and mother, **Johanna Galligan**, at Castle Garden, New York.

November 26, 1859

Of **Hanorah Sullivan**, a native of RILAH, Parish of TUSSIST, County KERRY, Ireland, who was left with her aunt's husband, **William Palmer**, on the Central R.R. in NEW JERSEY, on their way to SAVANNAH, GA. When last heard from they were in TENNESSEE. Any information of her will be thankfully received by her mother, **Mary Sullivan**, ELIZABETHPORT, N.J.

Of **Mary Sweeny**, a native of the Parish of ODORNEY, County KERRY, Ireland. She left Liverpool about 6 years ago, and landed in New York. When last heard from she was living in YORKVILLE, NEW YORK. Any information of her will be thankfully received by her sister **Catherine Sweeny**, by writing to her in care of **James McElligott**, MILWAUKEE, WISCONSIN.

Of **John Condon**, a native of BALLINAMONA, Parish of MITCHELSTOWN, County CORK, Ireland, who emigrated to this country nine years ago. When last heard from (6 years ago), was in the State of KENTUCKY. Any information of him will be thankfully received by his sister **Mary Condon**, by writing to **William Turner**, 40 WEST BROADWAY, NEW YORK.

December 3, 1859

Of **Joseph O'Connel**. When last heard from was living with **Samuel C. Kayes**, EMINENCE, LOGAN County, ILLINOIS, up to the latter part of April last. Any information of him will be thankfully received by his father, **Joseph O'Connell** 22 JAMES STREET, NEW YORK CITY, or **Patrick Perry**, 22 JAMES STREET. Illinois papers please copy.

Of **James Mahon**, a native of CASTLETOWNDELVIN, County WESTMEATH, Ireland, who came to this country twenty-three years ago. Any information of him will be thankfully received by his sister **Bridget Mahon**, who now resides at 119 LAURENS STREET, NEW YORK.

Of **Thomas Merry**, a native of the County ARMAGH, Ireland. When last heard from on year ago, he was in CANADA WEST. Any information of him will be thankfully received by his sister **Mary** by writing to her in the care of **James Devine**, No. 111 WEST 21st STREET, NEW YORK, near 7th Avenue. Canada papers please copy.

Of **Susan McCabe**, a native of BILLBERRY, ARDLOGHER, County CAVAN, Ireland. Any information of her will be thankfully received by her sister, **Bridget** by writing to her in care of **Patrick Glan[b]y**, 105 BROOME STREET, NEW YORK. Albany papers please copy.

Of **Michael** and **James McMorrow**, natives of the City of SLIGO, Ireland, who lived with **Mr. Quail**, in Bruckle Street, KINGSTON, CANADA. Any information of them will be thankfully received by their sisters, **Ann** and **Bridget**, by writing to them in care of **Thomas Stanford**, No. 58 WHITEHALL STREET, NEW YORK. Canada papers please copy.

Joana Quan, a native of the County of LIMERICK, Ireland. When last seen was in NEW YORK, about seven years ago, and about that time went to WATERBURY, CONN. Any information of her will be thankfully received by her sister, **Ellen Quann**, at **Michael Walsh's**, No. 3 CATHERINE SLIP, NEW YORK. Connecticut papers please copy.

Of **Mary Cally**, a native of RYE-HILL, Parish of ABBEY, County GALWAY, Ireland, who left Liverpool on the 7th of last June, in the ship *Agnes*, for Boston. Any information of her will be thankfully received by her uncle, **Patrick Devany**, by addressing a note to Bay View Post-office, CLIFTON, STATEN ISLAND, State of NEW YORK. Boston papers please copy.

December 10, 1859

Of **Mayanne Doherty**, from WATERSIDE, LONDONDERRY; 11 years in America. When last heard from was with **Mrs. Crowly**. Her address was care of **Mr. Mahon**, 17 CHESTNUT STREET or 31 JAMES STREET, NEW YORK. Any information respecting her will be thankfully received by her sister **Catherine** and **Susan Doherty**, 6 STAPLE STREET, NEW YORK.

Of **John Hunt**, of CLOONSHRAAN, County ROSCOMMON, Ireland. When last heard from was living in NEWGARDEN, WAYNE County, State of INDIANA. Any information of him, living or dead, will be thankfully received by his brother, **William Hunt** address, **William Binkerman**, BRIDGEPORT, CONN. Western papers please copy.

Of **Martin** and **William Casey**, of TURYANBREEN, County TIPPERARY, Ireland (laborers), who came to New York in 1858; boarded same Summer with **James Toole**, 18th Street, SOUTH BROOKLYN; they left there and worked with a farmer in FLATLANDS for some time; they afterwards left as is supposed, to go out West. Any information of them will be thankfully received by their sister **Mary Casey**, care of **George Riggs**, 25 PARK ROW, NEW YORK. Western papers please copy.

Of **Arthur** and **Hugh Mahon**, from CALLAN, County TYRONE, Ireland. When last heard of they were residing in NEW YORK. Address **Mary Mahon** (their sister), 731 Sampson Street, PHILADELPHIA.

December 17, 1859

Of **William Cotter**, who emigrated from FRANCE to this country about eight years ago, and when last heard of was at HICKMAN'S FERRY, N.Y., and is supposed to have gone to BOSTON about six years ago. Any information of him will be thankfully received by his daughter, **Jane Walsh**, Columbia Street, corner of Mill Street, BROOKLYN, N.Y. [Appeared Dec. 24, 1959 with the surname **Cotter** changed to **Coulter**.]

Of **Eliza** and **Hanah O'Connor**, daughters of **Edmond** and **Mary O'Connor**, natives of ASHVALE, MOG[ILIE], County CLARE, Ireland. They left Ireland about 10 years ago, and when last heard from they were in NEW YORK CITY. Any information of them will be thankfully received by their sister, **Kate O'Connor**, NORWICH, CONN., at the office of the Irish American.

Of **Michael** and **Humphrey Lynch**, natives of the Parish of CROMONAN, KENMARE, County KERRY, Ireland. When last heard from, were in the State of NEW YORK. Any information of them will be thankfully received by their brother **John Lynch**, who lately arrived and who is most anxious to hear from them, as he has no friends in New York. Address in care of Lynch & Cole, 32 Beekman Street, New York.

Of **Catherine Conroy**, a native of WOODFORD, County GALWAY, Ireland. When last heard from she was in NEW ORLEANS. Any information of her will be thankfully received by her mother and sister, by writing to them to No. 254 14th STREET, NEW YORK. New Orleans Catholic Standard, please copy.

December 24, 1859

Of **John McCarthy**, who left NEW YORK in August, 1858, for CINCINNATI. It was reported he was lost on his way to NEW ORLEANS, on the 2nd of Nov., 1858. It is now said he is in ST. LOUIS. Any information of him will be thankfully received by his sisters. Please direct to **James McCarthy**, Painter, No. 208 EAST 19th STREET, NEW YORK. Boston Pilot and Western papers please copy.

Of **William McKim**, a native of the Town of SLIGO, Ireland, who left Ireland about fifteen years ago. When last heard from he was in LOUISVILLE, Ky. Any information of him will be thankfully received by his brother **Philip McKim** by writing to him to KATORAH, WESTCHESTER County, N. Y. Louisville papers please copy.

Of **Michael Kenery**, Parish of KILBALLYOWEN, County CLARE, Ireland. When last heard from was in BINGHAMTON, N.Y. Any information of him will be thankfully received by his children, **John** and **Margaret**. Direct to **E. Geraghty**, HANCOCK, DELAWARE County, N.Y.

Of **Sylvester Mooney**, who left NEW YORK in August 18[5]8. He is a native of the Parish of EAST ANNAMULLEN, County MONAGHAN, Ireland. Any information respecting him will be thankfully received by his mother, **Elizabeth Mooney**, Direct to **Felix Boylen**, 474 THIRD AVENUE.

Of **Edward Day**, a native of CASTLEGREGORY, County KERRY, Ireland. When last heard from he lived in LEESBURG, OHIO. Any information of him will be thankfully received by his brother, **James Day**, Van Buren St. corner of Bedford Avenue, BROOKLYN.

Of **Patrick**, **John** and **Bridget Kelly**, natives of BALLYGLASS, Parish of RAHARA, County ROSCOMMON, Ireland, who arrived in New York about sixteen years ago. When last heard from they were in PITTSBURGH, PA. Any information of them will be thankfully received by their brother or sister, **James** and **Mary Kelly**, by writing to them at 157 FERRY STREET, N.Y.

December 31, 1859

Of **Patrick Cotter**, son of **Michael Cotter**, from the Parish of CONNY, County CORK, Ireland; he sailed from Waterford seven years ago. When last heard from, five years ago, he was in CINCINNATI, OHIO. Any information of him will be thankfully received by his father and his brother, **James Cotter**, WASSAIC, DUTCHESS County, State of NEW YORK.

Of **Thomas Geraghty**, a native of the Town of SLIGO, Ireland, cooper by trade. When last heard from he was in LOUISVILLE, KENTUCKY, 3 years ago. Any information of him will be thankfully received by his cousin, **Bessy Tuohey**, by writing to her in care of **Mr. John N. Robbinson**, WILMINGTON, DEL. Louisville papers please copy.

Of **Hannah O'Connor**, daughter of **Edmund** and **Mary O'Connor**; and of **James Butler**, tailor, a native of TUBBER, County CLARE. Hannah O'Connor is a native of ASHVALE, MOGOLIE, County CLARE, Ireland: They left Ireland about eleven years ago, and when last heard from they were in NEW YORK (which was last Summer). Any information of them will be thankfully received by **Kate O'Connor**, NORWICH, CONN, who has lately arrived, and is anxious to hear from them, as she has no friends here. Address to **John McCloud**, NORWICH, CONN.

[No ads from 1860 available.]

January 5, 1861

Of **Patrick Brophy**, a native of the County KILKENNY, Parish of CALLAN, Ireland; who arrived in New York, November, 1856, and went to his son-in-law, **James Rice**, in the neighborhood of ALBANY or TROY. Any information respecting him will be thankfully received by his son, **Patrick Brophy**, by addressing a few lines to **Edward Brennan**, 33 FORSYTH STREET, NEW YORK. Albany or Troy papers please copy.

Of **Johanna Donoghue**, a native of the Parish of SCREEN, County WEXFORD, Ireland. When last heard from she arrived in New York at Castle Garden, on the 6th of last July. Any information of her will be thankfully received by **Peter Connors**, by writing to him in care of **Mr. Thomas Maguire**, GREAT NECK, QUEENS CO., L.I., MANHASSETT Post-office.

Of **Patrick Conlen**, of MULLAGHBY, Parish of BALLINTEMPLE, Co. CAVAN, Ireland. When last heard of he was working on a railroad, forty miles from BEAUMONT, JEFFERSON CO., TEXAS. If he should see this advertisement by addressing a few lines to **John Delaney**, 59 SHERIFF ST., NEW YORK, he will hear something to his advantage. There are three letters for him in Beaumont Post-office. Texas papers please copy.

Of **Hugh McLaughlin**, a native of ST. JOHNSTON, County DONEGAL, Ireland. Any information of him will be thankfully received by his cousin, **Thomas McLaughlin**, in care of **Mrs. Mary Reiley**, Grant St., SOUTH TRENTON, N.J.

Of **Patt**, **John**, **Nancy** and **Mary O'Brien**, natives of BREAKNAY, Parish of KILFILE, County MAYO, Ireland. When last heard from, John, Nancy and Mary were in some part of ILLINOIS. Patt was in QUEBEC. Any information of them will be thankfully received by their sister **Catherine O'Brien**, by writing to her in the care of **Captain A. C. Lyon**, TOTTERSVILLE, STATEN ISLAND, N.Y.

Of **Margaret Kelly**, also her son and Daughter, **Thomas** and **Bella Kelly**, natives of POMEROY, County TYRONE, Ireland, who sailed from Belfast for Quebec, in 1837. When last heard from they were in TORONTO, CANADA. Any information respecting them will be thankfully received by **James Kelly**, No. 91 WEST 46th STREET, NEW YORK. Toronto papers please copy.

Of **Patrick Gormly**, who came to this country about twelve years ago, and a native of CASTLEREA, County OF ROSCOMMON, Ireland. Any information of him will be thankfully received by **Mrs. Carroll**, 189 FIRST AVENUE, NEW YORK. When last heard from he was in LOWELL. Boston, Lowell and Providence papers, please copy.

Of **Owen**, **Michael**, **Mary** or **Bridget Bruen**, natives of the County of ROSCOMMON, within four miles of STROKESTOWN, Ireland. They came to America about nine or ten years ago. They are supposed to be in the State of MARYLAND. Any information [?] of the Parish of KILLGLASS, County ROSCOMMON.

Of **Patrick Bracken**, blacksmith a native of the Parish of KILGLASS, County ROSCOMMON, Ireland. Who sailed from Liverpool about the middle of October last, on board the ship *James Foster*, bound for New York, from which time no account has been heard of him. Information of him is earnestly solicited by his Sister-in-law, **Winefred Gannon**, No. 304 17th Street, above Vine, PHILADELPHIA.

Of **Patrick Glinnan**, from MOUNT PLUNKET, County of ROSCOMMON, Ireland, who arrived in New York, on or about the 28th of October last. Direct to **Patrick Kelly**, PHILIPSVILLE, ALLEGHANY County, N.Y.

January 12, 1861

Of **John Murray**, who left PHILADELPHIA, PENN., about a year ago for CHARLESTOWN, S.C. Any information of his whereabouts will be thankfully received by his brother, **Thomas Murray**, at 1447 North Tenth St., PHILADELPHIA, PENN.

Of **John Tierney**, a native of the Parish of BARNA, KING'S County, Ireland. When last heard from he was in NEW YORK, and is supposed to have gone to ST. LOUIS, MO. Any information of him will be thankfully received by his brother **Roger Tierney**, by writing to him to BABYLON, L.I. or **Mrs. Maher**, No. 577 PITT STREET, NEW YORK.

Of **James** and **George Henry**, of the County FERMANAGH, Townland of DUNANNY, Ireland. When last heard from seven years ago, they were in NEW YORK CITY. If this should meet their eye, they will hear of something to their benefit by addressing their sister, **Sarah Henry**, TOM'S RIVER, N.J.

January 19, 1861

Of **John**, **Patrick** and **Bridget Hanly**, who emigrated from County LIMERICK, Ireland. When last heard from was in ST. CHARLES County, State of MISSOURI. Any information of them will be thankfully received by their brother **Thomas Hanly**, or by **John Lynch**, 32 SCAMMELL STREET, NEW YORK CITY. Missouri papers please copy.

If this should meet the eye of **Sarah** or **Eliza McHugh** (supposed to be living in NEW ORLEANS), daughter of the late **Bernard McHugh**, who emigrated from the Parish of DUNMORE, County GALWAY, Ireland, to the United States in 1838, settled in New Orleans and died about the year 1846, they will please send their address to **Mrs. Elizabeth McHugh**, RALLAGH, DUNMORE, County GALWAY, Ireland, and they will hear something to their advantage. New Orleans papers please copy.

January 26, 1861

Of **Edward Duffy** and **Eliza Love**, natives of Ireland, who left Ireland, for America, in June last. Any information of them will be thankfully received by addressing G. R., Box 1460, P.O., NEW YORK, or **Mrs. Duffy**, mother of Edward, LANCHA PLANA, CALIFORNIA.

Of **James** and **Ellen Campion**, of KILKENNY, Ireland. When last heard from were residing near JOLLIET, ILLINOIS. Any person knowing their present residence will confer a favor by writing to **Anthony Campion**, No. 241 Hudson Avenue, BROOKLYN, N.Y., in care of **Michael Mulhall**. Illinois papers, please copy.

Of **Michael** and **Patrick Gafney**, natives of LOUTH, Ireland. When last heard from (about 18 months ago) were in MOBILE, ALA. Any intelligence of their present whereabouts will be thankfully received by their mother, **Mrs. Bridget Gafney**, by addressing to the care of **Patrick Cummings**, corner of 45th ST. and 1st AVENUE, NEW YORK.

Of **Daniel K** and **John O'Neil**, natives of DRUMMOD MORAN, Parish of KILTUBRIDE, County LEITRIM, Ireland. When last heard from Daniel was in BUFFALO and John in SYRACUSE, N.Y. Should this come under the observation of either of the above mentioned, they will learn of something to their advantage by addressing their friend **Anthony McKiernan**, No. 7 WOOSTER STREET, NEW YORK CITY.

Of **John Connor**, and **Elizabeth**, his sister, natives of FORTHLAND, Parish of EASKEY, County SLIGO, Ireland. John came to this country about four years ago, and Elizabeth a year ago last June. When last heard from John lived in No. 135 AVENUE C, between 8th and 9th Streets and Elizabeth lived with a **Mr. Smith** No. 113 7th STREET, N.Y. Any information of them will be thankfully received by their sister, **Bridget** and her husband, by writing to **John Carden**, KENOSHA, WISCONSIN.

February 2, 1861

Of **Mary Eccles**, of COAL ISLAND, County TYRONE, Ireland, wife of **William Corrigan**, of the County of ARMAGH. When last heard from lived in JOHN STREET, NEW YORK. Any information of her will be thankfully received by her sister **Sarah Eccles** by addressing a letter to her at No. 816 Market Street, PHILADELPHIA.

Of **Thomas**, **Michael**, and **Bridget Cryne**, all natives of KILCOOLY, Parish of KILCROAN, County GALWAY, Ireland. When last heard from they were in MIDDLETOWN POINT, NEW JERSEY. Any information of them will be thankfully received by writing to their sister, **Mary Cryne**, in care of **John Brennan**, NORTH ORANGE, N.J. New Jersey papers please copy.

February 9, 1861

$20 Reward. Information wanted of **Lawrence** and **Hugh McShane**, who left home on Saturday night, January 26th. Age of Hugh 10 years and Lawrence, 13 years. Lawrence had red rings on his ears, a round jacket and grey pants, and a southwestern hat on. Hugh had a blue cloth sack and brown pants and a light colored cap. Address **Hugh McShane**, MORRISANIA post office, WESTCHESTER County, N.Y. Boston and Western papers please copy.

Of **Patrick Campbell**, who emigrated from the Zoological Gardens, LIVERPOOL, in October, 1854. When last heard from, about three years ago, he was near NATCHEZ, ADAMS Co., MISSISSIPPI. Any information of him will be thankfully received by his mother, **Mary Campbell**, who came to this country four months ago, or his uncle, **John Rogan**. Address, in care **Mr. R. Smith** for Mary Campbell or John Rogan, AUBURN, MASS. Mississippi papers please copy.

Of **Mary Supples**, who left the Parish of MINO, SCARIFF, Ireland, in September 1848. When last heard from was in KNOXVILLE, CONNECTICUT, married to one **Thomas Blake**. Any information thankfully received by her brother, **John Supples**, Company K, 2nd Cavalry, CAMPWOOD, TEXAS. [Appeared under County CLARE]

February 16, 1861

Of **Charles** and **John Mooney** (dead or alive), sons of **Charles Mooney**, 155 Garngad road, GLASGOW, SCOTLAND. There last letter was dated September 18, 1855, and their address at that time was Western Post-office, LEWIS Co., VIRGINIA. Address to **Miss Sarah McMullen**, 38 Ferry St., FALL RIVER, MASS. Virginia papers please copy.

Of **Mary**, **Bridget**, or **Margaret McDermott**, natives of the County ROSCOMMON, Ireland. Any information of them will be thankfully received by **Patrick McGrath**, Saloon, No. 216 BROADWAY, NEW YORK, who has a letter from their brother **Peter** for them.

Of **Connor Roe**, who left the County MEATH, Ireland, August 1851, and sailed for New York. When last heard from was in LONG ISLAND, N.Y. Any information of him will be thankfully received by his brother **Michael Roe**, No. 128 Marshall Street, PATERSON, N.J., or to **B. O'Neil**, Justice of the Peace, 81 Congress St., PATERSON, PASSAIC CO., N.J.

February 23, 1861

Of **Mary Falvey**, or **Mrs. Mara**, a native of KILARNEY, County KERRY, Ireland, who left England about 23 years ago. When last heard from was in NEW ALBANY HILL. Any information of her will be thankfully received by her sister, **Mrs. Donohue**, 18 CHERRY STREET, NEW YORK.

Of **Daniel** and **Timothy Foley**, natives of KENMARE, County KERRY, Ireland, who came to this country in 1851; when last heard of they were in CHICAGO. Any information of them will be thankfully received by their brother, **James Foley**, No. 31 BAXTER STREET, NEW YORK. Chicago and St. Louis papers please copy.

Of **Margaret O'Brien**, a native of KILDYSART, County CLARE, Ireland, married to **Simon Fairchild**. When last heard from was in YIPSILANTY, MICHIGAN, said to be going West. Her mother, who lives here in CLYDE, would be glad to hear from her. Direct to **D. E. Flynn**, CLYDE, WAYNE County, NEW YORK.

Of **John Mack**, a native of the Parish of FEAKLE, County CLARE, Ireland. When last heard from was in WASHINGTON, D.C. Should this reach him, he is requested to come immediate to his brother, **Patrick Mack**, NEW BRITAIN, CONNECTICUT.

Of **James Grenen**, native of KING'S County, Ireland. When last heard from he was in MOUNT MORRIS, LIVINGSTON County, State of NEW YORK. He will hear of something to his advantage by addressing a few lines to **James Marshal**, No. 11 JACOB STREET, NEW YORK

Of **Mary Hughes**, daughter of **Patrick** of CASTLENODE, STROKESTOWN, County ROSCOMMON, Ireland. She was married in ENGLAND, to a shoemaker, named **Patrick Ryan**, and came to this country about 13 years ago. When last heard from, about five years ago, she was living in EAST 18th STREET, in this City. Any information of her or her family will be thankfully received by her sister **Bridget Hughes**, 145 WEST 35th STREET, NEW YORK.

March 2, 1861

Of **John** and **Brine Brady**, of SALAKEN, Parish of SCRABBY, County CAVAN, Ireland. When last heard from John was in Algiers at NEW ORLEANS. Any information of them will be thankfully received by their brother, **James Brady**, at No. 171 EAST 32nd ST., NEW YORK CITY. New Orleans papers please copy.

Of **Kate O'Brien**, whose maiden name was **Kate Rooney**, a native of South King Street, DUBLIN, Ireland. In 1848 she was married to **Edward O'Brien**, a tailor. When last heard from she lived in LONDON, ENGLAND. Any information in regard to her will be thankfully received by her brother, **John Rooney**, No. 161 LAURENS STREET, NEW YORK.

Of **Martin Gibbon**, of the Parish of BOYLE, County ROSCOMMON, Ireland. When last heard from, was in LACHINE, CANADA. Any information respecting him will be thankfully received at No. 626 Shippen Street, PHILADELPHIA, by his brother-in-law, **Bernard Lynch**. [Appeared March 9, 1861 with the surname **Gibbon** changed to **Giblin**.]

March 9, 1861

Of **Henry Nolan**, who lived in 1856, in 107 GREENWICH STREET, NEW YORK, and was a member of the Society of Longshoremen of NEW YORK. Any information concerning him will be thankfully received by his niece, **Mrs. Maria Wilson**, MONTEZUMA, FLATT TUOLUMNE County, CALIFORNIA.

Of **Johannah McGuire** and **Mary Rourke**, of the Parish of BRUFF, County LIMERICK, Ireland. When last heard from, Johannah was residing in WARSAW County, NEW YORK, and the other was in NEW ORLEANS. Any information of them will be thankfully received by their sisters, **Catherine** and **Bridget Rourke**, or **Thomas Green**, LYNN MASSACHUSETTS.

Of **Elizabeth Gaffeny**, alias **McCabe**, and her daughter, **Margaret Gaffeny**, the former of the Parish of BALLINACRE, County of MEATH, Ireland, who came to this country twice: the last time was in 1845, and were then supposed to be living in the DISTRICT OF COLUMBIA, or in COLUMBUS, OHIO. Any information respecting them will be gladly and thankfully received by their daughter, or sister **Elizabeth Gaffeny**, by directing in care of **John Burke**, carpenter, NEW BRIGHTON, STATEN ISLAND. Washington, and Columbus, Ohio, papers please copy.

Of **Hugh** and **John Mulreeny**, natives of ENVER, County DONEGAL, Ireland. When last heard from Hugh was in LANCASTER, PENN. John was in ILLINOIS. Any information concerning them will be thankfully received by their brother, **George Mulreeny**, by writing to him in care of **Henry McGill**, GLEN COVE, Long Island.

Of **John Gleeson**, a native of FANLAUGH, Parish of NENAGH, County TIPPERARY, Ireland. When last heard from he was at LOCKPORT, WILLIS County, INDIANA. Any information of him will be thankfully received by his brother **Patrick**, by writing to him in care of **Edward Gleeson**, 135 WEST 28th STREET, NEW YORK.

Of **Thomas Brogan**, a native of the Town of ROSCOMMON, County ROSCOMMON, Ireland. When last heard from was in MILFORD, PENNSYLVANIA. Any information of him will be thankfully received by his sister, **Mrs. Rourke**, 77 ALLEN STREET, NEW YORK.

March 16, 1861

Of **John Tracy**, by his sister **Mrs. Daniel Coughlan**, a native of the Parish of DENENKERK, County GALWAY, Ireland. Any information of him will be gladly received by his sister, Mrs. Daniel Coughlan. Address 234 WEST STREET, cor. of Beach, NEW YORK.

Of **Thomas** and **John Cloney**, of the Parish of DONAMAGGIN, County KILKENNY, Ireland. When last heard of were in ST. LOUIS. Any information of them will be thankfully received by their sister, **Mary**, who lately landed. Direct to **Mr. Cummingham**, No. 267 EAST 12th STREET, NEW YORK, for Mary Cloney. St. Louis papers please copy.

Of **Martin Duggan**, a native of the County CORK, Ireland. When last heard from he was in NEW YORK, with **James Gare**. Any information of him will be thankfully received by his sister, **Kate Duggan**, by writing to her in care of Lynch & Cole, 32 Beekman St., New York.

Of **Honora McCarthy**, whose maiden name was **Honora Murphy**, a native of ROCK HILL, County CORK, Ireland; who married a man by the name of **Thomas McCarthy**, She came to this country about 9 years ago. Any information of them will be thankfully received by her niece, **Kate Duggan**, daughter of **Patt Duggan**, of the County CORK, Ireland, at the office of this paper.

March 23, 1861

Of **Edward Philip** and **Peter Clarke**. When last heard from Edward was in MONTREAL, and Philip was in the Southern States. Any information of their present whereabouts will be thankfully received by their brother, **Arthur Clarke**, 129 GOEREK STREET

[GOERCK ST.], NEW YORK, of whom they will hear something to their advantage. Montreal papers please copy.

Of **Mrs. Hayes** (formerly **Johannah Moloney**), **Michael Moloney** (Smith), **Patt Maloney** and **John Maloney**, from BOHERBUOY, LIMERICK. Any information of them will be thankfully received by their sister, **Ellen Moloney**, GREENFIELD, Long Island, care of **Patrick Guarin**. She is there at present.

March 30, 1861

Of **Martin Murphy**, a native of ATHENRY, County GALWAY, Ireland. When last heard from was in PHILADELPHIA, PA. Any information of him will be thankfully received by his brother **John Murphy**, by writing to him at No. 195 EAST TWELFTH STREET, NEW YORK.

Of **Edward** and **John Quinn**, natives of CARIGEENSHINAE, Parish of GLENDALOUGH, County WICKLOW, Ireland. When last heard from were in ROCHESTER, MONROE County, N.Y. Any information of them will be thankfully received by their nephew, **Michael Quinn**, by writing to him in care of **Mr. Edward Byrnes**, 19 WASHINGTON STREET, N.Y.

Of **Mary Anne Fennelly**, a native of the City of KILKENNY, Ireland, who left Ireland for BOSTON about nine years ago, and left Boston for NEW YORK in 1857, to go West. Any information will be thankfully received by her brother, **John Fennelly** by writing to him to No. 81 HENRY STREET, NEW YORK.

Of **Thomas White**, a native of BIRR, KING'S Co., Ireland. When last heard from, last July, was in NEW YORK. It is supposed he now resides in POUGHKEEPSIE, N.Y. Any information of him will be thankfully received by his sister, **Jane White**, 266 WEST HOUSTON ST., NEW YORK.

Of **Frank Higgins**, a native of ABBEYLEIX, QUEEN'S Co., Ireland. When last heard from he was working at CASCADE BRIDGE, PENN., on the Erie R.R., in May, 1859. Any information of him will be thankfully received by his sister, **Ann Higgins**, by writing to her in care of **Mrs. Brogan**, NORTH EVANS, ERIE Co., N.Y.

Of **Thomas** and **James Liston**, of BALLYLIN, Parish of COOLCAPPA, County LIMERICK, Ireland. When last heard from, about three years ago, they were in CINCINNATI, OHIO. Any information of them will be thankfully received by their sister, **Mrs. Mary Hanrahan**. Address **J. Connolly**, Box 211 WASHINGTON CITY, D.C. Cincinnati papers please copy.

April 6, 1861

Richard Dunphy, aged 14, recently arrived whose father, **Patrick**, and mother, **Judith Downey**, reside at CRUTT, County KILKENNY, near BALINAKILG Parish of QUEEN'S County, Ireland, wishes to find his uncle, **John**, or aunt **Eliza Dunphy**. Apply at the office of the Irish Emigrant Society, 51 Chanbers Street.

Of **James Morrisey**, by his daughter **Mary**. He came from GOWRAN, County KILKENNY, Ireland, about four years. When last heard of was working in a stone quarry, near RONDOUT, ULSTER County, State of NEW YORK. Address **William R. Lait**, painter, 120 Atlantic Street, SOUTH BROOKLYN.

Of **Maria Walsh**, late of GOREN, County KILKENNY, Ireland. Who emigrated to America in August, 1852. Any information of her will be thankfully received by **Michael T. Reddings**, SQUAN VILLAGE, NEW JERSEY, who has a communication for her from her sister **Bridget** in AUSTRALIA.

Of **John** and **Michael Hart**, natives of the Parish of DRUMCLIFF, County SLIGO, Ireland. When last heard from was in LOUISVILLE, KY. Any information of them will be thankfully received by their brother, **Patrick Hart**, by writing to him to No. 79 MULBERRY ST., NEW YORK.

Of **Mary McManus**, a native of CRUMMY, Parish of KILTUBRIDE, County of LEITRIM, Ireland. When last heard from she was in Castle Garden. Any information of her will be thankfully received by her cousin **Charles Gratton**; or by sending her address to Charles Gratton; No. 349 1st AVENUE and 21st STREET, in care of **Mr. Thomas Keenan**. New Jersey papers please copy.

Of **Richard Reilly**, a tailor, a native of the Parish of AHAGOUR, Townland of MASSE, County MAYO, Ireland, who sailed from Stockport, England, about five years ago. when last heard from was in FALL RIVER, MASS. Any information of him will be thankfully received by his brother, **Laurence Reilly**, by writing to him to No. 58 Adam Street, BROOKLYN, N.Y., who lately arrived from England, and wishes to hear from him.

April 13, 1861

Of the present residence of **Mary Ferguson**, wife of **John Connelly**, living at SYRACUSE, State of NEW YORK seven years since. The husband died there, leaving a son named **James Connelly**. The grandmother of James is desirous of learning where he and his mother now live. Any information from, or of, Mary Ferguson will be gratefully acknowledged. **Bridget Costello**, a niece of the subscriber, will please let her aunt know her present residence. **Bridget Ferguson**. Direct to the care of **Michael Ferguson**, HOOSICK FALLS, RENSSELAER County, NEW YORK.

Of **William Phelan**, a native of BALLYVERA, Parish of BALLYBACON, County of TIPPERARY, Ireland. When last heard from he was in JACKSONVILLE, MORGAN County, State of ILLINOIS. Any information respecting him will be thankfully received by his brother **Thos. Phelan**, by writing to him in care of **Thomas Wall**, 401 Columbia Street, SOUTH BROOKLYN, NEW YORK.

Of **James Tracy**, also his wife **Anne Gallagher**. When last heard from they were in NOVA SCOTIA. Any information of them will be thankfully received by brothers **Charles** and **John Gallagher**, of the County FERMANAGH, Parish of WHITEHILL, Ireland. Please direct to 96 WEST 24th STREET. St. John's and Nova Scotia papers please copy.

Of **Arthur Riley**, a native of KILLOTER, Parish of ANNA, County CAVAN, near REDHILLS. When last heard from he was working in a shovel factory in MIDDLEBORO', MASSACHUSETTS. Any person knowing of his whereabouts will please write to **Andrew McKee**, No. 50 SPRING STREET, NEW YORK, as his father in the old country is anxious to hear from him.

Of **Edward Finn**, Parish of BALLYDUFF, County WATERFORD, Ireland. When last heard of he was in ALBANY. Any information of him will be thankfully received by his brother, **Patrick**, who landed in New York on the 12th of May, 1860. Address **Wm. Power**, 144 PEARL STREET, NEW YORK.

April 20, 1861

Of **George Lester** and **Michael Sullivan**, natives of the Parish of KILCASKIN, County CORK, Ireland. Any information will be thankfully received by their sister, **Mary Sullivan**, by writing in care of the **Rev. Isaac Orchard**, 17 BEDFORD STREET, NEW YORK. Canada and Western papers, please copy.

Of **John Carroll**, from the Parish of LACKIN, County of MAYO, who came to this country about ten years ago. When last heard from he was in CARBONDALE,

PENNSYLVANIA. Any information will be thankfully received by his sister, **Bridget Carroll**. Address **Mrs. Cronikin**, corner of 61ˢᵗ STREET and 2ⁿᵈ AVENUE. Pennsylvania papers, please copy.

April 27, 1861

Of **Peter Fagan**, who left the Hibernia Gas works, DUBLIN, nine or ten years ago. Any information of him will be thankfully received by **John Reilly**, No. 6 ROSEVELT ST. [Roosevelt Street], N.Y.

Of **Thomas Millet**, a native of the County of TIPPERARY, Ireland. When last heard from in 1852, was in OHIO. Any information of his whereabouts will be thankfully received by his brother **Mathew Millet**, at 77 ROBINSON ST. N.Y. Ohio papers please copy.

Of **Catherine Kerans**, a native of the Parish of KILMOVEE, County MAYO, Ireland. When last heard from was in BROOKLYN, WINDHAM Co., State of CONNECTICUT. Any information concerning her will be thankfully received by her brother, **John Kerans**, No. 186 AVENUE A, NEW YORK.

May 4, 1861

Of **John Hogg**, (goes by the names of **John Hague**) who came to this country 17 or 18 years ago, from the Townland of KILLCOCK, Parish of KILMORE, County ROSCOMMON, Ireland. When last heard from, he was living in AUBURN FOUR CORNERS, CAYUGA County, State of NEW YORK. Any information of him or his sister, **Annie Hogg**, who got married to a shoemaker, (name not known) and who is supposed to be living in the City of NEW YORK, will be thankfully received at **Thomas J. McDonald's** 23 State Street, BROOKLYN, by his daughter, **Mary Hogg**, who landed here last harvest.

Of **Jane Campbell**, who left CAVAN, Ireland, about fourteen years ago. When last heard of, about four years ago, she was in employment in the Protestant Half-Orphan Society, FIFTH AVENUE, NEW YORK, since which time there had been no account from her. If this should meet the eye of any of her cousins, **Mary Farley**, or her sisters, they will please write to her at 311 Union Street, PHILADELPHIA, PA., for **Rose Campbell**, who arrived in America about nine months ago.

May 11, 1861

Of **Bridget Burgess**, who arrived in this City March 28, per ship *Amora*, native of SHEDS of CLONTARF, County DUBLIN, Ireland, and whose father lives in ST. THOMAS' Parish, DUBLIN. Apply to A. Carrigan, Prest. Irish Emigrant Society, 57 Chamber Street, NEW YORK.

Of **Mathew Colwell**, a native of ORISTOWN, County MEATH. Any person who knows of his whereabouts will confer a lasting favor by informing his brother, **William Colwell**, No. 7 South Margin Street, BOSTON, MASS.

May 18, 1861

Of **Ellen Toole**, a native of CLIFTON, STATEN ISLAND, daughter of **Michael Toole**, who left her home on the 27ᵗʰ of April. Any information of her will be thankfully received by her father, Michael Toole, who is most anxious to see or hear from her. Address BAYVIEW Post-office, STATEN ISLAND; or at the office of the Irish-American.

Of **Daniel Reilly**, native of SHEENS, KNUCKAHAPPEL, County KERRY, Ireland. When last heard from was at MIDDLEGRANVILLE, WASHINGTON County, State of NEW YORK. Any information will be thankfully received by writing to his sister **Johanna**, in care of **James Donoghue**, No. 27 OLIVER STREET, NEW YORK. Irish-American papers, please copy.

Of **James Dillon**, a native of ODORNEY, County KERRY, Ireland, who left BALLYROBERT in 1848. When last heard from was in ST. LOUIS, MO. Any information of him will be thankfully received by his first cousin, **John Egan**, who went to LONDON before he left Ireland, by writing to him to RYE Post-office, WESTCHESTER County, NEW YORK.

Of **Patrick Lyons**, son of **Thomas Lyons**, of MONASTER, County WESTMEATH, Ireland. When last heard from was in the neighborhood of ST. LOUIS. Any information respecting him will be thankfully received by his brother **Mallick**, at No. 566 GREENWICH STREET; or, No. 6 COLUMBIA STREET, NEW YORK.

May 25, 1861

Of **John Fahey**, of KILKEESHAN, County CLARE, who came to this country about three years ago, and is supposed to be living in NEW YORK CITY. Any information of his whereabouts will be thankfully received by his sister, **Mary Fahey**, in care, of **Michael Carmody**, No. 161 PERRY STREET, NEW YORK.

Of **Martin Farrell**, from TOUR. Co. ROSCOMMON, Ireland. When last heard from (about two months since) he was residing in the vicinity of NEW YORK, probably on LONG ISLAND. Any information of him will be thankfully received by his cousin, **Michael McGann** (of BOKER), now in HUDSON CITY, NEW JERSEY.

June 1, 1861

Of **Mary Howard**, of the Parish of DRUM, County TIPPERARY, Ireland. She left on the 11th of March 1857. Her sister is stopping at 165 MADISON ST., NEW YORK.

Of **Michael Curran**, from FURBOUGH, County GALWAY, Ireland, who sailed for America on June 24, 1860; stopped in BOSTON for two months and came to NEW YORK with the intention of going home. Any information of him will be thankfully received by his brother, **Martin Curran**, 382 FIFTH AVENUE, NEW YORK.

Of **Michael**, **Patrick** and **Dan Kelleher**, from near SCARIFF, County CLARE, Ireland, who left Galway for America about ten years ago. Any information of them will be thankfully received by **Michael Horan**, Calvary Cemetery, WILLIAMSBURGH, L.I.,; or, by their mother in Ireland, who is most anxious to hear from them.

June 8, 1861

Of **Mary Gleeson** and **Thady Ryan**, from SHALLEE, County TIPPERARY, Ireland, who landed in New York on the 25th of April, by the ship *Guif Mamelsinley*. If this should meet the eye of any one that can give an account of them, please write to her sister and brother, **Margaret** and **Michael Gleeson**, MOUNT WASHINGTON, BALTIMORE County, MD.

Of **John Coffee**, of the Parish of ROSCREA, County TIPPERARY, Ireland. When last heard from, about two years ago, he was steamboating from ALBANY to BUFFALO. Any information of him will be thankfully received by his brother **Cornelius** by writing to him in care of **Stephen Rushman**, NORTH HEMPSTEAD, Long Island, N.Y.

Of **James** and **Patrick O'Brien**, natives of COOLEEN, Parish of BORRISOLEIGH, County TIPPERARY, Ireland. When last heard from they were in REYNOLD'S BASIN, State of NEW YORK. Any information of them will be thankfully received by their cousin, **Timothy Egan**, by writing to him to 69 Wright Street, JERSEY CITY, State of NEW JERSEY.

Of **Susan McDonnell**, daughter of **Thomas McDonnell**, a native of DERRYGORSH, Parish of CURRIN, County of FERMANAGH, Ireland. She resided in NEW YORK CITY when heard from, in August 1860. Any information of her sent to the care of **Thomas Loaram**, No. 135 EAST 11th STREET, NEW YORK, will be thankfully received.

June 15, 1861

Of **John O'Neil**, a native of NEWTOWN, BALLINAKILL, County GALWAY, Ireland; also, **James Kilroy**, native of GLINECK, BALLINAKILL, same County. Any information of them will be thankfully received by the brother of James Kilroy, by addressing a note to No. 27 SIXTH AVENUE, NEW YORK. Boston papers please copy.

Of **Thomas G. Lavin**, a native of BALLYMOATE, County SLIGO, Ireland. When last heard from, four years ago, he was in NEW YORK, and is supposed to be there still. Address his sister, **Mary Lavin**, care of **Mrs. Anna M. Bourke**, 302 Union Street, PHILADELPHIA, PA.

Of **Michael** and **Dennis Ryan**, natives of the Parish of GREAN, County LIMERICK, who left BUSKIRK'S BRIDGE four years ago. When last heard from they worked in ST. JOSEPH'S, MISSOURI in 1857. Any information from them will be thankfully received by their cousin, **Dennis Ryan**, by addressing **Edward Hayes**, BUSKIRK'S BRIDGE, NEW YORK.

Of **John Fox**, who came to this country four years ago, from the County WESTMEATH, Parish of CASTLETOWNGEOGHEGAN, Ireland. Any information of him will be thankfully received by his brother **Thos.** at **Mr. Thomas Hughes**, Benson St., MELROSE, WESTCHESTER County, N.Y.

June 22, 1861

Of **John Dillon**, aged 33, native of DUBLIN. He sailed in the bark *Fortune*, from Dublin, on the 13th May, 1851. He is supposed to be in NEW YORK CITY. Any information of him will be thankfully received by his brother, **James Dillon**, 83 North Dearborn St., CHICAGO, ILL.

Of **Patrick Riley**, a native of the Parish of GRAINE, County KILKENNY, Ireland. Any information of him will be thankfully received by his daughter, **Mary Riley**, who is after landing. Address 544 HUDSON STREET, NEW YORK CITY. Albany and Troy papers please copy.

June 29, 1861

Of **James, Daniel, Thomas, Edward** and **Alexander McDermott**, natives of SHANTONA, Parish of CLOGHER, County TYRONE, Ireland. When last heard from they were in EAST MENDEN, State of OHIO. Any information of them will be thankfully received by their sister, **Bridget McKenna**, by writing to her to FAR ROCKAWAY, QUEENS County, Long Island, N.Y. Western papers please copy.

July 6, 1861

Of **Thomas, James,** or **Mary Ann Murty**, of LONGFORD, Ireland, who came to this country some ten years since. Mary was in MILFORD, CONN, in 1855. Their brother **William** is very anxious to her from them. Direct letter to Irish American Office.

Of **Roseanna Noon**, a native of BALLINAHACKA, KING'S Co., Ireland. When last heard from was in BALTIMORE. Any information of her will be thankfully received by her brother **Patrick Noon**, at No. 29 Amity Street, BROOKLYN, N.Y. Baltimore papers please copy.

Michael Fallon, aged 24 years, a native of CARROWERIN, Parish of KILBRIDE, barony of BALLINTUBBER and County of ROSCOMMON. Who came to this country about eight years ago; was residing in PHILADELPHIA about two months ago since. Any information of his whereabouts will be thankfully received by his sister **Mary** by directing to the care of **Mrs. Bridget C. Duffy**, at her residence, 129 EAST 19th STREET, NEW YORK. Philadelphia papers, please copy.

July 13, 1861

Of **John Lawler**, a native of LIMERICK, Ireland. When last heard from was in FALMOUTH, KENTUCKY. Any information of his whereabouts will be thankfully received by his brother **Patrick** and sister **Bridget Lawler**. Please direct to **Patrick Kenny**, EAST 19th STREET, NEW YORK.

Of **Mary Burke**, a native of the Parish of CASTLE CONNELL, County LIMERICK, Ireland, who came to America about two years ago. She is married to a man of the name of **Michael Boland** from BROADFORD, County CLARE. Any information of her will be thankfully received by **Bridget Burke**, by writing to her in care of **Mr. George Gorege**, HAMTONSBURGH [Hamptonburgh], ORANGE County, N.Y.

July 20, 1861

Of **Patrick** and **Edward McEvoy**, Moulders by trade. Patrick to BALTIMORE, MD., from NEW JERSEY, about three years since; and Edward to CHICAGO, ILL. Any information of them will be thankfully received by their mother, at **Michael Duffy's**, 312 STANTON STREET, NEW YORK.

Of **Ellen Barry**, daughter of **Thos. Barry**, native of BALLINOE, County CORK, Ireland. When last heard of, was in PORTLAND, CONN.; she may be now in HOLYOKE, MASS. Any information of her will be thankfully received by her father. Direct to **Daniel O'Brien**, corner of Cumberland Street and Park Avenue, BROOKLYN, N.Y.

Of **Patrick** and **James Rourke**, a native of the Parish of RIESTOWN, County LOUTH, Ireland. When last heard from they were in NEW YORK CITY. Any information of them will be thankfully received by **Peter Rourke**, by writing to him in care of **Francis Sharkey**, No. 19 Park Avenue, BROOKLYN, N.Y.

Of **Michael Doyle**, a native of the Parish of COLERY, County WESTMEATH, Ireland. When last heard from he was in the State of PENNSYLVANIA. Any information of him will be thankfully received by **John Williams**, by writing to him at No. 140 Tillary Street, BROOKLYN, N.Y.

July 27, 1861

Of **Ellen Cassidy**, by her brother **James Cassidy**, or of his father, **James Cassidy**. Have not seen or heard anything of them for ten years. Any information concerning their whereabouts will be thankfully received by addressing **James Cassidy**, SALEM (Mannington), NEW JERSEY.

Of **Ellen Long**, daughter of **John Long**, of WOODQUAY, GALWAY, Ireland, who landed in this country in 1854. Any information of her will be thankfully received by her sister, **Mary Conway**, by writing to **John Fahy**, 75 WASHINGTON STREET, N.Y. Boston papers please copy.

August 3, 1861

Of **John Gallagher**, a carpenter by trade, who left PHILADELPHIA, about three years ago. When last heard from was in NEW ORLEANS. Any information of him will be thankfully received by his sister **Sarah**, at 1413 Tilbert St., PHILADELPHIA, PENN. [Appeared August 10, 1861 with additional information.]

Of **Dr. John Hession**, a native of GALWAY, Ireland. When last heard from was in NEW YORK. Any information of him will be thankfully received by his sister **Margaret Hession**, by writing to her to No. 275 AVE. A, NEW YORK.

Daniel Kelly, of LIMERICK, would be glad to hear from **John Sexton**, of LIMERICK, who was in NEW YORK six years ago. Direct to D. K., at **James O'Donoghue's** BANGOR, MAINE.

Of **David Steward**, of SALT HILL, Parish of INVAR, County DONEGAL, Ireland, who left there in last October, by the ship *Great Western*. Any information of him will be thankfully received by his friend **Jane McNeely**, No. 353 WEST 22nd ST, NEW YORK. Western papers, please copy.

Of **Owen Tierney**, a native of SCOTCH TOWN, County MONAGHAN, Ireland, who left OLD BERRY, in ENGLAND, about ten years ago, and arrived in New York. It is supposed he is living out West. Any information of him will be thankfully received by his brother, **John Tierney**, by addressing a letter to him to No. 2 Twentieth Street, Third Avenue, BROOKLYN, NEW YORK. Western Papers, please copy.

August 10, 1861

Of **William Gleeson**, a native of KILLENAULE, County TIPPERARY, Ireland, who came to America about eight years ago. When last heard from was living in CHERRY STREET, NEW YORK. Also of **John Kenny**, a native of LISMON, Parish of CALLONGAY, Co. KILKENNY, Ireland. When last heard from was in GLOBE VILLAGE, MASS. Any information of them will be thankfully received by **Michael Kenny**, by writing to MORRISTOWN, N.J.

Of **Hugh** and **Anna Connolly**, natives of the County LEITRIM, Ireland, who emigrated to the United States in the year 1850 or 1851. When last heard from they were at or near the City of BOSTON, MASS. Any information concerning their whereabouts will be thankfully received by their cousin, **Hugh Hoey**. Address to the care of the office of the Belle Plaine Enquire, MINNESOTA.

Of **John Gallagher**, a carpenter by trade, a native of LONDONDERRY, Ireland, who left PHILADELPHIA about three years ago. When last heard from was in NEW ORLEANS. Any information of him will be thankfully received by his sister, **Sarah**, at 1413 Filbert St., PHILADELPHIA, PENN. [Appeared Aug. 3, 1861 with less information.]

Of **Mary Ann Purdin** and her daughter, who came to NEW YORK CITY about sixteen years ago. Any information in regard to them will be thankfully received by her daughter, **Rosy Purden**, who lives at No. 95 Rutler Street, BROOKLYN. If **Miss Ellen Stone** sees this advertisement she will please call as above.

August 17, 1861

Of **Margaret Fitzgerald** (her maiden name), native of the City of LIMERICK, Ireland. Was first Married to **Mr. O'Flaherty**; second to a **Mr. Gallagher**, who kept a wood or lumber wharf foot of PINE STREET, NEW YORK; and last, to whom I forget. Had one daughter by the first husband, who was taken to her by Mr. Gallagher, from Limerick, where her mother resided about 30 years since. Any information will be thankfully received by writing to **Patrick Sullivan**, 43 Minot Street, BOSTON [Appeared under County CORK]

August 24, 1861

Of **Jeremiah Callanan**, a native of CLONAKILTY, County CORK, Ireland, who left there for London about the year 1829 or 1830, and resided in LONDON about two years. From thence he is supposed to have emigrated to SYDNEY, VAND[I]EMAN'S LAND. The surviving members of his family-with the exception of his eldest brother **Thomas**, who is in London-are all in the United States, since 1849, and understand that he has caused inquiries to be made for them through Irish papers some three years ago. Any intelligence of his present address, or the advertisement referred to, will be thankfully received by his youngest brother, **Michael Callanan**, PORT JERVIS, N.Y.; or his brother, **Patrick**, 612 WATER STREET, NEW YORK. Sydney Empire and Freeman's Journal will oblige us by copying the above.

Of **Patrick** and **Ellen Callaghan**, children of **Thomas Callaghan**, of SKEHAN, near MITCHELLSTOWN, County CORK, Ireland, by their Uncle, **John Callaghan**. Address a letter to him, ARICHAT, NOVA SCOTIA.

Of **Thomas Pearl**, a native of the Parish of TAGMON, County WEXFORD, Ireland. He sailed from Ross, for Quebec, about four years ago. When last heard from was in MONTREAL. Any information of him will be thankfully received by his brother-in-law, by addressing a letter to **Michael Byrnes**, BULL'S HEAD, CLINTON, DUTCHESS County, N.Y. Canada papers please copy.

Of **Mark O'Donnell**, a native of TARBERT, County KERRY, Ireland, who landed in New York on the 7th of June. Any information of him will be thankfully received by his Uncle **Stephen O'Donnell**, No. 1440 2nd Street, below Jefferson, PHILADELPHIA.

Of **John Loughnan** and wife, from the County of TIPPERARY, village of CLERIHAN, Ireland. They emigrated to the State of New York seven years ago. Any information regarding them will be thankfully received by **Mary Casey**, sister of **Mrs. Loughnan**. Direct to **John Casey**, No. 250 Fourth Street, SOUTH BOSTON, MASS., for Mary Casey.

September 7, 1861

Of **William Blake**. He landed in New York, November, 1859. Any information of him will be thankfully received by his friend **John Horgan**, PLANO, ILLINOIS.

Of **Patrick McKenna**, carpenter, a native of the Parish of INNISKEAN, Townland of BLITOGUE, County of MONAGHAN, Ireland, who left NEW YORK for California in 1853. When last heard of (about two years ago) he was said to be in or near SAN FRANCISCO. Any intelligence of him will be thankfully received by his cousin, **Peter McKenna**, 178 EAST 36th STREET, NEW YORK.

Of **John Mack**, of TULLA, County CLARE, recently of SPRINGFIELD, MASS., but now of CALIFORNIA. Any information of him will be thankfully received by his mother, **Mrs. Mack**, Chester Factory, SPRINGFIELD, MASS. California papers please copy.

September 14, 1861

Of **Joseph Deams** or his wife, maiden name, **Bessy Forbus**, natives of the Parish of CROUGHAN, KING'S County, Ireland. When last heard from were in BROOKLYN, NEW YORK. Her cousin **Stephen Lowry**, would wish to hear of them. Direct to 24 Coates St., Spring Garden Post-office, PHILADELPHIA, PA.

Of **John** and **William Nanry**, sons of **Patrick Nanry**, of BARRY, County LONGFORD, Ireland and cousins of the late **Charles M. Nanry**, well and extensively known in this City. John it is said, held a position on the Watch in NEW ORLEANS, LA., some years ago, and William a situation in the Custom-house, in this City, some four or five years ago. If either be living, they will hear something to their advantage by addressing the undersigned; and if any friend can furnish any such information they will subserve a philanthropic cause by addressing **John Hoey**, 154 WEST 30th STREET, NEW YORK CITY.

Of **John Linihan**, a native of GLINMORE, Parish of RAWCAHILL, NEWCASTLE WEST, County of LIMERICK, Ireland. When last heard of was in CHICAGO, ILL. Any information of him will be thankfully received by his sister **Mary Linihan**. Address to BETHLEHEM Post-office, NORTHAMPTON CO., State of PENNSYLVANIA.

Of **John Maguire**. Carpenter, a native of MANORHAMILTON, County LEITRIM, Ireland. Any information of him will be thankfully received by his wife **Catherine Maguire**, by writing to her in care of Lynch & Cole, Irish-American Office, 32 Beekman St., New York.

September 21, 1861

Of **Andrew Byrne**, a native of DUBLIN, Ireland, who came to New York with his mother and brother **Matthew**, in the ship *James Nesmith*, nine years ago. When last heard from was living near NEWARK, N.J., with a farmer named **Williams**. Any information of him will be thankfully received by his father, **Andrew Byrne**, No. 43 Second St., Harbor Hill, City of ALBANY; or, at the office of the Irish-American, New York.

Of **Morris Murphy**, of DUNMORE EAST, County of WATERFORD, Ireland. When last heard from he was in ALBANY. Any information will be gladly received by his cousins, the daughters of **James Powers**, of WOODSTOWN, at 37 Warren Street, or 14 Douglas St., SOUTH BROOKLYN, N.Y. Albany and Troy papers, please copy.

Of **James Wallace**, of HOLY CROSS, County TIPPERARY. When last heard from was living in CINCINNATI, State of OHIO. Any information of him will be thankfully received by his niece, **Mary Ryan**, who lately landed here, and daughter of **Widow Ryan**, of the Parish of DRUMBANE, County TIPPERARY, Direct to Mary Ryan, care of **David Lane**, cor. Of Erie and North Third Streets, JERSEY CITY, N.J. Cincinnati papers, please copy.

September 28, 1861

Of the whereabouts of the sisters, of **Bernard Farrell**, deceased, late of the Town of VICTORIA, VANCOUVER ISLAND. Deceased was a native of the County of ARMAGH, Ireland, and aged about twenty four years. One sister is supposed to reside in NEW YORK CITY. Address to **Patrick Kelly**, care Office British Colonist, VICTORIA, VANCOUVER ISLAND.

Of **William Farley**, formerly of DUBLIN CITY, tailor, by his mother, **Mrs. Murphy**, North Howard Street, near Catharine Street, BALTIMORE, MD. When last heard from he lived in BROOKLYN, NEW YORK.

Of **Thomas Connoly**, a native of DURAS, Parish of KINVARRA, Co. GALWAY, Ireland; supposed to have left home this Spring. Any information of him will be thankfully received by his sister, **Margaret Hearken**, by writing to **Patrick Hearken**, ALTOONA, BLAIR County, PA.

Of **Michael Curtin**, a native of the Parish of BANTEER, County CORK, Ireland. When last heard from was in the State of OHIO. Any information of him will thankfully received by his brother, **Cornelius Curtin**, by writing to him to YORKVILLE, NEW YORK.

Of **Henry McAnaley**. He is from the Parish of RAPEY, County DONEGAL, Ireland. When last heard of he was in WARREN, TRUMBULL County, OHIO. He is supposed to be in NEW YORK or PHILADELPHIA. He has two sisters in Philadelphia City. Any person knowing of his whereabouts will confer a favor by writing to me, where he will here of something to his advantage. Please address ORANGE Post office MAHONING Co., OHIO, for **Thomas Gallen**.

October 5, 1861

Of **John Fay**, a native of the Town of TRIM, County MEATH, Ireland, who left NEW YORK five years ago last May, for CHICAGO. Any information of him will be thankfully received by his brother **James Fay**, by writing to him to KING'S BRIDGE PARK P.O., N.Y.

Of **Mary Considine**, of KILRUSH, County CLARE, Ireland. When last heard from was in NEW YORK CITY. Any information respecting her will be thankfully received by her brother and sister **Michael** and **Bridget Considine**, ELIZABETH PORT, NEW JERSEY.

October 12, 1861

Of **Johanna Curtin**, who left BIRMINGHAM, CONN., on the 30th of August last, for BRIDGEPORT, where she was expected to have taken the Bridgeport boat to NEW YORK. She is about seventeen years old, and not long in this country. She came from the Town of FERMOY, County CORK, Ireland. Any information of her whereabouts will be thankfully received by her Brother, **Patrick Curtin**, No. 109 E. 16th ST., NEW YORK.

Of **Isabella McCormick**. Widow of **William Doyle**, native of BALLYCASTLE, County ANTRIM, Ireland. Any information of her, or any of the family will be thankfully received by her daughter **Isabella**. Please direct to **Patrick M. Hayes**, 304 Walnut Street, PHILADELPHIA. North of Ireland papers will please copy.

Of **John MacAlwee**, who landed in Canada fourteen or fifteen years ago, or any of his daughters, **Mary, Jane**, and **Doreanna**. Information of them will be thankfully received by **James Gillaspie**, 216 BROADWAY, NEW YORK.

October 19, 1861

Of **John Mahoney**, TOUBER, Parish of BEAGH, County GALWAY, Ireland. When last heard of in 1857, he was in OHIO. Any person knowing his whereabouts will confer a favor by addressing a note to his daughter **Margaret**, care of **Mr. Andrew Keane**, 316 MONROE STREET, NEW YORK. Ohio papers please copy.

Of **John Sisk**, late of MITCHELSTOWN, County of CORK, Ireland; supposed to be in NEW YORK. By addressing a letter to **Captain W. O. Sullivan**, SAN FRANCISCO, CAL., he will hear of something to his advantage.

Of **James McManus**, a native of STRADONE, County CAVAN, Ireland, who came to this country two years ago. When last heard from he was on board the United States Mail Steamship, commanded by **Captain John Robinson**, plying from NEW YORK to SOUTHAMPTON. Any information of him will be thankfully received by addressing **James Monaghan**, 201 Union Street, PHILADELPHIA.

October 26, 1861

Of **Mrs. Sarah Abel**, formerly **Mrs. Sarah Law** of CAVENDISH, VT. If she or any of her friends will write to her daughter **Elizabeth**, she will hear of the death of a very near relative, that will be greatly to her interest to know. Please write soon, as I am going to England next month. Address **Miss Elizabeth Law**, CAVENDISH, VT.

Of **Jane Stokes**, a native of the Townland of SHANBOLARD, Parish of BALLINAKILN County GALWAY, Ireland. She left Clifden ten years ago last August, and landed in Boston. Her only brother, **Anthony**, was then in ENGLAND. Any information of her will be thankfully received by her brother, **Anthony Stokes**, NEW BRITAIN, CONN.

November 2, 1861

Of **William Kelly**, from Ireland (part not known). When last heard from lived at service either as coachman or gardener, with **Mr. Roswell C. Smith**, HARTFORD, CONN, about the year 1854. Any information which will lead to his whereabouts left with **Mrs. Mitchell** at the furniture store, 288 HUDSON STREET, will be duly rewarded.

Of **John McNally**, formerly of DUNGANNON, County of TYRONE, Ireland, by his brother, **Frank McNally**, 322 PEARL STREET, NEW YORK.

Of **Edward Sweeney** and his daughter **Mary**. They are from near BOYLE, County ROSCOMMON, Ireland. Some years ago they lived in GREENWICH STREET, NEW YORK CITY. Edward Sweeney is a tailor by trade and fourteen years ago worked for Howard & Scofield, NEW YORK. He had a brother name **Bernard M. Sweeney**, who went to LOGANSPORT, INDIANA, some years ago, and died there in December last. Edward Sweeney, or his daughter Mary, or their heirs, will hear of something greatly their advantage by calling or writing to **Patrick Foley**, 722 WASHINGTON STREET, NEW YORK CITY, or **Arthur McGovern**, Administrator of Bernard M. Sweeney's estates, LOGANSPORT, CASS County, INDIANA. Any person knowing anything of the said Sweeneys will confer a favor by writing to either of the above parties.

Of **Sarah Hartigan**, and **Catherine** her sister natives of the County CLARE Parish of TRENGH. Sarah left Ireland about seven years since. When last heard from she was in MASSACHUSETTS. Any information of the will be thankfully received by their sister **Ellen**. Direct to Convent Sisters of Mercy, HOUSTON STREET, NEW YORK.

November 9, 1861

Of **Mary Murphy**. About five years since, she lived with a family of the name of **Robertson**, in 166 WALKER STREET, NEW YORK. She will hear of something to her advantage by writing to **John Stedman**, Union Coast Guards, in care of **Lieut. Millward**, Harbor Master, FORTRESS MUNROE, VA.

November 16, 1861

Francis Clark, a native of RACK WALLACE, County MONAGHAN, Ireland. When last heard from he was in the PHILLIPSBURGH MINES, AUSTRALIA. Any information of him will be thankfully received by his brother, by writing to him to 206 GREEN STREET [Greene Street], NEW YORK.

Of **Ellen Roache**, from the Townland of LAUGHTS, Parish of GLANWORTH, County CORK, Ireland. Came to this country last Spring; and when last heard from was somewhere in GREENWICH STREET, NEW YORK. Any information of her will be thankfully received by her brother, **Frank Roache**, to whom direct letter, care of **Mr. Mitchel**, PECKTOWN, N.J.

November 23, 1861

Of **Patrick McCreaith**, by his brother **Jeremiah**. When last heard from he went from JERSEY to LONG ISLAND. Any information of him will be thankfully received by his brother, at the PHILADELPHIA Marine Barracks.

Of **Patrick Martin** a native of the Parish of MULEHOVER, County CAVAN, who went to MORGAN County, State of ILLINOIS. Any information will be thankfully received by his sister, **Ann Martin**, 237 ELIZABETH STREET, NEW YORK.

Of **Jeremiah Meagher**, a native of BALLYQUIRK, Parish of LORHA, County TIPPERARY, Ireland. When last heard of about seven years ago, he was in MASSACHUSETTS. Please direct to **Thomas Meagher**, 1720 Walnut Street, PHILADELPHIA.

Of **John Murphy**, a native of SILVER GROVE, County CLARE, Ireland. When last heard from he was in PETERSBURGH, UPPER CANADA, and worked on the railway. Any information of him will be thankfully received by his sister, **Ann Murphy**, by writing to her to No. 3 Tiffany Place, BROOKLYN, N. Y. Canada papers, please copy.

Of **James Keenan**, of FOOBAGH, Parish of TYDAVENET, County MONAGHAN, Ireland. Who came to this country about eleven years ago. When last heard of he was employed by **Mr. James Henderson**, JERSEY CITY, and is supposed to have gone to the country.

Any information of him will be thankfully received by his sister, **Mary Keenan**, 22 Brunswick Street, JERSEY CITY. Western papers, please copy.

November 30, 1861

Of **Anthony Devitt**, who left home about four years since. When last heard from he was in the State of ILLINOIS, in the employment of a farmer. Any information of him will be thankfully received by his mother **Susan Devitt**, at ASHLAND, SCHUYLKILL County, PENNSYLVANIA.

Of **Mary Carlon**, a native of the City of DUBLIN, Ireland, who came to America about seven years ago. Any information of her will be thankfully received by her cousin, **Ann Halpin**, by writing to her at 96 HENRY STREET, NEW YORK.

December 7, 1861

Of **Patrick Sullivan**, who arrived in this country, from LONDON, in the beginning of July, 1857. Was last employed in the Pacific Hotel, LAWRENCE, MASS. Any information concerning him will be thankfully received by his brother, **John Sullivan**, Co. A, 31st Regt., N.Y.S.V., Camp near ALEXANDRIA, VA.

December 14, 1861

Of **Mary** and **Bessy Martin**, County LEITRIM, Townland of GLINAN, by their sisters, **Rose** and **Catherine**. Direct to them at YONKERS, NEW YORK.

Of **John Blake**, who emigrated from CORK five or six years ago. When last heard from, about 18 months ago. he was in NEW ORLEANS. He is about 35 years of age; height, between 5 and 6 feet; hair between dark and light; sandy whiskers; long features; blue eyes and is slightly pock-marked. Any information of him will be thankfully received by directing to "J.J.C." at the office of this paper.

Of **John MacShane**, a native of Ireland, Parish of ANNACLONE, near BANBRIDGE. Was last heard from was at NEW ORLEANS, in 1847. Any information of him-dead or alive-will be thankfully received by his sister, **Mary MacShane**, Box, No. 431, CINCINNATI, OHIO.

Of **James McKugh** and wife, **Bridget McKugh**, both natives of Ireland, County ROSCOMMON, Parish of KILLTRISTON and Townland of CULMORE. When last heard from was in CASCADE, DUBUQUE County, IOWA. Any information of the said parties will be thankfully received by their brother, **Dennis Brannan**, at ELIZABETHPORT, UNION County, NEW JERSEY.

December 21, 1861

Of **John**, **Patrick** and **Thomas Purcell**, natives of the County CLARE, Parish of MEELICK, near LIMERICK, Ireland. When last heard from, eight years ago, was in HARTFORD, CONN. Any information of them will be thankfully received by writing to their sister, **Anne Purcell**, DETROIT, MICHIGAN.

Of **John Madden**, from the County LIMERICK, Parish of DRUMEN, BALINCOLOO. When last heard of he was in the State of WISCONSIN. Any information of him will be thankfully received by his sister **Margaret**, or brother **David Madden**. Direct to David Madden, 88th Street, YORKVILLE P.O., NEW YORK CITY.

Of **Thomas Sweeny**, eldest son of **Michael Sweeny**, SHRUEL, MAYO, who enlisted in the 88th Regiment, and afterwards volunteered to the 45th. When last heard from was Commissary Conductor at KING WILLIAMS TOWN, CAPE OF GOOD HOPE. Address, **Miles Sweeny**, 767, South Sixth St., PHILADELPHIA, PENNSYLVANIA, U.S. British Army Gazette, please copy.

Of **John Cogan**, of PASSAGE WEST, CORK, Ireland. When last heard from he was in ST. LOUIS, MISSOURI, with his cousin, **James Cogan**, who has a widowed mother in Passage West, who is in great affliction about him; a reward of ten dollars will be given to any person giving any information about him, by addressing to his sister, **Hannah M'Cureey**, MEDFORD, MASS. Western papers, please copy.

If **John Kelaghan**, formerly of the County of MONAGHAN, Parish of AUGHNAMULLEN, Ireland, will call or send his address to 70 HESTER STREET, he will oblige his brother **Patrick**, who has lately arrived.

December 28, 1861

Of **Francis McCabe**, when last heard from was in TROY, N.Y., supposed to have went to the State of WISCONSIN; two years ago. Any information of him will be thankfully received by his brother, **James**. Direct to PROVIDENCE, R.I. Western papers please copy.

Of **Thomas Finneron**, who left London in the *Devonshire*, for New York, May 15th, 1857. Any information of him will be thankfully received by his mother, 6 Samuel Street, St. George's, East, LONDON.

Of **James Williams**, who left London and landed at New York about seven years ago, a native of the County LIMERICK, Parish of RATHKEALE, Ireland; his brother **Nicholas Williams**, wishes to hear from him. Any person knowing of him will please to write to BROWNSBURGH, BUCKS County, PA., in care of **Thomas Lawless**.

January 4, 1862

Of **Mary Herrety**, or **Heraughty**, niece to **Patrick Francis**, of the Town of GALWAY, Ireland. She was married to a man named **Thomas Burke**, and emigrated to the United States in 1834 or 35. By addressing a note to **P. F. Harrington**, 25 HAMMOND STREET, N.Y., she will hear of a near relative.

January 11, 1862

If **Mary Anne O'Connell**, now **Mrs. Gillis**, a native of the City of CORK, Ireland, and now, or lately, was residing in the City of DERRY, Ireland, or its vicinity, will write or address her sister **Ellen**, now **Mrs. Matthew Dwyer**, LENNOXTOWN, CAMPAIS, near GLASGOW, SCOTLAND; or, to **John Buckley**, 311 EAST TENTH STREET, NEW YORK, she will hear of something to her advantage. Glasgow (Scotland), Derry (Ireland), and other Irish papers, please copy.

Of **James**, **John** and **Patrick Lynch**, natives of COOLYFINCHING, County WICKLOW. Any information regarding them will be thankfully received by their sister **Jane**. In care of **John Lambert**, 161 WEST 18th STREET, NEW YORK. Irish papers, please copy.

January 18, 1862

Of **Catherine Lundy**, who left **Michael Morley's** Store, MONTREAL, in September, with **Mr. Kelly**, for ST. ANTHONY'S FALLS, MINNESOTA. Information will be thankfully received by her sisters at **J. Mullin**, 172 WEST 18th STREET, NEW YORK.

Of **Richard Maguire**, of KILLEAGH, County CORK, Ireland, will be thankfully received by his brother **James**, of whom he may hear something to his advantage by addressing **James Carroll**, No. 3, CATHERINE SLIP, NEW YORK.

January 25, 1862

Of **George Hagen**, carpenter and hand-rail maker, supposed to have died in NEW YORK, January, 1858. Five hundred dollars will be given to any person who will give correct information. Address **William Woodland**, No. 505 Fitzwater Street, PHILADELPHIA.

Of **James Daly**, of INOUGH, County of CLARE, Ireland, supposed to be in NEW YORK. Any information of him will be thankfully received by his cousin, **John Daly**, by addressing **M. Madden**, No. 33 Main Street, BROOKLYN.

Of **Charles Reilly**, a native of the Parish of MULLAHORAN, Townland of LISNEY, County CAVAN, Ireland. Who landed in this country on the 8th of March, 1853. When last heard from was in ILLINOIS. – Any information from him will be thankfully received by his brother, **Pat Reilly**, by writing to him in care of **John Smith**, No. 422 WEST 16th Street, NEW YORK.

Of **Catherine Davis**, who married **William Stanton** – she is a native of the Town of BALLYMAHON, County LONGFORD. When last heard from was in KINGSTON, UPPER CANADA. Any information of her will be thankfully received by her sisters **Maria** and **Jane**, by writing to Maria (now **Mrs. Ryan**) to WEEHAWKEN Post office, State of NEW JERSEY; or in care of Lynch & Cole Irish-American Office, 32 Beekman Street, New York

Of **Mary Hall**, a native of the Parish of KILLINNADANAGH, Townland of SONAGH, County GALWAY, Ireland. When last heard from was in NEW YORK. Any information of her will be thankfully received by her brother, **Patrick Hall**, by writing to him in care of **Mr. John Reilly**, Carroll St., between 4th and 5th Avenues, BROOKLYN, L.I.

February 1, 1862

If **James McCabe**, of PROVIDENCE, R.I., who advertised for his brother, **Francis McCabe**, whom he supposed to be in WISCONSIN, will write to **John McCabe**, Co. D., Seventeenth Regiment, Camp Butterfield, HALL'S HILL, VIRGINIA, he will hear some news respecting his brother, Francis, as John thinks he is brother of both. Rhode Island papers, please copy.

Mrs. Sherman, KILKENNY, Ireland, wishes to hear from her son, **Francis Xavier Sherman**, When last heard from he was in ROCHESTER, N.Y.

February 8, 1862

Of **John Myers**, who left England in 1856; supposed to be in CANADA; a native of County CLARE, Ireland. Any information of him will be thankfully received by his sister, **Bridget Myers**, at 49 GREENWICH AVENUE, NEW YORK.

Of **Dan Considine**, who left BALLYVAUGHAN, County CLARE, about three years ago. When last heard from, was employed in or near NEW YORK. He is about 20 years of age. Any information of him will be thankfully received by his mother, who resides in Ballyvaughan, County Clare, Ireland; or by his well wisher, **Martin Dolan**, Company E, 17th Regt, N.Y.V., HALL'S HILL, Camp Butterfield, VA.

Of **Anne Fitzpatrick**, 23 years of age, a native of County CAVAN, Ireland, who left NEW YORK about 12 years ago. When last heard from, she was in COLCHESTER, CONNECTICUT. Any information of her will be thankfully received by her brother, **Barney Fitzpatrick**, or her sister, **Mary**. Address, 121 MULBERRY STREET, NEW YORK.

Of **Esther Quinn**, maiden name, **Young**, who, with her husband, **Henry Quinn**, left BALLYRONEN, County DERRY, Ireland, twenty years ago. Henry died six years after in PHILADELPHIA; had a family of four children, whose names were **Mary**, **James**, **Catherine** and **Henry**. Any information of her would be thankfully received by her daughter Mary, by addressing **Joseph O'Malley**, FISHKILL LANDING, DUTCHESS County, State of NEW YORK. Philadelphia papers, please copy.

Of **Honora Griffin** alias **Fitzgerald**, wife **Edmund Fitzgerald**, from DINGLE, County KERRY, When last heard from, four years ago last March, she was in HAMILTON,

CANADA WEST. Anyone one knowing of her whereabouts will confer a favor on her husband, by writing to him to CHICOPPE FALLS, MASS; or, **John Brick**, SOUTH HADLEY FALLS, MASS. Canada papers, please copy.

Of **Mary McLaughlin**, a native of NEWRY, County DOWN, Ireland, who emigrated to New York in the ship *Margaret Tison*, in 1857. Any information of her will be thankfully received by her brother, **Henry McLaughlin**, Newkirk Street, Post Richmond, PHILADELPHIA, PA.

February 15, 1862

Of **John** or **Mary Bowles**; will be thankfully received by her sister, **Ellen Flynn**, or **Patrick Cummings**, 6 AMITY PLACE, NEW YORK. Buffalo papers please copy.

Of **Julian Sexton**, who married a printer (name not known) in LONDON, and came to New York a year and a half ago, and inquired at the Convent in Mulberry Street for her sister **Sarah**. Her sister will be thankful for any information about her, and address me to box 174, YORKVILLE Post office.

Of **Thomas White**, a native of GARINDERK, County LIMERICK, Ireland. When last heard from he was in SUGAR LOAF, ORANGE County, N.Y., and worked for a man by the name of **Rourke**, from NEWBURGH. Any information of him will be thankfully received by his mother, **Hanora Collins**, by writing, to her in care of **John Powers**, 364 WASHINGTON STREET, NEW YORK.

Of **Mrs. O'Connell**, (maiden name **Mary Foley**,) a native of the Parish of CORDANGAN Town of TIPPERARY, Ireland. When last heard from was in BOSTON. Any information of her will be thankfully received by her stepdaughter, **Anne O'Connell**, by writing to her in care of **Mr. Patrick Harvey**, cor. of Plymouth and Adams Street, BROOKLYN, L.I.

February 22, 1862

Of **William Walsh**, a native of BALLYRAGGETT, County KILKENNY, Ireland, who is supposed to be in the Union Army. Any information of him will be thankfully received by his sister, **Winifred Walsh**, by writing to her to No. 158 Atlantic Street, BROOKLYN, L.D.

Of **Patrick Heyden**, of GRANGE Parish, LISDOWNEY, County KILKENNY, Ireland. When last heard from, some thirteen years ago, he was in NEW HAVEN, CONNECTICUT. Any one knowing of his whereabouts will confer a favor on his brother **Michael Heyden**, by writing to him to 240 Fulton Avenue, BROOKLYN. New York and New Haven papers, and Boston Pilot, please copy.

Of **Michael Grady**, son of **Michael Grady** and **Mary Lynch** of the Parish of TEMPLEROACHE, Co. SLIGO, Ireland. He left NEW HAVEN in June, 1857, and went PLAINFIELD, NEW JERSEY. Any information of him will be thankfully received by his brother, **John Grady**, NORTHAMPTON, MASS. New Jersey Papers please copy.

Of **Eliza McKin**, daughter of **Susan** and **Thomas McKin**, of COLLOONEY, County SLIGO, Ireland, who is supposed to be married, and living in NEW YORK. Any information of her will be gratefully received and suitably rewarded by her mother at 538 THIRD AVENUE, NEW YORK.

March 1, 1862

Of **William Ahern, Sr.**, who left the London Docks, on board of the *Rhine*, on the 22nd of May, 1859, and sailed for America. He went by the name of **William Hubbard**. Any information of him will be thankfully received by his uncle, **Denis Ahern**, TOWNSEND Post-office, NEW CASTLE County State of DELAWARE. Boston papers please copy.

Miss Ellen Mackey, daughter of **Mr. Andrew Mackey**, formerly of City Quay, DUBLIN would thank the charitable and kind hearted for intelligence of **Mr. Lawrence Mackey**. He formerly resided in TULLAMORE, as far as she recollects, and in DUBLIN. She applied to relatives in Ireland for information of his address more than once, but received no reply, owing to a selfish and unkind motive. Any information of the above named gentleman, whether living or dead will be thankfully received. Please direct to NEW YORK Post office, Box 680; or, the Irish American Office, 32 Beekman Street.

Of **Mary A. Brosnan**, CASTLE ISLAND, County KERRY, Ireland. She lived in SAN FRANCISCO and vicinity from 1855 to the Fall of 1857, when last heard of. She is supposed to be dead; and her unknown fate sorely distresses her relatives. Will the good sisters of Charity of San Francisco be kind enough to make inquiry regarding her and give comfort to this excellent and most dutiful daughter's parent, **Andrew Brosnan**, MOONVORE, CASTLE ISLAND, KERRY, Ireland; or to her brother, **Daniel A. Brosnan**, WASHINGTON CITY, D.C.

March 8, 1862

Of **Stephen Leonard**, who left ENNIS eight years ago last June. When last heard from (3 years ago) he was in ROCHESTER. Any information of him will be thankfully received by his sister-in-law, **Mary Leonard**, at the office of this paper. [Appeared under County CLARE]

March 22, 1862

Of **John McCombs**, or **Thomas Lloyd** his cousin, natives of MOHILL, County LEITRIM, Ireland. When last heard from was in ST. LOUIS. Any information of them will be thankfully received by **Thos. McCombs**, GARRISON'S STATION, PUTNAM County, NEW YORK. St. Louis and Cincinnati papers, please copy.

Of **Mrs. Heaphy**, maiden name **Ellen Mulcahy**, who left TALLOW, County WATERFORD, Ireland, about five years ago, and came to this country. Any information of her will be thankfully received by her niece, **Mary Mulcahy**, by writing to her to No. 130 WEST 21st STREET, NEW YORK. Boston Pilot, please copy.

Of **Mary Anne Keeffe**, a native of the Parish of EGLISH, KING'S County, Ireland. When last heard of she was living in ALBANY. Any information of her will be thankfully received by addressing **Mr. Timothy Keeffe**, COLUMBUS, BURLINGTON County, NEW JERSEY. Albany papers, please copy.

Of **Hugh Fannin**, who emigrated to this country ten years ago. Left NEW YORK about five years ago for WISCONSIN, VERAQUE, BADEAUX County. Any intelligence of him will be thankfully received by his uncle and brother, **Patrick** and **John Fannin**, 117 KING STREET, NEW YORK.

Of **Martin Feeney**, son of **Anthony Feeney** and **Sarah Murphy**, native of BALLYBOCKOUGH, near SHRUEL, County MAYO, Ireland, sailed from Galway about 14 years ago, supposed to be in MAYSVILLE, State of KENTUCKY. Any information of him will be thankfully received by his sister, **Judy Feeney**, by writing to her in care of the **Rev. George Montgomery**, Catholic Priest, WEDNESBURY, STAFFORDSHIRE, ENGLAND; or send his address to **James Boyle**, 168 EAST 24th STREET, NEW YORK CITY. Kentucky papers, please copy.

Of **Michael Morris**, formerly of LUCAN, County OF DUBLIN, Ireland, will hear from his brother and sisters by writing to **Maria Morris**, care of **Mrs. Rachel Toole**, Church Street, NEW HAVEN, CONN. Melbourne Argus, of Australia, please copy.

Of **Alexander Read**, a native of CURNANOAL, near CASTLEBAR, County MAYO, Ireland. When last heard from was working in the mines in PENNSYLVANIA. Any information will be thankfully received by addressing a few lines to **Hugh Duffy**, UNIONTOWN, MIDDLESEX County, NEW JERSEY.

Of **Elizabeth** or **Patrick Mitchell** and **Mary Brenen**, sister of Elizabeth, supposed to be in TORONTO, CANADA. They were natives of MOUNTRATH, QUEEN'S County, Ireland. Any information will be thankfully received by their sister, **Margaret Hurly**, 411 Girard Avenue, PHILADELPHIA, PA.

Of **Michael Dwyer** and his Wife. (her maiden name was **Ellen Walsh**), a native of CARRICK-ON-SUIR, County TIPPERARY, Ireland. When last heard from they were in NEW HAVEN, CONN. Any information of them will be thankfully received by their niece, **Margaret Cotter**, by writing to her to 105 Academy Street, NEWARK, N.J.

March 29, 1862

Of **Patrick McCue**, a native of KILLRAIN, Parish of INISHKEEL or GLENTIES, County DONEGAL, Ireland. He is twenty years old, and will be in this country three years next May. He went to peddle with a man of the name of **Neal Keeney**. When last heard from he was in MISSOURI, with a farmer by the name of **O'Donnell**, from the County DONEGAL; heard since that he enlisted in the Union Army in Missouri. Any information of him, dead or alive, will be thankfully received by his mother, **Rose McCue**, 126 MOTT STREET, NEW YORK. Missouri papers, please copy.

Of **William Wallace Martin**, formerly of BELFAST, County ANTRIM, Ireland, who emigrated to America in 1836. He or his heirs will hear of something to their advantage by addressing **John D. Collins**, Box 1097 Post Office, PHILADELPHIA.

Of **Mary McGough**, from near CARRICKMACROSS, by her brother, **Patrick**. She is supposed to be in LOWELL, MASS. Any person knowing her whereabouts would confer an everlasting favor by addressing her brother, Patrick McGough, General Post Office, NEW YORK. Boston and Lowell papers please copy. [Appeared under County Monaghan]

Of **James Cox**, a native of the Parish of KILLKEVEY, County ROSCOMMON, Ireland, who emigrated from WAKEFIELD, ENGLAND, in 1856. Any information of him will be thankfully received by **Phillip Duffy**, No. 1729 South 4th Street, PHILADELPHIA.

Of a soldier named **John Dunn**, son of **Mary Dunn**, formerly of CLONDUFF, QUEEN'S County, Ireland. When last heard from November 1856, he was in the 6th Regiment of Infantry, U.S.A., Co. H, **Captain Henderson**, NEWPORT BARRACKS, KENTUCKY. Any information concerning him will be thankfully received by his mother. Address **Mrs. Mary Dunn**, MECKLENBURG, SCHUYLER County, NEW YORK.

April 5, 1862

Of **Kezia Haworth**, a native of the Town of BURY, LANCASHIRE, ENGLAND; is 18 years of age; said to have left England with her mother, **Mrs. R. Haworth**, in company with **Mathew Astley**, and his two daughters **Rebecca** and **Hannah**, for AUSTRALIA, about the year 1852. Any information of the aforesaid Kezia Haworth, alive or dead will be thankfully received by her Father **Richard Haworth**, private, Cavalry Detachment, WEST POINT, NEW YORK, and **L. C. Fell**, 103 Bolton Street, BURY, LANCASHIRE, ENGLAND.

Of **Patrick McCabe**, a native of the Parish of MULAHORAN, Co., CAVAN, Ireland. When last heard from was in PATERSON, N.J. Any information of him will be thankfully received by his mother. **Rose McCabe**, by writing to her at No. 168 EAST 32nd STREET, N.Y., or at the office of the Irish American.

Of **James Pedigan**, a native of the Parish of ARTONSTOWN, Co. LOUTH, Ireland; who emigrated to NEW YORK about twelve years ago. Any information of him will be thankfully received by his brother, **Patrick Pedigan**, WOBURNE CENTRE, MASS. [Appeared April 12, 1862 with the surname **Pedigan** changed to **Fedigan**].

Margaret Shine!: There is a letter for you from CALIFORNIA, at no.2 Beach Street, BROOKLYN.

If this should meet the eye of **Mrs. Isabella Sullivan**, formerly **Gibbons**, of the City of DUBLIN, she will hear of an old friend who is anxious to see her, by addressing **Mrs. Reilly**, 145 WEST 31st STREET.

Of **Mrs. Carroll**, formerly **Lewis**, who left DUBLIN about 1847, and when last heard of resided in BROADWAY about 15th St. Her friend **Mr. Chas. O'Hara**, of Wellington St., DUBLIN, would be thankful to hear from her. Should this meet her eye she will confer a favor by addressing **Mrs. Mortimer**, BROADWAY, P.O., NEW YORK.

Of **Michael Ryan**, of the City of CASHEL, Co. TIPPERARY, Ireland, who left NEW YORK in the fall of 1855, for MELBOURNE, AUSTRALIA, and who, after arriving there, left for the gold mines. If this should happen to meet his notice he will write directly to his brothers **Thomas** and **John Ryan**, 331 HUDSON STREET, N.Y., U.S.A.

Of **James Cox**, native of DRIMDULEN, Parish of KILLKEVEN, a son to **Patrick Cox** and **Catherine Flyn** (maiden name), County ROSCOMMON, Ireland, who left WAKEFIELD, ENGLAND, in 1856. Any information of him will be thankfully received by his friend, **Phillip Duffy**, No. 1720 South 4th Street, PHILADELPHIA.

April 12, 1862

Of **Robert, John** and **James Reid**, natives of the Parish of DUNLUCE, County ANTRIM, Ireland. When last from they were working with a farmer named **Peeke**, in SCHENECTADY, WEST GLENVILLE CORNERS, State of NEW YORK; and who left there about six or eight years ago to go to the State of ILLINOIS. Since that time nothing has been heard of them. Any information of either of them will be thankfully received by their brother, **Maurice**, who came to this country two years ago. Please address **Maurice Reid**, care of **John B. Farrell**, Irish American Office, New York.

Of **Alice O'Rourke**, native of RATHJORDAN, Parish of HERBERTSTOWN, County LIMERICK, left Queenstown October 25th, in the steamer *City of Baltimore*, and landed in New York City some three months ago. Her sister is very impatient until she hears from her. Address her sister **Johanah O'Rourke**, care of **Nicholas J. Lynch**, West 12th Street, between Clinton & Jefferson Streets, CHICAGO, ILL.

April 19, 1862

Of **Dennis McCauley**, a native of the County ANTRIM, Ireland. When last heard from he was at 684 Germantown Road, PHILADELPHIA. Any information of him will be thankfully received by his brother, **James McCauley**, by writing to him in care of Lynch & Cole, Irish American Office, 32 Beekman Street, New York.

Of **Mr. John Healon**, a native of KILLURAN, within five miles of TULLAMORE, KING'S County, Ireland, who landed in PHILADELPHIA in May, 1860, where he worked until the 26th of August, 1861, at which time he and wife left for MONTREAL, CANADA, since which time he has not been heard from. Any information of him or is whereabouts, will be thankfully received by brother-in-law, **Mr. Terence Dempsey**, at Willard's Hotel, WASHINGTON, D.C. Toronto papers, please copy.

Of **Thomas Patrick Tuohy**, late of LIMERICK. Was in MIDDLEBORO, MASS., in August, 1855; and in 1856, in GENEVA, ONTARIO Co., N.Y. Should this meet his notice, he will hear of something to his advantage by addressing **Geo. Carey**, 190 3rd AVENUE, cor. 18th Street, NEW YORK; or any person knowing his whereabouts, will confer a favor by communication to the above address.

Of **Thomas Kenny**, son of **Bryan Kenny**, a native of the Townland of KEEL, Parish of LEGAN, barony of ARDAGH, County LONGFORD, Ireland. He came to this country twenty or twenty one years ago. –When last heard from, ten years ago, he was in ILLINOIS. Any information of his whereabouts, dead or alive, will be thankfully received by **Thomas Kelly**, 37 York Street, JERSEY CITY, N.J.; or his brother-in-law, **Thomas Kelly**, BALLYMAKEEGAN, County LONGFORD, Ireland. By communication with them, he will hear of something to his advantage. Boston Pilot and Illinois papers please copy.

April 26, 1862

Of **Patrick Murphy**, a native of SPRINGFORD, Parish of CHARLEVILLE, County CORK, Ireland, who emigrated to this country about 13 years ago, when last heard from was living in BUFFALO, State of NEW YORK. Any information of him will be thankfully received by his sister **Johanna**, or his cousin, **William Simms**, at No. 155 EAST 21st Street, N.Y. Pennsylvania papers please copy.

Of **Mary Reed**, a native of the City of DUBLIN, Ireland, who arrived in New York about nine years ago, and boarded with a **Mrs. Fitzsimons**, in CHERRY STREET, and then left to see her brother, who was then living in RICHMOND, VA. Any information of her will be thankfully received by Messrs. Lynch & Cole, Irish-American office, 32 Beekman Street, New York.

Of **John Murvihill**, a native of the Parish of ATHLEAGUE, County ROSCOMMON, Ireland. When last heard from he was with his uncle in BALTIMORE, MD. Any information of him will be thankfully received by his friend **John Mee**, by writing to him at 71 SPRING STREET, N.Y.

May 3, 1862

Of **Hugh Clark**, County of CAVAN, Parish of LOURIGAN, Township of MURMID, who left Ireland about fifteen years ago. When last heard from, about ten years ago he was in south ORANGE County, State of NEW YORK. Any information of him will be thankfully received by his brother, **Bernard Clark**. Address ANDELUSID Post Office, BUCKS, PA.

Of **David Fitzgerald**, a native of KINGWILLIAMSTOWN, Co. CORK. He landed in America about ten years ago. Also of **Julia Walsh**, his sister, who came to this country at the same time. Any information of them will be thankfully received by **James Fitzgerald**, David's son, as his mother and sister are both dead. He wishes to meet his father and aunt as soon as possible. Direct to James Fitzgerald, care of **Wm. Porter**, 46th ST., corner of First Avenue, N.Y.

Of **Patrick Murray**, a native of MONEVEA, Co. GALWAY, Ireland, who landed in New York on the 15th of April, 1862. Any information of him will be thankfully received by his brother, **Thomas Murray**, by writing to him, in care of **Samuel Roberts**, MOORSTOWN Post Office, BURLINGTON County, N.J.

Of **Mary Ann McDermott**, a native of the QUEEN's County, Ireland. Who left Dublin in 1854, in company with her cousin, **Mary Brady**. Since she landed she went to live in HOBOKEN, and since there nothing has been heard of her. Any account of her will be most thankfully received by her sister, **Kate McDermott**, now **Mrs. Spratt**, 194 Mill Street, POUGHKEEPSIE, N.Y.; or **William Spratt**, at Brewster's Corner of MOTT and BROOME STREETS, NEW YORK. [Appeared May 10, 1862 with **Mary Ann** changed to **Ann**.]

May 17, 1862

Of **John Brophy**, who remained in Liverpool about four weeks with his brother, **William**, when coming to this country, and sailed for New Orleans on the 17th of March, 1851. He worked on the ILLINOIS Central Railroad in UNION County, and is said to have been employed in CINCINNATI, on a steamboat, with **Mr. Southern**. His wife **Anne** (maiden name **Quill**) is very anxious to hear from him. Address care of **Mr. Bernard Cahill**, No. 2 Sidney St., PHILADELPHIA, PA.

Of **John Boyrus**, of CLONASLEE, QUEEN'S County, Ireland; or of his brother-in-law, **Frank Herman**, will be thankfully received by **Michael Culliton**, Co. F, 1st Regt. N.Y.V., NEWPORT NEWS, VA.

Of **Peter**, **James** and **Patrick Kenny**, natives of the Townland of FREEL; Parish of ARDAGH, County LONGFORD, Ireland, children of **Thomas** and **Margaret Kenny**. When last heard from were living in BROOKLYN, L.I. Any information of them will be thankfully received by their sister, at No. 601 WASHINGTON ST., N.Y.

May 24, 1862

Of **Mrs. John Watson**, widow with three children; said to have left ENGLAND about the year 1852 for AUSTRALIA, in company with her father, **Matthew Astley**, late of HEYWOOD, W. BURY, LANCASHIRE, ENGLAND. Any information by letter of the family enquired for, alive or dead, will be thankfully received by her brother-in-law, **Richard Haworth**, private, Detachment of Cavalry, WEST POINT, NEW YORK.

Of **Robert Rodney**, When last heard from he was a soldier in the United States service. Any information of him will be thankfully by his wife and child, **Mary Rodney**, 84 Greene Street, TROY, NEW YORK.

Of **Patrick Bush**, a native of BENNETT'S BRIDGE, County KILKENNY, Ireland. When last heard from, two years ago, he was in SOUTHWICK, State of MASSACHUSETTS. There was an account of a man of the same name in the Irish American of June 22, 1861, being killed at Bull's Run, who belonged to a regiment of the New York S[t]ate Militia, Co. E. If **Lieut. Dempsey**, of the 2nd knows anything about him he will confer a great favor by writing to **Jeremiah Bush**, SOMMERS Post-office, TOLLAND County, State of CONNECTICUT.

May 31, 1862

Of **Michael** and **Margaret Mulcahy**, formerly of Gardiner St., DUBLIN. Address, **Mrs. Margaret Moran**, 394 EIGHTH STREET, NEW YORK. **Margaret Doyle** enquirer. Boston papers, please copy.

Of **Barney Gunn**, a native of the Parish of CLONES, County FERMANAGH, Ireland. When last heard from was in GALENA, ILLINOIS. Any information of him will be thankfully received by his sister, **Ellen Gunn**, by writing to her to 34 ½ PRINCE STREET, NEW YORK.

Of **Edward** and **Dennis Ginnaw**, of the Parish of COOLL, County of KERRY, Ireland. When last heard from they were living in the State of OHIO. Any information of them will be thankfully received by their sister, **Honora Ginnaw**, by writing to her to 255 WEST 26th STREET, NEW YORK. Ohio papers, please copy.

Of **Edward Doyle**, a native of CLOONGOONA, about three miles from ATHLONE, in the County of ROSCOMMON, Ireland. When last heard from, about seven or eight years ago, he lived and worked in a lumber yard in GREENBUSH, near ALBANY, N.Y. Any information of him dead or alive, will be thankfully received by his nephew, **Edward Lennon**, FITCHBURG, MASS.

Of **Owen Kilmurray**, a native of the Townland of DONIEL, Parish of KILLEAR, County WESTMEATH, Ireland. When last heard from, one year ago, was in NEW ORLEANS. Any information of him will be thankfully received by his wife and child, by writing to them in care of **Mr. Patrick Carney**, 85 Tillary Street, BROOKLYN.

June 7, 1862

Of **Hannah Anna Maria O'Sullivan**, a native of KILLARNEY, County KERRY, Ireland, who married a man named **John Howard**, of LAUGHSIE, County CORK. When last heard from were in NEW YORK. Any information of them will be thankfully received by **Mrs. Kennedy**, 530 Columbia Street, BROOKLYN, L.I.

Of **Hugh O'Connor**, a native of the Parish of FERMOY, County CORK, Ireland, who arrived in this country about ten years ago. When last heard from, was living in the State of CONNECTICUT. Any information of him will be thankfully received by addressing a line to his brother, **Thomas O'Connor**, care of **Judge Strong**, SETAUKET, Long Island.

Of **Archibald Hanlon**, a native of LEITRIM, County LOUTH, Ireland. When last heard from was in NASHVILLE, TENN. Any information of him will be thankfully received by his wife, **Bridget Hanlon**, by writing to her in care of **Captain Spinny**, 296 Pearl St., BROOKLYN, L.I.

June 14, 1862

Of **George McKeon**, a native of the County ANTRIM, Ireland. When last heard from six years ago, he was in CLINTON County, IOWA. Any information of him will be thankfully received by his brother-in-law, **Joseph Tait**, by writing to him to RAHWAY, NEW JERSEY, **George McKeown**, his son, is also anxious to hear from him, who is stopping with his brother-in-law, **Abraham Tait**, at COLD SPRING, NEW YORK.

If **Mrs. Catherine Foley**, of the Parish of FERMOY, County CORK, Ireland, will call at the house of **Thomas Morley**, 155 Willoughby Street, BROOKLYN, she will receive money from her friends in Ireland.

Of **Thomas Burke**, a native of the Parish of LEADMORE, KILRUSH, County CLARE, Ireland, who arrived lately in the steamship *Kangaroo*. Any information of him will be thankfully received by his brother, **John Burke**, by writing to him to SALEM, WASHINGTON County, N.Y., or by **Michael Fitzpatrick**, 327 FIRST AVENUE, NEW YORK.

Of **Thomas** and **Edward Walsh**, natives of the Parish of THOMASTOWN, County KILKENNY, Ireland. When last heard from, in 1852, they were living in SPRINGFIELD, OHIO. Any information of them will be thankfully received by their brother, **Michael Walsh**, in care of **James Macgarr**, corner of South First and Provost Streets, JERSEY CITY, HUDSON County, N.J.

Of **James Coffey**, a native of the Townland of BALLYBRIT, KING'S County, Ireland. When last heard from, about one year ago, he was in ROCHESTER, N.Y. Any information of him will be thankfully received by his sister, **Ellen Coffey**, by writing to her to No. 50 HOUSTON STREET, NEW YORK.

Of **Catherine Shea**, a native of the City of CASHEL, County TIPPERARY, Ireland. When last heard from she was in NORTH WALES, England. She emigrated to New York in January, 1859. Any information of her will be thankfully received by her brother **Patrick**, at No. 84 NINTH AVENUE, NEW YORK CITY.

June 28, 1862

Of **Michael** and **Mary Cadecan**, natives of GENEMADDY, County GALWAY, Ireland, who went to CANADA in 1847. Any information of them will be thankfully received by their brother, **Patrick Cadecan**, by writing to him in care of **James Reilly**, 115 EAST BROADWAY, NEW YORK.

July 5, 1862

Of **Edward Hare**, a native of the Parish of ARDAGH, near the post Town of BALLINA, County MAYO, Ireland, who left Ireland for AUSTRALIA about 28 years ago. Any information of him will be thankfully received by his brother-in-law, **Patrick Hope**, by writing to him to 2033 Market Street, PHILADELPHIA, PENN, U.S.: or, at the Office at the Irish American, 32 Beekman St., New York.

July 12, 1862

Of **Bridget Finnelley**, a native of KILMENEY, MARYBOROUGH, QUEEN'S County, Ireland. When last heard from about three years since she lived in Henry Street, BROOKLYN. Any information of her will be thankfully received by her Aunt, **Ellen Malone**, by addressing **John Ford**, WEST MERIDEN, CONN.

Of **Anne McCluskey**, a native of the Parish of KILLINO, Townland of KILLIKEARNEY, County CAVAN, who landed in New York eight years ago this July. She lived with a family in BATAVIA STREET, with the family of **Hugh O'Reilly**. When last heard from was married to **Thomas Davy**, a carpenter, in NEW JERSEY. Any information of her will be thankfully received by her sister, **Alice McCluskey**, care of **Thomas E. G. O'Shea**, 273 GREENWICH STREET, NEW YORK.

Of **Margaret King**, a native of the Parish of ANNAGH, Townland of MULLACROKER, County CAVAN, Ireland. When last heard from five years ago, was in NEW YORK CITY. Any information of her will be thankfully received by her sister **Catherine King**, by writing to her, to No. 40 Page Street, LOWELL, MASS.

July 19, 1862

Of **Master Walter Dignan**, son of **Walter Dignan**, leader of the Manchester Cornet Band, now with Fourth Regt. N.H.V., stationed at ST. AUGUSTINE, FLA. He left his home, at MANCHESTER, N.H., Friday, June 6; is 14 years old, light complextion, light brown hair, dark hazel eyes; rather tall and slim of his age. Was dressed when he left in a spencer of drab cloth with a black velvet collar, dark trousers, small blue and black check, blue cap, congress boots. Appears when in conversation rather shy and diffident. Any information of him will be gladly received by his mother, **Eliza Dignan**, Laurel St., MANCHESTER, N.H.

Of **Patrick Brusnihan**, of ARDAGH, County LIMERICK, Ireland, who landed in New York in September, 1857. Any information of him will be thankfully received by his sister, **Ellen Kelley**. Address, in care of **Michael Sheahan**, 208 WEST SIXTEENTH STREET, NEW YORK. Boston papers please copy.

Of **Matthew Keaty**, aged about 20, a native of THURLES, County TIPPERARY, Ireland. When last heard from was in NEW YORK CITY. Any information of him will be thankfully received by his brother, **Thomas Keaty**, 190 Ewing St., CHICAGO, ILLINOIS.

July 26, 1862

Of **Philip Owens**, of BELTURBET, Parish of DRUMALEE, County CAVAN, Ireland, shoemaker. Any information of him will be thankfully received by **Patrick O'Brien**,

Townland of DRUMGART, Parish DRUMLANE, County CAVAN, Ireland, at 94 OLIVER STREET, in liquor store.

Of **Charles Murray**, Townland of MULLINEWARA, Parish DRUMLANE, County CAVAN, Ireland, coachmaker. Any information of him will be thankfully received by **Patrick O'Brien**, same Parish Townland, DRUMGART, at 94 OLIVER STREET, in liquor store.

August 2, 1862

Edward Deane, of CASTLEREA, Ireland, aged seventy. Any person who can give information regarding the death and burial of the above is requested to address **Geo. M. Knevitt**, 65 WALL STREET, NEW YORK.

Of **Cornelius Curley**, about sixty years of age. He left his home on the 20th of June last, and has not since been heard from; had on when he left home a black silk hat, black cloth coat, black vest, black satinet pants, grain leather boots and woolen stockings. Any person giving any information of him will be liberally rewarded, and receive the thanks of his anxious children, by calling at 85 Wyckoff St., BROOKLYN.

Of **John Scannel**, a native of the Parish of CARRIGALINE, County CORK, Ireland, who left there about twenty years ago. When last heard from he was in CAPE COD, State of MASSACHUSETTS; he is now supposed to be in the United States service, in the 9th Massachusetts Regiment. Any information of him will be thankfully received by his brother, **Thomas Scannel**, WAPELLA, DE WITT County, State of ILLINOIS.

Julia Connor (maiden name, **Julia Walsh**), wants information as to where her husband, **Maurice Connor**, is. Previous to her landing in New York he wrote to her, but the letter has been lost or mislaid. Also, of her cousin, **John Lyne**, all natives of the Parish of LISTOWEL, County KERRY, Ireland. Any information of them will be thankfully received at **Mr. John Casey's**, No. 12 ½ WASHINGTON STREET, NEW YORK. [Appeared August 16, 1862 with the name **Walsh** changed to **Nash**]

Of **Matthew**, **Thomas** and **William Blackburne** brothers from the Parish of GALBALLY, County LIMERICK, Ireland. Emigrated here about 12 years ago. Supposed to be in ILLINOIS, or WISCONSIN. Any information of them will be thankfully received by addressing a few lines to the Office of the Irish American, for **Frances Blackburne**, from TALLOW. Western papers please copy.

Of **James McDermott**, son of **Francis**, native of the Parish of EDGWORTHSTOWN, County LONGFORD, Ireland, later of COVENTRY, ENGLAND, was in BROOKLYN, NEW YORK, nine years ago. He will hear of something much to his advantage by calling on or addressing his aunt, **Anne** Johnson Street, corner of Navy Street, BROOKLYN, N.Y.

Of **Michael Lyons**, who arrived at New York, in ship *London*, from the County ROSCOMMON, Ireland, about five and a half years ago. By writing to his wife **Maria**, he will hear of something to his advantage. Address to **Maria Lyons**, ST. LOUIS, MO.

Of **John Devine**, a native of GORTYCRUMB, Parish of LACK, County TYRONE, when last heard from had left NEW YORK, March 17th, 1856 for CALIFORNIA. Any information of him will be thankfully received by his brother **Hugh**, at N.W. Cor. 15th and Filbert Streets, PHILADELPHIA, PA.

August 9, 1862

If **Miss Mary McGrath**, a school teacher by profession, and formerly of CLOYNE, County CORK, Ireland, will make known her address, through the Irish American, or the "personals" of the *NEW YORK Herald*, she will hear from a friend whom she met about two years ago on board a Hudson River Passenger boat, while in company with another young lady named **Maggy**.

Of **Hannah Barry**, of CASTLETOWNROCHE, County CORK, Ireland, who came to New York about eighteen years ago, and went to PHILADELPHIA. She has not been heard from for seven years; also, of **John Sheehan**, of the same place. Any information concerning them will be thankfully received by directing to **Richard Barry**, in care of **David Pierce**, BURLINGTON P.O., N.J.

Of **James O'Shea**, a native of KERRY, by his son **John O'Shea**. When last heard from he was in PERU, ILLINOIS. Any information of him will be thankfully received at 209 FULTON ST., NEW YORK.

Of **Michael Jordan**, who came to New York in 1852, since which time nothing has been heard of him. He is a native of JONESBOROUGH, County LOUTH, Ireland. Any person knowing anything about him will confer a great favor on his brother, **Dennis Jordan**, by writing to SAN FRANCISCO Post Office, CALIFORNIA.

Mrs. Maria Lyons, of ST. LOUIS, Mo., who advertised for her husband, **Michael Lyons**, from the County ROSCOMMON, Ireland, who arrived in the ship *London*, his address is 7 CLARK STREET [Clarke Street], between Broom and Spring Streets, NEW YORK.

August 16, 1862

Of **Mary Shay**, of SOUTH WALES. When last heard of was living in NEW YORK. Any information of her whereabouts will be thankfully received by her sister, **Margaret Shay**, No. 2,417 Callowhill Street, PHILADELPHIA, PA.

Of **Honora Murnane**, of LETTERLICCA, Parish of DURUS, County CORK, Ireland, who emigrated to America in 1837. When last heard from was in INDIANAPOLIS, INDIANA, and married to **Jeremiah Murnane** of the Parish of IVELEARY. Any information of her will be thankfully received by her brother, **Michael Murnane**, care of **Dennis Driscoll** 64 MONTGOMERY ST., NEW YORK. Western papers, please copy.

Of **Michael Fleming** and **Dennis Kinnelly**, cousin and brother of **Margaret Kinnelly**, of PETER'S WELL, Parish of KILTOMISH, County GALWAY, Ireland. The last heard of **Michael Flemming's** address was LYNDON Post Office, WHITESIDE County, ILL. Dennis Kinnelly came out about six years since – residence not known. Margaret has been in New York some weeks, and is very anxious to hear from one or both. She has written five letters to Flemming, but has received no answer. Please address any information to Margaret Kinnelly, No. 8 ELIZABETH STREET, NEW YORK.

Of **Patrick Cosgrove**, a native of the Parish QUEENSBOROUGH, County GALWAY, Ireland. When last heard from was in NEW ORLEANS, LA. Any information of him will be thankfully received by his brother, **Arthur Cosgrove**, by writing to him to 99 NINTH AVENUE, NEW YORK.

August 30, 1862

Of **Thomas McCrudden**, who is supposed to be in BOSTON, MASS. Any information of him will be thankfully received by his brother, **James McCrudden**, QUINCY, ILLINOIS.

September 6, 1862

Of **David Burke**, of the Parish of KILMALY, County CLARE, Ireland. When last heard from he resided in YORKVILLE, State of NEW YORK. Any information of his present residence will be thankfully received by his anxious sister, **Margaret Burke**, NORFOLK, CONNECTICUT.

Of **Hanora McGuire**, **Catherine McGuire**, **Patrick Page**, and **Martin Connors**, who came to this country between fifteen and seventeen years ago. P. Page was in YORK

STREET. M. Connors in FAIRFIELD, CONN; natives of County CLARE, Parish of ABBY. Any information of them will be thankfully received by their niece, **Bridget Kerins**, who lives in 112 College Street, NEW HAVEN, CONN.

Of **Thomas** and **James Honan**, natives of BALLINAHINCH, County TIPPERARY, Ireland, who arrived in New York in 1857. Any information of them will be thankfully received by their brother, **John Honan**, 121 Atlantic Street, BROOKLYN, LI.

Of **Michael Byrnes**, a native of ROSCREA, County TIPPERARY, Ireland, who left CHICAGO on the 25th of March last, and is supposed to have enlisted in some regiment of the U. S. Volunteers. Any information of him will be thankfully received by his wife, **Mary Byrnes**, by writing to her to 327 CATHARINE STREET, NEW YORK, or at the office of the Irish American, 32 Beekman Street.

September 13, 1862

Of **Joseph A. Quinn**, who came to this country from Liverpool in the steamship *City of Washington*, October, 1860. Any information of him will be thankfully received by writing to **Francis Coyle**, 122 GREENWICH STREET, NEW YORK, or to **Mathew Fogarty**, 19 Halston Street, DUBLIN, Ireland. Boston and Philadelphia papers please copy.

Of **Miss Mary Egan**, who resided in TROY ST., NEW YORK, over a year ago, will send her address to **James Harrenn**, 199 WEST 37th ST., he will be happy to communicate intelligence of her brother, received from **Mr. George Daly**, of TULLAMORE.

September 20, 1862

Of **Edward Connell**, of MALDEN, MASS., Who was born at CLOHANE, County KERRY, Ireland. He is a blacksmith by trade, and is about 20 years of age. He worked for **Mr. Michael England**, IRVINGTON, NEW JERSEY, and was seen in NEWARK last Fall, and is supposed to have enlisted either in the 8th or 9th New Jersey Regiment. Any information of him will be thankfully received by his mother, brothers, and sisters. Address **Patrick Connell**, MALDEN, MASS.

Of **Jeremiah Manion**, a native of the Town of ROSCOMMON, Ireland. When last heard from, was in OTISVILLE, ORANGE CO., N.Y. Any information of him will be thankfully received by his brother, by writing to the **Rev. James O'Beirne**, FLUSHING, L.I.

Of **Alexander Reynolds**, from the Town of GOREY, Co. WEXFORD, Ireland, who emigrated to America, 1798, or of any of his family. Any information of them will be thankfully received by **James Reynolds**, 10 WEST STREET, NEW YORK.

September 27, 1862

J.J.H-, can hear his friend, Miss Mary Mc-, by addressing a note to her at TARRYTOWN, N.Y.

Of **Francis Gallagher**, or his brother, **Michael**, or his sisters **Anne** and **Mary**, natives of TUAM, Parish of DRUMRILEY, County LEITRIM, Ireland. When last heard from they were in NEW YORK CITY. Any information of their whereabouts will be thankfully received by their brother, **James**, at **John Coynes**, No. 1 Willow Street, SOUTH BROOKLYN.

Of **William Mackin**, a native of GRANARD, County LONGFORD, Ireland, who left NEW YORK for Ireland in May, 1861. Any information of him will be thankfully received by his brother, **Michael Mackin** by writing to him in care of **Thomas Brennan**, 7 WASHINGTON STREET, NEW YORK.

Of **James Shannon**, of Parish of ELPHIN, Townland of CLONNEYEFFER, County ROSCOMMON, Ireland. When last heard of he was living in MULBERRY ST., N.Y. Any information of him will be thankfully received by his brother, **Luke Shannon**, TOLEDO, OHIO.

Of **Anne Dolan**, of LACKAGH, Parish of COLLOONEY, County of SLIGO, Ireland, who left home for New York on the 1ˢᵗ of May, 1862, in company with **Peter McGouldrick** and **Bridget Higgins**. She is supposed to be in NEW YORK or vicinity. Any information of her will be thankfully received by her uncle, **Edward Fitzwilliam**, 73 Charles St., LOWELL, MASS.

Of **Thomas Sparrow**, who had a spilt lip, formerly of COOLS and WEXFORD, in the County of WEXFORD, Ireland, cabinet-Maker, who sailed from Liverpool for New York in or about the year 1840, and if living is now entitled to property in consequence of his father's death. Any person knowing anything of said Thos. Sparrow, and the locality where he resides, if living, or the time of his death, will confer a favor by writing to M. W. STARIN, Commission Merchant, 29 Duane St., N.Y.

October 11, 1862

Of **John Hale**, who left HUDSON STREET, NEW YORK, as a United States soldier, on the 21ˢᵗ of June, 1861, and was not heard from since the 3ʳᵈ of August, 1861; is about 21 years of age; a native of KILGLASS, County SLIGO, Ireland; is supposed to be in the 3ʳᵈ Cavalry or a light Battery. Any information of him will be thankfully received by his brother **Thomas**, at 161 EAST 25ᵗʰ STREET, NEW YORK.

If **Richard Doyle**, lately from MALLOW, County CORK, Ireland, or **Ellen Doyle**, his daughter, will call on **Mr. John Hennessy**, No. 9 LISPENARD STREET, NEW YORK, they can obtain information of interest to them.

Of **John Molloy**, formerly of LOUGHENROE, in the Parish of TYNAGH, County GALWAY, Ireland. He is supposed to have arrived at New York in August last. Any information of him will be thankfully received by his sisters **Ann**, **Mary**, **Bridget**, and **Hanora Molloy**, No. 1713 Moravian Street, PHILADELPHIA, PA.

Of **John** and **Thomas Horan**, from SHRAUGH, Parish of PARTRY, Co. MAYO, Ireland. Any information of them will be thankfully received by their cousin, **Bridget Horan**, daughter of **Matthew Horan**, by writing to **Michael Gibbons**, 121 WORTH ST., NEW YORK.

If **Jane** or **Ally Taffe**, from the County SLIGO, Ireland, wish to hear of their sister BRIDGET TAFFE they can do so by addressing her at No. 1 Commerce Street, SOUTH BROOKLYN.

October 18, 1862

Of **Johanna** and **Kate Kelleher**, natives of the Parish of DONAGHMORE, County CORK, Ireland, who left Cork in 1849 for AUSTRALIA. Any information of them will be thankfully received by their brother, **John Kelleher**, by writing to him in care of Lynch & Cole, Irish American office, 31 Beekman St., New York.

Of **Michael Fitzpatrick**, a native of the Parish of ATHY, County KILDARE, and who landed at Newfoundland about eighteen years ago. Any information of him will be thankfully received by his sister, **Elizabeth Fitzpatrick**, MYSTIC RIVER, CONN.

Of **James Pender**, a sawyer by trade; a native of the City of LIMERICK, Ireland, who landed in the ship *Ganges*, at Quebec, in 1849. When last heard from he was at PERTH AMBOY, N.J. It is supposed he now resides in CHICAGO, ILLINOIS. Any information of him will be thankfully received by his brother, **Robert Pender**, by writing to him in care of **Mr. E. Looney**, No. 693 FOURTH ST., N.Y. CITY. Chicago papers, please copy.

November 1, 1862

Of **Patrick, James**, and **David Fitzgerald**, natives of the Town of CHARLEVILLE, Parish of NEWTOWN, County CORK, Ireland, who arrived in New York in April, 1841. When last heard from, were living in 39th STREET, near 3rd Avenue. Any information of them will be thankfully received by their brother, **Denis Fitzgerald**, by writing to him, in care of **Michael Donovan**, 141 READE STREET, NEW YORK.

Of **John Donovan**, a native of BANTRY BAY, County CORK, Ireland, who sailed for this country in the ship *Victory*, on the 13th of April last. Any information of him will be thankfully received by his uncle **Timothy Donovan**, VALLEY FALLS, RENSSELAER County, State of NEW YORK.

November 8, 1862

Of **Mrs. Mary Moore**, a native of the County of LONGFORD, Ireland, who arrived in America in 1847. Her husband left her in October, 1850, in WAREHOUSE POINT, CT., and went to sea. Since that time he has heard nothing of her. Any information of her will be thankfully received by her husband, **Michael Moore**, in care of **Mr. James O'Neill**, NATICK, MASS., or by her mother, **Mrs. Margaret Moore**, BLACKINTON, MASS.

Of **Richard Bourke**, a native of TINAKELLA, Parish of CARRICK-ON-SUIR, County TIPPERARY, Ireland. Who arrived in New York, Oct. 20, in the ship *Adelaide*. Any information of him will be thankfully received by **Nicholas Britton**, Florence, NORTHAMPTON, MASS. If he will call at Castle Garden, he will be sent to his friends in Massachusetts.

Of **Michael Crean**, a native of the Parish of FETHARD, County TIPPERARY, Ireland. Eight years ago he and I boarded at the house of **John Beechman**, at EASTON, PENN. When last heard from, five years ago, he was in LONG ISLAND, State of NEW YORK. Any information of him will be thankfully received by his brother, **Lawrence Crean**, by writing to him in care of **S. E. Decon**, TRENTON, NEW JERSEY.

November 15, 1862

John Carmody, formerly of CROSS, County of CLARE, Ireland, wants to know where his brother-in-law, **Daniel Sullivan**, ship carpenter. Formerly from CORK, Ireland, now is, Carmody heard, he left NEW ORLEANS, for NEW YORK, before the blockade was put on. He will give a handsome reward to any person giving information to Lawrence & Ryan, 10 Broad Street, Boston, or to the office of the Irish American, 32 Beekman Street, New York.

November 22, 1862

Of **Mary Griffin**, a native of the City of GALWAY, Ireland. She sailed from Galway in the bark *Albion*, of Galway, bound to New York, and arrived there about the first of May, 1853. She is of fair complexion, and about thirty-one years of age. Any information of her whereabouts will be thankfully received by her brother, **John Griffin**, Township of EMMET, County ST. CLAIR, MICHIGAN, TOURASHALL Post Office.

Of **Sally Cornally**, a native of the village of KNOCKAWALLEY, Parish of SPIDEL, County GALWAY, Ireland. When last heard of she was in PHILADELPHIA. Any information will be thankfully received by her sister's daughter. Direct No. 178 EAST 35th STREET, care of **Mrs. Callaghan**.

Of **Michael, Timothy** and **William Doyle**, natives of LISTOWELL, County KERRY, Ireland. When last heard from they were in PITTSBURGH, PA. Any information of them will be thankfully received by their sister, **Catherine Doyle**, by writing to her to 187 LEWIS STREET, NEW YORK, in care of **James Riordan**, cooper.

Of **James Murray**, a native of DUNDALK, County LOUTH, Ireland, who left NEW YORK on the 28th of August in the ship *Thornton*, for Liverpool. Any information of him will be thankfully received by his wife, **Annie Murray**, by writing to her to No. 65 GREENWICH STREET, NEW YORK.

December 6, 1862

Of **John**, **Timothy**, **Denis**, **James** and **Martin Driscoll**, natives of COURTMACSHERRY, County CORK, Ireland, who arrived in America about 34 years ago. Any information of them will be thankfully received by their nephew, **Daniel McCarthy**, Co. H. 170th Regiment N.Y.V., Corcoran Legion, NEWPORT NEWS, VA.

Of **Jane Strokes**, a native of SHAMBOLARD, Parish of BALLINAKILLY, County GALWAY, Ireland. She left Clifden about eleven years ago, and sailed for Boston. Also, of **Catherine Ryan** and **Norrey Grace**, natives of the Townland of BALLYWILLIAM, Parish of BURGIS, County TIPPERARY, Ireland. Norrey was a widow, and had four children. They were last seen by Catherine's sister, **Mary Ryan** (now **Mrs. Stokes**) in NEW YORK, about eight years ago. Any information of them will be thankfully received by their sister, by writing to **Anthony Stokes**, NEW BRITAIN, State of CONNECTICUT. Pennsylvania papers and Boston Pilot please copy.

Of **John Power**, a native of the Parish of GRANE, County LIMERICK, Ireland, who arrived in this country last April. When last heard from (Oct 26,) he was staying at **Timothy Dillon's**, GRANVILLE CORNERS, WASHINGTON County, N.Y. Any information regarding his present whereabouts will be thankfully received by his aunt, **Mrs. T. Murphy**, corner of Carroll Street and 3rd Avenue, BROOKLYN, L.I.

Of **John** And **George Butler**, natives of KILCOOLAN, County LIMERICK, Ireland; first cousins of the **Rev. Dr. Butler**, Bishop of LIMERICK. Any information respecting them will be thankfully received by their sister, **Ann Butler**, No. 222 WEST 19th STREET, NEW YORK, and also by their cousin, **Thaddeus B. Carey**, No. 3 Caroll Street, BROOKLYN. Kansas and California papers, please copy.

December 13, 1862

Of **Ann Morrisey**, daughter of **Edward Morrisey**, GRAIGUE, County KILKENNY, Ireland. When last heard from she was in PHILADELPHIA. She landed in this country about 13 years ago. Any information of her will be thankfully received by her brother, **James**, who lately landed in this country, and now resides at No. 580 Columbia Street, BROOKLYN. Philadelphia papers, please copy.

Of **Elizabeth Conley**, a native of the Parish of FENEGH, County LEITRIM, Ireland. When last heard from was in PROVIDENCE, R.I Any information of her whereabouts will be thankfully received by **Thomas McTaggert**, No. 243 9th AVENUE, NEW YORK.

December 20, 1862

Of **Thomas** and **Mary Revelle**. When last heard from about two years ago, they were living in 7th AVENUE, between 29th and 30th Streets, NEW YORK. Any information respecting them will be thankfully received by their brother **John Revelle**. Address Quartermaster's Department, FORT UNION, NEW MEXICO.

Of **Margaret Nugent**, daughter of **James Nugent**, a native of the Townland of AUGHMORE, County LONGFORD, Ireland; she married a man named **Bartholomew Shay**, about seven years ago, and left NEW YORK for the State of ILLINOIS. Any information of her will be thankfully received by her father **James Nugent**, HASTINGS ON THE HUDSON, WESTCHESTER County, State of NEW YORK; or her cousin, **Mary O'Hara**, No. 75 EAST 23nd ST., NEW YORK CITY.

Of **Mary Gelsenan**, alias **Carroll**, a native of the County MEATH, Ireland. When last heard from she was employed at French's Hotel, NEW YORK. Any information of her will be thankfully received by her brother, **Christy**, at Castle Garden.

January 3, 1863

Of **Mary Crowley**, alias **Byrne**, wife of **Paul Crowley**, both natives of CLONAKILTY, County CORK, Ireland. She left NEW YORK nineteen years ago, and went to BALTIMORE, MD. Any information of her will be thankfully received by her cousin, **Mrs. Mary Crowley**, alias **Donovan**, of No. 9 NEW STREET, NEW YORK. Baltimore papers, please copy.

Of **Dennis McEvoy**, of No. 2 Proud's Lane, DUBLIN, Ireland. When last heard from was in TEXAS. Any information concerning him will be thankfully received by **Anne Curley**, MANHATTANVILLE, NEW YORK.

Of **Michael** and **Julia Keeffe**, natives of the City of KILKENNY, Ireland. Any information of them will be thankfully received by their brother **John** who is landed in this country. Address **Mr. James Fitzgerald**, No. 21 MORRIS STREET, NEW YORK.

January 10, 1863

Of **Mary**, **Michael**, **John** and **James Butler**, natives of ENNISCORTHY, County WEXFORD, Ireland.-When last heard of they were in NORTH HARTFORD, CONN. Information of them will be thankfully received by their brother, at 14 South Front Street, BALTIMORE, MD.

Of **Thomas William** and **Dennis Murray**, natives of RATHKEALE, County LIMERICK, Ireland, who came to America (by way of Canada) in 1849. William was in BUFFALO about six years ago. Any information of them will be thankfully received by their brother, **Michael**, at No. 3 PECK SLIP, NEW YORK.

If **Bridget Melvin**, a girl (15) fifteen years of age, whose parents died on board of the ship *Webster* on her passage to this port, and who eight years ago was adopted from WARD'S ISLAND by one **Mr. Murphy** will send her present address, or apply, to Mr. Casserly, Superintendent of Emigration Castle Garden, she will hear of something to her advantage. N.B. The above mentioned girl was born in BOHALLOW, near BALLINA, County MAYO, Ireland, and was, when taken 7 years old. NEW YORK, January 5, 1863.

January 17, 1863

Of **John Dunlap**, late of BALLYVERSAL, County ANTRIM, Ireland. Should he or any of his friends see this, he will hear of something to his advantage by applying to W. & H. Glenn, INDIANAPOLIS, IND.

Of **Francis**, **James**, and **Margaret McCann**, natives of the City of BELFAST, Ireland. When last heard from they were in NEW YORK CITY. Any information of them will be thankfully received by their friend, **Patrick Keenan**, by writing to him to 126 South Third Street, WILLIAMSBURGH, L.I.

Of **Michael Galvin** and his four sisters, **Bridget**, **Catherine**, **Ellen**, and **Elizabeth**, natives of the Parish of ST. PETER'S, ATHLONE, County ROSCOMMON, Ireland. Any information of them will be thankfully received by their sister, **Mrs. Mary Cain**, No. 347 WEST 16th ST., NEW YORK, between 8th and 9th Avenues.

January 24, 1863

Of **Patrick Mc Ellistrim**, mason by trade, a native of KERRY, who is supposed to be in NEW YORK.—His brother **John** is anxious to hear from him. Direct to the care of **Francis Fitzgerald**, No. 8 VANDEWATER ST., NEW YORK.

Of **Mary Hands**, a native of BALLINAMORA, Co. LEITRIM. When last heard of she was in NEW YORK.- Any information of her will be thankfully received by her friend, **Jane Flynn**, at St. Vincent's Hospital, 11th Street, near 7th Avenue.

Of **Thomas Flanagan**, a native of QUEEN'S County, Ireland. When last heard from he was living at No. 103 BROOME STREET, NEW YORK. Any information concerning him will be thankfully received by his sister, **Theresa Flanagan**, at 29 EAST 28th STREET, NEW YORK.

Of **Bernard Madden**, a native of the Parish of OUGHNAUGH, County SLIGO, Ireland. When last heard from he was in EAST CAMBRIDGE MASS. Any information of him will be thankfully received by his brother **John Madden**, by writing to him to 156 Navy Street, BROOKLYN, N.Y.

January 31, 1863

Of **John Dowling**, formerly of KILRUSH, County CLARE, but late of the City of LIMERICK, Ireland, who arrived in New York a year ago last May or June, and is supposed to have enlisted in the 42nd Tammany Regt., N.Y.S.V., about eight or nine months ago. Any information of him will be thankfully received by his afflicted family, at he Irish American Office, 32 Beekman Street, New York

February 7, 1863

Of **Aubrey Mountagne**, a native of CORK, Ireland. Any information of him will be thankfully received by **Richard O'Shea**, by writing to him to 177 EAST 12th STREET, NEW YORK, or to his father, **James Mountagne**, 72 North Main Street, CORK, Ireland. [Appeared February 14, 1863 with surname **Mountagne** changed to **Mountayne**]

Of **John**, **Patt** and **James Kennedy** and sisters **Catherine** and **Margaret**. When last heard from they were in the State of VIRGINIA. Any information of them will be gladly received by their sister, **Johannah Kennedy**, who arrived in New York in September last from CLAHANBEG, County CLARE, Ireland. Address Johannah Kennedy, JEFFERSON VALLEY, WESTCHESTER County, N.Y.

February 14, 1863

Of **John Bouhan**, who left NEW YORK January 9th, 1862, and when last heard of was in CHICAGO, ILLINOIS. Any information concerning him will be thankfully received by his sister, **Margaret Bouhan**, at No. 18 EAST 14th STREET, NEW YORK CITY.

Of **Denis McCashin**, born in DOWN County, Ireland; 50 years of age; 5 feet 10 inches high; stoutmake; ruddy complexion; blue eyes, and hair originally sandy. Emigrated to Canada, with wife and two children, in '46 or '47. Family at present, probably large, settled in MONTREAL. Was there in ' 52. Heard he since left for CANADA WEST. Occupation uncertain – supposed transporting logs or rafts in navigable streams. Was a farmer; probably is so still. Intelligence respecting him will be thankfully acknowledged by his nephew, **Daniel McCashin**, who is the bearer to him of dispatches of paramount importance. Address Lynch, Cole & Meehan, 32 Beckman Street, New York. Montreal, Canada West, and Canadian papers generally, please copy.

Of **Patrick Murphy**, son of **Bernard Murphy**, attorney, native of the Town of GALWAY, Ireland. They moved from there to WOOD QUAY, County GALWAY. When last heard from Patrick Murphy, he was leaving for some part of America. Any information of them will be thankfully received by **Mary Kelly**, by writing to her in care of Lynch, Cole & Meehan, Irish American Office, 3[ ] Beekman Street, New York.

Of **John McCormick**, a native of NEWCASTLE, County OF LIMERICK, Ireland (son of **Margaret McCormick**), who sailed from London, England, about seven years ago, at which time his mother received a letter from him after landing in New York; but since then nothing has been heard of him. Any person knowing his whereabouts will confer a favor by writing to his brother **Dennis McCormick**, WINCHESTER, MASSACHUSETTS.

February 21, 1863

Of **Ellen Mangan**, from AMAGAN, County LIMERICK, Ireland, who came to this country thirteen years ago. When last heard of was in EAST TROY, N.Y. Any information of he will be thankfully received by **Mary Ann Collins**, SOUTH NORWALK, CONN.

Of **Bridget Carney**, a native of the County MAYO, Ireland, who left Ireland about ten years ago. When last heard of was in NEW YORK. Information of her will be thankfully received by her brother and sister, **Michael** and **Catherine Carney**, by addressing to **John McCarron**, 1264 BROADWAY, NEW YORK.

Of **James Galvin**, late of GALWAY, and a native of the County of ROSCOMMON, Ireland. When last heard from was in PORTLAND, State of MAINE. Any information concerning him will be thankfully received by is wife, **Agnes Galvin**, by addressing to **Mrs. Martyn**, No. 56 HENRY STREET, NEW YORK CITY. Portland papers, please copy.

February 28, 1863

Eugene Connellan seeketh information of his brother, **Michael Connellan**, of the Parish of SKREEN, County SLIGO, Ireland. He will be most thankful to any person who would favor him with any tidings of him, at **Mrs. Tulte's**, 215 DELANCEY ST., NEW YORK. [Ad is also written in Irish].

Of **John** and **Patrick Stanton**, from LIMERICK, Ireland, who came to this country about thirty years ago. When last heard of they were in LONDON, ENGLAND. Also, **Christopher Farrell**, from CLAINE, County KILDARE, who came from LEEDS, in YORKSHIRE about eighteen years ago. Any information respecting the above will be thankfully received by their nephew, **D.F. Tierney**, at 21 WEST 44th STREET, between 5th and 6th Avenues, NEW YORK.

March 7, 1863

Of **Robert Quinn** and his daughter, **Susan Quinn**, who emigrated from the City of BELFAST, Ireland, in May, 1841, to this country. His occupation, at that time, was a butler. Heard in 1852 he was in NEW YORK. Should this meet his eye or that of his cousin, **Bernard Quinn**, SPRINGFIELD, BELFAST, correspondence or any of the above named will be most thankfully received by **Robert Quinn**, son of the first-name, at DOLPHIN MILL, PATERSON, NEW JERSEY.

Of **Johannah Hartigan**, a native of the Parish of ELFIN, County LIMERICK, Ireland. When last heard from was in the employ of **Mr. Potter**, Washington Hotel, NEW YORK CITY. If she will call at the office of the Irish American she will hear of something to her advantage.

Of **Mrs. Miller**, of BANAHER, KING'S County, Ireland. If she will send her address to the office of the Irish American she will hear of something to her advantage.

March 14, 1863

Of **Alfred Howell**, aged sixteen years, a native of PATERSON, N.J. He went out West with his Uncle **James**. Any information of him will be thankfully received by his uncle, **Robert McLaughlin**, PATERSON, N.J.

Of **Patrick Clampit**, of the City of LIMERICK, who left Ireland in April, 1854, and landed in Quebec, and has not since been heard from, except that his mother heard he is at present at work in a tobacco factory in NEW YORK. Any information respecting his whereabouts will be thankfully received by his mother, at **Mr. John Doody's** at 137 CHERRY STREET, NEW YORK.

Of **Michael Fean**, from the Parish of ROCKHILL, County LIMERICK, Ireland. When last heard from he was in ALBANY, N.Y. Any information of him will be thankfully received by his sister, **Catherine Fean**, in care of **Maurice Flynn**, 15 Chestnut St., BALTIMORE, MD. Boston Pilot, please copy.

Of **Patrick Kearns**, late of BELFAST, but formerly of BLACKRAW, County MONAGHAN, Ireland. He left NEW YORK about two and a half years ago and has not since been heard from. He is a clerk by profession. Address D.K., care of **John O'Mahony**, 6 CENTRE STREET, NEW YORK.

Of **John** and **James Henigan**, natives of the Parish of TUBERCURY, County SLIGO, Ireland. When last heard from they were in CHICAGO, ILLINOIS. Any information of them will be thankfully received by their sister, **Bridget**, by writing to **John McCarrick**, 49 MOTT STREET, NEW YORK. Illinois papers, please copy.

March 21, 1863

Of **Catherine Driscoll**, a native of GLANDIN, County CORK, Ireland. She was married to **Charles McCarthy**, of Glandin, County Cork. When last heard from, seven years ago, she was in HASVILLE, NEW YORK. Any information of her will be received by her daughter, **Mary Donovan**, by writing to her in care of **Mrs. Yorkston**, 14 FOURTH AVENUE, NEW YORK.

Of **Patrick Conohan**, a native of the Parish of INVA, Townland of CRANAH, County DONEGAL, Ireland. He is about 48 years of age. Any information respecting him will be thankfully received by his daughter, **Ellen**, at 604 South 7th Street, PHILADELPHIA, PA.

Of **Patrick Curran**, a native of LOUGHREA, Co. GALWAY, Ireland, who enlisted in the 63rd Regt. N.Y.V., Irish Brigade, under **Brigadier General T. F. Meagher**. When last heard from he was in general hospital, FREDERICK CITY, MD. Any information of him will be thankfully received by his aunt, at the office of the Irish American. [Appeared March 18 and April 4, 1863 with the surname **Curran** changed to **Cullan**]

Of **Daniel** and **Mary O'Keeffe**, natives of MOUNT BROWN, Parish of CROAGH, County LIMERICK, Ireland. When last heard from, were in BOSTON, MASS., and left there, with their brother **Patrick** and family, about four years ago for WISCONSIN. Also, of his brother, **John O'Keeffe**, from the County WEXFORD, who arrived in New York about three years ago, and when last heard from, was near ALBANY, N.Y. Any information of them will be thankfully received by their brother, **Michael O'Keeffe**, by writing to him, in care of Messrs. Lynch, Cole & Meehan, Irish American office 32 Beekman Street, New York.

Of **Michael Quin**, a native of GEASHIL, KING'S County, Ireland. He left PHILADELPHIA, December 26, and took the boat at the Walnut Street Wharf to see a friend of his in NEW YORK, named **Maria Deroy**; since that time nothing has been heard of him. Any information of him will be thankfully received by **James Mallen**, 909 Alden Street, above Poplar, between 10th and 11th Streets, PHILADELPHIA, PA.

March 28, 1863

Of **Thomas Tierney**, a discharged member of Co. E. 37th New York, "Irish Riffles," Who left NEW YORK, on the 2nd of February last, and is supposed to be in the company of **Captain O'Beirne**; since then nothing has been heard from him. Any information concerning him, or his whereabouts, will be thankfully received by his uncle, **Andrew Tierney**, 221 CHERRY ST., or the office of the Irish American.

Of **James Carroll**, a native of CLOHELA, Parish of COWRAN, County KILKENNY, Ireland. Landed in New York in September, 1852. When last heard of nine years ago, was working on the ILLINOIS Central Railroad, at EWINGTON, EFFINGHAM County. Supposed to be in some part of ILLINOIS. Any information of him will be thankfully received by addressing his brother, **Andrew Carroll**, 940 Manilla Street, PHILADELPHIA. Illinois papers, please copy.

Of **Dermoth McMurray**, a native of the Parish of BALLINAGLARIUGH, Townland of CURRAGLASS, County LEITRIM, Ireland. When last heard from was in ALBANY, N.Y. Any information of him will be thankfully received by his sister, **Margaret McMurray**, by writing to her, in care of her uncle, **Michael Ford**, No. 5 Beaver Street, NEWARK, N.J.

Of **Catherine McDermott**, a native of DROGHEDA, County LOUTH, Ireland. When last heard from, about seven years ago, she was hired from 41st Street and 7th Avenue, with a gentleman from DOVER PLAINS, WESTCHESTER County, NEW YORK, since which time nothing has been heard from her. Any information of her will be thankfully received by addressing **John McCormack**, No. 183 WEST 33rd STREET. Readers of the Irish American will please notice.

Of **Peter Quirk**, a native of DERRY, County WEXFORD, Ireland. If he will call at 232 TWELFTH STREET, NEW YORK, he will get some money that has been left him.

April 4, 1863

Of **William O'Keefe**, of DROMORE, County CORK, Ireland, by his nephew, **Arthur O'Keefe**. He left Ireland some 26 years ago. When last heard from, some 12 or 14 years since, he was in PHILADELPHIA keeping a confectioner's store. Please address **Arthur O'Keefe**, BERGEN POINT, N.J.

Of **John Driscoll**, a native of the County of CORK – wife's maiden name **Ellen Walsh** – and of **John Walsh**, her brother, a native of CLONEA, Parish of MOTHILL, and County of WATERFORD. Any information of them will be thankfully received by their brother, **Patrick Walsh**, at **Mr. James O'Donnell's**, COLLEGE POINT, L.I., N.Y.

Of **Jeremiah Collins**, a native of BANDON, Co. CORK. He was lately discharged from the 1st U.S. Infantry. He can hear from his brother by writing to **John Dempsey**, 1721 Wood Street, PHILADELPHIA.

April 11, 1863

Of **Catharine Dossey**, a native of the County of MEATH, Ireland, who arrived in New York about fourteen years ago; she lived in PATERSON, NEW JERSEY, in 1856, and when last heard from was in ST. LOUIS, MO. Any information respecting her will be thankfully received by her sister, **Margaret Dossey**, at No. 185 Main Street, PATERSON, N.J.

Of **Bernard Garrity**, a native of the Parish of KILLIGLASS, County of ROSCOMMON, Ireland, who landed in New York about a year ago. Let him write, or call in person to his sister-in-law, **Mrs. Peter Garrity**, or his cousin **John Cain**, EAST RUTLAND, VERMONT.

April 18, 1863

Of **Thomas Halloran**, a native of the Parish of BALLYHIGH, County KERRY, Ireland, by his sister-in-law, **Ellen Sweeney**. When last heard of, he and mother, and brothers and sister, lived in SCHUYLHKIL County, State of PENNSYLVANIA. Any information of them will be thankfully received by **Ellen Sweeney**, 479 CHERRY STREET, NEW YORK.

April 25, 1863

Of **John Kiernan**, who left his home on the 2ⁿᵈ of April, at 87ᵗʰ STREET, between 3ʳᵈ and 4ᵗʰ Avenues. He has left a wife and four children to mourn his absence. Any information of him will be thankfully received at his sister's, 100 EAST 12ᵗʰ STREET; or by his old acquaintance, **Michael Maguire**, 143 1ˢᵗ AVENUE.

Of **Daniel Shea**, a native of BEREHAVEN, County CORK, Ireland, who emigrated from Youghal in the year 1835. When last heard from he was a resident of North Main Street, ROCHESTER, NEW YORK State. Any person or persons having any account of him, either dead or alive, would very much oblige by addressing a few lines to his brother **Patrick**, at No. 9 MULBERRY ST., (rear building), NEW YORK CITY.

Of **John McEnroe**, of OLDCASTLE, County MEATH, Ireland, a baker by trade, who came to this country about fourteen years since. Also, of his sister, **Madge McEnroe**, who, at the age of seventeen, married **Thomas Lowndes**, and came to this country about fourteen years since. Any information thankfully received by their sister, **Anne E. McEnroe**, 48 WEST 47ᵗʰ ST.

May 2, 1863

Of **Michael Pentony**, brother of **John Pentony**, LIVERPOOL, ENGLAND. He left Liverpool for New York seven years ago. Any person knowing his whereabouts will confer a favor by addressing Coakley Bros, Leather Dealers, 18 South Calvert Street, BALTIMORE., MD Other papers, please copy.

Of **Patrick** and **Peter Flinn**, of BALLINA, County MAYO, Ireland, by their nephew, **James Flinn**. When last heard of, Patrick worked in NEW YORK, between 10ᵗʰ and 11ᵗʰ AVENUES. Both are blacksmiths by trade. Any information of them will be thankfully received by their nephew, **James Flynn**, Co. D. 69ᵗʰ Regt, N.Y.S.N.G., Corcoran's Irish Legion, SUFFOLK, VA., or elsewhere. Pennsylvania papers, please.

Of **Patrick Henry**, a native of the Parish of KILMORE MOY, Townland of ARDNAREE, County SLIGO, Ireland, a cooper by trade, and having been brought up in the City of BELFAST. When last heard from he was in BALTIMORE, MD. Also, of his uncles, **Patrick** and **Michael O'Hara**, from ARDNAREE, County SLIGO, sons of **Arthur O'Hara**. They are twenty years in America. -When last heard from, in 1857, they were in CARBONDALE, LUZERNE County, PENN. Any information of them will be thankfully received by **Patrick Henry**, at No. 71 10ᵗʰ AVENUE, near West 15ᵗʰ Street, NEW YORK.

May 9, 1863

Of **Peter Dunne**, a native of SHANKHILL, County of DUBLIN, Ireland. Wife's maiden name, **Jane McAneney**; and of her niece, **Elizabeth Kiernan** a native of Harrold's Cross, City of DUBLIN. Any information of them will be thankfully received by their nephew, **George Kiernan**, at **Messrs. T. T. & C. W. Church**, FORT HAMILTON, Long Island, N.Y. New York and Brooklyn papers, please copy.

Of **Ellen Broderick**, a native of the Parish of ARDMORE, County of WATERFORD, Ireland. She was married to **James Dwyer**, of the Parish of ARDMORE, County of WATERFORD. When last heard from about 14 months ago, she was in the State of NEW YORK. Any information will be thankfully received by addressing her nephew, **Thomas Dee**, Co. L, 3ʳᵈ Regt., R.I.V., HILTON HEAD, S.C.

Of **Anne Fleming**, of KILDRUM, near KILBEGGAN, County WESTMEATH. When last heard of by the advertiser, was in BOSTON. Any information concerning her will be thankfully received by **Jeseph [sic] M. Jones**, Light Battery "D," 4ᵗʰ U.S. Artillery, SUFFOLK, VA.

Of **Ellen Sheehan**, from the County CORK, Ireland, who landed in New York on the 30th of April, in the ship *Edinburgh*, from Queenstown. Any information of her will be thankfully received by her cousin, **John Buckley**, No. 10 STATE STREET, NEW YORK.

May 16, 1863

Of **Thomas Hearn**, a native of the Parish of CARRICKBEG, County WATERFORD, Ireland, who emigrated to this country in the Fall of 1852; lived subsequently at ZANESVILLE, OHIO. When last heard from he was at ST. LOUIS, and intended going into ILLINOIS. Any information relative to him will be gratefully received by his brother **William**, at 285 EIGHTH AVENUE, NEW YORK. St. Louis and Illinois papers, please copy.

May 23, 1863

Of **Barnard Kelly**, who left WASHINGTON on the 9th of April, to come to PHILADELPHIA. Any information of him will be thankfully received by his distressed wife, at No. 10 Gaffney's Avenue, Fitzwater St., below Seventh St., PHILADELPHIA.

Of **Mary** and **Catherine Collins**, of FETHARD, County TIPPERARY, Ireland. Mary left about 16 years ago. Their father died one year ago last Easter, and left them some money. By calling on their cousin, **Mary Collins**, at 14 Hamilton Avenue, BROOKLYN, they will receive all particulars. Philadelphia papers, please copy.

Of **Ellen Hardiman**, a native of BALLINASLOE, County GALWAY, Ireland. When last heard from was in PHILADELPHIA. Any information of her will be thankfully received by **Mr. Thomas Lynch**, 774 South 6th St., PHILADELPHIA, PA.

Of **Thomas Strudgeon**, from the County of GALWAY, Ireland. When last heard from was at BARN HILL., SARATOGA Co., MARSELLES FALLS, N.Y Any information of him will be thankfully received by **Mr. John Lynch**, 774 South 6th Street, PHILADELPHIA, PA.

Of **James Monahan**, blacksmith, a native of RATHNALLY, County MEATH, Ireland. When last heard from (in 1851), he was in KENOSHA, WISCONSIN. Also, of **Thomas McDonnell**, machinist, a native of DROGHEDA, County LOUTH, Ireland. When last heard from (in 1856), he was working in the Eagle Foundry, ST. LOUIS, MO. Any information of either of them, or their wives, whose maiden names were **Teresa** and **Kate McCann**, will be thankfully received by the sister of the latter, **Rose M. McCann**, 33 EAST 25th STREET, NEW YORK. Wisconsin and Missouri papers, please copy.

Of **Dan** and **David Sheahan**, natives of BALLYCLOUGH, near MALLOW, County CORK, Ireland. When last heard from, they were in AUCKLAND, NEW ZEALAND. Any information of them will be thankfully received by their mother, **Mary Sheahan**, by writing to her, in care of Lynch, Cole & Meehan, Irish American Office, 32 Beekman Street, New York.

Of **Timothy Kelly**, late of CLONLISK, KING'S County, near ROSCREA, Ireland; or his heirs, if any. He or they (if living) will hear of something to their advantage, by addressing a letter to **John Fitzpatrick**, 154 EIGHTH AVENUE NEW YORK CITY.

Of **Ann, Maria**, and **John Trapp**, natives of the Town of MOATE, County WESTMEATH, Ireland. They will hear of something to their advantage by calling on or addressing **Thomas O'Brien**, No. 73 WATTS STREET, NEW YORK CITY.

May 30, 1863

Of **John Dowling**, tinsmith, late of Bridge St., in the City of BROOKLYN, supposed to be in the 69th Regiment, Irish Brigade. If he will call on **Thos. Rowan,** Real Estate Agent and Insurance Broker, No. 10 Mill St., Brooklyn, he will hear of something to his advantage.

Of **Bridget Murray**, a native of RATHMORE, County ROSCOMMON, Ireland, who arrived in New York, in the ship *North America*, on the 11th of May, and stopped at Castle Garden for two days, and then left. Any information of her will be thankfully received by her aunt, **Ann Tiernan**, by writing or calling at 75 Third Place, BROOKLYN, L.I.

Of **Bridget Ryan**, a native of CLOVERFIELD, in the County of LIMERICK Ireland. When last heard from she left Ireland on the 14th of March for New York. Any information of her will be thankfully received by her brother, **Patrick Ryan**, by writing to him to Swan Street, BUFFALO., N.Y, or to **Oliver Ryan**, Hamilton St., NEW HAVEN, CONN.

Of **Thomas Curley**, a native of ATHLONE, County WESTMEATH, Ireland, who arrived in New York on Monday, May 18th, in the ship *New World*, and stopped at Castle Garden. Any information of him will be thankfully received by **Edward Kelly**, by writing to him to Miller Street, GERMANTOWN., PHILADELPHIA Co, PENN

Of **Patrick, Mary** and **Kate Skehan**, and of **Henry Skehan**, natives of CARRICK-ON-SUIR, County TIPPERARY, Ireland. Any person knowing of their whereabouts will confer a favor by writing to their sister, **Bridget Skehan**, who arrived in this country eighteen months ago. Please direct in care of **General James A. Moore**, BELLEVILLE, ESSEX Co., NEW JERSEY, for Bridget Skehan.

Of **John Sullivan**, a native of MALLOW, County CORK, Ireland, who arrived in the *City of Washington* at New York on the 12th May, where he is supposed to be. Through accident, he got separated from his wife and left in NEW YORK, while she came on to BOSTON. Any one knowing anything of him will confer a great favor on a distressed family by writing to his son, **John Sullivan**, No. 63 Nashua Street, BOSTON, MASS.; or let him call on **John G. Dale**, No. 15 BROADWAY, who will pay his fare to BOSTON.

June 6, 1863

Of **Patrick, James** and **Margaret O'Sullivan**, natives of KILCROHAN, County KERRY, Ireland. When last heard from they were in WEST STOCKHOLM., ST. LAWRENCE County, N.Y Any information of them will be thankfully received by their brother, **Daniel O'Sullivan**, by writing to him in care of **Jas. Fitzgerald**, No. 7 NORTH WILLIAM STREET, NEW YORK.

Any person knowing the present location of **John** or **Michael O'Loghlen**, formerly of MOYHILL, Parish of RATH, County CLARE, Ireland, will confer a lasting favor on their brother, **Andrew O'Loghlen**, of 142 EAST 32nd STREET, NEW YORK CITY, by informing him of it. John emigrated to this country in 1846, and was supposed to be at NIAGARA FALLS, N.Y., lately; Michael in 1848, and was supposed to be at TIDOUCH, PENNSYLVANIA, lately.

Of **Thomas Cunningham**, a native of ANAGHAVACKEY, County of LOUTH, Ireland. When last heard of, ten years ago, he was in CINCINNATI, OHIO. Any information of him will be thankfully received by his brother, **Michael Cunningham**, by writing in care of **Mr. G. B. Hubbell** & Co., SING SING, WESTCHESTER County, State of NEW YORK. New Orleans papers, please copy. [Appeared July 18, 1863 and Jan. 23, 1864 with slightly different information.]

June 13, 1863

Of **Mary Anne Wren**, (maiden name **Young**), and **Julia Dwyer** (maiden name **Wren**), both natives of the City of DUBLIN, Ireland, and came to this country about twelve years ago. Any information of them, or their whereabouts, will be thankfully received by writing to **Joseph Wren**, Co. M, 9th N.Y. Vol. Cavalry Regt., Army of the Potomac, WASHINGTON, D. C. Other papers, please copy.

Of **Charles Phayer**, a native of the Parish of GALBALLY, County LIMERICK, Ireland. When last heard from, about ten years ago, he was in WISCONSIN. Any information of him will be thankfully received by his nephew, **Robert Phayer** (in care of **Edmund Lynch**) at 236 Hudson Avenue, BROOKLYN; or at the office of the Irish-American, 32 Beekman Street, N.Y.

Of **John Reynolds**, Currier, who left LIMERICK, Ireland, in 1847. Would very much favor and oblige his sister-in-law, **Mrs. Hanah Dwyer**, by writing or calling to see her at No. 6 Tappen-place, off Green Street, above 7th, PHILADELPHIA, PENNSYLVANIA, who has business of importance to relate to her sister **Margaret**. When last seen or heard of they were at PEEKSKILL, State of NEW YORK, in 1852. Other papers please copy.

Of **Pat, Thomas**, and **Edward Kenny**, natives of the Townland of LIS, Parish of TUBBER CLARE, County WESTMEATH, Ireland. When last heard from they were in COLCHESTER., CONN Any information of them will be thankfully received by their brother, **John Kenny**, by writing to him, in care of Lynch, Cole & Meehan, Irish-American Office, 32 Beekman-st., N. York.

Of **Thomas Ryan**, shoemaker by trade, a native of CASHEL, County TIPPERARY, Ireland. When last heard from, he landed in New York on the 9th of May, in the ship *Excelsior*, and stopped at Castle Garden two days. Any information of him will be thankfully received by **Daniel Kennedy**, by writing to him to No. 1 Spring St., WORCESTER, MASS.

Of **Maurice Dwyer**, who left the Parish of NEWCASTLE, County TIPPERARY, Ireland, in 1860, aged 30 years. When last heard of, two years ago, he was at MANHATTANVILLE, NEW YORK. Any information of him will be thankfully received by his sister, **Ellen Dwyer**, in care of **David Leonard**, ROCKFORD, WINNEBAGO County, State of ILLINOIS.

Of **Michael O'Donnell**, or either of his sons, **Thomas** or **John**, natives of ENNISTYMON, County CLARE, Ireland. When last heard of, they were in NEW YORK. Any information of them will be thankfully received by writing to **Thomas Barrington**, Co. K, 93rd Regt., N.Y.V. Headquarters Army of the Potomac.

Of **Timothy Whealan** and **Mrs. Whealan**, of YOUGHAL, County CORK, Ireland. When last heard from (13th of June, 1862), they were in BOSTON, MASS. Any information of them will be thankfully received by writing to **Eliza Canty**, ELIZABETHPORT, NEW JERSEY.

June 20, 1863

Of **Mary Weeks**, a native of the Parish of GRANGE, County of LIMERICK, Ireland. When last heard from, fourteen years ago, was in NEW YORK. Any information of her will be thankfully received by her nephew **George Weeks**, No. 9 Bank-street, PHILADELPHIA, PENNSYLVANIA.

John Ganley wishes to ascertain the whereabouts of his brother **Michael Ganley**, native of BALLYMORE, County of WESTMEATH, Ireland. When last seen by him, he was in NEW YORK CITY. Any information tending to the discovery of his present abode will be duly appreciated. Please address John Ganley, NEVADA, COLORADO Territory.

Of **Ned Moore** (husband of **Mary Higgins**), ROUND STONE, CONNEMARA, born in CURDAROON, County MAYO, Ireland. Any information of him will be thankfully received by his sister **Bridget Moore**, 112 EAST BROADWAY, City of NEW YORK.

Of **Michael, William** and **Thomas Ryan** (sons of **Mary Mackesy**), natives of the Town of TIPPERARY, Ireland. When last heard from, nine years ago, were in the gold diggings, CALIFORNIA. Any information of them will be thankfully received by their sisters, **Mary** and **Catherine Ryan**, by writing to them in care of **John Mullan**, 326 PEARL-STREET, NEW YORK.

Of **Honora Ryan** (daughter of **Mary Mackesy**), who was married to a man by the name of **Hackett**, a native of the Town of TIPPERARY, Ireland. When last heard from, eight years ago, was living in ST. LOUIS, Mo Any information of her will be thankfully received by her sisters, **Catherine** and **Mary Ryan**, by writing to them to 326 PEARL-STREET, NEW YORK, in care of **John Mullen**.

Of **Ellen O'Brien**, native of DUNGARVAN, County WATERFORD, Ireland, who arrived in Halifax, Nova Scotia, about two years ago. Any information of her will be thankfully received by her sister **Ann O'Brien**, who landed in New York about six weeks ago. Please direct your letter in care of **William Wade**, 38 CHERRY-STREET, NEW YORK. Halifax papers please copy.

Of **Alice Rogers**, a native of MINNEHENEN, County TYRONE, Ireland, who arrived in New York on the 21st of May, in the ship *Minehaha*, and stopped at Castle Garden. Any information of her will be thankfully received by her sister **Barbara Rogers**, by writing to her to WATERTOWN, MASS.; or to George W. Wheeler, Esq., Castle Garden, New York, who will send her on to her sister in Massachusetts.

Of **John Fallon**, of BRYERFIELD, Parish of ORAM, County ROSCOMMON, Ireland. When last heard from he was in BROOKLYN. Any information of him will be thankfully received by his cousin, **Michael Ward**, care of **T. B. Chase**, 111 FULTON-STREET, NEW YORK.

Of **Julia** and **Mary Barry**, natives of BANTRY, Parish of KILLKRINE, County of CORK, Ireland. When last heard from, fourteen years ago, they were in NEW YORK. Any information of them will be thankfully received by their brother **Michael Barry**, by writing to him to FORT COLUMBUS, NEW YORK HARBOR.

June 27, 1863

Of **Mr. Thomas Keane**, his son **Thomas**, and daughters **Mary** and **Easther**, who sailed from the City of Dublin about the year 1847; supposed to have arrived and residing in some part of the United States. If this should meet their eyes, and they wishing to see their brother **John**, that was left behind, they can address **John MacDonald**, 129 4th AVENUE, NEW YORK; or if any person knowing their whereabouts will confer a great favor or will be paid for their trouble.

Of **James** and **Owen Farrell**, natives of the County LONGFORD. When last heard from, in 1854, they were in NEW YORK. Any information concerning them will be thankfully received by their brother, **Thomas Farrell**. Address Ordnance Department, FORT UNION, NEW MEXICO.

Of **John, Margaret, Michael** and **Robert Purtell**, of the Parish of CROW, County LIMERICK, Ireland. When last heard from, were in DETROIT, MICH Any information of them will be thankfully received by their brother, **William Purtell**, WEST TROY, N.Y.

Of **John Fitzgibbons**, of RINGLEA, County CLARE, by his niece, **Mary Kelly**, daughter of **John Kelly** and **Margaret Fitzgibbons**, of TUBBOR. Call at 490 6th AVENUE, NEW YORK, between 29th and 30th Streets, Room 9.

Of **John Hennessy**, of YOUGHAL, County CORK, Ireland, who left Liverpool for Boston in 1852, aged about 49 years. When last heard from was in the State of ILLINOIS. Any information of him will be most thankfully received by his old friend, **Catherine Foley**, 939 North Second Street, PHILADELPHIA, PA.

July 4, 1863

Of **Thomas Minnick**, who arrived in New-York on last Friday week, by ship *Ontario* from Liverpool. Any information of him will be thankfully received by his brother **Hugh**, at **Mr. John McGuire's**, cor. of 34th STREET and FIRST AVENUE, NEW-YORK.

Of **Mary Anne Walsh**, alias **McDonnell**, daughter of **Owen** and **Ann McDonnell**, of the Canal Bank, next to Old Brewery, LIMERICK. When last heard from, in 1859, she was residing with her husband, **Michael Walsh**, at No. 20 Rose Street BALTIMORE, MARYLAND. Any information of her will be thankfully received by her friends if addressed to the care of **Rev. Michael Malone**, C.C., St. Michael's, LIMERICK, Ireland.

Of **James Cummins**, miller, formerly of ASKEATON, Ireland. He is requested to forward his address to or call at the office of the Irish American, as a niece of his, who lately arrived from LIMERICK, wishes to hear from him.

Of **Mary Carrol (Mrs. Burns)**, a native of EGLISH, County TIPPERARY, Ireland. When last seen by her husband, **Martin Burns**, was in FISHKILL LANDING, DUTCHESS County, NEW YORK. Please address **Thomas Maher**, 609 Lombard Street, PHILADELPHIA.

Of **Michael Nolan**, a native of COROFIN, County CLARE, Ireland; also of his nephew and niece, **Daniel** and **Bridget Neylan**. The former served in the British Army, and lived some years in RHODE ISLAND, U.S., the latter arrived in New-York by the steamship *Washington*, on the 6th April, 1863. Their passage was paid to the City of OTTAWA, CANADA WEST. Please address **Anne Nolan**, COBOURGH, CANADA WEST.

Of **Ellen, Mary Anne** and **Cornelius Sweeny**, natives of Ann Street, City of CORK, Ireland. Ellen left home in 1847, Mary Ann in 1848. They came to New York, and went on to MOUNT MORRIS, LIVINGSTON County, N.Y. When last heard from, Ellen resided in BOSTON, MASS. Any information of them will be thankfully received by their sister, **Margaret Sweeny**, by writing to her in care of **Mrs. Riordan**, 104 ELEVENTH STREET, between 1st and 2nd Avenues, NEW YORK. Boston papers, please copy.

July 11, 1863

Of **Thomas Gloster**, carpenter, who left TORONTO, CANADA WEST, about four years ago. When last heard from, he was residing in NEW YORK CITY. Any information respecting his whereabouts will be thankfully received by his brother, **James Gloster** 29th Battery, N.Y.S.V., CAMP BARRY, WASHINGTON, D. C or his father, **Thomas Gloster**, 13 Melinda Street, CANADA WEST.

Of **James McAnnally**, from near VERNER'S BRIDGE, County ARMAGH, Ireland. He left PHILADELPHIA on the 1st of April, 1848, to go to WASHINGTON or GEORGETOWN, to work on railroads for a contractor named **MacIntire**. Any information of him will be thankfully received by his aged mother, who has just arrived, and is living at 520 South Street, PHILADELPHIA. Direct in care of **Peter Molloy**, 520 South Street, PHILADELPHIA, for **Mary McAnnally**.

Of **Mr. Ambrose Folliott**, formerly of OLD-CASTLE, Ireland. When last heard from, he was going with a **Mr. Gustavus Kelly** to the silver mines of WASO or WASH RIVER from STRINGTOWN, BUTTE County, CALIFORNIA. The decease of his uncle makes his immediate return home necessary. He can get further information by addressing his brother-in-law, **Mr. Darby**, Box 906 WASHINGTON, D. C. [Appeared under County MEATH]

Of **Mary Ann Norris**, a native of BALLINLOUGH, County MEATH, Ireland, who arrived in New York in May. Her brother, **Thomas Norris**, arrived in New York on the 17th May.

Any information of her will be thankfully received by him at **John Fagan's** confectioner store, 32ⁿᵈ STREET, near 1ˢᵗ Avenue, NEW YORK.

Of **Mary** and **Ellen Mackey**. Mary was born in SIX-MILE BRIDGE, County CLARE, Ireland. Ellen was born in NEW YORK. Any information of them will be thankfully received by their father, **Patrick Mackey**, by writing to him in care of **Thomas Griffin**, No. 240 WATER STREET, NEW YORK

July 18, 1863

Of **Mary Molony**, by her son **Michael**, or of **Martin Hayes** and **James Dougherty**. When last heard from they were in NEW-YORK CITY. Direct to **Michael Molony**, U.S. Hospital, Ward, 36, Chestnut St., PHILADELPHIA.

Of **Michael Dunn**, a native of EDENDERRY, KING'S County, Ireland. When last heard from, was in CINCINNATI, OHIO. Any information of him will be thankfully received by his nephew, **John Dunn**, by writing to him to 295 Degraw Street, BROOKLYN, N.Y.

Of **Thomas Cunningham**, a native of ANNAHAVACKEY, County of LOUTH, Ireland, who came to this country about 14 years ago. When last heard of him, ten years ago, he was in CINCINNATI, OHIO. Any information of him will be thankfully received by his brother, **Michael Cunningham**, by writing in care of **Mr. G. Hubbell** & Co., SING SING, WESTCHESTER County, N.Y. Cincinnati papers, please copy. [Appeared June 6, 1863 and Jan. 23, 1864 with slightly different information.]

July 25, 1863

Of **Hugh McDonough**, a native of ARRAN, Co. GALWAY, who landed in New York in June last. Any information respecting him will be thankfully received by his uncle, **Thomas McDonough**, FOX CURT, CORTLAND, MAINE.

Of **Michael Kenealey**, aged 26 years, and **Mary Kenealey**, aged 24 years. They lived in MASSTOWN, County CORK, Ireland. Their parents came to this country with them, and died one week after landing. They arrived in CONNECTICUT April 22, 1846. Mary was a dressmaker. Any information of them will be thankfully received by their sister Hannah, who arrived in Boston April 22, 1863, addressed to **Hannah Kenealey**, care of **E. Moffett**, American Bank Note Co., 39 State Street, BOSTON, MASS.

Of **Edmund Power**, a native of BOULAH, Parish of BALLYGORMICK, County WATERFORD, who left Ireland two years ago last April. When last heard from he was in NORTHWHITE CREEK WASHINGTON County, State of NEW YORK. Any information concerning him will be thankfully received by his wife, **Catherine**, who is after landing in this country. Address Mrs. Power, No. 76 Flatbush Avenue, BROOKLYN. California papers, please copy.

August 1, 1863

Of **Bridget Murphy**, who arrived in this country in April last, per ship *Thornton*, from Liverpool, and whose friends reside in DELPHI, INDIANA. Also, of **Johanna Cantwell**, from FETHARD, County TIPPERARY, Ireland, who arrived in New York per *Vanguard*, June 1863. Apply to Andrew Carrigan, President, Irish Emigrant Society, 51 Chambers Street, New York.

August 15, 1863

Of **Margaret Ganahan**, a native of the Parish of EMPER, County WESTMEATH, Ireland, who was married to a man, named **John Floyd**, from the same place. When last heard from, eight years ago, were in BROOKLYN. Any information of them will be thankfully received by their sister, **Bridget Ganahan**, by writing to her to No. 32 ROOSEVELT STREET, NEW YORK, in care of **John Carroll**.

Of **Patrick, Edward** and **Catherine Quinne**, and also their mother, **Elizabeth McDermott**, from CLONEE, Parish of DUNLEVIN, County MEATH, Ireland, who emigrated to New York about ten years ago. When last heard from (about four years ago), they were in NEW YORK. Patrick and Edward were blacksmiths by trade. Any information of them will be thankfully received by their affectionate brother, **Michael Quinne**, care of **Mr. Robert Walsh**, 69 St. Eustache Street, QUEBEC, CANADA.

Of **Thomas Tarpy**, who landed in New York last May, from the ship *Bridgewater*. He there received railroad tickets through to INDIANAPOLIS, but since that time has not been heard from. He is nineteen years old, is the son of **William** and **Mary Tarpy,** of ST. BRANDON'S, Parish of KILLYON, County GALWAY. Any information of him will be thankfully received by his sister, **Mary Tarpy**, care of **J. L. Ketchum**, Esq. Indianapolis, Ind.

Of **James Scully**, formerly of KING'S County, Ireland. When last heard from, was in CINCINNATI, O. Any information of him will be thankfully received by his brother, **Wm. Scully**, WATERBURY, CONN.

Of **Bridget Carmody**, of the Parish of TROUGH, County CLARE, Ireland, who sailed from Liverpool and landed in New York about seven or eight years ago. -When last heard from, she was in BERKSHIRE County, MASS Any information of her will be thankfully received by her brother **Tom**, and uncle, **James Carmody**, LANCASTER. Post-Office, GRANT County, WIS

Of **Anthony O'Hara**, who left the Parish of BACKS County MAYO, two years ago, and came to the United States. When last heard from, he was in the United States Army, Battery G., 5th Artillery, FORT HAMILTON, NEW YORK harbor. Any information of his whereabouts will be thankfully received by his brother, **Michl. O'Hara**, MEADVILLE, CRAWFORD County, PA.

Of **James** and **Margaret Calnan**, natives of MACROOM, OMEADON, County CORK, Ireland. When last heard from, they were in MALDEN CENTRE, MIDDLESEX County, MASS. Any information of them will be thankfully received by their sisters **Ellen** and **Mary**, by writing to them, in care of **Henry Wolten**, No. 116 CENTRE STREET, cor. Franklin Street, NEW YORK.

Of **Johanna Riordan**, of KNOCKROE, Parish of KILNAMARTARA, County CORK, Ireland, who landed in New York the 1st of May, and is supposed to be in NEW YORK or its vicinity. Any information of her will be thankfully received by her brother **Timothy**, in care of **John Quill**, NEWBURYPORT, MASS

August 22, 1863

Of **Edward, Peter** and **John Mellely**, who were in PENNSYLVANIA six years ago, and have not been heard from since. Any information respecting them will be thankfully received by their sister, **Catherine Mellely**, 113 Elliott Place, BROOKLYN, N.Y. Illinois and St. Louis papers, please copy.

Of **Patrick** and **Mary McCade**. When last heard from were in FLEMING HILL, CAYUGA County, NEW YORK. Direct to **Julia McNamarra**. THOMPSONVILLE., CONNECTICUT. *Boston Pilot*, please copy.

Of **Mary O'Claughessy** (daughter of **Timothy O'Claughessy** and **Ellen O'Cleary**, of BALLINTUBBER, Parish of GLENROE, County LIMERICK, Ireland,) who came to this country about 15 years ago, and when last heard from was in the State of OHIO. Any intelligence of her will be thankfully received by her brother, **David O'Claughessy**, who arrived here last May. Direct to him at FALL BROOK, TIOGA County, PA

Of **Patrick Keys**, a native of the Parish of MOYNE, County TIPPERARY, Ireland, who came to this country in 1849. When last heard from, eleven years ago, he was in CHICAGO, ILLINOIS. Any intelligence of him will be thankfully received by his brother-in-law, **Simon Wall**, 617 South Front Street, PHILADELPHIA.

Of **Mrs. Mary Scully**, a native of TIPPERARY, Ireland, who is missing from her home since the 30th of July; aged 67 years, long features, gray hair, a little silly, but quiet, had on a black alpacca dress, and black shawl with a broche border, also, a red and black woolen shawl, a small cross barred calico skirt and sack, and leather shoes. Any information of her will be thankfully received by her husband, **William Scully**, No. 95 WEST 27th STREET, NEW YORK.

Of **John Callaghan**, a native of KILRUSH, County CLARE, Ireland. He was a member of Co. G, 88th Regiment, Meagher's Irish Brigade, was taken prisoner at the battle of FREDERICKSBURG, and has not been heard of since. Any intelligence respecting him will be thankfully received by his brother, **Patrick Callaghan**, 602 SIXTH AVENUE, NEW YORK.

August 29, 1863

Of **Denis McEvoy**, a native of DUBLIN, aged 30 years, horseshoer by trade. When last heard of, in 1859, was in HOUSTON, TEXAS. Any information will be thankfully received by **M. Dempsey**, 39 Kent Avenue, EAST BROOKLYN, L.I.

Of **Mary Magovern**, a native of the Parish of KILLINA, County CAVAN, Ireland, who came to the United States, fifteen years ago. She had left PHILADELPHIA for CINCINNATI about eight years ago. Any information will be thankfully received by her uncle, **Mr. Thomas Magovern**, 714 Stafford Street, between Shippen and Fitzwater Streets, PHILADELPHIA.

Of **Joseph**, **Maria**, **Annie** and **Elizabeth Dillon**, of BALLYGAR, County GALWAY, Ireland, by their brother, **Robert Dillon**. Address, Box 3656, BOSTON Post office.

Of **Bridget** and **Edmond Hogan**, natives of TORY HILL, in the Parish of CROOM, County LIMERICK, Ireland. When last heard from they were in CANADA EAST. Any intelligence of them will be thankfully received by their youngest brother, **Michael Hogan**, who came to this country a short time since. If this should come under the notice of **Patrick** or **John Buckley**, natives of the same place, they will confer a great favor on their cousin Michael Hogan, by writing to him to 311 EAST BROADWAY, NEW YORK, in care of **John McLaughlin**. Canada papers, please copy.

September 5, 1863

Of **Patrrick** [sic] **McTernan**, who emigrated from No. 101 James Street, in the City of DUBLIN, and who was born in the County LEITRIM, Ireland. He left Dublin about the year 1849. Any person knowing anything of him will confer a favor by writing to **Myles Gerald Keon**, 15th Street, between 5th and 6th Avenues, GOWANUS, SOUTH BROOKLYN, L.I., NEW YORK.

Of **Edward O'Rourke**, a native of the Parish of DURROW, QUEEN'S County, who left Ireland in 1854. When last heard from he was serving in the Second Regt., U.S. Cavalry, Company D, FORT MASON, TEXAS. Any information respecting him will be thankfully received by his brother, **Daniel O'Rourke**, 141 BOWERY, NEW YORK. [Appeared Sept. 12, 1863 with the name Daniel O'Rourke changed to **Samuel O'Rourke**. Also appeared Feb. 27, 1864, with additional information]

Of **Ellen Barry**, daughter of **Patrick Barry** and **Ellen Roberts**, of KILLARNEY, County KERRY, Ireland, who left BOSTON about 1852 or '53 to come to NEW YORK to her cousin, **Mrs. Healy**. It is supposed she got the wrong directions from a friend in Boston. Any information concerning her will be thankfully received by **Frank Roberts**, 142 MAIDEN LANE, or her brother, **Thos. Barry**, DANVILLE, VERMILION County, ILL

Of **Mary Sheridan**, a native of DUNGARVAN, County WATERFORD, Ireland, who landed in this country about nine years ago. Any information will be thankfully received by her brothers, **Denis** and **Michael Sheridan**, by writing to them in care of **Timothy Brosnan**, 78 WASHINGTON STREET, NEW YORK.

Of **William McGinty**, a native of the Parish of RAPHOE, County DONEGAL, Ireland, who came to this country about 14 years ago. When last heard from (about 8 years ago) he was in NEW YORK CITY. Any information of him will be kindly received by his brother, **Anthony McGinty**, at the cor. of Warren and Chatham Streets, NEWARK, N.J

September 12, 1863

Of **Terence McGirr**, a butcher, or his brother **James**, a shoemaker, or their brother-in-law, **Thomas Brooks**, who left STRABANE, County TYRONE, Ireland, for NEW YORK about the year 1835 or '36. Anyone knowing of their address would confer a lasting favor by sending it to **Susan McManus**, otherwise **Mrs. Beatty**, 27 Lee Street, BALTIMORE, MARYLAND.

Of **James McMullen**, a native of LOUGHIN ISLAND, County DOWN, Ireland. When last heard from, last December ten years ago, he was in BATON ROUGE, LA Any information of him will be thankfully received by his sister **Agnes McMullen**, by writing to her in care of **Mr. Richard Fitzsimons**, 121 FIRST AVENUE, NEW YORK.

Of **Anthony Gaffney**, a native of the County CAVAN, Townland of CARRICKATUBBER, near CROSS KEYS, Parish of DENN, Ireland. When last heard of (about thirteen years ago), he was on his own farm in some part of the State of INDIANA. Any account from himself or any other person will be thankfully received by his brother, **James Gaffney**, 13 Rose Street, NEW HAVEN, CONN.; or by **John Smith**, 172 WEST 32nd STREET, NEW YORK.

September 19, 1863

Of **Walter Power**. When last heard from, he was employed in **Mr. G. C. Boynton's** factory, St. Gabriel Locks, MONTREAL, CANADA EAST. Any person knowing his whereabouts will confer a favor by writing to his wife, **Rosanna Power**, 44 RIVINGTON STREET, NEW YORK; or at the office of the Irish-American, 32 Beekman St., New York. Canada papers, please copy.

Of **Mrs. Burns** (maiden name, **Mary Sullivan**), from the Parish of BALLYHAGRAN, County LIMERICK, Ireland, who emigrated to New York about eight years ago. When last heard from (about five years ago), was living in GEORGETOWN, D. C. Her whereabouts will be thankfully received by her sister, **Johannah Sullivan**, in care of **J. B. Dayton**, CAMDEN, N.J. Washington papers, please copy.

Of **Martin Adams**, or wife (maiden name, **Catherine Robinson**), from the Parish of AUGHAMORE, County MAYO, Ireland. When last heard from, he was in the State of OHIO, HAMILTON County, COLLEGE GREEN-Any information of his whereabouts will be thankfully received by his nephew, **Patrick Adams**, OLNEYVILLE, R.I. Ohio papers, please copy.

Of **William Pratt**, who left Ireland about the 1st of July, 1863, for the City of NEW YORK. He is a native of RATHDOWNAWAY, EAST, QUEEN'S County, Ireland, and about sixteen years of age. Any information respecting him will be thankfully received by his uncle, **John Pratt**, PATERSON, N.J, or address **Bernard O'Neill**, Justice of the Peace, PATERSON, N.J.

Of **Patrick Manning**, who left DUNGARVAN, County WATERFORD, Ireland, about 15 years ago. Any intelligence respecting him will be thankfully received by his brother, **E. Manning**, who lately landed in New York, by writing to **Mr. Michael Cavney**, 191 CHERRY ST., NEW YORK. Boston papers, please copy.

Of **Sarah McGee**, a native of GOLOUGH, County DONEGAL, Ireland, daughter of **Edward** and **Winnifred McGee**. When last heard from, she was living with either **Mr. Willie People** or **Mr. James Sweeny**, at GOLOUGH, County DONEGAL, Ireland. Any information of her will be thankfully received by her sister, **Margaret McGee**, No. 448 4th STREET, NEW YORK.

September 26, 1863

Of **Bridget Connor**, a native of the Parish of TIEBOHAN, Townland of CLOONCHANVILLE and County of ROSCOMMON, Ireland. When last heard from was in HALIFAX, CANADA. Any information of her will be thankfully received by her sister, **Mrs. Mary Regan**, 508 CANAL STREET, NEW YORK. Canada papers, please copy.

Of **Patrick Moran**, a native of GORTHNACLOY, Parish of ELPHIN, County ROSCOMMON, Ireland, who emigrated to this country last Spring, and is supposed to be either in NEW YORK, or WASHINGTON, D. C. Any information of him will be thankfully received by addressing a few lines to his brother-in-law, **Patrick Morris**, corner of Market and Catherine Streets, NEWARK, N.J., in care of **Messrs. Halsey & Tucker**. New York and Washington papers, please copy.

Of **John Ryan**, of BOURISHOLEIGH, County TIPPERARY, Ireland, who landed at New York, April 22, 1860. Address **Bridget Ryan**, Box No. 1380, BALTIMORE Post-office.

Of **John Shannon**, a native of FEEAHOE, Co. MONAGHAN, Ireland, and who left there about thirty-five years ago. When last heard of he was in NEWBURGH, ORANGE County, NEW YORK. Any information of his whereabouts will be thankfully received by his nephew, **Nicholas Shannon**, by writing to him in care of **Mr. Pat McGowan**, American Street, three doors below Jefferson, PHILADELPHIA.

October 3, 1863

Of **Mary, Catharine, Walter, Dennis**, and **Edward Jordan**, formerly of CURSKA, Parish of KILTRUSTEN Co. ROSCOMMON, Ireland, who emigrated with their father, **Edward Jordan**, in 1847, and have not been heard from in 8 years. Any information of them will be thankfully received by their sister, **Margaret Jordan**, by writing to her in care of **John Waldron**, 18 Vandam St., Pedan's Avenue, house 5, PHILADELPHIA, PA, or at the office of the Irish-American, 32 Beekman St., N.Y. [Appeared Oct. 10, 1863 with John Waldron's address as No. 5 Pedan's Avenue, Nandain-st., between 18th and 19th-sts., PHILADELPHIA, PA. Also on the 10th the ad included the following copy request: Canada and California papers, please copy.]

Of **Mr. Wm. Hogan**, of the County TIPPERARY, Ireland, who came to the States 10 years ago. When last heard from he was in CANADA. Any information of him will be thankfully received by his daughter, **Honora Hogan**, No. 183 CHERRY STREET, NEW YORK. Canada papers, please copy.

Of **George Ketcheside**, late of the Constabulary Force of KILMACRENAN, County DONEGAL, Ireland. If he applies by letter or in person to **Charles Rogers**, of the Girard House, he will hear of something to his advantage.

Of **Edward Campbell**, a native of the Parish of KILLATHDURNEY, County DONEGAL, Ireland. When last heard from was in PEORIA County, ILLINOIS. Any information of him will be thankfully received by his mother, **Mary Campbell**, or his brother, **George Campbell**, 1825 Jones Street PHILADELPHIA. PA

October 10, 1863

Of **Patrick Molony**, son of **James** and **Mary Molony**, of ASHTON-UNDER-LYNE, LANCASHIRE, ENGLAND, who left there (seven years ago) for the United States. When last heard from (four years ago) he was in BROOKLYN, NEW YORK. Any information of him or his wife, **Catherine Meehan**, will be thankfully received by his sister, **Bridget Molony**, at 102 Common St., LAWRENCE, MASS

Of **William Lynd**, a native of the Parish of ARDBOE, County TYRONE, Ireland. When last heard from he was in ORANGE County, State of NEW YORK. Any information of him will be thankfully received by his brother, **John Lynd**, at No. 68 Grand Street, NEW HAVEN, CT. California papers, please copy.

Of **John Shea** and **Ellen McQuinn**, who left RATONY, County of KERRY, Ireland, fifteen years ago. When last heard from they were in CLINTON County, State of NEW YORK. Any information of them will be thankfully received by their daughter, **Margaret Shea**, 532 Columbia Street, BROOKLYN, for **Thomas Brosnan**.

Of **Mary Hynes** and **Nanny Lyden**, who left Galway in the steamer *Anglia*, and arrived in Boston on Saturday, September 26. Any information of them will be thankfully received by **Joseph Anderson**, by writing to him to 20th Street, between M and N, WASHINGTON, D. C.

Of **Patrick Moohan**, son of **Terence Moohan**, of KILLEEN, near BALLYSHANAN, County DONEGAL, Ireland. Any information of him will be thankfully received by **P. Daly**, 82 FULTON STREET, NEW YORK CITY, and his enquiring parents.

Of **Hugh Cassidy**. When last heard from was in PHILADELPHIA. Also of **William J. Cassidy**. When last heard from was in the Government service in TEXAS. Also of **James Cassidy**. When last heard from was in the United States service. All are sons of the late **Michael Cassidy**, Esq., Castle Street, BALLYSHANAN, County DONEGAL, Ireland. Any information of them will be thankfully received by **P. Daly**, 82 FULTON STREET, NEW YORK CITY.

October 17, 1863

Of **Mary Gallagher**, a native of the Parish of HORSE LEAP, Townland SELIEVE, County WESTMEATH, Ireland, who arrived in New York in May, 1855; when last heard from, in April, 1862, her residence was No. 226 EAST 22nd STREET, NEW YORK CITY. Also of her brother, **Hugh**, who arrived in January, 1863. Any information of them will be thankfully received by their sister, **Bridget**, by writing to her in care of **Mr. Waiter**, No. 40 William-street, SOUTH BROOKLYN, L.I., or at the office of the Irish-American.

Of **Mrs. Mary Lennon**, maiden name **Brennan**, a native of TERENACHREE, DERRYNOOSE, County ARMAGH, or MIDDLETOWN, TYNAN, Ireland. When last heard from, was in AUBURN, intending to visit her brother, **Hugh Brennan**, HAGERSTOWN, WAYNE County, INDIANA. Any information of her whereabouts will be thankfully received by her widowed son and daughter, **John Lennon** and **Eliza Johnston**, corner Liberty and E Sts. GREENPOINT, L.I Indiana papers, please copy.

Of **Patrick Melia**, a native of the County MEATH, Parish of BYERSTOWN, Ireland; who landed in New York, in the ship *Cornelius Grinnell*, in May, 1854; when last heard from he was in SULLIVAN County with one **Dr. Livingston**. Any information of him will be thankfully received by his nephew, **Thomas Stanton**, who has lately arrived in this country, at 77 7th-AVENUE, NEW YORK CITY.

Of **Patrick Reily, Thomas Reily**, and **Ellen Reily**, alias **Ellen Brennan**, all natives of the County KERRY, Ireland. When last heard from, Patrick and Thomas were in CHICAGO, ILL., and Ellen was in JEFFERSON CITY, MO Any information of them will be thankfully received by their mother, **Mary Reily**, by writing to her in care of **Daniel Connor**, 89 WASHINGTON STREET, NEW YORK CITY.

October 24, 1863

Maria Lawler, please leave or send your address to the office of this paper.

Of **Mary Donahoe**, a native of the Parish of KILLMACKTRANY, Townland of KILLAMY, County SLIGO, Ireland, who left Liverpool in August last for New York. Any information of her will be thankfully received by her brother **Patrick Donahoe**, WEST RUTLAND, VERMONT.

Of **James McBrerty**, a native of the Parish of KILLATEE, County DONEGAL, Ireland. When last heard from, was in PHOENIXVILLE, PA Any information of him will be thankfully received by his wife, **Bridget McBrerty**, 1828 Barker Street, or **George Campbell**, 1825 Joines Street, PHILADELPHIA, PA.

October 31, 1863

Of **Eliza Burns**, a native of Grange Gorman Lane, City of DUBLIN, Ireland, who left there 13 years ago, in company with **Mr. Joseph Dempsey**, from JOBESTOWN, County DUBLIN. Any information of her will be thankfully received by her sister, **Mrs. Wilson**, by writing to her to 477 DIVISION-STREET, NEW YORK. [Appeared Nov. 7, 1863 with Mrs. Wilson's address changed to 47 ½ DIVISION STREET, NEW YORK.]

Of **Jane Lavelle**, of CASTLEBAR, County MAYO, Ireland, who married **John Madden**, from CASTLEREA, County ROSCOMMON. They came to America about 16 years ago, and landed in New York. Any information of them will be thankfully received by her son, **Michael Madden**, by writing to him in care of Messrs. Lynch, Cole & Meehan, Irish-American Office, 32 Beekman St., New York. [Appeared Nov. 14, 1863 with more information]

If **Dennis Miskill**, formerly of CORK, Ireland, should see this notice he will please write to his brother **Thomas**, at 10 BATTERY PLACE, N.Y; or if any acquaintance of his knows of his whereabouts they will confer a great favor by informing me. He was a miller by occupation, and had a blue mole on his cheek.

Of **Mary Molony**, a native of the County LIMERICK, Ireland. When last heard from she was in OGDENSBURG, N.Y. in June, 1862. Any information of her will be thankfully received by her sister **Anne**, by writing to her to Pavilion, No. 13, U.S. General Hospital, DAVID'S ISLAND, N.Y.

Of **Michael Hickey**, a native of KILLONAN, County LIMERICK, Ireland. When last heard from was in NEW YORK State. Any information of him will be thankfully received by **John Fitzpatrick**, by writing to him to No. 200 Columbia Street, BROOKLYN, L.I.

Of **James Walsh**, who left MORTALSTOWN, KILFINANE, County LIMERICK, Ireland, on the 6th of October for New York. Any information respecting him will be thankfully received by **William Murphy**, 250 BOWERY, NEW YORK.

Of **Philip Griffin**, of the Parish of INVER, County DONEGAL, Ireland. When last heard from was in the South. Left Ireland about six years ago. Any information of him will be thankfully received by his wife, **Jane Griffin**, at No. 623 WASHINGTON STREET, NEW YORK.

Of **Mark Donohue, Cesily Donohue, Honora Donohue, Mary Folan**, wife of **Patrick Curran**, and **Catherine Folan**, wife of **William Madden**, who came out in the bark *Barbara* in 1856, from PARK, near SPIDDELL, County GALWAY, Ireland. Any intelligence of them will be thankfully received by writing to **Walter Donohue**, 73 CANAL STREET, NEW YORK.

November 14, 1863

Of **Mrs. Jane Wilson** or **Lucy Kavanagh**, PIIKINGTON, THORPSVILLE, P.O., CANADA. Direct to Castle Garden, New York, for **Anne Kavanagh**. Canada papers, please copy.

Of **Michael** and **Paul Egan**, late of the County CLARE, Ireland; last residence WATERLOO, NEW HOPE, CANADA WEST. Direct **Winnifred Egan**, 183 HOUSTON ST., NEW YORK. Canada papers, please copy.

Of **Catherine** and **Bridget Connors**, natives of the Parish of LURRA, COOLAGOWN, MOATFIELD, County TIPPERARY, Ireland. When last heard from were in NEW YORK. Any information of them will be thankfully received by their sister, **Mary Connors**, by writing to her to No. 89 East Baltic Street, BROOKLYN, N.Y. Also, of **William Connors**, blacksmith, from the same place, who left MOUNT MELLICK for New York. Address Mary Connors as above.

Of **Jane Madden** (maiden name, **Jane Lavelle**), a native of CASTLEBAR, County MAYO, Ireland, who sailed from Sligo for this country about 16 years ago. She was accompanied by her brother, **Edward Lavelle**, and three of her children named **Mary, Jane** and **Patrick Madden**. They are supposed to be in DUNKIRK or the neighborhood. Any information of them will be thankfully received by her son, **Michael Madden**, who landed in New York about three weeks ago, by writing to him to the Irish-American office, New York. [Appeared Oct. 31, 1863 with less information.]

Of **James Rafferty**, a native of the Townland of KNOCKANORNY, Parish of GLEN, near NEWRY, County DOWN, Ireland, who came to this country about 4 years ago. When last heard from, two years since, was residing at FLATLANDS, near BROOKLYN, Long Island, NEW YORK. Any information regarding him will be thankfully received by addressing his brother, **Charles Rafferty**, in care of the Falls Co., NORWICH, CONN

Of **John, Michael** and **Simon Kelly**, natives of the Parish of QUANSBOROUGH, Townland of CLONAMASKA, Village of RAHEEN, County GALWAY, Ireland. When last heard from, Simon parted with his sister **Ellen**, who came in the ship *Thornton* from Liverpool Any information of them will be thankfully received by their sister Ellen, by writing to her to No. 39 Morris St., JERSEY CITY, N.J Boston papers, please copy.

November 21, 1863

Of **Patrick Everard**, or **Everitt**; who left Ireland about the year 1850; and of his wife, whose maiden name was **Catharine McEnemy**, and of his children. He was a brother of the **Rev. Richard Everard**, Parish Priest of CLOGHER HEAD, County LOUTH, Ireland. Any information as to Patrick Everard, or his wife or children, is requested by O'Gorman & Wilson, No. 8 Pine-street, NEW YORK CITY.

Of **Mary Tierney**, a native of the Parish of GONEDING, County TIPPERARY, Ireland; who married **Patrick McCarthy**, of BALLYSLATEEN, same County. When last heard from, were in BOSTON, MASS Any information of them will be thankfully received by **Patrick Tierney**, brother of Mary, by writing to him in care of **John McCool**, to ENGLEWOOD Post Office, BERGEN County, State of NEW JERSEY.

Of **Mary McIntyre**, a native of the Parish of KILMACTIGE, County SLIGO, who married **Hugh McGlauhin**, of County MEATH, Ireland. Also of her sister **Bridget**, who married **Samuel Smith**, an American by birth. When last heard from, they resided in the State of NEW YORK. Any information of them will be thankfully received by their brother, **Patrick McIntyre**, who lately arrived, by writing to him in care of **Patrick Foy**, 81 BAXTER STREET, NEW YORK.

November 28, 1863

Wanted from the driver of the load of lumber, which was going along 13th Avenue in the direction of 12th Street, about the 28th of July last, when a horse and wagon was upset, and a man named **Little** drowned. If he would call at No. 548 PEARL STREET, he would do a great favor to the drowned man's family.

Of **Patrick Short**, a native of SWINEFORD, County MAYO, Ireland, who left Galway about the year 1844. Direct to his step-brother **Dominick Cogan**, from LONDON, ENGLAND, at this Office.

Of **Sarah Currigan**, of BALLANDINE, County ROSCOMMON, Ireland, who left London, England about 1853. Direct to her cousin **Nancy Currigan**, from White Cross-street, LONDON, at this Office. [Appeared Dec. 5, 1863 with some additional information.]

Of **Thomas Doyle**, COOLSDERRY, CARRICKMACROSS, County MONAGHAN, Ireland. When last heard from was at the Ohio Exchange, NEW ORLEANS. Any information respecting him would be thankfully received by his brother **James Doyle**. Address **P. Doyle**, 215 HESTER-STREET, NEW YORK. New Orleans papers please copy. [Also appeared Dec. 5, 1863, with some changes.]

Of **John Daly** (son of **Jeremiah Daly**), a native of the Parish of CAHARRAGH, County CORK, Ireland, who left home in 1847, by his mother, **Mary Daly**. Address her at 17 MULBERRY-STREET, NEW YORK. [Appeared Dec. 5, 1863 with some additional information.]

Of **Michael Hayes**, from HOLYCROSS, near BRUFF, County LIMERICK, Ireland. When last heard from he was living in the State of INDIANA. His wife, **Margaret Hayes** (maiden name **Kenny**) has arrived in this country, and is anxious to hear from him. Address care of **Daniel Riordan**, 437 Columbia-street, BROOKLYN, NEW YORK.

Of **Betsy Brady** (maiden name **Dervekin**), a native of the Parish of DARTRY and NEWHAMPTON, County LEITRIM, Ireland, who lately left home and her children, and has not since been heard of. She is of middle size, greyish blue eyes, and has the mark of a cross on her forehead. Her husband, **Patrick Brady**, is now at the seat of war. Any intelligence of her, alive or dead, will be thankfully received by **Philip** or **Julia Anne Brady**, at No. 75 WEST 25th-street, NEW YORK.

Of **Mr. Thomas Monaghan**, a native of the County GALWAY, Ireland. When last heard from was in ORVILLE, BUTLER County, California. Any information of him will be thankfully received by his sister-in-law **Julia Sullivan**, by writing to her to 472 PEARL-STREET, NEW YORK.

December 5, 1863

Stop.- Wanted to know the whereabouts of **Patrick** and **James Dillon**, from GURTGURANE, near LIMERICK, Ireland. Their sister and her husband await an answer. Address **Thomas Doody**, 8 Furman Street, BROOKLYN, N.Y., for **William O'Connor**.

Of **Mrs. Jane Dudgeon** (maiden name, **Perrin**) from DUBLIN. She resided at 86 WEST 16th STREET, NEW YORK. Also, of any of the **DeZouche** family, or any of the **Misses**

Barry, all of DUBLIN. Information respecting any of them will be thankfully received by **William Mason,** at the office of this paper, or No. 50 FRANKLIN ST., NEW YORK.

Of **Peter** and **Rose McGuire**, natives of the County TYRONE, Ireland, who left PHILADELPHIA about eight years ago. Peter was in SAVANNAH when last heard of. Any information from them will be thankfully received by their brother, **John McGuire**, 724 S. 6th Street, PHILADELPHIA.

Of **William James Mills** and **Margaret Anne Mills** natives of CASTLEDERG, County TYRONE, Ireland. When last heard from was in NEW YORK, in December, 1862. Any information of their whereabouts will be thankfully received by their brother, **Richard J. Mills**. Address to B. K. Fallon's Intelligence Office, 10 American Row, HARTFORD, CONN.

Of **Thomas Doyle**, a native of COOLDERRY, CARRICKMACROSSLY, County MONAGHAN, Ireland. When last heard from was in the State of ILLINOIS. Any information respecting him would be thankfully received by his brother **James Doyle**. Address **Peter Doyle**, 215 HESTER-STREET, NEW YORK. Illinois papers, please copy. [Also appeared Nov. 28, 1863 with some different information.]

Of **John Daly,** son of **Jeremiah** and **Mary Daly**, a native of the Parish of CAHARRAH, County of CORK, Ireland, who left Ireland in about the year 1847, with his sister **Catherine**. Any information of him will be thankfully received by his sister **Ellen** and his mother, **Mary Daly,** 17 MULBERRY STREET, NEW YORK. [Appeared Nov. 28, 1863 without some information.]

Of **Mrs. Sarah Carrigan**, a native of BALLANDINE, County ROSCOMMON, Ireland, who left London, England with her sister, **Bridget Burke**, about the year 1853. When last heard of was in ST. LOUIS, MISSOURI. Any information of her or her sister will be thankfully received by her cousin **Nancy Carrigan**, from White Street, St. Luke's, LONDON, ENGLAND. Direct to the office of this paper. [Appeared Nov. 28, 1863 without some information.]

December 12, 1863

$20 Reward. Information wanted of **Mrs. Margaret Maloney**, (Maiden name **Margaret McCabe**.) She has not been seen by the advertiser since she left Smithfield Street, LIVERPOOL, ENGLAND, some twenty-three years ago. The above reward will be paid to any one who will give information of her present whereabouts, by calling or sending to No. 660 Myrtle Avenue, BROOKLYN, NEW YORK.

Of **Bridget Quin**, aged 15 years, who landed at Castle Garden, on Thursday, 19th November last, in the ship *Escott*. Address **Margaret Quin**, 12 HAMMOND STREET, cor. Greenwich Avenue, or **William Quin**, 13 MOTT STREET, NEW YORK.

Of **William Lamb**, youngest son of **William Lamb** deceased, formerly of DOON, near BALLINAHOUN, Parish of LEMANAGHAN, KING'S County, Ireland, who sailed to this country from England about four years since. Any information respecting him will be thankfully received by his brother, **Patrick Lamb**, TRENTON Gas Works, MERCER County, NEW JERSEY.

December 19, 1863

Of **Kate** and **Mary Griffin**. When last heard from they were in NEW YORK CITY. Any information of them will be thankfully received by their brother, **John Griffin**, in care of **John Kelleher**, BUFFALO P.O., NEW YORK.

NOTICE.- **Edward Stokes** (son of **Mr. James Stokes**, late of DUBLIN, deceased), who resided at DRY RIDGE, GRANT County, KENTUCKY, in the year 1857, is hereby informed that he has been left a legacy by his mother's will. By communicating to the undersigned he will get every information as to this legacy. Any information as to the above-named Edward Stokes will be thankfully received by Messrs. O'Gorman & Wilson, 8 Pine Street, NEW YORK; or Messrs. D. & T. Fitzgerald, 20 St. Andrew Street, DUBLIN, IRELAND.

Of **Hugh, Gus.** and **Michael Cowley**, of the County WICKLOW, Parish of RATHDRUM, Ireland, who came to the United States a short time ago. By addressing a note to **John Woodburn**, ELKTON, CECIL County, MD, they will hear of something to their advantage.

Of **Mary Donnellan**, a native of the Parish of DUNMORE, Village of CARRAROE, County GALWAY, Ireland, who married **Nicholas Haverin**, of CARRAROE, and who left Ireland in 1849 for New Orleans. Any information of her will be thankfully received by her brother, **John Donnellan**, from SHEFFIELD, who lately arrived in New York, at 250 EAST 14th STREET, NEW YORK.

Of **Eliza Blunett**, a native of CLANILA, QUEEN'S County, Ireland, who landed in New York last July. When last heard from she resided in WEST 34th STREET, NEW YORK CITY. Any information of her will be thankfully received by her mother and brother, by writing to them in care of **Mr. James Gleeson**, PRINCE'S BAR, STATEN ISLAND, NEW YORK.

December 26, 1863

Of **Michael Lannan**, a native of the Parish of BRIEVE, County of ROSCOMMON, Ireland. Any information of him will be thankfully received by his niece, **Mary Cunningham**, 329 10th AVENUE, NEW YORK.

Of **Edmond** and **Thomas Ryan**, formerly of LIMERICK (nephews of **Mrs. David Fitzgerald**). When last heard of they were in ST. LOUIS, MO. Any information as to their present address may be sent to the Irish-American office, or to **Mr. John Ryan**, hatter, 53 ½ Union Street, NEWARK, N.J

Of **Patrick Reidy**, a native of the Townland of ATTICOLE, Parish of CLOONA, County CLARE, Ireland. When last heard from was in BINGHAMTON, BROOME County, N.Y. Any information of him will be thankfully received by his brother, **Thomas Reidy**, who has lately arrived in New York, by writing to him in care of **Thomas Mongan**, No. 34 GREENWICH STREET, NEW YORK.

January 2, 1864

Of **Ellen Phelan**, who left home on Thanksgiving Day, aged 7 years. Had on, when lost, a brown dress and drab hood with a red border; has dark hair and dark eyes, and is slightly pockmarked. Any information of her will be thankfully received by addressing her parents, 18 Van Brunt Street, BROOKLYN. [Appeared Jan. 16, 1864, identifying her father as **Nicholas Phelan**, No. 18 Van Brunt Street, BROOKLYN, N.Y.]

Of **Ann Flesh**, who landed here on the 9th of July. If she is in the City she will please write to her cousin, **James Robinson**, on board the U.S.S. *Howatonic*, off CHARLESTON HARBOR, or elsewhere.

Of **Morgan Nolan**, stone cutter; when last heard of he was at ST. JOSEPH, MO; also of **Mary Kelly** (maiden name **Nolan**), both of the County DUBLIN. Any information of them will be thankfully received by their sister, **Eliza Nolan**, who has just landed, by addressing to 199 EAST 112th STREET, rear building, NEW YORK.

Of **Owen Fox**, a native of the Parish of BALLINTEMPLE, County CAVAN, Ireland. He was a member of the Ancient Order of Hibernians of NEW YORK, and is said to have driven a brick-cart for **Patrick Lynch**, the Contractor. Any intelligence of him will be thankfully received by his first cousin, **Patrick G. Brady**, 69th Regiment, N.Y. Artillery, Corcoran's Irish Legion, FAIRFAX, ALEXANDRIA P.O., VA

Of **Jeremiah Manion**, a native of the Town of ROSCOMMON, County of ROSCOMMON, Ireland. When last heard from was in NEW YORK CITY. Any information of him will be thankfully received by **Patrick Manion**, 246 Grand Street, JERSEY CITY, N.J

Of **Mary Brennan**, alias **Whelan**, and **Dennis Brennan**, her brother, both from KILLAGH, KENMARE Parish, County KERRY, Ireland; and of **Daniel Brennan**, their cousin, from BANTRY, County CORK, Ireland, who is the subscriber's brother. When last heard of, Dennis was in CANADA, Mary at DANBURY, CONNECTICUT, and Daniel was at the mines, CALIFORNIA. Any information of them will be thankfully received by **James Brennan**, CLARKSVILLE, PIKE County, MISSOURI.

Of **Edward Daley**, a native of BRUFF, County LIMERICK, Ireland, by trade a wood carver; who left BOSTON in 1861, and is supposed to be in NEW YORK or thereabouts. His wife and child, **Johanna Daley**, maiden name **Walsh**, are very anxious to hear from him and her two children. Any person knowing of his whereabouts will confer a favor on his wife and child by addressing Johanna Daley, No. 3 Tinkhan Court, Brackett Street, PORTLAND, MAINE.

Of **Lucy Russell**, of the Parish of RINS, County CLARE, Ireland. When last heard from, was in FULTONVILLE, MONTGOMERY County, NEW YORK, five years ago. Any information of her will be thankfully received by her sister, **Catherine Russell**, in care of **C. K. O'Hara**, No. 140 Camp Street, NEW ORLEANS, LA

January 9, 1864

If **Michael O'Grady**, who worked on a farm in King Street, near PORTCHESTER, N.Y., during the month of July, 1863, will apply to **Samuel Lyon**, GREENWICH, CONN., he will hear of something to his advantage.

Of **Mary Kayla** by her sister **Johannah Kayla**. She is a native of CAPPOQUIN, County WATERFORD, Ireland, and arrived in this country about eleven years ago. Any information of her will be thankfully received by her sister Johannah, at the Water Cure, SARATOGA SPRINGS, N.Y.; or **Mr. Daniel Langan**, Mansion House, Hicks Street, BROOKLYN.

Of **Harriet Anderson**, a native of KILLFINANE, County LIMERICK, Ireland; who married **Thomas Kerwin**, from the same place, by trade a Boot and Shoe Maker. When last heard from she resided at No. 269 AVENUE A., NEW YORK CITY. Any information of her will be thankfully received by her brother, **James Anderson**, by writing to him to CLIFTON, STAPLETON P.O., STATEN ISLAND, N.Y

If **Charles Page, Maria Page** or **Nannie Page** (otherwise **Fowles**), children of the late **William Page**, formerly of the County WEXFORD, Ireland, will communicate with **Mr. James Addison**, No. 1 Duke St., DUBLIN, Ireland, they will hear of something to their advantage.

Of **Patrick O'Keeffe**, of KILLAMONA, County CLARE, Ireland, aged about 50 years. He lived with his father, **Danial O'Keeffe**, at TOUREEN, near SHALLEE, under **Mr. Tomkins** Brew. For a short while before leaving Ireland he held a farm called Gurtavalla. He was married to a woman named **Cullinan**, and left with his wife's family a daughter who was sent to him a short while ago. Any intelligence of him will be thankfully received by **John Sexton**, care of **M. H. Bird**, Bookseller, 129 West 5th Street, CINCINNATI, OHIO.

January 16, 1864

If **Mary McCarron**, who lived a few years since at No. 2 UNION SQUARE, will call at that place, she will oblige **Mrs. Pelton**.

Of **Mrs. Sayers** (maiden name, **Mary Maguire**), a native of RUSSELTOWN, County WATERFORD, Ireland.- Any information concerning her will be thankfully received by her sister, **Hannah Maguire**, at the South American Hotel, No. 36 HOUSTON STREET, NEW YORK.

Of **James Hughes**, a native of the Parish of KILTRUSTAN, STROKESTOWN, County ROSCOMMON, Ireland. Any information of him will be thankfully received by his brother, **John Hughes**, in care of **Mr. John Fallon**, 326 PEARL STREET, NEW YORK.

Of **John Carroll**, a native of ANAHARVEY, KING'S County, Ireland. When last heard from, he was in CINCINNATI, OHIO. Any information of him will be thankfully received by his brother, **Michael Carroll**, by writing to him to No. 48 Railroad Avenue, JERSEY CITY, N.J

Of **James Foley**, a native of AUNAGARRY, Parish of KILLORGLINN, County KERRY, Ireland, who left for America in 1850, and arrived in New Orleans. When last heard from was in OHIO. He intended to become a Roman Catholic clergyman. Any information of him will be thankfully received by his brother **Bartholomew** and sister **Mary Foley**, by writing to them to No. 80 JAMES STREET, NEW YORK.

Of **Mary** and **Margaret Hurley**, natives of the Parish of FIDAGH, County of CORK, Ireland.- Mary married a man by the name of **Timothy Murphy**; Margaret married **Arthur Gotsell**. When last heard from, they were in the State of VERMONT. Any information of them will be received by their sister, **Ellen Hurley**, by writing to her, in care of **John Connor**, her husband, No. 36 THOMAS STREET, NEW YORK. [Appeared Jan. 23, 1864 with the Parish name of FIDAGH changed to ORDAUGH.]

Of **Mary Davy**, a native of the Parish of ST. JOHN'S County SLIGO, Ireland, who left home seven years ago, and lived three years at TUCKAHOE, WESTCHESTER County, N.Y Her sister Eliza will be thankful to any person who can give her information of her whereabouts. Address **Eliza Davy**, care of **J. Stewart**, corner of Atlantic Avenue and Clove road, BEDFORD, BROOKLYN, N.Y

Of **Mary Walsh**, a native of BRUREE, County LIMERICK, Ireland, who emigrated to this country last April or May. Any information of her will be thankfully received by her brother, **John Walsh**, No. 141 MOTT STREET, NEW YORK.

January 23, 1864

Of **John Gegan**, who arrived at Victoria, Australia, in the year 1853. When last heard from, in 1854, he was thinking of coming home by the next steamer. He used to have his letters directed to the care of **Mr. Usher**, Shamrock Hotel, Moorabool Street, GEELONG, and afterwards in care of **Mr. Jackson**, wine merchant. -Any information of him will be thankfully received by his brother, **M. Gegan**, by writing to him to 110 North 15th Street, PHILADELPHIA, PA.

Of **Mary O'Grady**, a native of BALLYGRIFFIN, near CROOME, County LIMERICK, Ireland, who arrived in New York about twelve years ago. When last heard from, was in the State of NEW YORK. Any information of her will be thankfully received by her niece, **Mary Grady**, by writing to her to 147 EAST 11th STREET, NEW YORK.

Of **Thomas Cunningham**, a native of ANNAGHAVACKEY, County LOUTH, Ireland. When last heard of (twelve years ago), he was in CINCINNATI, OHIO. Any information of him will be thankfully received by his brother, **Michael Cunningham**, by writing in care of

J. Horner & Co., POMPTON, N.J.; or to his brother, **John Cunningham**, LYONS, CLINTON County, IOWA. Cincinnati papers, please copy. [Appeared June 6, 1863 and July 18, 1863]

January 30, 1864

Of **Joseph P. Carey Morrison**, who left BALLYNOE, County CORK, Ireland, about fourteen years ago; is a carriage builder by trade. When last heard from was in NEW HAVEN. Any information as to his whereabouts will be thankfully received by addressing his brother, **Redmond Morrison**, 84 MADISON STREET, NEW YORK. Connecticut papers, please copy.

Of **Patrick** and **Thomas Sweeny**, natives of the Parish of MILICK, Townland of KILLGUINE, BALLYCANANE, County CLARE, Ireland. When last heard of (eight years ago), Patrick was in BOSTON. Any information of them will be thankfully received by their father, **Thomas Sweeny**, by writing to him to 448 CHERRY STREET, NEW YORK.

Of **William Corcoran**, a native of BRUFF, Co. LIMERICK, Ireland, who left ALLEGHANY SPRINGS MONTGOMERY County, VIRGINIA, September, 1858, and went to RIDGWAY FARM, ELK County, PENNSYLVANIA. He is requested to inform his brother, **Michael Corcoran**, of his present whereabouts. A letter to him should be addressed to Michael Corcoran, Second Massachusetts Battery, WASHINGTON, D. C.

Of **John McHugh**, of GLENTEES, Parish of INISHKEEL, County DONEGAL, Ireland, who left home last June, and landed in Quebec, Canada, on July 12, 1863, and was not heard from since. Any information of him will be thankfully received by his brother, **Andy McHugh**, by addressing a letter to him to SUMMITHILL, CALHOUN County, State of PENNSYLVANIA, in care of **Michael O'Donnell**. Canada papers, please copy.

Of **Patrick Hyland**, a native of the Parish of MEELICK, near SWINEFORD, County MAYO, Ireland. When last heard from (about two years since) he was living in POTTSVILLE, PENNSYLVANIA. Any information of him will be thankfully received by his brothers, **James** and **John Hyland**, who arrived in this country about two months since, by writing to them to YONKERS, Post Office, WESTCHESTER County, NEW YORK.

Of **Michael McIlduff**, a native of DROMORA, County DOWN, Ireland, who is supposed to have settled in BOSTON. Any information of him will be thankfully received by **John McIlduff**, 207 WEST 26th STREET, NEW YORK.

February 6, 1864

Of **Thomas Armstrong**, a native of the City of DUBLIN, Ireland, who arrived in New York in the *City of Edinburgh*, on the 24th December. Any information of him will be thankfully received by his brother-in-law, **Lawrence Ostenburgh**, by writing to him to 28 HAMILTON STREET, or 45 LAURENCE STREET, NEW YORK CITY.

Of **Ann Elizabeth Murday**, a native of the Parish of KILLMORE, Townland of CLANOGONEL, Co. CAVAN, Ireland, who left home, 8 years ago. If this should meet her eye, or any of her relatives, they will find something to their advantage by calling or writing to **Mrs. Maryann Stanley**, 237 WEST 15th STREET, NEW YORK. Newburgh and New Jersey papers, please copy.

Of **Michael Molloy**, a native of RAHEEN, Parish of LOCHLIN BRIDGE, County CARLOW, Ireland. He left home in the year 1852 or 1853. When last heard of was in NEW YORK. Any information of him will be thankfully received by his sister, **Mary Molloy**, by writing to her in care of **Mr. Fardy**, 125 EAST 38th STREET, NEW YORK.

Of **Richard Kavanagh**, a native of INISTIOGA, County KILKENNY, Ireland. When last heard from he was in the Quartermaster's Department, at ST. LOUIS, MO Any information concerning him given to his father, **Francis Kavanagh**, 22 North 7th Street, WILLIAMSBURGH, Long Island, N.Y., will be thankfully received.

Of **John** and **James Clearey,** natives of CALEEN, KING'S County, Ireland. When last heard from, John was in PHILADELPHIA, PA, and James was in ST. PAUL, MINNESOTA. Any information respecting them will be thankfully received by their nephew, **Joseph Clearey**, on board U.S. steamer, *New Ironsides*, off CHARLESTON, S.C.

Of **Bryan Brody**, formerly of FOMERLA, near NEWGROVE, Co. CLARE, and **James McNamarra**, a native of the Parish of CLUNA, CROWHILL, NEWGROVE, County CLARE. They left home for AUSTRALIA in the year 1841. Any information of them will be thankfully received by **Patrick McNamarra**, CLIFTON, STATEN ISLAND, N.Y, or at the Irish-American Office, 29 Ann Street, New York City.

Of **Bridget** and **Ann Nolan**, natives of KILTEVAN, County ROSCOMMON, Ireland. When last heard from, they lived in NEW YORK CITY. Any information of them will be thankfully received by their brothers, **James** and **Frank Nolan**, at HANNIBAL, MARION County, MISSOURI.

February 13, 1864

Thomas O'Grady, of CANANDAIGUA, N.Y., desires information of his son, who left CANANDAIGUA on the 19th of May, 1859. When last heard from (3 years ago) he was in CHICAGO, ILL. He is 27 years old, black hair, dark eyes, about 5 feet 10 inches high. Any information respecting him will be thankfully received by his father, **Thomas O'Grady**, CANANDAIGUA, N.Y. Chicago papers, please copy. [Appeared Feb. 20, 1864, with the son identified as **Patrick O'Grady** instead of Thomas, and the spelling of Canandaigua changed to Canandaguo.]

Of **John** and **Elisha Moore**, natives of Ireland, who left STEALYBRIDGE, ENGLAND, for this country about 15 years ago. Elisha is a tailoress by trade, and when last heard from was living in BLACKSTON, MASS; John is a jackspinner, and worked in the MANCHESTER Mills about 9 months ago. Any intelligence of them will be thankfully received by their sister **Cecilia Moore**, by writing to her to No. 8 Kidders Block, MANCHESTER, N.H

Of **Nicholas Dempsey**, a native of DUBLIN, Ireland. When last heard from was in BROOKLYN, N.Y. Any person knowing of his whereabouts will please address **N. Glennon**, No. 9 Portland Avenue, BROOKLYN, N.Y., as he will hear of something to his advantage.

Of **Thomas Mahon**, son of **Patrick Mahon**, of NEWCASTLE, Parish of OLDCASTLE, County MEATH, Ireland, who came to America in 1855. Any information of him will be thankfully received by his sister, **Bridget Mahon**, by addressing her at 51 Jefferson Street, NEWARK, NEW JERSEY. Boston papers, please copy.

Of **Thomas Pendergast**, a native of the Townland of CRAUGHATOURE, Parish of BALALOOBY, County TIPPERARY, Ireland. When last heard of (about two years ago) he was in ST. JOSEPH, MISSOURI. Any information of him will be thankfully received by his sister, **Mary Pendergast** (wife of **James O'Brien**), by addressing her at GLEN COVE Post Office, Long Island, N.Y

Of **Denis Guinan**, of MOUNTMELICK, QUEEN'S County, Ireland. When last heard from he was in ROCK ISLAND, State of ILLINOIS. Any information of his whereabouts will be thankfully received by his mother, **Dorah Guinan**, by addressing her at 18 Bedford Avenue, EAST BROOKLYN, N.Y. Western papers, please copy.

Of **Daniel Purtill**, a native of the Parish of CROOM, County LIMERICK, Ireland. He is supposed to be at present in TROY, N.Y. Any information of him will be thankfully received by his cousin, **Ellen Brown**, by writing to her in care of **Mr. Fritwine**, 100th STREET, between 10th and 11th Avenues, BLOOMINGDALE, NEW-YORK. [Also see Dec. 10, 1864, for slightly different information.]

Of **Robert** and **Johm** [sic] **Wiseman**, natives of the County CORK, Ireland. When last heard from (which was in 1855) they were in BALLARAP Diggings, AUSTRALIA. Any information respecting them will be thankfully received by their mother and sister, **Mrs.** and **Miss Esther Wiseman**, No. 20 Canal Street, FALL RIVER, MASS

February 20, 1864

Of **Thomas Hogan**, aged 18 years, who left BROOKLYN., N.Y, on the 22nd of September, 1863, and has not been since heard from. Any information of him will be thankfully received by his mother, **Margaret Hogan**, SAUGERTIES, ULSTER County, N.Y

Of **Sarah** and **Bridget Carron**, natives of ENNISKILLEN, County FERMANAGH, Ireland. When last heard from, about six years ago, they were in DECATUR County, ILL. Any information of them would be thankfully received by their brother, **Hugh Carron**, at 401 North 11th Street, PHILADELPHIA, PA Illinois papers, please copy.

Of **Ellen, Eliza** and **Bedelia Sweeney**, who arrived in this country from GALWAY about 12 years since. When last heard from (about 4 years ago), they were residing in BROOKLYN. Eliza got married here to a gentleman named **Keogh**. Any intelligence of them will be thankfully received by **Joseph F. Crowley**, No. 7 COENTIES SLIP, NEW YORK.

Of **John Carroll**, a native of ANNAHARVEY, KING'S County, Ireland. When last heard from, two months ago, he was in ST. PAUL, MINNESOTA. Any information of him will be thankfully received by his brother, **Michael Carroll**, by writing to him to 48 Rail Road Avenue, JERSEY CITY, N.J. [Appeared 16 Jan. 1864 with a different last known location.]

Of **John Barry**, a native of the Parish of KILDORARY, County CORK, Ireland. When last heard from was a teamster in the army at COLUMBUS, KENTUCKY. Any information of him will be thankfully received by his brother, **Richard Barry**, WASHINGTON HEIGHTS, NEW YORK.

Of **Mathew Britton**, who left CHARLEVILLE, Co. CORK, Ireland, about 18 years ago. When last heard from was in GRAHAM, NODAWAY County, MISSOURI. Any information of him will be thankfully received by his brother, **Patrick Britton**, 176 MADISON STREET, NEW-YORK Boston and Missouri papers, please copy.

Of **John Chanery**, a native of KANTURK, County CORK, Ireland. When last heard from, twelve years ago, he resided in SYRACUSE with his brother **Owen**. Any information of him will be thankfully received by his sister **Mary**, by writing to her to 80 JAMES' STREET, NEW YORK CITY.

Of **John Mannion**, who left CARRICKBOY, County LONGFORD, Ireland, and came to this country about seven or eight years ago. When last heard from he was in BROOKLYN, N.Y. Any information of him will be thankfully received by his brother, **Thomas Mannion**, HOPKINTON, MASSACHUSETTS.

Of **Denis Downing**, a native of the County KERRY, Ireland; he was a resident of BOSTON in Aug., 1863. When last heard of he was in NEW BRUNSWICK, NOVA SCOTIA. Any information of him will be thankfully received by his friend, **Daniel Murphy**, on board of the United States gunboat, *Chippewa*, PORT ROYAL, SOUTH CAROLINA, or elsewhere.

Of **James Watson**, a native of NEWTOWN, County ROSCOMMON, Ireland. When last heard from he was in the State of PENNSYLVANIA. Any information of him will be thankfully received by his step-brother, **Edward Watson**. Address **David M. Marvin**, Esq., WESTPORT, CONNECTICUT.

February 27, 1864

Of **Andrew Fitzpatrick**, or his wife **Margaret**, her maiden name was **Heaney**. When last heard from, they lived in 28th STREET, between Second and Third Avenues, NEW YORK. Any information of them will be thankfully received by addressing **James** and **Patrick Heaney**, in MUSCATINE, IOWA.

Of **James Keating**, a native of ENNISCORTHY, County WEXFORD, Ireland, who came to America in February, 1861. When last heard from, in May, 1863, he was in one of the New York Regiments with the Army of the Potomac. Any information of him will be thankfully received by his father, **John Keating**, by writing to him in care of the Irish-American, 29 Ann Street, New York.

Of **James Hamilton**, of the Town of MULLAGHDUE, Parish of KILLINUNNA, County of LEITRIM, Ireland, who came to this country and landed in New York about 16 years ago, and when last heard from he was working in the tunnel at BERGEN HILL, about seven or eight years ago. Any information of him will be thankfully received by his wife, **Mary Mulrooney**, of MOUNT HOPE, GRANT County, WISCONSIN.

Of **John Molloy**, formerly a resident of Tullow-street, CARLOW, Ireland, who came to America about 12 years ago. When last heard from was working in PITTSBURGH, PENNSYLVANIA. Any information of him will be thankfully received by his brother **James Molloy**, No. 181 Kent Avenue, BROOKLYN, Eastern District, NEW YORK.

Of **Edward O'Rourke**, a native of the Townland of KNOCKANORAN, in the Parish of DURROW, QUEEN'S County, Ireland. He sailed from Wexford to America in the year 1854. When last heard from he was serving in the 2nd Regiment, U.S. Cavalry, Co. D, SAN ANTONIO, TEXAS, U.S. America. Any information respecting him will be thankfully received by his brother, **Samuel O'Rourke**, No. 141 BOWERY, N.Y. Other papers please copy. [Appeared Sept. 5, 1863 and Sept. 12, 1863 with less information.]

Of **Patrick** and **John McCain**, natives of the Parish of DRUMCULLEN, KING'S County, Ireland, who landed in New York 13 years ago. When last heard of Patrick was in ROCHESTER, State of NEW YORK, and John in CHARLESTON, S.C. Any information of them will be thankfully received by their parents, **John** and **Margaret McCain**, by writing to No. 215 Orange-street, WILMINGTON, DELAWARE.

March 5, 1864

MISSING, since Feb. 8th, 1864, a girl named **Sarah Jane Hughes**, nearly 15 years of age, rather good-looking; had on a plaid dress; supposed to be kidnapped, or sent to place from the Wilson School, in AVENUE A, near 10th Street, N.Y. Her father is at the war. Any information of her will be thankfully received by her Uncle, **Frank Hughes**, at 161 EAST 11th STREET, NEW YORK.

Of **Andrew** or **Kitt Quinn**, from DUBLIN. When last heard of (in 1855), they were in READING, PENN.- Any information of them will be thankfully received by their afflicted mother. Address **Patrick Quinn**, 49 VESEY STREET, NEW YORK.

Of **Timothy Callian**, a native of County CLARE, Ireland. When last heard of (twelve months ago) he was in NEW YORK. Any information of him will be thankfully received by his sister, **Bridget Callian**, MYSTIC RIVER, CONNECTICUT.

Of **John, Eliza** and **Sarah Eagan**, natives of the Parish of ROSCREA, County TIPPERARY, Ireland. When last heard from (six years ago) they were in CINCINNATI, OHIO; John was living in the Burnet House. Any information of them will be thankfully received by their sister **Mary**, at 2017 Hand Street, PHILADELPHIA, PA. Cincinnati papers, please copy.

Of **Bridget Conaughton**, who emigrated from the County GALWAY, to AUSTRALIA, in 1846, and married a man named **Delafield**. When last heard from, was in No. 15 Victoria place, AUCKLAND, NEW ZEALAND. Any information of her will be thankfully received by her mother, **Ellen Conaughton**, at 144 Cottage Street, PHILADELPHIA, PA.

Of **Edward Perry**, of the Parish of BALLYLONGFORT, County KERRY, Ireland, who is supposed to be living in CARLISLE STREET, NEW YORK CITY. Information of him, sent to the Parish of St. Peter's Church, MEMPHIS, TENNESSEE, will reach his friend, **Dennis Breen**.

Of **John Stokes**, of TRALEE, who sailed from Queenstown, in the *City of New York*, on the 14th of January. If he will call at his uncle's, No. 78 EAST 41st STREET, NEW YORK CITY, he will hear of something to his advantage. [Appeared under County KERRY]

March 12, 1864

Of **Mary O'Claughessy**. When last heard of was in CINCINNATI, OHIO. Any information of her will be thankfully received by her brother, **David O'Claughessy**, ANSONIA, CONNECTICUT. Boston *Pilot* and New Orleans papers, please copy.

Of **William Howard** (formerly revenue officer) and his wife **Martha**, also of their children, **William** and **John**, natives of West Street, CALLAN, County KILKENNY, Ireland. Any information of them will be thankfully received by **Jane Howard**, daughter of William and Martha Howard, and sister of William and John, by writing to her in care of **Mrs. Ditmas Duryea**, FLATBUSH, KING'S County, L.I.

Of **Edward Armstrong**, a shoemaker by trade, and his wife, **Catherine Armstrong** (maiden name **Grace**), natives of the Townland of BALLYTARSNA, Parish of BOHARLAHAN, County TIPPERARY, Ireland. When last heard of, about six years ago, they were living in PHILADELPHIA, PA. Any information of them will be thankfully received by her sister, **Margaret Holihan**, by writing to **Patrick Holihan**, prentice, MORGAN County, ILLINOIS.

Of **Catherine Downs** (maiden name **Gilroy**), who, with her husband, **Patrick Downs**, moved West, some time ago, from DANSVILLE, LIVINGSTON County, N.Y, and when last heard from they were living in a place called AURORA, PORTAGE County, OHIO, about two years ago. She had along with her a daughter by her former husband, named **Mary Mulderrig**, now about fourteen years old. She is about thirty-two years of age, a native of the Parish of LACKEN, County MAYO, Ireland, and came to this country with her mother and sisters about 17 years ago. Any information of them will be thankfully received by addressing **Michael Gilroy**, DANSVILLE, LIVINGSTON County, N.Y.

Of **Kate, Mary** and **Michael Moran**, or their cousin, **Joseph Hughes**, all of whom left GALWAY, Ireland, for the United States, about the month of September, 1856, accompanied by their aunt, **Esther Hughes** (since dead). If they will send their address to J. B. C., Box 329, Post Office, NEW YORK, they can hear of an old friend now in this City.

March 19, 1864

Of **Margaret Renaghan**, a native of FORK HILL, County ARMAGH, Ireland, daughter of the late **Daniel Rice**. Any information of her will be thankfully received and liberally rewarded by **Michael Begley**, No. 92 Penn Street, near Shippen Street, PHILADELPHIA, PA.

Of **John** and **Timothy Flynn**, natives of GAGGIN, near BANDON, County CORK. John came to America about 12 years ago, and when last heard from was on the Mississippi River; Timothy, who is a carpenter by trade, came out about eight years ago; when last heard from he was in MONTREAL, LOWER CANADA, residing with his sister, **Mrs. Collins**. Any information respecting them will be thankfully received by their brother, **James Flynn**, No. 30 High Street, BOSTON, MASS. [Appeared under County ARMAGH.]

Of **Ellen Mahoney**, a native of BENGOUR, Parish of MORAGH, County CORK, Ireland. When last heard from, she had left BOSTON and was living in MILWAUKEE or some other part of WISCONSIN. Any information of her will be thankfully received by her sister, **Mrs. Giles**, No. 10 PEARL STREET, NEW YORK.

Of **Margaret Dolan**, a native of the Parish of KEASH, County SLIGO, Ireland. When last heard from (about four years ago,) she resided at WEST 12th STREET, NEW YORK. Any information concerning her would be thankfully received by **P. Jordan**, 172 WEST STREET, NEW YORK, as she can hear of something to her advantage.

Of **Susan Roach**, a native of CRAGBRIEN, County CLARE, Ireland, who came to BOSTON 11 years ago, and is, for the past few years, living in some of the western States. Any information of her will be thankfully received by **Thomas Healy**, 131 Federal Street, BOSTON, MASS. Chicago papers, please copy.

Of **Michael Hally**, from NEWCASTLE, County TIPPERARY, Ireland. Any information of him will be thankfully received by his sister, **Margaret Hally**, who landed in New York about nine months ago, by addressing **Mr. Wm. Scholes**, glasscutter, No. 63 ELIZABETH ST., NEW-YORK CITY. [Appeared March 26, 1864 indicating, "When last heard from was in JERSEY" and "New Jersey papers please copy."]

March 26, 1864

Andrew Fitzpatrick and his wife **Margaret Heany**, are living at 163 EAST 26th-STREET, NEW YORK, and have written several letters to **James Heany**, MUSCATINE, IOWA, and have got no answer. Please address in care of **James H. Drake**, cor. 9th-street and 4th AVENUE, NEW YORK CITY. [An advertisement for Andrew and Margaret appeared Feb. 27, 1864]

Of **Timothy Griffin**, who came in the ship *Orion*, and arrived here on the 12th of January. Any information of him will be thankfully received by his sister, **Mrs. M. Henry**, No. 327 8th STREET, NEW YORK. Canada papers please copy.

Of **John** and **Anna Maria Kennedy**, natives of PARSONSTOWN, KING'S County, Ireland. When last heard from were in BYTOWN, UPPER CANADA. Any information of them will be thankfully received by their first cousin, **Patrick Kennedy**, by writing to him to No. 36 Gold-street, BROOKLYN, N.Y.

Of **William, Mary** and **Margaret Condon**, natives of the County LIMERICK, Ireland, who came to this country and landed in New York about seven years ago. When last heard from was in STATEN ISLAND. Any information of them will be thankfully received by their brother, **Thomas Condon**, by writing to him in care of **Mr. Smith Montgomery**, OLNY. Post Office, via PHILADELPHIA, PA

April 2, 1864

Of **Bridget** and **Catherine Forestall**, natives of the Parish of MULINAVAT, Townland of SLEEVEBEGG, Co. KILKENNY, Ireland. Bridget was married to a man named **Martin Keefe**, who is now dead, and Catherine is married to **Michael Wall**. They are supposed to be living in ST. LOUIS, State of MISSOURI, for the last thirteen years. If any of the above mentioned persons will communicate with **John Rigby**, Sergeant of the City

Police, QUEBEC, CANADA, they can get information of their deceased brother, **James**, that will be of benefit to them. Boston and St. Louis papers, please copy.

Of **Michael Frawley**, a native of BANOGUE, Parish of CROOM, County LIMERICK, Ireland, who came to this country about 15 years ago. When last heard from he was at SMITH FALLS, N.Y His afflicted mother, his brother **James**, and his sister **Bridget** (now **Mrs. Ryan**) are most anxious to hear from him. Any intelligence respecting him, whether dead or alive, will be thankfully received by his brother-in-law, **Thomas Ryan**, WESTTHOMPSON, WINDHAM County, CONN.

April 9, 1864

Of **Thomas Garvey**, who left ENGLAND for NEW YORK in June, 1863, and has not been heard of since. Any information of him will be thankfully received by his sister, **Mary Garvey**, by writing to her to No. 104 Front Street, WILMINGTON, DELAWARE, in care of **Patrick Christy**.

Of **Luke Lee**, a native of the Parish of DRUMLUMON, County CAVAN, Ireland, who landed in New York, Dec. 31, 1863, from the ship *Constellation*. Any information concerning him will be thankfully received by his brother **Walter**, North-East corner of Dillwyn and Willow Streets PHILADELPHIA, PENN.

Of **John Moran** and **Catherine** his wife (maiden name **Gilroy**), who left BALLINA, County MAYO, Ireland, about ten years ago. When last heard from (two years ago) was at FOUR PLAINS SEMINARY, State of NEW YORK. Any information of them will be thankfully received by Mrs. Moran's brother, **Patrick Gilroy**, care of **Alderman Gafney**, 27 Montgomery Street, JERSEY CITY, N.J.

Of **James Keating**, a native of ENNISCORTHY, County WEXFORD, Ireland, who came to America in February, 1861. When last heard from, in May, 1863, he was in one of the New York Regiments with the Army of the Potomac. Any information of him will be thankfully received by his father, **John Keating**, by writing to him in care of the Irish-American, 29 Ann Street, New York.

Of **Patrick Kilroy**, a native of the Parish of ROSCOMMON, County ROSCOMMON, Ireland, who came to this country about six years ago. When last heard from was in NEWPORT, R.I. He was in the American Army, and got wounded in the battle of BULL RUN. Any information of him will be thankfully received by his sister, **Anne Kilroy**, by writing to **Mr. Justice Morris**, ELIZABETH CITY, N.W

Of **Robert Claby**, a native of the Parish of KILGLASS County ROSCOMMON, Ireland. When last heard from was at GLEN COVE, Long Island, N.Y Any information will be gratefully received by his cousin, **Nicholas Claby**, corner of Smith and Consiliea Streets, WILLIAMSBURGH, Long Island, N.Y

Of **Mary Furlong**, (maiden name **Mary Nash**), and of her husband, **William Furlong**, both from BALLYHOOLY, County CORK, Ireland. They came to NEW YORK about 13 years ago. Any person knowing their whereabouts will oblige her sister by addressing **Eliza Nash**, care of **Ralph Dawson**, Esq., No. 36 First Street, WILLIAMSBURGH, N.Y

Of **John, Joseph** and **Morris Burns**, natives of the County LIMERICK, Ireland, who arrived in this country about 15 years ago, and who are supposed to be at present in NEW YORK. Any information of them will be thankfully received by their sister, **Alice Burns**, by writing to her in care of Lynch, Cole & Meehan, Irish-American Office, 29 Ann Street, New York.

April 16, 1864

Of **Edward Watson**, a native of NEWTOWN, County ROSCOMMON, Ireland. When last heard from he was in WESTPORT, CONNECTICUT. Any information of him will be thankfully received by his step-brother, **James Watson**, DUNNINGS, LUZERNE County, PENN

Of **William** and **John Long**, who came to this country from GORTROA, County LIMERICK, Parish of APHENA. Any information relative to their whereabouts will be thankfully received by their brother, **Thomas Long**, care of **Patrick Hanrihan**, 57 BETHUNE ST., NEW YORK.

Of **Patrick Byrne**, carpenter by trade, and his sister, **Anne Byrne**, from NEWTOWN, Parish of FRESHFORD, County KILKENNY, Ireland. When last heard from, they were both living in BROOKLYN, N.Y. Any account of them will be thankfully received by their brother, **Michael Byrne**, who lately arrived here, at **Patrick Reagan's**, corner of Bank and Bergen Streets, NEWARK, N.J.

April 23, 1864

Of **John, Martin**, and **Patrick Duffy**, brothers. When last seen they were at HAVERSTRAW, N.Y. Any information of them will be most thankfully received by their brother, **Mark Duffy**. Address Mark Duffy, Co. E, 4th N.Y. Cavalry, 2nd Brigade, 1st Cav. Division, WASHINGTON, D. C.

Of **Andrew Sweeny**, otherwise **McSuiggan**, Blacksmith by trade, a native of GULLADUFF, County DERRY, Ireland. When last heard from he was in CANADA. Any information of him will be thankfully received by his nephew, **James Sweeny**, by writing to him in care of **John McCloud**, ELIZABETH TOWN, N.J.

Of **Patrick Hicks**, a native of CREEMULLEY, Parish of FURTY, County ROSCOMMON, Ireland. When last heard from he went to live in KINGSTON, ULSTER Co., N.Y Any information of him will be thankfully received by his cousin, **William Mannings**, by writing to him to 164 EAST 31st ST., NEW YORK CITY.

Of **Patrick McNamara**, a native of KILMURRY-MACMAHON, County CLARE, Ireland, who came to this country about 13 years ago. When last heard from was in LAKE PROVIDENCE, INDIANA. Any information respecting him will be thankfully received by his brother, **John McNamara**, at **Charles Barry's**, 533 CANAL STREET, NEW-YORK. Indiana papers, please copy.

Of the relatives of the deceased, **Michael Moran**, who was a member of Co. H, 108th Illinois Volunteer Infantry. He last saw his brother and sister in 1853 or 1854; his brother, **James Moran**, was then living in 52nd STREET, between 10th and 11th Avenues, and his sister, **Bridget Kelly** (maiden name **Moran**), was living in 43rd STREET, between 10 and 11th Avenues, NEW YORK. His father's name is **William Moran**, and lived in the Parish of KILLO, County LONGFORD, Ireland. If any of the above parties will write to **Sergeant Michael Glasheen**, Co. H, 108th Ill. Vol. Infantry, MEMPHIS, TENNESSEE, they will hear of something to their advantage.

Of **Michael Collopy**, of GLIN, County LIMERICK, Ireland. When last heard from he was in ALEXANDRIA, VA., in 1857; was a little out of his mind; a farmer took him about 10 miles in the country. Any information of him will be thankfully received by his cousin, **John Normile**, NORMANVILLE, DONIPHAN County, KANSAS.

April 30, 1864

Of **Jane Dixon**, born in LONDON, daughter of **Frederick Dixon** and **Kate Supple**. When last heard from she was in NEW YORK CITY. Any information of her will be thankfully received by **James G. Smith**, at the office of the Irish-American.

Should this meet the eye of **Ignatius Carr**, late of KINGSTOWN, County DUBLIN, he will hear of his sister, **Anne Woods**, by writing to her in care of **James Lanigan**, *Sun* Office, NEW YORK, as his brother **Daniel** wishes most particularly to get his address.

Of **Margaret Galvin**, a native of CLARA, KING'S County, Ireland. When last heard from, in 1861, she was in NEW YORK CITY. Any information respecting her will be thankfully received by her brother, **James Galvin**, Co. G, 10th Kansas Vols., ALTON, ILL.

May 7, 1864

Of **Jeremiah** and **John Twomey**. When last seen, in May, 1855, they left their cousin's house (**Johannah Leavy**) in NEW YORK CITY. Any information of them will be thankfully received by their father and sister, **Timothy** and **Johannah Twomy**, by writing to them in care of **Daniel J. O'Sullivan**, No. 2 MISSION PLACE, NEW YORK CITY.

Mary Bryce, from BRIDGE-OF-WEIR, SCOTLAND, wishes to know the whereabouts of her uncle, **Patrick McNelis**, and her friends, **Bridget Daly, James, John, William** and **Mary Askin**, all supposed to be in NEW YORK. Please address Mary Bryce, OAKVILLE, CONNECTICUT.

Of **Jeremiah Madden**, from KILLENAN, County LIMERICK, Ireland. When last heard from he worked in a sugar house in NEW-YORK. By calling at No. 83 10th AVENUE, NEW-YORK, he will see his friend, **James Madden**.

Of **Sarah McGee** and daughters, **Mary Husey**, and **Bridget** and Son, natives of the Townland of CARGIN, County ARMAGH, Ireland; who sailed from Queenstown about the 15th of February, 1863, their destination being to CHICAGO, ILLINOIS. Any information of their whereabouts will be thankfully received by **Nicholas Shannon**, by writing to him in care of **Thomas Cullen**, Warer's Court, No. 2 Jermontown-road, PHILADELPHIA, PENN.

Of **Lawrence Doyle**, a native of BALLYDUGGAN, Parish of MULLINAHONE, County TIPPERARY, Ireland, who emigrated to the United States of America in September, 1851. When last heard from he worked in the City or suburbs of ALBANY, N.Y. If this should meet his eye or the eye of any person knowing his whereabouts, they would not only oblige but confer a great favor on his youngest and most anxious brother, **John Doyle**, by writing to John Doyle, in care of **Mr. Henry O'Neill**, No. 711 South Broad St., PHILADELPHIA, PENN. Boston *Pilot*, and Western and San Francisco papers, please copy.

May 14, 1864

Of **Sarah** and **Mary Kerens**, who left Ireland about two years past, from QUEEN'S County, Town of MOUNT MELLICK, Ireland. Any information respecting them will be thankfully received by their brother, **John Kerens**, No. 51 Jersey-street, PATERSON, NEW JERSEY.

Of **Michael** and **William Mulshennick**, or their cousin, **Michael Casey**, of the Parish of RATHCORMAC, Co. CORK, Ireland. Any information of them will be thankfully received by their sister **Ellen**, by sending word to **Pat Daly**, 14 CHERRY ST., NEW YORK. Ohio papers, please copy.

Of **John, Mary** and **Ellen Daly**, natives of the Parish of SCORTAGLIN, County KERRY, Ireland. When last heard from they were in OHIO. Any information of them will be thankfully received by their brother, **Eneas Daly**, by writing to him in care of **Mr. J. M. Pruden**, ELIZABETH CITY, NEW JERSEY.

Of **Robert Smith**, of STRADBALLY, County KERRY, Ireland. When last heard from he was in WARE VILLAGE, ILLINOIS. Any information of him be thankfully received by his brother, **Michael Smith**, by addressing his friend, **Patrick Dean**, GREENPOINT, Long Island, N.Y

Of **James Hopkins**, a native of the Parish of TIERNASKA, County GALWAY, Ireland, who arrived in New York about 15 years ago. When last heard from he was in CHICAGO. Any information of him will be thankfully received by his mother, **Mary Hopkins**, at 204 EAST 17th STREET, NEW-YORK, or at the Irish-American Office, 29 Ann Street, New-York. [Appeared May 28, 1864 saying James was "a native of LONGFORD, Parish of TIERNASKA, County GALWAY, Ireland, who left this City nine years ago."]

Of **McCabe Brothers**, natives of the County GALWAY, Ireland. When last heard from were in BATON ROUGE, LOUISIANA. Any information of them will be thankfully received by **John McCabe** by writing to him in care of Lynch, Cole & Meehan, Irish-American Office, 29 Anne Street, New York. Louisiana papers please copy.

Of **Michael Ford**, native of the County GALWAY, Ireland, who arrived in New York about six years ago; when last heard from was in the State of NEW YORK. Any information concerning him will be thankfully received by his brother, **Patrick Ford**, No. 926 Market-street, PHILADELPHIA, PA.

May 21, 1864

Of **Larry Brennan** and his wife, **Mary Brien**, from the Parish of GRAIN, County KILKENNY, Ireland, who came to this country about eleven years ago; also of **James Brien**, who landed here last Summer, and went to PENNSYLVANIA. Any information of them will be thankfully received by their father, **Thomas Brien**, at **Thomas Mitchell's**, No. 4 GREENWICH STREET, NEW YORK.

Of **Patrick** and **Bridget Kean**, natives of CAHIRCANIVAN, Parish of KILMICHAEL, Co. CLARE, Ireland. When last heard of were in CATTARAUGUS County, State of NEW YORK. Any information of them will be fondly received by their brother, **John Kean**, at **Mr. David Roche's,** 258 WEST STREET, NEW YORK CITY.

Of **Mary Fleming**, a native of KILRUSH, County CLARE, Ireland. When last heard from (5 years ago) she was in PATERSON, NEW JERSEY. Any information of her will be thankfully received by her brother, **John Fleming**, by writing to him in care of **J. P. Miller**, Esq. at No. 67 Congress Street PATERSON, NEW JERSEY.

Of **David Linehan**, a native of MOONAMRAHER, Parish of ARDAGH, County CORK, Ireland. When last heard from (5 years ago) was in BOSTON, MASS. Any information of him will be thankfully received by his sister, **Mary Linehan**, by writing to her to 111 53rd STREET, between Broadway and Eighth Avenue, NEW YORK CITY, in care of **Jeremiah Kerrigan**.

Of **Coleman Ahern**, a native of BALLYNOCK, Parish of DONGOURNEY, County CORK, Ireland. He left Ireland 11 years ago. Any information of him will be thankfully received by his brother, **Michael Ahern**, by addressing him care of **Thomas Downing**, to No. 335 WEST 26th ST., NEW YORK.

Of **Mary Caudy**, of CLONMEL, County TIPPERARY, Ireland, who came to this country about 14 years ago. When last heard from she was in NEW YORK CITY. Any information of her will be thankfully received by her sister, **Catherine Caudy**. Address **James R. Cantwell**, 250 North Front Street, PHILADELPHIA, PA.

May 28, 1864

If **Mr. George McCullough**, who left LARGYMORE, LISBURN, Ireland, for NEW YORK, about seven years since, call on me, or write, giving his address, stating the name of his mother, &c., he will hear of something to his advantage. **Walter O'Donoghue**, 73 CANAL STREET, corner of Allen, N.Y [Appeared under County ANTRIM.]

Of **Thomas Delmer**, a native of the Parish of EDGWORTSOWN. Co. LONGFORD, Ireland, who left home on the 22nd of March, for PROVIDENCE, RHODE ISLAND. Any information of him will be thankfully received by his brother, **John Delmer**, by writing to him in care of **Mr. John Soughrum**, SPOTTSWOOD, MIDDLESEX County, NEW JERSEY.

Of **Nicholas Lovely**, a native of TUBAQUAIL, near MULLINGAR, County WESTMEATH, Ireland, who resided in DUBLIN for nearly 15 years. When last heard from he was in WATERTOWN, MASSACHUSETTS. Any information of him will be thankfully received by his brother **Bernard**, by writing to him to No. 102 North 6th Street, between 3rd and 4th Streets, WILLIAMSBURGH, Long Island

Of **Thomas Heveren**, a native of the Town and Parish of CONG, County MAYO, Ireland who embarked for the United States of America in October 1851 and has not been heard of since. Any information of him will be thankfully received by his father **Peter Heveren**, by writing to him in care of **Patrick Mackin**, North-East corner of Tenth and Carpenter Streets, PHILADELPHIA, PA.

Of **John Riordan**, millwright by trade, a native of RIVERSTOWN, Parish of GLANMIRE, County CORK, Ireland, who emigrated to the United States of America some 14 or 16 years ago. If this should meet his eye or the eye of any person knowing his whereabouts, they would confer a great favor on his nephew, **James Riordan**, by writing to him to LEAVENWORTH CITY, State of KANSAS.

June 4, 1864

Of **James Breen**, born in MONTREAL, CANADA; married on the 4th day of September, 1860, in MOBILE, ALABAMA. Direct, **Margaret Breen**, care of the Catholic Priest, St. Peter's Church, MEMPHIS, TENNESSEE.

Of **Tim** and **James Ahearn** and **Catharine Enright**. When last heard from were in WOODSPORT, NEW YORK. Any information of them will be thankfully received by their cousin, **Mary Enright**. Address **D. McCarthy**, 35 GREENWICH STREET, NEW YORK.

Of **Mrs. Catharine Foye** and **John, William** and **Bernard Foye**, natives of GALWAY, Ireland. When last heard from were in GLOSSOP, ENGLAND. They came to this country about one year ago. Any information of them will be thankfully received by **James Hogan**, WEST NEWBURY, MASS. or by **James Foye**, Co. E, 1st Mass. Heavy Artillery, FORT CASS, VA., via WASHINGTON, D. C.

Of **Thomas Tighe**, a native of CASTLEREAGH, County ROSCOMMON, Ireland. He left Ireland in the year 1848 or 1849, and landed in New Orleans, La. When last heard from he was in the State of OHIO. Any information concerning him will be thankfully received by his brother, **Bartholomew Tighe**, who has just landed from England. Please address Bartholomew Tighe, Irish-American Office, 29 Ann Street, New York.

Of **Ann Keayes**, maiden name **Ann Ryan**, but who is now married (second marriage) to a man named **James Hanly**, of CINCINNATI, OHIO. She emigrated to this country about 13 or 14 years ago; is a native of BALLYBROOD, Parish of BALLYBREEN, County LIMERICK, Ireland. Any information of her or her son **John Keayes**, who landed here about six years ago, will be thankfully received by her youngest son, **William Keayes**, at **Mrs. Murphy's**, 50 VANDAM ST., NEW YORK, in the rear. Cincinnati, Ohio, and California papers, please copy.

Of **Miss Mary** (now **Mrs. Ryan**) and **Catharine Laffan**, of HERBERTSTOWN, County LIMERICK, Ireland. They can hear from their cousin **John M. Clancy**, by sending their address to **John McMahon**, care of **R. J. Riley**, ROWLESBURG, PRESTON County, WEST VIRGINIA.

June 11, 1864

Of **Thomas, Bridget, Ann** and **Mary Trainor**, who, when last heard from, were in BROOKLYN, N.Y. Any information of them will be thankfully received by their brother, **James Trainor**, who has enlisted in the 59th Mass. Regiment. Further information will be received by writing to **Patrick Reynolds**, 2 Ice Court, Water Street, CHARLESTOWN, MASS [Appeared under County LONGFORD]

Of **Ellen Regan**, of GLANBEG, County KERRY, Ireland, who came to this country on board the packet ship *Sir Robert Peel*, and landed in New York on or about the 21st day of May last. Any intelligence of her, addressed to Washington House (Williams & Enright, Proprietors), 82 GREENWICH STREET, NEW YORK, or to the TOMPKINSVILLE, Post Office, STATEN ISLAND will confer a great favor on her sister, **Catherine Regan**.

Of **Thomas Buckley**, a native of the County KERRY, Ireland. When last heard from (three years ago) he was in GRANTSTOWN school, County WATERFORD, Ireland. Any information of him will be thankfully received by his sister, **Margaret Buckley**, by writing to her in care of Lynch, Cole & Meehan, Irish-American Office, 29 Ann Street, New York.

Of **Terence Grimes**, a native of the Parish of TURLOUGH, Townland of TOWNICKANAFF, CASTLEBAR, Co. MAYO, Ireland. When last heard from (ten years ago) was in WOOLWICH County, WISCONSIN. Any information of him will be thankfully received by his brother, **James Grimes**, by writing to him in care of Lynch, Cole & Meehan, Irish-American Office, 29 Ann Street, New York. Also, of his sisters, **Ellen** and **Betsy**. When last heard from both were in NEW ORLEANS, LA

I would be grateful for any information of my nephew, **Patrick O'Maley**, from LEGAN, near LOUISBURGH, County MAYO, Ireland, who left NEW YORK for CALIFORNIA about three years ago, and has not since been heard from. He intended going to the mines, as far as my brother-in-law, **Patrick O'Connor**, SOUTHFORK, NEVADA County, and of whom also I am very anxious to obtain some intelligence. Please address **Thomas Gibbons**, 315 BOWERY, NEW YORK CITY. California papers, please copy.

June 18, 1864

Intelligence is wanted of a daughter of the late **Capt. Cunningham**, from QUEEN'S County, Ireland (formerly of the 89th Infantry Regt. British Army). She was married to a **Dr. Charles McCosker**, from the Parish of DROMORE, County TYRONE, Ireland, who disappeared from NEW YORK some 16 or 17 years ago. Her husband's brother, **Thomas**, has died intestate; and as she and her heirs have a claim on his property, if this should meet the eyes of any of them they will find it to their advantage to communicate immediately with **John McCosker**, SHULLSBOROUGH, LAFAYETTE County, WISCONSIN.

Of **James Comerford**, who landed in this City about 12 years ago; also, his brother **Tim**, who landed in New York about 7 years ago; and his sister **Mary**, who also arrived in New York about 5 years ago, natives of BIRR, KING'S County, Ireland. Any information of them will be thankfully received by their brother **William Comerford**, at

130 CLINTON PLACE, near 6th Avenue, or at **Rodey Mooney's**, 169 EAST 12th STREET, NEW YORK CITY. [Appeared July 2, 1864 with some new information.]

Of **Timothy Kennedy**, and his brother **Martin**, formerly of KNOCKALTON, Parish of NENAGH, County TIPPERARY, Ireland. When last heard from they were residing in JO DAVIESS County (Post Office Address VINEGAR HILL,) State of ILLINOIS. Any intelligence of them will be thankfully received by their nephews **Timothy** and **Bryan**, sons of the late **Simon Kennedy**, of GURTNAHALLA, Parish of UPPER CHURCH, County TIPPERARY. Address **Patrick Quinana**, 300 SEVENTH AVENUE, NEW YORK CITY. Illinois papers, please copy.

Of **Mr. Patrick Magill**, or **McGill**, who was employed in the Treasury Office, WASHINGTON, D. C., when last heard of in March, 1863. Any information of him will be thankfully received by **Daniel C. O'Connor**, son of the late **William O'Connor**, at 247 ELIZABETH STREET, NEW YORK. Said P. Magill resided in THOMASTOWN, County KILKENNY, Ireland, about 28 or 30 years since.

Of **Miss Bridget Doran**, Parish of BALLYRAGGET, BYRNS GROVE Townland, County KILKENNY, Ireland. She emigrated to this country about two and a half years ago, in company with **John Padie**, a young man from the same place, and **Martin Berigan** and family, from BALLYRAGGET. It is supposed she is living in or around the City of NEW YORK. Any information of her will be thankfully received by **Patrick Kenna**, WATERVILLE, LE SUEUR County, MINNESOTA.

Of **Mary McCarthy**, of the Parish of OOLA, of KILITY, Co. LIMERICK, Ireland, who, it is supposed, sailed from Liverpool on the 4th of April 1864. Any information of her will be thankfully received by her sister **Margaret**, at 47 East Street, NEW HAVEN, CONN., or to **Y. Murphy**, 464 WASHINGTON STREET, NEW YORK. Boston *Pilot*, please copy.

June 25, 1864

Of **James, John**, and **Honora Glinny**, natives of MILTOWN MALBAY, County CLARE, Ireland. When last heard from were in LONG POINT, ADAMS County, State of ILLINOIS. Any information of them will be thankfully received by their brother, **Matt Glinny**, by writing to him in care of **James Walsh**, 99 Hamilton Avenue, BROOKLYN, L.I. Chicago papers, please copy.

Of **John Bailie**, a native of RASSAN, Parish of CREGGAN, County LOUTH, Ireland, who left RICHMOND, VA, in 1863. Any information of him will be thankfully received (as his wife has been heard from lately) by writing to **Owen Gorman**, 26th and G Streets, care of **Mr. Morgan**, WASHINGTON, D. C.

Of **John Duffy**, a native of the Parish of STRANORIER, County DONEGAL, Ireland. When last heard from four years ago, he left PHILADELPHIA for CONNECTICUT. Any information of him will be thankfully received by his brother, **Patt Duffy**, by writing to him to No. 20 LEONARD STREET, NEW YORK.

Of **Thomas** and **Andrew Whalen**, natives of BALLYROANE, QUEEN'S County, Ireland. Andrew came here about 16 years ago, and Thomas 10 years. When last heard from Thomas was in WATERBURY, and Andrew was in CHICAGO. Any information of them will be thankfully received by their niece, **Bessey Buckley**, at **William O'Reilly's**, cor. of Grand and Pacific Streets, BROOKLYN, Long Island, N.Y. Boston and Chicago papers, please copy. [Appeared July 9, 1864 with William O'Reilly changed to **William O'Neill**.]

Of **John Steele**, from the County TIPPERARY, Ireland, who left Ireland last April, and came to PHILADELPHIA. Any information of him will be thankfully received by **Mary Patterson**, No. 4, BATTERY PLACE, NEW YORK CITY.

Of **James Dalton**, a native of GRANARD, Parish of COLUMKILL, County LONGFORD, Ireland, who enlisted for three years in the United States gunboat O. Wasko, and left for the blockade of GALVESTON, TEXAS. When last heard from, ten months ago, he was on board the O. Wasko, being off the port of GALVESTON doing blockade duty. Any information of him will be thankfully received by his brother, **Edward Dalton**, by writing to him to No. 260 EAST 14th ST., NEW YORK CITY.

Of **John Kiely**, of CASTLEMAHON, Co. LIMERICK, Ireland. When last heard from, two years ago, he was living in BLUEGRASS, VERMILION County, ILL Any information of him will be thankfully received by his brother, **Michael Kiely**, at 144 Wallace St., NEW HAVEN, CONN

Of **Widow of Patrick O'Leaky** (maiden name **Catharine O'Connor**), a native of BLACKWATER, County KERRY, Ireland. She came to this country in the Spring of 1845; she was married in NEW YORK, and is now supposed to be residing somewhere in NEW YORK State. Any information of her will be thankfully received by **Mrs. Jones**, No. 30 Maple Street, LAWRENCE, MASS.

July 2, 1864

Of **Thomas O'Connor**, a cooper by trade, who left MONTREAL, CANADA EAST, in 1848, and when last heard from (in the same year) was in or about TROY, N.Y. Any information of him, or any of his family, will be thankfully received by his nephew, **John O'Connor**, 395 River Street, TROY, N.Y.

Of **James Comerford**, who arrived in CINCINNATI, and is supposed to be in OHIO, about twelve years ago; also, of his brother **Tim**, who landed in New York about 7 years ago, and his sister **Mary**, who also arrived in New York about 5 years ago, natives of BIRR, KING'S County, Ireland. Any information of them will be thankfully received by their brother, **William Comerford**, at 130 CLINTON PLACE, near 6th Avenue, or at **Rodey Mooney's**, 169 EAST 12th STREET, NEW YORK CITY. [Appeared June 18, 1864 with less information and slightly different wording.]

Of **Mary Wilson**, late of CLONMEL, County TIPPERARY, Ireland. When last heard from was in BROOKLYN, N.Y. Her father has arrived, and would wish to hear from her. Address, **William Wilson**, No. 12 VANDEWATER STREET, NEW YORK.

Of **Mary Malone**, of MUNGRETT, County LIMERICK, Ireland, who came to this country about nine years ago, and when last heard from was in BOSTON, MASS. Any information of her will be thankfully received by her sister, **Johanna Malone**, at No. 9 Summit Street, SOUTH BROOKLYN, N.Y.

Of **Mary Ryan**, a native of BALLYCABIS, County KILKENNY, Ireland. When last heard from she was in CHICAGO, ILLINOIS. Any information of her will be thankfully received by her sister, **Catherine Murphy**, at No. 17 WEST STREET, NEW YORK.

July 9, 1864

Of **Thomas Bowes**, a native of DUNGARVAN, County WATERFORD, Ireland. When last heard of (about 16 years since) was in SYDNEY, CAPE BRETON. Any information of him will be thankfully received by his son, **Edward Bowes** at Girard Bolt Works, 23rd Street, between Race and Vine Streets, PHILADELPHIA, PA. Canada papers, please copy.

Of **Michael O'Keefe**, a native of YOUGHAL, County CORK, Ireland. When last heard from (seven years ago) he resided in NEW YORK. Any information of him will be thankfully received by his brother, **James O'Keeffe**, by writing to him to 116 CEDAR STREET, NEW YORK.

Of **Mrs. Ann McHugh**, (maiden name **McMackan**,) of TULLYMUCK, County TYRONE, Ireland, who is supposed to be in LOWELL, MASS. If this should meet her notice, or any one knowing her address, they will confer a favor by communicating with her husband, **James McHugh**, care of **Mr. Wm. Caffrey**, FAR ROCKAWAY, Long Island, N.Y Lowell, Mass., papers, please copy.

Of **Thomas Lannon**, a native of the Townland of CARRICKMULLEN, Parish of KNOCKBRIDGE, County LOUTH, Ireland. He was a member of the Irish Constabulary, and left for NEW YORK in June, 1853. Any information of him will be thankfully received by his brother, **Michael Lannon**, by writing to him in care of **George W. Melvil**, No. 42 HAMILTON STREET, NEW-YORK. Irish and American papers, please copy.

July 16, 1864

F. Z. Vincent, Jr., WASHINGTON, D. C., received both: replied. Be explicit with your address; will promptly reply. **D. C. O'Connor**, 247 ELIZABETH STREET, NEW YORK.

Of **Catherine Malley**, who left Ireland twelve years ago. When last heard from (five years ago,) was in CONNECTICUT. Her husband's name was **George Balley**. Her father and mother live in 149 Plymouth St., BROOKLYN. Any information concerning her will be thankfully received by **Edward Malley**, at the above address.

Of **James Conroy**, of Townsend Street, City of DUBLIN, Ireland. When last heard from, was in the 26th Penn. Vols. Any intelligence of him will be thankfully received by his brother, **Christopher Conroy**, by writing to him on board the U.S. steamer *Hydrangea*, James River squadron, *via* FORTRESS MONROE, VA., or elsewhere. Dublin papers, please copy.

Of **Edward Brennan**, a native of NEWTOWN, Parish of CROOK, County WATERFORD, Ireland, who left SPENSORPORT, MONROE County, N.Y, about five years ago, and moved to JEFFERSON. County, N.Y Any information of him will be thankfully received by his sister, **Mary Troy**, by writing to her to No. 134 Plymouth St., BROOKLYN, N.Y. Jefferson County, N.Y. papers, please copy.

Of **John McGrath**, a native of KILGARVEN, Co. KERRY, Ireland. When last heard of, he lived at 18 or 19 BRUNSWICK STREET, NEW YORK. His brother **Cornelius** wishes to hear from him at his earliest convenience. -Direct, in care, to **Mr. Ed. Kelly**, No. 18 Blue Anchor Alley, Parish of St. Luke's, LONDON.

Of **Timothy Sheehan**, a native of CAHIRCIVEEN, County KERRY, Ireland, who arrived at Castle Garden in the ship *Progress*, on the 24th of June, and who wrote to his brother in SPRINGFIELD, MASS, for some money to bring him to SPRINGFIELD. Since that time nothing has been heard from him. Any information of him will be thankfully received by his brother, **Daniel Sheehan**, by writing to him to SPRINGFIELD, MASS.

Of **Robert, Thomas** and **George Roe**, natives of QUEEN'S County, Ireland. When last heard from, Thomas was at NEW HAVEN CONN.; George in the Federal service; Robert's whereabouts unknown. Any information respecting them will be thankfully received by their brother, **Dr. J. F. Roe**, JEFFERSON, MARION County, Oregon.

Of **Margaret Fahey**, aged 14, a native of the Parish of BALLINAKILL, County GALWAY, Ireland, who arrived in New York on the 9th of April, in the ship *Webster*, from Liverpool. Any information of her will be thankfully received by her brother and sister, **John** and **Ellen Fahey**, by writing to them to No. 19 Stone Street, NEWARK, N.J

Of **Mary Normyle**, a native of KILBRIGET, Parish of KILMICHAEL, County CLARE, Ireland. When last heard from, about fourteen years ago. Any information of her will be thankfully received by her sister **Margaret**, at **Mr. John Cunningham's**, 131 HUDSON ST., NEW YORK.

July 23, 1864

Of **Mary Anne** and **Catherine Fay**, natives of the City of NEW YORK, who were born in CHAMBER STREET and then moved to CLINTON STREET, and whose father was killed by falling from a building. Mary Anne was sent to one of the Half-Orphan Asylums; Catherine lived with her aunt in another part of the City. Any information of them will be thankfully received by their brother, **Thomas Fay**, Co. B, 5th Regiment, V. R. Corps, INDIANAPOLIS, IND.

Of **Hanora Stapleton**, who, when last heard from was in NEW YORK. Any information of her will be thankfully received by her brother, **Patrick Stapleton**, at **Michael Murphy's**, cor. Esplanade and Church Streets, TORONTO, CANADA WEST.

Of **Margaret Flood**, a native of the Town of STRADONE, Co. CAVAN, Ireland. When last heard from she lived in NEW YORK. Any information concerning her will be thankfully received by her mother or sister, **Mary**, by writing to them to 53 ORCHARD STREET, NEW YORK.

If **Charles Hunt**, who left Queenstown on the 14th or 15th of March, 1863, in the steamship *Etna*, will write, giving his address to **T. J. Ryan**, 59 New Street, NEWARK, N.J., he will confer a favor. [Appeared under County CORK]

Of **James Cullen**, a native of the Parish of CALRY, County SLIGO, Ireland. Any information of him will be thankfully received by his brother and sister, **Brian** and **Cathesine** [sic], by writing to them to No. 18 23rd STREET, NEW YORK.

Of **Ann Ryan**, a native of the Parish of UPPERCHURCH, County TIPPERARY, Ireland. When last heard from was in the Town of ERIE, PENN. If this should meet her notice or any one knowing her address, they would confer a favor by communicating with her brothers, **Michael** and **Edward Ryan**, in care of **Mr. William Peters**, Fourth Street, SOUTH TROY, N.Y. Canada papers, please copy.

Of **Lawrence Mullally**, of ATHENRY, County GALWAY, Ireland, who arrived in New York on the 29th of June, 1864, in the ship *Gallatin*, from Liverpool. Any information of him will be thankfully received by **Margaret Mullally**, No. 70 Summit Street, BROOKLYN.

July 30, 1864

Of **Michael Farrell**, a native of the City of DUBLIN, Ireland. He arrived at New York, in the ship *Emerald Isle*, on the 16th of May, 1863, and is supposed to be in the naval service. He is five feet four inches in height, has a fair complexion, light sandy hair, blue eyes, and is rather stout. He is in his 20th year. Any information of him will be thankfully received by his father, **P. Farrell**, 85 Lower Gardiner Street, DUBLIN, Ireland, or the Editors of the *Catholic Telegraph*, CINCINNATI, OHIO.

Of **Dennis Daly**, a native of GALBALLY, County LIMERICK, Ireland. When last heard from he was in LOCKPORT, NIAGARA County, N.Y. Any information of him will be thankfully received by his brother, **Timothy Daly**, by writing to him to 122 Elm Street, LAWRENCE, MASS.

Of **Thomas Walsh**, a native of TRALEE, County KERRY, Ireland. When last heard from, about twenty years ago, he was in ST. LOUIS, MISSOURI. Any information of him will be thankfully received by his nephew, **Patrick Walsh**, by writing to him to No. 283 WEST 27th ST., NEW YORK CITY.

Of **John, Austin**, and **Bridget Durkin**, natives of the County SLIGO, Ireland, who came from LANCASHIRE, ENGLAND, to BOSTON, where they resided for many years. Information is also wanted of **James Carrabine** and family, of the same place. If this advertisement meets the eyes of any of the above-named persons, or their friends or acquaintances, they will confer a great favor on the advertiser by addressing **Sergt. James Durkin**, Co. G, 17th Regt., N.Y.V.V., 4th Division, 16th Corps, DECATUR, ALABAMA.

Patrick Mackeague, of SHRULE, TUAM, Ireland, is anxious to get tidings of his brother, **John Mackeague**, alias **McCabe**, who, when last heard from, eight or nine years ago, was living in GRAPE-HILL, ST. LOUIS. St. Louis papers, please copy. [Appeared under County TIPPERARY]

Of **Thomas Holland**, a native of CLARINBRIDGE, County GALWAY, Ireland, who left Ireland about 18 years ago. When last heard from he was in CINCINNATI, OHIO. Any information of him will be thankfully received by his nephew, **Patrick Leonard**, SPRINGFIELD, MASS.

Of **Richard Gerraty**, of HEADFORD, County GALWAY, Ireland. When last heard from he was in DUNBAR, WASHINGTON County, State of OHIO. Any information of him will be thankfully received by his wife and family by writing to his son, **Thomas Gerraty**, LOCKHAVEN, CLINTON County, PENN, or to **Thomas Tully**, 347 WATER ST., NEW YORK.

August 6, 1864

Patrick McCarthy who, in July, 1843, gave a child of the name of **Mary Mallen** in charge of the N.Y. Commissioners of Public Charity, the parents of this child, or any person who could give any information of said child, and the persons connected with this affair, are respectfully requested to address as soon as possible W. Ch., Post Office, Box 5290.

Of **John McLaughlin**, a native of BRIXTON, LONDON, ENGLAND. When last heard from (last August) he arrived in New York City. Any information of him will be thankfully received by **Thomas Northage**, by writing to him to GLEN COVE, L.I., in care of **Mr. Lyston**.

Of **Joseph O'Neil**, a native of the Parish of BELL DOYLE, County DUBLIN, Ireland, who left home in the year 1853, for AUSTRALIA. Any information concerning him will be thankfully received by his brother and sister, **John** and **Maryann O'Neill**. Address, **John O'Neil**, 16 JONES STREET, NEW YORK CITY, U.S. Australia papers, please copy.

Of **Michael Hoban**, from County MAYO, Ireland, who went to New York, in March, 1863, from Liverpool. His sister Margaret would be very thankful to hear of him. Address **Margaret Hoban**, No. 420 South Third Street, PHILADELPHIA, PA.

Of **Margaret Redden**, and her daughter **Catharine**, natives of the Parish of CAPPA, County LIMERICK, Ireland, who arrived in New York on the 17th of June, 1863. When last seen (about 12 months ago) they were in this City. Any information of them will be thankfully received by her son, **Patrick Redden**, by writing to him to 635 WASHINGTON STREET, NEW YORK.

Of **Daniel Clancy**, of the Parish of BRUFF, County LIMERICK, Ireland. When last heard from was in PUTNAM County, INDIANA. Any intelligence of him will be thankfully received by his nephew, **Michael Corbett**, 125 GREENWICH STREET, NEW YORK, in care of **Patrick Clancy**. Indiana papers, please copy.

Of **Mrs. Thomas Clancy** and **Dennis Whelan**, of BALLYPOREEN, County TIPPERARY, Ireland, who left there 10 and 13 years ago respectively, and landed in New York - are in the neighborhood of NEW YORK still. Any information concerning them will be thankfully received by their cousin, **Bridget Fitzgibbon**, by writing to her at 223 Second Street, SOUTH BOSTON, MASS.

Of **Thomas Shea**, from the County TIPPERARY, Ireland, who was a passenger on board the *Tonawonder*, and landed in Philadelphia, Pa., in April, and left on the 14th of May, and has not been heard of since. Any information of him will be thankfully received by his brother, **Richard Shea**, by addressing to No. 631 Fistswatter St., PHILADELPHIA, PA.

August 13, 1864

Of **Edward** and **Patrick Siney**, natives of the Parish of MOUNTMELICK, QUEEN'S County, Ireland. Edward came to this country in 1849; Patrick, about 1852 or '53. When last heard from they were living in PHILADELPHIA, PENN. Any intelligence of them will be thankfully received by addressing a note to their cousin, **John Siney**, ST. CLAIR, SCHUYLKILL Co., PENN

Of **Maurice Spillane**, a native of the Parish of KILGOPPIN, County KERRY, Ireland, who arrived in New York about nine years, and left for CALIFORNIA about seven years since, and when last heard of was in SAN FRANCISCO. Any information of him will be thankfully received by his brother, **John Spillane** - who arrived here on the 1st of last July - by writing to him, in care of **Maurice Spillane**, New York Gas Works, EAST 21st STREET, NEW YORK CITY. California papers, please copy.

Of **Timothy Harnett**, a native of the Parish of ISLANDDONNY, County KERRY, Ireland. When last heard from (about 12 months ago) he was at MINNESOTA MINES, LAKE SUPERIOR, State of MICHIGAN. Any information of him will be thankfully received by his sister, **Bridget Barret**, by writing to her in care of **Squire Callaghan**, CLIFTON, STATEN ISLAND, N.Y

Of **John** and **Patrick Green**, Parish of KENMARE, County KERRY, Ireland. They were in ST. LOUIS, MO, about six years ago. Their father, **Frank Green**, will gratefully acknowledge any information of them. Address to **Daniel A. Brosnan**, WASHINGTON, D. C.

Of **Margaret Gibson,** a native of COOLANY, Parish of KILLORAN, County SLIGO, Ireland, who came to this country in April, 1861. She was said to be travelling with a lady who went to South America. Any intelligence of her will be thankfully received by her sister, **Bridget Gibson**. Address Henderson's Intelligence office, 80 Nassau Street, NEW YORK.

August 20, 1864

Of **John Kennedy**, who left DUBLIN, Ireland, eleven years ago. Any information of him will be thankfully received by his sister, **Mrs. Bridget Caulfield**, by writing to her, in care of **Mrs. Lockhart**, 90 CLINTON PLACE, NEW YORK.

Of **Michael** and **Patrick Kieley** and their sister, **Mrs. Moloney**, natives of BALLINACANA, County LIMERICK, Ireland. When last heard from, 8 years ago, they were in CHICAGO, ILL Any information of them will be thankfully received by their brother **William**, at **Laurence Tuomy's**, 402 CHERRY ST., NEW YORK.

Of **Mary Coffee**, wife of **Thomas Coffee**, maiden name **Mary Shannon**, who left Parish of HOSPITAL, OLDHAM, County LIMERICK, Ireland, about eleven years ago, for NEW YORK; has not since been heard from. Information of her will be thankfully received by her nephew, **Michael Shannon**, 63 Worthington Street, SPRINGFIELD, MASS

Of **Thomas, Daniel, Patrick** and **Edward McGrath**, who emigrated to this country from BALLYDUFF, Parish of TALLOW, County WATERFORD, Ireland. When last heard from they were in the State of OHIO. Any information of them will be thankfully received by their brother **William**, in care of **Peter Hancock**, 23 Congress Street, NEWARK, NEW JERSEY.

Of **John Martin**, a native of the Parish of BALLINAKILL, County of GALWAY, Ireland, who left his wife and family in FRANKLIN, WARREN Co., OHIO, on the 15th of July. He is about forty years of age, dark complexioned, has the little finger of his right hand crooked, and is given to whistling. Any intelligence of him, or of a girl named **Mary Allen**, who is supposed to have accompanied him, will be thankfully received by **John Goonane**, FRANKLIN, OHIO.

August 27, 1864

Of **William, James, Catherine** and **Ann Mooney**, who were in NEW YORK when their sister Nora left there in February, 1851. She had been in the Home for Orphans. She was informed that her brother had advertised for her in the Irish-American, and that he belonged to a New York Regiment. Any information of them will be thankfully received by their sister, **Nora Mooney**, by writing to her at 28 Elm Street, SPRINGFIELD, MASS, in care of **John Cassidy**.

Of **Mary Anne Doran**, daughter of **Patrick Doran** (or **Dolan**), 91st Regiment, N.Y.S.V., lately deceased. When last heard of was supposed to be living with her grandparents in EIGHTH AVENUE, NEW YORK. Any information of her will be thankfully received at 84 WOOSTER STREET, NEW-YORK, where she will hear of something to her advantage.

Of **Michael Newman**, from CASTLE POLE, Parish of CAREN, County MEATH, Ireland, who sailed for Boston, thirteen or fourteen years ago. Any information of him will be thankfully received by his stepbrother, **John Shaw**. Address **Patrick Carroll**, WESTPORT, CONN. Boston papers, please copy.

Of **Edward** and **Mary Donahue**, who sailed from AUGHOOMAR, County LONGFORD, Ireland, and came to NEW YORK in the year 1844. Any information respecting them will be thankfully received by their brother, **Thomas Donahue**, No. 51 Pine Street, PATERSON, NEW JERSEY, or to **Bernard O'Neill**, Justice of Peace, PATERSON, NEW JERSEY.

Of **Margaret King**, a native of the Parish of KILLMORE, County MAYO, Ireland. Any intelligence of her will be thankfully received by her brother, **Patrick King**, by writing to him in care of **Peter Perrin**, No. 14 South Front Street, BALTIMORE, MD.

Of **James Feighery**, or his uncle, **James Feighery**, natives of the Parish of FERLEANE, KING'S County, Ireland. The former was in PHILADELPHIA about seven years ago, and the latter was living some time since in GLASSBERRY, TIOGA County, PENN. Any information of them will be thankfully received by his brother and nephew, **Daniel Feighery**, by writing to him in care of **John Brazel**, 241 Cuthbeart Street, PHILADELPHIA, PA.

Of **Dennis O'Connell**, a native of MUHER, near DIRNAGREE, Parish of DROUNSHARIFF, County CORK, Ireland, who came to this country about ten or twelve years ago. When last heard from was in BALTIMORE, MD. Any information of him will be thankfully received by his brother, **John O'Connell**. Please address, **Jeremiah Galvin**, 24 Chelsea Street, CHARLESTOWN, MASSACHUSETTS.

Of **Margaret Ryan** and her daughter **Catharine Flemming**, natives of the Parish of FETHARD, County TIPPERARY, Ireland. When last heard from they were in NEW YORK. Any information of them will be thankfully received by her sons, **Edward** and **John Flemming**, by writing to them to CAMDEN Post Office, NEW JERSEY.

September 3, 1864

Of **Mrs. Ann Purcell** (maiden name **Bryan**) who came to this country 10 years ago. When last heard from was in YONKERS. Should this come under her notice she will please address **Mrs. Mary Kealey**, IRVINGTON, WESTCHESTER County, NEW YORK.

Of **John Kitson**, who left ENNIS, County CLARE, Ireland, about seven years ago. When last heard of (about two years since), he was in the Corcoran Legion. Any intelligence of him will be thankfully received by his mother, **Mary Kitson**, SPRINGFIELD, MASS.

Of **Bridget** and **Elanor Bingham**, natives of BALLINROBE, County MAYO, daughters of **Denis Bingham**, a soldier in the United States Service, who departed this life June 16, 1864, and who has left some money to be divided between said children. Any information will be thankfully received by **Michael Gibbons**, 94 BAXTER STREET, NEW YORK CITY.

Of **James Driscoll**, a native of CORK, who emigrated from Cork about two years ago, and went to UPPER CANADA; he stopped there for some time working at his trade, a cooper; was seen in MEMPHIS about 12 months ago. Any information of him will be most thankfully received by his wife, **Mrs. Driscoll**. Foster's Place, BLACKPOOL, CORK. Memphis papers, please copy.

September 10, 1864

Mrs. Dempsey, the widow of **James Dempsey**, who left KEY WEST about five months ago, will hear something to her advantage by sending her address to **Mrs. Catharine Ennis**, No. 259 WILLIAM-STREET, NEW YORK. St. Louis papers please copy.

Of **William Murphy**, who enlisted in the neighborhood of OSWEGO County, N.Y., a year ago last July. He has dark hair, large blue eyes, and two large teeth in the front of his mouth. Any person who can give the requisite information will confer a great favor on his afflicted mother. Address **Mrs. Murphy**, 326 EAST-8th STREET, NEW YORK CITY.

Of **Patrick Connor**, a native of the County MEATH, Ireland, who arrived in this City, in the ship *James Foster*, on the 3rd of August, 1864. Any information of him will be thankfully received by his brother, **Matthew Connor**, HART'S VILLAGE, DUTCHESS County, NEW YORK, or at the Irish-American Office, 29 Anne Street, New York.

Of **Dennis Crimming, Kate Crimming**, and **Margaret Kinnea**, ASHFORD, NEWCASTLE WEST, County LIMERICK, Ireland, who are supposed to have left home about the 2nd day of June, 1864, and sailed in the ship *Cenasure* from Liverpool, and arrived in New York July 22, 1864. Any information of them will be thankfully received by **Mrs. Jordan**, DUNKIRK, CHAUTAUQUA County, NEW YORK, care of **Thomas N. Hayes.**

Of **Mrs. Mary Hannigan**, maiden name **Mary Maguire**, native of County FERMANAGH, Parish of AUGHALAIGHER, Townland of KINMORE, Ireland. Any information of her will be thankfully received by her only son, **Patrick McBerrin**, No. 52 Bridge Street, BROOKLYN, NEW YORK. Canada papers please copy.

Of **David, Edward**, and **Mark Fitzgibbon**, tailors by trade, and natives of MALLOW, County CORK, Ireland. Edward was in NEW YORK ten years ago. Any information respecting them will be thankfully received by their sister. Address to **Eugene Ryan**, corner of Fifth and Washington Streets, EAST TROY, NEW YORK. Philadelphia papers please copy.

Of **Mary Flannery**, a native of TEMPLEMORE, County TIPPERARY, Ireland, when last heard from, nine years ago, she was at HYDE PARK (NATCHES), NEW YORK. Any information of her will be thankfully received by her brother **John**, who has lately arrived in New York, 93 EAST 11th-street, NEW YORK CITY.

September 17, 1864

$50 REWARD - For any information that will lead to the recovery of **Tommy Kennedy**, aged 8 years, who strayed or was stolen from No. 6 Union St., BROOKLYN, on the evening of April 20th. He had on, when last seen, a blue flannel jacket, gray pants, soldier's blue cap, also shoes; hair and features fair; front teeth decayed. Any information of him will be thankfully received by his father, **Edward Kennedy**, at 49 BEEKMAN ST., NEW YORK, or at the office of this paper.

Of **Mrs. Slattery** (maiden name **Julia Woods**), a native of the Parish of HOSPITAL, County LIMERICK, Ireland, or of her husband, **Patrick Slattery**, a blacksmith by trade. When last heard from they were in BALTIMORE, MD. Any information of them will be thankfully received by their daughter, **Catharine Enright**, care of **John Woods**, 235 MULBERRY STREET, N.Y.

Of **Michael Carney** and his wife **Bridget** (maiden name, **Bridget Neagle**,) who left MORRIS'S MILLS, County CLARE, Ireland, about twenty years ago. When last heard of they were in ST. JOHN, NEW BRUNSWICK, BRITISH AMERICA. Any intelligence of them will be thankfully received by their son, **Patrick Carney**, by addressing him at New Bedford Copper Works, NEW BEDFORD, MASS.

Of **Patrick Gillen**, who left the Parish of DRUMCLIVE, County SLIGO, Ireland. When last heard from was in ST. JOHN'S, on his way to NEW YORK. Any information of him will be thankfully received by his sisters, **Mary** and **Catherine Gillen**. Address **Mary Gilmartin**, in care of **T. D. Hercey**, PORTLAND, MAINE.

Of **Patrick Lavelle**, a native of TYRAWLEY, County MAYO, Ireland, who left England for America in 1858. When last heard from (in 1861) he was in NEW ORLEANS, LA. Any information of him will be thankfully received by his brother, **Michael Lavelle**, by writing to him to No. 42 Montgomery Street, JERSEY CITY, N.J.

Of **Thomas Lalor**, a native of NEWTOWNBARRY, County WEXFORD, Ireland, who emigrated to this country in the year 1848. Any information of him will be thankfully received by his brother, **Michael Lalor**, by writing to him to RAHWAY, N.J.

Of **Nicholas McCaffery**, a native of Boat Street, NEWRY, County DOWN, Ireland, who landed at Quebec in 1863. When heard from in June last he was in QUEBEC. Any information of him will be thankfully received by his wife, **Bridget McCaffery**, who lately arrived in New York. Please address in care of **John Harndon**, No. 4 MORRIS STREET, NEW YORK CITY.

Of **Patrick Cronin**, a native of GLYBE, County KERRY, Ireland. When last heard of was in SEGERTON, CRAWFORD County, PENNSYLVANIA. Any information of him will be thankfully received by his sisters, **Ellen** and **Mary Cronin**, at 13 PELL STREET, NEW YORK.

Of **Thomas Mannion**, a native of the Townland of ESKER, Parish of BEVENAGH, County of GALWAY, Ireland. He is a son of **Patrick Mannion**. The last time left home was in 1847, being previously in this country. When last heard of, in April, 1864, was in the City of NEW YORK. His brother, **William Mannion**, who landed here last April, is very anxious to hear from him. Address in care of **W. J. Lally**, WOONSOCKET, R.I.

Of **Robert Murphy**, otherwise **Robert Fitton**, who arrived in the City of New York about 14 years ago. He was a native of the City of CORK, a carpenter, and worked for **Joseph Doyle**, CLIFTON, STATEN ISLAND. When last heard from was in the City of NEW YORK. If this should meet his eye it would be to his advantage to write to **William Burns**, No. 3 Vanbrunt Street, SOUTH BROOKLYN, as he can inform him about his income in the old country. If any person knows about him or where he is they would very much oblige his friends by writing to the above address.

Of **Cornelius Cotter**, a native of SCHABREENE, County CORK, Ireland, who emigrated to PHILADELPHIA, PA., about 15 years since, and was in the employment of **Mr. McGowen**, an inn-keeper. Any information of him will be thankfully received by his daughter, who lately arrived in this country. Address **John Driscoll**, U.S. Hospital, BEVERLY, N.J., Ward 8.

September 24, 1864

Of **Cornelius** and **Mary Gallavin**. When last heard of they were residing in COOPER County, MISSOURI. Any information of them will be thankfully received by their son, **Timothy Gallavin**, U.S. Tug *Alert*, JAMES RIVER, VA.

Of **Patrick Lynch**, baker, who left the City of LIMERICK, in 1857, for NEW YORK; wrote once after landing and never heard from since. Any information of him will be thankfully received by his son, **Michael Lynch**, baker. Address **Mr. Patrick Feron**, 404 Hudson Avenue, BROOKLYN.

Of **Margaret Walsh**, of CAHERELLY; also of her cousins, **Thomas, John, David, Mary, Johannah** and **Catherine Connor**; also their aunt, **Mrs. O'Connor**, all of the Parish of GRANGE, County LIMERICK, Ireland. They emigrated about the year 1848; when last heard from they were in NEW YORK. Any person knowing of their whereabouts will confer a lasting obligation by addressing **Patrick Kennedy**, MILWAUKEE, WISCONSIN, as they will hear of something much to their satisfaction.

Should this meet the eye of **Stephen Kelly**, formerly of ROSCOMMON, Ireland, he will please call or address his nephew, **James Kelly**, at 197 6th AVENUE, NEW YORK.

Of **Patrick Geraughty**, a native of WESTPORT, County MAYO, Ireland. When last heard from was in PENNSYLVANIA. Any information of him will be thankfully received by **Sarah Geraughty**, 180 ELIZABETH ST., NEW YORK. Philadelphia papers, please copy.

Of **Patrick** and **Mary Gallagher**, from CROSSMOLINA, County MAYO, Ireland. Any information will be thankfully received by their brother **Edward**, at 125 WEST 33rd STREET, NEW YORK.

Of **Peter** and **Michael McCormick,** natives of SCOTCHTOWN, County MONAGHAN, Ireland. When last heard from (8 years ago) they were in NEW YORK CITY. Any information of them will be thankfully received by their niece, **Sarah McCormick**, daughter of **John McCormick**, by addressing her at 535 SIXTH AVENUE, cor. of 22nd Street, NEW YORK. Exchange papers, please copy.

Michael McElligott, late from LISTOWELL or TARBERT, County KERRY, Ireland. Any intelligence of him will be thankfully received by his sister, **Catherine Shea**, who is anxious to hear from him. Direct to 155 Congress Street, BOSTON, MASS.; or to the care of **Joseph Kearney**, 69 OLIVER STREET, NEW YORK.

Of **Catherine Clashy**, a native of the Town of KINVARRA, Parish of BALLYDERIEN, County GALWAY, Ireland. When last heard from, in April, 1860, she lived with **Mr. S. Hammond**, in NEW HAVEN, CONNECTICUT. Any information of her will be thankfully received by her brother, **James Clashy**, by writing to him to SING SING, WESTCHESTER Co., N.Y. [Appeared Oct. 1, 1864 as Catherine Clasby and with some different information.]

Of **Thomas Dennehy**, a native of KILLATTY, Parish of BALLYHOOLY, County CORK, Ireland, who left Cork in or about March, 1842, for SIDNEY, and has not since been heard from, but is supposed to be in SAN FRANCISCO, CALIFORNIA. If this should meet the eye of any person knowing his whereabouts, they will please communicate the same to his brother, **John Dennehy**, No. 20 Burnt Lane, CORK, or to his nephew, **Thomas Dennehy**, 628 Cherry St., PHILADELPHIA, PA. California papers, please copy.

October 1, 1864

Of **Thomas** and **Hugh Quinn**, of the Townland of DERRYCREW, Parish of LOUGHGALL, County ARMAGH, Ireland. When last heard of Hugh was at GEORGETOWN, C.W., about 10 years ago; Thomas, when last heard of, was in ST. PAUL, MIN Any information of them will be thankfully received by addressing Lynch, Cole & Meehan, Irish-American Office, New York.

Of **Mrs. Mary Harrigan** (maiden name **Rairdon**) of the Parish of CROOM, County LIMERICK, Ireland, who emigrated to America about 10 years ago. When last heard from she was in LAWRENCE. County, PENN Any information of her will be thankfully received by her niece, **Maryann Conway**, at Mr. Carroll's Intelligence Office, 69 Sixth Avenue, NEW YORK.

Of **John King** or his wife, **Ellen Behen**, of the Parish of COURLOUS, County CLARE, Ireland. When last heard from they were living in DETROIT, MICHIGAN. Any information of them will be thankfully received by their sister, **Bridget Behen**, by writing to her in care of **John Ahearn**, corner of Vanbrunt and Elizabeth Streets, SOUTH BROOKLYN, N.Y.

Of **Charles Bradly**, a native of TYRONE, Ireland. He came to America some twelve years ago. When last heard of he was in LOUISVILLE, KENTUCKY. Any information concerning him will be thankfully received by his brother, **Patrick Bradly**, at 1010 Passyunk Road, PHILADELPHIA, PA.

Of **Thomas Dwyer**, a native of the Parish of LULEY, County TIPPERARY, Ireland, who arrived in New York, by the ship *Neptune*, about three weeks since. Any information of him will be thankfully received by his mother, **Ellen Quirk**, at **Dennis McCarthy's**, No. 35 GREENWICH ST., NEW YORK.

Of **Thomas Horn**, son of **Richard Horn**, who left BALLINATUBBER, County MAYO, 16 years ago. When last heard of, he was in NEW YORK. If he will send his address to the office of this paper he will hear of his mother and sister, **Winefred**. New York and Brooklyn papers, please copy.

Of **Patrick Ferriter**, of BEHNOUGH, Parish of CAMP, County KERRY, Ireland, who landed in New York City in the year 1851, and has not since been heard from. Any information concerning him will be thankfully received by addressing **Edmond Farrell**, 28 Wapping Street, CHARLESTOWN, MASS.

Of **Catherine Clasby**, a native of the Townland of BALLYCLARERE, Parish of BALLINDERRINE, Co. GALWAY, Ireland. When last heard from, she was in NEW YORK CITY about nine months ago. Any information of her will be thankfully received by her brother, **James Clasby**, SING SING, N.Y. [Appeared Sept. 24, 1864 with as Catherine Clashy and giving slightly different information.]

October 8, 1864

Of **James McBrian**, who sailed from New York about five years ago for CALIFORNIA, and has not been heard from since September, 1862. Any information leading to the discovery of him will be thankfully received by his loving brother, **Patrick McBrian**, HUNTINGTON, Long Island, N.Y., in care of **Henry F. Conklin**, Esq.

Of **Michael Corcoran**, a native of the Parish of KILMESSAN, County MEATH, Ireland, who arrived in New York about six months ago, and left about the same time for

BALTIMORE, MD. Any intelligence of him will be thankfully received by his brother, **Patrick Corcoran**, by writing to him to ELIZABETHPORT, NEW JERSEY.

Of **Mary O'Connor**, who left Ireland about 17 years ago. When last heard from (four years ago) she was in CANADA WEST. She is a native of the County of SLIGO, Ireland, and left that place a widow, with two children. Any information of her will be thankfully received by her brother, **Morris O'Connor**, and daughter, **Mary Gughin**. Post Office address, 168 Bay Street, JERSEY CITY, N.J.

Of **Richard Green**, who left STRATFORD, County of WICKLOW, Ireland, about twenty years ago, and is supposed to be either in BOSTON or NEW YORK. Any information regarding him will be thankfully received by his nephew, **Thomas Linen**, by addressing him at No. 20 Smith Street, JERSEY CITY, N.J.

Of **Edward Sheah**, GRANGE ROWER, County KILKENNY, Ireland. When last heard of he was in BALTIMORE, MARYLAND. Any information of him will be thankfully received by **Morgan Dreelan**, 76 CANNON-ST., NEW YORK.

Of **John Cahill**, formerly of THOMASTOWN, County KILKENNY, Ireland, where he was in the Constabulary. He left there in March, 1863. If this should meet his eye or that of anyone knowing his present address, they will hear of something to his advantage, by writing to **William Keeffe**, 232 Market-street, NEWARK, N.J.

Of **Mary Kenny**, a native of the Parish of KILLABEGS, County DONEGAL, Ireland, who married **Luke McCann**, and when last heard from was in NEW YORK CITY. It is supposed she now lives near ST. LOUIS, State of MISSOURI. Any information of her will be thankfully received by her sister, **Bridget Kenny**, by writing to her in care of **James Byrnes**, No. 37 ROSE-STREET, NEW YORK CITY.

Of **Timothy Southwell**, native of CRAGGS, Parish of KILBEGNET, County GALWAY, Ireland; also, his sister **Celia**, who left home in 1846. They will hear of something to their advantage through their sister **Caroline**, by calling or addressing to 53 WEST 22nd-street, NEW YORK, care of **Mr. Morrison**. Boston papers please copy.

October 15, 1864

Of M. J. C., who left home for MANCHESTER, ENGLAND, on the 2nd of January last, and sailed from Cork on the 3rd of the same month, per the *Scotia*, to New York, is requested to write to his poor, broken hearted mother and afflicted family, who are in the deepest distress. A line addressed to T. M. (his old friend), *Freemans Journal*, DUBLIN, will be duly forwarded to its destination.

Of **Thomas Foley**, formerly of COHOES, ALBANY County, N.Y Mr. Foley is between 35 and 40 years of age; black hair, dark eyes, rather dark complexion, and about 5 feet 10 inches high. He is supposed to have gone to seek employment in the mines of PENNSYLVANIA. Any information of his whereabouts will be gratefully received by his wife, **Affa Foley**, by writing to her to COHOES, ALBANY County, N.Y.

Of **Bridget O'Neill**, who lived with a teacher at NEW ROCHELLE, N.Y., in 1862. Address S. D. C. at the office of the Irish-American. [Appeared Nov. 26, 1864, adding that New Rochelle is in WESTCHESTER County, and, "Call at No. 11 MORTON STREET, NEW YORK, or address S. D. C., at this office."]

Of **Mary McGovern**, who landed in New York, Dec. 24, 1863, per ship *Ontario*; also her daughter **Margaret**. Any information of her will be thankfully received by her son. Address **George Black**, Co. E, 63rd Regt., N.Y.V., 2nd Brigade, 1st Division, 2nd Corps, WASHINGTON, D. C.

Of **Thomas Sheehy**, formerly of RATHKEALE, County LIMERICK, Ireland. When last heard from was in LA SALLE County, State of ILLINOIS. Any information respecting him will be thankfully received by his brother and sister, **Edward** and **Mary Sheehy**, by addressing a letter to the office of the Irish-American, 29 Ann St., New York.

Of **John McCormack**, of LIMERICK, Ireland. When last heard of was in GRASS VALLEY, NOVEDIA County, N.Y. Any information of him will be thankfully received by his father, **John McCormack**, at 407 Columbia Street, BROOKLYN, N.Y. California papers, please copy.

Of **Hanora Hynes**, a native of the Town of GALWAY, Ireland, who arrived in New York in the year 1854. When last seen she was living in STATEN ISLAND, N.Y. Any information respecting her will be thankfully received by her sister, **Mary Myres**, alias **MOGAN**, at No. 494 PEARL STREET, NEW YORK. [Appeared Oct. 29, 1864 with the name **Myres** changes to **Hynes**.]

Of **James McHugh**, a native of BARONSCOURT, Townsland of KIESTY, Parish of ARDSTRAW, County TYRONE, Ireland, who left home about 1835, was then about 22 years of age, and when last heard of was in a printing establishment at FALL RIVER, MASS, 18 or 20 years ago. Any information of him will be thankfully received by **Claudius Bradley**, at 197 Myrtle Avenue, BROOKLYN, N.Y., who can tell him of something to his advantage.

Of **Peter Connell**, a native of the County of CORK, Ireland. When last heard from he was living at 71 Erie Street, JERSEY CITY, N.J. Any information of him will be thankfully received by **John C. Howard**, U.S. steamer Shamrock, ALBERMARL SOUND, N.C., or elsewhere.

Of **James Flanigan**, a native of the County of LEITRIM, Ireland, is pock marked, was in BORDENTOWN, N.J., about seven years ago. Any information respecting him will be thankfully received by addressing **Rev. Father Biggio**, Pastor of St. Mary's Church, BORDENTOWN, N.J.

Of **Michael Murphy**, a native of the Parish of BALLA, County MAYO, Ireland, who landed in New York in Nov. 1848. When last heard from, he was in OHIO. Any information of him will be thankfully received by his daughter **Mary** (who has been in this country three years), at her residence, 326 Adelphi St., BROOKLYN, N.Y.

October 22, 1864

Of **Miss Anne McCardle**, by her aunt, of the same name, now at the New York Hotel, Room 159. The former arrived from Ireland some months since, intending to go to her aunt in HAVANA, and is supposed to have remained in BROOKLYN.

Of **James Cummings**; was in NEW YORK about 3 months ago. Address, **Christy Keenan**, care of **Thomas Kelly**, corner of Hudson and York Street, JERSEY CITY, N.J.

Of **James** and **Martha Fare**, who left CARENTHRONE, LISNASKEA, County FERMANAGH, Ireland, about 12 years ago. When last heard from they were in the City of NEW YORK. Any information of them will be thankfully received by their nephew, **William Henry Clendining**. Address William Henry Clendining, CONCHOHOCKEN Post Office, MONTGOMERY County, PENNSYLVANIA.

Of **Thomas**, **William** and **Mary Ram**, natives of the Townland of KILBRIDE, Parish of RIVER CHAPPEL, County WEXFORD, Ireland. Mary married a man by the name of **Patrick Duff**. When last heard from all were living in BANGOR, State of MAINE. Any information of them will be thankfully received by their sister, **Catherine Ram,** by writing to her to No. 51 EIGHTH ST., Clinton Place, NEW YORK CITY.

Of **Thomas Monaghan**, of KILLOE, County of LONGFORD, Ireland. When last heard of, in 1859, he left the U.S. service in WALLA, Oregon Territory. Any intelligence of him will be thankfully received by his sister, **Bridget Monaghan**, who has lately arrived in this City. Please direct to care of **Michael McKenna**, 360 WEST 43rd ST., NEW YORK.

Of **Teresa Flynn**, a native of BAYLOUGH, ATHLONE, Ireland. Eight or nine years ago, she lived in PEARL STREET, NEW YORK. Advertiser is informed she was seen in NEW JERSEY a short time since. She will hear something to her advantage by sending her address to **Mr. William Langan**, GREEN POINT, KINGS County, Long Island, N.Y. [Appeared under County WESTMEATH]

Of **Lawrence Farrell**, a native of the Parish of LADY'S BRIDGE, County CORK, Ireland, who emigrated to this country in 1836. When last heard from he was in BROOKLYN, N.Y. Any information of him will be thankfully received by his brother, **James Farrell**, Town of GENT, COLUMBIA County, N.Y.

October 29, 1864

If **Patrick Flood**, late of Eustace Street, DUBLIN, Ireland, will call at the office of Messrs. O'Gorman & Wilson, No. 8 Pine Street, in the City of NEW YORK, he will find a confidential communication from H. C. S. and W. M.

Of **John Deacon**, a carpenter, formerly of BALLYCASTLE, County ANTRIM, Ireland, who emigrated to America in 1845. When last heard from he resided in NEW YORK. Any information of him will be thankfully received by his brother, **William**, now a prisoner of war on GOVERNOR'S ISLAND, NEW YORK HARBOR.

Of **Mary Moriarty**, a native of DINGLE, County KERRY, Ireland, who sailed from Tralee, in the ship *Lady Russell*, May, 1854, landed in Quebec, and left thence for NEW YORK CITY. When last heard of (last Christmas) she was living in WATER STREET, NEW YORK. Any information concerning her will be thankfully received by her sister, **Ellen Moriarty**, at BONDSVILLE, MASS., or to **Patrick Downes**, 148 CHERRY STREET, NEW YORK.

Of **Thomas Barry**, a native of the Town of KILKENNY, Ireland. When last heard from he was in NEW ORLEANS. Any information of him will be thankfully received by his sister **Bridget**, by writing to her in care of **Thomas Toner**, 160 WEST 38th STREET, NEW YORK CITY.

Of **John Morrow**, a native of the Parish of CARRICKERMAN, County LONGFORD, Ireland. When last heard from he was living in BROOKLYN, N.Y. Any information of him will be thankfully received by his brother, **James Morrow**. Address, Company D., 2nd Battalion, HART'S ISLAND, NEW YORK HARBOR.

Of **James Cleary**, a native of MOATE, County WESTMEATH, Ireland. He left NEW YORK on the 28th of April for MASSACHUSETTS, to learn a trade. Any information of him will be thankfully received by his stepbrother, **Thomas O'Brien**, at No. 308 EAST 32nd STREET, NEW YORK CITY.

Of **Hanora Hynes**, a native of the Town of GALWAY, Ireland, who arrived in New York in the year 1854. When last seen she was living in STATEN ISLAND, N.Y. Any information respecting her will be thankfully received by her sister, **Mary Hynes**, alias **Mogan**, at No. 494 PEARL STREET, NEW YORK. [Appeared Oct. 15, 1864 with Mary's surname **Myres**]

Of **John** and **Roger Sheehan**, natives of BROUGHAL, CHARLEVILLE, County CORK, Ireland, who were in NEW YORK about nine years ago, and is supposed to be in DUNKIRKE, OHIO. Any information of them will be thankfully received by their sister and cousin, **Mary** and **James Sheehan**, care of **Mr. O'Connell**, 180 28th STREET, NEW YORK. Cincinnati, Ohio, papers please copy.

November 5, 1864

Of **James Broomfield**, who landed in New York about 9 years ago. When last heard from he was in NEW MADRATH, MISSOURI. Any information of him will be thankfully received by his brother **Michael**, at 126 South Third St., WILLIAMSBURGH, L.I.

Of **Bridget Lowry**, who arrived in this country three years ago, from near EYRECOURT, Ireland. Address or call on her sister, **Elizabeth Lowry**, 7 WEST 25th ST., NEW YORK. [Appeared under County GALWAY]

Of **Patrick** and **Martin Healy**, and their brother **Thomas** and mother, who landed in this country about 20 years ago, from near BOYLE, County ROSCOMMON, Ireland. Any information of their whereabouts will be thankfully received by their brother, **Denis Healy**, by writing to him to 16 French St., BALTIMORE, MD.

Of **James** and **Daniel Murphy**, natives of the Parish of TEMPLE TUOHY, Townland of LISTUHLEEN, County TIPPERARY, Ireland. When last heard from they were in NEW YORK CITY. Any information of them will be thankfully received by their cousin, **James Leahy**, by writing to him to NEWBURGH, State of NEW YORK.

November 12, 1864

Of **Ellen Edgell**, or her cousin, **George Edgell**, natives of the Town of BURR, Parish of LONGFORD, KING's County, Ireland. Any information of them will be thankfully received by her sister, **Ann Edgell**. Address No. 52 PITT STREET, NEW YORK CITY.

Of **Martin Dyer** (or **Dwyer**) a native of the Parish of KILCORKY, County ROSCOMMON, Ireland, who lived with the late **Right Rev. Bishop Brown** for several years, and came to this country in 1861. Any information of him will be thankfully received by his sister, **Ellen Dyer**, in care of **Mr. Peter Muldoon**, 61 North Broad Street, NEWARK, N.J.

November 19, 1864

If **Mrs. Elizabeth John Mitchell** - supposed to be living in WILLIAMSBURGH, N.Y. -will call or send her address to this office she will hear of her brother, (who is after returning from the war,) **Stephen Mitchell**, late of Co. H., 6th Mass. Vol. Militia.

Of **Mr. John Mulhall**, who emigrated to America about three years since. When last heard of (about fifteen months ago) was Lieutenant in the 69th New York Regiment. Any intelligence of him will be thankfully received by addressing **Mr. Hugh O'Donnell**, 87 North King Street, DUBLIN, or the Irish-American, 29 Ann Street, New York.

Of **Mary Walsh**, a native of CASTLEBAR, County MAYO, Ireland, who arrived in New York, on Wednesday the 9th inst., in the ship *Resolute*, from Liverpool, and stopped at Castle Garden. Any information of her will be thankfully received by her brother, **Michael Walsh**, by writing to him in care of **Patrick Coghill**, Church Street, POUGHKEEPSIE, N.Y.

Of **John Liden**, a native of NAIL, near the Town of BALLINGROBE, County MAYO, Ireland. Any information will be thankfully received by his niece, **Bridget Sullivan**, daughter of **Patrick** and **Bridget Sullivan** writing to her in care of **Patrick McDermott**, 16 Pacific Street, BROOKLYN, N.Y.

Of **Catherine Clasby**, daughter of **Michael Clasby**, BALLYCLARA, Parish of BALLINDERRINE, County GALWAY, Ireland. When last heard of was in NEW HAVEN, CONNECTICUT. Any information of her will be thankfully received by her brother (who arrived lately in this country) **James Clasby**, SING SING. [Appeared Sept. 24, 1864 and Oct. 1, 1864 with slightly different wording]

Of **Robert Murphy**, otherwise **Fitton**, a house carpenter, and a native of CARRIGROHANE, County CORK, Ireland, who came to this country about twelve years ago. He was left one hundred pounds a year by the death of his father, who died last July. By writing to **John McCartny**, THOMSONVILLE, HARTFORD County, CONNECTICUT, he will learn all particulars. [Appeared Sept. 17, 1864 with different wording.]

November 26, 1864

Of **Sarah Harty**, or her daughter **Jane**. The daughter is about 12 years of age, and was for some time in the Half Orphan Asylum in this City. At the same time the mother was an inmate of one of the charitable hospitals of the City. Any person knowing of their whereabouts will confer a great favor by addressing a note to "A. B.," care of the Editor of the NEW YORK *Tablet*, 31 Barclay Street.

Of the relatives of **Philip Brady**, who, when near thirteen years of age (about fourteen years since) came to the United States, from County CAVAN, Ireland. Said Philip Brady has lately died in the United States' Government service. His legal representative is requested to address **Captain David B. Elliott**, Box 214, NASHVILLE, TENN., U.S. All papers in County of Cavan, Ireland, please copy.

Of **John Johnson**, Esq., of ST. JOHN'S WELL, County MEATH, Ireland. Any intelligence of him will be thankfully received by **Elizabeth Johnson**, NEW YORK, U.S.

Of **John McKeon**, stone mason, of CONG, County MAYO, Ireland, by his brother, **Michael McKeon**, who is after landing. Any information given will be thankfully received by **Patrick McKeon**, No. 399 Columbia Street, BROOKLYN, N.Y.

Of **James Fitzgibbon**, a native of CROOME, BELLEREIN, YIELDING'S DOMAIN, County LIMERICK, Ireland. -He went to CANADA in 1832. When last heard from, three years ago, he was in KINGSTON, CANADA. Any information of him will be thankfully received by his sister, **Bridget Fitzgibbon**, by writing to her, in care of **Mr. Carroll**, SIXTH AVENUE, near St. Joseph's church, NEW YORK CITY.

Of **Michael Sullivan** and his wife, **Julia Lovelt**, natives of KILLARNEY, Ireland, who came to this country about thirteen years ago. When last heard from, were in PROVIDENCE, R.I. Any information of them will be thankfully received by her son, **John Slattery**, 85 ELDRIDGE STREET, NEW YORK CITY. [Appeared under County KILKENNY.]

Of **Daniel, Mary** and **Rose Ryan**, natives of the County DOWN, Ireland. Mary and Rose both lived in the Weddle House, CLEVELAND, OHIO. Mary got married and went to live to ALLEGHANY County, OHIO. Any information of them will be thankfully received by their brother, **John Ryan**, by writing to him to 114 FRANKLIN STREET, NEW YORK CITY.

Of **Jeremiah Buckley**, a native of LISTOWEL, County KERRY, Ireland, who was conscripted into the rebel service at AUGUSTA, GA., and who deserted from said service sometime in July. It is supposed that he is a prisoner in some part of the North, or has come North to live. Any person that knows anything of him will oblige his wife and four small children, who have lately arrived from the South, by writing to **Margaret Buckley**, 10 VANDEWATER STREET, NEW YORK CITY.

If **Edward Ryan**, of KELLS, County CORK, Ireland, and late of NEW YORK, will call at or address **James O'Donnell**, Esq., 50 WALKER STREET, NEW YORK, he will hear of something unexpected and to his advantage. Any information respecting him will be thankfully received at the above address. Boston *Pilot* and Baltimore *American*, please copy.

Of **Martin Corcoran**, son of **Thomas Corcoran**, of CAGGLESTACK, Parish of CLONFINLOUGH, County ROSCOMMON, Ireland. When last heard from he was living in ROCHESTER, State of NEW YORK. Any information of him will be thankfully received by his brother **Daniel**, residing on the corner of 31ˢᵗ and Chesnut Street, West, PHILADELPHIA.

December 3, 1864

Of **Mrs. Margaret Mary O'Brien**, formerly **Mrs. Wm. H. Collins,** who sailed from New York in the Brig *John Scott*, for MELBOURNE, AUSTRALIA, in 1852. Any person who knows of her whereabouts will confer a great favor on her sister, **Jane** by sending word to the office of this paper. Melbourne (Australia) and Dublin (Ireland) papers, please copy. [Appeared under County DUBLIN] [Appeared Dec. 24, 1864, with additional information.]

Of **Joseph Smith**, late of NAVAN, County MEATH, Ireland, who arrived in New York per ship *Luisiana*, in September 1863, in company with his brother **Bernard**. When last heard of, in March last, was employed at the Delevan Hotel, ALBANY CITY, NEW YORK State. Any information of him will be thankfully received by his brother Bernard, Clerk, in care of **Lieutenant Stephens**, A.Q.M., Cherry Street, NASHVILLE, TENN.

Of **Frank Moran** and **James Tunny** and wife, from CASTLEBAR, County MAYO, Ireland, who came to America about 16 years ago. Frank is supposed to be in or about SYRACUSE, State of NEW YORK. James Tunny is supposed to be in the City of PHILADELPHIA. Any information of them will be thankfully received by their sister **Bridget** and her sons, **Martin** and **P. Durkan**, No. 408 Adam Street, cor. of Carrol Street, KENSINGTON, PHILADELPHIA, PA.

December 10, 1864

Of **Timothy Murphy**, of the Parish BECAN, County MAYO, Ireland. When last heard from he was in BOSTON, MASS. Any information of him will be thankfully received by his nephew, **Patrick Healy**, 101 Queen St., PHILADELPHIA, PA.

Of **William** and **Patrick Hanify**, of the Parish of ATHENRY, County GALWAY, Ireland. When last heard from, in July, 1862, they were living in MENDON, MASS. Any information of them will be thankfully received by **Patrick Fahey**, WINDSOR LOCKS, CONN.

Of **Mary Torpey**, a native of KILKEE, County CLARE, Ireland. When last heard from, 3 years ago, she was in CORNWALL, ORANGE County, N.Y., and is now supposed to be in NEW YORK or vicinity. Any information of her will be thankfully received by her brother, **Patrick Torpey**, by writing to him to SCARSDALE, WESTCHESTER Co., N.Y.

Of **Daniel Purtell**, a native of CROOM, County LIMERICK, Ireland. When last heard from, 6 months ago, he was in WEST TROY, State of NEW YORK. Any information of him will be thankfully received by his friend, **Ellen Brown**, by writing to her in care of **Mr. John S. Andrews**, PEEKSKILL, WESTCHESTER County, N.Y. [Appeared Feb. 13, 1864, with some different information.]

Of **Mrs. O'Brien**, maiden name **Bridget Hassett**, from the Parish of TRUAGH, County LIMERICK, Ireland, by her brother, **John Hassett**. When last heard from he was in MICHIGAN. Address **Dennis McCarthy**, No. 35 GREENWICH ST., NEW YORK.

Of **Thomas McKeown**, formerly a resident of BELFAST, County ANTRIM, Ireland. When last heard of, 3ʳᵈ March, 1860, he resided in NEW YORK. Any information of him will be thankfully received by his friend, **Robert Carrigan**, 38 Atlantic St., SOUTH BROOKLYN.

December 17, 1864

Of **John, Owen, Eliza, Bridget**, and **James Daley**, children of **John Daley** and **Anne Clarke,** natives of CASTLEBLANEY, County MONAGHAN, Ireland. Any information of them, or their whereabouts, will be gratefully received by **Susan Moane**, 242 6th AVE., between 15th and 16th-streets, in the rear, N.Y.

Of **John Caulan**, and three brothers and sister, who came to this country twenty years ago, from near FERMOY, County CORK. Any information of them will be thankfully received by their brother **Thomas Caulan**, 623 Shipping-street, PHILADELPHIA, in care of **Mr. Fitzgibbon**.

Of **Patrick M'Donagh** and his sister **Mary**, natives of CASTLEBALDWIN, County SLIGO, Ireland, who came to this country about forty years ago. When last heard from, they were in NEW YORK CITY. Any information of them will be thankfully received by their sister **Anne M'Donagh**, by writing to her in care of **Mr. Thomas Bowen**, 2138 P.O. Box, CHICAGO, ILL.

Of **Mary O'Connell**, of the County CAVAN, Ireland. She landed in America about a year and a half ago, in the ship "*New World*," and since that time is supposed to have been living in NEW YORK CITY. Any information of her will be thankfully received by her sister, **Catherine**, who has just arrived from Cavan, in the ship "*Isaac Webb*," and who is now stopping with **Mrs. McAdams**, 86 7th-street, between 1st and 2nd Aves., NEW YORK.

Of **Michael Ford**, a native of TUAM, County GALWAY, Ireland, who left ASHTON-UNDER-LINE, ENGLAND, on March 9th, 1863, for NEW YORK; went from there to PENNSYLVANIA, and returned to NEW YORK last Spring. Any information of him will be thankfully received by his wife, **Sarah Ford**, care of **J. R. Smith, Jr.**, RAHWAY, N.J., or 77 PEARL ST., N.Y.

December 24, 1864

Of **Thomas Gallagher**, by trade a puddler, lived at No. 75 Point Street, PROVIDENCE, R.I., about 3 years ago. Any information respecting him will be thankfully received by his brother, who recently arrived in this country. Address, **John Gallagher**, 225 ELIZABETH STREET, NEW YORK. Providence and Boston papers, please copy.

Of **Mrs. Peter O'Brien**, formerly **Mrs. M. M. Collins**, (maiden name **Margaret M. North**), of the City of DUBLIN, who sailed from New York, in the Brig *John Scott*, for MELBOURNE, AUSTRALIA, in 1852. Any person who knows of her whereabouts will confer a great favor on her sister, **Jane North**, by sending her address to the office of the Irish-American, 29 Ann Street, NEW YORK. Melbourne (Australia) and Dublin (Ireland) papers, please copy. [Appeared Dec. 3, 1864 with less information and different wording.]

Of **Mary O'Keefe**, a native of the Parish of COLLIGAN, Townland of GARRYDUFF, near DUNGARVAN, County WATERFORD, Ireland. When last heard from (11 years ago) she was living in NEW YORK CITY. Any information of her will be thankfully received by her brother, **Thomas O'Keeffe**, by writing to him to No. 76 MADISON STREET, NEW YORK CITY.

Of **Ann Byron**, a native of the Townland of BALLYCARRON, County TIPPERARY, Ireland. When last heard from she was in PORTLAND, State of MAINE. Any information of her will be thankfully received by her brother, **William Byron**, by writing to him to 49 RECTOR STREET, NEW YORK CITY.

December 31, 1864

Of **Thomas Devine**, a native of the Town of ATHLEAGUE, County of ROSCOMMON, Ireland, who landed in this country 18 or 19 years ago. He lived with **Mr. Kelly**, of BALLYMURRY, before coming to this country. Any information of him will be thankfully received by his nephew, **Peter Galvin**, at the Irish-American office, 29 Ann Street, New York.

Of **Mr. William Walsh**, baker, who had left Quaker Road, CORK, Ireland, in 1852, for America. When last heard from he was in SANTIAGO, on the Colorado River, LOWER CALIFORNIA. Any information of him will be most thankfully received by his brother **James**, who is now living with **Cornelius Sullivan**, 345 WATER STREET, NEW YORK.

Of **Mary Lunney**, of DRUMGOW, near KILLASHANANE, County CAVAN, Ireland. When last heard of was in MANCHESTER, N.H, and is supposed now to be in NEW YORK CITY. Any information of her will be thankfully received by her cousin, **Ann Riley**, in care of **P. P. Lonergan**, ST. JOHNSBURY, State of VERMONT.

Of **Patrick, Thomas** and **William Fowler**, natives of the Parish of MINUTOWN, NEW GRANGE, County MEATH, Ireland. Information sent to their sister **Ann**, at 169 South Ninth Street, WILLIAMSBURGH, Long Island, N.Y, will be thankfully received.

Of **John Naughtin**, a native of BELCERRA, County MAYO, Ireland. When last heard from (seven years ago) he was in CHICAGO. Any information of him will be thankfully received by his brothers, **Martin** and **Austin Naughtin**, by writing to them in care of **Anthony McHale**, 93 MARKET STREET, NEW YORK CITY. Chicago and Buffalo papers, please copy.

January 7, 1865

John MacPherson, carpenter, in NEW ORLEANS, is requested to send his address to his mother in LONDON, ENGLAND. Same address as before. A letter was addressed to him to the Post Office, New Orleans, in June 24, 1864.

Of **Bridget Riley**, who, when last heard from, was in service with **Mr. Riley,** in the Merchants' Cafe, PINE STREET, NEW YORK CITY, in 1850. She will hear of something to her advantage by calling on **Mr. John McMahon**, at No. 8 VANDEWATER STREET, NEW YORK.

Of **Patrick Cuff**, a native of the Parish of KILTRUSTON, County ROSCOMMON, Ireland, who left ENGLAND, in May last, for NEW YORK, and left thence in last August, for the Coal Mines of PENNSYLVANIA. Any information of him will be thankfully received by his father, **Michael Cuff**, by writing to him in care of **Sarah Gorman**, 285 MOTT STREET, NEW YORK CITY.

$50 Reward. - Of **John Horgan** or **Hogan**, a native of the City of CORK, Ireland, who left his house on the 5th of July, 1864. When last seen he wore brown pants, red plaid undershirt, blue outside shirt, glazed cap and shoes. Five feet one and a half inches high, gray eyes, brown hair, dark complexion and sandy goatee, and had a cast in one of his eyes; he was about 37 years of age and is a sailor. Any person giving information of his whereabouts to his sister, **Catherine Murphy**, 66 ½ CARMINE STREET, NEW YORK, will receive the above reward. Boston and St. John, N.B, papers, please copy.

Of **Thomas Sweeny** (late of KINGSTOWN, DUBLIN,) a native of the County LEITRIM, Ireland. He left Dublin about June or July last for New York, and is at present supposed to be either in JERSEY CITY, BROOKLYN, or NEW YORK. By leaving his address at the office of the Irish-American, he will hear of something to his advantage.

January 14, 1865

Of **Thomas A. Delany**, DRUMCONDRA, DUBLIN, a sailor, about 19 years of age. When last heard from (17th of March, 1862), was on board the ship *Corinne*, from Cardiff, to York. Supposed to be in the Navy. Any information of him will be thankfully received by his sister **Maria**, 5 MONROE STREET, NEW YORK CITY. Houston (Texas) papers, please copy.

Of **William McGrath**, a native of BALLYPOREEN, County TIPPERARY, Ireland, who arrived in New York, in 1862. When last heard from (about 12 months ago) he was in FLATROOT, State of NEW YORK. Any information of him will be thankfully received by his brother, **Rody McGrath**, by writing to him in care of **Quartermaster William Logan**, FORT SCHUYLER, N.Y.

Of **Cornelius Bradley**, a native of the Parish of ADAIR, County LIMERICK, Ireland. When last heard from, about eight years ago, he was in the State of VERMONT. Any information of him will be thankfully received by his sister, **Ellen Bradley**, by writing to her to 378 Atlantic Street, BROOKLYN, in care of **Mr. William Schaefer.**

Of **Ellen Dunn**, wife of **James Flaherty**, of KNOCKNAGUR, Parish of KILBANNON, County of GALWAY, Ireland, who arrived in New York last June or July, and has not been heard from since her arrival. Any information of her will be thankfully received by her husband, James Flaherty, at CARLISLE STATION, WARREN County, OHIO.

Of **Felix Farrell**, a native of the Parish of BRAY, County CARLOW, Ireland. When last heard from, three months ago, was at NORTH CURRENT, SARATOGA County, State of NEW YORK. Any information of him will be thankfully received by his wife, **Ann Farrell**, by writing to her to 59 MULBERRY STREET, NEW YORK CITY.

Of the children of **Peter** and **Fanny Doyle**, of BALLANVALLEY, Parish of MONAMOLIN, or of the children of **William Sommers** of MOUNTOUERD, by their cousin, **Anna**, daughter of **James** and **Catherine Doyle**, BALLYREAGAN, County WEXFORD, now living at 115 WEST 24th STREET, NEW YORK.

Of **John Tobin**, a native of CELBRIDGE, County KILDARE, Ireland. He came to America, from ENGLAND, in 1863, and enlisted in the 16th Maine Volunteers, but was discharged in April, 1864, to enter the Navy. Any information of his whereabouts will be thankfully received by **Joseph Murray**, 54 Vanbrunt Street, SOUTH BROOKLYN, N.Y

Of **Timothy Curtin** and family, natives of FORTGRADY, Parish of BANTYRE, County CORK, Ireland. When last heard from was in the State of NEW YORK. Any information respecting him or any of the family will be gratefully received by his son-in-law, **Keady Burke**, UXBRIDGE Woollen Mills, MASS.

Of **Daniel** and **Timothy Coleman**, natives of UMMERA, MACROOM, County CORK, who emigrated from WOOLWICH, ENGLAND, to America, in the year 1858. Any information regarding them will be thankfully received by their sister, **Margaret Coleman**, residing at 13 Newark Avenue, JERSEY CITY, N.J.

January 21, 1865

Of **Catherine** and **Mary Russell**, natives of KILKISHEN, County CLARE, Ireland. When last heard from (8 years ago) they were in the State of NEW YORK, with their uncle, **Michael Blake**. Any information of them will be thankfully received by their sister, **Elizabeth Russell**, by writing to her in care of **Henry Haraan**, No. 24 South 12th Street, PHILADELPHIA, PA.

January 28, 1865

Of **Patrick O'Connor**, brother-in-law of **James Craney**. When last heard from he was in NEWARK, N.J. Any information of him will be thankfully received by James Craney, NEW ROME, ADAMS County, WISCONSIN.

Of **Patrick Butterly**, baker by trade, son of **John Butterly**, who left DUBLIN, Ireland, 14 years ago. When last heard from he was in BOSTON, 13 years ago. If this should meet his eye, or any of his friends, they would confer a great favor on his father by addressing a note to 128 8th AVENUE, to his father, in care of **Mr. McCabe**, NEW YORK. Boston papers please copy.

Of **Kate Sliney**, native of KILMURRY, County WATERFORD, Ireland. When last heard from was in CINCINNATI. Any information of her whereabouts will be thankfully received by **James Sliney**, Colt's Armory, HARTFORD, CONN.

$50 REWARD - For information of **Mary** and **Bridget Leo**, whose parents were **Michael** and **Sally Leo**, natives of the Parish BALLINA, Co. TIPPERARY, Ireland, who died at FALL RIVER, MASS., leaving three children very young. Any person giving information of where they are to their brother, **Michael Leo,** will receive the above reward. Direct to Michael Leo, U.S. Gunboat *Commodore Barney*, CITY POINT, VA. Fall River papers, please copy.

Of **Michael Bryan**, of MADESHILL, Parish of MULLINAHONE, County TIPPERARY, Ireland, by his wife, **Margaret**, now at Castle Garden.

Of **James O'Dea**, who left COROFIN, near ENNIS, County CLARE, Ireland, about 12 years ago for LONDON, and afterwards came to this country. When last heard from, ten years ago, he was in CANADA. Any information of him will be thankfully received by his sister, **Fanny O'Dea**, No. 74 WEST 43rd STREET, NEW YORK. Canada and Western papers, please copy.

$20 REWARD - For information of **John Riely**, a native of County CAVAN, Ireland. Was married to **Sarah Cavanagh**, at COOLLYUNE, near NEW ROSS, County WEXFORD. He left his home, Headly Street, LIVERPOOL, in the Fall of 1849, and came to this country. When last heard from, November, 1863, he was working on a U.S. steamboat on the Mississippi River. The above reward will be paid to any person who will give information of his present address, if living, or a satisfactory Statement of his death and place of burial, if dead. Address **Joseph Crabtree**, Post-Office Box 252, WOONSOCKET, R.I.

February 4, 1865

Of **Catherine Cunningham**, a native of either the Parish of MULLINABREENA or CLOONACOOL, County SLIGO, Ireland. She came to this country about ten years ago; is supposed to be somewhere in the State of NEW YORK. She will hear of something to her advantage by addressing a line to **John Flynn**, 156 North St., BOSTON, MASS. [Appeared Feb. 11, 1865, showing Catherine as a native of the Parish of ACHONRY, County SLIGO, Ireland.]

Of **Catherine B. Crowley**, and her brother, **Arthur B. Crowley**, both formerly of CROSSFIELD, near MALLOW, County CORK, Ireland. Catherine lived at **Mr. Parker's**, ROXBURY, MASS., about six years ago. Arthur landed at Boston about four years ago. Any information of them will be thankfully received by their brother, **Timothy B. Crowley**, ATCHISON, KANSAS.

Of **Mary Riely**, a native of the County CLARE, Ireland, who arrived in New York City in March, 1864. Any information of her will be thankfully received by her brother, **Patrick Riely**, at the office of the Irish-American, 29 Ann Street, New York.

Of **Michael**, **William**, **Ann**, **Mary**, **Kitty**, **Judy**, and **Ellen Clerkin**, children of **Phillip** and **Mary Clerkin** (maiden name **Gormley**). Michael came to America over thirty years ago, and William about 24; the girls all came at different times since. They settled in ALBANY, N.Y. Also, of **Michael Clerkin**, cousin to the above, and son of **Patrick Clerkin**, all from the Townland of CUREROUGH, near BUNNOW, Co. CAVAN, Ireland. Any information of them will be thankfully received by their cousin, **John Clerkin**, son of **Michael Clerkin**, Sen., of RED HILL, in the same County, at **Joseph Nolan's**, Van Buren St., between Franklin and Bedford Avenues, BROOKLYN, L.I. Albany Papers, please copy.

February 11, 1865

$100 Reward. - Of **William Ingham**, who left his home on the 5th of January, 1864. He is a native of ENGLAND, aged 40 years, dark complexioned, black eyes, 5 feet 8 inches in height, was a boot and shoemaker by trade. The above reward will be given for any information of him dead or alive by his troubled wife, **Bridget Ingham**, at 215 WEST 26th STREET, NEW YORK.

Of **Michael Carey**, from the Townland of MOUGHROW, County WESTMEATH, Ireland. When last heard from he was in CALIFORNIA. Any information of him will be thankfully received by his brother, **Neil Carey**, or his sisters, by writing to 23 WEST 17th STREET, or 15 EAST 22nd STREET, NEW YORK. California papers, please copy.

Of **Eliza O'Brien**, aged 17 years, a native of ARDFINNAN, County TIPPERARY, who came to NEW YORK about a year since, and is supposed to be still living there. Her mother's maiden name was **Mary Page**. Any information concerning her sent to Colonel **John O'Mahony**, 22 DUANE STREET, NEW YORK, will be forwarded to her father, **Daniel K. O'Brien**, who is now in CALIFORNIA, and is most anxious to hear from her.

Of **Michael Cronan**, of RACOWN, Parish of CASHEL, County TIPPERARY. He went to CALIFORNIA about five years ago. When last heard from (a year since) he was living near the Post Office in SAN FRANCISCO. Any intelligence of him would be gratefully received by his sister, **Margaret Cronan**. Address, care of **Edmond J. O'Neill**, 331 Market St., PHILADELPHIA, PA.

Of **Daniel McSwiney**, who came to this country from the City of CORK, in 1857, or any of his friends is requested to communicate with his brother, **John McSwiney**, No. 28 Dawson St., BALTIMORE, MD. Boston papers, please copy.

February 18, 1865

Of **Annie Monahan** (now **Mrs. Riley**), of the Parish of LICKBLAY, County WESTMEATH, Ireland. When last heard from, about 15 years ago, she lived in TROY, NEW YORK, and is supposed to be there at present. Any information of her will be thankfully received by her brother, **Francis Monahan**, WEST THOMPSON, WINDHAM County, CONNECTICUT. Troy papers please copy.

Of **Martin O'Melia**, native of the island of ARRAN, County GALWAY, Ireland. When last heard from was in MINNESOTA. Any information of him will be thankfully received by his brother **Peter**, who has lately arrived in this country, at PORTCHESTER, WESTCHESTER County, N.Y.

Of **James Weire**, of the Parish of CLIFFORD, Town of MONIN, County DONEGAL, Ireland. Arrived at Castle Garden on the 19th of October, 1864. Any information regarding him will be thankfully received by addressing **Anne Campbell**, at **T. Mitchel's**, No. 4 GREENWICH STREET, NEW YORK

Of **Hugh Meighan**, or his brother **Thomas**, formerly of MAYNE ESTATE, CASTLE BELLINGHAM, County LOUTH, Ireland. When last heard from was in NEW ORLEANS. Should he, or any of his friends, communicate with **Philip McKenna**, No. 61 MARION-STREET, NEW YORK CITY, he will hear of something that will add greatly to his interest. New Orleans papers please copy.

Of **Edward Doolan**, a native of LACKE, Parish of LISELTON or BALLYDONOHUE, County KERRY, Ireland. When last heard from was in FORT SMITH, ARKANSAS, September 14, 1864, in Co. I, Second Arkansas Cavalry; and from thence he was to proceed to WASHINGTON, D. C., to be honorably discharged. Nothing heard from him since. Any information of him will be thankfully received by addressing a few lines to his cousin, **Maurice Doolan**, COXSACKIE, GREENE County, State of NEW YORK; or to his sister **Ellen**, of the same place.

Of **Timothy Sullivan**, a native of COROBEG, VALENTIA ISLAND, County KERRY, Ireland. When last heard from he was in Mount Direy Agricultural Institute, GERMANTOWN, PA. Any information of him, dead or alive, will be thankfully received by his sister, **Mrs. Mary Murphy**, NORFOLK, VIRGINIA.

February 25, 1865

Of **Joseph Murphy**, who left NEW YORK about 8 years ago; a native of GARRYDUFF, Parish of AUGHABOE, QUEEN'S County, Ireland. Any information of him will be thankfully received by his mother **Catherine Murphy**, (maiden name **Catherine Fitzpatrick**,) by writing to 220 Water St., BROOKLYN, N.Y, for Catherine Murphy; or to his sister, **Mary Hall**, 23 Jay St., BROOKLYN.

Of **James Kelley**, of High Street, GRAIGUE, County KILKENNY, Ireland. He came to this country in 1850, and resided in the New England States for 5 or 6 years, when he removed to the western States. When last heard from, in 1859, he was in VIRGINIA. Any information of him will be very thankfully received by his son, **Edward Kelley**, 53 Salem Street, LOWELL, MASS.

Of **Walter Healy**, of the Parish of BOHERMEEN, OATLAND, County MEATH, Ireland. He came to this country in the year 1846, in the ship *New World*. When last heard from he was in ROCHESTER, State of NEW YORK. Any information of him will be thankfully received by his brother, **Patrick Healy**, MANHATTANVILLE, NEW YORK. Rochester papers, and Boston *Pilot*, please copy.

Of **Edward Martin Dillon**, a native of MOATE, County WESTMEATH, Ireland, who came to America in June, 1836. When last heard from, he was in ST. LOUIS, MO. Also of **Joseph Ross**, from same place. Any information of them will be thankfully received by their niece, at the office of the Irish-American, 29 Ann St., New York.

Of **Catherine Ross**, widow of **Henry Ross**, formerly of MOATE, County WESTMEATH, Ireland. Also of her children, **Henry, Francis** and **Eliza**. When last heard from, in 1855, were in DUBLIN. Any information of Mrs. Ross will be thankfully received by her daughter, at the office of the Irish-American, 29 Ann St., New York City.

Of **Julia Sweeney**, of the City of CORK, Ireland. When last heard from, 8 years ago, she was living with her brothers, in the City of NEW YORK, in 32nd STREET, between 7th and 8th Avenues. Any information respecting her, or her brothers, will be thankfully received, through **Rev. J. Ireland**, ST. PAUL, MINN., by persons anxious to hear about them.

March 4, 1865

Of **John Birminghham**, a native of the City of DUBLIN, Ireland, and a carpenter by trade, who came to this country about 15 years ago. When last heard of was in SAN DIEGO, CALIFORNIA. Any information respecting him will be thankfully received by his sister, **Mrs. Catherine O'Beirne**, 458 WEST 42 STREET, N.Y. Boston and California papers, please copy.

Of **Mary Kelly**, a native of KINGSCOURT, County CAVAN, Ireland. She left the City of DUBLIN, for America, in the year 1847. When last heard from she lived with her husband, **John Neary**, in BROOKFIELD, CONN. Any intelligence of her will be thankfully received by her brother, **John Kelly**, at the office of the Irish-American, 29 Ann Street, New York.

Of **Margaret Duffy**, of County MONAGHAN, Ireland, who came to this country about the year 1845. Any information of her will be thankfully received by her brother, **John Duffy**. Address, **Edward Cosgrove**, No. 589 GRAND ST., NEW YORK.

Of **Bridget Neylon**, of CLONROAD, County CLARE, Ireland. She was married to a man named **James Nash**, of CLONMEL, County CORK. When last heard from (about 8 years ago) she lived in CHERRY ST., NEW YORK. Any information of her will be thankfully received by her nephew, **Patrick Neylon**, SPRINGFIELD, MASS.

Of **Patrick Kain**, a native of TUAM, County GALWAY, Ireland, mason by trade, who landed on the 26th of December, per steamer *Erin*. Any information of him will be thankfully received by his sister, **Catherine Kain**, at 110 ROOSEVELT ST., NEW YORK.

March 11, 1865

Of **Mrs. John McMahon**, who sailed from Liverpool for New York on the 6th of February, 1864, in the ship *Wisconsin*. Intelligence of her will be received at the office of the Irish-American, 29 Ann Street, New York.

Of the whereabouts of **Matthew Pigott**, a native of FERMOY, County CORK, Ireland, who left Cork, for New York, in or about the year 1858, and is now supposed to be in NEW YORK. Any person knowing anything of him will please communicate the same to his brother, **Patrick Pigott**, No. 2 Martindale Place, between Broad and 15th, Spring Garden Street, PHILADELPHIA, PA.

Of **William Fleming**, a native of the Town of NEW ROSS, County of WEXFORD, Ireland, who came to America about eight years ago, and landed in New York. When last heard from he was in CHICAGO, ILL. Any information of him will be thankfully received by his brother, **Nicholas Fleming**, by writing to him in care of **Nicholas Wall**, No. 1 WASHINGTON STREET, NEW YORK CITY.

Should this meet the eye of **William Cassidy**, a native of TAGHMON, County WEXFORD, Ireland, boilermaker, supposed to be working in this City, he will please communicate with **Capt. Wm. Miliner**, foot of 110th STREET, HARLEM, E.R., for **William Eagan**, WARD'S ISLAND.

Of **Anthony, Annie** and **Bridget McGeever**, brother and sisters of **Patrick McGeever**, who was killed, December 3, 1864, at TUNNEL GRANDE, near RIO DE JANEIRO, BRAZIL. When last heard from, Anthony and Annie were in PHILADELPHIA; Bridget was in the County DONEGAL, Ireland. Important communications will be made, on addressing **J. A. McMaster**, *Freeman's Journal*, NEW YORK.

March 18, 1865

$50 Reward - Of **Alice Butterfield**, who, with her mother, left ENGLAND, in the ship *Argo*, with the Latterday Saints or Mormons, for NEW ORLEANS, in the year 1849. Her mother, **Hester Butterfield**, died in the year 1850 or 1851, in New Orleans. Any information of her will be thankfully received, as she was left an orphan at the age of nine or ten years. The above reward will be received from her brother, **Charles Butterfield**, store keeper, COUNCIL BLUFFS, IOWA. St. Louis and New Orleans papers, please copy.

Of **Patrick Walsh**, a native of DUNGANSTOWN, Parish of BARNDERG, County WICKLOW, Ireland. When last heard from (four years ago) he was in the English Army. Any information of him will be thankfully received by his sister, **Catherine Kavanagh**, by writing to her to No. 33 Congress Street, NEWARK, N.J. [Appeared April 15, 1865, adding that Patrick was a native of "Townland of BALLINAPARK," and changing Catherine's address to No. 38 Congress Street, Newark, N.J. Also, a request for Irish papers to copy was added.]

Of **Patrick** and **Mary Hasset**, brother and sister, natives of CAPPAMORE, County LIMERICK, Ireland. The former left home about 12 years ago, and the latter 15 or 16 years. When last heard of Mary lived in BROOKLYN, CITY, N.Y., and Patrick lived in Mount (rear house), ALBANY. Any information of them will be thankfully received by addressing their brother, **James Hasset**, at No. 59 WASHINGTON STREET, NEW YORK CITY.

Of **Mrs. Catherine Mernin**, a native of the City of CORK, Ireland. When last heard from (six years ago) she was in NEW YORK. Any information of her will be thankfully received by her cousin, **Ellen Kennedy**, at 65 Prospect St., NEW BEDFORD, MASS.

Of **Maurice** and **David Walsh**, natives of CHARLEVILLE, County of CORK, Ireland. When last heard from (eight years ago) they were in BLAIRSVILLE, INDIANA County, PENNSYLVANIA. Any information of them, living or dead, will be thankfully received by their brother, **Michael Walsh**, who has lately arrived from ENGLAND. Address **Mr. John Ryan**, No. 76 JAMES STREET, NEW YORK. Western papers, please copy.

Of **James Hunt**, a native of the Parish of NEWTOWN SANDS, County KERRY, Ireland. When last heard from he was in KNOBNOSTER, JOHNSON County, MISSOURI. Any information of him will be thankfully received by his niece, **Johannah Hunt**, daughter of **Laurence Hunt**, of TULLAHILL, in the same County, by writing to her in care of Lynch, Cole & Meehan, Irish-American, 29 Ann Street, New York.

Of **John Broderick**, a native of the Parish of FIERIES, County KERRY, Ireland. When last heard from he was in WAYNTOWN, MONTGOMERY County, INDIANA. Any information will be thankfully received by his nephew, **Daniel Day, Jun.**, SAVANNAH, GEORGIA.

Of **Catherine Carenough**, of the Parish of DRUM, County MAYO, Ireland, who married **Mr. J. Rankin**, and lived, in 1861, in 9th or 10th AVENUE, NEW YORK. Address **M. Carenough**, care of **Dr. Healy**, IDAHO CITY, IDAHO TERRITORY. [Appeared July 1, 1865, with the surname "Carenough" changed to "CAVENOUGH".]

Of **James Lynch**, of the Parish of MULLECHORAN, Townland of KILCOGY, County CAVAN, Ireland, who advertised his brother Michael in the *Public Ledger*, in the City of PHILADELPHIA, on the 25th and 26th of May, 1863. His brother Michael is now anxious to know of his whereabouts. Any information will be thankfully received by addressing **Michael Lynch**, RIVERTON, PALMYRA Post Office, BURLINGTON County, N.J.

Of **William Dougherty**, a native of the Parish of CARNDONAGH, County DONEGAL, Ireland. When last heard from (two years ago) he was in the State of PENNSYLVANIA, working on a Railroad. Any information will be thankfully received by his brother **John**. Also, his son **John**, who arrived in NEW YORK last June, and is working at the printing business. Please address, **John Dougherty**, 344 First Street, WILLIAMSBURGH, N.Y.

March 25, 1865

Of **Michael Dempsey** and **Catherine Sweeney**, who came to this country, from LONDON, in August 1863, and left Castle Garden. Nothing has been heard of them since. Any information of them will be thankfully received by **Catherine Dempsey**, at 273 HENRY STREET, NEW YORK. [Appeared April 1, 1865, with changes to the above information.]

Of **Charles** and **Isaiah Downing** or **Downey**, father and son, from MARGHILL, near GLASGOW, SCOTLAND. Address the son and brother, **Thomas Downey**, Cambrian Mills, BRIDGEPORT, CONN.

Of **Susan Smith**, who came to this City about 12 or 15 years ago, from MONTREAL, CANADA, with a family of the name of **Dempsey**. Any information of her whereabouts will be thankfully received by her sister, **Mary Smith**. Address, **C.D. Peacock**, CHICAGO, ILL., P.O. Box 191.

Of **John Dooley**, a native of the Parish of PORTARLINGTON, QUEEN'S County, Ireland. When last heard from sixteen years ago was in NEW YORK. Any information of him will be thankfully received by his sister, **Eliza Dooley**, by writing to her in care of the **Rev. James M. Hunting**, JAMAICA, L.I., State of NEW YORK

Of **Michael Lynch**, a native of TRALEE, County KERRY, Ireland, who landed here about six months ago, and is supposed to be working in a tobacco factory in BROOKLYN. Any information of him will be thankfully received by his brother, **John Lynch**. Direct to the care of **M. O'Connell**, 76 NASSAU ST., NEW YORK.

April 1, 1865

$25 Reward. - For information of **Michael Dimpsey**, who came with his wife, **Catherine Sweeney**, from LONDON; arrived at Castle Garden, N.Y., August, 1863; he left Castle Garden, and nothing has been heard from him since. Any information of him will be thankfully received, and the above reward paid, by his wife **Catherine Dimpsey**, 273 Henry Street, BROOKLYN, L.I. [Appeared March 25, 1865 with the surname **Dempsey** and some different information.]

If **Susan Friel**, wife of **Morris Friel**, who came from BONESS, SCOTLAND, to NEW YORK, about 11 years ago, and when last heard from was in PENNSYLVANIA, will send her address to **Robert Coddington**, 366 BOWERY, NEW YORK, she will hear of something to her advantage.

Of **Michael J. Cronin**, bricklayer, who left KEY WEST last July for NEW ORLEANS; since then has not been heard of. Any information of him will be thankfully received by his distressed wife, **Mrs. Annie Cronin**, FAR ROCKAWAY, L.I., NEW YORK.

Of **Joseph Cleary**, a native of CLONASLEE, QUEEN'S County, Ireland, who emigrated to AUSTRALIA in the year 1855. When last heard from (about ten months ago) he was in NEW ZEALAND. Information of him will be thankfully received by his brother, **James Coyne**, by writing to him to 99 WEST HOUSTON STREET, NEW YORK, United States of America. Australian papers please copy.

Of **Johanna Cummins**, daughter of **Ned Cummins**, from DONERAILE, County of CORK, by her sister, **Ellen Wall**,. Address box 956, CHICAGO, ILLINOIS.

April 8, 1865

Of **Michael Barry**, who when last seen was in the City of NEW YORK, February 15th, 1865, being *en route* from his home in SOUTH BOSTON, MASSACHUSETTS, for CINCINNATI, OHIO. Said Barry was by trade a carpenter, five feet seven inches in height, blue eyes, fair complexion, and aged 45 years. Any information of him will be thankfully received by addressing his wife, **Annie L. Barry**, 60 Gold Street, South Street, MASS.

Of **Patrick Boyle**, a native of the Parish of DRUMNESKIN, County LOUTH, Ireland. When last heard from twelve years ago was in Ireland. Any information of him will be thankfully received by his first Cousin, **Lawrence Boyle**, by writing to him in care of **John Barry**, No. 47 MARKET STREET, NEW YORK. [Advertised under County TIPPERARY (probably switched with the following advertisement)]

Of **Thomas Joye**, a native of the Parish of BANSHA, County TIPPERARY, Ireland. When last heard from in June, 1855, was in APPLETON, WISCONSIN. Any information of him will be thankfully received by his father, **James Joye**, by writing to him to No. 147 FIRST AVENUE, between 9th and 10th Streets, NEW YORK CITY. [Advertised under County LOUTH (probably switched with the previous advertisement)]

Of **Michael Pemrick**, a native of BALLINROBE, County MAYO, Ireland, who left ENGLAND on the 6th of May last. When last heard of he was supposed to have left PHILADELPHIA for POTTSVILLE, about November last. Any information of him will be thankfully received by **Richard Pemrick**, at 15th and Willow, Streets, PHILADELPHIA, PA. Boston *Pilot*, please copy.

April 15, 1865

Of **Jeremiah J. Carroll**, by his mother, who is very anxious to hear from him. Should this meet his view or any one acquainted with him, they will confer a great favor by informing his mother of his whereabouts. Address, **Mrs. Carroll**, 12 ROOSEVELT STREET, NEW YORK CITY.

Of **David White**; supposed to have joined the Army of the James, last September two years; and **Mathew McParlan**, of NEW YORK, by his brother, **Maurice White**. Address LEAVENWORTH CITY, KANSAS

Of **Catherine O'Hare**, wife of **James O'Hare**, who left PROVIDENCE, R.I, some thirteen years ago. Any information of her will be thankfully received by her sons, **William** and **Andrew**, corner of Cross and McKenna Streets, PROVIDENCE, R.I. Western papers, please copy.

Of **Mrs. Adelia T. Ryan**, a native of NENAGH, County TIPPERARY, Ireland. When last heard from, about eight years ago, was living at No. 48 JAMES ST., NEW YORK. Any information of her will be thankfully received by writing to **P. T. Ryan**, Glesboro Point, WASHINGTON, D. C., Box 50.

Of **John Cahill**, a native of the Parish of BALLYHILL, County KILKENNY, Ireland. When last heard of, he was in ALBANY, N.Y., about 6 months ago. Address A.B., Irish-American Office, 29 Ann St., New York.

Of **Thomas McKeab** and **Ellen McKeab**, formerly **Sullivan**, daughter of **Peter Sullivan**, of SHANBALLYMORE, County CORK, Ireland. Her mother is now here. Direct to **Margaret Sullivan**, 142 Washington St., JERSEY CITY, N.J.

April 22, 1865

Of **Patrick** and **Thomas Walsh**, natives of the Townland of LOWER MOOR PARK, Parish of ORCATH, County DUBLIN. When last heard of Patrick was living in ROUNDOUT, and Thomas was living in PENNSYLVANIA. Any information of them will be thankfully received by their brother, **William Walsh**, No. 225 WEST 21st ST., NEW YORK.

If this should meet the eye of **Michael** and **John Scott**, of LIMERICK, Ireland, their two sisters- **Catharine Scott** and **Mary Ann Cain** - will be most happy to hear from them. Address to either of them, in care of **Mr. W. W. Gearn**, Oil Cloth Manufacturer, NEWBURGH, ORANGE County, N.Y

April 29, 1865

Of **James Alexander Boyle** (*alias* **James Alexander**), and **Frederick Boyle**, who left Ireland in 1848 and lived for sometime in JEFFERSON CITY, MO., also at HARMONY, BROWNSVILLE, ST. JOSEPHS, ST. LOUIS, &c. A reward of $50 will be paid for well authenticated information of them, either dead or alive. Address **H. G. Maw**, 40 17th St., SOUTH BROOKLYN; or **Wm. Walsh**, Esq., 8 Lower Mount St., DUBLIN, Ireland.

Of **Catherine Kelly**, daughter of **Theady** and **Margaret Kelly**, natives of CORDRUMM, Parish of BUMLIN, County ROSCOMMON, Ireland. She came to America about 24 years ago. When last heard from, in December, 1863, she was at Messrs. Evens & Swift, CINCINNATI, OHIO. Any information of her will be thankfully received by her mother, in care of **Patrick Ryder**, TAMLAUGHT, MOHILL, County LEITRIM, Ireland. Ohio papers, please copy.

Of **James McCool**, a native of the Parish of STRANORLAR, County DONEGAL, Ireland. He went to CALIFORNIA about 10 years ago. When last heard from, about 3 years since, he was in WASHINGTON TERRITORY. Any information of him will be thankfully received by his father, **Alexander McCool**, No. 150 WEST 30th ST., NEW YORK CITY. [Appeared Sept. 2, 1865, with a different contact person and different information.]

If **James Whalen** or **Christy Dillon**, formerly of ATHY, County KILDARE, Ireland, will write to **Stephen Whalen**, at present on board the U.S. Receiving Ship *North Carolina*, BROOKLYN Navy Yard, N.Y., they will confer a favor on Stephen Whalen. P.S. - Or any others from that part.

Of **James Sheridan** or **William Spellman**, of County MAYO, Ireland. Supposed to be in ILLINOIS. If they should see this advertisement, or any one knowing their whereabouts, they would confer a great favor by informing **Mrs. Hagan**, SAINT CLAIR, SCHUYLKILL County, PA. Boston *Pilot*, please copy.

May 6, 1865

If **James Cunneen**, who left **Mr. Coomey's** service in LIMERICK, about a year ago, will call at once at **Major Clark's** Hotel, 110 CHATHAM ST., he will hear of something to his advantage. Any one knowing where he lives in BROOKLYN, and seeing this, will please acquaint him of it.

Of **Paul Dunne**, a native of the Parish of KILMANNION, near CLONASLEE, QUEEN'S County, Ireland, who emigrated to this country in 1850. Any information of him will be thankfully received by his son, **Mcchael** [sic] **Dunne**. Address, **John Conroy**, FORT COLUMBUS, NEW YORK HARBOR.

Of **Mathew McDermott**, and **Bessy Brennan**, of the Parish of BUNNANADEN, County SLIGO, Ireland. When last heard from, about 18 years ago, lived in the City of MONROE, State of OHIO. Any information of them will be thankfully received by her sister, **Mrs. Nanny Brennan**, GLENS MILLS, DELAWARE Co., PENN. Monroe papers, please copy.

Of **Ellen Stoney**, a native of the Town of BALCAROW, Parish of DRUM, County MAYO, Ireland. When last heard of, 10 years ago, was in HUDSON, OHIO. Any information of her will be thankfully received by her father, **John Stoney**, SOUTH BEND, ST. JOSEPH Co., IND.

May 13, 1865

Of **Mary Mahan**, wife of **Michael Helay**, who left ENGLAND, in January 1864. Any information of her will be thankfully received by her husband, Michael Helay, at 63 WASHINGTON STREET, NEW YORK, care of **Mrs. Cooney**.

Of **Henry O'Brien**, from LARAGAN, DRUMSHANBO, County LEITRIM, Ireland, who came to this country about twenty years ago. When last heard of he was in STATEN ISLAND, NEW YORK. Any information of him will be thankfully received by his nephew, **Thomas O'Brien**, LAFAYETTE, MCKEAN County, PENNSYLVANIA.

Of **Charles, James, Patrick, Ann, Mary** and **Alice Fitzsimmons**, children of **Dr. Patrick Fitzsimmons** of the Parish of CARRIGALLAN, Town of CARRIGALLAN, County of LEITRIM, Ireland, all supposed to be in the United States. If this should meet their eye, by addressing a few lines to the *Monitor* office, SAN FRANCISCO, CALIFORNIA, giving their address, they will hear of something to their advantage. Any person knowing anything concerning them will please give information as above.

Of **Daniel Murray**, of MOYLOUGH, County GALWAY, Ireland, who came to America in April 1840, and is thought to be in the U.S. Marine Corps or Army. Any information concerning him will be most thankfully received by his brother, **Michael Murray**, at No. 10 Little Water Street, BALTIMORE, or by his Niece, **Mrs. Mary Ward**, 750 South Sixth Street, PHILADELPHIA.

Of **Jamee** [sic] **Lee**, a native of the Parish of KILLDARRIRIE, County CORK, Ireland. When last heard from (two years ago) he was in CLEVELAND, OHIO. Any information of him will be thankfully received by his nephew, **John Coughlin**, by writing to him to No. 42 RUTGERS STREET, NEW YORK CITY

Of **Robert Flahire**, a native of the Parish of BALLYLONGFORD, County KERRY, Ireland. When last heard from (three years ago), he was in PENNSYLVANIA. Any information of him will be thankfully received by his brother, **Michael Flahire**, by writing to him to PENN YAN, YATES County, NEW YORK.

May 20, 1865

Of **Patrick Coyle** and family, of 56 Watlin Street, DUBLIN City, Ireland. If they should see this advertisement, or any one knowing their whereabouts, they would confer a great favor by informing their brother, **Joseph Coyle**, or sister, **Jane O'Brien**, at 128 MOTT STREET, NEW YORK CITY. Dublin papers, please copy.

Of **Mark Kealy**, a native of BENNETT'S BRIDGE, Parish of DEANSFORT, County KILKENNY, Ireland. Also, of his sister **Ellen**. They came to this country about sixteen years ago. When last heard of, Mark was in NEW YORK CITY. Any information of them will be thankfully received by their cousin, **Nicholas Quirk**, Stone-yard, Plymouth Street, BROOKLYN, L.I.

Of **Lawrence Brennan**, of the Town of SLIGO, Ireland, who landed in New York in May, 16, 1859, served his time in the New York State Volunteers, was discharged in May, 1863, and has not been heard from since. Any information respecting him will be thankfully received by his sister, **Ann Fennon**, 6 Cove Street, cor. of Kneeland St., BOSTON, MASS.

Of **Patrick** and **Edward McHugh**, natives of GLENISLAN, Parish of ISLANDEADY, County MAYO, Ireland, sons of **Bryan McHugh**, the poet. Any information of them will be thankfully received by addressing their cousin, **Thomas McHugh**, Station A, Post Office, NEW YORK CITY. Boston *Pilot*, please copy.

May 27, 1865

Of **Patrick** and **Michael Larken**, sons of **John** and **Elizabeth Larken** of BIRR, KING'S County, Ireland. Any information of them, either dead or alive, would be thankfully received by their brother, **Joseph Larken**, who is still in BIRR, and is most anxious to hear from them.

Of **Mary McGenn**, a native of the Parish of CLIMRONEY, County LONGFORD, Ireland. When last heard of was in NEW YORK CITY, 13 years ago. Any information from her or any of her friends will be thankfully received by her brother, **John McGenn**, JAMAICA, QUEENS County, N.Y

Of **David Fitzgerald**, a cooper, from CASTLE GREGORY, County KERRY, Ireland, who arrived in this country about 12 months ago. It is believed he went to the State of CONNECTICUT. Any information will be thankfully received by his brother-in-law, **John Callaghan**, baker, 551 WEST 26th STREET, in care of **William Sullivan**.

June 3, 1865

Of **Michael Cassidy**, son of **Michael** and **Sarah Cassidy**, late of READING, PENNSYLVANIA. When last heard from (about three months ago) he was in KITTARNING, ARMSTRONG County, PA. His parents are anxious to hear from him. Address, **Michael Cassidy**, READING, PA. Western papers, please copy.

Of the whereabouts of **John Sheridan**, of KILRUSH, Parish of DUNGARVAN, County WATERFORD, Ireland. Information will be thankfully received by directing a letter to **Thomas Whalan**, BOSTON Post Office, MASS.

Of **James Finnegan**, or brother, of CARRICK MCCLEM, County MONAGHAN, Ireland. By sending their address to 370 Court Street, BROOKLYN, N.Y, they will hear of an old friend, **George McKittrick**.

Of **Ann Elliget**, who left CROOM, County LIMERICK, Ireland, about nine years ago. When last heard from she was in UPPER CANADA. Any information of her whereabouts will be thankfully received by her mother, **Margaret Elliget**, by addressing her at 2[0]6 EAST 17th STREET, NEW YORK. Canada papers, please copy.

Of **John Flynn**, a carpenter, late of Pope's Quay, City of CORK, Ireland, who left that City about the 23rd of May, 1862, in the steamship *St. George*, for Quebec. When last heard from (about two years and a half ago) he was in TORONTO, UPPER CANADA. Any information of him will be thankfully received by his father, **Timothy Flynn**, at 153 MADISON ST., NEW YORK.

June 10, 1865

Of **Michael Sheridan**, who emigrated to America in the year 1846, on board the *Jennet*, of Drogheda, commanded by **Captain Moore**. When last heard of he was on GOVERNOR'S ISLAND in the year 1848. The said Michael Sheridan was born on the North Road, in the Town of DROGHEDA, County LOUTH, Ireland. His father, **John Sheridan**, was in the employ of the owner of the *Jennet*. Any information of him will be thankfully received by his distressed father, John Sheridan, in care of **Terence Monaghan**, STRADONE, County CAVAN, Ireland, or to **James Monaghan**, 725 Cherry Street, PHILADELPHIA, PA.

Of **James Lyons**, a native of BELFAST, County ANTRIM, Ireland, and nephew of the late **Wm. O'Shea**, of the Ordnance Department, Belfast. He left Ireland in 1848. Any information of him will be thankfully received by "A Friend," by calling at or addressing a letter to 111 ½ WEST 24th STREET, N.Y. CITY.

Of **Miss Kate Dargan**, a native of CLONMEL, County TIPPERARY, Ireland, who landed in New York on the 21st of October, 1864. Any information of her will be thankfully received by her friend, **Michael O'Mahony**, by calling on, or addressing him at 40 BOND STREET, NEW YORK. P.S. - Any one who may inconveniece themselves by writing or calling will be liberally rewarded. Boston *Pilot*, please copy.

Of **Matthew McNamara**, a native of the Parish of ST. PATRICK, City of LIMERICK, Ireland, who left NEW YORK in March, 1864. When last heard from he was in GERMANTOWN, PA. Any information of him will be thankfully received by his brother, or uncle, at **Patrick O'Neil's**, 48 ROOSEVELT STREET, NEW YORK. Germantown papers, please copy.

June 17, 1865

Of **Bernard Cain**, of OLDBURY, ENGLAND. When last heard from he was in CHARLESTON, S.C. Any information of him will be thankfully received by **William Hamill**, by writing to him to 272 Hicks St., BROOKLYN, N.Y., where he will hear of something to his advantage.

$100 Reward. - For any information that will lead to the recovery of **Tommy Kennedy**, aged eight years, who strayed, or was stolen from No. 6 Union Street, BROOKLYN, on the 20th of April, 1864. He wore a blue soldier cap and blue flannel jacket, trimmed with red, and gray pants. Any information of him will be thankfully received by his father, **Edward Kennedy**, No. 49 BEEKMAN STREET, NEW YORK.

Of **Bridget Finan**, and her daughter **Margaret Fallon**; also of **Margaret** and **Bessy Finan**, daughters of **Hugh Finan,** natives of CASTLEREAGH, CLOUNTRASK, County ROSCOMMON, Ireland. Any information of them will be thankfully received by their brother, **Hugh Finan**, 42 Montgomery Street, JERSEY CITY, N.J.

Of **Mary Devine**, a native of GRANGE, Parish of KILBRIDE, County ROSCOMMON, Ireland; or **James Burke**, from the same place. Mary was married to **James Reagan**. Any information of them will be thankfully received by **Luke Devine**, by writing to him to Machine Shop, Illinois C. R. R., CHICAGO, ILL.

Of **Anne Connellyy** [sic], daughter of **Martin Connelly**, from the County KILKENNY, Ireland. When last heard of was in ORANGE County, N.Y Any information will be thankfully received by her father, Martin Connelly, No. 8 Oliver Street, PATERSON, N.J.

Of **Michael Noon**, formerly of MILTOWN, near TUAM, County GALWAY. When last heard from was Porter in a store in NEW YORK CITY. Information of him will be thankfully received by his niece, **Bridget Morgan**, late from Tuam. Address 85 Henry Street, BROOKLYN City, Long Island.

Of **Stephen** and **Edwaed** [sic] **McEnroe**, natives of the Parish of BALLINLOCK, County MEATH, Ireland. When they were last heard from Stephen was in HARTFORD, INDIANA, and Edward was in ST. LOUIS, MISSOURI. Any information of them will be thankfully received by their brother, **Thomas McEnroe**, by writing to him to the St. Nicholas Hotel, NEW YORK CITY. Hartford, Indiana, papers, please copy.

June 24, 1865

Of **Stephen Gilderoy**, of Co. I, 185th Regt., N.Y Volunteers, a native of GLENCAN, County LEITRIM, Ireland. Any person that can give information of him will please write to his brother, **Peter Gilderoy**, ELIZABETH PORT, N.J

Of **Thomas McIntyre**, a native of SKAALTY, County DONEGAL, Ireland. When last heard from he was in NEW YORK CITY. Any information concerning him will be thankfully received by his brother, **Robert McIntyre**, care of **W. B. Mann**, 22nd and Wood Streets, PHILADELPHIA, PA.

July 1, 1865

The parents or nearest akin of **John Brown**, late a sergeant of Co. H., 164th Regt., N.Y.S. Vols., will hear of something to their advantage by calling on or addressing **M. O'Rorke**, for two weeks, at 71 SUFFOLK ST., NEW YORK CITY. Utica papers, please copy.

Of **Michael** and **Anne Fagan**, natives of ARCHESTOWN, County WESTMEATH, Ireland. When last heard from they were in LEECHFIELD, CONNECTICUT, 10 months ago. Anne left Ireland 8 years ago. Any information of them will be thankfully received by their brother, **Patrick Fagan**, by directing in care of **Samuel Sloan**, Esq., GARISON, PUTNAM County, NEW YORK.

Of **Edward Lunny**, a native of INCHINORE, Co. FERMANAGH, Ireland. When last heard from he was living in ENGLAND. Any information of him will be thankfully received by his sister, **Mary Lunny**, by writing to her in care of **E.L. Bushnell**, Esq., No. 38 Sands Street, BROOKLYN, Long Island, N.Y.

Of **John, Thomas** and **Edmund Burke**, also mother and sister, of CURABAHAN, BURRESSLEE, County TIPPERARY, Ireland. Any information of them will be thankfully received by their sister, **Mary Mahar**. Direct to **Mr. James Roe**, WEST TROY, N.Y.

July 8, 1865

Of **Michael Welch**, who left Ireland nineteen years ago. When last heard from he was in WASHINGTON, D. C. Any information concerning him will be thankfully received by his brother, **Anthony Welch**, No. 3 Clymer Street, above 6th Street, between Fitzwater and Catherine, PHILADELPHIA, PA.

Of **Sarah Gaffney**, maiden name **Sarah Melliot**, a native of ENGLAND, who left NEW YORK in January last, from No. 8 MULBERRY STREET. Any information of her will be thankfully received by her husband, **John Gaffney**, No. 25 PELL STREET, NEW YORK CITY, who was lately discharged from the 16th U.S. Infantry.

Of **Dr. James Fitzpatrick**, formerly of DUBLIN. When last heard of was in BRIDGEPORT, CT. If this advertisement should be seen by the Doctor he will hear of something to his advantage by addressing immediately C. F, 390 CANAL STREET, NEW YORK. Any one having any information as to his whereabouts will confer a favor by dropping a line to the above address.

Of **Mrs. Mary Corrigan**, maiden name **Mary Deniffe**, a native of the City of KILKENNY, Ireland. When last heard from was living in OHIO. Any information respecting her will be gratefully received by either of her sisters, **Ellen** or **Elizabeth**, or her brother-in-law, **Michael Bradley**, SARATOGA SPRINGS, NEW YORK. Ohio papers, please copy.

Of **Sarah Grames**, a native of the Parish of DONAGHEADY, County TYRONE, Ireland, who arrived in New York on the 24th of June, 1865, on board the ship *Village Belle*.

Any intelligence of her will be thankfully received by her brother, **Patrick Grames**, VERPLANKS' POINT, WESTCHESTER County, N.Y

Of **Patrick, Lawrence** and **Michael Nugent**, natives of the Parish of FEDEMORE, County LIMERICK, Ireland, sons of **William** and **Catherine Nugent**. Patrick came to America fifteen years ago, the others came about eight years ago. Any information of them will be thankfully received by their aunt, **Catherine Nugent,** or otherwise **Catherine Downey**, by writing to AMBOY Post-office, LEE County, ILLINOIS.

Of **Patrick Doyle**, a native of the Parish of CAHIR, County TIPPERARY, Ireland. When last heard of he was in the State of CONNECTICUT. Any information of him will be thankfully received by his brother, **John Doyle**, in care of **John Holeran**, 347 WEST 39th STREET, NEW YORK.

July 15, 1865

Of **Margaret Carden**, a native of the Parish of LACKEN, County MAYO, Ireland. She is supposed to be in NEW YORK, and when last heard from was in the FIFTH AVENUE. She is a daughter of **Thomas Carden** and **Bridget Ford**. Her brother, **Anthony Carden**, of PITTSTON, PA., offers $25 Reward to any person that will inform him where she now resides. Address, Anthony Carden, Pittston, Pa.

Of **John Rodgers**, a sadler by trade, who arrived here from the County TYRONE Ireland, about two years ago. He will hear of his sister by calling on **James Douglass**, at 33 SOUTH ST., NEW-YORK.

Of **Sarah Ellis**, a native of the Parish of ARVAH, County CAVAN, Ireland. When last heard from she was in BROOKLYN, N.Y. Information of her will be thankfully received by her brother, **James Ellis**, by writing to him in care of **Joshua S. Edell**, OYSTER BAY, Long Island, N.Y.

Of **Philip Kilroy** and his wife **Catherine** (maiden name **Riley),** natives of MOUNT PALACE, County CAVAN, Ireland. When last heard of they were in GREENBUSH, N.Y. Any information will be thankfully received by **Margaret Riley**, NEWBURYPORT, MASS.

Of **William Mack**, a native of RATHBEG, KING'S County, Ireland, who landed in New York in 1864 and left BROOKLYN, May 10, 1865. Information of him will be thankfully received by his uncle, **Michael Carroll**, at No. 167 WEST ST., NEW YORK. Any person giving information, by writing or calling, will be liberally rewarded. [Appeared July 22, 1865 with Michael Carroll's address as No. 167 WEST 25th ST., NEW YORK.]

July 22, 1865

Of **Margaret Sawey** and **Mary Rocks**, who came to this country in the year 1860. Any information as to their whereabouts will be thankfully received by **William Hogan**, at U.S.A. Gen. Hospital, HILTON HEAD, S.C.

Of **Edmund Ashton Hicks**, who left DUBLIN in June, 1863, for NEW YORK. Any intelligence of him will be thankfully received by **M. Rafter**, at 49 MARKET STREET, NEW YORK CITY.

Of **William Price** (a printer by trade), who left DUBLIN in September, 1861, and, it is believed, joined the U.S. Army shortly after landing here. When he left home he was 20 years old, 5 feet 9 or 10 inches in height, and made in proportion, fair hair and complexion, and rather good-looking. Any information will be thankfully received by his father, **James Price**, Lad Lane Police Station, DUBLIN, Ireland, or by **Michael Pearse**, U.S.S. *Memphis*, BROOKLYN. Navy Yard, N.Y Boston *Pilot*, please copy.

Of **James B. Reilly**, of the City of DUBLIN, Ireland, machinist by trade. When last heard from, 3 years ago, he was in HAVANA, CUBA. Address, **B. Mullvany**, 159 Broad Street, PROVIDENCE, R.I Cuban papers, please copy.

Of **Patrick McEneany**, a native of the County LOUTH, Ireland. When last heard of he was in COLUMBUS, GEORGIA. Any one having any information as to his whereabouts will confer a favor by dropping a line to his sister, **Mary McEneany**, 1712 Wood Street, PHILADELPHIA, PA.

Of **James Moore**, a native of KNOCKBRANDON, County WEXFORD, Ireland, who arrived in the United States from ENGLAND in 1842. When last heard from about 4 years ago, he was living in WASHINGTON, near OPELOUSAS, LA. Any information of him will be thankfully received by his sister, **Catherine Creighton**, 51 Cedar Street, SPRINGFIELD, MASS Louisiana papers, please copy.

July 29, 1865

Of **Mrs. Maria Joyce**, her brothers **Patrick, John A., William**, and her sisters **Lucinda, Elinor** and **Margaret O'Meara**, formerly of CLI[F]DEN, County GALWAY, Ireland. Within the last few years they have resided in Atlantic St., Bedford Avenue and Spencer St., BROOKLYN. About a year ago, they are said to have moved to the vicinity of 3rd AVENUE and 26th ST., NEW YORK. Further information of them is solicited by Messrs. O'Gorman & Wilson, 8 Pine St., or Lalor & Hollahan, 82[6] Broadway, cor. 12th St., N.Y

Of **Edward McCarron**, of CLONMANY, County DONEGAL, Ireland, who got his discharge from the U.S. Ship *Neptune* or *Heptune*. Any information regarding him will be thankfully received by his sisters, **Margery** and **Ellen McCarron**, corner of C and 4th sts., SOUTH BOSTON, MASS., in care of **Mr. Charles Smyth**.

Of **William Lamb**, a native of DOON, near BALLINAHOUN, Parish of LEMANAHAN, KING'S County, Ireland, who left TROY Iron and Nail Factory, State of NEW YORK, about 18 months ago, to go to CHICAGO. When last heard from (about 4 months since) he was in TENNESSEE. Any information of him will be thankfully received by addressing his brother, **Patrick Lamb**, TRENTON Gas Works, MERCER County, State of NEW JERSEY.

August 5, 1865

Of the wife of **Timothy Hayes**; when last heard of she was living in TROY, N.Y. By writing to her sister-in-law, **Mary Hayes**, she will hear of something to her advantage, as there has been some money left to her by her brother-in-law, **James Hayes**, who died in the army. Write to Mary Hayes, 110 WEST 31st ST., NEW YORK.

Edward Higgins left his wife at WASHINGTON, CONNECTICUT, July 4, 1865. Was last seen in NEW YORK CITY. Any information of him will be thankfully received, and all expenses paid, by writing to **Mrs. Mary Higgins**, Washington, Conn., or **J. Edwards**, WASHINGTON HEIGHTS, N.Y.

Of **Patrick** and **Hanora Koonan**, who did reside in NEW YORK CITY. Any one will confer a great favor by sending their address to their cousin, **Bridget Higgings**, No. 832 W. Baltimore St., BALTIMORE, MD.

Of **Michael Connor**, who left PHILADELPHIA on last November, 1864; supposed he went to POTTSVILLE; he has not been heard from since; his sister Bridget is very anxious to hear from him. Any one knowing anything of him as to his present residence, will confer a favor by addressing a note to **Bridget Connor**, Pennsylvania Hospital Philadelphia.

Of **Hanora Hayes**, who came to this country about 15 years ago, from DUNGARVAN, County of WATERFORD, Ireland. When last heard from, she was in HARRISBURG,

PENNSYLVANIA. Any information of her will be thankfully received by her brother, **Richard Hayes**, by writing to 51 North 7th Street, WILLIAMSBURGH, Long Island, N.Y. Pennsylvania and Richmond papers, please copy.

Miss Annie Manging wants information of her brother, **Timothy Manging**, from LIMERICK, Ireland, the son of **Mary Manging**, of BALEY COMENA. Any information of him will be thankfully received by Miss Annie Manging, Alleghanny House, 814 Market Street, PHILADELPHIA, PENN.

By **Mary Maguire**, of her mother, **Catherine**, from ENNISKILLEN, County FERMANAGH, Ireland, who married **Mr. Carr** at ELIZABETHPORT, N.J., about 16 or 17 years ago, and who went with her husband to the State of ILLINOIS. Any information concerning her will be thankfully received and will reach her by addressing **T. S. Gray**, American Meter Works, No. 512 WEST 22nd ST., NEW YORK. Illinois and St. Louis papers, please copy.

August 12, 1865

Of **John** and **Matthew McCarthy**, natives of the Parish of DRUM, County ROSCOMMON, Ireland. When last heard from Matthew was in the State of IOWA. Any information will be thankfully received by their sister **Maria** and mother, who are very anxious to hear from them. Please direct to 143 WEST 25th STREET, NEW YORK CITY. Indiana and Western papers, please copy.

If **Mr. P. McGlone** or **Mr. Giblin**, late of GLENFARNE, County LEITRIM, Ireland, will address a note to "T. M," SACRAMENTO Post Office, CALIFORNIA, they will hear from their old friend "**Terry**."

Of **Jane Crooks** (**Mrs. Kiernan**), of the Parish of KILDALKEY, County MEATH, Ireland, who is supposed to be either in the States of NEW JERSEY or NEW YORK. Her husband was killed in the Army. When last heard from she was in WASHINGTON, D. C. Her brother, **Thomas Crooks**, is most anxious to hear from her. Address, **James Bligh**, 239 D Street, Washington, D. C.

Of **Martin** and **Michael Fitzmaurice**, natives of the Parish of CREG, County GALWAY, Ireland. When last heard from, in 1855, they were living in MANITOWOC, WISCONSIN. Any information of them will be thankfully received by their niece, **Mary Conway**, by writing to her in care of **Mrs. Habbit**, No. 93 OLIVER STREET, NEW YORK CITY.

Of **Michael Walsh**, of the Parish of TYNORE, County MAYO, Ireland. When last heard from (about nine months ago) he was in WASHINGTON, D. C. Any information concerning him will be thankfully received by his brother, **Anthony Walsh**, in care of **Wm. Cronin**, No. 117 S. 11th Street, PHILADELPHIA, PA.

Of **Lawrence Roach** and family, natives of the County MAYO, Ireland, who formerly lived in CANADA. When last heard from they were in BELOIT, ROCK County, WISCONSIN. Any information of them will be thankfully received by his daughter, **Mary Davidson**, widow, by writing to her in care of **Samuel Lavery**, No. 141 FULTON STREET, NEW YORK CITY. Wisconsin papers, please copy.

Of **Patrick Molloy**, a native of the Parish of RAHAN, KING'S County, Ireland. When last heard from (about four years ago) he was in CHICAGO, ILL. Any information of him will be thankfully received by his brother, **Joseph Molloy**, at 33[6] WEST 27th STREET, N.Y. Chicago papers, please copy.

August 19, 1865

Of **William McAneney**, a native of SHANKHILL, County DUBLIN, and of **Patrick Kiernan**, a native of the City of DUBLIN, Ireland. William, when last heard from (about two years ago), was in PIQUA INLAMA County, OHIO, and Patrick was in the British Army in CANADA WEST. Any information of them will be thankfully received by **Geo. W. Kiernan**, 769 Indiana Avenue, CHICAGO, ILL. Ohio and Canada papers, please copy.

Of **Patrick Fleming**, of the City of LIMERICK, Ireland, who came to this country in May, 1856. He was in CHICAGO, ILL., when last heard from. Any information of him will be thankfully received by his brother, **Thomas Fleming**, No. 37 Little Street, between Plymouth and John Streets, BROOKLYN, N.Y. Chicago papers, please copy.

Of **William Dooly**, a native of Fish Street, City of CORK, Ireland. When last heard of (six years ago) he was in CHICAGO, ILL. Any information of him, sent to **Michael Foley**, SUFFOLK STATION, Long Island, N.Y., will be thankfully received by his mother, **Mary Dooly**.

Of **Cornelius Mahony**, a native of MILLSTREET, County CORK, Ireland, who left NEW YORK on the 4th of April last. Any information of him will be thankfully received by his brother, **John Mahony**, who has lately arrived in New York, by writing to him in care of **John Kearney**, No. 5 MULBERRY STREET, NEW YORK CITY.

Of **John** and **James Lynch**, natives of ALTLOUGH, Parish of LARA, County CAVAN, Ireland, who arrived in New York in 1854. When last heard from they were in MORRISTOWN, N.J. Information concerning their present whereabouts will be thankfully received by **Patrick Colwell**, 72 First Place, BROOKLYN, N.Y. New Jersey papers, please copy. [Appeared Aug. 26, 1865 with "Altlough" changed to "ALTBEAUGH. "]

August 26, 1865

Of **Daniel Sheridan**, seaman, a native of NEW YORK aged about 38 years; only son of the late **Farrell Sheridan**, County FERMANAGH, Ireland. Any information of him will be thankfully received by his sister **Mary**, No. 2 Pierpont Place, BROOKLYN, N.Y. [Appeared Sept. 2, 1865 with 'Pierpont" spelled "Pierrepont."]

Of **John Driscoll**, late of NOTTINGHAM, ENGLAND. When last heard from he was nurse in BEVERLY Military Hospital, under **Ward Master General Quinn**. Any information of him will be thankfully received by his brother **James**, at Franklin Avenue, near Vanburan St., BROOKLYN, N.Y. Philadelphia and Germantown papers, please copy.

Of **John Carmody**, a native of BALLINGOWN, within 1 mile of TRALEE, County KERRY, Ireland. He served 10 years in the United States Regular Army, and, when last heard of, was living in 140 Broad Street, PHILADELPHIA, PA. Any information of him will be thankfully received by his brother, **Thomas Carmody**, 14 Carroll Street, SOUTH BROOKLYN, L.I., and all expenses freed.

If **James, Denis**, or **Thomas Woods**, from ENNISTYMON, County CLARE Ireland, will write to **Louis Hummel**, GOLDSBORO, NORTH CAROLINA, they will hear from their brother.

Of **Thomas Doyle**, of COOLDERRY, CARRICKMACROSS, County MONAGHAN, Ireland. When last heard from he was at the Ohio Exchange, NEW ORLEANS, LA. Any information respecting him will be thankfully received by his brother, **James Doyle**, by addressing **Peter Doyle**, No. 215 HESTER ST., NEW YORK.

Of **Dan Duane**, a native of the Parish of SKIR, QUEEN'S County, Ireland, who came to America 15 years ago. When last heard from about 6 years ago, he was in ST. LAWRENCE County, State of NEW YORK. Any information of him will be thankfully received by his brother and sister, **Edward** and **Anne Duane**, 52 PITT ST., NEW YORK. Canada papers, please copy. [Appeared Nov. 11, 1865, with some different information.]

$30 Reward. - For information of **Mary Benson**, maiden name **Moloney**, granddaughter of **James Heffernan**, shop keeper, THURLES, County TIPPERARY, Ireland. Any information her, living or dead, will be thankfully received by her mother, or by addressing **Mrs. Bridget Moloney**, OMAHA, N.J. Ohio and Boston papers, please copy.

Of **Kate Walker**, who left NEWCASTLE WEST, County LIMERICK, Ireland, on the 16th of July last. Any information of her will be thankfully received by her brother, **Thomas Walker**, 262 MONROE ST., NEW YORK. Buffalo papers, please copy.

Of **Bridget Conly**, maiden name **Bridget Tully**, a native of County CAVAN, Ireland. Her nephew, **Patrick Tully**, would be glad to receive any information respecting her or her children. Any person knowing anything of them or their whereabouts will confer a particular favor by addressing a line to Patrick Tully, care of **Hugh Riley**, corner of 35th ST., and 2nd AVENUE, NEW YORK [Appeared Sept. 16, 1865 with the following added: "Boston and Philadelphia papers, please copy."].

Of **James Commins**, a native of the Parish of ARDAGH, County MAYO, Ireland, who emigrated to America about the year 1840, supposed to be in the State of NEW YORK. Any information of him will be thankfully received by his nephew, **James Commins**, care of **M. W. Morris**, PITTSTON P.O., LUZERNE County, PENN.

September 2, 1865

Of **James McCool**, a native of Ireland, who left this City 10 years ago. When last heard from he was in PEARSE MINES, CALIFORNIA. Any information of him will be thankfully received, and a liberal reward paid, by his sorrowful mother, **Mrs. McCool**, 150 WEST 30th STREET, N.Y. CITY. California papers, please copy. [Appeared April 29, 1865 with a different contact person and some different information.]

Of **Thomas, Michael** and **John Griffin**, natives of the City of DUBLIN, Ireland. When last heard from, John was at CITY POINT, VA., and Michael was in PENNSYLVANIA, a time-keeper on the railroad. Any information of them will be thankfully received by their mother, **Mary Griffin**, by writing to her to 205 Columbia Street, BROOKLYN, N.Y.

Of **John Mullen**, who left DUBLIN, Ireland, 17 years ago, and, when last heard from (5 years ago), was in LAMBERTVILLE, HUNTERDON County, N.J.; also, of **Dan Mullen**, potmaker for a glass factory, who left Dublin about the same time. Any information of them will be thankfully received by John's sister, **Mrs. Ellen Noller**, General Post Office, ALBANY, N.Y.

Of **Ellen, Christian**, and **Margaret Reilly**, natives of CHURCHTOWN, County WESTMEATH, Ireland. Information of them will be thankfully received by their sister, **Catherine Reilly**, by writing to her in care of **Mr. Michael Griffin**, corner of South 8th and Monmouth Streets, JERSEY CITY, N.J.

Of **Mary Manning** and **Bridget Ennis**, natives of FARTHINGSTOWN, County WESTMEATH, Ireland. When last heard from, about a year ago, they were in MERCER County, N.J. Any information concerning them will be thankfully received by writing to **Richard New**, 105 MORTON STREET, NEW YORK.

Of **James** and **Thomas Fitzpatrick**, who belonged to STRAFFAN, County KILDARE, Ireland. James, when last heard from, was in JAMESTOWN, CONN., and Thomas was in BUFFALO, N.Y. Information of them will be thankfully received by their sister **Esther**, No. 44 MARKET STREET, N.Y.

Of **Alexander McAvitt**, a native of County DOWN, Ireland, who arrived here about six years ago. When last heard from (about two years ago) he was in NEW YORK, and was about going to CALIFORNIA. Information of his whereabouts will be thankfully received by **Peter Devlin**, 16 Pacific, corner of Novation Street, LAWRENCE, MASS.

Of **John, Michael, Luke, Patrick, Thomas** and **Ellen Kelley**, natives of the Townland of RUSHPORT, Parish of KILLMORE, County ROSCOMMON, Ireland. Information of them will be thankfully received by **Patrick Kelley**, HEBRONVILLE, MASS.

Of **Maurice Foley**, a waggon maker by trade, a native of the Parish of KILLORGLIN, County KERRY, Ireland. When last heard of (last October) he was in the State of INDIANA. Information of him will be thankfully received by his sister, **Mrs. Bridget Falvey**, by writing to her to No. 80 JAMES STREET, NEW YORK. [Appeared Jan. 6, 1866 with some additional information.]

Of **Mary Foley**, daughter of **Michael Foley**, a native of BALLYTROSNA, Parish of VENTRY, County KERRY, Ireland. She was married to **Thomas Bowler**, Parish of LOCK, and lived, about 10 years ago, in CIRCLE VILLA, OHIO. Information respecting her will be thankfully received by **Daniel Donohoe**, MIDDLETOWN, CONN.

Of **Martin Molony**, a native of CAPPAFEUNE, Parish of INCHICRONAN, County CLARE, Ireland, who came to this country 7 years ago. Information of him will be thankfully received by his cousin, **Michael Glynn**, ATHENS, GREENE County, N.Y.

Of **Patrick Mahony**, a native of NENAGH, County TIPPERARY, Ireland, who sailed from Limerick for America about 16 years ago. When last heard from he was in the State of OHIO. Intelligence of him will be thankfully received by his sister **Margaret**, wife of **Dennis Callahan**, at 62 High Street, BOSTON, MASS. Ohio papers, please copy.

Of **Michael O'Keeffe**, a native of RATHKEALE, County LIMERICK, Ireland, who left ENGLAND in August, 1864, and arrived in New York. When last heard from he left the Morris and Essex Railroad Company to go to PHILADELPHIA, PA. Any information of him will be thankfully received by his wife, **Bridget O'Keeffe**, by writing to her to No. 215 HESTER STREET, NEW YORK CITY.

Of **Pat**, son of **Mr. John McEvey** and **Catherine Palmer**, deceased, of CARROWMORE, RATHLACKAN, near KILLALA, County MAYO, Ireland. He is supposed to have sailed, in July, 1865, on board the steamer *City of Washington*, from Liverpool, for New York. Should this meet his notice, he is earnestly requested to correspond with, or come at once to see, the undersigned. Any person giving satisfactory information of him, and his address, will be liberally rewarded by **N. Duncan**, LASALLE, LA SALLE County, ILL.

September 9, 1865

Of **Mary Toothe** (maiden name **Waters**), from near ANNAGHAPORE, County LOUTH, Ireland; or of any of her boys, if any. Information of them will be thankfully received by **Michael Kelly**, ST. JOHNSVILLE, MONTGOMERY County, N.Y. Fall River, Providence, papers, please copy.

Of **Thomas Plunkett**, a native of CASTLETOWN DELVIN, County WESTMEATH, Ireland, who left NEW YORK on the 4th of May. Any information of him will be thankfully received by his wife at 327 9th AVENUE, NEW YORK.

Of **Patrick Donovan**, a native of the Parish of CURRE, County KERRY, Ireland, who immigrated to CALIFORNIA about 25 years ago. His friends heard he was in NEW YORK CITY about 12 months since. Any information of him will be thankfully received by **Timothy Donovan**, 80 NASSAU STREET, NEW YORK CITY. California papers, please copy.

Of **Ellen Behan**, who married a man by the name of **Patrick King**; also of her sister, **Catherine**, and her two cousins, **Mary** and **Margaret Heatherman**, and their two sisters; also of **Martin Hayes**, all from the Parish of CARRIGAHOLT, County CLARE, Ireland. Any information of them will be thankfully received by **Bridget Behan**, by writing to her in care of **Mr. Alexander Sweeney**, Commerce Street, between Vandyke and Elizabeth Street, SOUTH BROOKLYN, N.Y. [Appeared Sept. 16, 1865, with the place of nativity for Martin Hayes as "from the Parish of DUNBEG, County CLARE, Ireland." All others are still said to be from the Parish of Carrigaholt, County Clare. The following sentence was added at the end: "As Bridget is about going home soon, she is the more anxious for information."]

Of **Phillip Quigley**, of CORINCHAGO, near CASTLEBLANEY, County MONAGHAN, Ireland. When last heard of he lived in BOSTON, MASS. His cousin, **Patrick Connelly**, who lately arrived in this country, would be thankful to know where to find him. Address, **Edward Duffy**, STAMFORD Cove Mills, CONN. Boston *Pilot*, please copy.

Of **Rodger Sheedy**, of KILFENANE, County LIMERICK, Ireland. His son **John**, who came to this country about two years ago, is very anxious to hear from him. Any person knowing of his whereabouts will confer a great favor by writing to his brother, **Michael Sheedy**, Pacific Iron Works, BRIDGEPORT, CONN.

Of **John Flanagan**, of the Townland of BORNAHILL, County CAVAN Ireland, who left GREENPOINT, Long Island, about a year ago, aged fifty years. Any one giving information of him would confer a great favor on his sister, **Bridget Flanagan**, by addressing her at 264 Gold St., BROOKLYN, Long Island, N.Y.

September 16, 1865

If **Michael** or **Daniel Doyle** should see this notice, they will please to write to **Martin Donahoe**, in care of **Mr. James A. Dickson**, WAYNESBORO Post Office, BURKE County, GEORGIA.

Joseph Fox, who landed at the Castle Garden about the 1st of August, can hear from his brother **Jas. H. Fox**, by calling or writing to him at the Irish-American Office.

Of **Patrick Cavanagh**, of the Parish of DISERCALE, near POMEROY, County TYRONE, Ireland, who came to this country about 30 years ago, and has not been heard of for about 16 years. Any information of him will be thankfully received by **Peter Cavanagh**, corner of Partition and Van Brunt Streets, SOUTH BROOKLYN, N.Y.

Of **John Ward**, from the County GALWAY, Ireland, a traveling agent for the sale of books. He has lived in the State of ALABAMA for 24 or 25 years. When last heard from (at the beginning of the war) his address was ZERO post office, LAUNDERALE, MISSISSIPPI. Any information of him will be gladly received by his sister, **Mrs. Bridget Boylan**, at No. 76 Orchard and Martin Streets, NEW HAVEN, CONN.

Of **Michael O'Loughlin**, a native of the Parish of KILLANY, KNOX, County MAYO, Ireland. When last heard from (about a year ago), he was in CANADA. Any information of him will be thankfully received by his nephew, **John O'Loughlin**, by writing to him to 123 WEST 33rd STREET, NEW YORK. Canada papers, please copy.

September 23, 1865

Of **James Bradley**, son of **James Bradley** and **Ann Doolen**, who came to this country from GLASGOW, SCOTLAND, about 14 years ago, and is supposed to be working at FALL RIVER, MASS. Information of him will be thankfully received by his brother, **Patrick Bradley**, MAHONY CITY, SCHUYLKILL County, PA. Boston *Pilot*, please copy.

Of **John Hoey**, formerly of MONTREAL, CANADA. He was last heard from June, 1863, when in the 18th Regiment, N.Y.V. Information of him will be most thankfully received by his brother, **James Hoey**, Customs, QUEBEC, CANADA.

Of **Michael Connors**, of LARD CAPPOQUIN, County WATERFORD, Ireland, who is supposed to be in NEW YORK. Information of him will be thankfully received by his cousin, **Michael K. Condon**, ANNAPOLIS JUNCTION, A.[nne] A.[rundel] County, MD, who has something to his advantage to communicate, having just received a letter from his father from Lard Cappoquin.

Of **Morris Coogan**, of RATHANGAN, County KILDARE, Ireland, who came to this country about ten years ago, and when last heard of was in LANCASTER, PA., or WILMINGTON, DEL. Information of him will be thankfully received by his daughter, **Bridget Coogan**, 1238 Howard St., KENSINGTON, PHILADELPHIA, PA. California papers, please copy. [Appeared Nov. 11, 1865, identifying Morris Coogan as "the harness maker."]

Of **Peter Levins** of the Town of DUNDALK, County LOUTH, Ireland, who sailed in the ship *Braemar* from Liverpool, for Monte Video, in 1857. When last heard from (3 months since) he was in BOSTON. Information of him will be thankfully received by his cousin, **Mrs. Bernard Brady**, NEW BRITAIN, CONN. Boston papers, please copy.

Of **James Johnston**, from MULCURRY, Parish of DUNLEER, County LOUTH, Ireland, who arrived in this country on the 1st of May, 1846. When last heard from he was in SYRACUSE, N.Y. Information of him will be thankfully received by his nephew, **James Johnston**, at No. 16 Herbert St. WILLIAMSBURG, N.Y. Western papers, please copy.

Of **Michael Murray**, a native of WESTPORT, County MAYO, Ireland, who emigrated to this country in 1853. When last heard from he was in LOUISVILLE, KY. Any person knowing of his present residence will confer a favor on his afflicted parents by communicating the same to **Patrick Lavelle**, 9 Hamilton Ave., BROOKLYN, N.Y. Louisville papers, please copy.

September 30, 1865

Of **Patrick Mahony** and his sister **Mary**, who belong to INCHIGOGIN, near the City of CORK, Ireland. They have not been heard from since 1859. Mary is supposed to be married to a German. Information of them will be thankfully received by their sister **Julia**, at 88 MOTT STREET, NEW YORK. [Appeared Oct. 7, 1865 with Julia's address changed to 88 WATT STREET [WATTS ST.], NEW YORK.]

Of **David, Mark** and **Edward Fitzgibbon**, tailors by trade, and sons of **Mark Fitzgibbon**, who lived at PARSON, TOWNSENDS, as gardener, at BANTER, MALLOW, County CORK, Ireland. They are many years in America. If any friend should know their whereabouts they would confer a particular favor on their sister, by writing to **Eugene Ryan**, 32 Washington Street, EAST TROY, NEW YORK.

Of **Patrick O'Neill**, of the Parish ARRIGLE, County TYRONE, Ireland, who left about fourteen years ago for the United States. When last heard from he was in PHILADELPHIA about five years ago. Any information of him will be thankfully received by his brother, **Bernard O'Neill**, 37 LISPENARD STREET, NEW YORK, or at the office of this paper.

Of **John Ryan**, or relatives, who left the County TIPPERARY, (near THURLES), about 14 or 15 years ago, and who, when last heard of, was living in NEWARK, N.J. By addressing **Joseph Smith**, No. 7 MONROE STREET, NEW-YORK, they will hear of something to their advantage. Jersey City and Newark papers, please copy.

Of **John** and **Peter Lynch**, who left County CARLOW, Ireland, some eight years ago, and are supposed to be either in CHICAGO, ILL., or BRIDGEPORT, CT. Information of them will be thankfully received by their niece, **Catharine Doyle**, SOUTH SIDE, STATEN ISLAND, N.Y. Chicago and Bridgeport papers, please copy.

Of **Daniel Houlahan**, a native of WILLIAMSTOWN, Parish of CLONRUSH, County GALWAY, Ireland. When last heard of he was at No. 46 Cherry Street, PHILADELPHIA, PA., about 5 years ago. Any information concerning him, whether dead or alive, will console his aged mother, and be thankfully received by his friends, if addressed to his cousin, **Mr. Martin Hartnedy**, 15 EAST HOUSTON STREET, NEW YORK. Pennsylvania, New York and New Jersey papers, please copy.

Of **Thomas Mee**, or **Mary Mee**, his wife, who came to this country about 15 or 16 years ago; also of **Patrick Crane** and **John Egan** all natives of the County GALWAY, Ireland. When last heard from they were in BALTIMORE, M.D. Any information of them will be thankfully received by **Thomas Mee**, who came to this country a short time ago. Address, **Henry Corkey**, WEST FARMS P.O., WESTCHESTER County, N.Y.

October 7, 1865

Of **Patrick Carr**. When last heard from was in ST. LOUIS. Any intelligence concerning him will be thankfully received by his sister, **Betty Carr**, 1122 North Front Street, PHILADELPHIA, PA.

If this should meet the eye of **Patrick, Mary**, or **Elizabeth Mahady**, of MELCONOUGH, GRANARD, Co. LONGFORD, they will hear of an old friend by addressing **John Farrell**, office of the Irish-American, New York.

Of **Michael** and **Patrick Regan**, from the Parish of LISDALE, County KERRY, Ireland. When last heard from they were in ALBANY, N.Y. Information of them will be thankfully received by their sister, **Mary Regan**, at 40 CLARKSON ST., N.Y.

October 14, 1865

Of **John Taylor** and Child, late of Her Majesty's 84th Regiment Foot, who left ENGLAND on the 27th of July, 1865. Should this meet the eye of any person knowing his whereabouts, they will confer a great favor on his wife, **Bridget**, by sending a few lines or directing him to her. **James Joyce**, 183 SPRING ST., NEW YORK CITY.

Of **John Granfield**, formerly a member of Co. C. (**Capt. Lynch**) 63rd Regt. N.Y. Vols. He was captured before RICHMOND on the 14th day of October, 1863, and when last heard from (February 14th, 1864,) was confined at BELLE ISLAND as a prisoner. Any information respecting him will be most thankfully received by his mother. Address, **William Downes**, Attorney At Law, NEW HAVEN, CONN.

Of **John Gallagher**, a native of RATHSCANLON, near TUBBERCURRY, County SLIGO, Ireland. He left BRADFORD, YORKSHIRE, ENGLAND, on board the ship *Arctic* on the 14th Oct., 1856, for New York, in company with a man named **Thomas Gilmore**. He has not been heard from since. Any information of him will be most thankfully received by his father, **John Gallagher,** near BULL'S HEAD. Post Office, CLINTON, DUTCHESS County, N.Y Country papers, please copy.

Of **Daniel Blake**, of the Parish of KILLOUGHEY, KING'S County, Ireland. When last heard from (ten or eleven years ago) he was working at COLUMBIA STATION, OHIO. Any information of him will be thankfully received by his sister, **Ann Blake**, in care of **James Doody**, COLLINSVILLE, CONN.

Of **Tim Comerford**, who came to this country from the City of MANCHESTER, ENGLAND, in 1856, stopped a while in NEW JERSEY, then moved to the City of LOWELL, MASS., in company of **Patrick Cosgrove**, and was since heard from in 1861, by **Michael Flannigan**. Also, of **James, Pat** and **Mary Comerford**, all natives of BIRR, KING'S County, Ireland. Any information of them will be thankfully received and liberally rewarded by an interesting brother and sister, who now reside in the City of NEW YORK.

Address **William Comerford**, No. 500 THIRD AVENUE, NEW YORK CITY. Boston and Ohio papers please copy.

Of **Mary** and **William Kenney**, natives of the Parish of KILTOMASH, PETER'S WELL, County GALWAY, Ireland. Mary emigrated to this country about two years ago, and William one. When last heard from both were living in LOUISVILLE, KY. Any information concerning them will be thankfully received by addressing their cousins, **Michael** and **Ciscely Hearn**, No. 837 Mountain Street, PHILADELPHIA. Louisville papers, please copy.

October 21, 1865

Of **John O'Brien**, a native of STRADBALLY, QUEEN'S County, Ireland, who emigrated from PROSPEROUS, County KILDARE, about 15 years ago; was employed at the laying of the Atlantic Cable seven or eight years ago. Any information of him will be thankfully received by his mother, **Margaret Darcy**, care of **Rev. Dr. Taylor**, P. P., MARYBORO', QUEEN'S County, Ireland.

Of **William Murphy**, a native of the Parish of AHERBOY, Townland of KILNAHARVY, County MONAGHAN, Ireland, who is about 25 years in America, and a tailor by trade. He left MILWAUKEE about six years ago, and is now supposed to be in NEW YORK. Any information of him will be thankfully received by his cousin, **Hugh Rilley**, at FORT HAMILTON, NEW YORK. [Appeared Oct. 28, 1865, with "Aherboy" changed to "AUGHBOY;" appeared Nov. 4, 1865 with "Aughboy" changed to "AUGHBOG."]

Of **George Kew**, or **Ellen**, his wife, of the Parish of MULLABRACK, County ARMAGH, Ireland, who left about twenty years ago, for the United States. When last heard from they were living in ST. LOUIS; supposed since to have gone to MINNESOTA. Information of them will be thankfully received by his cousin, **John Kew**, OSWEGO, N.Y.

Of **Mr. L. Dargan**, a native of CLONMEL, County TIPPERARY, Ireland, who arrived in New York about a month ago. Information of his whereabouts will be thankfully received by his friend, **Michael O'Mahony**, at 40 BOND STREET, NEW YORK.

Of **Patrick Torpy**, a native of the County CLARE, Ireland. When last heard from he was in SANDY HOOK, WASHINGTON County, MD. Information of him will be thankfully received by his father, **Michael Torpy**, PEEKSKILL, WESTCHESTER County, N.Y.

Of **John** or **Hanora Griffin**, who left GLEN, County LIMERICK, Ireland, about 18 years ago; also of **Tobias** or **Richard Fitzgerald**, or any of the family, who left RATHKEALE, County LIMERICK, Ireland, about 16 years ago. Information of them will be thankfully received by **Mary Crimmin**, in care of **John Sullivan**, 10 WASHINGTON ST., NEW YORK. Massachusetts papers, please copy.

Of **Nancy, Bridget** and **Margaret Carney**, natives of the Parish of HERBERTSTOWN, County LIMERICK, Ireland. When last heard from were in GERMANTOWN, PHILADELPHIA, PA. Any information of them will be thankfully received by their brother, **Maurice Carney**, HAVERSTRAW, ROCKLAND County, N.Y., care of **George Washburn,** Esq.

Of **Edward** and **James Callahon**, of BUNNEDEN, County SLIGO, Ireland. When last heard from they were in MADISON TOWN, MADISON County, N.Y. Any information of them will be thankfully received by their brother's son, **Thomas Callahon**. Direct to No. 180 North First Street, JERSEY CITY, N.J.

Of **Patrick, Edward** and **David Cain**, sons of **Denis Cain**, of the Parish of HORSELIP, KING'S County, Ireland. When last heard from, in 1859 they were in ALBANY. Any information of them will be thankfully received by their brother, **Thomas Cain**, ORO FINO, IDAHO TERRITORY.

Of **Catherine Doherty**, who sailed from Londonderry 21 years ago, in the ship *Columbus*. She married the second mate of the ship; his name is **William Hunt**. They were through the New England States. Five years ago he sailed as captain under a shipping merchant named **Jones** of NEW YORK. Any information of her will be thankfully received by her sister, **Mrs. Devine**, care of **Denis Martin,** Esq., 16 Roseville Street, LONDONDERRY, or to the office of the Irish-American. [Appeared under County DERRY]

of **James Clasby**, a native of BALLYCLARE, Co. GALWAY, Ireland. When last heard from was at SING SING, N.Y. State. (Advertised for his sister Kate in the Irish-American about six months ago). Any information concerning him will be thankfully received by the said sister, **Kate Clasby**, in care of **Mrs. Shelly**, No. 5 Fair Street, NEW HAVEN, CONN.

October 28, 1865

Of **Mary Anne Griffin**, daughter of **Philip Griffin**, late of SKERRIES, County DUBLIN, who left there about 16 or 18 years ago, and who, when last heard from (near two years since), was at 41 Public-square (North side), CLEVELAND, OHIO. Any information of her will be thankfully received by her sister, **Jane Griffin**, at 44 MARKET STREET, NEW YORK. Cleveland, Ohio, papers, please copy.

Of **Eugene** and **Malachy McAuliffe**, and sister **Mary**, who married a man named **John O'Connor**. They are natives of NEWMARKET, County CORK, Ireland. When last heard from they were in MEMPHIS, TENN. Any information of them will be thankfully received by their brothers, **Cornelius** and **Henry**, by writing to them to No. 24 CITY HALL PLACE, N.Y.

Of **Patrick Bruen**, a native of the County ROSCOMMON, Ireland, who landed at Castle Garden, in the packet ship *Excelsior*, about the 4th of October, inst. Information of him will be thankfully received by his brother, **John Bruen**, at 224 10th AVENUE, N.Y. Pennsylvania papers, please copy.

Of **Laurence Quinn**, who came to this country about four months ago, in the ship *Atmosphere*. It has been reported that he was killed in NEW YORK, together with two other persons. He is 17 years of age. Information of him, dead or alive, will be thankfully received by his brother, **Martin Quinn**, care of **Mr. McGuire**, 120 EAST 28th STREET, NEW YORK. [Appeared under County KILKENNY]

November 4, 1865

Of **John Coughlin**, a native of the Parish of TAGMON, County WEXFORD, Ireland. When last heard from he was in ALBANY, N.Y. Information of him will be thankfully received by his brother, **James Coughlin**, at 94 FULTON STREET, NEW YORK. Western papers, please copy.

Of **John Delaney**, a native of the Parish of MOUNTMELLICK, QUEEN'S County, Ireland. When last heard from was in LEBANON County, PA. Information of him will be thankfully received by his sister, **Ann Delaney**, by writing to her to School St., GERMANTOWN, PHILADELPHIA County, PA., in care of **Mrs. Boarden**.

Of **Patrick Driscoll**, a native of VALENCIA, County KERRY, Ireland aged 24 years, who left home on the 10th of April, 1864. He wrote home from NEW YORK about six months ago, and has not been heard from since. Information of him will be thankfully received by his friend, **Mary J. Sullivan**, at 212 BOWERY, NEW YORK.

Of **Jeremiah Sullivan**, a native of the County KERRY, Ireland, aged about 40 years, who went to CALIFORNIA in June 1862, and was in SAN FRANCISCO when last heard from.

Information of him will be thankfully received by his friend, **John B. Shea**, 33 VANDEWATER STREET, NEW YORK California papers, please copy.

Of **Dennis Berry**, a native of the Parish of AUGHRAM, County ROSCOMMON, Ireland. When last heard from he was living in BROOKLIN, F.Y. Information of him will be thankfully received by his nephew, **William Glancy**, by writing to him in care of **Mr. Kelleher** to No. 132 LEONARD ST., NEW YORK.

Of **Daniel Molin**, a native of the Parish of BALLYPORENE, County TIPPERARY, Ireland, who is supposed to have landed in New York in July last. Information of him will be thankfully received by his brother, **Thomas Molin**, by addressing him at TORRINGTON, CONNECTICUT.

Of **Jane Hammond**, maiden name **Jane Long**, a native of KING'S County, Ireland, and lived in the City of DUBLIN for many years. She came to America with her nephew, **Michael Williams**, about 15 years ago. When last heard from she was living in 12th ST. cor. of 5th AVENUE, NEW YORK. Information of her will be thankfully received by her son, **William Carey**, care of Messrs. Lynch, Cole & Meehan, Irish-American office, 29 Ann St., New York.

Of **Ann** and **Mary Conroy**, natives of WOODFORD, County GALWAY, Ireland. Mary is supposed to be married to a German. When last heard from (eight years ago) they were in MELBOURNE, AUSTRALIA. Information of them will be thankfully received by their mother, **Mary Conroy**, by writing to her to No. 199 AVENUE A., NEW YORK, U.S.A. Melbourne papers, please copy.

November 11, 1865

Of **Michael Murphy**, aged about 28 years, 5 feet 8 inches high, fair hair, who left his wife and child in WOONSOCKET, R.I., on the 7th day of February, 1860, since which time she has had no account of him. If this meets his eye or that of any person knowing his present whereabouts, will confer a great favor on his young and sorrowing wife and little daughter, by writing to **Kate Murphy**, in care of **W. J. Lally**, Woonsocket, R.I.

Of **Charles Connolly**, of EDGE-HILL, LIVERPOOL, LANCASHIRE, ENGLAND, who has been in America about 18 years, and is supposed to have settled in NEW ORLEANS. Any information of his whereabouts will be thankfully received by his brother, **Edward Connolly**, U.S.S. *Tacony*, CHARLESTON, S.C.

Of **Rebecca Baxter**, who recently arrived in the *Minnehaha* from Ireland. Address her sister, **Jane Baxter**, No. 1627 Arch St., PHILADELPHIA.

Of **William Lacey**, a native of the County WEXFORD, Ireland. Came to this country nine years ago. Any information of him will be thankfully received by his brother, **Richard Lacey**, 121 WEST 20th STREET, near 7th Avenue, NEW YORK. [Appeared Nov. 24, 1866 with a different contact person.]

Of **Richard Hughes**, of CALLANA, TYRAWLEY, County MAYO, Ireland; or his children, **John, Thomas, Mary** and **Joseph**. When last heard from they were living in Crosby Street, LIVERPOOL, ENGLAND. John and Thomas were painters by trade, and served their time in Liverpool. John and Thomas are supposed to be in the City of NEW YORK. Any information of them will be thankfully received by their brother, **James Hughes**, No. 32 Phelp's Court, SALEM, MASS.; and ten dollars reward paid for the information. [Appeared Nov. 18, 1865 with "Tyrawley" spelled "TERAULY" and "Ten Dollars Reward" as a heading to the ad.]

Of **Patrick Carey**, a native of the Parish of KILKARNEY, County LOUTH, Ireland, aged about thirty or forty years, and is now supposed to be residing in NEW YORK. When last heard from, seven years ago, he was in New York; he is a bricklayer by trade, and was at that time working for a man named **Kilpatrick**, a builder. Any information of him will be thankfully received by his sister, wife of **Mr. Cascarlay**, whose address is BELLBROOK, GREENE County, OHIO.

Of **Charles Doyle**, SEVEN CHURCHES, County WICKLOW, Ireland. When last heard from was in RICHMOND, VA., about 18 months ago. Any information concerning him will be thankfully received by his friend **John Lee**, Virginia and Tennessee Railroad, LYNCHBURG, VA.

Of **Dan Duane**, a native of the Parish of SKIRK, QUEEN'S County, Ireland. He went to CANADA about 15 years ago, and afterwards came to New York. When last heard of, about nine ago, he was in ST. LAWRENCE County, State of NEW YORK. Any information respecting him will be thankfully received by his brother and sister, **Owney** and **Edward Duane**, by writing to 52 PITT STREET, NEW YORK CITY, care of **John Connell**. Canada, Ohio and Kentucky papers, please copy. [Appeared Aug. 26, 1865, with some different information; appeared Nov. 18, 1865 with the spelling of "Duane" changed to **"Dwayne."**]

November 18, 1865

Of **Andrew O'Reilly**, late private in Co. A., 155th Regt. N.Y. Vols., who left PROVIDENCE, R.I., on July 3rd last for NEW YORK (to raise his pension), and has not been heard from since. Any tidings of him will be thankfully received by his two children, who arrived in Providence (from ENGLAND) on the 4th of last August. Address **John Whitney**, 166 Westminster St., Providence, R.I.

Of **Francis McNamee**, a native of GLANMORE, County LOUTH, Ireland. When last heard from, about 4 years ago, he was in or about HOURCK, CHAUTAUQUA County, N.Y. If this should meet his eye, he will please come right home to his father and mother, **Owen** and **Susan McNamee**, Glanmore, County Louth, Ireland.

Of **Philip Clarke**, a native of the Parish of DONAHCLONEY, Townland of LURGANTAMERY, County DOWN, Ireland. When last heard from was in OHIO. Any information of him will be thankfully received by his niece, **Eliza Clarke**, at No. 143 EAST 28th STREET, NEW YORK, in care of **Mr. Patrick Gillespie**.

Of **John McNally**, a native of OLD LOUGHLIN BRIDGE, County CARLOW, from which place he emigrated. When last heard from, in 1835, was working at farming at MURRY HARBOR, ST. JOHN, N.B. He or any of his heirs can hear of something to their advantage by addressing **M. J. Hoey**, 82 North 3rd Street, WILLIAMSBURGH, Long Island, N.Y. New Brunswick papers, please copy.

By **Honora Farrell**, 291 PEARL STREET, NEW YORK, youngest daughter of the late **Edmond Farrell**, of GARRAN ROW, County LIMERICK, of her sister **Mary**, married to **Daniel Hollahon**, of the same place in 1850, and emigrated to this country in 1855. Address Honora Farrell, 291 Pearl Street, New York.

Of **Bernard Shevlin**, a native of the Parish of CLOGHER, County TYRONE, Ireland, who came to America about 26 years ago, remained some time in PROVIDENCE, R.I., then went to CALIFORNIA. When last heard from he was in SAN FRANCISCO. Any information respecting him will be gratefully received by his nephew, **Patrick Campbell**, No. 273 Main St., POUGHKEEPSIE, N.Y. California papers, please copy.

Of **Bartholomew, James** and **Patrick McManus**, natives of BOYLE, County ROSCOMMON, Ireland, who came to this country about twenty years ago. - When last heard of (fifteen years ago) Bartholomew was in CINCINNATI, OHIO; James lived in LAFAYETTE, INDIANA; and Patrick came to this country about twenty months ago from

STALLYBRIDGE, ENGLAND. Any information of them will be thankfully received by their nephew, **Patrick McManus**, son of **Charles**, by writing to him to No. 137 SULLIVAN STREET, NEW YORK. Cincinnati papers, please copy.

Of **Thomas Brown**, a native of the County ROSCOMMON, Ireland, who left MILFORD, MASS., in January, 1855, and went as book-keeper to Marshall & Man, of PHILADELPHIA, and is supposed to be living in Philadelphiia or CAMDEN at present. Any information concerning him will be thankfully received by his brother, **James Brown**, MEDWAY, MASS.

Of **John Kelly**, a native of the Parish of ABBERGORMAN, County GALWAY, Ireland. When last heard from, in 1851, he was in GEELONG, PORTPHILLIP, NEW SOUTH WALES. Any information of him will be thankfully received by his sister, **Mary Kelly**, No. 26 Observatory Road, CINCINNATI, OHIO.

November 25, 1865

Of **Martin Ford**, who left WEDNESBERY, STAFFORDSHIRE, ENGLAND, three years ago, for the United States. He is now supposed to be in PITTSBURGH, PA. Any information of him will be thankfully received by his sister, **Mary Ford**, by addressing a letter to her to MAPLEVILLE, RHODE ISLAND.

Of **Alexander, Charles** and **Mary Ann McDonald**, who left COLDRAIN, County DERRY, on the 15th of September, 1865. Information of them will be thankfully received by their brother, **John McDonald**, at the rear of 1328 Passyunke Road, PHILADELPHIA, PA.

Of **Kate O'Leary**, a native of PROHUS, near MILLSTREET, County CORK, Ireland, who came to NEW YORK in the Spring of 1863. Any information of her will be thankfully received by her brother, **John O'Leary**, at 528 Arch street, PHILADELPHIA, PA., in care of **S. S. White**.

Of **Honora** and **Julia Fitzgerald**, of DROUMANARIGLIE, County CORK, Ireland, who sailed to Boston 14 years ago, and are now living in MINNESOTA. Honora is married to **Daniel Guinea**. Information of them will be thankfully received by their brother, **Edmond Fitzgerald**, at 100 MOTT STREET, NEW YORK.

Of **William Tumilty**, a native of CASTLEWELLIN, County DOWN, Ireland, who left LIVERPOOL, ENGLAND, in March, 1863, for America. When last heard from, in May, 1863, he was in PORTLAND, CONN. Any information of him will be thankfully received by his brother, **James Tumilty**, NORTH BELLVILLE, ESSEX County, N.J. [Appeared Nov. 24, 1866 with a different contact person and less information.]

Of **Laurence** and **Miles Burke**, and their children, **Michael**, **John**, **Ellen** and **Ann**, or of **Michael Ryan**, their cousin, or of any of the family, from CAPPAWHITE, County TIPPERARY, Ireland. Information of them will be thankfully received by their cousin M.F. by calling or addressing at No. 80 WEST 43rd ST., NEW YORK.

Of **Martin Connolly**, a native of the Townland of TULLY, County GALWAY, Ireland, who left LIVERPOOL about the 23rd of last June, for America. Any information of him will be thankfully received by his sister, **Bridget Connolly**, 49 MARKET STREET, NEW YORK CITY, care of **Mr. Thomas Dunphy**.

Of **Joseph Leech**, of FERMONFECKIN, County LOUTH, Ireland, who came to this country, from DUBLIN, in February last. Supposed to be in NEW YORK CITY. Any information of him will be thankfully received by his brother, **James Leech**, DUDLEY Post-office, HUNTINGDON County, PA.

Of **Patrick Murphy**, a native of the County ROSCOMMON, Ireland who came to this country about one year ago. When last heard of he was in the State of PENNSYLVANIA.

Information of him will be thankfully received by his daughter, **Maria Murphy**, care of **Admiral Bell**, Navy Yard, BROOKLYN, N.Y. Pennsylvania papers, please copy.

December 2, 1865

Of **Charles Stone**, who emigrated from TULLAMORE, KING'S County, Ireland, about 10 years ago. When last heard from he was in MARY County, MARYLAND. Any communication from him will be gratefully received by his father, **John Stone**, Burg Quay, TULLAMORE, or by **P. O'Brien**, 98 Amity St., BROOKLYN, N.Y. Baltimore papers, please copy.

Of **Hugh Reynolds**, a native of the County LONGFORD, Ireland. He left MANCHESTER, ENGLAND, about 16 years ago and came to America, and no proper account of him has been heard since. He is a plasterer by trade. If this should meet his eye, or any friend of his, they will confer a favor on his brother, **Patrick Reynolds**, who lives in LONSDALE, RHODE ISLAND, by writing. Direct to Lonsdale Post-Office, R.I. California papers, please copy.

Of **Patt, James**, and **Michael Moloney**, natives of County CLARE, Ireland. When last heard from they were between TERRE HAUTE and INDIANAPOLIS, IND. Any information of them will be thankfully received by their brother, **John Moloney**, 141 Plymouth St., BROOKLYN, N.Y.

Of **William Lane**, a native of CAREYSVILLE, Parish of FERMOY, County CORK, Ireland, who came to this country when quite young, about 15 years ago. When last heard from, about 4 years ago, he was in St. Mary's Hospital, ROCHESTER, N.Y. Any information of him will be most thankfully received by his brother **Daniel**, or cousin **John Lane**, by writing to them to ANSONIA, CONN.

Of **Michael, Mary** and **Bridget Hogan**, natives of the Parish of MULLINAHONE, County TIPPERARY, Ireland. It is supposed they are in some part of the State of NEW YORK. Any information of them will be thankfully received by their brother, **John Hogan**, by writing to him to STAPLETON, STATEN ISLAND, N.Y.

Of **Mathew Gannon**, a native of the Parish of ACHONRY, Townland of CLOONVEHER, County of SLIGO, Ireland. When last heard from was in WINOSKIE County, WISCONSIN. Information of him will be thankfully received by his sister, **Bridget**, in care of **Mr. Martin Hogan**, No. 12 PELL STREET, NEW YORK. Western papers, please copy.

December 9, 1865

Of **William, Bernard, Matthew, Christopher** and **Charles Fagan**, who, when last heard from, were in NEW YORK. Any information of them will be thankfully received by their brother, **Joseph Fagan**, by writing to him in care of **Thomas Parrington**, ROSSVILLE, STATEN ISLAND.

Of **Michael Lynch**, by trade a pork butcher, a native of the City of DUBLIN, Ireland, and who came to this country in 1863. When last heard from he lived at 227 EAST 12th STREET, NEW YORK. Any information of him will be thankfully received by his brother and sister, **Thomas** and **Anne**. Please address Thos. Lynch, care of **Patrick Ryan**, CARMANSVILLE, WASHINGTON HEIGHTS, N.Y

Of **John, Mary** and **Kate Mulvey**, natives of HIGHWOOD, County SLIGO, Ireland, who came to this country about 15 years ago. When last heard from, about 8 years ago, they were in CHICAGO, ILLINOIS. Any information of them will be thankfully received by their sister, **Bridget Sharkey**, at No. 223 ELIZABETH ST., NEW YORK. Chicago papers, please copy.

Of **George Hussey**, a native of County MEATH, Ireland. When last heard from, in May last, he was in Co. C. Fifth New York Heavy Artillery. Any information of him will be thankfully received by his brother, **Michael Hussey**, BRIDGEPORT, CONN.

Of **Bridget Gallagher**, a native of the Parish of KILDALKY, County MEATH, Ireland. When last heard of she was in HAVERSTRAW, ROCKLAND County, State of NEW YORK. Any information of her will be thankfully received by her brother, **Nicholas Gallagher**, SAINT CLAIR, SCHUYLKILL County, PENNSYLVANIA. Rockland County papers please copy.

Of **James Larken**, a native of the Parish of KILLALON, WESTMEATH, Ireland. When last heard from was a hand on one of the boats running between NEW YORK and ALBANY. Any information concerning him will be thankfully received by his brother, **John Larken**, by addressing a letter to him to No. 8 Comes Street, NEWARK, NEW JERSEY.

Of **John** or **James Finegan**, natives of the Townland of CARRICKMACLIN, County MONAGHAN, Ireland. Supposed to be somewhere in this country, from an advertisement in the Irish-American three or four months ago. Any information of them will be thankfully received by their Cousin, **Owen Finegan**, of DUNCARROW, by writing to **James McKittrick**, 143 FIFTH STREET, NEW YORK CITY. Boston *Pilot* and Western papers please copy.

December 16, 1865

Of **Eliza Donnelly**, wife of **James Donnelly**, of MONTREAL, and her three children; supposed to be in NEW YORK or BROOKLYN. Any information thankfully received by **Patrick Donnelly**, Station D, New York Post Office.

If any of the friends of **Martin Gore**, of DUBLIN, Ireland, know where he resides, would they be so kind as to inform him that his wife died on the 7th of February, 1865; also his mother, who died in August. He will learn the particulars by writing to his friend, **Michael O'Neill**.

Of **William Maher**, a native of the Parish of RATHKEALE, County LIMERICK, Ireland. He enlisted in 1847, in the English army, in the 70th Regt. He went to the EAST INDIES in 1849. When last heard from, in 1855, he was in CAMPHER, EAST INDIES. Any information of him will be thankfully received by **John N. Blasi**, 52 WEST BROADWAY, NEW YORK.

Of **Dubbey Sullivan**, daughter of **Denis Sullivan**, of CLOUGHFUNE, Parish of GLANCARE, County KERRY, Ireland, who came to this country 12 or 13 years ago. Any information of her will be thankfully received by her sister, **Johanna Sullivan**. Or of her uncle, **Denis Sullivan**, CRONE BALLEY LEADER, Parish of TONE, County KERRY, Ireland. Direct to Johanna Sullivan, 16 FRANKLIN ST., NEW YORK.

Of **Michael Mangan**, and his uncle **Rodger Hunt**, a native of BALLYGLASS, Parish of LOUGHGLYNN, County ROSCOMMON, Ireland; are supposed to be in the State of NEW JERSEY. Information of them will be thankfully received by their brother, **Patrick Mangan**, HEBRON VILLE, MASS.

Of **Bernard** and **Edward Kernan**, natives of MOUNT NUGENT, Parish of KILBRIDE, County CAVAN. When last heard from they were in HASTINGS, MINN. Information of them will be thankfully received by their sister, **Elizabeth Kearnan**, or her son, **Michael Briody**, No. 326 EAST 32nd ST., NEW YORK.

Of **James Ward**, son of **Wm. Ward**, Parish of FOHENY, Townland of CAPPA, County GALWAY, Ireland, who came to NEW ORLEANS about 10 or 11 years ago, to his sister **Elizabeth**; is about 23 or 24 years of age. Any information of him, living or dead, will be gratefully received by his sister **Catherine**, by addressing her husband, **Sergeant Sullivan**, Bridesbury Arsenal, PHILADELPHIA, PA. New Orleans papers, please copy.

Of **Mary** or **Margaret Judge**, natives of CRUSHEEN, County CLARE, Ireland. When last heard from Mary was at **Peter McDonnell's**, GRAND ST. Information of them will be thankfully received by their sister, **Honora Judge**, at 53 CANNON ST., NEW YORK.

December 23, 1865

Of **John Miller**, who emigrated from GLASGOW in August, 1864, for MASSACHUSETTS, as pudler in a rolling mill, and left SQUABBETY, EAST TAUNTON, MASS., on the 24th of last July, to look for his brother, **George Miller**, to SPUYTEN DUYVEL rolling mill, N.Y., and left there for SYRACUSE, N.Y., or for PENNSYLVANIA. Any information of him will be thankfully received by his wife, **Sarah Miller**. Direct care of **Mrs. Wallace**, No. 1625 Mervin Street, above Oxford, PHILADELPHIA, for Sarah Miller.

Of **James Coakley**, son of **John Coakley** and **Catherine Lynch**, who left CHICAGO, ILL., on or about Oct. 10th, 1863. When last heard from was in LEAVENWORTH CITY, KANSAS. Any information concerning him will be thankfully received by his mother, **Catherine Coakley**, No. 29 Chicago Avenue, Chicago, Ill.

Of **Christopher Brannan** and his children, **Charles, Bartley, Michael** and **Rose Ann Brannan**, natives of the Parish of SURDS, County DUBLIN. When last heard from, five years ago, they were in NEW YORK CITY. Any information of them will be thankfully received by his son, **Mathew Brannan**, JEFFERSONVILLE, CLARK County, INDIANA.

Of **Michael Cooney**, a native of the Parish of MULLIN, County CAVAN, Ireland. When last heard from he was living in TENNESSEE. Any information of him will be thankfully received by his brothers, **Patrick** or **John Cooney**, by writing to them to NEW UTRECHT, Long Island, N.Y. Tennessee papers, please copy.

Of **Anthony Baker**, a native of BALLINA, Co. MAYO, Ireland, who landed in New York about a year ago, or light complexion, and about 24 years of age. When last heard from (a year ago last August), he was in NEW YORK CITY. Any information of his whereabouts will be thankfully received by his sister, **Fannie Baker**, 95 Summer Street, LAWRENCE, MASS.

Of **Catherine Gilligan**, from PARSONSTOWN, near BIRR. When last heard from was in UPPER CANADA. Address **Wm. Gallagher**, care **D. Gells**, corner 1st STREET and 2nd AVENUE, NEW YORK. [Appeared under KING'S County]

Of **Thomas Rafter**, son of **James Rafter**, of BROWNSTOWN, one mile from the City of KILKENNY, Ireland, who was murdered on his way home from the City of Kilkenny about 20 years ago. His son Thomas was left in charge of **Mrs. Tom Meaney**, of KILDERRY, at the time, by his mother, she having departed for America in the year 1848, accompanied by her younger son, **Patrick**, and a daughter only two years old. Any information will be thankfully received by his brother, **Patrick Rafter**, TRENTON, WAYNE County, MICHIGAN, United States of America. Kilkenny papers, please copy.

Of **Nicholas Carey**, of County WICKLOW, Ireland, late of ALBANY, N.Y, who, when last heard from (2 years ago), was in NEVEDA. Any person giving information of his whereabouts will confer a favor on his sister, **Mrs. J. Thompson**, 369 BLEECKER STREET, NEW YORK.

Of **John Ryan**, tailor by trade, a native of the City of CORK, Ireland. When last heard from he was living in BROOKLYN, Long Island, N.Y. Any information of him will be thankfully received by his cousin, **John Broderick**, by writing or calling at 3[6]5 WEST 35th STREET, between 8th and 9th Avenues, NEW YORK CITY.

Of **Patrick Conway**, of the Parish of DONERAILE, County CORK, who arrived in New York last July. He will please inquire for his uncle, **Patrick Conway**, at **Mrs. Ray's**, 163 EAST 29th STREET, NEW YORK. He is supposed to be a dry goods clerk.

December 30, 1865

Of **James** (commonly called **Joe**) and **William Costelo**, natives of the Parish of FEDMORE and BRUFF, County LIMERICK, Ireland. William is supposed to be in ROUSE'S POINT, or somewhere in NEW YORK State. James worked eight years ago in the NEW YORK and NORWICH boat; also of **John Wise**, of the Parish of Bruff, who is somewhere in CANADA. Information of them will be thankfully received by their cousin, **Michael C. Hayes**, Wason's Manufacturing Company, SPRINGFIELD, MASS.

Of **Bridget Flaherty**, a native of the QUEEN'S County, Ireland. She left Ireland nine years ago and came to NEW YORK. Information of her will be thankfully received by her brother, **Peter Flaherty**, CHENGEWATER, WARREN County, NEW JERSEY.

Of **Edward McManus**, a native of BALLYSHANNON, County DONEGAL, Ireland, who left in July, 1854. He lived in NEW YORK CITY up to 1857. When last heard from, in 1858, was in BOSTON. It is supposed that he either went to CALIFORNIA or some of the western States. Information of him will be thankfully received by his brother, **Hugh McManus**, by writing to him in care of **Mr. John Cleary**, 517 Columbia Street, BROOKLYN, L.I.

Of **Winifred, Ellen, Patrick** and **Bridget Monaghan**; also, of their nephew, **William**, and **Mary Brennan**, all natives of the Parish of ST. JOHN'S, County ROSCOMMON, Ireland. Information of them will be thankfully received by **John Monaghan**, 77 Orange St., ALBANY, N.Y Hartford papers, please copy.

Of **James McDonald** and his son **William McDonald**, natives of BLOOMFIELD, BALLYHOOLY, County CORK, Ireland. When last heard from five years ago, they were in KENTUCKY. Address **Richard O'Connor**, WILKESBARRE, PENNSYLVANIA.

January 6, 1866

Of **Maria Lamb**, a native of LONGFORD, Ireland. She emigrated from the above town about five years ago, and is now supposed to be living in NEW YORK CITY. Any information concerning her will be thankfully received by her brother, **Patrick Lamb**, No. 82 Morgan Street, ST. LOUIS, MISSOURI.

Of **Michael Shiels**, of GARRYOWEN, LIMERICK, Ireland. When last heard from was in QUEBEC, CANADA. Any information of him will be thankfully received by his brother, **Patrick Shiels**, 918 Ernst Street, below Elsworth St. PHILADELPHIA, PA.

Of **Joseph Dee**, a native of CLONMEL, County TIPPERARY, Ireland, who came to America 16 years ago. Any information of him will be thankfully received by his son, **Thomas Dee**, by writing to him in care of **Mr. Thomas Finton**, 41 CHERRY ST., NEW YORK. Boston Papers, please copy.

Of **Maurice Foley**, coach and waggon maker by trade, a native of the Parish of KILLORGLIN, County KERRY, Ireland, who arrived in America in 1848. When last heard from, in October, 1864, he resided in INDIANAPOLIS, INDIANA. Any information of him will be thankfully received by his sister, **Mrs. Bridget Falvey**, by writing to her to No. 80 JAMES STREET, NEW YORK CITY. [Appeared Sept. 2, 1865 without as much information.]

Of **Eugene Callaghan** and his sister, -, **(Mrs.) Mary Fogarty** (maiden name **Callaghan**), natives of the Parish of TRALEE, County KERRY, Ireland. When last heard from, about five years ago, they lived within one mile of the Town of PARIS, CANADA

WEST. Any information of them will be thankfully received by their brother, **John Callaghan**, by writing to him to No. 31 Pasaic Street, PATERSON, N.J.

Of **Mary Woreskey**, who left CRISLOW, County DONEGAL, Ireland, in the year 1861, and set sail for America. When last heard from, by her brother, **Francis Worreskey**, she was in BROOKLYN, Long Island, N.Y. The above is the widow of **John Boyce**, of Crislow, County Donegal. Any information respecting her will be thankfully received by her Nephew, **James Boyce**, No. 54 Jersey Street, PATERSON, N.J., or to **B. O'Neill**, Judge, 81 Congrrss [sic] St., Paterson, N.J.

January 13, 1866

Of **Andrew Dunlevy**, or relatives. Any person knowing their present address in Ireland will greatly oblige -, **(Mrs.) Mary Jackman** (maiden name **Dunlevy**) by addressing her at BELLEZANE, WASHINGTON County, State of PENNSYLVANIA, U.S.A. Irish papers, please copy.

Of **Patrick Martin**, a ship-carpenter, who served his time in Barr & Sheares, shipbuilders, ARDROSSEN, SCOTLAND, and came out to this country in 1860. When last heard from (in June or July, 1863), a was a Captain in Breckenridge's Division, La. Batallion Sharpshooters Southern Army. Any information of him will be thankfully received by his brother, **James Martin**, care of Lynch, Cole & Meehan, Irish-American Office, 29 Ann Street, New York, or by his sister, **S. A. Martell**, No. 2 Arch St., PHILADELPHIA, PA.

Of **James Roddy**, who has not been heard of during the last nineteen years. By applying at No. 199 SOUTH STREET, NEW YORK, he will hear of something to his advantage.

Of **Edward O'Connor**, a native of the Parish of COLUMBKILL, County LONGFORD, Ireland, who arrived in New York about 14 years ago. When last heard from, five years ago, he resided in OREGON County, VIRGINIA. Information of him will be thankfully received by his brother, **Charles O'Connor**, by writing to him in care of Mr. **Peter Ledridge**, No. 49 Willow St., BROOKLYN, Long Island, N.Y.

Of **Michael Maher**, a native of the City of LIMERICK, Ireland, and a ropemaker by trade, aged 23 years, who left MOTT HAVEN, N.Y., about 9 weeks ago, for NEW YORK CITY. Any information of him, dead or alive, will be thankfully received by his father, **Daniel Maher**, by writing to him to New Rope Walk, Mott Haven, N.Y.

Of **John Leheney**, his wife **Bridget** (maiden name **Naughton**) and their daughter, formerly of the Town of ROSCOMMON, Ireland, who, it appears, lived in WALLERTOWN, N.Y. When last heard from they were in CANADA. Information of them will be thankfully received by their son, **Thomas Leheney**, SWEETWATER, MENARD County, ILLINOIS.

Of **William** and **Michael Carney**, natives of the Parish of KILLINA, County ROSCOMMON, Ireland. William left STOCKPORT, ENGLAND, about 20 years ago, and when last heard from he was in NEW ORLEANS, LA.; Michael left the same place 18 years ago, and when last heard from he was in ST. LOUIS, MO. Any information of them will be thankfully received by their sisters, **Mary** and **Fanny Carney**, HEBRANVILLE, MASS.

January 20, 1866

Of **James Flaherty**, who left QUEEN'S County, Ireland, for NEW YORK, and landed at Castle Garden, on board the ship *Chancellor*, on the 3rd of November, 1865. Information of him will be thankfully received by his wife, **Bridget Farrell**, at 54 Stanton St., BROOKLYN, Long Island, N.Y.

Of the whereabouts of **Patrick, Daniel, Dennis** and **Margaret Rosney**, from TULLAMORE, KING'S County, Ireland. Address **Ann Rosney**, CLINTON HOLLOW, DUTCHESS County, N.Y.

Of **John Dundon**, a native of PHILLIPSTOWN, CAPPAWHITE, County TIPPERARY, Ireland, who came to this coutry 15 years ago. When last heard of, in March, 1863 he was in LOUISVILLE, KY. Any information concerning him will be thankfully received by his brother, **Michael Dundon**, by writing to him in care of **Laurence Higgins**, Erie St., four doors from corner of North Third St., JERSEY CITY, N.J.

January 27, 1866

Of **Cornelius** and **Daniel Mangan**, brothers, who left KILCOSGRIFF, SHANNAGOLDEN, County LIMERICK, Ireland, about 25 years ago. When last heard from they were in the State of MICHIGAN. Any information of them will be thankfully received by their sister, **Ann Mangan**, 218 SECOND AVENUE, between 13th and 14th Streets, NEW YORK. Western and Canadian papers, please copy.

Of **Dan O'Connor**, a native of the Parish of BRUFF, County LIMERICK, Ireland, who sailed from Queenstown on the 12th of January, 1860, in the *City of Baltimore*. When last heard from, in August, 1861, he resided in 10th AVENUE, NEW YORK. Any information of him will be thankfully received by his brother, **Michael O'Connor**, by writing to him to No. 204 Columbia Street, BROOKLYN, Long Island, N.Y.

Of **Hannoria** and **Julia Hurley**, natives of the Parish of KILMURRY, County of CORK, Ireland. Julia is supposed to be married to **Timothy O'Mahony**. Any information of them will be thankfully received by their brother, **John Hurley**. Direct to KANSAS CITY, JACKSON County, MISSOURI.

Of **John B. Haire**, C.E., who sailed from Liverpool in March, 1848. When last heard from in '51 or '52 was then staying at NASHVILLE or EVANSVILLE, State of INDIANA, at said time conducting some public works. Information of his whereabouts will be thankfully received by his brother in ENNISTIMON, County CLARE, Ireland, or **John Flynne**, SAVANNAH, State of GEORGIA. [Appeared Feb. 3, 1866 under County KILKENNY although reference to County Clare is made in the text; appeared Feb. 24, 1866, again placed under County Clare.]

Of **John Brassill**, a native of BALLYLONGFORD, County KERRY, Ireland. When last heard from, about fourteen years ago, he was at CLEVELAND, OHIO. Any information of him will be thankfully received by his brother, **James Brassill**, DOWAGIAC, CASS County, MICHIGAN.

Of **George, Charles** and **Ann Moran**, from the County DONEGAL, Ireland. If they will send their address, or call at 65 SPRING STREET, NEW-YORK, to their sister, **Catherine Moran**, they will hear of something to their interest. All Catholic papers, please copy.

Of **Thomas Cavanaugh**, of the Townland of LECARROW, Parish of CREEVE, barony of BOYLE, County ROSCOMMON, Ireland, who left home in 1848. When last heard of he was in NASHVILLE, TENN. Any information of him will be thankfully received by addressing his brother, **Edward Cavanaugh**, *Catholic Telegraph* Office, CINCINNATI, O.

February 3, 1866

Of **Miles Sheehy**, who, when last heard of, was in NEW YORK. Any information respecting him will be thankfully received by his brothers, **Thomas** and **James Sheehy**, by writing to them to WOODSTOCK, MCHENRY County, MO., in care of **John Donnelly**. Boston *Pilot*, please copy.

Of **Ann** and **Ellen Golden**, of the Townland of TULLYLEGFINN, Parish of TEMPLEPORT, County CAVAN, Ireland. When last heard from they were in TROY, N.Y. Any one knowing of their whereabouts will oblige their sister by writing to **Thomas McGovern**, No. 1,128 York Street, Port Richmond, PHILADELPHIA, PA.

Of **Norry Connell**, daughter of **James Connell**, a native of CASTLEMARTYR, County CORK, Ireland. She will confer a favor by calling on **Jeremiah McCarthy**, No. 15 THAMES STREET, NEW YORK.

Of **Patrick Kitson** of ENNIS, County CLARE, Ireland. When last heard from, about three or four months ago, he was in ILLINOIS. Any information of him will be thankfully received by his mother, **Mary Kitson**, or his sister **Ann**, by addressing her at the Massasoite House, SPRINGFIELD, MASS.

Of **Mary Buggy**, a native of the Townland of BALLYUSKILL, Parish of BALLYRAGET, County of KILKENNY, Ireland. When last heard from, in December, 1851, she was living in NEW HAVEN, CONN. Any information of her whereabouts will be thankfully received by her father, **John Buggy**, at 35 John Street, BROOKLYN, Long Island, N.Y.

February 10, 1866

Of **Patrick** and **William Clancy**, and **Owen Heffernan**, who are supposed to be in BROOKLYN, N.Y.; also of **Patrick Dawson**, **Simon Ryan** and -,**Mrs. O'Hara** (maiden name **Bridget Condon**), supposed to be in ILLINOIS. Any information respecting them will be thankfully received by **Michael Condon**, BIRMINGHAM, NEW HAVEN, CONN. Chicago papers, please copy.

Of **Michael Drumgoole**, a native of the Town of ARDEE, County LOUTH, Ireland, who arrived in New York about two years ago, in company with a first cousin, maiden name, **Anne Burns**, but for the last twenty-five years a resident of LIVERPOOL, ENGLAND, where he conducted the business of shoemaking. Information concerning him will be most thankfully received by his brother, **Patrick Drumgoole**, No. 46 Orleans Street, BALTIMORE, MARYLAND, where he is residing for the last twelve years.

Of **Patrick Hanratty**, also of his daughter **Margaret**, natives of CHURCHTOWN, County LOUTH, Ireland. When last heard from, about 5 years ago, they were in POWELL'S FORT, SHENANDOAH VALLEY, VA. Any information of him will be thankfully received by his daughter, **Catherine Hanratty**, by writing to her in care of **Thomas Carroll**, to No. 42 CEDAR STREET, NEW YORK CITY.

Of **Michael O'Sullivan**, son of **Patrick** and **Mary O'Sullivan**, of the City of LIMERICK, now in NEW YORK. When last heard of he was on a canal boat with one **Captain Burke**, who left for BUFFALO, N.Y. Any person knowing of his whereabouts would confer a great favor on his anxious father and mother, by addressing a few lines to his uncle, **R. P. Burke**, 6 MORRIS STREET, NEW YORK CITY. Buffalo papers, please copy.

Of **Honora Gleeson**, a native of LISMOYNAN, in the Parish of DRANGAN, County of TIPPERARY, Ireland, who came to this country about 35 years ago, and when last heard from, about 12 years ago, her address was LITTLEFORTH, CHICAGO, LAKE County, ILLINOIS. She was married to **Edward Gleeson**, from the Parish of MCCARKEY, in the same County. Information concerning her will be thankfully received by her nephew, **William Greer**, who came to this country in June, 1865, by writing to **John Gleeson**, No. 161 Green Street, ALBANY, for William Greer. Chicago papers, please copy.

Of **Thomas** and **Margaret Conlon**, who immigrated to this country about the year 1845, from ELPHIN, County ROSCOMMON, Ireland. Information relative to both, or either of them, will be thankfully received by their sister, **Mary Conlon**, 91 Washington Street, NEWARK, NEW JERSEY.

February 17, 1866

Of **Michael Malone**, a native of the County CLARE, Ireland, who was raised close by PLASSEY MILL, on the River Shannon, two miles from LIMERICK; has been in this country about twelve years. When last heard from he was in CHICAGO, ILL., and was a short time before in PEORIA, in the same State. Also, of **Anna** and **Mary Malone**, sisters to Michael, who had once lived in SALMONDS FALLS, NEW HAMPSHIRE. Any information of them will be thankfully received by their brother, **Thomas Malone**, by writing to him, in care of **William Hutton** & Brother, RONDOUT, ULSTER County, N.Y.

February 24, 1866

Of **Frank McGann**. When last heard from, about 8 years ago, he worked in a Brewery in BROOKLYN, N.Y. Any information will be thankfully received by his brother, **Richard McGann**, 114 Shippen Street, PHILADELPHIA, PA.

Of **John Smith**, a native of the Parish of BALLINTEMPLE, County CAVAN, Ireland. When last heard from, in July, 1863, he was in NEW ORLEANS, LA. Any information of him will be thankfully received by his cousin, **Philip Smith**, by writing to him to No. 512 WEST 22nd ST., NEW YORK CITY.

Of **Joseph Burns**, a boot and shoemaker by trade, a native of TULLOW, County CARLOW, Ireland. When last heard from, about six months ago, was in Everton Road, MANCHESTER, ENGLAND. Any information of him will be thankfully received by his sister, **Mary Burns** (now **Mrs. Morrissey**), by writing to her to No. 10 PRINCE STREET, NEW YORK CITY.

Of **John Doyle**, formerly of WHITAND BOY, Co WATERFORD, Ireland who resided in YONKERS, N.Y. about seven years ago. When last heard from he was in a western State Any information respecting him will be thankfully received by his brother, **Patrick Doyle**, Yonkers, N.Y.

Of **James Boyle**, a native of KILRUSH, County CLARE, Ireland, who arrived in Halifax, Nova Scotia, in 1853, and when last heard from in 1853, he was residing in BOSTON, MASS. Any information of him will be thankfully received by his brother, **Francis Boyle**, by writing to him to No. 34 Passaic Street, PATERSON, N.J.

Of **Michael Carroll**, aged about 30 years, a native of the City of KILKENNY, Ireland, who left NEW ORLEANS for ST. LOUIS in May, 1860. Any information concerning him will be thankfully received by his sister, **Mrs. Johanna Fitzpatrick**, New Orleans, Louisiana.

Of **Miles Sheehy**, from the Parish of PATRICK'S WELL, County LIMERICK, who left Ireland about 17 years ago. When last heard from, he was in the City of NEW YORK. Any information of him will be thankfully received by writing to his sister, **Bridget Sheehy**, WOODSTOCK Post Office, McHENRY County, State of ILLINOIS.

Of **Hannah Welsh**, or **Edward**, or **Morris Welsh**, of BRUFF, County LIMERICK, Ireland. When last heard from Hannah was in NEW YORK, with **Thomas Lee**, of CHERRY STREET, and Edward in OHIO, about eleven years ago. Any information of them will be thankfully received by their sister, **Ellen Welsh**, NEWTON Post-office, SUSSEX County, NEW JERSEY.

Of **Honora Fitzmaurice** of KILLARNEY, County KERRY, Ireland, who came to this country about 20 years ago. Particulars will be gratefully received by addressing **J.F. Towell**, PORTSMOUTH, OHIO.

Of **John Power**, son of the late **John Power**, Esq., of TRALEE, County KERRY, Ireland. When last heard from, about three years ago, he was in QUEENSTOWN, about taking passage for New York. Any information of him will be thankfully received by his brother, **James D. Power**, Surgeon General's Office, WASHINGTON, D. C., or by his sister **Kate**, by writing to the office of the Irish-American. Other papers, please copy.

Of **Timothy Thornton**, and his wife **Honorah Thornton**, maiden name, **Hays**, both natives of the Parish of LISTOWELL, County KERRY, Ireland. When last heard of were in NEW YORK CITY, or suburbs. Any information given of them will be thankfully received by their cousin, **Mary McElligott**, No. 39 Orange Street, ROCHESTER, MONROE County, N.Y

Of the whereabouts of **Thomas Stanley**, a native of the Parish of BALLINTUBBER, County ROSCOMMON, Ireland, who left the quay of BARNA, GALWAY, about 17 years ago for America. Information of him will be thankfully received by his uncle's son, **John Stanley**, No. 20 South St., PHILADELPHIA, PA. Boston and Western papers, please copy.

March 3, 1866

Of **John Sullivan**, who enlisted in the U.S. Army, 1st Delaware Vet. Vols, 3rd Brigade, [3]d Division, 2nd Corps. and who was mustered out of service previous to the 12th of July, 1865. Any information of him will be thankfully received by his father, **Humphrey Suchrue**, 109 MOTT STREET, N.Y. Washington papers, please copy.

Of **John Keogh**, of KILKENNY City, Ireland, who is supposed to be working in a bacon yard in the City of BROOKLYN, N.Y. Information of him will be thankfully received by his brother, **James Keogh**, at 2 Hartwell Street, FALL RIVER, MASS.

Returned Soldiers, Attention! - Can any one of you give any information as to death, discharge or present whereabouts of **William Kenely**, who, when last heard from, April 22, 1865, held a situation as Clerk in the U.S. Hospital at POINT LOOKOUT, MD. He is a native of the County LIMERICK, Ireland. Address **John J. Clancy**, 152 South Market St., NEWARK, N.J.

Of **John Hayes**, a native of PALLASKENRY, County LIMERICK, Ireland, who arrived in this country 17 years ago. When last heard from he was in the State of CONNECTICUT. Any information of him will be thankfully received by his brother, **Daniel Hayes**, care of **John Synan**, EAST TROY, N.Y.

Of **Timothy Maguire**, a native of the Parish of CAHARAGH, near SKIBBEREEN, County CORK, Ireland. He left STATEN ISLAND in Sept. 1861, and when last heard from, in October following, he was in the employment of **John P. Dillion**, contractor, ST. LOUIS, MO. He is supposed to have joined the Army. If this should meet the eye of Mr. Dillion or anybody who has made his acquaintance they would confer the greatest favor by making it known to his widowed mother, **Ellen Maguire**, STAPLETON Post Office, STATEN ISLAND, N.Y. St. Louis, Mo., papers, please copy.

Of **Ellen Hannon**, a native of YOUGHAL, County CORK, Ireland, who was married to **William Healy**, of the same place. When last heard from, five years ago, she resided at GREENPOINT, Long Island, N.Y. Information of her will be thankfully received by her brother, **Richard Hannon**, by writing to him in care of **Mr. John Kane**, 79 ROOSEVELT STREET, N.Y.

Of **Mrs. Rose Naughten** (maiden name **Rose Mannion**), a native of CASTLE BLEAKNEY, County GALWAY, Ireland. When last heard from, twenty-three years ago, she was living between Rice and Vine Streets, PHILADELPHIA, PA. Any information of her will be thankfully received by her niece, **Mary Waldron**, by writing to her to 148 7th AVENUE, between 20th and 21st Street, NEW YORK, in care of **Mr. Francis McCabe**. Philadelphia papers, please copy.

Of **Margret Coleman**, of the Parish of KILLOREN, County SLIGO, Ireland. When last heard of, 9 years ago, she was in JERSEY CITY, N.J. Any information of her will be thankfully received by her brother and sisters, **Owen, Bridget** and **Onney Coleman**, by addressing her brother Owen, at 115 WEST 15ᵗʰ STREET, NEW YORK.

Of **Mrs. Mooney** (formerly **Sabina McGuire**), of BURR, QUEEN's County, Ireland. She came to this country, with her husband about sixteen years ago. Any information of her may be left at the office of this paper, 29 Ann Street, New York, and will be gratefully received by her friends.

Of **Philip Shea**, a native of the Parish of STRADBALLY, County WATERFORD, Ireland. When last heard from he was in NEW YORK CITY, where he landed about October, 1865. Any information of him will be thankfully received by his brother, **John Shea**, at SPRINGFIELD, ILL.

Of **Arthur McKenna**, who left the County ARMAGH, Ireland, about 20 years ago. When last heard from he was in RHINEBECK, N.Y. Any information of him will be thankfully received by his sister, **Eliza McKenna**, Sweeny's Hotel, NEW YORK. Boston Pilot, please copy.

Of **James Gorman** and his son **James**, natives of the Parish of BELCARA, County MAYO, Ireland, who sailed from Liverpool, in March, 1847, in the ship *Great George*, and landed in Quebec. Any information of them will be thankfully received by his daughter, **Mary Gorman**, by addressing **Owen Hannan**, 24 MULBERRY ST., NEW YORK. Canada papers, please copy. [Appeared March 16, 1867 with the Parish name of BELLERA, County MAYOand Hannan's address changed to 52 MADISON ST.]

Of **Joseph Lavery**, a native of WARRENSTOWN, County DOWN, Ireland. When last heard from he was in PORT CHESTER, WESTCHESTER County, N.Y. Any information of him will be thankfully received by his sister, **Mary McNally** (now **McCabe**), at 59 EAST HOUSTON STREET, NEW YORK.

Of **John Moynihan**, of the County of KERRY, Ireland. When last heard from he was in NEW YORK CITY, in the Summer of 1858; also of his sisters, **Julia** and **Mary**, who resided in BOSTON in the same year. Any information of them will be thankfully received by **Mrs. Jane Davis**, of 19[6] MADISON ST., NEW YORK CITY, sister-in-law of the above-named John Moynihan. Boston *Pilot*, please copy.

Or **Timothy** and **Patrick Crowley**, natives of TRALEE, County KERRY, Ireland. When last heard from, two years ago, they were living in AMBOY, LEE County, ILL. Any information of them will be thankfully received by their brother, **Dan Crowley**, by writing to him in care of **John Crowley**, 17 WEST ST., NEW YORK.

March 10, 1866

Of **James Sullivan** who left NEW YORK last August. When last heard from, on the 15ᵗʰ of October, he was in SIDNEY, OHIO, working on a railroad. Information of him will be thankfully received by his wife, **Ellen A. Sullivan**, by addressing her in care of **James Agen**, 108 11ᵗʰ Street, between 1ˢᵗ and 2ⁿᵈ Avenues, NEW YORK. Sidney, Ohio, papers, please copy.

Of **Dennis Murphy**, a native of CLONAKILTY, County CORK, Ireland, who left DELAWARE County, PA., in the Summer of 1859, and is now supposed to be in the State of NEW YORK. Information of him will be thankfully received by his brother and sister, **Daniel** and **Ellen Murphy**, at No. 961 Franklin Street, PHILADELPHIA, PA.

Of **Thomas Ward**, stone mason by trade, a native of the Parish of BALLINACOUR[L]Y, near ORANMORE, County GALWAY, Ireland; also of his daughter **Mary**, who was married to **John Hanniffey**, of the same place. Thomas and Mary lived some time in LIVERPOOL, ENGLAND, the former having left for America 16 years ago, and the latter 11 years. When last heard from, 5 years ago, they were in MILLSBORO, KY. Information will be gladly received by his daughters, **Bridget** and **Elizabeth Ward**, in care of **Daniel Berrane**, Rockingham Place, ROXBURY, MASS [Appeared March 24, 1866 with "Thomas" changed to **John Ward.**]

Of **Michael Rielly**, a native of the County LONGFORD, Ireland. When last heard from, on the 25th of April, 1864, he was at ST. PAUL, MINN, and was supposed to have left for MONTANA TERATORY, VIRGINA CITY or CALIFORNIA. Any information of him will be thankfully received by writing to his father, **Patrick Reilly**, ANALOMINK Post Office, MONROE County, PA. California and St. Paul papers, please copy.

Of **John Kenny**, son of **James** and **Mary Kenny**, of LISNACUSHA, Parish of LECLOYNE, County LONGFORD, Ireland. When last heard from he resided at No. 37 Little Street, BROOKLYN, Long Island, N.Y. Any information of him will be thankfully received by his sister **Bridget**. Address **Frank P. Blair, Jun.**, ST. LOUIS, MO.

Of **John Flanagan** and wife, son of **James Flanagan**, a native of BALANDERRY, County MEATH, Ireland. He came to America 21 or 22 years ago, and when last heard from was in ORANGE County, N.Y. Information of him will be thankfully received by **James M.**, PORT RICHMOND, STATEN ISLAND, N.Y. [Appeared March 17, 1866, with John's father named as **Thomas Flanagan.**]

Of **Patrick Nealon**, who left LISTOWEL, County KERRY, Ireland, about 10 years ago. When last heard of he was in NEW YORK. Any information will be thankfully received by his brother, **Thomas Nealon**, 220 North Deleware [sic] Avenue, PHILADELPHIA, PA. [Appeared March 17, 1866, with Thomas identified as Patrick's nephew rather than his brother.]

By **James Connolly**, of his two sisters, **Ann** and **Bridget Connolly**, and three cousins, **John, Patt** and **Michael McDermott**, natives of RABBIT BURROW, BALLINLOUGH, Parish of CALLTULLOUGH, County ROSCOMMON, Ireland. Sister Bridget left home 8 years ago. When last heard from they were in ROCK ISLAND, State of OHIO. Any information of them will be thankfully received by their brother, **James Connolly** of NEWBURGH, ORANGE County, State of NEW YORK, who left home the 1st of February, 1866. Direct to **Mr. Patt Dunnegan**, Washington Iron Works, Newburgh, Orange County, N.Y.

March 17, 1866

Of **Thomas Bolgar**, who, when last heard from, was in SAN FRANCISCO, CAL., employed by **J. C. Bideman**, deceased, about seven months ago. Any information of him will be thankfully received by his father, **Bryan Bolgar**, by addressing **M. Dreelan**, No. 76 CANNON STREET, NEW YORK CITY.

Of **John Kelly**, bookbinder, late of DUBLIN; Ireland. Information will be thankfully received by his brother. Direct to **William Kelly**, General Post Office, WASHINGTON, D. C., to be kept until called for.

Of **Patrick Cassin**, of DUBLIN, who left QUEENSTOWN in May, 1863; was in employment at Linnoman & Co.'s Spirit Store, NEW YORK, for some time. His parents, not having heard from him for the last two years, would thankfully receive, through Messrs. Willmer & Rogers, New York, or direct to **Thomas Cassin**, 28 Talbot Street, DUBLIN, such information as would lead to his whereabouts.

Of **James Connors**, a native of SHANBALLYDUFF, Parish of CASHEL, County TIPPERARY, Ireland. When last heard of he was in PARIS, EDGAR County, ILLINOIS, working in a brick yard, eight years ago, and his letters were directed to **John Walsh**, Paris Post

Office, Edgar County, State of Illinois. Any information of him will be thankfully received by his mother and brothers, by addressing **Michael Connors**, 39 Spruce St., or **Stephen Connors**, 18 Elm Street, HARTFORD, CONN. Western papers, please copy.

Of **Thomas, Michael, Maria** and **Kate Phelan**, children of **James Phelan**, COOLINUNHA HOUSE, near BANSHA, County TIPPERARY, Ireland. They are supposed to be in CANADA. Information wanted by **Major Phelan**. Direct to the office of the Irish-American.

Of **William Moloney**, who sailed from Limerick twenty years ago, a native of LIMERICK, Parish of ARDAGH, Ireland. Any information concerning him will be thankfully received by **John** or **James Moloney**, Railroad Shop, ROCK ISLAND, CHICAGO, ILL.

Of **Bridget Dogherty**, a native of the City of LONDONDERRY, Ireland. She was married to a man named **James Dolan**, who was in the employment of **Mr. William Kendall** at the time of his death, fourteen years ago. Any information of her will be thankfully received by her sister **Margaret**. Direct to **Mrs. Margaret Moore**, FORT RILEY, KANSAS.

Of **Elizabeth Lawless**, who, when last heard from (seven years ago) was in NEW YORK. Any information respecting her will be thankfully received by her sister, **Margaret Lawless**, SPRINGFIELD, WALMOUTH County, WISCONSIN; or her mother, **Mary Lawless**, of MOORTOWN near NAVAN, County MEATH, Ireland. Boston *Pilot*, please copy.

Of **Michael, William, Mary** and **Catherine Wiley**, natives of BALLINASKEA, County MEATH, Ireland, who emigrated to America between the years 1838 and 1843. By writing to **Samuel Wiley**, C. and R.I.R.R. Freight Office, CHICAGO, they may communicate with their brother.

Of **Mary Cairney**, aged about forty-five years, daughter of **Charles Cairney** and **Alice O'Donnell**, of NEWTOWN, near DONEGAL, Ireland. She sailed from Donegal in a vessel called the *Susan Maria Brooks*, for New York, about twenty six years ago, and when last heard of was living in PHILADELPHIA. Any intelligence of her whereabouts will be thankfully received by **Captain Hugh Rogers**, 1,840 Catherine Street, Philadelphia, Pa.

Of **Patrick O'Conner**, harness maker by trade, a native of College Street, KILLARNEY, County KERRY, Ireland, who served his apprenticeship to **Samuel** and **John Huggard**, High Street, Killarney. When last heard from in 1860 he was in ST. LOUIS, MO. Any information of his whereabouts will be thankfully received by his mother, **Mary O'Conner**, or his brother, **Jeremiah O'Conner**, No. 71 Salem Street, BOSTON, MASS.

March 24, 1866

Of **Miss Margaret Lyons**, aged 16 years. When last heard from, two years ago, she was in ROCHESTER, NEW YORK. Any information leading to her whereabouts will be thankfully received by her aunt, **Miss Sophia Sullivan**, CHICAGO, ILLINOIS. Rochester papers, please copy.

Of **James Dillon**, of OLDBURY, ENGLAND. - When last heard from, he was with his brother-in-law, **John Wallas**, in BLOOMINGTON, ALLEGANY County, MARYLAND. Any information of him will be thankfully received by his brother, **Joseph Dillon**, by writing to him to SOUTH BERGEN Post Office, HUDSON County, NEW JERSEY.

Of **Honora Keough**, who left LIMERICK, Ireland, for America about ten years ago. When last heard from she was in the Town of ADELPHI UPPER CANADA. She married a man by the name of **John McGowern**. Any information of her will be thankfully received by her brother, **John Keough**, NASHUA, NEW HAMPSHIRE.

Of **Margaret, Ellen**, or **Mary Hand**, natives of RAFERAGH, County MONAGHAN, Ireland. When last heard from, they were in DETROIT, MICH. Any information of them will be thankfully received by their cousin, **Patrick Hand**, by writing to him to 1280 BROADWAY, cor. 33rd Street, NEW YORK.

Of **Ellen Perry**, of EDENBURT, Parish of LORIGAN, County of CAVAN, Ireland, who landed in New York about 7 or 8 years ago and has not been heard from since. Information of him [sic] will be thankfully received at the office of the Irish-American, 29 Ann St., New York, or to box 652, AKRON, SUMMIT County, OHIO.

Of **Anne Carrol**, who married **James Hall**, carpenter by trade, of MOUNTRATH, QUEEN's County, Ireland. She landed in New York in 1836. Also, of her brother, **Daniel Finley**, shoemaker, who came to this country from CARLOW in 1838. When last heard from he was serving in the Mexican Volunteers. Also, of **Robert** and **Finton Fitzpatrick**, stone masons, who left Mountrath in 1848. Information of any of the above parties will be thankfully received by **James Finley**, at 707 Hubble Street, off Fetywater, PHILADELPHIA, PA. Boston *Pilot*, please copy.

Of **Patrick Sullivan**, a native of ROUGHTY KENMARE, County KERRY, Ireland, who emigrated to NEW ORLEANS about seven years ago; heard, lately, he was living in WASHINGTON, D. C. Any information of him will be thankfully received by his mother, **Mary Sullivan** (maiden name **Murphy**), 44 OLIVER STREET, NEW YORK CITY. New Orleans papers, please copy.

March 31, 1866

If **Michael Moran**, who arrived in the *Harvest Queen* March 1, 1866, will apply to the Treasurer at Castle Garden, he will be sent to his brother in MASSACHUSETTS.

Of **Patrick Sweeny**, a native RAHORINE, Parish of BALLINROBE, County MAYO, Ireland. He went to ENGLAND in the year 1848, and left LIVERPOOL in September, 1852, and landed in New York in October, 1852. When last heard from, about seven years ago, he was in CINCINNATI, OHIO. Any information of him will be thankfully received by his brother, **Michael Sweeney**, CALLAO, MACON County, MISSOURI.

Of **James Carroll**, of BAGNALSTOWN, County CARLOW, Ireland, who arrived in New York about November last, from YUNSTON, ENGLAND. He worked for a time at NEWBURGH, N.Y. Any one knowing his present abode will confer a great favor by addressing his wife, **Bridget Carroll**, care of **Hugh McNally**, 220 Van Buren Street, CHICAGO, ILL.

Of **Robert Lynett**, a native of DROMORE WEST, County SLIGO, Ireland. When last heard from, five years ago, he was in MEMPHIS, TENN. Any information of him will be thankfully received by his brother, **Thomas Lynett**, by addressing **Michael O'Reilly**, No. 135 CROSBY STREET, NEW YORK CITY.

Of **Thomas** and **John McGuinness**, natives of NEWTOWN, DROGHEDA, County of LOUTH, Ireland. Thomas left Ireland 26 years ago, and John about 20 years. When last heard from they were in NEW JERSEY. Any information of them will be thankfully received by their niece, **Catherine Tierney**, and daughter of **Jane Tierney**, by writing to her to No. 70 BAXTER STREET, NEW YORK.

Of **Edmond Morrisey**, a native of BALLYGURIHEA, DONOUGHMORE, County CORK, Ireland, who emigrated to this country about 13 years ago. When last heard from, in November 1860, he was at No. 94 Pehoupitoulas Street, NEW ORLEANS. Any information of him, or of his wife (who is a native of the City of CORK) will be thankfully received by his brother, **Michael Morrisey**, in care of the Irish-American, 29 Ann Street, New York.

Of **John Keating**, a native of BANTRY, County CORK, Ireland. When last heard from, in 1859 or 1860, he was in NEW ORLEANS. Any information of him will be thankfully received by his brother, **William Keating**, MOUNT STERLING, BROWN County; ILLINOIS or his father, **Jeremiah Keating**, Bantry, County Cork, Ireland. Southern papers, please copy.

Of **James Horan**, brother to **Mary** and **Anne Moran**, of BALLYDRENNAN, County TIPPERARY, Ireland - He is a sawyer by trade. Any information of him will be thankfully received by **John Dowling**, 41 Union St., BROOKLYN, N.Y.

Of **Betty Riley**, a native of the County MONAGHAN, Ireland, and who left home about five years ago. When last heard from, a year ago, was living in NEW YORK. Any information of her will be thankfully received by her sister, **Bridget Riley**, by writing to **John McBride**, No. 30 Vine Street, SPRINGFIELD, MASS.

Of **Catherine Graham**, who left the Parish of KNOCKBRIDE, County CAVAN, Ireland, about the year 1845, and set sail from Liverpool for New York. When last heard from, she was in NEW YORK. Any information respecting her will be thankfully received by her sister-in-law, **Catherine Graham**, and family, at No. 34 John Street, PATERSON, N.J.

Of **Cornelius Griffin**, a native of LOWER LETTER, Parish of GLENBEAGH, County KERRY, Ireland. When last heard of he was near CORINTH, State of MISSISSIPPI, and is now supposed to be working on a railroad at MAD RIVER, OHIO. If this should meet his eye or any person knowing of his whereabouts, will confer great favor by informating his anxious mother, **Mrs. Ellen Griffin**, and his sisters, **Abby, Mary** and **Catherine**, now living in MEMPHIS, TENN. Direct to **Thos. J. Griffin**, No 12 St. Marin St., MEMPHIS, TENN.

April 7, 1866

Of **James Hayes**, of the County of WATERFORD, Ireland, who left his home in August 1859, for America, and when last heard from was in HALIFAX, NOVA SCOTIA. Any information regarding his whereabouts will be thankfully received by his brother, **Michael Hayes**, by addressing him in care of **Dennis Hacket**, YONKERS, WESTCHESTER County, N.Y.

Of **Thomas Kenny**, a native of the Parish of STAPLESTOWN, County KILDARE, Ireland, who came to America about ten years ago. Any information of him will be thankfully received by his brother, **Patrick Kenny**, SOUTH ORANGE, ESSEX County, State of NEW JERSEY.

Of **Eliza Farrel**, a native of the Parish of KILCOCK, County KILDARE, Ireland, who came to America about 3 years ago; she is a daughter of **James** and **Ann Farrel** (maiden name **McDonald**). Any information will be thankfully received by her brother **James Farrel**, SOUTH ORANGE, ESSEX County, N.J.

Of **Miss Mary Lathim**, who was married to **Dick Korough**, from the Parish of BALLINGARRY, County TIPPERARY, Ireland. When last heard from (eight years ago) she was in NEW YORK. Information will be thankfully received by her brother **Patrick Lathim**, AKRON, SUMMIT County, OHIO.

Of **Patrick Ryan**, son of **John** and **Mary Ryan**, of the City of LIMERICK, Ireland. When last heard from he was in NEW YORK CITY, after being mustered out of Battery G, of the

13th N.Y. Heavy Artillery, about six months ago. Any information of his whereabouts will be gratefully received by his brother, **Michael Ryan**, tailor, St. Joseph, Mo.

Of **Michael Finn**, a tailor by trade, from Kilfinane, County of Limerick, Ireland, who came to New York City about eight years ago. Any information of his whereabouts will be thankfully received by his brother, **John Finn**, by addressing him in care of **Michael Hannan**, Box 302, Crawfordsville, Indiana.

April 14, 1866

Of **James Meagher**, who came to this country in 1846, from the City of Cork to Quebec in the ship "*Eliza*," and was in the Mexican war. He enlisted in Buffalo, and he came back again and went to Rochester, September, 1848, and then went from Rochester to Buffalo to see after the government land that he was to get; also, **John Maher**, who enlisted in New York, May, 1855, in the United States army, for California, and has not been heard from since. Any information of them will be thankfully received by their sister **Margaret**, by writing to **Mrs. Margaret Hines**, Key Port, or the Office of the Irish-American. Boston *Pilot*, New Jersey, and Western papers, please copy.

Of **William O'Brien**, Parish of Ballyline, Co. Kilkenny, Ireland. When last heard from he was at work one mile from Wilmington, Delaware, in August, 1865. Any information of him will be thankfully received by his brother, by addressing, **L. Quinlan**, 27 Hickey Street, between Market and Chestnut Streets, Philadelphia, PA. Delaware and Baltimore papers, please copy.

Of **John** and **Patrick Ryan**, natives of Gortecarman, Parish of Killbakendry, County Galway, Ireland. Any information of them will be thankfully received by **P. Christy**, proprietor of the Sorrell House, 104 Front St., Wilmington, Del.

Of **John Walsh**, a native of Athlacca, County Limerick, Ireland who was in the State of Missouri six years ago. Any information of him will be thankfully received by his father, **Patrick Walsh**, in care of **John Ryan** No. 76 James St., New York. Also of **David Walsh**, a native of Charleville, County Cork, Ireland, who was supposed to be in New Orleans in April, 1865, on his way to Mobile, Ala. Any information of him will be thankfully received by his uncle, Patrick Walsh, by addressing him as above. [Appeared April 21, 1866 with the following added: "Western and Southern papers please copy."]

A Fenian wants information of **John Flanagan** and wife, natives of Ballenderry, County Meath, Ireland. When last heard from, were in Orange County, State of New York. Any information respecting them will be thankfully received by their nephew, **Jas. Malone**, Factoryville Post Office, Staten Island, New York.

April 21, 1866

Of **John Smithes** who left Ireland in June 1863. When last heard from he was working on the North Central Railroad. Any information of him will be thankfully received by **Henry Molony**, 103 East Broadway, New York.

Of **Michael Small**, who left Philadelphia one year ago. Any information of him will be thankfully received by his wife, **Mary Small**, No. 222 South Front Street, Philadelphia, Pa.

Of **William McLaughlin**, formerly spirit merchant in the Cowceddens, Glasgow, Scotland; or his nephew, **William**. Property is left in the family - Address 99 Avenue D, New York.

Of **Jane McCullagh**, a native of OMAGH, Co. TYRONE, Ireland. When last heard from, about ten years ago, resided in NEW YORK CITY. Any information of her will be thankfully received by her brother, **Peter McCullagh**, by writing to him to No. 9 WASHINGTON ST., NEW YORK CITY.

Of **Thomas, Hugh, Mary** and **Rose Keoghgan**, natives of the Parish of GRANARD, County LONGFORD, Ireland, who left LIVERPOOL, for NEW YORK in the month of March, 1861, and when last heard of were in the City of NEW YORK. Any information respecting them will be thankfully received by their brother **Philip Keoghgan**, in care of **Patrick Kennie**, No. 100 Marshall Street, PATERSON, N.J.

Of **Matthew Cunningham**, a native of the Townland of BRACKNEY, near KILKEEL, County DOWN, Ireland. When last heard from, about nine years ago, he was in CHICAGO, ILL. Any information of him will be thankfully received by his sister, **Elizabeth Cunningham** (now **Mrs. Sawey**), by writing to her in care of the **Rev. P. O'Neill**, St. Joseph's Church, Pacific St., BROOKLYN, Long Island, N.Y.

Of **Michael Clifton**, a native of BROHILL, Parish of CHARLEVILLE, County CORK, Ireland. When last heard from about five years ago, he was in ERIE, State of PENNSYLVANIA. Any information of him will be thankfully received by his brother, **Patrick Clifton** by writing to him to 442 EAST 13th STREET, NEW YORK CITY.

Of **John Glynny**, a native of the Parish of MILTOWN MOLBAY, County CLARE, Ireland, who left LASSELL, ILLINOIS, three years ago. Any information of him will be thankfully received by his brother, **Matthew Glynny**, GALESBURG Post Office, KNOX County, State of ILLINOIS.

April 28, 1866

Of **John Lee, Edward Lee, William Lee** and **Eliza Lee**, who left DUBLIN in 1848, for NEW YORK. They will hear something to their advantage by communicating with **Mr. John Harrison**, Book-binder, No. 13 Bishop Street, DUBLIN. American papers, please copy.

Of **John Boland**, formerly of BALLYMORE, County WESTMEATH, Ireland. He is supposed to be in MELBOURNE, AUSTRALIA. Any information of him will be thankfully received by his brother, **Lawrence Boland**, TROY, N.Y. Melbourne papers please copy.

Of **Michael Darcy**, a native of CORK City, who emigrated to this country in 1860 and when last heard of was serving in the U.S. schooner, *George Manghan*, South Atlantic Squadron. Any person or persons knowing of his whereabouts would confer a favor by addressing his sister, **Catherine Darcy**, in care of **John Teyhin**, 432 EAST 13th STREET, NEW YORK CITY. Boston *Pilot*, please copy. [Appeared May 5, 1866 with the surname Darcy changed to **Dacy**.]

Of **Patrick Malone**, a native of SUMMERHILL, County MEATH, Ireland. When last heard from he lived in NEW JERSEY; has been in America nine years. Any information of him will be thankfully received by his brother, **Christopher Malone**, No. 8 Dock Street, SCHENECTADY, NEW YORK.

May 5, 1866

Of **Mrs. Flynn** (maiden name **Ellen Power**), a native of the County WATERFORD, Ireland. When last heard from she was living in NEW YORK. Any information of her will be thankfully received by her niece's daughter, **Ellen Ryan**, No. 8 WEST 35th STREET, NEW YORK CITY.

Of **William McNamee**, who left Bond Street, City of BROOKLYN, in October, 1865, for HACKETSTOWN, N.J. Any information of him will be thankfully received by his wife,

Mary McNamee, or **Edward Donohue**, 108 Warren Street, BROOKLYN, N.Y. [Appeared under County WESTMEATH]

Of **John Cashman**, a native of the City of CORK, Ireland, who was in the English Navy, and afterwards the year 1860 or '61; then went to CALIFORNIA and has not been heard from since. Any information of him will be thankfully received by his loving brothers, **Jeremiah** and **Michael Cashman**. Address Jeremiah Cashman, 1,005 Washington Street, BOSTON, MASS. California papers, please copy. [Appeared May 12, 1866, with a line added.]

Of **Dr. Thomas F. Keher**, a native of CASTLEREA, County ROSCOMMON, Ireland. Any information of him will be thankfully received by his brother, **Tim**. Post Office, MONTREAL, CANADA. St. Louis papers please copy.

May 12, 1866

Of **Richard Dwyer**; he worked at the LAKES with his brother-in-law, **Michael Ryan**, about September or October, and is supposed to have left for the PENNSYLVANIA mines. His wife and children will for ever feel thankful to any person knowing his whereabouts and informing her by addressing **Nathaniel Hawke**, DOVER, N.J. Pennsylvania and Western papers, please copy.

Of **John McCarthy**, who sailed from Liverpool on the 1st of July, 1855; and his father, **Benjamin McCarthy**, and brother, **Robert McCarthy**, who came in the same vessel with him, and landed 5th of August. The father and Robert went home. John McCarthy's age was 20 years. Lived in MONTGOMERY, State of NEW YORK. Last letter sent in September, 1857; he was then in the State of ILLINOIS. Any information of him will be thankfully received by his father, Benjamin McCarthy, 2056 Sansom St., PHILADELPHIA, PA.

Of **Patrick J. Coffey**, son of the late **Matthew M. Coffey**, deceased, of BROOKFIELD, DUBLIN; also, of his son, **John Francis Coffey**, born in the year 1845. When last heard from, in 1853, Patrick was in NEW ORLEANS. Information regarding either of the above-named persons will be thankfully received by **Matthew J. A. Coffey**, No. 20 Wicklow Street, DUBLIN, Ireland; or, at the office of the Irish-American. New Orleans papers, please copy.

Of **Michael** and **Hugh Donnell**, or of **Johanna** and **Ellen Donnell**, who left the Parish of FETHARD, County TIPPERARY, about 18 years ago. When last heard from, about four years ago, they were living between ALBANY and TROY. Information of them will be thankfully received by **Lawrence Connell**, NEWBURGH, ORANGE County, State of NEW YORK. Troy papers, please copy.

Of **John Evans** and his two sons, **John** and **Michael**, and two daughters, **Mary** and **Margaret**, from GLEN, County LIMERICK, Ireland. When last heard from they were all in ST. JOHN, NEW BRUNSWICK. - Any information of them or their whereabouts will be thankfully received by their sister, **Kate Evans**, daughter of the above John Evans. Address, Kate Evans, MAHANY CITY, SCHUYLKILL County, PA. Canada papers, please copy.

Of **Owen Murphy**, from the Parish of TOGHER, County LOUTH, Ireland. When last heard from, in December, 1860, was in JONESVILLE, TEXAS. Any information of him will be thankfully received by his brother-in-law, **John Darby**, WASHINGTON, D. C.

Of **Ellen Fitzgerald**, daughter of **Michael Fitzgerald** and **Ellen Wallace**, of KILBREE, Parish of CLOYNE, Barony of IMIKELLY, Diocese of CLOYNE, County CORK, Ireland, who arrived in New York two weeks ago in the *City of New York*, from Queenstown, Ireland. Her uncle's son, **David Wallace**, of MIDDLETOWN, CONN., would be thankful to any one who would inform him of her whereabouts. Any information of her will be received at the office of this paper.

Of **John Cashman**, a native of the City of CORK, Ireland, who was in the English Navy, and afterwards came to the United States, and was in BOSTON in about the year 1860 or '61; then went to CALIFORNIA, and has not been heard from since. Any information of him will be thankfully received by his loving brothers, **Jeremiah** and **Michael Cashman**. Address Jeremiah Cashman, 1,006 Washington Street, Boston, Mass. California papers, please copy.

Of **Patrick Keal**, a native of the Parish of KILLMORE DALY, County GALWAY, Ireland, and husband of the late **Margaret Cunniffe**. When last heard from he was in GALWAY, and left for NEW YORK. Any information of him will be thankfully received by his brother-in-law, **C. Cunniffe**, by writing or calling at 21 Butler Street, BROOKLYN, L.I.

May 19, 1866

Of **Kate Fallon** and her three uncles, **Michael, James** and **John Doyle**, natives of BORTAL, County WICKLOW, Ireland, who came to this country 14 years ago. When last heard from they were in GAINSVILLE, PRINCE WILLIAM County, VA. Any information of them will be thankfully received by **Essy Fallon**, who came to this country five weeks ago. Address to 726 WASHINGTON STREET, NEW YORK CITY, in care of **Mr. John Mooney**. Western Papers, please copy.

Of **Michael** and **Patrick McArdle**, a native of the Townland of LOWRATH, near MULLACREW, County of LOUTH, Ireland, who emigrated to this country twelve or fourteen years ago. Information of them will be thankfully received by their brother, **Thomas McArdle**, who landed in this country last month, by writing to him in care of **Denis Byrns**, No. 24 27th Street, corner of K Street, WASHINGTON, D. C.

May 26, 1866

Of **Vall** and **Laurence Burns**, natives of the Parish of MULLAGH, County CAVAN, Ireland, who came to this country in 1849. When last heard from, in 1856, they were in WESTMORELAND County, PA. Any information respecting them will be thankfully received by their brother, **Matthew Burns**, at 43 Newark Street, NEWARK, N.J.

Of **Patrick McNamara**, a native of County CLARE, Ireland. When last heard from he was in MADORA, INDIANA. Any tidings of him will be thankfully received by his brother, **Michael McNamara**, in care of **Patrick Leddins**, DUNKIRK, N.Y.

June 2, 1866

Of **Daniel Leahy**, who, when last heard from, was in INEGOES, MARYLAND, Promotic Flotile Street. Information of him will be thankfully received by **John Leahy**, at MIDDLETOWN, CONN. [Appeared June 30, 1866, with additional information.]

Of **Patrick, Richard** and **Thomas White**, natives of the Parish of HOLEYWOOD, County DUBLIN, Ireland. When last heard of, were in RICHMOND, MILLICAN'S BEND and KIRK FERRY, LA. Any information of them will be thankfully received by their father, **Thomas White**, at Fifth St., GREENPOINT, Long Island, N.Y. Louisiana papers, please copy.

Of **Andrew, Margaret** and **Bridget Quinn**, from LOUGHPARK, near CASTLEPOLLARD, County WESTMEATH, Ireland, who left Ireland in the year 1832. When last heard from they were in NEW YORK. Information will be thankfully received by **Andrew Quinn**, at 126 Boyden St., NEWARK, N.J.

Of **John Grims**, of the Parish of LOUGHLIN, County ROSCOMMON, Ireland. Any information will be thankfully received by his brother, **Thomas Grims**, by addressing him in care of **George Spottiswoode**, ORANGE, N.J.

Of **Margaret Shanahan**, and of her sons and daughters - namely, **William, Morris, Mary, Ellen** and **Anne Shanahan**, natives of the Parish of KILLEA, County WATERFORD, Ireland, and is supposed to have arrived in this country in 1857. Any one knowing their whereabouts will confer a favor on the undersigned by addressing a few lines in care of **Rev. Father Gilligan**, LOCK HAVEN, CLINTON County, PA., for **Thomas Shanahan**.

Of **Margaret, Jane, Lebecca** and **James Turner**, of the Parish of LOWER PATONEY, Townland of ALLAHAMSEY, County TYRONE, Ireland. Information will be thankfully received by **Alice Turner**, at 247 10th AVE. cor West 26th Street.

Of **William Curtin**, only brother of **Mary Curtin** (deceased), of the County LIMERICK, Ireland. When last heard from, after said sister's death, he was in SYDNEY, AUSTRALIA, 19 or 20 years ago. Any information of him or his daughter **Mary**, or any of his family, will be thankfully received by his niece, only child of his sister Mary, who is now residing in GEORGETOWN, S.C. Address **Miss Margaret J. Moore**, Georgetown, S.C. Sidney papers, please copy.

Of **Jeremiah Dismond**, from the Parish of KILMURRY, County CORK, Ireland. Information of him will be thankfully received by his sister, **Johannah Dismond**, at 1,333 Filbert Street, PHILADELPHIA, PA.

Of **Kate Hanrohan**, daughter of the late **Andrew Hanrohan**, of LAHINCH, County CLARE, Ireland. She was married to a man named **John Sheahan**. When last heard from she was in SPRINGFIELD, MASS. Any information of her will be thankfully received by her brother, **Martin Hanrohan**, by writing to him to No. 26 OLIVER STREET, NEW YORK CITY.

June 9, 1866

Of **John Gamben**, of DUBLIN, Ireland. When last heard from he was at the CAPE of GOOD HOPE, on board a British man-of-war. Any information of him will be thankfully received by his brother, **Michael Gamben**, at Sanford Street, WILLIAMSBURGH, Long Island, N.Y.

Of **Edward Sherlock**, a native of the Town of TRIM, County MEATH, Ireland. When last heard from he was either in TROY, or LITTLE FALLS, N.Y. Any information of him will be thankfully received by **Silvester Halpin**, by writing to him to LINDEN Post office, NEW JERSEY.

Of **Johanna** and **Mary Corbett**, natives of NEWCASTLE WEST, County LIMERICK, Ireland, who are supposed to be at present in CANADA. Any information regarding them will be thankfully received by their brother, **Michael Corbett**, at 47 ESSEX STREET, NEW YORK CITY.

Of **John** and **James McMannis**, sons of **James McMannis**, of MILTOWN DRYLIN, County FERMANAGH, Ireland, who left the above-named place 14 years ago. Any information of them will be thankfully received by their sister, at 325 WEST 17th STREET, NEW YORK. St. Louis papers, please copy.

Of **Mary Doyle**, a native of BALLYDAUGHAN, Parish of BAGLINSTOWN, County CAVAN, Ireland, who sailed from Liverpool, about the month of April, 1856. When last heard from she was residing in the City of NEW YORK. Any information concerning her will be thankfully received by her sister **Kate**, and brother, **Patrick Doyle**. Address **Peter**

Tiernan, TOMPKINSVILLE, STATEN ISLAND, N.Y. [Appeared June 16, 1866 with County Cavan changed to County CARLOW.]

June 16, 1866

Of **Mary Bryan**, daughter of **Richard** and **Catherine Bryan**, of the Parish of BOOTERSTOWN, BLACKROCK, County DUBLIN, Ireland. When last heard from, in 1857, she was at **Mr. Sutton's**, 102 EAST 14th STREET, NEW YORK CITY; since then married; her husband's name not known by any of her friends. Information of her, dead or alive, will be thankfully received by her brother, **Richard Bryan**, 31 Sussex Street, JERSEY CITY, N.J.

Of **George Gillmer**, a native of the Parish of BALLINTOUGHER, County SLIGO, Ireland. When last heard from he was in NEW YORK CITY. Any information of him will be thankfully received by his sister **Mrs. Ann Wallace** (maiden name **Ann Gilmer**), by writing to her to BUFFALO Post Office, N.Y.

Of the certainty of day and date of the death of **Patrick Fitzpatrick**, a native of the Parish of DRUMBANE, near BALTURBET, County CAVAN, Ireland. He left BROOKLYN, N.Y., in 1854, for SAVANNAH, GA., and married a widow, named **Mrs. Mary Teerney**, in 1855, who died in the same year, and he left thence in 1856. He was a baker by trade, about 26 years of age when he left, 5 feet 8 or 9 inches high, sandy hair, blue eyes, a mark on his under lip, and was of drinking habits. It is understood he died in the State of LOUISIANA or in the City of NEW ORLEANS. Information will be thankfully received by his sisters, **Ellen** and **Mary Fitzpatrick**. Address **Mr. John Maleag**, Savannah, Ga.

Of **Michael Murphy**, of BALLYHUSKARD, near ENNISCORTHY, County WEXFORD, Ireland, who arrived at New York in the *City of Paris*. He will hear of his wife by addressing **Walter Cullen**, 418 North Tenth St., PHILADELPHIA, PA.

June 23, 1866

Of **Denis Flynn**, who left WOODBRIDGE, N.J., on the 2nd of February, 1864. Any information of him will be thankfully received by his wife, **Ellen Flynn**, RAHWAY, N.J.

Of **Kate McGeeney**, who left WASHINGTON, D. C., one year ago, for NEW YORK. Any information of her will be thankfully received by her sister, **Mary McGeeney**, at 16 Armsted Lane, Federal Hill, BALTIMORE, MD. Philadelphia and Boston papers, please copy.

Of **Mary Doran**, of BALBRIGGAN, County DUBLIN, Ireland. If any person knowing her whereabouts will communicate with **Ellen McGlew**, they will confer an everlasting favor. Please call on or address Ellen McGlew, in care of **James Poynan**, 430 WEST 32nd ST., NEW YORK CITY.

Of **William Miller**, a native of DUBLIN, Ireland; gardener by trade. He landed on 3rd of February, 1864. Information of him wanted by his uncle, **Robert Miller**, No. 32 Reyon St., BALTIMORE, MD.

Of **Ann Dougherty**, who came to this country about nine years ago. She lived a short time in BROOKLYN, N.Y., and then went to BRANDYWINE, PA. When last heard from she was in DELAWARE, four years ago. Also of her sister, **Catherine**, who landed in Philadelphia, Pa. about seven years ago; she also lived in Brandywine. The above were natives of the Town of GORTMULLEN, Parish of GLENCOFF, County of DONEGAL, Ireland. Any information respecting them will be thankfully received by their brother, **Owen Dougherty**, No. 131 Marshall St., NEWARK, N.J. Pennsylvania papers, please copy.

Of **Michael Fitzgerald**, a native of QUEENSTOWN, County CORK, Ireland. Information of him will be thankfully received by his brother, **John Fitzgerald**, PORTLAND, CONN.

Of **Lizzie Roach**, a native of SHANBALAMORE, County CORK, Ireland, who embarked for America, with her mother, in 1851. When last heard from she was living with one **John Treasey** in NEW YORK CITY. Any person giving information of her present residence will be amply rewarded. Information will be received by addressing her cousin, **P. McDonald**, 9 Washington Street, FALL RIVER, MASS. Other papers, please copy.

Of **Patrick McBrine**, a native of the Parish of NEWTOWN BUTLER, County FERMANAGH, Ireland. When last heard from, five years ago, he was in NEW YORK. Any information of him will be thankfully received by his sister, **Bridget McBrine**, by writing to her in care of **Mr. John Bard**, 11 WASHINGTON STREET, NEW YORK CITY.

June 30, 1866

Of **Thomas Lynch**, aged 25 years, who arrived in Philadelphia, Pa, in January, 1863 from LEEDS, YORKSHIRE, ENGLAND. When last heard from he was in NEWPORT, KY, in the year 1864. Information will be thankfully received by his brother, **Michael Lynch**, 403 North 16th Street, PHILADELPHIA, PA.

Of **Martin Meehan**, who sailed from New York for SAN FRANCISCO, CAL., in April, 1865. Any information of his whereabouts will be thankfully received by his brother, **Patrick Meehan**, SPRINGFIELD, MASS. California papers, please copy.

Of **Robert McCool**, a native of the Parish of ARMOY, County ANTRIM, Ireland, who came to this country about six years ago, and is now supposed to be living in, or convenient to, INDIANAPOLIS, INDIANA. Any information of him will be thankfully received by his brother, **Alexander McCool**, 1749 North Second Street, PHILADELPHIA, PA. Indianapolis papers, please copy.

Of **Michael O'Rourk**, a native PHILIPSTOWN, KING'S County, Ireland. Who landed in New York, December 24, 1865. Any information concerning him will be thankfully received by addressing a few lines to **William Molloy**, HONESDALE, WAYNE County, State of PENNSYLVANIA.

Of **Daniel Leahy**, a native of the Parish of DOUGLAS, BALLINCURRIG, County CORK, Ireland. He joined the United States Navy in September, 18, 1865, on board the *George Buckingham* steamer, and was at FORT FISHER on Christmas Day, 1865. When last heard from he was in the Potomac Flotilla, ST. INGOS, MARYLAND. Information of him will be thankfully received by his brother, **John Leahy**, MIDDLETOWN, CONN. California papers, please copy. [Appeared June 2, 1866 with less information.]

Of **Thomas Doran**, of the County KILKENNY, Ireland, by his brother, **William Doran**. Any information concerning him will be thankfully received at **Nicholas Quirk's**, 133 Plymouth Street, BROOKLYN, N.Y.

Of the whereabouts of **Catherine McDonald**, supposed to be in BROOKLYN, daughter of **Daniel McDonald**, formerly of NEWRY, and niece of **Patrick Collius**, late of BRIGHTON, ENGLAND, but a native of DARABY, County ARMAGH, Ireland. By applying to the **Rev. Thomas Kieran**, PORT RICHMOND, PHILADELPHIA, she will hear of something to her advantage.

Of **Simon** and **Catherine Houlihan,** and **Mary** and **Thomas,** also their mother, **Honor Houlihan,** late of KILLARD, County CLARE, Ireland. When last heard of, Mary and Simon were is OSWEGO, and Catherine at ROCKAWAY or NORTH HAVERSTRAW, State of NEW YORK. By applying to P.W.G., 29 BROADWAY, NEW YORK, they will hear of something to their advantage.

July 7, 1866

Of **Michael Clarke**, aged 14, a native of SYDNEY, near BELLVILLE, CANADA WEST, who strayed from his parents in BUFFALO, on the 10th of last April. Any information respecting him will be thankfully received by his father, **Patrick Clarke**, who works in a gravel pit near KILLBRECK Post-office, GREAT VALLEY, CAT[TARAUGUS] County, N.Y.

Of **James Keogh**, a native of BARRETTSTOWN, County KILDARE, Ireland, a butler by trade, who left home about twelve years ago. When last heard from he was on the FALL RIVER boats traveling. Any information of him will be kindly received by his nephew, **Lawrence Keogh**, by writing to him to WILLIAMSBRIDGE Post Office, WESTCHESTER County, N.Y.

Of **Eliza** and **Mary Nolan**, natives of BARRETTSTOWN, Parish of CARRIGH, County KILDARE, Ireland. When last heard from they were living in DERBY, CONN. Any information of them will be thankfully received by their brother, **Patrick Nolan**, by writing to him to No. 150 JANE ST., NEW YORK CITY.

Of **Peter McCahill** and wife, who came to this country about 25 years ago, and when last heard from were in NEW YORK State. They were natives of the Town of DRIMGORMAN, Parish KILLYMARD, County DONEGAL, Ireland. Any information of them will be thankfully received by their son, **Patrick McCahill**, at No. 1303 Moyamensing-avenue, PHILADELPHIA, PA. New York papers, please copy.

July 14, 1866

Of **Bernard McGovern**, who left the residence of his parents, in PHILADELPHIA, on the 14th of June; aged 14 wearing light coat and vest. Any information respecting him will be thankfully received by his parents, **Hugh** and **Catharine McGovern**, 1012 Richmond Street, Philadelphia, Pa. New York papers, please copy.

Of **William Illidge**, a native of the City of DUBLIN, Ireland. When last heard from he was in HAVERSTRAW, NEW YORK. Any information of him will be thankfully received by his brothers, **Richard** and **Thomas Illidge**, by writing to them to MORRISANIA Post-Office, State of NEW YORK.

Of **George Fleming**, a native of the Townland of BECTIVE, Parish of KILMESSIN, County MEATH, Ireland. When last heard from, in June, 1862, he was in FORT HAMILTON, Long Island. Information of him will be thankfully received by his son, **Thomas Fleming**, by writing to him in care of Lynch, Cole & Meehan, 29 Ann Street, New York.

Of **John O'Rourke**, a native of CALLEN, County KILKENNY, Ireland. When last heard from he was in MILWAUKEE, WISCONSIN. Any information of him will be thankfully received by his cousin, **William Butler**, at 265 WEST 28th STREET, NEW YORK. Western papers, please copy.

Of **Micheal** [sic] **Maloy**, a native of the County KILKENNY, Ireland. When last heard from about six months ago, he was in ALLEGHENY County, PENNSYLVANIA. Information will be received by his sister **Alice** by addressing her in care of **M. P. Mason**, 39 NASSAU STREET, NEW YORK CITY. [Appeared July 21, 1866 with the surname **Maloy** changed to **Malay**.]

July 21, 1866

Of **Margaret Power**, a native of HOLY CROSS, County TIPPERARY, Ireland, who married a man of the name of **Francis**. When last heard from was living near RIDGE STREET, NEW YORK CITY. Information of her will be thankfully received by her sister, **Mary McCray**, by writing to her to GOSHEN, CAPE MAY County, NEW JERSEY.

Of **Ellen Donovan**, a native of the Parish of KILGARVAN, County KERRY, Ireland. When last heard from, in March last, was in GERMANTOWN, PA. Information of her will be thankfully received by her cousin, **Timothy Donovan**, by writing to him to 326 EAST 54th STREET, NEW YORK CITY.

Of **Thomas** and **John O'Maley**, natives of STOKEFIELD, Parish of SHANAGOLDEN, County of LIMERICK, Ireland, who emigrated to this country about sixteen years ago. When last heard from John was in PHILADELPHIA, in '64; previous to that time was for some years in NEW ORLEANS. Information respecting them will be gratefully received by their brother, **William O'Maley**, by addressing **Patrick Sloan**, Box 396, BRIDGEPORT, State of CONNECTICUT. Philadelphia and New Orleans papers, please copy.

Of **Nicholas Conner**, a native of the Parish of LOUTH, County of LOUTH, Ireland, who arrived in the steamship *Caledonia*, last April. Information of him will be thankfully received by his sister, **Catherine Power**, by writing to her in care of **Mr. D. J. Willett's**, FLUSHING, Long Island.

July 28, 1866

Of **Mrs. Hanora Brennan**. When last heard from (about 15 months since) she wrote that she was then living with her friends in HANNIBLE, MO., but said she was going to ST. LOUIS. Her husband died last August, at his mother's residence, in the old country. If Mrs. Brennan is living she will please write to **Mary Brannen**, PHILADELPHIA Post-Office. Hannible, Mo., papers, please copy.

Of **Bridget Riely**, a native of the Townland of CLOONRABER, Parish of CURRY, County SLIGO, Ireland. When last heard from (about 8 years ago), she was in NEW YORK. Information of her will be thankfully received by her sister, **Margaret Reily**, by addressing **Thomas Dunne**, BREWSTER STATION, PUTNAM County N.Y.

Of **Edward McGettigan**, a native of GLENERERAUGH, Parish of MEEVAGH, County DONEGAL; he left home about 11 years ago, and when last heard from (in 1861), he was in NEW ORLEANS, LA. Information will be thankfully received by addressing **Anthony McGarvey**, 1707 Pine St., PHILADELPHIA, PA.

Of **Thomas Flynn**, of BALLYBRADO, near CAHIR, County TIPPERARY, Ireland. Information of him will be thankfully received by addressing J.O.B., office of the Irish-American, 29 Ann St., New York.

August 4, 1866

Of **Bridget Gorman**, a native of the Parish of KILLARD, County CLARE, Ireland, who came to this country about 15 years ago, and was married to **James O'Loughlin**. When last heard from she was in the State of NEW YORK. Information of her will be thankfully received by her brother, **John Gorman**, NORTH ADAMS, MASS.

Of **Julia Boland**, a native of MUNSTREVEN, County KILDARE, Ireland. Information of her will be thankfully received by her brother, **Patrick Boland**, who is lately landed, and is stopping at No. 78 TRINITY PLACE, NEW YORK. [Appeared Aug. 11, 1866 with different contact information.]

Of **Michael Walsh**, a native of the Townland of AHANISH, Parish of ROBERTSTOWN, County of LIMERICK, Ireland, who emigrated to this country, from ENGLAND, in 1849 or 1850. When last heard from he was in WELTON, CLINTON County, IOWA. Any information as to his whereabouts will be thankfully received by his brother, **Patrick Walsh**, by addressing in care of the Editors of the Irish-American, 29 Ann Street, New York, or No. 2 Washington Square, WORCESTER, MASS. Boston Pilot, please copy.

August 11, 1866

Of **John Denehy**, a native of the City of CORK, Ireland; tailor by trade. He arrived in New York about 25 years ago. Any information of him will be thankfully received by his brother, **Michael**, and his sister, **Martha Denehy**, by writing to them to No. 47 CROSBY STREET, NEW YORK CITY.

Of **Patrick Boland**, a native of MONASTREVAN, County KILDARE, Ireland. Any information of him will be thankfully received by his sister, **Julia Boland**. Call on **Peter Black**, 85 FRONT STREET, NEW YORK. Pennsylvania and New Jersey papers, please copy. [Appeared Aug. 4, 1866 with different contact information.]

Of **Thomas Travers**, shoemaker, of the County GALWAY, Ireland; supposed to be in CANAAN, State of CONNECTICUT. He will confer a favor on a friend by sending his address to J. T., office of the Irish-American, 29 Ann Street, New York. Connecticut and other papers, please copy.

Of **Patrick Laherty**, who left KILKENNY, some 17 years ago, for the United States, in the ship *Meteor* (supposed). When last heard of he left NEW YORK for some of the western States. Information of him will be thankfully received by his mother, **Rose Laherty**, care of **David Davis**, No. 11 FRANKFORT STREET, "Leader" office, New York.

Of **Thomas, David** and **Denis O'Keeffe**, natives of the Parish of EFFIN, County LIMERICK, Ireland. When last heard from Thomas resided in CHARLESTON, S.C. Any information of them will be thankfully received by their nephew, **Henry O'Keeffe**, (son of **Jeremiah**,) by writing to him to 194 Partition St., BROOKLYN, L.I.

August 18, 1866

Of **John Fulton**, who came from Ireland, and went to CANADA 21 years ago. Any information of him will be thankfully received by his daughter, **Sally Fulton**, 1439 Marshal Street (KENSINGTON DISTRICT), PHILADELPHIA, PA.

Of **Jane Nolen**. When last heard from, three years ago, she was living in the City of DUBLIN, Ireland. Information of her will be thankfully received by her parents, **Michael** and **Wilhelmine Nolen**, living at 79 Forrest Street, BALTIMORE, MD.

Of **Michael Roach**, son of **William Roach**, carpenter, Gilverts, or any of his family. They came to this country about 12 years ago, from LONDON. His aunt, **Margaret Birdseye**, would like to hear from him. Write to 156 Willow Street, PHILADELPHIA.

Of **William McLoughlan**, a native of the County DONEGAL, near BALLYBOFAY, Ireland. When last heard from, about four years ago, he was in BOSTON, MASS. Information of him will be thankfully received by his niece, **Mary Marley**, 244 Marshall St., BROOKLYN.

Of **Rosanna Horan**, a native of the Parish of GILLEN, KING'S COUNTY, Ireland, who emigrated to America about 16 years ago. When last heard from, in October, 1865, she was living in WEST TROY, N.Y. If this should meet the eye of her, or any of her brothers, **Kieran, Patrick,** or **John Horan**, or any one who knows of their whereabouts, they will confer a favor by writing to her daughter, **Maria Mealy**, in care of her uncle, **Michael Mealy**, 959 Somerset Street, above Belgrade Street, PORT RICHMOND, PHILADELPHIA, PENN.

Of **Patrick Herlihy**, tailor, a native of INCHABEG, County CORK, Ireland. When last heard from, in March, 1857, he was in ST. LOUIS, MO. Any one knowing of his whereabouts would confer a favor by dropping a line to his nephew, **William Hallissy**, Sweeny's Hotel, CHATHAM ST., NEW YORK. Southern and Southwestern papers, please copy.

Of **Mary Bennett**, a native of the Parish of FEDAMORE, County LIMERICK, Ireland, daughter of **Edmond Bennett** and **Bridget Moore**. When last heard from she was in the City of NEW YORK. Any information of her will be thankfully received by her brother, **David**, by writing to **William Bennett**, GERMANTOWN, PHILADELPHIA, PENN.

August 25, 1866

Of **Patrick Joyce**, aged about twenty years, who left his home in TORONTO, C.W., in the latter part of July, 1863. When last heard from (about two years ago) he was in CINCINNATI. Any information of him will be thankfully received by his grieved mother, **Bridget Joyce**, ALLIANCE, STARKE Co., OHIO. Cincinnati and Western papers please copy.

Of **Hugh Hart**, a native of BUNDORAN, Parish of INNISMACSAINT, County DONEGAL, who left Ireland last April. Any information of him will be thankfully received by his brother, **John Hart**, at No. 19 Benton Street, PHILADELPHIA, PA. Boston papers, please copy.

of **Patrick Reynolds**, of CULFURE, between DROGHEDA and CULLEN, County LOUTH, Ireland. When last heard from, which was previous to the war, he was residing on LONG ISLAND. Any intelligence of him will be thankfully received by **Ellen McGlew**. Please call on or address Ellen McGlew, in care of **James Poynon**, No. 430 WEST 32nd STREET, NEW YORK.

Of **Maurice Walsh**, a native of the Town of TRALEE, County KERRY, Ireland. When last heard from, 8 months ago, he was sick in hospital, at NORFOLK, VA. Any information of him will be thankfully received by his brother and sister, **Patrick** and **Mary Walsh**, by writing to them to No. 283 WEST 27th ST., NEW YORK. Canadian papers, please copy.

Of **John Leary**, a native of SKIBBEREEN, County CORK, Ireland. He left home about 15 years ago. When last heard from, about one year ago last May, he resided in BROWN County, ILLINOIS. Please direct to **Florence Leary**, BLOSSBURG, TIOGA County, PENN.

September 1, 1866

Of **Patrick Murray**, a native of the County WATERFORD, Ireland, who left SPRINGFIELD, ILL., in November, 1859. When last heard from he was in the State of TEXAS. Any information of him will be thankfully received by his nephew, **Mathew Clancy**, Springfield, Ill.

Of **Mary, William, Anne** and **Thomas Cline**, who lived in the Parish of KILLOW, and recently MOYDOW, and in the Townlands of BOHER and CLONKER, County LONGFORD, Ireland. Their mother, sister and two brothers emigrated to America in the Spring of 1847, and left the above named brothers and sisters after them in Ireland, and have not since heard from them. If this should meet the eye of any person from the above named place, who could give any information of them, either in Ireland or America, or of their sister, **Catherine Cline**, who was in NEW ORLEANS in 1849, an everlasting favor would be conferred on their brothers, **Peter** and **John Cline**, by addressing a letter to them at SAN FRANCISCO, CALIFORNIA, Washington St., between Leavenworth and Hyde.

Of **Ellen, Patrick, Catherine**, and **Edmund Sweeny**, of LISTERICK, Parish of TRALEE, County KERRY, Ireland. The first named embarked March 17, 1846, from the cove of Cork for New York; Patrick and Catherine sailed from Tralee to Baltimore, Md., in the "*Jennie Johnson*," in 1848; and Edmund in the same vessel, and from and to the same ports, May 10, 1849. Any information of their whereabouts will be thankfully received by their nephew, **Thomas O'Shanahan**, care of **Philip J. Ryan**, 157 Main St., SPRINGFIELD, MASS.

Of **John Barry**, a native of the Townland of GLENOE, County KERRY, Ireland. When last heard from he was in MONTGOMERY, N.Y. Any information of him will be thankfully received by his sister, **Hanora Barry**, by writing to her to the corner of Pierce and Atlantic Avenues, BROOKLYN, L.I.

September 8, 1866

Of **James McCabe**, and his wife **Margaret McCabe**. When last heard from they were on the Hempfield Railroad, twenty miles from PITTSBURGH. Information of them will be thankfully received by **Sylvester Kennedy** and his wife, **Mary Kennedy**. Address Sylvester Kennedy, SUNPRARIE, DANE County, WISCONSIN.

Of **Andrew, Mary** and **Sarah Dougherty**, who left Ireland as follows: - Andrew about 14 years ago, Mary about 12, and Sarah about 10, for PHILADELPHIA, PENN., and when last heard from was in LANCASTER, PENN. Information respecting them will be thankfully received by their sister, **Ann Dougherty**, No. 38 Passaic St., PATERSON, N.J.; or by **Bernard O'Neill**, Justice of the Peace, No. 81 Congress Street, PATERSON, N.J.

Of the whereabouts of a young man named **James Gill**. He left WEXFORD, Ireland, about eleven years ago, and followed the sea. Any information concerning him will be thankfully received by his anxious father, **Patrick Gill**, No. 510 South Front St., PHILADELPHIA, PA.

Of **Kate Fox**, who came to NEW YORK in March, 1862. If any person knowing her address will please send it to **Joseph Young**, ALBIA, MONROE County, IOWA, she will hear of a friend. [Appeared under County MEATH]

Of **Thomas Coleman**, a native of the Parish of CLOUNBEG, County TIPPERARY, Ireland, who has been in this country eight years. Two years ago he went to NASHVILLE, TENN., and after that went to the CLARKSVILLE Iron Works, KENTUCKY. Information of him will be thankfully received by his brother, who arrived here on the 7th of August. Address **John Coleman**, 23rd Street, corner 5th Avenue, GOWANUS, BROOKLYN.

Of **John** and **Cornelius Maguire**, natives of the Town of THURLES, County TIPPERARY, Ireland. John left a wife and two children in LEWISTON eight years ago, and has not been heard from those four years, and then he was supposed to be in MEMPHIS, TENNESSEE; his brother, Cornelius, is now supposed to be in CINCINNATI. Information concerning them will be thankfully received by their sisters, **Sarah** and **Bridget Maguire**, LEWISTON, MAINE.

Of **Patrick D. Mahon**, from GLANAFOSHE, CLARE TUAM, County GALWAY, Ireland, by his sister, **Sarah**, at No. 13 STANTON STREET, NEW YORK; or by H. D. Glynn, Castle Garden.

Of **James Moloney**, a native of NEWCASTLE WEST, County LIMERICK, Ireland, who emigrated to this country about the year 1852. When last heard from was in NEW YORK CITY. Information as to his whereabouts will be thankfully received by his nephew, **Denis Moloney**, by addressing in care of **Patrick Walsh**, for Denis Moloney, No 2 Washington Square, WORCESTER, MASS.

Of **Thomas** and **John Sheridan**, of TERMANPECKIN, County LOUTH, Ireland. When last heard from Thomas was in NEW YORK, and John in NEW ORLEANS. Information of them will be thankfully received by their brother, **Peter Sheridan**, at 316 Battery Street, SAN FRANCISCO, CALIFORNIA.

September 15, 1866

Of **Julia Hughes**, who landed in New York on the 6th July, per ship "*Universe.*" When last heard of she was living as a servant with **Mr. P. Cogan**, 109th STREET, NEW YORK.

Any information of her would be thankfully received by **Thomas Maddon**, ORRSVILLE. P.O., ARMSTRONG County, PA

Of **Maria Casady**, daughter of **James Casady** and **Sarah Dooras**, or of her sister **Margaret**, from the County LONGFORD, Parish of KILLOW, Ireland. Call at No. 3 HANOVER STREET, NEW YORK, office of **S. B. Cole.**

Of **Thomas Ward**, a native of GREENAN, DRUMCONRA, County MEATH, Ireland. He left BELFAST about five years ago and came to NEW YORK. When last heard of he was living with a **Mr. Boyer**, of LONG BRANCH, N.J. He is supposed to have joined the army. He is about 2[4] years of age. Any information of him will be thankfully received by his brother, **Joseph Ward**, 155 AVENUE C, NEW YORK.

Of **Julia Donovan**, (maiden name, **Julia Coughlin**,) a native of CLONALTY, Parish of CASTLEVENTRY, County CORK, Ireland. Any information of her will be thankfully received by her brother, **John Coughlin**, SOUTHPORT, CONN. When last heard of was in ALBANY, N.Y.

Of **Daniel Lane**, of GURTEENNACLOONA, Parish of CASLTEMAGNER, County CORK, Ireland. He left home about twelve or thirteen years ago. When last heard from (last November,) he was married and resided in BALTIMORE, MD. Any person knowing of his whereabouts will confer a great favor by addressing a few lines to his brother, **Anes Lane**, care of **Michael Judge**, LAWRENCE, MASS.

Of **John McHugo**, a native of ATHLONE, County ROSCOMMON, Ireland, a carpenter by trade. Supposed to have been a member of the Jackson Guard, NEW ORLEANS. Any information concerning him will be thankfully acknowledged by his nephew, **John Joseph Monaghan**, corner Turk and Mason sts., SAN FRANCISCO, CALIFORNIA. New Orleans papers, please copy.

September 22, 1866

Of **John Ryan**, who sailed from Dublin on the 11th of April, 1863, in the ship *St. Andrews*, for America. When last heard from he was in WILL County, ILLINOIS. Information will be received by **William Mason**, Irish-American office, 29 Ann Street, New York.

Of **Simon Buckley**, of BALLYDENANE, Parish of KILMIHEL, County CLARE, Ireland. When last heard from, 10 or 12 years ago, he was living in BROOKLYN, N.Y. Boot and shoemaker by trade. Any information concerning him will be thankfully received by his brother, **Thomas Buckley**, living in GORDONSVILLE, ORANGE County, VIRGINIA.

Of **John McCullough**, a native of the County TYRONE, Ireland. When last heard from he was at OAK HILL, PEORIA County, ILLINOIS. Information of him will be thankfully received by his wife, **Hanora McCullough**, by writing to her in care of **Dr. Carey B. Gamble**, 198 North Howard Street, BALTIMORE, MARYLAND.

Of **John Kearins**, a native of the Parish of BOYLE, County of ROSCOMMON, Ireland, who left home three years ago. When last heard from he was in RICHLAND County, OHIO. Information of him will be thankfully received by writing to his sister and brother-in-law, **Bartley Trustnan**, NORTH ORANGE, ESSEX County, N.J.

September 29, 1866

Of **James Colquin**, a member of the 7th N.H., who died in hospital at LAKE CITY, FLA. It is supposed his mother resides in CANADA. Any information will be thankfully received by **Mrs. D. Jones**, LAKE CITY, FLA.

Of **Bridget Breheny**, a native of MOUNT-BELLEW, County GALWAY, who arrived in Quebec about fourteen years ago. Any information of her will be thankfully received by her brother, **Michael Breheny**, by writing to him in care of **William Nolan**, 118 Railroad Avenue, JERSEY CITY, N.J.

Of **Michael Keenan**, who emigrated to NEW YORK six years ago last June, from CASTLETOWN, near MANORHAMILTON, County LEITRIM. Two years ago he had a liquor store on the corner of Hicks and Sacket Streets, BROOKLYN. When last heard of he worked in a lead factory, cor. DUANE and ELM STREETS, NEW YORK. Any information of him will be thankfully received by his brother, **Patrick Keenan**, at **John Cleary's**, 517 Columbia Street, BROOKLYN.

October 6, 1866

Of **James** and **Patrick Costelloe**, late of Butts Green, City of KILKENNY, Ireland. When last heard of James was in NEW ORLEANS; he served in the U.S. Army, from which he now draws a pension. The last heard of Patrick, about 10 months ago, he was in SPRINGFIELD, ILLINOIS. Any communication as to their whereabouts will be thankfully received by their brother, **Richard**, and sister, **Anne**, at 284 SEVENTH-AVENUE, cor. 28th St., NEW YORK. New Orleans and Illinois papers, please copy.

Of **Mrs. James Power**, (maiden name, **Margaret Malone**,) a native of the Parish of ROSBARACON, County KILKENNY, Ireland, who emigrated to QUEBEC about 15 years ago. When last heard from, about 7 years ago, she lived with her husband and family in COBURGH, CANADA WEST. Any information of her or her husband will be thankfully received by writing a few lines to her brother, **Michael Malone**, HOOKSTOWN P.O., BALTIMORE CO., MD.

Of **James McGinness**, a native of KILLYBEGS, County DONEGAL, Ireland. When last heard from, 8 months ago, he was pedling in the State of MICHIGAN. Any information of him will be thankfully received by his sister, **Catherine**, by writing to her at No. 80 Talcot St., HARTFORD, CONN. Boston papers, please copy.

October 13, 1866

Of **Christopher Byrne**, who left Dublin in September, 1850, in the ship *"Enterprise."*- Any information of him will be thankfully received by **Charles Quigley**, 25 Augusta Street, NEWARK, N.J., for his brother **William**. Mobile and San Francisco papers, please copy.

If **Margaret McCarthy**, who for several years was a servant at No. 9 Lower Ormonde St., DUBLIN, and who, when last heard of, in March, 1866, was in TOLEDO, OHIO, will send her address to the office of the Irish-American, she will hear of something to her advantage.

Of **Ann McKenna** (maiden name, **Ann Walsh**) of KILCARN, Parish of NAVAN, County MEATH, Ireland, who came to this country in 1848 or '49. Her cousin, **Thomas Reilly,** would be glad to hear from her. Address, Thomas Reilly, UNION HILL, P.O., BERGEN, N.J.

Of **Stephen Ryan**, a native of the Parish of CASTLECONNELL, Townland of LISHNAGRINE, County LIMERICK, Ireland, who emigrated to this country on the 6th of March, 1861. Any information of him will be thankfully received by his wife, **Ellen Kelley**, a daughter of **Michael Kelley**, from DRUMBANNA. Direct to **John Fleming**, PIEDMONT, MINERAL County, WEST VIRGINIA.

Of **Michael McCool**, a native of CULLINBUY, near the Town of DONEGAL. He left Ireland in March, 1864, for BOSTON. When last heard from he was in ILLINOIS.

Information of him will be thankfully received by his brother-in-law, **George Boyle** by writing to him in care of **Anthony O'Donnell,** No. 7 MARION STREET, NEW YORK CITY. Illinois papers, please copy.

October 20, 1866

Of **John Rogan**, from the Co. MEATH, Ireland, and **Ann Smith**, of DONNOVER, Ireland. Any information of them will be thankfully received by **Bridget McGennis**, care of **A. Davidson**, BRIDGEPORT, CONN.

Of **Patrick Hore**, of GALBALLY, County LIMERICK, Ireland, who left home in November, 1863. When last heard from he was in FRANKLIN, OHIO. Any information of him will be thankfully received by his brother, **Maurice Hore**, by writing to him in care of **Mr. Peter Garvey**, 488 10th AVENUE, NEW YORK. Southern and Western papers, please copy.

Of **James** and **Michael Byrns**, natives of the County MONAGHAN, Ireland. When last heard from, James was in CHICAGO, and Michael is presumed to be in CINCINNATI, OHIO. Information of either of them will be thankfully received by their brother, **Patrick Byrns**, care of **Michael Flood**, Catholic Bookseller, 727 Market Street, SAN FRANCISCO, CAL.

October 27, 1866

Of **William C. Brown**, who left home March 30th, 1865. He generally followed the sea; his occupation was fireman. The last vessel he was on was the steamship *Ashland*. When last heard from, May 7th, 1865, he was boarding with **Mr. John Connell**, No. 146 LIBERTY ST., NEW YORK CITY. Any information of him will be thankfully received by addressing a few lines to his mother, **Mrs. Catherine C. Brown**, GEORGETOWN Post Office, D. C.

Of **Patrick Leech**, a native of TERMONFECKIN, County LOUTH, Ireland, who sailed for Australia in June, 1862. When last heard from he was convenient to the City of MELBOURNE. Any information of him will be thankfully received by his brother, **James Leech**, DUDLEY, HUNTINGDON County, PA. Melbourne and Australian papers, please copy.

Of **John Kenniley**, a native of KILBEHENNY, County CORK, Ireland. When last heard from, about 2 years ago, he lived in NEW YORK CITY. Also of **Simon Kenniley's** children. Any information concerning them will be thankfully received by his nephew, **John Kenniley**, who at present resides in SCHENECTADY, N.Y.

Of **John O'Neill**, of the Parish of EFLIN, County LIMERICK, Ireland, who arrived in this country about twenty-two years ago. When last heard of was in the neighborhood of PITTSBURGH, PENNSYLVANIA; supposed to be at present in the neighborhood of WASHINGTON, D. C. Any information of him or his family will be thankfully received by his brother, **Florence O'Neill**, 21 PELL STREET or 128 PEARL STREET, NEW YORK CITY.

Of **David Fitzgerald**, a native of the Parish of CAHERDANIEL, County KERRY, Ireland, who went to AUSTRALIA about 11 years ago, and from there to America. When last heard from, in December, 1865, he was in ST. LOUIS, MO. Any information concerning him will be thankfully received by his brother, **Thomas Fitzgerald**, City of LYNN Post Office, MASS. Missouri papers, please copy.

Of **Peter Tully**, a native of COOTEHILL, County CAVAN, Ireland. When last heard from, in March last, he was living in the State of NEW JERSEY. Any information of him will be thankfully received by his brother, **Charles Tully**, No. 126 Fifth St., WILLIAMSBURGH, L.I., N.Y.

November 3, 1866

Of **Patrick, Thomas, Alice, Margaret** and **Jane Conner**, natives of MULLAPHIN, County MEATH, Ireland, who came to this country about twelve or fifteen years ago. They lived in ALEXANDRIA at that time, Patrick being then married. Information of them will be thankfully received by their friend, **Walter Casey**, by addressing him at MADISON, MORRIS County, N.J. Southern papers, please copy.

Of **Thomas Corcoran**, who left DROGHEDA, County LOUTH, Ireland, four years ago, and went to BUFFALO, N.Y. Information of him will be thankfully received by his sister, **Mrs. Jane Coony**, No. 70 3rd AVENUE, NEW YORK. [Appeared Nov. 10, 1866 with some different information.]

Of **Catharine English**, and **Nancy Malone**, wife of **Patrick English**. Catharine came to this country about 4 years and Nancy about 13 ago, both being from the Parish of LOUTH, County LOUTH, Ireland. When last heard of, about two years ago, they were in the State of MICHIGAN. Information will be thankfully received by their brother-in-law, **Peter Lyons**, WEST STOCKBRIDGE, BERKSHIRE County, MASS. Western papers, please copy.

Of **Catharine** and **Ellen White**, of the Parish of BALLANUDE, near BANDON, County CORK, Ireland. When last heard from they were living in BOSTON, and were married to men of the name of **Martin**. Information of them will be thankfully received by their brother **John's** daughter, **Mary White**, care of **J. Hagy**, 416 North Second St., PHILADELPHIA, PA.

Of **Michael Costelo** and **John** and **Patrick Rohan**, who left the Townland of KISHIKIRK, in the Parish of BOHER, County LIMERICK, Ireland, about 20 years ago. When last heard from Michael Costelo was in SINKERS RUN, ROLESTON County, PA., 14 years ago, and John and Patrick Rohan were in CLEVELAND, OHIO, or in SPRINGFIELD, MASS., 13 years ago. Information of them will be thankfully received by writing to their sister, **Bridget Rohan**, or her husband, **Timothy Hayes**, to WOODSTOCK P.O., MCHENRY County, ILL.

Of **Mary Hussey**, a native of SCOTLAND, near GLANNAVADDY, County GALWAY, Ireland. When last heard from she was in the employment of **Mr. Jonathan Spaulding**, LOWELL, MASS. Information of her will be thankfully received by her brother, **Lackey Hussey**, by writing to him to 109 LIBERTY ST., NEW YORK CITY. Massachusetts papers, please copy.

Of **Patrick, Mary, Jane, Ann, Bessy,** and **Katy Harden**, natives of the County of SLIGO, Ireland, who sailed for America in 1847. When last heard of they were in OHIO. Information of them will be thankfully received by their brother, **Timothy Harden**, by addressing a letter to **Patrick Fleming**, CONSHOHOCKEN, MONTGOMERY County, PA. Ohio papers, please copy. [Appeared Nov. 9, 1847 saying they "came to America in 1846" instead of "sailed for America in 1847." Also specified CINCINNATI, OHIO as the place they were last heard from, and requested Cincinnati papers to copy.]

Of **John Kelly**, of the Parish of THOUGHEM, Townland of AHENA, County MAYO, Ireland. When last heard of he was working with **Peter Dunne** in TENNESSEE. Information of him will be thankfully received by his sister, **Maryanne Kelly**, 103 South Broad St., NEWARK, N.J. Tennessee papers, please copy.

November 10, 1866

Of **Miss Maria Holden**, who came from Ireland by the steamship *City of London* in the year 1863. She will confer a favor upon an old friend by sending her present address to the Editors of this paper or to the Editor of the New York Herald.

Of **Margaret** and **Sarah Gray**, of ATHY, County KILDARE, Ireland. They prepaid their brother Patrick's passage by the National Steam Navigation Line last April. He has not yet found them, and will be thankful for any information of them. Sarah then lived with **Mr. Philip Smith**, corner of Pacific and Columbia Streets, BROOKLYN, N.Y. Address **Patrick Gray**, care of **Philip J. Ryan**, bookseller, 157 Main St., SPRINGFIELD, MASS.

Of **William Crinigan**, of the County LONGFORD, Ireland. When last heard from he was living on LONG ISLAND. Information of him will be thankfully received by his uncle, **Patrick Brown**, Vanburen Street, between Franklyn and Bedford Avenues, BROOKLYN, Long Island, N.Y. [Appeared Nov. 17, 1866 with the second sentence changed as follows: "When last heard from he was living in LA SALLE CO., ILL."]

Of **Thomas Corcoran**, who left DROGHEDA, County LOUTH, Ireland, 14 years ago, and when last heard from (four years ago) was in BUFFALO, N.Y. Information of him will be thankfully received by his sister, **Mrs. Jane Coony**, No. 70 3rd AVENUE, NEW YORK. [Appeared Nov. 3, 1866 with different wording.]

Of **Bartholemew Donovan**, from the Parish of BALLYMARTLE, County CORK, Ireland, and of his sons, **Patrick, Michael, Timothy** and **Jeremiah**, and his daughters, who came to this country about sixteen years ago. When last heard from, about twelve years since, they were in WATERBURY, CT. Any intelligence of them will be thankfully received by **Bartholemew Donovan** (son of Bartholemew), who has just arrived from WALES. Direct to the office of the Irish-American, New York.

Of **Patrick Murphy**, a native of MILTOWN MALBAY, County CLARE, Ireland, who landed at Castle Garden last May, and stopped one week at **Wm. McMahon's**, in NEW YORK CITY. He is now supposed to be working in JERSEY CITY. By calling immediately on Wm. McMahon, at 89 HENRY STREET, NEW YORK CITY, he will get a letter from his friends in CALIFORNIA, informing him that his passage money is paid.

Of **Richard F. Paisley**, formerly of LOUGHREA, County GALWAY, Ireland. When last heard from, about 13 years ago, he was in BRIDGEVILLE, SULLIVAN County, N.Y., at a saw mill. He was then thinking of going to CALIFORNIA. If he or any of his friends will write to **John Ryan**, 43 ½ Union Street, NEWARK, N.J., he will hear of something greatly to his advantage.

Of **Edward Morley**, a native of LISANISKA, Parish of BAKEN, County MAYO, Ireland, who emigrated to this country in December, 1864, from LEEDS, YORKSHIRE, ENGLAND. When last heard from he was in BUFFALO, N.Y., on the 31st of May last; he stopped for a time in CINCINNATI; he is about 21 years of age. Information of him will be thankfully received by his cousin, **William Morley**, carpenter, HACKENSACK, BERGEN County, N.J Cincinnati papers, please copy.

November 17, 1866

Of **Matthew Glaster**, a native of MOORSTOWN Parish of KEELQUAN, west of DINGLE, County KERRY, Ireland, who left home 15 years ago. When last heard of he was in WISCONSIN. Information respecting him will be thankfully received by his sister, **Mary Glaster**, 6th Street, between I and K Streets, Island, WASHINGTON, D.C.

Of **Martin Devany**, a native of BELLAGHY, Townland of BUSHFIELD, County of MAYO, Ireland, who left home about 14 or 16 years ago, and supposed to be in SCRANTON, PA., in the month of May or June, 1866; he was very badly sick, and was not expected to live. Any information of him or his wife and family will be thankfully received by his brother, **John Devany**; also, of **Bridget Gallagher**, a native of the same place, Townland of BULKANE, who left home about the same time; supposed to be in SING SING, NEW YORKAny information of them will be thankfully received by their brothers,

John Devany and **Thomas Gallagher**, by addressing John Devany, SHOEMAKERTOWN Post-office, MONTGOMERY County, PENNSYLVANIA.

November 24, 1866

Of **John McGauley**, a native of NAVAN, County MEATH, Ireland. He came to America in 1861, and remained in GERMANTOWN, near PHILADELPHIA, PA., until May, 1866, with the exception of five months, which he served in the Fifth Pennsylvania Cavalry, in 1865. He is a weaver by trade, and 25 years of age. Information will be thankfully received by his brother, **Thomas McGauley**, GERMANTOWN Post Office, near PHILADELPHIA, PA. Western papers, please copy.

Of **William Lacey**, a native of the County WEXFORD, Ireland, who arrived in New York about nine years ago. Information of him will be thankfully received by his wife, **Fanny Lacey**, by writing to her in care of Lynch, Cole & Meehan, 29 Ann Street, New York. [Appeared Nov. 11, 1865 with a different contact person.]

Of **Edward J. Whelan**, who left ENNISCORTHY, County WEXFORD, Ireland, about the 20th of last June; was in NEW YORK CITY in July. Any person knowing his whereabouts will confer a great favor on his wife, by addressing a letter to her in care of **Connolly Rroddy**, Esq., 43 Willow Place, BROOKLYN, N.Y.

Of **Bernard** and **John Gogerty**, natives of the Townland of BALLYHENEVY, County LOUTH, Ireland. The former, when last heard from, was supposed to be in BLACCO ALTONA, MARSHALL County, IOWA, and the latter in ST. LOUIS, MISSOURI. They will confer a great favor on their very much bereaved sister **Margaret**, alias **Gorman**, by addressing a line to her residence, TOMPKINSVILLE P.O., RICHMOND County, N.Y. Marshall County, Iowa, and St. Louis papers, please copy.

Of **John Sanders**, of CLONAKILTY, County CORK, Ireland. Information of him will be received by his sister **Jane**. Address **Daniel Donovan**, 25 VANDEWATER STREET, NEW YORK.

Of **William Dunlea**, a native of KANTURK, County CORK, Ireland, who sailed from Queenstown on the 7th of June, per steamship *City of Paris* (Inman line), and landed at New York; he went to BROOKLYN on the 30th of June, 1866, and hired at an office there as waiter in the army. Information of him will be thankfully received by his brother, **Maurice Dunlea**, by addressing a letter to **Mr. Patrick Carmody**, 81 BAXTER STREET, NEW YORK CITY.

Of **William McInerney**, a son of **James** and **Catherine McInerney**, of the Parish of CASTLE CONNELL, County LIMERICK, Ireland. He left BOSTON, MASS., for NEW ORLEANS, in 1855, and has not been heard from since. Information of him will be thankfully received by his mother, brothers and sisters at No. 5 Oswego Street, BOSTON, MASS.

Of **John, Con, Mary, Catherine, Margaret** and **Ann Fitzgerald**, natives of the Parish of RAHEEN, County LIMERICK, Ireland. When last heard from they were in BROADHEAD GREEN, State of WISCONSIN. Information of them will be thankfully received by their sister and brother **Bridget** and **Thomas Fitzgerald**. Address Lynch, Cole & Meehan, Irish-American office, 29 Ann Street, New York, for Mrs. Bridget Fitzgerald. Wisconsin papers, please copy.

Of **William Tumilty**, a native of CASTLE WILLIAM, County DOWN, Ireland. When last heard from was in PORTLAND, CONN. Any information of him will be thankfully received by his brother **James**, by writing to him in care of **Mr. Henry Van Winkles**, NORTH BELEVILLE, N.Y. [Appeared Nov. 25, 1865 with a different contact person and some additional information.]

December 1, 1866

Of **Patt Stack**, his son **James**, and daughter **Ellen**. When last heard from, in 1861, they lived in ST. JOSEPH City, MO. Any information of their whereabouts will be thankfully received to the following address: - **Edmund Stack**, THORNTON'S FERRY, MERIMAC, N.H. St. Joseph Dispatch, please copy.

Of **Thomas Brady**, who landed in New York about nine years ago. He worked about ten months in NEW YORK, and left to go to OHIO, and that was the last that was heard of him. He is a native of the County MAYO, Parish of KELOGUES, near CASTLEBAR, Ireland. Any one knowing anything of his whereabouts will confer a great and everlasting favor by addressing his brother, **Henry Brady**, now residing in LAWRENCE County, OHIO. Ironton and other papers, please copy.

Of **Thomas Fagan**, late of 80 Lower Camden Street, DUBLIN, Ireland. When last heard from, April 14th, 1865, he was at COACHLAND Court House, two miles from RICHMOND, VA. Any person knowing him will please address **Patrick Fagan**, 11 ½ WASHINGTON STREET, NEW YORK, care of **Thomas Mutchell**.

Of **Timothy McGowan**, of the County WESTMEATH, Ireland. When last heard of he was in ALBANY, N.Y. Any information concerning him will be most thankfully received by his brother, **Peter McGowan**, VAILS GATE, ORANGE County, N.Y.

Of **Michael Powers**, from CORBALLY, County KILKENNY, Ireland. When last heard from, about eight years ago, he was in QUEBEC, CANADA EAST. Any intelligence of him will be thankfully received by his brother, **John Powers**, 21 COURTLAND ST. [Cortlandt St.], NEW YORK.

Of **Owen, Mary** and **Ellen Melan**, who were last seen by their brother, **James Melan**, in the Parish of GLOUNTHAN, County CORK, some five or six years ago, when they were going to NEW YORK, and have not been heard of since. Any information of them will be thankfully received by their brother. - Direct to James Melan, in care of **Mrs. Bleak**, 71 Railroad Avenue, JERSEY CITY, N.J.

Of **Thomas Sheehy**, a native of NEWCASTLE WEST, County LIMERICK. When last heard from, in 1860, he was in MEMPHIS, TENN., engaged as fireman on a railroad. Information concerning him will be thankfully received by his father, **Daniel Sheehy**, PAQUETTE P.O., MANITOWOC County, WIS.

Of **Michael, Patrick** and **Catherine Heagney**, natives of CARROCRIN, Parish of BALLINAKILL, County GALWAY, Ireland. When last heard from, seven years ago, Michael was in SAVANNAH, GA., and Patrick and Catherine were in CLINTONVILLE, MASS. Information of them will be thankfully received by **James Heagney**, SAVANNAH Post Office, GA. Boston Pilot, please copy.

December 7, 1866

Of **Edward McCurley**, formerly of OTTAWA C.W., now supposed to be in HOPKINSVILLE, KY. If this should meet his eye or that of any one knowing his present whereabouts, by sending his address to the office of the Irish-American, he will hear of something to his advantage.

Of **Philip, Edward, Michael** and **Ellen Hanrahan**, natives of the County KILKENNY, Ireland. When last heard of they were in PHILADELPHIA. Information will be thankfully received by their brother, **John Hanrahan**, 128 WEST 33rd STREET, NEW YORK. Philadelphia papers, please copy.

Of **Bridget Murray**, who left Water Street, LONGFORD, Ireland, last March, for New York. Any information of her will be thankfully received by addressing **William Murtagh**, Box 628 PHILADELPHIA Post Office, PHILADELPHIA, PA.

Of **Mary, Hanorah, Ellen, Catherine, Margaret** and **John Hourigan**, of the City of CORK, Ireland. Margaret and family emigrated to this country 14 years ago, and when last heard of were in ALBANY, N.Y. Information of any of them will be thankfully received by their sister **Johanna's** son, **John Murphy**, LAURY'S STATION, LEHIGH County, PA. New York and Massachusetts papers, please copy.

Of **Johana, Mary** and **Margaret** (maiden name) **Sheehan**, natives of BALLYNOSKING, County CORK, Ireland, came to this country about 20 years ago. When last heard from (about 5 years ago) they were in MAYSVILLE or WASHINGTON, KENTUCKY. Information of them will be thankfully received by their sister, **Hanora O'Hern**, NEW OHIO, BROOME County, N.Y. Kentucky papers please copy.

Of **Patrick Ready**, shoemaker, a native of CREE, County CLARE, Ireland. He worked for **Stephen Rinaoh**, of 22 HOUSTON ST., NEW YORK, when last heard of. He arrived on the 22nd of June, 1862, in New York. Any person knowing of his whereabouts will oblige by informing his brother, **James Ready**, Decalb St., NORRISTOWN, MONTGOMERY County, PA., in care of **Michael Scanlan**.

Of **Catherine McDermott**, daughter of **Patrick McDermott** and **Jane Burns**, of DUNAMON, County ROSCOMMON, Ireland. When last heard of she was at 94 RIVINGTON ST., NEW YORK. Information of her will be thankfully received by her father, by directing a letter to **Francis Bacon**, Woolen Company, PITTSFIELD, MASS., for Patrick McDermott.

December 15, 1866

Of **William Lacy**, a native of the County WEXFORD, Ireland, who came to NEW YORK about 9 years ago, and called at 15 EAST 33rd STREET, on the 28th of November last. He is requested to call at 121 WEST 20th STREET, near 7th Avenue, NEW YORK, for his anxious wife, **Fanny Lacy**. [Also see Nov. 24, 1866.]

Of **Lawrence Kent**, or any of his heirs, who emigrated to CANADA upwards of 40 years ago from County TIPPERARY, Ireland, by a near relative. Information of their whereabouts will be thankfully received by addressing **Mary Murphy**, 1514 Carlton Street, PHILADELPHIA, PA. Canada papers, please copy.

Of **Henry, Mary** and **Rose Hagan.** When last heard from Henry was in CHARLESTON, S.C., and Mary and Rose were in PHILADELPHIA, PA. Any information of them will be thankfully received by their brother, **Charles Hagan**, by addressing him at NECADA, GUNIA County, WIS [Appeared under County DERRY]

December 22, 1866

Of **Richard Walsh**, who left DEWSBURY, YORKSHIRE, ENGLAND, last Spring. When last heard from he was in SCRANTON, PA., with **Luke Kennedy**. Any information concerning Richard Walsh will be thankfully received by his brother, **Patrick Walsh**, at 509 South 19th St., PHILADELPHIA, PA.

Of **Bridget Tunney,** a native of WOLVERHAMPTON, ENGLAND, who arrived in New York in October last. Any one knowing her address will please write to **Edward Kirkham**, Messrs. Hodges & Coleman, 106 Sudbury Street, BOSTON, MASS.

Of **Patrick Ahern**, who left PATERSON, N.J., about the 15th of January, 1866. When last heard of was in NEW YORK CITY. Any information respecting him will be thankfully received by his parents, **Patrick** and **Mary Ahern**, 31 Godwin Street, PATERSON, N.J.; or **Bernard O'Neill**, Justice of the Peace, No. 81 Congress Street, PATERSON, N.J.

Of **William Flood**, a carpenter by trade, formerly of DUBLIN, Ireland, who came to this country in the year 1852, since married. He will hear of something to his advantage by calling on **James Hayes**, at **Mr. Connolly's**, 165 WOOSTER ST., NEW YORK.

Of **John Grace**, who emigrated from ROSS, WEXFORD, in 1856, to NEW YORK (the second time). When last heard of, in 1861, was in PEORIA, ILL. His uncles are supposed to be in NEW YORK CITY. Any information of him, or any of his friends, will be thankfully received by his step-brother, **David Walsh Grace**, Battery H, 5th U.S. Artillery, FORTRESS MONROE, VA.

Of **William Lacey**, a native of County WEXFORD, Ireland, who came to NEW YORK CITY about nine years ago. Information of him will be thankfully received by his anxious wife, **Fanny Lacey**, who is a native of County DUBLIN. Address, 121 WEST 20th STREET, near 7th Avenue, NEW YORK. [Appeared 11 Nov. 1865 and Nov. 24, 1866 with different information]

Of **Mary** and **Johannah Cahill**, of GLENDRAGH, near BARNA, Parish of RATHCAHILL, County LIMERICK, Ireland, who came to America in 1852 or 1853. When last heard from were in CANADA. Any information of them will be thankfully received by their brother, **Cornelius Carmody**. Address in care of **Mr. Patrick Flanigan**, for Cornelius Carmody, No. 141 EAST 29th STREET, NEW YORK.

Of **Mary** and **Julia Larkin**, daughters of **Patrick Larkin**, Parish of KILLAAN, County CAVAN, Ireland. When last heard of were married, and residing at JOLIET, ILL. A letter directed to their brother, **Patrick Larkin**, in care of **John Farrell**, cor. 40th ST. and 2nd AVENUE, NEW YORK CITY, will be thankfully received.

December 29, 1866

Of **James McClean**. When last heard of, in 1864, he was on HART'S ISLAND, N.Y. Information appertaining to his whereabouts will be thankfully received by his father, **James McClean**, PITTSFIELD, MASS.

Of **Thomas Mitchell**, shoemaker, a native of the City of CORK, who sailed from there 12 or 14 years ago, for ST. JOHN, N.B. If this should meet his eye, he is advised to write immediately to **James Hagerty**, Esq. J.P., CORK, Ireland, and he will hear of something to his advantage; or in case of his death, his next heir will do well to write as above directed. St. Johns, N.B., papers, please copy.

Of **Bryan Dignan**, a native of the County CAVAN, Townland of CLONKEEFEY, Ireland. He left about 20 years ago. Information concerning him will be most thankfully received by his sister's son, **Henry Nugent**, by addressing a letter to him to 183 North Halsted St., CHICAGO, ILL.

January 5, 1867

Of **John Meehan**, who resided near OMAHA, NEBRASKA TERRITORY, in the year 1857, and pre-empted a quarter section of land in WASHINGTON County, NEBRASKA, about that time. Said Meehan is about 34 years old, light complexion, and about five feet six inches in height. Should he, or any one who may know him, see this notice, they will confer a favor by sending his Post-office address to **Timothy Donovan**, OMAHA CITY, NEBRASKA TERRITORY.

Of **Patrick Clinch**, a drover, or of his sons, natives of CLONEE, County DUBLIN, Ireland, who came to this country about 25 years ago; supposed to be farming in PENNSYLVANIA.

Any information of them will be thankfully received by his nephew, **Hugh Clinch**, No. 78 JAMES ST., NEW YORK CITY. Pennsylvania and Ohio papers, please copy.

Of **John Leonard**, a native of LUCAN, County DUBLIN, Ireland. Six years ago he was living at BAYRIDGE, Long Island. Any information of him will be thankfully received by his brother, **Joseph Leonard**, No. 35 Oneida St., BOSTON, MASS.

Of **Michael Hopkins**, a native of RATHCOFFEY, County KILDARE, Ireland. When last heard from he was in ROME, ONEIDA County, N.Y. Any information of his whereabouts will be thankfully received by his brother, **Thomas Hopkins**, CRESCENT CITY, POTTAWATTAMIE County, IOWA.

Of **Patrick, James, Conner**, and **Denis Hallinan**, all of NEWMARKET-ON-FERGUS, County CLARE, Ireland. Any information of them will be thankfully received by their nephew, **James Murray**, at LAURY'S STATION, LEHIGH County, PA. Massachusetts papers, please copy.

Of **Peter Collins**, who left BELFAST, County ANTRIM, Ireland, about 14 years ago. The last place he worked there was in Leper's Mill, Belfast, before he came to NEW YORK. The last account of him was that he was on board a Propeller, trading between NEW ORLEANS and VIRGINIA. Any information of him will be thankfully received by his brothers, **Patrick** and **John Collins**. Address, care of J. Graham & Co., Booksellers and Emigration Agents, No. 102 East Madison St., CHICAGO, ILL.

Of **Andrew Dugdale**, horseshoer, a native of GALWAY, Ireland, who left there about 28 years ago, with his wife, **Margaret Looky**. When last heard from he was in TROY, N.Y. Any information of him will be thankfully received by his brother, **John Dugdale**. Direct to **John Bright**, Horseshoeing Establishment, 883 Perth St., between Peach and Poplar sts., PHILADELPHIA, PA.

January 12, 1867

Of **Charles Harnett**, an engine-maker by trade, who sailed from Dublin in July, 1865, in the Montreal ocean steamship *St. George*, to Quebec, and then came by railroad cars to NEW YORK. Information respecting him will be thankfully received by applying to Lynch, Cole & Meehan, Irish-American Office, New York.

Of **James Banaghen**, a native of the Townland of GREENEAN, Parish of MOHILL, County LEITRIM, Ireland. His father's name was **Denis Banaghen**. When last heard from, he was living in CHICAGO, ILL. He is supposed to have left there nine years ago and went to CALIFORNIA. Any information of him will be thankfully received by his brother, **Michael Banaghen**, 216 Hamilton Street, NEW HAVEN, CONN., in care of **Mrs. Kennedy**. California papers, please copy.

Of **Patrick, Daniel, Denis** and **Margaret Rosney**, of the Parish of KILLEY, KING'S County, Ireland, who sailed from Dublin in the ship *Kingston*, in June, 1850, and landed in New York. - When last heard from, they were in the City of NEWARK, N.J. Any information respecting them will be thankfully received by their sister, **Ann Rosney**, CLINTON HOLLOW, DUTCHESS County, N.Y., care of **Alexander Wing**.

Of **William McNamara**, a native of the City of CORK, Ireland. Last seen, in June, 1866. Any information of him will be thankfully received by his brother, **J. McNamara**, room 9, 124 8th Street, CLINTON PLACE, NEW YORK.

Of **John Cautillion**, a native of MILLTOWN, County KERRY, Ireland. When last heard of he was residing in CUMMINGSVILLE, HAMILTON County, OHIO. His sister-in-law, **Mrs. Margaret Quill**, of No. 7 Moore, Street, BUFFALO, N.Y., is anxious to hear from him.

January 19, 1867

Of **John Lewis**, who left DUBLIN in February, 1866, for NEW YORK. Intelligence of him will be thankfully received by **Michael Lynch**, who left DUBLIN, for America, last April. Address Michael Lynch, ROCKVILLE, CONN.

Of **Sarah Lawless** and **Margaret Nolan** (maiden name, **Penrose**), natives of the Parish of BARRENDARRIG, County WICKLOW, Ireland, who came to this country 1[4] years ago. Information of them will be thankfully received by their sister's daughter, **Annie Fisher**. Address **John Hatton**, 285 WEST 24th STREET, NEW YORK.

Of **Michael Filand**, a native of KILBEGGAN, County WESTMEATH, Ireland. When last heard from (about 16 years ago) he was in BROOKLYN, Long Island, N.Y. Information of him will be thankfully received by his sister, **Margaret Madden** (maiden name, **Filand**), by writing to her to No. 168 Front Street, HARTFORD, CONN. Brooklyn papers, please copy.

Of **John Ryan**, of Chapel Lane, LISMORE, County WATERFORD, Ireland, who left PHILADELPHIA, PA., in 1865, for NEW YORK, where he has been last heard of in 1866. Intelligence of him will be thankfully received by his sister, **Mary Ryan**, at No. 226 North Front Street, PHILADELPHIA, PA. Boston and Canadian papers, please copy.

January 26, 1867

Of **Edward** and **Thomas Redden**, who emigrated to this country - Edward in 1852, and Thomas in 1846 - natives of CULLEN, Parish of DURROW, County TIPPERARY, Ireland. When last heard of they were both in the City of RICHMOND, VA. Thomas left the United States and went to AUSTRALIA, but returned in the year 1862, and went to some of the western States. Edward is about 43 and Thomas about 40 years of age. $10 Reward will be given for information of the above-mentioned men, which will be thankfully received by their brother, **Patrick Redden**, NORWICH, CHENANGO County, State of N.Y. Western papers, please copy.

Of **Cornelius Cotter**, of SKIBBEREEN, County CORK, Ireland, who came to America, in 1847. When last heard from he was in PHILADELPHIA, PA, working with a contractor named **McGowan**, 18 years ago. Also of his nieces **Catherine** and **Mary Cotter**, of the same place. Catherine got married to the Mate of the vessel she sailed in, and is supposed to be in NEW YORK. Information of them will be thankfully received by his daughter and their cousin, **Margaret Cotter**, at **John Driscoll's**, Vanburen Street, between Franklin and Bedford Avenues, BROOKLYN, Long Island, N.Y. Pennsylvania papers, please copy.

Of **William** and **John Lee**, natives of KILEVEG, HEADFORD, County GALWAY, Ireland. When last heard of they lived in PENNSYLVANIA. Also, of **Patrick** and **Mary Connell**, of Kileveg, son and daughter of **John Connell** and **Bridget Faugheye**, who came to this country about four years ago. Information of them will be thankfully received by **Bridget Connell**, BRIDGEPORT, CONN.

February 2, 1867

Of **Timothy Lydon**, a hatter by trade. Intelligence of him will be thankfully received by his sister, **Margaret Lydon**, at 59 BAXTER STREET, NEW YORK CITY.

Of **John Walsh** and **Mary**, his wife, maiden name **Mary Gaul,** natives of SMITHSTOWN, Parish of THOMASTOWN, County KILKENNY, Ireland, who landed in New York, June 9, 1865. Information of them will be thankfully received by their sister, **Johanna Gaul**, at **Mr. J. Griffin's**, PERTH AMBOY, MIDDLESEX County, N.J. Boston Pilot, please copy.

Of **Thomas Flynn**, bootmaker; also of **Thomas, Catherine** and **Mary Dean**, who left DOONAS, County CLARE, Ireland, about 1848. When last heard from (nine years ago) they were in NEW YORK. Information of either of the above will be thankfully received by their nephew, **John McInerney**, 151 Broadway, ALBANY, N.Y.

Of **William Daniel** and wife, natives of the County TIPPERARY, Ireland. When last heard from they were in ST. LOUIS, MO. Information of them will be thankfully received by addressing **Henry Jones**, Box 19, WEST FARMS Post Office, WESTCHESTER County, N.Y., or by sending a note to the Irish-American Office, New York.

Of **John** and **Catherine McGovern**, who came to this country about 17 years ago along with their mother, **Eliza McGovern**, who hast since died. Their father, **Michael McGovern**, was then working in a glass house in NEW YORK, but had got killed. They are natives of AUGHRIM, near BALLINASLOE, County GALWAY, Ireland. Information will be thankfully received by their cousin, **Michael Egan**, 22 Wara Allens lane, MOUNT AIRY, PHILADELPHIA, PA.

February 9, 1867

Of **Patrick** and **John Morris**, natives of ATHBOY, County MEATH, Ireland. Any information of them will be thankfully received by their brother, **James Morris**, by writing to the Irish-American office, 29 Ann St., New York.

Of **Michael Brenan**, from the Parish of TULLAROAN, County KILKENNY, Ireland. When last heard from, about three years since, he was in ADAMS County, ILLINOIS. Any intelligence of him will be thankfully received by his sister, **Bridget Brenan**, care of **Patrick Power**, 308 EAST 24th ST., NEW YORK.

Of **Mary** and **Catherine Quinn**, of BRICKFIELD, Parish of EFFIN, County LIMERICK, Ireland. Mary married **William Hanley**, of BALLINVREENA, County LIMERICK, and Catherine married **Michael Ryan**, of EMLY, County TIPPERARY. Mary and husband sailed from Cork, and Catherine and husband sailed from Limerick, about twenty-six years ago. When last heard from, they were in the vicinity of BOSTON, MASS. Any information of them will be thankfully received by their brother, **Edmond Quinn**, who came to CHICAGO in April, 1866. Address care of **John Fitzgerald**, No. 554 South Halsted Street, CHICAGO, ILL.

Of **Thomas Casey**, a native of BALLYMOTE, County SLIGO, Ireland. When last heard of he was in SHERMAN, CHAUTAUQUA County, N.Y. Any information of him will be thankfully received by his sister, **Ellen Casey**, at No. 222 Bridge St., (first floor) BROOKLYN.

February 16, 1867

Of **Eliza LeDuage**, a native of ARDEMAGH, County MEATH, Ireland. When last heard from she was in the State of NEW YORK. Any information will be thankfully received by her cousin, **John Quigley**, THROGG'S NECK, WESTCHESTER County, N.Y.

February 23, 1867

Of **Mrs. Sarah Donohoe**, (maiden name **Graham**), a native of the Parish of DURROW, KING'S County, Ireland, who landed in this country from Dublin, about the month of May, 1865. When last heard from she lived with her niece, **Mrs. Thompson**, in INDEPENDENCE, JACKSON County, MISSOURI. She will hear something deeply interesting to her by writing to her cousin, **Francis Kenny**, 115 Elliott Street, CANTON, BALTIMORE, MD.

Of **Lawrence** and **Richd. Sexton**, sons of **Thomas** and **Johannah Sexton**, of LICKAWN, Parish of TEMPLEORUM, County KILKENNY, Ireland. Lawrence left NEW YORK about eight years ago. Richard, when last heard from (about seven years ago) was in lower TENNESSEE. Information of them will be thankfully received by their mother, **Mrs. Johannah Sexton**, No. 100 WEST 19th STREET, NEW YORK.

Of **Michael Powers**, a native of CORBALLY, County KILKENNY, Ireland. When last heard of he was in QUEBEC, CANADA. Information of him will be thankfully received by his brother, **John Powers**, at 21 COURTLAND ST. [Cortlandt St.], NEW YORK.

Of **Charley Delahunty's** family, natives of CASHEL, County TIPPERARY, Ireland. Any person knowing the whereabouts of any member of his family will confer a favor on the subscriber by addressing a line to **Joseph Casey**, Asst. Supt. City Temp. House, Charles Street, BOSTON, MASS.

Of **Patrick Moloney**, of CLOUNMACON, Parish of LISTOWEL, County KERRY, Ireland, who came to this country in the year 1854, and is now supposed to be in PITTSBURGH, PA. Information of him will be thankfully received by his brother, **John Moloney**, 74 OLIVER STREET, NEW YORK. Pittsburgh papers, please copy.

Of **William Meally**, from CULLINAMUCK, Parish of MYCULLEN, County GALWAY, Ireland, who came to this country about 14 years ago. His nephew is most anxious to ascertain any information of his whereabouts. Address **Mark Sarsfield**, No. 414 North 22nd Street, PHILADELPHIA, PA.

March 2, 1867

Of **John Gerrety** or **John Tiernan**, or their wives, whose maiden names were **Mary** and **Elizabeth O'Connor**. Any information of them will be thankfully received by their brother, **Bernard O'Connor**, OTTAWA, LA SALLE County, ILLINOIS.

Of **James McDonnell**, who, when last heard from (in August, 1866), was in BROOKLYN, running the Fulton House, in partnership with a man named **George Ward**. Anybody giving information concerning him will confer a great favor on his brother-in-law, **John Johnson**, NIAGARA FALLS, N.Y. Brooklyn papers, please copy.

Of **Mary McCaul**, a native of CARRICKMACROSS, County MONAGHAN, Ireland. When last heard from (about five years ago) she was in MICHIGAN County, State of MICHIGAN. Information will be kindly received, and $5 Reward will be given, by her brother, **Bernard McCaul**, at 214 East Lumber and Bethel Streets, BALTIMORE, MD.

Of **Brien, John** and **James Cunnaghan**, sons of **Martin Cunnaghan** and **Bridget Killday**, from the village of DRUMINDUFF, Parish of OUGHAUNE, WESTPORT, County MAYO, Ireland. Brien left Ireland about 17 or 18 years ago. Intelligence of them will be most thankfully received by their cousin, **Mary Killday**, by writing to her in care of Lynch, Cole & Meehan, Irish-American Office, 29 Ann Street, New York.

Of **Phillip McGovern**, who came from the County of CAVAN, Ireland, 15 or 16 years ago, and worked in a tailor's shop in NEW YORK. Any information of him will be thankfully received by his sister, **Mary Greenwood**, HALLOWELL, MAINE.

Of **Thomas Ryan**, son **Patrick** and **Johanna Ryan**, of TINETERIFFE, Parish of CAPPAMORE, County LIMERICK, Ireland, who left home on the 15th of July, 1853. When last heard of he was working on one of the steamboats running between ST. LOUIS and CAIRO. Information of him will be most thankfully received by his brother, **STEPHEN RYAN**. Address Ryan's house, 30 MADISON STREET, NEW YORK. St. Louis and Chicago papers, please copy.

Of **John Flynn**, from NEWMARKET, County CLARE, Ireland, by his sister **Margaret**. When last heard from, October 27, 1865, he was with **Mr. Nash**, PETERSBURG, VA Apply to H. D. Glynn, Castle Garden, New York.

Of **Richard Hogan** and **Richard Morgan**, formerly of George Street, CASTLEDURROW, QUEEN'S County, Ireland, who came to this country 10 or 11 years ago. When last heard from they were living in NEW YORK. Also, of Richard Hogan's wife **Catherine** (maiden name **Mack**). Any information of them will be thankfully received by **Judith** or **Maryann Hogan**, or by their cousin, **Dennis Devine**, 559 SIXTH AVENUE, between 33rd and 34th Streets, NEW YORK.

Of **John** and **Edmund Stapleton**, who left TIPPERARY, Ireland, about 16 years ago; both were at SYRACUSE, N.Y., about one year since. Information of them will be thankfully received by **John Ryan**, care of **William B. Burnett**, LYONS, WAYNE County, N.Y.

March 9, 1867

Of **Thomas Travers**, a peddler, with horse and buggy. When last heard from he was in ADRIAN, MICHIGAN. Any information will be thankfully received by writing to **Michael Mullen**, AUBURN, N.Y.

Of **Margaret** and **Ann Hayes**, of the Parish of TIMLAGE, County CORK, Ireland. Married **Thos. Prutcherd**, of BRITISH SOUTH WALES, and arrived in this country about 11 years ago. Ann married **William Hickey**, of County CORK, and left WALES for this country about 7 years ago. When last heard from they were in the vicinity of BOSTON, MASS. Information of them will be thankfully received by their sister, **Ellen Anderson**, who came to this country about 10 months ago. Address Ellen Anderson, PHARON, MERCER County, PA.

Of **Patrick Nolan**, a native of BERT, County KILDARE, Ireland. When last heard of he was in MEMPHIS, TENN. Information of him will be thankfully received by **Wm. Nolan**, 118 Railroad Avenue, JERSEY CITY, N.J., or by his brother, **John Nolan**, at BERT, ATHY, County KILDARE, Ireland.

Of **James Maloy**, a native of the Parish of STRANORLAN, County DONEGAL, Ireland, aged 23 years. When last seen he was in BROOKLYN, N.Y. Information of him will be thankfully received by his sister, **Bridget Maloy**, 41 Skillman Street, BROOKLYN, N.Y. California papers, please copy.

Of **Michael** and **Patrick Quinn**, from ATHLONE, County ROSCOMMON, Ireland. Michael came to this country 21 years and Patrick 18 years ago. When last heard from, 14 years ago, were in COXSACKIE, GREENE County, N.Y. They are supposed to be somewhere in the west. Any intelligence of them, or of their cousin **James Quinn**, will be thankfully received by their brother, **Andrew Quinn**, who arrived in this country last July. Direct to Lynch, Cole & Meehan, Irish-American Office, New York.

Of **Patrick Collins**, a native of the County WICKLOW, Ireland, formerly of TORONTO, C.W When last heard from was in WEST TROY, NEW YORK. He then said he was going to PHILADELPHIA, PA. Any information of him will be thankfully received by his father, **John Collins**, or his brothers **Dennis** and **Andrew Collins**, 188 Race St., CINCINNATI, OHIO.

Of **John Maher**, of the Parish of CONAHY, County KILKENNY, Ireland. He came to this country in 1847, and when last heard of he was in BROOKLYN, L.I. Any information of him will be thankfully received by his brother, **Thomas Maher**, 34 JACKSON STREET, NEW YORK, who lately came to this country.

Of **William, John** and **Thomas McGlenn**, of BLENEVILL, County KERRY, Ireland. When last heard from they were in the State of NEW YORK, after the close of the war. Address **Patrick McGlenn**, DAYTON, OHIO.

Of **Michael Mannon**, a native of the County GALWAY, Ireland, who left WIGGAN, LANCASHIRE, ENGLAND, in July, 1864. When last heard from he was in NEW YORK CITY, in August, 1864. Information of him will be thankfully received by his wife, **Margaret Mounton**. Address **Michael P. Damson**, 64 Anaman Street, FALL RIVER, MASS., for Margaret Mounton. [Appeared March 16, 1867 with the surnames Mannon and Mounton changed to **Manton**, and the surname Damson changed to **Dawson**.]

Of **Patrick, Bridget, Mary** and **Catherine Leonard**, from RAHEEN, Parish of CARABANE, County GALWAY, Ireland. When last heard of, four years ago, Catherine was in ALLEGHANY, PA. Information of them will be thankfully received by their brother, **John Leonard**, who came to this country one year ago, by addressing him in care of **Patrick Monahan**, Classon Avenue, between Pacific and Dean Streets, BEDFORD, BROOKLYN, Long Island, N.Y. Pennsylvania papers, please copy.

March 16, 1867

Of **Michal** [sic] **Hanly**, a native of the County of DURHAM, ENGLAND, who arrived at Philadelphia, Pa., about April, 1866. Information of him will be thankfully received by **John Reeve's**, at 23 Clymer Street, WILLIAMSBURG, Long Island, N.Y.

Of **Mrs. Ellen Callahan**, who left BOSTON, for NEW YORK in 1957, [sic] and lived in the family of a gentleman who kept an office at 3 COENTIES SLIP, NEW YORK CITY. Her former husband, **Mr. Wm. Callahan**, was proprietor of the Fresh Pond House, CAMBRIDGE, MASS., between the years 1849 and 1852. Information of her will be thankfully received by her brother, **John J. O'Brien**, Marlboro Hotel, BOSTON, MASS.

Of **John Daly**, and his children, **William** and **Teresa Daly**, who, when last heard of, were in WEST HOBOKEN, N.J. Also of **Patrick** and **Mary Sherry**, or their children, who, when last heard of, were in FREE PORT, ARMSTRONG County, PA. They can hear of some of their relatives by writing to **James Daly**, at 225 Hudson Avenue, BROOKLYN, N.Y.

Of **James, Andrew** and **Elizabeth O'Neil**, of BALLYCOMANDE, Parish of DORUS, County CORK, Ireland. Elizabeth was married to a man of the name of **Conely**; she lived in ST. LOUIS, MO. Information of them will be thankfully received by their sister's son, **Henry Farr**, at WINSTED, N.Y.

Of **Mary Sullivan**, alias **Mary Fitzgerald**, a native of CORK City, Ireland, who is supposed to be living at the house of her sister's husband, **Ignatius O'Callaghan**, also a native of Cork City. Information of her will be thankfully received by **John Sullivan**, at 161 LEONARD STREET, NEW YORK.

Of **Walliam** [sic], **John** and **Eliza Moran**, natives of ATHY, County KILDARE, Ireland, and of their uncle, **Hugh Gaffney**, from the Parish of STRAFFAN, County KILDARE, Ireland. Information of them will be thankfully received by their uncle, **Matt Gaffney**, at MIDDLETOWN, CONN. Brooklyn papers, please copy.

Of **Patrick Murphy**, a native of BALLYCASTLE, County MAYO, Ireland. He left New York for HAVANA, by the steamer *The Empire City*, on the 2nd of May, 1859. Information of him will be thankfully received by his brother, **Philip Murphy**, at 55 PITTS STREET [Pitt Street], NEW YORK.

Of **Bridget Coughlin** and family, natives of RAHEEN, County LIMERICK, Ireland, who came to this country about 13 years ago. When last heard from, about six years since, they were in WASHINGTON County, OHIO. Information of them will be most thankfully received by their aunt, **Ellen Coughlin**, at WEST TROY, ALBANY County, N.Y.

Of **Mary Conners**, a native of GURTLIEN, Parish of KEEL, County KERRY, Ireland. When last heard from she was in SHOREHAM, ADDISON County, State of VERMONT.

Information of her will be thankfully received by her cousin, **Patrick Flaherty**, at HANNILAE, MARION County, MISSOURI.

March 23, 1867

Of **Michael Keating**, who left LEVERN BANKS, VELLSTON, GLASGOW, SCOTLAND, for this country in the Summer of 1859. When last heard from he was in CHICAGO, ILL. Information of him will be thankfully received by his brother, **John Keating**, Diamond Flax Spinning Mill, Paterson Street, PATERSON, N.J., or by **B. O'Neill**, Justice of the Peace, 81 Congress Street, Paterson, N.J. Chicago papers, please copy. [Appeared Sept. 21, 1867 with some changes.]

Of **Eliza Dogherty**, who arrived in New York, per steamer *Virginia*, on the 8th of Sept. last, and has not been heard of since. Information of her will be thankfully received by her sister **Bridget**, and brother-in-law, **Patrick Shanly**, by writing to them to No. 183 North Desborn Street, CHICAGO, ILLINOIS.

Of **James Cusack**, who arrived in New York, in the steamship *City of Washington*, on the 1st day January, 1867. His brother, **John Cusack**, would be glad to hear from him at PORT RICHMOND, STATEN ISLAND, N.Y.

Of **Robert McDermott**, a native of ANNAMULLEN, County MONAGHAN, Ireland. When last heard from he was in SAN FRANCISCO, CAL. Information of him will be thankfully received by his brother, **Patrick McDermott**, at 54 North 2nd Street, WILLIAMSBURGH, N.Y. California papers, please copy.

Of **James Dods** and sister **Mary**, who, twenty years ago, were in the State of PENNSYLVANIA, having come from LURGANEARLY, County MONAGHAN, Ireland. Any information of them will be thankfully received by **Margaret Dods**, alias **Whittle**, care of **William Whittle**, NEPONSET, BUREAU County, ILLINOIS.

Of **Dennis O'Connor**, a native of the Parish of DROMARD, County SLIGO, Ireland. When last heard from he was in the English Service. Any person knowing of his whereabouts will confer a great favor by informing his sister, **Eliza O'Connor**, TROY, N.Y.

Of **Peter Morrin**, a native of the Parish of CROOKSTOWN, County KILDARE, Ireland. When last heard from (in October '65) he was in QUEEN ANNE'S County. He then Stated himself in bad health. Information of him will be thankfully received by **James Nolan** in care of **William Nolan**, 118 Railway Avenue, JERSEY CITY.

Of **John Gallin**, formerly of the County DONEGAL, Ireland. When last heard from he was in NEW ORLEANS, LA. Intelligence of him, whether dead or alive, will be thankfully received by his brother and sister, **Charles** and **Sarah Gallin**. Please address Charles Gallin, 431 Munroe Street, PHILADELPHIA, PA.

Of **Luke Greham**, son of **John Greham** and **Mary Geraghty**, from CLONGOUND, Parish of DRUM, County ROSCOMMON, Ireland. Luke left Clongound about 7 years ago, and, when last heard from, was in BALTIMORE, MD. Intelligence of him will be thankfully received by his brother, **Patrick Greham**, by writing to him in care of **Mr. Bernard Fallon**, Brookline Street, CAMBRIDGEPORT, MASS. Baltimore, Md., papers, please copy.

Of **Patrick** and **Michael Washington**, from the Townland of DERAMORE, Parish of KILBECANTY, County GALWAY, Ireland. Patrick left home 14 years and Michael 13 years ago. When last heard from, Patrick was supposed to be residing in the State of INDIANA 3 years ago. They are sons of **John Washington** and **Catherine Connors**. Any one knowing of their whereabouts will confer a great favor by writing to their brother, **John Washington**, LAWRENCE, MASS.

March 30, 1867

Of **John O'Brien**, a blacksmith, formerly of DELHI, DEL., who went to NEW YORK on the 10th of July, 1846. Also of **William Maher**, coal merchant, who lived on the corner of Relay and West Streets, Delhi, Del. Intelligence of them will be thankfully received by **Patrick McMeel**, DELHI, DELAWARE.

Of **Margaret Loughary**, by her brother, **William Loughary**. When last heard from was in the City. Information of her will be thankfully received. Address, William Loughary, PEEKSKILL, WESTCHESTER County, N.Y., care of **Wm. M. Dayton**, Box 160.

Of **John, James** and **Lawrence Dwyer** and sisters, of CARROWREAH, near TUBBERCURRY, Parish of CLOONACOOL, County SLIGO, Ireland, who came to this country about 20 years ago. Also of their sister, **Catherine Kennedy**, who emigrated from MANCHESTER, ENGLAND, in November, 1865, and landed in New York in the ship *Chancelor*. Information of them will be thankfully received by their uncle's son, by addressing **W. P. Coleman**, 119 MULBERRY STREET, NEW YORK. Western papers, please copy.

Of **James Collins**, a native of the County CORK, Ireland, who left FALL RIVER, MASS., in 1857, and went West. When last heard from, about 2 years ago, he was in PORT WASHINGTON, WISCONSIN. Information of him will be thankfully received by his father, **David Collins**, No. 7 ½ Washington St., FALL RIVER, MASS. Western papers, please copy.

Of **Thomas** and **Mary Lynch**, natives of SHIRCOCK, County CAVAN, Ireland, who emigrated to this country about 13 or 14 years ago. When last heard from, about 7 years ago, they were in BROOKLYN. Information of them will be thankfully received by their brother **James**, who arrived here in April, 1866. Address **James Lynch**, FALL RIVER, MASS.

Of **Patrick O'Brien**, of KILBENRY, County LIMERICK, Ireland, aged 24 years. When last heard from, last Christmas 12 months, he lived with a gentleman named **Jones**, in LAWRENCEVILLE, ALLEGHENY County, PA. Information of him will be thankfully received by **Mrs. O'Brien**, COEYMAN'S LANDING, ALBANY County, N.Y.

April 6, 1867

Of **Michael, John** and **Mary Anne Byrnes**, who were sent to America about 12 years ago, by **Mr. John Kennedy**, of PAYMOUNT, County DUBLIN. Any information of them will be thankfully received by their sister, **Margaret Byrnes**. Address F, Box 2295, NEW YORK P.O.

Of **Bridget** and **Johanna Moore**, natives of THOMASTOWN, County KILKENNY, Ireland. When last heard from they were in PITTSBURGH, PA. Information of their whereabouts will be thankfully received by their sister, **Ellen Moore**. Address, **Richard Coady**, ST. JOSEPH, BUCHANAN County, MO.

Of **John** and **Michael Murphy**, natives of KILFANE, Parish of TOLLO, County KILKENNY, Ireland. When last heard from, one was in BELFONTE, CENTRE County, PA., and the other in ST. LOUIS, MO. Information of their whereabouts will be thankfully received by their brother, **Edward Murphy**. Address Edward Murphy, ST. JOSEPH, BUCHANAN County, MO., care of **Richard Coady**.

Of **John Keliher**, who left CAHIRCIVEEN, County of KERRY, Ireland, in August, 1863. When last heard from was in MILFORD, MASS. His brother **Timothy**, who arrived in steamer *Malta*, March 18th, in New York, wishes to hear from him. Address Box 4,860, Post Office, NEW YORK.

Of **John, James** and **Robert Prendergast**, brothers who emigrated to this country in 1847, from the Parish of GAMMONSFIELD, County TIPPERARY. When last heard from, James was with Engineers on the Mississippi, and Robert was in IOWA. - Any information of their whereabouts will be thankfully received by their sister. Address **Mary Prendergast**, 287 Prospect Street, CLEVELAND, OHIO. Boston and Iowa papers, please copy.

Of **Catherine Lawler**, or her uncles, **Patrick, James** and **Austin Mooney, natives of** ENNISTYMON, County CLARE, Ireland. When last heard from they were in MELBOURNE, AUSTRALIA. Any information of them will be thankfully received by their sister, **Mary Lawler**, No. 2 Wooster Place, NEW HAVEN, CONN. Canada papers, please copy.

Of **Michael, Frank, Bridget** and **Alice Lawler**, natives of ENNISTYMON, County of CLARE, Ireland, and who left about the year 1845. Any information of them will be thankfully received by their sister, **Mary Lawler**, No. 2 Wooster Place, NEW HAVEN, CONN. St. John's, N.B, papers, please copy.

April 13, 1867

Of **Michael, Phillip, Bridget, Catherine** and **Eliza McIntyre**, all of whom are supposed to be in NEW YORK. Information of them will be thankfully received by their sister, **Margaret McIntyre**, LEAVENWORTH CITY, KANSAS.

Of **Michael, Patrick** and **James Mulvey**, and also of their sisters, **Jane, Maria, Eliza** and **Susan Mulvey**, natives of SHEEBUG, Parish of KILTURBET, County LEITRIM, Ireland. They are supposed to reside in NEW YORK or its vicinity. Information of either of them will be thankfully received by their sister, **Teresa Mulvey**. Address **John Whitney**, 186 Westminster Street, PROVIDENCE, R.I.

Of **Michael McCarthy**, and of his wife **Mary** (whose maiden name was **Mary Hudson**), natives of GOREY, County WEXFORD, Ireland. When last heard from (about nine years ago) they were in DAYTON, OHIO. Information of them will be thankfully received by **Jas. Hudson**, care of **Martin Riley**, cor. Kent and Flushing Avenues, BROOKLYN, Long Island, N.Y. Ohio papers, please copy.

Of **Daniel Gannon**, a native of ROSCOMMON, Ireland, who left the City of NEW YORK about seven years ago, and has not been heard of since. Information of him will be thankfully received by his wife, **Elizabeth Gannon**, JAMAICA, QUEENS County, Long Island, N.Y.

Of **Michael Cawley**, a native of the Parish of BUNNINNADDEN, County SLIGO, Ireland, who moved from XENIA, OHIO, in 1853, to ST. PAUL, MINN. When last heard from he was running on a steamboat from St. Paul, south. Information will be thankfully received by his brother, **John Cawley**, GREENCASTLE, PUTNAM County, INDIANA.

April 20, 1867

Of **Michael McKendra**, who, when last heard from, was somewhere in NEW YORK or PENNSYLVANIA. Any information of him will be thankfully received by his father, **James McKendra**, EAST LONGMEADOW, MASS.

Of **Henry Hurll**, a native of BALLYMENA, County ANTRIM, Ireland. He arrived in this country, at New Orleans, in 1832. When last heard of he was in NEW BRUNSWICK, N.J. Information of him will be thankfully received by his sister, **Teresa Hurll**, at No. 280 FIRST AVENUE, NEW YORK CITY. New Orleans and New Brunswick papers, please copy.

April 27, 1867

Of **Mary Ann Ford**, who left MERIDEN, CONN., in October, 1863, to go to her uncles in NEW YORK. Information of her will be thankfully received by her brother **Patrick**. Address **P. Ford**, MERIDEN, CONN.

Of **Thomas, Patrick**, and **Joseph Mullaly**, natives of the County LONGFORD, Ireland. About five years ago they left DUBUQUE, IOWA, for PIKE'S PEAK. Information of them will be thankfully received by their sister **Bridget**. Address **John Bridgett**, Box 916, POKEEPSIE Post Office, N.Y. California papers, please copy.

Of **Patrick Ahern**, who left BALLYMACODA, Co. CORK, Ireland, about 19 years ago. When last heard from, he was in ALBANY, N.Y. Information of him will be thankfully received by his sister **Margaret**. Direct to **Patrick Leary**, STAUGHTON, DANE County, WISCONSIN.

Of **Patrick Langan**, a native of the Parish of STAMULLAN, County MEATH, Ireland, who emigrated to this country about 12 years ago. When last heard from he was in one of the western States. Information of him will be thankfully received by his brother, **Michael Langan**, PHILADELPHIA, PA. Address **Patrick Davis**, 1903 Pearl Street, PHILADELPHIA, PENNSYLVANIA.

Of **Daniel Conroy**, a native of the Parish of REARY, near the Town of MOUNTMELLICK, QUEEN'S County, Ireland. He is 21 years of age, and a mason by trade. He sailed from Cork for New York in the steamer *City of Washington*, in the month of April, 1864. When last heard from he was in NEW JERSEY. Information of him will be thankfully received by his sister, **Mary Anne Conroy**, 138 Preston Street, BALTIMORE, MD.

Of **James O'Neill**, from AUGHRIM, County ROSCOMMON, Ireland. Intelligence of him will be thankfully received by his sister **Eliza** (who arrived on the 19th ult., in the steamship *Great Eastern*), at **Thomas B. Mitchell's** SCHENECTADY, NEW YORK.

Of **John Connell**, of the Town of TIPPERARY, Ireland, who emigrated to this country in May, 1865. When last heard from he was in PENNSYLVANIA. Any information of him will be thankfully received by his brother, **Dennis Connell**, No. 2 Mill St., BROOKLYN, N.Y. [Bottom of page is illegible.]

May 4, 1867

Of **Martin J. Pye**, formerly of CLIFDEN, County GALWAY, Ireland, who came to this country about three years ago, and spent some time in NEW YORK CITY. Intelligence of his present whereabouts will be thankfully received by **Patrick J. Meehan**, Irish-American Office, New York.

Of **Jerry Tuohey**, a native of FEAKLE, County CLARE, Ireland. When last heard of (about two years ago), he was in OIL CITY, PA. Information of him will be thankfully received by his sister, **Mary Tuohey**, at 240 MONROE STREET, NEW YORK, in care of **Thady Moloney**.

Of **Patrick O'Keefe**, from the County of CLARE, Ireland, who left NEW YORK CITY in January, 1866, to go to PENNSYLVANIA. Information of him will be thankfully received by his only sister, at 63 WASHINGTON STREET, NEW YORK. Western papers, please copy.

May 11, 1867

Of **John McKeowen**, who was taken out of the Catholic Orphan Asylum of PHILADELPHIA about ten or eleven years ago, and bound out to a man named **Patrick O'Donnell**, a blacksmith by trade, residing in some part of SUSQUEHANNA County,

PENN. Information of him would be thankfully received by his mother, **Isabella McKeowen**, at No. 214 Columbia Avenue, PHILADELPHIA, PENN.

Of **Patrick Carty**, a native of County LEITRIM, Ireland, who left HENCE, near WIGGING, LANCASHIRE, ENGLAND, on the 17th of November, 1863. When last heard from he was in NOBLESTOWN, ALLEGHENY County, PA. Information of him will be thankfully received by his brother-in-law, **Paul Nuel**, BLOSSBURG, TIOGA County, PA.

Of **Patrick Davey**, of the Parish of DRUMISKABOLA, County SLIGO, Ireland. When last heard from he lived in BROOKLYN, L.I., about a year ago. Any information regarding his whereabouts will be thankfully received by his brother, **John Davey**, in care of **Patrick McGuinn**, 146 Hamilton Avenue, BROOKLYN, N.Y.

Of **Maria Turnbull**, daughter of **John** and **Elizabeth Turnbull**, Merrion-square, DUBLIN, who, in company with her cousins, **Dennis** and **Bessy McGee**, emigrated from BALLYMAHON, County LONGFORD, Ireland, to the United States, in 1851 or 1852. When last heard from, in 1854, she was in NEW ORLEANS, LA. Information of her will be gratefully received, and a reward of $10 given, by her sister, **Elizabeth Flannery**, BENICIA, SOLANO County, CAL. New Orleans papers, please copy.

Of **Patrick McLoughlin**, a native of the Town of ATHY, County KILDARE, Ireland, who arrived in New York last March, and is supposed to be still residing there. Information of him will be thankfully received by his wife, **Mrs. McLoughlin**, at 59 MOTT STREET, NEW YORK.

May 18, 1867

Of **Rose Kenney**, late of WAKEFIELD, Parish of BLUNT, WESCOTT, Ireland. When last heard from was in the City of NEW YORK. Please address **Michael Kenney**, No. 7 South Calhoun Street, BALTIMORE, MD.

Of **John Wasson**, who left RAHWAY, N.J., on the 6th of November, 1853. When last heard from, in 1865, he was in NEW YORK City. Any information of him will be thankfully received by his son **George**, or his wife, **Ellen Wasson**, No. 254 Union St., RAHWAY, N.J.

Of **William Henderson**, of DUBLIN, boot and shoemaker, who left MANCHESTER, ENGLAND, in 1856. Was in BOSTON in 1858. Intelligence of him, given to **Mr. Maurice Kiely**, United States Arsenal, WASHINGTON, will be gratefully and substantially rewarded by his wife, **Ann Morrissey**.

Of **Ellen McLaughlin** - second name, **Ellen Keefe** - a native of the Parish of BALLINACOURTY, near DINGLE, County KERRY, Ireland, who came to NEW YORK about thirty years ago. When last heard of was in the neighborhood of ALBANY. Address her sister, **Johanna Flahiff**, or **Patrick Flahiff**, TIVOLI Post Office, DUBUQUE County, IOWA. Albany papers, please copy.

Of **Stafford Kane**, a native of KADY, County DERRY, Ireland, who left PHILADELPHIA some eight or nine years ago, and served in Co. D, 3rd Infantry, U.S. army. Any information of him will be thankfully received by his sisters, **Margaret** and **Mary Kane**, by addressing **R. W. Hamilton**, DOYLESTOWN, BUCKS County, PA.

Of **Bridget Kerin**, aged 25 years, of BALLYVAUGHAN, County CLARE, Ireland. When last heard from, in 1861, she was in NEW ORLEANS. Her sister, **Mrs. Honora Higgins**, will be thankful for information of her, addressed to D. A. Brosnan, Foreign Passage and Exchange Agent, WASHINGTON, D. C.

May 25, 1867

Of **Thomas Foley**, by his wife **Susan**. It will be thankfully received at 63 18th STREET, North-West corner of 6th Avenue, NEW YORK. New Orleans and St. Louis papers, please copy.

Of **Edward Riordan**, carpenter, who left BANDON, County CORK, Ireland, 19 years ago, for NEW YORK; went to ILLINOIS in 1855, left BLOOMINGTON, ILL., in May, 1866, and has not since been heard from. Information of him will be thankfully received by his son **Daniel**, and a reward of $10 will be given to the person who gives information as to his whereabouts (if alive), and (if dead) where and when he died. Address **Daniel Riordan**, corner of 90th STREET, and 4th AVENUE, NEW YORK. Irish and American papers, please copy.

Of **Arthur Murphy**, a native of BELTUCHBUNO, County LOUTH, Ireland. When last heard of, in 1846, he was in CAMBRIDGEPORT, near BOSTON, MASS. Information of him will be thankfully received by his nepehws, **John** and **Joseph Hoy**, at 69 York Street, JERSEY CITY, N.J.

Of **John Duffy**, a native of BRUFF, Parish of AUGHAMORE, County MAYO, Ireland. When last heard from, about five years ago, he was in SUMMERVILLE, GEORGIA. He has lost one arm, and has one son, a Counselor-at-Law. Information of him will be thankfully received by his niece, **Mary Duffy**, by addressing her at DUNKIRK, CHAUTAUQUA County, N.Y.

Of **Dougal White**, a native of KILMACRENAN, County DONEGAL, Ireland. When last heard from he was in PHILADELPHIA, PA. Information of him will be thankfully received by his brothers, **Hugh** and **Michael White**, at 223 WEST 27th STREET, NEW YORK, care of **Mr. Bernard Toner**. Philadelphia papers, please copy.

June 1, 1867

Of **William Murphy**, a native of BROOKLYN, N.Y. When last heard of he lived with **Mr. Edward Houns**, MELBOURNE, N.J. Information of him will be thankfully received either by writing to the Irish-American office, New York, or to **Thos. Sheridan**, 234 Wain Street, JERSEY CITY, N.J. His sisters, who live in NEW YORK CITY, will confer a favor, should they know of his whereabouts, by writing to either of the above addresses.

Of **William Keating**, of BALLYGRIFFIN, County TIPPERARY, Ireland, who emigrated to this country several years ago. When last heard from he was in the State of ILLINOIS. Any person knowing of his whereabouts will confer a great favor on his sister **Mary** by addressing her at 24 BANK STREET, NEW YORK.

Of **Catherine Preston**, a native of BALLINA, County MAYO, Ireland, who landed at Castle Garden on the 27th of April last, and while there wrote to her brother to MIDDLEFIELD, MASS., for money, who forwarded $10 to Castle Garden for her. A few days before the money arrived she strolled out and has not been seen or heard of since. Her disappearance is so mysterious (added to the fact of her not again calling to get the money) as to arouse the serious apprehensions of her brother as to what may have befallen her. Information of her will be thankfully received by writing either to J. W. Wheeler, Castle Garden, or to **Edward Dowdeen**, No. 145 LEONARD STREET, NEW YORK CITY.

Of **Austin Gaughan**, a native of TURLOUGH, County MAYO, Ireland, who left LIVERPOOL for this country about 18 years ago, and when last seen (about nine years ago) was in ALTON, ILL. Information of him will be thankfully received by his poor, troubled mother, **Mary Gaughan**, by addressing her in care of **B. O'Neill**, Justice of the Peace, PATERSON, N.J.

Of **Charles, Catherine, Nancy** and **Sarah Tenney**, son and daughters of **Neil Tenney** and **Catherine Doherty**, of DRUMQUIN, Parish of RAPHOE, County DONEGAL, Ireland, who are residing in or around PHILADELPHIA. Information of them will be thankfully received by their sister **Margaret,** by addressing **Mrs. Margaret Liardi**, 314 MONROE STREET, NEW YORK. Philadelphia papers, please copy.

Of **Daniel Cunningham**, a native of BALLYBUNION, County KERRY. He was in PORTLAND, MAINE, at the time of the conflagration. Information of him will be thankfully received by his brother, **Timothy Cunningham**, Patent-office, WASHINGTON, D. C.

Of **John** and **William Borns**, natives of THOMASTOWN, Parish of SOONCRAFT, County KILDARE, Ireland, who left home about 16 years ago. When last heard from they were in MENDOTA, LA SALLE County, ILL. They will find something to their interest by addressing **James Hoye**, AKRON, SUMMIT County, OHIO.

June 8, 1867

Of **Charles Borromeo**, who came as steerage passenger in the *Virginia*, a year ago. Any information of him will be thankfully received by **Bernard Conway**, care of **E. Van Wagenen**, P.M., NEW PALTZ, ULSTER County, N.Y. The ship was put in quarantine, and the passengers transferred to a cholera receiving ship, supposed to be the *Falcon*. Borromeo might be remembered by a black ebony flute he played. A large reward will be given for authentic information. [This ad seems to refer to the same man called **Charles B. McDermot** in an ad which Appeared June 22, 1867.]

Of **Cornelius O'Brien**, a native of the Parish of SKULL, County CORK, Ireland, who emigrated about 20 years ago. He sailed from Balledhob in a ship called the *Tryagain*, and landed in Quebec, and went to KINGSTON, in CANADA. When last heard from, about 18 years ago, he was in NEW YORK. Any information of him will be thankfully received and $5 reward given, by his father and sister. Address **Daniel O'Brien**, ROXBURY, CHALLYBEES Post-office, LITCHFIELD County, CONN.

Of **Patrick Carrick**, who came to this country from GOWER, County CLARE, Ireland, about 3 years ago. When last heard of (about 2 years since) he was living in NEW JERSEY. Information respecting him will be thankfully received by **John Hassett**, care of **J. P. Harbison**, HARTFORD, CONN.

June 15, 1867

Of **Mrs. Caroll** and her son **Mike**. When last heard of (in 1862) her address was 341 (at the store) MADISON STREET, NEW YORK. They will hear of something to their advantage by immediately writing to their friend in NEW LONDON.

Of **Thomas Mulligan**, who left DUBLIN in February, 1865. When last heard of he was in NEW YORK. Any information will be thankfully received by his brother, **Daniel Mulligan**, at **Mr. Brower's**, FLUSHING, Long Island, N.Y.

Of **John Walton** (son of **Frank Walton**), formerly of MACROOM, County CORK, who came to this country some 15 years since, and is supposed to be in ST. LOUIS, MO. His brother, **Cornelius Walton**, has arrived in this country, and is anxious to hear from him. Address him care of **Timothy Hogan**, 410 PEARL STREET, NEW YORK.

Of **Timothy Conway**, of CAHIRCIVEEN, County KERRY, Ireland. When last heard from was in CHICAGO, ILLS. Any information of his present whereabouts will be thankfully received by his brother, **Michael Conway**, No. 497 PEARL STREET, NEW YORK CITY.

June 22, 1867

Of **Charles B. McDermot**, who left for America, on board the *Virginia*, about twelve months since, as a steerage passenger. He arrived in New York Bay, and has not since been heard of. Any one who knows what has become of him will confer a favor by writing to **Bernard Conway**, NEW PALTZ, ULSTER County, N.Y., care of **E. Van Wagenen**. [This ad seems to refer to the same man called **Charles Borromeo** in an ad which Appeared June 8, 1867.]

Of **Bridget Martin**, of KNOCK, Parish of KILMAIN, County ROSCOMMON, Ireland, who sailed from Liverpool, on the 30th of April, in the ship *Victory*, and landed at Castle Garden on 11th of June, 1867. Information of her will be thankfully received by her sister, **Mary Martin**, at 127 Ward Street, PATERSON, N.J., or at the Irish-American Office. If any of the passengers of the *Victory* know anything concerning her, they will confer a great favor by sending it to either of the above addresses.

Of **Michael Pyne**, of the Parish of CASTLELYONS, County CORK, Ireland, who landed in New Haven, State of Connecticut, in the year 1846, where he worked for seven years, and then left for INDIANA, about 14 years ago, with a railroad contractor, name **John Boyle**. Information will be thankfully received, and a reward of $5 will be given, by his brother, **Edward Pyne**, ALEXANDRIA, VA. Indiana papers, please copy.

Of **Bartly Heaher**, of COROFIN, County CLARE, Ireland, who left there 16 years ago. When last heard of (three years ago), he was in the State of CALIFORNIA. Intelligence of him will be thankfully received by his sister, **Mary Collins**, and her two sons, **Thomas** and **Patrick Collins**, at AMSTERDAM, MONTGOMERY County, N.Y. California papers, please copy.

June 29, 1867

Of **Bridget Carr**, who left Ireland in the year 1844. Her brother, **Patrick Carr**, resides in PORTER County, INDIANA. Bridget Carr is supposed to reside in the adjoining County of LAKE. Any letters giving intelligence of her, directed to **H. Norton**, VALPARAISO, PORTER County, IND., will be promptly answered.

Of **Thomas Dyer**, from BALLYMOTE, Co. SLIGO, Ireland, by his wife, **Mary**, and her children, at Castle Garden. When last heard from, three and a half years ago, he was in YOUNGSTOWN, OHIO.

July 6, 1867

Of **Edward Nolan**, a native of KILDARE, Ireland, who left Dublin, on the 18th of September last for New York, by one of the Cunard line of steamers. He was last employed as fireman in Pine's Flour Mills, RINGSEND Drawbridge, DUBLIN. Intelligence of him will be thankfully received by his sister. Address or apply to **Bridget Caufield**, 30 Sussex Street, JERSEY CITY, N.J.

Of **Joseph McCabe**, a native of KILDUFF, County MONAGHAN, Ireland, by his brother, **Thomas McCabe**, at 127 LIBERTY STREET, NEW YORK.

Of **Patrick Harvey**, a native of DONEGAL, Ireland, who left his brother's house, on Germantown road and 8th Street, PHILADELPHIA, PA., about nine months ago. Any information of his whereabouts will be thankfully received by his sister, **Litia Harvey**, at 611 South 4th Street, PHILADELPHIA, PA.

July 13, 1867

Of **John Madden**, who lived at No. 25 BROADWAY (Stevans House), NEW YORK CITY. Was last heard of, in January, 1867. Information of him will be kindly received by his brother, **Hugh Madden**, who lives at **Mr. Brower's**, FLUSHING, Long Island, N.Y.

Of **Peter Donohoe**. Any one knowing of his whereabouts will confer a favor on **Catherine Donohoe** and child, by writing to them in care of **James McDonald**, ROUNDOUT, N.Y.

Of **James, Ann** and **Bridget McCann**, of the Townland of MULLAY, Parish of KILLASS, County LEITRIM, Ireland, who came to this country 17 years ago. When last heard from they were in BOSTON, MASS., about 15 years since. Information of them will be thankfully received by their brother, **Patrick McCann**, BRIDGEPORT, CONN.

Of **James Hanlon**, who joined the 6th Pa. Cavalry in 1863. When last heard from, in October, 1864, he was in the Gutherian Hospital, MARTINSBURG, VA. Information of him will be thankfully received by his mother, **Mrs. Bridget Hanlon**, 1930 Belgrade Street, PHILADELPHIA, PA.[Appeared under County LONGFORD]

Of **Jeremiah O'Leary**, a native of the County CORK, Ireland. When last heard from he was in CHICAGO, ILL., about 14 months ago. Information of him will be thankfully received by his sister **Ellen Rain**, QUINCY, ILL., Post Office Box 1158. New York papers, please copy.

July 20, 1867

Of **Kate Fox**, a native of the County MEATH, Ireland, who came to NEW YORK in March, 1862. Any person knowing her present address will confer a favor by sending it to **James Mathews**, care of **Maurice Lynan**, No. 32 Depuyster Street, CHICAGO, ILLINOIS.

Of **Jane Cleary**, a native of LIMERICK, but for about three years a resident of CREGG CASTLE, County GALWAY, Ireland. Should this meet her eye she will learn something to her advantage by addressing **F. Keogh**, Box 64, NEWBURGH, N.Y., giving her address in full.

Of **David, Cornelius, Pat**, and **Daniel Leahy**, natives of BALLYREGAN, County of LIMERICK, Ireland. When last heard from (about 11 years ago) they were in ILLUMINATED ISLAND, LOWER CANADA. Intelligence of them will be thankfully received by their brother, **James Leahy**, care of **John Feaghney**, 145 EAST 9th STREET, NEW YORK. Canada papers, please copy. [Appeared July 27, 1867 with the name John Feaghney changed to **Michael Faghney**, and his address changed to 415 EAST 19th STREET, NEW YORK.]

Of **Martin** and **James O'Farrell**, natives of the Parish of CLONDIGAD, County CLARE, Ireland, who emigrated to this country - Martin in 1850, and James in 1856. When last heard from (in August, 1858,) they were in LASALLE, ILL. Intelligence of them will be thankfully received by their brother, **William O'Farrell**, No. 5 Hudson Avenue, BROOKLYN, L.I., in care of **Wm. Lennon**.

Of **Mary Kane** or **Hagerty**, and her daughter, **Mary Kane**, natives of BALLINA, Co. MAYO, Ireland. The former arrived in New York 18 years ago, and the latter 11 years since at the same port. Information of them will be kindly received by **Henry Kane**, at 131 Lock Box, INDIANAPOLIS, IND.

Of **James Bourke**, a native of CLONMEL, County TIPPERARY, Ireland, who landed in New York 8 months ago. When last heard from (a month ago) he was in EAST NEW

YORK. Intelligence of him will be thankfully received by his wife, **Bridget Bourke**, at 36 CHERRY STREET, NEW YORK.

Of **Francis Donoghue**, a native of BALLYSHANNON, County DONEGAL, Ireland. When last heard from he was in CAMP NELSON, KENTUCKY, in February, 1865. Information of him will be thankfully received by his sister, **Catherine Donoghue**, at 16 WEST 21st STREET, NEW YORK. Kentucky papers, please copy.

July 27, 1867

Of **Thomas Leary**, who left No. 6 Sleaters Court, Bluanker Yard, Royal Mint Street, LONDON, ENGLAND, about three years ago. When last heard from he was in PORT JERVIS, ORANGE County, N.Y. Intelligence of him will be thankfully received by his friend, **Timothy Mahony**, by writing to him in care of **Patrick Feelley**, North Third Street, between Grove and Prospect Streets (Connolly Building), JERSEY CITY, N.J.

Of **Ellen Flynn**, who arrived in this country in June last, per steamer *Helvetia*, and was going to PEORIA, ILL., and missed her friends at the NEW JERSEY Central Depot. Call at Thompson's Passage Office, 73 BROADWAY, NEW YORK.

Of **John Byrne**, a native of the Parish of BALLINAMEAN, County ROSCOMMON, Ireland, who left home 3 years last February, and was in NORTH ORANGE, N.J., the first year after landing. When last heard from he was in PENNSYLVANIA. Information of him will be thankfully received by his sister, **Margaret Byrne**, at NORTH ORANGE, ESSEX County, N.J.

Of — **McCabe**, a native of the Townland of DRUMNAVEEL, Parish of DRUMGOON, County CAVAN, Ireland, who came to this country about five years ago. Also of her brother, **Patrick McCabe**, from the same place, who, it was heard died lately somewhere in this country. Any person giving information of the above will confer a great favor on their brother, **John McCabe**, and friends. Please direct to John McCabe, VICKSBURG, MISS.

Of **Thomas** and **Edward Flynn**, from the Town of CARLOW, Ireland, bricklayers by trade. When last heard from (about twelve years ago), they were in NEW YORK CITY. Information of them, addressed to their brother, **James Flynn**, GLOUCESTER, CAMDEN County, N.J., will be thankfully received.

Of **Patrick McGinn**, a native of WESTPORT, County MAYO, Ireland. Any person knowing his present address will confer a favor by sending it to **Martin McGinn**, SAN FRANCISCO Post Office, CALIFORNIA.

Of **Mrs. Catherine Walsh**, maiden name **Neary**, widow of the late **James Walsh**, boot and shoe maker; also of her son, **John Joseph Walsh**. When last heard from, 2 years ago, Mrs. Walsh was in NEW YORK. Information of them will be thankfully received by her brother, **Michael Neary** (late of BURNFURZE, County KILKENNY, Ireland,) by writing to him in care of **James Newhall**, Esq., DYE HOUSE VILLAGE, LYNN, MASS.

Of **Margaret Walsh**, a native of CARREGTWOHILL, County CORK, Ireland. When last heard from (about 8 years ago), she was in NEW YORK CITY. Intelligence of her will be thankfully received by her sister, **Ellen Walsh**, at No. 102 Sixth Street, HOBOKEN, N.J.

Of **Michael Shiels**, a native of GARRYOWEN, LIMERICK, Ireland. When last heard of he was in Dexter's Hotel, QUEBEC, CANADA. Information respecting his whereabouts will be thankfully received by his brother, **Patrick J. Shiels**, 918 Ernst Street, PHILADELPHIA, PA. Canada papers, please copy.

August 3, 1867

Of **John Sullivan**, a native of KENMARE, County KERRY, Ireland. When last heard from he was in NEW ORLEANS, LA. Intelligence of him will be thankfully received by his brother **Patrick**, at 21 Hudson Street, NEWARK, N.J.

Of **William Ready**, a native of LISTROY, County KERRY, Ireland. He landed in New York in June, 1866. Any information of him will be thankfully received by his sister, **Margaret Ready**, at 81st ST., between 9th and 10th Avs., NEW YORK.

August 10, 1867

Of **Bernard William Hughes**, a native of the Parish of DONAH, County MONAGHAN, Ireland, who came to MILWAUKEE, WIS., on the 1st day of June, 1867, in search of his sisters. Information of him will be thankfully received by his sisters, **Bridget** and **Mary Hughes**, at 418 Clybourne Street, MILWAUKEE, WIS.

Of **Bessie Golligly**, a native of BALLYBAY, County MONAGHAN, Ireland, who left for this country in April, 1864, since which time she has not been heard from. Intelligence of her will be thankfully received by her brother, **Michael Golligly**, by addressing him in care of **William Geary**, 520 State Street, NEW HAVEN, CONN.

Of **Patrick Harney**, a native of the Parish of BALLYNAIL, County TIPPERARY, Ireland. When last heard from he was in NEW YORK CITY. Information of him will be thankfully received by his brother, **John Harney**, at BATTLE CREEK, CALHOUN County, MICH.

Of **John McCarty**, a native of BALLYSHEEN, Parish of ODORNEY, County KERRY Ireland. When last heard from he was in WILKESBARRE, PA. Information of him will be thankfully received by his father and brother, **Cornelius** and **James McCarty**. Address, **Catherine Moloney**, BINGHAMTON, BROOME County, N.Y.

Of **Margaret Renan**, (maiden name, **Stephens**), and her sister **Ann**, natives of the Parish of STRAY, County MAYO, Ireland, who left LANCASHIRE, ENGLAND, about 11 years ago, for NEW YORK. Information of them will be thankfully received by their sister **Hellen**, at MORRIS RUN, TIOGA County, PA.

August 17, 1867

Of **John Mulcahy**, of the 88th Regt. Irish Infantry, a native of LIMERICK City, Ireland. He will hear of his sister **Jenny**, by calling at No. 643 BROADWAY, NEW YORK, in the gallery.

Of **Patrick Desmond**, of CLONAKILTY, County CORK, Ireland. When last heard from (about 15 years ago) he was in SAULT ST. MARY, LAKE SUPERIOR, MICH. He was in the dry-goods business in both places. Information of his present whereabouts will be thankfully received by his brother, **Jeremiah Desmond**. Direct to **Daniel Fleming**, horseshoer, 112 CLINTON STREET, NEW YORK.

Of **James Whelan**, a native of CLUNMINES, County WEXFORD, Ireland. When last heard from he was in NEW JERSEY. Information of his whereabouts will be thankfully received by **Thomas Stafford**, HALLOWELL, ME.

Of **James Hefferan**, formerly of the County WESTMEATH, Ireland. When last seen by advertiser he was working in PATERSON, N.J. It is now supposed he is working in some of the coal mines in PENNSYLVANIA. Any information of him will be thankfully received by his sister-in-law, **Anne English**, 35 New Street, NEWARK, N.J.

August 24, 1867

Of **Bridget Smith**, a native of LAVE, County CAVAN, Ireland. When last heard from (about four years ago) she was in ST. LOUIS, MO. Any intelligence of her will be thankfully received by her sister **Ellen**, at 128 29ᵗʰ STREET, NEW YORK CITY.

August 31, 1867

Of **Ed. Ward**, who left ST. LOUIS in 18[6]4 for CALIFORNIA. If this should meet the eye of any of his friends they will please send his address to **E. McCormack**, 16 St. Felix Street, BROOKLYN, Long Island, N.Y. St. Louis, California and Montana papers, please copy.

Of **Wm. Fletcher Bournes**, a native of CASTLEBAR, County MAYO, Ireland. He served in the 11ᵗʰ Michigan during the war; went to CANADA with the Fenians in June, 1866, and was amongst the number arrested by the U.S. authorities, since which time nothing has been heard from or of him. Intelligence of him will be thankfully received by his brother, **George C. Bournes**, at NEW YORK CITY Post Office.

Of **Timothy** and **Mary Durkin**, from BALLINA, County MAYO, Ireland. Intelligence of them will be thankfully received by their mother, **Margaret Durkin**, PLATTSBURGH, N.Y.

Of **Thomas Kielly**, from BANSHA, County TIPPERARY, Ireland. When last heard from (about 18 months ago), he was in the U.S. Army. Since then it is supposed he has left the Army, and is now living in CHARLESTON, S.C. Information of him will be thankfully received by his sister, **Johanna Kielly**, by writing to her in care of **John Allen**, 31 Hamilton Avenue (in the coal office) SOUTH BROOKLYN, Long Island, N.Y. Charleston, S.C., papers, please copy.

Of **Michael Freeman**, from the Parish of BEMNENADEN, County SLIGO, Ireland, who came to this country 16 years ago. He served three years in the Confederate army, and escaped to CINCINATTI before the war terminated. Ten Dollars Reward to any one who will give any information of his whereabouts, if alive. Please address to his brother, **James Freeman**, care of **Thomas O'Bryan**, 64 Seneca Street, BUFFALO, N.Y. Boston Pilot and Ohio and Missouri papers, please copy.

Of **Martin Davey**, a native of the Town of SLIGO, County SLIGO, Ireland. When last heard of he was said to be in TENNESSEE. Intelligence of him will be thankfully received by his brother, **Michael Davey**, at Van Brunt Street, rear of the Atlantic Foundery, BROOKLYN, Long Island, N.Y.

Of **John Fortune**, a native of ADAMSTOWN, County WEXFORD, Ireland. He last wrote on the 4ᵗʰ of July, 1867, from CHICAGO, ILL. Information of him will be thankfully received by his brother and sister, **Terrence** and **Mary Fortune**, back of No. 336 St. John's Street, PHILADELPHIA, PA. Chicago papers, please copy.

September 7, 1867

Of **Margaret, Catherine** and **Hanorah Desmond**, natives of MALLOW, County CORK, Ireland, who emigrated to this country about 18 years ago. When last heard from (about 8 years ago) they were in PHILADELPHIA, PA. Intelligence of them will be thankfully received by their nephew, **John Callaghan**, at 460 WEST 40ᵗʰ STREET, between 9ᵗʰ and 10ᵗʰ Avenues. New York and Philadelphia papers, please copy.

Of **Catherine Burke**, (maiden name, **Larkin**,) a native of NENAGH, County TIPPERARY, Ireland. When last heard of she was a resident of TROY, N.Y. Information of her will be thankfully received by her niece, **Catherine Larkin**, of 195 WEST 11ᵗʰ ST., NEW YORK.

September 14, 1867

Of **Mrs. Gaierty** (maiden name **Bridget Moloney**), who, when last heard from, was employed as cook on board of one of the BUFFALO canal boats. Any person knowing of her present whereabouts will confer a favor by writing to her sister, **Catherine Moloney**, care of **Daniel Moris**, Esq., NEWBURGH, ORANGE County, N.Y., Box 663.

Of **John O'Brien**, who left his home about the 17th of October, 1864. Is about six feet high, sandy complexion, blue eyes, sandy hair, and by occupation a tailor. Information of his whereabouts will be thankfully received by his wife, **Catherine O'Brien**, 20 CHERRY STREET, NEW YORK. Cleveland and Cincinnati papers, please copy.

Of **James Roan**, who, when last heard from, was in KATSKILL, N.Y. Information of him will be thankfully received by his mother, in care of **Mr. John Williamson**, ANALOMINK post office, MONROE County PA. Western papers, please copy.

Of **James Lawlis**, son of **Thomas Lawlis**, a native of CONEHEY, County KILKENNY, Ireland. When last heard of he was in CINCINNATI, OHIO. Intelligence of him will be thankfully received by **Richard Lawlis**, at HAVERSTRAW, ROCKLAND County, NEW YORK.

September 21, 1867

Of **Michael Keating**, who came from LEVERN BANKS, NELISTON, SCOTLAND, to this country, in the Summer of 1859. When last heard from he was in CHICAGO, ILL. $20 Reward will be paid for information of his whereabouts, and will be thankfully received by his brother, **John Keating**, Diamond Flax Spinning Mill, Paterson St., PATERSON, N.J. Chicago papers, please copy. [Appeared March 23, 1867 with some different information.] [Appeared under the heading of GLASGOW]

Of **Edward Gallaugher** and his wife (maiden name **Mary Doherty**); also, of their sons, **Patrick** and **James Gallaugher**, natives of TOOTHFIELD, near MANORHAMILTON, County LEITRIM, Ireland. They landed in this country about 16 or 17 years ago. When last heard from they were in the City of NEW YORK. Information of any of them will be thankfully received by **Kate Doherty**, wife of **John McNamara**, of CHERRY VALLEY, MASS.

Of **Patrick Lenahan**, a native of the Town of SLIGO, County SLIGO, Ireland, who left his home, No. 48 PRINCE STREET, NEW YORK, at ten O'clock on the morning of the 25th of May, 1866, since which time nothing has been heard of or from him. He is supposed to have gone with the Fenian soldiers to CANADA, or enlisted in the U.S. Regular Service. Information of him will be thankfully received by his wife, **Maryann Lenahan**, at 212 ELIZABETH STREET, NEW YORK.

Of **John, Dan, Jeremiah, Johanna, Catherine** and **Margaret Crowley**, natives of CLAURAUGH, County CORK, Ireland. Johanna landed in this country about five years ago, and Catherine and Margaret last Summer. Intelligence of them will be thankfully received by their sister, **Mary Crowley**, at 509 EAST 15th STREET, NEW YORK CITY.

September 28, 1867

Of **Thomas** and **John Cosgrove**, natives of the Town of GALWAY, County GALWAY, Ireland, who emigrated from WIGAN, ENGLAND, to this country about four years ago. When last heard from John was in SCHUYLKILL County, PA. Information of them will be thankfully received by their sister, **Mary Cosgrove**, who has lately arrived in this country, and is now residing at 53 Market Street, LOWELL, MASS., the house of **Edward Meaney**.

Of **Patrick Seahill**, from the Parish of Ross, County GALWAY, Ireland, who left Ireland about 25 years ago. When last heard of (8 years ago) he was in CHICAGO, ILL. Information of him will be thankfully received by **Michael Seahill** (his brother's son), CARBONDALE, PA. Western papers, please copy.

Of **John** and **Mary Ward**, natives of MORIL, Parish of MORIL, County DONEGAL, Ireland, who left Ireland about 17 years ago. When last heard from they were in PHILADELPHIA, PA. Information of them will be thankfully received by their sister, **Margaret Ward**. Address **John Leadin**, ELMWOOD, PEORIA County, ILL. Philadelphia papers, please copy.

Of **William Carlin**, from CASTLETOWN, County MEATH, Ireland. When last heard from (in March, 1866), he was in a hotel in ST. LOUIS. Information of him will be thankfully received by his sister, **Bridget Carlin**, at 123 Vine Street, CAPERS POINT, CAMDEN, N.J. St. Louis papers, please copy.

Of **Michael** and **Thomas Roche**, of KILLMEEDY, County LIMERICK, Ireland, who came to this country about 16 years ago. When last heard from, Michael was in SPRINGFIELD, ILL. Information of them will be thankfully received by their sister, **Mary Roche**, by addressing **Bernard O'Neill**, Esq., Justice of the Peace, PATERSON, N.J.

October 5, 1867

Of **Martin Nangle**, a shoemaker. He was in PITTSBURGH, PA., on the 1st of July. Information of him will be thankfully received by his mother at 37 South 18th Street, PHILADELPHIA, PA.

Of **James Dinigan**, who, when last heard of, was living in PENNSYLVANIA. Information of him will be thankfully received by either his sisters, **Catherine** or **Margaret Dinigan**, who are living at 152 42nd STREET (between 2nd and 3rd Avenues), NEW YORK.

Of **Rose Murphy**, a native of WENSBURY, STAFFORDSHIRE, ENGLAND. When last heard from (about two years ago), she was in ROXBURY, MASS - Any intelligence of her will be thankfully received by her brother-in-law, **Patrick Fallon**, at 423 EAST 18th STREET, NEW YORK CITY. Boston papers, please copy.

October 12, 1867

Of **Eliza O'Malley**; also of **Mary Criban**, who came to this country in 1842, with **Mrs. Catherine Burke**, of LUCAN, County DUBLIN. When last heard of Eliza was in WILMINGTON, DEL., and Mary was in NEW JERSEY. Information of either will be thankfully received by "Querist," Station E, EIGHTH AVENUE, NEW YORK.

Of **Thomas Begley**, a native of the Parish of KILLAREAREN, County GALWAY, Ireland. When last heard from, about nine years ago, he was in ST. LOUIS, MO., and he intended to go to NEW ORLEANS, LA. Information of him, dead or alive, will be thankfully received by writing to his brother. Direct to **John Begley**, ST. JOSEPH, MO.

Of **Thomas Donohoe**, of GORTAHORNANE, Parish of KILLEEACOUTY, County GALWAY, Ireland. Intelligence of him will be thankfully received by his wife, **Mary Donohoe**, as also of her brother, **Martin Glynn**, of the Parish of KILTHOMAS, same County. Direct to Castle Garden, up stairs.

Of **John** and **Edmond Kinady**, natives of WARLINGFORD, County KILKENNY, Ireland. Also, of **Thomas Bracken**, tailor, a native of TULLAMORE, KING'S County, Ireland. Intelligence of them will be thankfully received by writing to **J. P. Bracken**, 130 Shippen Street, PHILADELPHIA, PA. [Appeared as separate ads on Nov. 2, 1867]

Of **Hugh Kelly**, a native of STRADBALLY, QUEEN'S County, Ireland. He landed in this country in Sept. 1862. When last heard from he was in the U.S. Army during the war. Intelligence of him will be thankfully received by his mother, **Eliza Kelly**, in care of **George Duval**, 40 Summit Street, SOUTH BROOKLYN, N.Y.

October 19, 1867

James Leahy, who advertised in the Irish-American, last August, for his brothers, **Daniel, Cornelius** and **Patrick**, can find them in GOUVERNEUR, ST. LAWRENCE County, N.Y. Any communication addressed to **Patrick Leahy**, GOUVERNER, ST. LAURENCE County, N.Y., will reach him.

Of **Edward Smith**, a native of DUBLIN, Ireland. Of **Thomas Smith** and wife (maiden name, **Ann Cowaly**), natives of KILMORE, County CARLOW, Ireland. Also of **John Conell**, a tailor, who left BOLTON, ENGLAND, some years ago, for NEW YORK. Intelligence of them will be thankfully received by writing to **Mary Mackgonering**, HALLOWELL, ME.

Of **Mary Connolly**, a native of the Town of DROGHEDA, County LOUTH, Ireland. When last heard from (in 1856) she was living with **Mr. Delaplane**, at 278 FIFTH AVENUE, NEW YORK CITY. Intelligence of her will be thankfully received by her brother, **John Connolly**, at 14 Laurence Street, NEWARK, N.J., in care of **Mr. Winters**, collar manufacturer.

Of **Ellen Nownan**, who left KILLMACOW, County KILKENNY, Ireland, and emigrated to NEW YORK about ten years ago. She then hired with a **William B. Rock**, of 78 North 6th Street, PHILADELPHIA, PA. Information of her will be most thankfully received by her mother, **Mary Christopher** (widow of **Michael Nownan**), Champlain Street, QUEBEC, CANADA.

Of **John Fitzpatrick**, who left Ireland some 30 or more years ago, a native of the Townland of TATAGHEE, CASTLEBLANEY, County MONAGHAN, Ireland. When last heard from he was in UPPER CANADA. Any information of him or his family will be thankfully received by his niece, **Susan Fitzpatrick**, No. 56 EAST 23rd ST., NEW YORK. Canada papers, please copy.

Of **Francis Timmins**, a native of GARRIROSS, County CAVAN, Ireland. When last heard from (in 1864) he was in Co. C, 30th Mo. Vol. Infantry, U.S. Army at VIDALIA, LA., opposite NATCHEZ, MISS. Any information concerning him will be thankfully received by his sister, **Anne Fagan**, 9 Halston St., DUBLIN, Ireland, or **Charles Fagan**, 279 6th ST., NEW YORK, America.

October 26, 1867

Of **Charles W. Courtenay**, a joiner by trade, who left LIVERPOOL, ENGLAND, about 16 years ago, and came to this country. When last heard from (in 1854) he was in NEW ORLEANS, LA. Information of him, alive or dead, will be thankfully received by **George Courtenay**, Box 70, CHAMPLAIN Post Office, CLINTON County, N.Y. New Orleans papers, please copy.

Of **Edward Moran**, who left QUEBEC in May, 1865, and, when last heard from, was in KERN County, CALIFORNIA. Information of his whereabouts will be thankfully received by his brother, **Michael Moran**, 265 SPRING STREET, NEW YORK. California papers, please copy.

Of **John Desmond**, now about 30 years of age, who left the City of CORK, Ireland, in 1854 or the beginning of 1855. By addressing **Michael Twohig**, HEBRONVILLE, MASS., he will know something of his brother **Jeremiah**. New Orleans and Southern papers, please copy.

Of **Catherine Clifford**, a daughter of **David Clifford**, of RAHEEN WOODS, Parish of CROUGH, County LIMERICK, Ireland, who left home about 13 years since. When last heard from (3 years ago) she was in NEW HAVEN, CONN. Information of her will be thankfully received by addressing her sister, **Maryann Clifford**, SCHENECTADY Post Office, N.Y.

Of **Edward O'Connor**, son of **Wm. O'Connor**, of GLENQUIN, County LIMERICK, Ireland, who left home about 19 years ago. When last heard from he was in River Street, CLEVELAND, OHIO. His brother **Terrance O'Connor**, who is at present in NEW YORK, would be thankful for any information concerning his whereabouts. Address **John O'Halloran**, corner of ANN STREET and PARK ROW, NEW YORK.

Of **Richard Gay**, aged about 55 years, who came to America, in 1847, from the County of WESTMEATH, Ireland. When last heard from (in 1858 or '59) he was in ALBANY, N.Y. Information of him will be thankfully received by his daughter, **Ellen Murray**, 25 Elm Street, HARTFORD, CONN.

Of **Michael O'Brien**, a native of DUNAMAGEN, County KILKENNY, Ireland. When last heard from (about 4 years ago) he was in MOUNT HOPE, GRANT County, WIS. Intelligence of him will be thankfully received by his nephew, **Thomas Whelan**, at Sixth Street, between 4th and 5th Avenues, GOWANUS, BROOKLYN, L.I., care of **Mrs. Comfort**. Wisconsin papers, please copy.

Of **James Mungavin**, and his wife, **Bridget Kain**, sister to **John Kain**, of OATFIELD, DERNAND, County CLARE, Ireland. If this happens to be seen by either of them, direct to **John Kain**, BUSHNELL, MCDONOUGH County, ILL.

Of **John Magaran**, of LISMORE, CROSSDOWNEY, County CAVAN, Ireland. Information of him will be thankfully received by his sister, **Annie Magaran**, at 40 First Street, GEORGETOWN, D. C.

November 2, 1867

Of **Mrs. Catherine O'Brien** (maiden name **Catherine Power**), who, when last heard of, was living in CONNECTICUT; she had one daughter. Information respecting her will be thankfully received by writing to **Michael Prindable**, SOMERSET, MASS., when she will be informed of something to her advantage.

Of **Rose Kenny**, wife of **Wm. Donnell**, of the Townland of ARTEBRACKE, County ANTRIM, Ireland, who emigrated to America in 1852; was married soon after either in NEW JERSEY or NEW YORK, and was heard from at home for a short time after her marriage, but not of late years. Her brother, **Miles Kenny**, will gratefully receive any information of her addressed to him at JENKSVILLE, MASS. [Appeared Nov. 9, 1867 with the County Antrim changed to County ARMAGH.]

Of **Mary Gibbons**, of the County MAYO, Ireland, who sailed from Liverpool, on board the *Minnesota*, on the 3rd of September last, and arrived in New York on the 18th. She is between 50 and 60 years of age, and hard of hearing. Information of her will be thankfully received by her daughter, **Mrs. Ann Carroll**, ST. CLAIR, SCHUYLKILL County, PA.

Of **Thomas Bracken**, a tailor by trade, and a native of TULLAMORE, KING'S County, Ireland. Information of him will be thankfully received by his brother, **J. P. Bracken**, 130 Shippen St., PHILADELPHIA, PA. Southern papers, please copy. [Appeared Oct. 12, 1867 with slightly different wording and in combination with Kinady.]

Of **William Hanrahan**, of GLEN OF AHERLOW, County TIPPERARY, Ireland. When last heard from he was in SOUTH BROOKLYN, L.I. Information of him will be thankfully received by writing to **John Hurley**, 21st Street, between 3rd and 4th Avenues, SOUTH BROOKLYN, Long Island, N.Y.

Of **Margaret Donaghey**, a native of LONDONDERRY, Ireland, who left Ireland in April, 1862, and sailed for Quebec. When last heard of she was living in MONTREAL, CANADA. Information respecting her whereabouts will be thankfully received by her brother, **George Donaghey**, 207 McGill Street, Montreal, Canada, care of **Mr. James O'Brien**. Boston papers, please copy.

Of **Michael Murphy**, and his wife, **Julia Kelly**, natives of the Parish of CLOHEEN, Co. CORK, Ireland. When last heard from they were at SARATOGA, N.Y. Information of their whereabouts will be thankfully received by their brother, **Michael Kelly**, at **John R. Handy's**, 196 CHERRY ST., N.Y. Boston and Western papers, please copy.

Of **John** and **Edmond Kinady**, natives of URLINGFORD, County KILKENNY, Ireland. Intelligence of them will be thankfully received by their sister and brother-in-law, **J. P. Bracken**, No. 130 Shippen Street, PHILADELPHIA, PA. California and St. Louis papers, please copy. [Appeared Oct. 12, 1867 with a different placename and in combination with Bracken.]

Of **William Brady**, a native of STRADONE, County CAVAN, Ireland, late Captain and Brevet Major of the 1st New Mexico Cavalry. When last heard from he was mustered out of service on the 19th of October, 1866, at FORT RENIOW, NEW MEXICO. Information of his whereabouts will be thankfully received by his bereaved mother, by addressing **Mrs. Dr. Brady**, STRADONE, County CAVAN, Ireland, or to **James Monaghan**, No. 1631 Market St., PHILADELPHIA, PA.

November 9, 1867

Of **Pat** and **Peter Killeen**, who, when last heard from, were in ILLINOIS. Information of them will be thankfully received by their brother, **Joseph Killeen**, at 448 WEST 16th STREET, NEW YORK CITY.

Of **Stephen** and **Elizabeth Donoghue**, who emigrated from BALLINASLOE, County GALWAY, Ireland, in 1860 or 1861. Intelligence of them will be thankfully received by **Martin F. Bruton**, 7 Atwell's Avenue, PROVIDENCE, R.I. Boston papers, please copy.

Of **Denis Sheehan**, of BALLYSHURDANE, Parish of KILDORORY, County CORK, Ireland, who came to this country 28 years ago. Intelligence of him will be thankfully received by his nephew, **Thomas O'Donnell**, 43 WEST ST., NEW YORK.

Of **James Cain**, of ALLICKEY, County LIMERICK, Ireland, who left home in August, 1867, on board the *City of Baltimore*, for New York. Information of him will be thankfully received by his uncle, **Thomas Cain**, at WEST CASTLETON, VT.

Of **James O'Conell**, a native of CROSSMAKEELEN, Parish of BAILIEBOROUGH, County CAVAN, Ireland, who came to this country 14 years ago. When last heard from, in 1859, he resided in CHICAGO, ILL., and in November of the same year left for the City of MEMPHIS, TENN. He was a mason by trade. Any person giving information of him will confer a favor on his father and brother, who lately arrived in this country. Address **Andrew O'Connell**, 71 Pennington Street, NEWARK, N.J. Western and Southern papers, please copy.

November 16, 1867

Of **James O'Brien**, of COOPERSTOWN, N.Y. When last heard from he was engaged in distilling for a **Mrs. Richardson**. Information concerning the present residence of himself or family will be thankfully received by his sister, **Harriet O'Brien**, in care of **Wm. Starkey**, NEW HAVEN, CONN.

Of **John Devlin**, who, when last heard from (in November 14, 1866), was in NEW ORLEANS, LA., in a situation as apothecary to the New Orleans Great Dispensary. Information of him will be thankfully received by his brother, **James Devlin**, Rockaway Street, LYNN, MASS.

Of **George Boyle**, from the Parish of BOHER, Townland of GRANGE, County LIMERICK, Ireland, who came to this country about 8 years ago. When last heard from he was living in LIMA in the State of NEW YORKIntelligence of him will be thankfully received by his brother, **John Boyle**. Direct to the office of the Irish-American.

November 23, 1867

Of **Ann Keenan**, of the Parish of CASTLETOWNGEOGHIGAN, Co. WESTMEATH, Ireland. Information of her will be thankfully received by her uncle, **James Keenan**. Address **Mrs. Gordens**, Barker St., between 17th and 18th, Market and Chesnut Streets, PHILADELPHIA, PA.

Of **John Carrig** and his sisters **Mary, Catherine, Ellen** and **Bridet** [sic] **Carrig**, natives of TULLA, County CLARE, Ireland. When last heard from (about fourteen years ago) John, Catherine and Bridget were in LIVONIA CENTER, LIVINGSTON County, N.Y. Intelligence of them will be thankfully received by their brother, **Patrick Carrig**, ELIZABETHPORT, N.J.

Of **Michael Rowley**, a native of the Parish of MOHILL, County LEITRIM, Ireland, who came to this country some time in 1860. When last heard of he was supposed to be in PROVIDENCE, R.I. Information of him will be thankfully received by his wife and child. **Maria** and **Anne Rowley**, by addressing a letter to them to NORWALK post office, CON.

Of **Samuel McElwee**, who left RAMELTON, County DONEGAL, Ireland, in September, 1858, for America, and was last seen in PHILADELPHIA about 5 years ago. Information of him wil be thankfully received by his brother, **James McElwee**. Address in care of Capt. **H. Rodgers**, 1840 Catherine Street, PHILADELPHIA, PA. Irish Republic and Boston Pilot, please copy.

Of **Mary McNulty**, a native of BALLINA, TYRAWLEY, County MAYO, Ireland, who came to this country about 14 years ago. When last heard from she was a servant with **Luke Clark**, GREENBUSH, ALBANY, N.Y. Since that she is supposed to have gone to PHILADELPHIA and to have got married. Intelligence of her will be thankfully received by **John Clark**, NISKAYUNA, SCHENECTADY County, N.Y.

November 30, 1867

Of **Catherine Scharco**, maiden name **Nugent**. When last heard from, in 1853, was at WHISTON, near PRESCOTT, ENGLAND, with **Richard Willis**, Esq. Information of her will be thankfully received by **Winney Carey** (maiden name **Nugent**), at the Irish-American Office, No. 8 North William Street, New York. Prescott (England) papers, please copy.

Of **Jonathan** or **John Kelly**, a native of DUBLIN, Ireland. When last heard from (1847) he was in Little's saw mills, on Grand River, CALEDONIA, CANADA WEST. Any intelligence of him will be thankfully received by his daughter, **Catherine Gilmore**, or his son, **Richard Kelly**, at Steuben St., west side, fourth house from DeKalb Av., BROOKLYN.

Of **Joseph Brett**, also of **Ellen Brett**, his sister, who left MAYNOOTH, County KILDARE, Ireland, in May, 1852. When last heard from, in 1854, Joseph was in GENESEE County, MICHIGAN, and Ellen in ALBANY, N.Y. Information of them, alive or dead, will be thankfully received by their mother, and brothers, **Samuel** and **William Brett**. Address, Samuel Brett, MAHONY CITY Post Office, SCHUYLKILL County, PENN.

Of **Peter Walsh**, a native of SALT MILLS, SUTTON'S Parish, County WEXFORD, Ireland. He left Ireland about 15 years ago. When last heard of he was residing in EAST BOSTON, MASS. Any information concerning him will be thankfully received by his nephew, **Martin Breen**, SOMERSVILLE, CONTRA COSTA County, CAL.

Of **Michael McTaggart**, a native of MOHILL, County LEITRIM, Ireland. When last heard from he was in CARBON County, PENN. Any information concerning him will be thankfully received by his brother, **Thomas McTaggart**, SAN FRANCISCO, CALIFORNIA.

Of **Mary Ferrick**, late of ROXBOROUGH and CURRAGHADOO, County MAYO, Ireland. She came to the United States about 15 years ago, and is now supposed to reside with her aunt, **Mary Hughes**, at KANKAKEE, ILL. Any information regarding her will be thankfully received by her brother, **James Ferrick**, No. 80 CANNON ST., NEW YORK. Boston Pilot, please copy.

December 7, 1867

Of **John Loftis**, who left NEW YORK about 8 years ago, and went to TOLEDO, State of OHIO. Information of him will be thankfully received by his sister, **Margaret Loftis**, by writing to her brother. Direct to 113 WEST 13th STREET, NEW YORK.

Of **Mary Kissane**, about 18 years of age, of CAPPOROUGH, BLACK VALLEY, County KERRY, Ireland, who left home in November, 3 years ago, and has not been heard from this last 14 months. She was then living in NEW YORK, with her cousin, **Mary Kissane**. Information respecting her whereabouts will be most thankfully received by her uncle, **Patrick Cassidy**, who is in this country about ten years. Address, Patrick Cassidy, HACKENSACK, BERGEN County, N.J.

Of **Thomas Cullan**, a native of the Parish of COLDREY, County WESTMEATH, Ireland. When last heard of he was in HARTFORD, CONN. Intelligence of him will be thankfully received by his children, **Thomas** and **Mary Cullan**, TROY, N.Y., care of **Thos. J. Jennings**.

Of **Michael Murphy**, a native of the County GALWAY, Ireland. When last heard from he was in PITTSBURGH, PA. Information of him will be thankfully received by his brother-in-law, **Patrick Flaherty**, 2003 Sand Street, BROOKLYN, N.Y. Boston Pilot, please copy.

Of **Patrick Heffernan**, of CORRABLE, Parish of CROOM, County LIMERICK, Ireland, who came to this country about eight years ago. When last heard of he was in JEFFERSONVILLE, IND. If this should meet the eye of him or any of his friends, they will please address a note to **Wm. Heffernan**, PHILADELPHIA Post Office, PA.

December 14, 1867

Of **Joseph Bowers**, formerly of the 14th (British) Regiment, Infantry. He was last heard from when his Regiment was stationed at QUEBEC, about 28 years ago. He is supposed to have left the army and settled in Quebec. Information of him will be thankfully received by his sister, **Catharine Mulligan**, 36 CENTRE STREET, NEW YORK. Canadian papers, please copy.

Of **Denis Collins**, from the City of CORK, who came to this country about two years ago, and is supposed to be in ILLINOIS. Any information of him will be thankfully received by his cousin, **Mary Daly**. Address care of Irish-American Office, New York.

Of **Susannah McMahon**, daughter of **Michael McMahon**, KNOCKNAGUN, near NEWMARKET, Co. CLARE, Ireland, who is supposed to have arrived in New York by the steamer *City of Washington*, on the 25th Nov., and hired from Castle Garden with a lady whose address is not known. Any one who may know of her whereabouts will relieve the anxiety of her friends by sending word of where she may be found to the office of the Irish-American.

Of **William Heaven** and **Ann Curren** (daughter of **Richard Curren** and **Catharine Whealon**), of DUNGARVAN, County WATERFORD. Information of them will be thankfully received by her sister, **Catharine Mansfield**, at 308 EAST 34th STREET, NEW YORK CITY.

December 21, 1867

Of **Mary O'Shea**, a native of INCACLONA, County KERRY, Ireland, daughter of **Patrick O'Shea**. When last heard from she was in MONTREAL, CANADA. Intelligence of her will be thankfully received by **Robert O'Shea**, 718 North Front Street, PHILADELPHIA, PA.

Of **Richard** or **Pat Stack**, a native of ODORNEY, County KERRY, Ireland. He was last seen in WHITE PLAINS, N.Y., by his nephew, **Michael Sheahan**, who was in his house in February, 1864. If this should chance to meet his eye he will hear of something of importance to him by writing to his brother-in-law, **Patrick Sheahan**, SALINA Post Office, ONONDAGA County, N.Y.

December 27, 1867

Of **Michael Ryan**, a native of FREEHOLD, State of NEW JERSEY, who left home on the 2nd of September last, and has not been heard of since. He is 16 years old. It is supposed he came to NEW YORK. Intelligence of him will be thankfully received by his parents. Address his father, **Michael Ryan**, in care of **Thomas Mulholland**, FREEHOLD, N.J.

Of **James** and **Thomas O'Neill**, natives of the Town of ANGLASS, County MONAGHAN, Ireland, who emigrated to IOWA some years since, and who brought thither, about seven years ago, their mother, **Mary O'Donnell**. If they will address a line in care of **James Dougherty**, 280 MADISON STREET (Coal Yard), NEW YORK, it will reach their brother, **Patrick O'Neill**. In fact, any information of the same will be thankfully received by him.

Of **Edward Cowley**, a native of BALREASK, County MEATH, Ireland. When last heard from, about 5 years ago, he was in PERRYSVILLE, MD., where he went with a cargo of corn for the government horses. Intelligence of him will be thankfully received by his brother, **John Cowley**, at Clark's Hotel, 110 CHATHAM ST., NEW YORK, or by directing a letter to the Irish-American office, New York. Trenton and New Brunswick papers, please copy.

Of **Thomas Fegan**, a native of the Parish of FAUGHANSTOWN, County WESTMEATH, Ireland. Also, of **Ann Clinton**, who sailed from Liverpool on the 12th of June, 1845, and landed in New York, July 27, 1845. Information of them will be thankfully received by **Michael Fegan**, 209 Taylor's Avenue, CAMDEN, N.J.

Of **Philip Loney**, son of **Thomas Loney**, of ERRYVALE, Co. TIPPERARY, Ireland, by his cousin, **John P. Walsh**, of the City of KILKENNY, Ireland. When last heard from he was in the State of NEW YORK. Address Irish-American office, New York City.

Of **James, Peter, Bridget** and **Catherine Crelly**, from BIRMEATH, County LOUTH, Ireland. When last heard from they were residing in DERBY, CONN., about 16 years since. Information of them will be thankfully received by their sister, **Mary Crelly**. Address **James Scally**, 489 PEARL ST., NEW YORK.

January 4, 1868

Of **John Spotswood**, son of the late **Captain Spotswood**, Carabeg House, VALENTIA, County KERRY; emigrated to America in 1859; served in the Union army; was discharged for physical debility, August 1864. When last heard from was in Bedloe's hospital. If living he will hear of something to his advantage by addressing **Edward Kennedy**, 29 ROOSEVELT ST., NEW YORK.

January 11, 1868

Of **Mrs. Gile**, a native of the City of DUBLIN, Ireland. When last heard from she was in CINCINNATI, OHIO. Information of her will be thankfully received by her father, **Peter Smith**, 21 Mary's-lane DUBLIN, Ireland, or by **John Mulhall**, 145 Main Street, HARTFORD, CONN.

Of **James Brady**, who left CLAREMORRIS, County MAYO, Ireland, about sixteen years ago. When last heard of, about three years since, he was in BARTON'S LANDING, VERMONT. Information of him will be thankfully received by his son, **John Brady**, at 94 Sha[ ]k Street, cor. of Conway, BALTIMORE, MD. Irish-American papers, please copy.

Of **Peter Green**, a native of QUEEN'S County, Ireland. When last heard from he was in GREEN County, WISCONSIN. Intelligence of him will be thankfully received by **Charles Green**, AMBOY, LEE County, ILL.

Of **Thomas** and **John Toole**, natives of QUEEN'S County, Ireland. Intelligence of their whereabouts will be thankfully received by **Charles Green**, AMBOY, LEE County, ILL.

Of **James, Matthew** and **Charles Parks**, of the County LEITRIM, Ireland. When last heard of they were in NEW YORK City. Information of them will be thankfully received by **Edward Synott, Jr.,** of SAINT GEORGE, NEW BRUNSWICK, in the Dominion of CANADA.

Of **William Shehan**, a native of MALLOW, County CORK, Ireland. His last place of residence in Ireland was KILBILANE, MILFORD; is now supposed to be in WISCONSIN. Information of him will be thankfully received by his brother, **Richard Shehan**, POUGHKEEPSIE, N.Y.

January 18, 1868

Of **Mary, Margaret** and **Bridget Lane**, natives of the County of LIMERICK, Ireland. When last heard from (about five years ago) they were in BROOKLYN, Long Island, N.Y. Intelligence of them will be thankfully received by their cousin, **Michael Shaw**, MATAWAN, MONMOUTH County, NEW JERSEY.

Of **Thomas, Michael, James, Anne, Julia** and **Janin Gaughran**, of the Parish of RUSHIVE, Township of SLANE, County MEATH, Ireland, who came to America about twenty years ago. Thomas is a mason by trade, and was in NEW YORK when last heard of. Information of them will be thankfully received by their cousin, **Thomas Henry**, by addressing him at MOUND CITY Post Office, PULASKI County, ILL.

Of **Peter Crowley**, a native of BALLYNAGRIN, County CLARE, Ireland. When last heard from (in August last) he was ESTAWCIA [ESTANCIA], SAN SALVADOR, or MONTEVIDEO, SOUTH AMERICA. Information of him will be thankfully received at the office of the Irish-American.

Of **James Hill**, a native of ROSSOWBRIDGE, Parish of KILMENA, County MAYO, Ireland. When last heard from (about two years ago) he was in BALTIMORE, MD. Intelligence of him will be thankfully received by his sister, **Bridget Hill**, corner of Becon and Oakland Avenues, HUDSON CITY, N.J., in care of **Hugh O. Johnston**.

January 25, 1868

Of **Edward McRoberts**, who, when last heard from, was in BLUFF HARBOUR, AUSTRALIA. Information of him will be thankfully received by his sister, **Jane Thompson**, in care of **Anthony Campbell**, 58 GOUVERNOUR STREET [Gouverneur Street], NEW YORK. Bluff Harbour and Melbourne papers, please copy.

Of **Mrs. Ann McDowell**, wife of **Charles McDowell**, deceased, and formerly of No. 2 Henrietta Place, DUBLIN, Ireland, who emigrated to this country. When last heard from, in 1865, her address was 100 or 101 LEXINGTON AVENUE, 53rd STREET, NEW YORK. Should this come under the notice of the above person or any one acquainted with her, they will confer a great favor by leaving her address at the office of the Irish-American, No. 8 North William Street, New York.

Of **Michael Prendergast**, a carpenter by trade, who sailed from Dublin, on board the bark *Franklin*, about twenty years ago, in company with his aunt, **Nancy Carton**, and his two children, **Jane** and **John** - Jane since deceased. He is supposed to be in NEW YORK CITY. Information of him will be thankfully received by his son, **John Prendergast**, CLEVELAND, West Side, OHIO.

Of **Miss Ellen Landy**, who left the Town of CARRICK-ON-SUIR, County TIPPERARY, Ireland, about 8 years ago. If she is living she will do her brother, Corporal **Richard Landy**, Her Majesty's 16th Regiment, MONTREAL, CANADA, a great favor by forwarding to him her address; or if any other person happens to know where she is they will greatly oblige by sending information to the above address.

Of **Mary McMahon**, a native of the Parish of BALLYEA, County CLARE, Ireland, who came to this country two years ago, on board the steamship *Louisiana*. When last heard from she was in LONG ISLAND. Information of her will be thankfully received by her brother, **John McMahon**, by addressing him at 252 WEST 29th STREET, NEW YORK.

Of **Patrick Sullivan**, a native of the Parish of MAGNOR, County CORK, Ireland. When last heard from he was in NEW YORK CITY. Information of him or of his friends will be thankfully received by his sister, **Mary Sullivan**, in care of **Michael Sweeney**, ROCK ISLAND, ILL.

February 1, 1868

Of **Michael Haney**, who left LEEDS, ENGLAND, about 14 years ago. When last heard from, in 1859, he was in OHIO. Information of him will be thankfully received by his cousin, **Michael Boyne**, at No. 125 Hudson Avenue, BROOKLYN, N.Y.

Of **Thomas Casey**, or any of his family, natives of the Parish of KILTHERONY, County CLARE, Ireland. Intelligence of them will be thankfully received by their cousin, **Patrick McMahon**, GALESBURG, ILL.

Of **Edward Conway**, **William Feeney** and **John Narry**, natives of the Townland of DOONEAL, near DROMORE WEST, County SLIGO, Ireland, who landed at New Orelans, La., in or about the month of June, 1848. Information of any of them will be thankfully received by their cousin, **John M. C. H. Rogers**, U.S.M.C. Navy Yard, CHARLESTOWN, MASS. Louisiana papers, please copy.

Of **Johannah Desmond**, a native of BANTRY, County CORK, Ireland, who arrived in New York about 15 years ago. When last heard from she was married and living in Pearl Street, ALBANY, N.Y. Information of her will be thankfully received by her sisters, **Mary** and **Julia Desmond**, No. 1307 Spruce Street, PHILADELPHIA, PA. Albany papers, please copy.

February 8, 1868

Of **Mary Scott**, who left LIMERICK about seventeen years ago. When last heard from she was in PHILADELPHIA. Information of her will be thankfully received by her brother, **Michael Scott**, 2 Dickson Place, Broad St., above Poplar St., PHILADELPHIA, PA.

Of **James Dignan**, a native of the Parish of TEEBOHAN, County ROSCOMMON, Ireland. He left CONGLETON, ENGLAND, in 1852, for NEW ORLEANS, LA. When last heard from, in 1867, he was in PITTSBURGH, PA. Information of him will be thankfully received by his brother, **Martin Dignan**, 612 Willow St., READING PA.

Of **Owen Cannavan**, a native of the County MONAGHAN, Ireland, who left NEWARK, N.J., in October last, for PHILADELPHIA, PA. Information of his present whereabouts will be thankfully received by his brother, **Michael Cannavan**, SOUTH BERGEN, HUDSON County, N.J. Philadelphia papers, please copy.

Of **Timothy Driscoll Feen**, a native of CLONAKILTY, County CORK, Ireland, who came to America in 1850. Information of him will be thankfully received by **Jeremiah Driscoll**, CAMERON Post Office, CAMERON County, PA., or by **J. Driscoll**, Station D, NEW YORK CITY. [Appeared April 4, 1868 with some additional information.]

February 15, 1868

Of **"The Brothers Price,"** or **Daniel O'Connell**, lately giving Dramatic Recitals in NEW YORK CITY. Their address will confer a favor upon **Thomas M. Derrick**, No. 1, Lafayette St., BOSTON, MASS.

Of **Hiram Moneypenny**, a native of the north of Ireland. When last heard from, three years ago, he was in NEW BEDFORD, MASS. Any information of him will be thankfully received by his wife, **Mrs. Moneypenny**, by writing to her in care of **John B. Farrell**, Irish-American Office, New York.

Of **John** and **Thomas Lewis**, who left BALLINTRIM, near CLOYNE, County CORK, Ireland, twenty-seven years ago. When last heard of, they were in NEW YORK CITY. **Maurice Lewis**, their brother, would be thankful for any information of them - He resides at EAGLE MILLS, RENSSELAER Co., N.Y.

February 22, 1868

Of **Edward Fleming**, a native of the Town of BALLINAGH, County CAVAN, Ireland. When last heard from he was living at 333 FIRST AVENUE, NEW YORK CITY. Information of him will be thankfully received by his cousin, **Charles Reilly**, OFFALLION Station, Union Pacific Rail Road, NEBRASKA.

Of **Mary** and **Timothy Campbell**, of BALLINDERRY, County WESTMEATH, Ireland. Information of their whereabouts will be received by addressing **Jacob Norris**, ROCK ISLAND, ROCK ISLAND County, ILLINOIS. By so doing the above parties will hear of something to their advantage.

Of **Ellen Hayes**, daughter of **Mary** and **Nicholas Hayes**, of CAHIR, Parish of BRUFF, County LIMERICK, Ireland, who lived some years in NORWALK, CONN., and afterwards went to QUINCY, ILL. Ellen was sent from ST. LOUIS to her uncle, in BALTIMORE; she left, and, it is supposed, went to Norwalk, Conn. Information of her will be gratefully acknowledged by her sister, **Maryanne Hayes**, 89 Greenmount Ave., BALTIMORE, MD.

February 29, 1868

Of **Patrick Guning** and his wife, **Ann Guning**, who resided in PHILADELPHIA, in Schuyler 3rd, between Lombard and South Streets, about eighteen years ago. Any information of her will be thankfully received by their daughter, **Catherine Guning**. Direct to 264 South 21st St., PHILADELPHIA, PA.

Of **Catherine McCabe**, of the Parish of TIERWORKER, Townland of CORMEEN, County MEATH, Ireland. When last heard from she was in MILWAUKEE, WISCONSIN. She came to this country about 9 years ago. Any information of her will be thankfully received by her brother, **John McCabe**, No. 517 WEST 38th ST., NEW YORK CITY. Milwaukee papers, please copy.

Of **Catherine Finegan**, a native of the Parish of ENNISKEAN, County CAVAN, Ireland. When last heard from about 3 years ago, she was in BOSTON, MASS. Any information of her will be thankfully received by her nephew, **John McCabe**, No. 517 WEST 38th ST., NEW YORK CITY. Boston papers, please copy.

Of **Margaret Carty**, from KEHORE, Parish of POOLDUFF, County WEXFORD, Ireland, who emigrated to this country about 18 years ago. When last heard from she was in PHILADELPHIAPA. Information of her will be thankfully received by her sister's husband, **John Dwyer**. Address, 356 EAST 13th STREET, NEW YORK.

Of **Patrick, Margaret, Edward, Catherine** and **Daniel Gallagher**, from the Townland of GRAIGUAGOWEN, County WATERFORD, Ireland. Information of them will be thankfully received by their brother, **James Gallagher**, who has lately arrived in NEW YORK, from CLONMEL, County TIPPERARY, Ireland. Address James Gallagher, No. 17 EAST 30th STREET, NEW YORK.

Of **Ellen Moran**, a native of the Townland of BALLYGUNNERMORE, County WATERFORD, Ireland, who landed in New York about three years ago. Her brother Patrick is anxious to learn her whereabouts. Address **Patrick Moran**, Rock Island Passenger Depot, CHICAGO, ILL.

Of **Jerome M. Guiry**, late of DUNGARVAN, County WATERFORD, Ireland, who sailed from Queenstown for New York on the 17th of January, 1868. He will hear of something to his advantage by sending his address to **Mr. James Smyth**, 442 WEST 42nd STREET, NEW YORK. Albany and Western papers, please copy. [Appeared March 7, 1868, with the advertiser changed to his wife, **Kate Mary Guiry**, at the same address.]

Of **Ann** and **Margaret Tracy**, who left PORTUMNA, County GALWAY, Ireland, accompanied by their mother, in September, 1855. When last heard of they were living in MUNDY or GENESEE, LIVINGSTON County, N.Y. By writing to **Edward Gillon**, 160 McCord Street, MONTREAL, CANADA, they will hear of something to their advantage.

Of **Edward Roark**, who landed in this country in 1860, from BALLYMAHON, County LONGFORD, Ireland. When last heard from he was in PENNSYLVANIA. Information of him will be thankfully received by his wife, **Ellen Roark**, by writing to her to 136 Buttler Street, BROOKLYN, N.Y. Pennsylvania papers, please copy.

Of **Mary Neil**, from the Parish of ORDAY, KENMARE, County KERRY, Ireland, whose son **Patrick** enlisted in the 66th British Regiment, at KINSALE, April 3, 1848, and transferred, April 1, 1849, to the 29th Regiment. He was originally a laborer. He died, October 29, 1867, in HAMILTON, CANADA. His mother is reported to be in the United States. Address **Rev. P. Bardon**, HAMILTON, ONTARIO, CANADA. Irish-American and U.S. papers, generally, please copy.

Of **Charles O'Connor**, who left GRANGE, County LIMERICK, Ireland, about 18 or 19 years ago. When last heard from he was supposed to be in SPRINGFIELD, ILL. Information of him will be thankfully received by his nephews, **Patrick C. O'Connor**, or **Patrick J. Hogan**, No. 6 Exchange, BALTIMORE, MD.

Of **John** and **Margaret Shaughnessy**, and of **Patrick Molone** and **Mrs. Molone**, all of the City of LIMERICK, Ireland, who, when last heard from, were in TRENTON, N.J. Information of them will be thankfully received by their sister, **Bridget Shaughnessy**, by writing to her at No. 117 East Baltic St., SOUTH BROOKLYN, N.Y.

March 7, 1868

Of **James Heffernan**, of County TIPPERARY, Ireland, who left NEW YORK on or about the 12th of March, 1866. When last heard of he was in HARRISBURG, PA. Intelligence of him will be thankfully received by his wife, **Catherine Heffernan**, Box No. 2, HOBOKEN, Post Office, N.J.

Of **John Campbell**, of CLONASLEE, QUEEN'S County, Ireland. When last heard from he was driving stage from MONTREAL, C.W., about eight years since. Information of him will be thankfully received by his brother, **Patrick Campbell**, 339 8th AVENUE, NEW YORK. Canadian papers, please copy.

March 14, 1868

Of **Mrs. Nathaniel Marks**, maiden name **Annie Shaw**, of the City of DUBLIN, Ireland. Came to America (N.Y.) about 4 years ago, a few days after marriage. When last heard from she was living in EAST 33rd ST., NEW YORK. She left New York about February, 1866, it is thought to go south. Should this meet the eye of any person knowing Mr. or Mrs. Marks, by calling their attention to it they will confer a lasting favor on a sorrowing family. Any information respecting them will be thankfully received by her (Mrs. Marks) brother, **Wm. Shaw**, 376 CHERRY ST., NEW YORK. Southern and Western papers, please copy.

Of **John Geoghegan**, son of **John** and **Catherine Geoghegan**, of ARDEN, TULLAMORE, KING'S County, Ireland, who left Ireland about 30 years ago for the United States. When last heard from he was in PENNSYLVANIA. Any information sent to **J. F. EUSTACE**, 51 CHAMBERS ST., NEW YORK, will be forwarded to his brothers and sister Catherine in BUENOS AYRES, S.A. Pennsylvania and Ohio papers, please copy.

Of **Mary Byrne**, (daughter of **James Byrne** and **Nancy Geraty**) a native of TONEYMAYES, Parish of KILMORE, County MAYO, Ireland. She sailed from Liverpool in the Spring of 1858. When last heard of (about four years ago) she was living in **Michael Quinlan's** house, in WATER STREET, NEW YORK. Information of her will be thankfully received by her sister, **Bridget Byrne**. Address **Anthony Dixon**, SCRANTON, LUZERNE County, PA.

March 21, 1868

Of **Catherine Sheridan** or, by marriage, **Catherine Kearnan**, a native of the Parish of NALTY, County MEATH, Ireland. When last heard of (about 6 years ago), she lived with a **Mrs. Ward**, GRAHAM STREET, NEW YORK. Information of her will be thankfully received by her sister, **Susiann Cawley**, LAMBERTVILLE, HUNTERDON County, N.J.

Of **James Kerins**, who sailed from Ireland in 1839, and landed in Quebec, Canada. He has not been heard of since 1840. He is a native of RUNBRACK, Parish of FOXFORD, County MAYO, Ireland; is about 44 or 46 years of age, 5 feet 7 ½ or 5 feet 8 inches high, light colored hair, light complexion and blue eyes, full shoulders and well educated. Any person giving information of him, if living, will receive $50 for their trouble with the utmost Satisfaction, or sent by post to any part of the world. Address **Thomas Kerins**, care of **Mr. Jonathan McGee**, ELIZABETH CITY, NEW JERSEY. Canada and Virginia papers, please copy.

Of **Geo. Casey** and wife (maiden name **Catherine Harrington**), natives of BALLANDING, County CORK, Ireland. Also, of **John, Daniel** and **Catherine Casey**, who have been in the States about 36 years. Intelligence of them will be thankfully received by **Mrs. Patrick O'Brien** (maiden name **Johannah Harrington**), COEYMANS, ALBANY County, NEW YORK.

Of **Charles Condlin** and **Thomas Power**, natives of CLONMEL, County TIPPERARY, Ireland. They landed in New York last October. Intelligence of their whereabouts will be thankfully received by **Maurice Collins**, DORCET COMER, VT.

March 28, 1868

Of **James Tierney**, a native of NEWMARKET-ON-FERGUS, County CLARE, Ireland. He arrived in America in September, 1851. When last heard from, he was in COLDSPRING, N.Y. Any intelligence of him will be thankfully received by his brother, **Rev. Denis Tierney**, at CHARLESTON, COLES County, ILL.

April 4, 1868

Of **Thomas Carr**, a native of DUBLIN, Ireland, who left home on the 13th of January last, without the consent or knowledge of his parents. He wrote from LIVERPOOL saying, by the time his letter was received, he would be crossing the Atlantic. He is about 5 feet 4 inches in height, slight and delicate in appearance, very light brown hair, long nose, grey eyes, a respectable and well-looking boy, and about 14 years of age. When he left home he wore a blue pilot coat, drab cloth trousers, and a black jerry hat. Should any person, seeing this, convey intelligence of his whereabouts to **James Nolan**, 638 GREENWICH STREET, NEW YORK, it will be esteemed as a great favor, or should the boy himself call there, he will hear of something to his advantage.

Of **Mary, Elizabeth** and **Matilda Ferguson**, natives of SHERCOCK, County MONAGHAN, Ireland. When last heard from (about two years ago) they were in NEW YORK State. Intelligence of them will be thankfully received by their brother, **Thomas Ferguson**, at 27 GREENWICH STREET, NEW YORK.

Of **Patrick Nee**, a native of the Parish of MILTOWNPASS, County WESTMEATH, Ireland. When last heard from (about three years ago) he was in BELL AIR, BELMONT County, OHIO. He is a stone mason by trade. Any person knowing of his whereabouts will confer a great favor on his afflicted mother by addressing a line to his sister, **Mrs. Mary O'Neill**, James' Street, third house off Orchard Street, FRANKFORD, PHILADELPHIA, PA. Ohio papers, please copy.

Of **Mrs. Bartholomew Sheehan**, (maiden name, **Hannah Greney**,) a native of the Town of NEWCASTLE WEST, County LIMERICK, Ireland. Information of her will be thankfully received by her sister, **Bridget Greney**, at [3]94 SECOND AVENUE, between 22nd and 23rd Streets, NEW YORK. Washington and Western papers, please copy.

Of **Timothy Driscoll Feen**, (Boxer), a native of CLONAKILTY, County CORK, Ireland, who came to America in 1850. Information of him will be thankfully received by his brother, **Jeremiah Driscoll**, CAMERON Post Office, CAMERON County, PA. or by **James Driscoll**, Station D, NEW YORK. [Appeared Feb. 8, 1868 with less information.]

April 11, 1868

Of **Martin McCorick**, or of any of his brothers, **John, Patrick**, or **Walter**. Martin and his brother Michael left the village of KILLATHINE, County MAYO, Ireland, about 21 years ago, and sailed for Boston; but, running short of provisions, the ship they sailed in stopped at the BERMUDA Islands, Michael remaining there and Martin going on to Boston. When last heard from he was in PERRY County, PA. Information of any of them will be thankfully received by their brother, **Michael McCorick**, or his daughter **Maria McCorick**, PORTDEPOSIT, CECIL County, MD.

Of **Thomas Carroll**, of County TIPPERARY, Ireland. When last heard of he was in GOLDSBOROUGH SAND CUT, WAYNE County, PA. Information of him will be thankfully received by his cousin, **Michael Gorman**, COOPERSTOWN, OTSEGO County, N.Y.

Of **Michael Corrigan** and wife (maiden name, **Allice Brady**,) of CARRICKMACROSS, County MONAGHAN, Ireland. When last heard from (11 years ago) they were in the State of PENNSYLVANIA. Information of them will be thankfully received by their sisters, **Jane** and **Catherine Brady**, in care of **Edward Crosby**, WABURN CENTRE, or to **Edward Carney**, STONEHAM, MASS. Western papers, please copy.

April 18, 1868

Of **Ambrose Mercier**, who arrived in New York, by the steamer *Kangaroo*, on the 1st of January, 1861. When last heard from (July 7th, 1864) he was in the employ of the Northern Transportation Company, DETROIT. Any information as to his location will benefit him materially, if addressed to **Joseph Cronelly**, Box 2494, P.O., NEW YORK.

Of **Thomas Klattey**, of LONDON, ENGLAND, a blacksmith, who left PHILIPSBURG 12 months ago to go west. Information of his present whereabouts will be thankfully received by his brother, **Thomas Rourke**, HOBOKEN Post Office, N.J. [Appeared May 2, 1868 with the surname **Klattey** changed to **Flatley**.]

Of **Richard Rooney**, otherwise **Nowlan**, a cabinet maker, and his brother, **Peter Rooney**, otherwise **Nowlan**, a draper's assistant, natives of SANDYMOUNT, DUBLIN. Their mother died recently leaving some property to them. Address **P. M. Haverty**, Publisher, 1 BARCLAY ST., NEW YORK.

Of **Andrew Doyle**, a native of MILLTOWN, Parish of TEMPLEMORE, County KILKENNY, Ireland. When last heard from (about 15 months ago) he was in MISSOURI CITY, MO. Intelligence of him will be thankfully received by his brother, **James Doyle**, Classon Avenue, Douglas Street, BROOKLYN, Long Island, N.Y., care of **Mr. Mooney**.

Of **John Delaney**, a native of the Township of MUCKLIN, County TIPPERARY, Ireland, son of **Con. Delaney** and **Mary Kennedy**. When last heard from (in 1851) he was employed by **Charles Adams**, a lawyer, in WELLINGTON, N.Y.; also of **Thaddeus Kennedy**, a native of the same place. Information of them will be gladly received by **Thomas Delaney**, brother to the former and cousin to the latter, by writing to him to CHEYENNE CITY Post Office, D.T. [DAKOTA TERRITORY]

Of **Thomas** and **John Caveney**, from the Parish of ARDCARNEY-ON-HILL, County ROSCOMMON, Ireland. Any person knowing of their whereabouts will confer a favor by writing to **Peter Fannon**, FRANKSTOWN Post Office, BLAIR County, PA. [Appeared May 2, 1868, with the surname **Fannon** spelled **Fannenn**, and adding that the Caveneys "landed in New York about 15 years ago, and who are now supposed to be in OHIO."]

Of **Michael Lally**, a native of ASKEATON, County LIMERICK, Ireland. When last heard from (a year ago last Christmas) he was in BATON ROUGE. Information of him will be thankfully received by **John Lally**, WEST TROY, ALBANY County, N.Y.

Of **Michael Spillane**, of CARRIGTWOHILL, County CORK, Ireland. When last heard from he was in MIDDLETOWN, CONN. Information of him will be gratefully received by his brother, **Cornelius Spillane**, who has just come to this country, at 62 Fayette Street, LOWELL, MASS.

April 25, 1868

Of **Alick McKinzy, Mathias** and **Joseph Maxwell**, natives of TUBBERCURRY, County SLIGO, Ireland. Intelligence of them will be thankfully received by their cousin, **Joseph Meredith**, at 15 Albion Street, SALEM, MASS. Philadelphia papers, please copy.

Of **James Griffin**, baker, a native of the Parish of INAGH, County CLARE, Ireland. When last heard of by his wife and child, he was staying with his sister, **Mrs. Carmody**, of CARROLLTON, GREENE County, ILL. Information of him will be thankfully received by **Rev. Michael Molone**, C.C., St. Michael's, LIMERICK, Ireland.

May 2, 1868

Of **John McDonnell**, of the Parish of CLOUGH, County KILKENNY, Ireland. When last heard from he was in POTTSVILLE, PA. Information of him will be thankfully received by his sister, **Mary McDonnell**. Address Irish-American Office, N.Y.

Of **John Long**, from the Parish of KILMURRY, County CORK, Ireland. His mother's maiden name was **Nance Crowly**. Information of him will be thankfully received by his cousin, **Mary Dremming**, who is most anxious to hear from him, at [114] Douglas Street, SOUTH BROOKLYN, Long Island, N.Y.

May 9, 1868

Of **Edward McCann**, a native of the Townland of GLENMACOFFER, County TYRONE, Ireland. When last heard from, two years ago, he was working in the PENNSYLVANIA coal mines; heard he went to CHICAGO, ILL. Information of him will be thankfully received by his sister, **Sarah McCann**, by writing to 272 MONROE STREET, NEW YORK, in care of **Mr. Patrick Smith**. Pennsylvania and Western papers, please copy.

Of **Bridget & Mary McCullough**, who came to this country about 20 years ago from the Parish of TALLONSTOWN, Co. LOUTH, Ireland. Information of them will be thankfully received by their brothers **Patrick** and **Peter**, by addressing **Peter McCullough**, 3706 Warren St. West, PHILADELPHIA, PA. New York papers, please copy.

Of **Thomas Cox**, a native of ARDEKELLUE, County ROSCOMMON, Ireland. Information of him will be thankfully received by his sister, **Mary Cox**, care of **Bernard McDermott**, 349 EAST 12th STREET, NEW YORK.

May 16, 1868

Of **Michael Ryan**, from BALLYCAHILL, County TIPPERARY, Ireland, who came to America 18 years ago. When last heard from he was in MONTREAL, UPPER CANADA. Intelligence of him will be thankfully received by his son-in-law, **Wm. Conroy**, No. 4 Clinton St., HOBOKEN, N.J. Also of his daughters, **Honorah** and **Jane**, and his son **John**, by the same party.

Of **James Moore**, of the Parish of CULMULLIN, County MEATH, Ireland, who came to America about 15 years ago. When last heard from he was in SANDUSKY, OHIO. Information of him will be gratefully received by his mother and his brothers, **John** and **Patrick**. Address **Patrick Moore**, in care of **John Sullivan**, MANITOWOC, WIS.

Of **George Moran**, from the County DONEGAL, Ireland, who arrived in this country 7 or 8 years ago. Information of him will be thankfully received by his sister, **Catherine Moran**, at 226 MULBERRY STREET, NEW YORK. Canada and Western papers, please copy.

Of **Patrick Kinnerny**, who left BALLAGOGUE, near DURROW, QUEEN'S County, Ireland, about the year 1830; also of **John Kinnerny**, who left the same place about 1854, and sailed for America. When last heard of were in DETROIT, MICH. Information of them will be thankfully received by their cousin, **Michael Maher**, at No. 340, cor. WEST 32nd STREET, and 10th AVENUE.

Of **John Kearney**, a native of LISAANISKA, Parish of BACKS, near BALLINA, TYRAWLY, County MAYO, Ireland. He was in PHILADELPHIA about 12 months ago, and is supposed to have gone west. If this should meet his eye or that of any body who knows his whereabouts, they will confer a favor on his sister, **Bridget Sherridan**, maiden name **Kearney**, by addressing her at No. 4 Loutey's Place, rear of 526 Christan Street, PHILADELPHIA, PA. Western papers, please copy.

$20 Reward. Of **Ann Shea**, maiden name **Ann Shannon**, a native of OMAGH, County TYRONE, Ireland, who came to this country 15 years ago. She got married to a man named **David Shea**, then residing in NEWARK, N.J. in the year 1855; her husband died in 1856. When last heard of she moved to ST. LOUIS, MO., in 1861, in company with one **Mr. Woods** and family. If this should come under the notice of any person knowing of her, dead or alive, they will confer a favor on her brother by notifying him of the same, and the above reward will be paid for reliable information of her present whereabouts, by addressing **Peter Shannon**, JESSUP, BUCHANAN County, IOWA.

May 23, 1868

Of **William Morgan**, from the Parish of KILGARVIN, County MAYO, Ireland. When last heard from he was in FALL RIVER, MASS. Information of him will be thankfully received by his brother **Thomas**, at **Mr. J. McMahon's**, No. 2 WASHINGTON STREET, NEW YORK.

May 30, 1868

Of **Mary McGough**, who, when last heard from, lived in the Colmore House, corner of SPRING STREET and BROADWAY, NEW YORK, with a **Mrs. Schanck**. She went with the same family about 15 years ago to CINCINNATI. Information of her will be thankfully received by her sisters **Ann** and **Catherine McGough**. Address **Robert Nixon**, MATAWAN, N.J. Irish-American and Cincinnati papers, please copy. [Appeared July 11, 1868, adding that Mary was a "native of the Parish of MONAGHAN, Co. MONAGHAN, Ireland." Appeared Aug. 22, 1868, adding a reward of $[2]0.]

Of **James McCormick**, a native of DRUMURY, Parish of DRUMARD, County LONGFORD, Ireland. When last heard of was in NEW YORK. Information of him will be most anxiously looked for and very thankfully received by his nephew, **James Reilly**, IRVINGTON-ON-HUDSON.

Of **John Gill**, aged 24 years, a native of the Parish of KILLTUBRED, County LEITRIM, Ireland, who came to this country in 1852. When last heard from was in POTTSVILLE, PA. Information of him, dead or alive, will be thankfully received by his mother and brothers. Address **Michael Gill**, SOUTHINGTON, CONN.

Of **Margaret** and **Ellen Driscoll**, of LISLIG, County CORK, Ireland, sisters to **Peter** and **Timothy Driscoll**, of SPRINGFIELD, MASS. Margaret was married to a **Mr. Manning**, and went, it is supposed, to CLEVELAND; Ellen was married to **John Sullivan**, in BOSTON, more than twenty years since; heard she was afterwards married in NEW YORK. If either of them or their heirs - if any - will address the Irish-American Office, they will hear of something to their advantage.

Of **James Dunlevy**, aged 40 years, about 5 feet 11 inches high, and a native of the Parish of INVER, County DONEGAL, Ireland. Whoever gives the first information about him will receive a handsome reward from his brother, **Ambrose Dunlevy**, 18 Hick Street, BROOKLYN, N.Y. Wisconsin, Iowa, Illinois and California papers, please copy.

June 6, 1868

Of **Andrew Fitzgerald**, who landed in the latter part of last April, and wrote to his brother-in-law, on the 30th of the same month; was stopping at **Owen Gleeson's**, GREENWICH STREET, NEW YORK, near Castle Garden. Information of his whereabouts will be kindly received by his brother-in-law, **Daniel Holland**, NORWICH, CONN.

Of **Ellen Hunt**, from SLIGO, Ireland. She arrived in New York in May, 1865, and lived with her Aunt, **Ann Rooney**, wife of **Michael Gearty**. **Bridget Hunt**, her sister, is very anxious to hear of her. Address 47 Sands Street, BROOKLYN, N.Y.

Of **Michael Gallagher**, who left the Townland of CARRICK MULLINGAR, County WESTMEATH, Ireland, on the 23rd day of January last and sailed in the ship *Harvest Queen*. Information of him sent to his sister, **Bessy Gallagher**, or to **John Reilly**, 395 SECOND AVENUE, NEW YORK, will be thankfully recieved. Neighboring papers, please copy.

June 13, 1868

Of **Patrick Donnelly**, a native of BELMULLET, County MAYO, Ireland. When last heard of (about fifteen months ago) he was met by a friend of his at PHILADELPHIA, PA. Intelligence of him will be thankfully received by his mother, who has lately arrived from Ireland, and who is at present living in BROOKLYN. Parties knowing of his present whereabouts will please send the desired intelligence to the Irish-American Office for **Mrs. Tolan**.

Of **James Hallihan**, late of YONKERS, N.Y., a native of WHITE CHURCH, County WATERFORD, Ireland. Intelligence of him will be thankfully received by his brother-in-law, **John Tobin**, of YONKERS, N.Y., who wishes to correspond with him.

Of **Denis Conner**, of CAMDEN, N.J., who left home on Saturday, May 31st. He is a puddler by trade, and was employed up to the time of his departure at the Rolling Mills, Camden, N.J. Parties knowing of his present whereabouts will confer a favor by addressing a few lines to his distressed and almost distracted wife, **Ellen Conner**, care of **John McAran**, CAMDEN, N.J. [Appeared under County WATERFORD]

June 20, 1868

Of **Patrick Clarke**, who came to this country from DUBLIN, Ireland, in 1863, and whose wife died suddenly in the month of September, same year, in NEW YORK CITY. Persons who know of his whereabouts will confer a favor by addressing **Clarke**, 79 CORTLANDT ST., N.Y.

Of **James Walsh**, of GARRYCOLLIN, Parish of TINTERN, County WEXFORD, Ireland, who left Liverpool on the 2nd of June, 1866, on board the ship *Elaranda*. When last heard from he was in CHRANTON, PA. Information of him will be thankfully received by his sister, **Margaret Revill**, by addressing her husband, **James Revill**, PLAINFIELD, UNION County, NEW JERSEY.

Of **Thomas McCormick**, or of his daughters, **Maryann** and **Bridget McCormick**, natives of the County CAVAN, Ireland, who came to this country about 10 or 12 years ago. Information of their whereabouts will be thankfully received by his son, **John McCormick**, at 192 Madison Avenue BALTIMORE, MD. New Orleans and neighboring papers, please copy.

Of **Thomas** and **Mary Mack**, natives of the Parish of DOONASS, County CLARE, Ireland. They emigrated about sixteen years ago to MELBOURNE, AUSTRALIA. When last heard from they were in ADELAIDE. If this catches the eye of the above mentioned, or any friend, they will bestow a favor on their sister, **Catherine Mack**, by writing to **Mr.**

Michael Darsey, No. 42 Bergen Street, SOUTH BROOKLYN, NEW YORK, America. Sydney Freeman's Journal and Australian papers please copy.

June 27, 1868

Of **Michael Hagerty**, of CROCKHAVEN, County CORK, Ireland. He is supposed to be either in the States of MICHIGAN or WISCONSIN, convenient to the copper mines. Information of him will be thankfully received by his brother's son, **Michael Hagerty**, who has lately arrived in NEW YORK, by addressing him in care of **James McCarthy**, 113 Sacket Street, BROOKLYN, N.Y.

Of **John McGowan**, a native of the Parish of CURRY, County SLIGO, Ireland, who sailed from Liverpool, in September, 1865. When last heard from he was living in the State of ALABAMA. Information of him will be thankfully received by his brother, **Thomas McGowan**, No. 1632 Camac Street, above Oxford, PHILADELPHIA, PA.

July 4, 1868

Of **Patrick Hayes**, a native of NENAGH, County TIPPERARY, Ireland. Also of **Peter Brady**, a native of DUBLIN, Ireland. Any intelligence of their present whereabouts will be thankfully received by **Mrs. Kate Hayes**, at No. 522 EAST 11th STREET, NEW YORK CITY. New Mexico papers, please copy.

July 11, 1868

Of **John Halpin**, formerly of BALLINAGARDE, Co. LIMERICK, Ireland, who left there about 30 years ago. When last heard from he was said to be living at 129 SPRING STREET, NEW YORK. Intelligence of him will be thankfully received by his stepbrother, **John Hogan**, 99 VANDAM STREET, NEW YORK.

Of **William Nicoll**, a native of KINGSCOURT, County CAVAN, Ireland, who emigrated to America in 1835. When last heard from (about five years ago), he was in MOBILE, ALA. Intelligence of his present whereabouts will be thankfully received by his sister, **Mrs. O'Brien** (maiden name **Fanny Nicoll**), at 31 Hamilton Avenue, SOUTH BROOKLYN, Long Island, N.Y. Alabama papers, please copy.

Of **John Tamplin**, a native of the County CLARE, Ireland. Also of **John Grennan**, a native of the County DUBLIN, Ireland. Intelligence of them will be thankfully received by **Bridget Tamplin**, at 323 EAST 21st STREET (rear building), between 1st and 2nd Avenues, NEW YORK.

July 18, 1868

Of **Cornelius Murphy** and his wife **Hanora** (maiden name **Maloney**), who left the Parish of MAGOURNEY, County CORK, Ireland, on April 1, 1848. When last heard of (in 1854) they were in COLUMBUS, OHIO. Information of them will be thankfully received by his brother-in-law **Daniel Mahoney**, KIRK'S MILLS, LANCASTER County, PA., or at the office of the Irish-American.

Of **Patrick Aldworth**, who left the County LIMERICK, Ireland, in 1854. When last heard from (about eight years ago) he was in INDIANA. Information of him will be thankfully received by his brother, **Joseph Aldworth**, MONTCLAIR, ESSEX County, N.J.

Of **Ellen Flaherty**, from near CURLISH, Parish of TULLYBRACK, County CLARE, Ireland, who came to NEW YORK on or about the 15th of June, 1868. Information concerning her whereabouts will be thankfully received by her sister **Mary**, if left with **R.P. Johnson**, 349 CANAL STREET, NEW YORK.

July 25, 1868

Of **John Corrigan**, a native of Leinster Market, in the Parish Of Saint Andrew, Westland Row, DUBLIN, who left Liverpool on board the steamship *City of London*, on July 12, 1865. When last seen was working in MILLERSBURG, PA., in February, 1866. Information of him will be thankfully received by his brother, **Michael Corrigan**, Pennsylvania Railroad, FORT WASHINGTON, MONTGOMERY County, PENNSYLVANIA.

Of **Patrick Sinnott**, of the Parish of MONNCOIN, CLONCUNNY, County KILKENNY, Ireland. When last heard from he was in NORTH ADAMS, MASS. Information of him will be thankfully received by his sister, **Mary Sinnott**, at 236 EAST 32nd STREET, NEW YORK. Boston and Illinois papers, please copy.

Of **Martin Mulrenin** and **Patrick Downs**, both natives of BOYLE, County ROSCOMMON, Ireland. When last heard from they were in HAGERSTOWN, MD., on their way to NEW YORK CITY. Downs came to the City, but Martin has not been seen or heard of since. Information of them will be thankfully received by **Edward Mulrenin**, Sterling Mines, SLOATSBURG, ROCKLAND County, N.Y., in care of **J. Crampton**. Philadelphia papers, please copy.

Of **Patrick** and **Martin O'Toole**, natives of the County GALWAY, Ireland, who, it is supposed, landed in New York about three years ago. Patrick is about 32 and Martin about 30 years of age. Information of them will be thankfully received if sent to **Martin Quinn**, No. 19 Barre Street, BALTIMORE, MD.

Of **Michael Keane**, tailor, a native of the City of WATERFORD, Ireland. When last heard from, in 1849, he was in his native City. Information of him will be gladly received by his sister, **Eliza Keane** (by marriage **Tracy**). Address **Richard Tracy**, carrier, Station D., Post Office, NEW YORK. Liverpool and Waterford papers, please copy. [Appeared Aug. 1, 1868, with the occupation of tailor changed to "sailor," and the surname **Tracy** changed to **Troy**.]

August 1, 1868

Of **Ann Bourke**, a native of the Parish of UPPERCHURCH, County TIPPERARY, Ireland, who emigrated to this country about 19 years ago. She is rather low in stature, and has dark hair. When last heard of she was somewhere in the State of NEW YORK. Information of her will be gratefully received by her sister and nephews. Address **Dr. Dwyer**, 9 Asylum Street, HARTFORD, CONN., Box 340. Catholic papers, please copy.

Of **Patrick** and **Timothy O'Regan**, of the Parish of CLOUNCAUGH, County LIMERICK, Ireland, who came to this country 23 years ago. When last heard from they were said to be in EAST TROY, N.Y. Intelligence of them will be gratefully received by their brother, **Jeremiah O'Regan**, by writing to him to COLUMBIA BRIDGE, BELMONT, PA.

Of **John O'Brien**, a native of LISBAWN, Parish of COOLMEEN, County CLARE, Ireland, who emigrated to BRANTFORD, CANADA WEST, 11 years ago. He left there seven years ago for ST. PAUL, MIN.; worked on board a steamboat on the Mississippi River, since when nothing has been heard of him. Information of him, either dead or alive, will be thankfully received by his mother, **Catherine O'Brien** (maiden name **Downs**), and his sister, **Alice O'Neil** (maiden name **O'Brien**). Address **John O'Neil**, 168 Bunker Street, CHICAGO, ILL.

August 8, 1868

Of **Michael Brennan**, of BRABSTOWN, TULLAROAN, County KILKENNY, Ireland, son of **Murtagh** and **Anastasia Brennan**, of same place. He answered an advertisement that Appeared in the Irish-American. He was at this time somewhere in MISSISSIPPI.

Information of him will be thankfully received by his sister **Bridget**, by addressing **Patrick Powers**, Irish-American Box 3025, N.Y. Post Office.

Of **Joseph McDermott**, of BELLEEK, Parish of DURROW, KING'S County, Ireland. Also of **Lawrence Finley**, of BRACK[L]IN. When last heard of were in NEW YORK CITY. If this should meet their eye they will please write to **James McDermott**, HOLLAND, LUCAS County, OHIO. Boston Pilot and New York papers, please copy.

Of **John Fahey**, a native of MOYLOUGH, County GALWAY, Ireland. When last heard of (about 13 years ago) he was at SALT LAKE, MICH. Intelligence of his present whereabouts will be thankfully received by his nephew, **John Morrissey**, 1128 2nd AVENUE, between 59th and 60th Streets, NEW YORK CITY.

Of **Patrick E. Naughton**, formerly of GALWAY, Ireland, who is supposed to have enlisted in NEW YORK in the Fall of 1861. Parties knowing of his whereabouts will confer a favor on his wife and children by sending information to **Edward Harrison**, NEW HAVEN, CONN.

August 15, 1868

Of **Patrick Sullivan**, of INCHIQUIN, County CORK, son of **William Sullivan** and **Mary Keeffe**. When last heard of (about 16 months since) he was in VIRGINIA, near RICHMOND. Intelligence of him will be thankfully received by his brother, **Wm. Sullivan**, care of P. J. Ryan, Emigration Agent, SPRINGFIELD, MASS.

Of **John Keenan**, formerly of KILGLASS, Parish of LEGAN, County LONGFORD, Ireland. Nine years ago he was living in ST. LOUIS, MISSOURI; but have just heard that he was at DIXON, ILL., a week ago, and left there for ROCKFORD, ILL., intending to go to MINNESOTA. He has been willed property worth $7,500 by his brother, **Peter Keenan**, deceased, in EUREKA County, CALIFORNIA, and he must appear in person on or before the 1[0]th of October next, or the property falls to the administrator, a total stranger. By addressing his cousin, **James Halligan**, CANAJOHARIE, N.Y., he can get all the necessary information. Western papers, please copy.

August 22, 1868

Will any of the officers of Co. D, 88th Regiment, N.Y. Vols., who is conversant with the facts of the death of Private **Charles Silverman**, or any of the soldiers who were in the Hospital at CITY POINT, VA., on or about the 14th day of July, 1864, and who know of the facts of his death, communicate with **Francis McGrath**, 7th Street, near 5th Avenue, BROOKLYN, N.Y., for the purpose of aiding **Mrs. Silverman** to obtain her pension.

Of **James Whelan**, of CAHIRON, Parish of KILL, County WATERFORD, Ireland; left in May, 1860. In 1863 he was in CANADA. Any information of him will be thankfully received by his brothers, **Patrick** and **Edward**, or his sister **Mary Whelan**, No. 813 Shippen St., PHILADELPHIA, PA.

Of **Pat.** and **Con. Mara**, natives of BALLYNACLOCH, near NENAGH, County TIPPERARY, Ireland. When last heard of (about six years ago) they were in NEW YORK CITY. Intelligence of them will be thankfully received by their brother and sister, **Tim** and **Norah Mara**, by addressing **Martin Tracey**, CHATHAM Post Office, N.J.

Of **Cornelius Sullivan**, tailor, of the Parish of KNOCKANE, near KILLARNEY, County of KERRY, Ireland, who left SPRINGFIELD, MASS., a few months since. If he will communicate with his friend, **John J. Coffey**, Bookkeeper, 123 Washington Street, BOSTON, MASS., he will hear of something of vital interest to him.

Of **Patrick Moran**, his wife **Catherine**, and her brother, **Dennis Moran**, all natives of TRALEE, County KERRY, Ireland. When last heard from they were residents of SPRUCE STREET, NEW YORK. Address **Ellen Moran**, care of Box 2536, ST. LOUIS Post Office.

Of **Dominick Hawd**, of the Parish of KILLCAREN, County GALWAY, Ireland, who landed in New York last March. Information of him will be thankfully received by his sister, **Mary Hawd**, at 102 PITT STREET, NEW YORK.

Of **Patrick Malley**, a native of LAYNAUN, County GALWAY, Ireland. When last heard of (about 18 months ago) he was in SCRANTON, PA. Intelligence of him will be thankfully received by his sister, **Catherine Malley**, HAVERSTRAW, ROCKLAND Co., N.Y., care of **Patrick Joyce**.

August 29, 1868

Of **Edward, Patrick** and **Peggy Loughlin**, of CLANRARUGHEN, County DOWN, Ireland. Edward left home in 1858, for WASHINGTON and when last heard from he worked on the railroad that went through to UTAH TERRITORY; Patrick left home in 1851, for NEW YORK, and Peggy is now **Mrs. Smith**; her husband is a blacksmith by trade; when last heard from they were in CHICAGO, ILL. Information of them will be thankfully received by their cousin, **Peter McPolen**, GARRISON STATION, PUTNAM County, N.Y.

Of **Ellen Curren**, a native of KANTURK, County CORK, Ireland. Her husband's name is **Thos. Barry**, a native of the County TIPPERARY, Ireland. When last heard from (about 8 years ago) they were at PORTAGE, HOUGHTON County, LAKE SUPERIOR, MICH. Intelligence of their present whereabouts will be thankfully received by **Thomas Bonworth**, nephew of Ellen Curren. Address **James Allen**, 57th STREET, between 2nd and 3rd Avenues, NEW YORK.

September 5, 1868

Of **Patrick Lunney**, of CARROWKEEL, Parish of DROMARD, County SLIGO, Ireland. When last heard from (two years ago) he was in LEAVENWORTH, KANSAS; served previously, during the war, in Company A, 8th Kansas Volunteers; is supposed to have gone to ST. LOUIS, with a man named **James Nicholes**, who resided there. Information respecting him will be gratefully received by his sister **Mary** and his brother-in-law, **Michael Gilgallon**, 220 WEST 36th STREET, NEW YORK. Western papers, please copy.

September 12, 1868

Of **Miss Mary Williams**, of STAFFORDSHIRE, ENGLAND. Intelligence of her will be thankfully received by **Thomas Casey**, 724 North Front Street, PHILADELPHIA, PA. [Appeared Dec. 12, 1868 with some different information.]

Of **Kate O'Brien**, of ENNIS, County CLARE, Ireland, who landed in this country about four years ago, and is supposed to have got married. She will receive her share of her brother's prize-money by applying to her mother, who came to NEW YORK two years ago, and who is now at **Mrs. Loftus's**, No. 12 GREENWICH STREET, NEW YORK CITY. New Orleans papers, please copy.

September 19, 1868

Of **Ann Fahey**, a native of COOLOO, Parish of MOYLOUGH, County GALWAY, Ireland. When last heard from (about 13 years ago) she was in BALTIMORE, MD., where she was married to a man named **George Gillingham**. Intelligence of her present whereabouts will be thankfully received by her nephew, **John Morrissey**, at 1[ ]32 2nd AVENUE, between 59th and 60th sts., N.Y., care of **Daniel Crimmins**.

Of **Daniel Nolan**, a native of NEWTOWNARDS, County KERRY, Ireland. When last heard from (about two years ago) he was living in WEST HICKORY, VENANGO County, PA. Information of him will be thankfully received by his brother, **Dennis Nolan**, FREISENSVILLE Post Office, LEHIGH County, PA.

September 26, 1868

Of **Patrick McManus**, who left GLASGOW, SCOTLAND, in June, 1861 and arrived in this country. He left NEWARK, N.J., in March, 1865, and it is supposed went to WEST VIRGINIA. When last heard of was employed as quarryman in PENNSYLVANIA. Information of him will be thankfully received by his brother, **John McManus**, 78 Market Street, NEWARK, N.J.

Of **Patrick Boyle**, a native of the Parish of ARDEE, County LOUTH, Ireland. When last seen (about eleven years ago) he was in NEW YORK CITY, from whence he went to the State of ILLINOIS. Information of him will be thankfully received by his mother **Bridget Boyle** in care of **Philip McIntee**, 551 WEST 26th STREET, NEW YORK.

Of **Elizabeth Mullen**, daughter of **Owen** and **Elizabeth Mullen,** a native of the Townland of CLARA, Parish of KI[L]L, County CAVAN, Ireland. When last heard of (in 1860) she lived in NEW YORK CITY. Information of her will be thankfully received by **John Hyar**, Co. K, Fifth U.S. Infantry, FORT RILEY, KANSAS. By making herself known she will hear of something to her advantage.

Of **Betty Cresswell**, (maiden name **Mulholland**) a native of the Parish of UPPER FAHAN, barony of INASHAWN, County DONEGAL, Ireland, who left home about 24 years ago. When last heard from she was in PHILADELPHIA. Information of her will be thankfully received by her brother, **Samuel Mulholland**, No. [4]02 Pine Street, or by **Bernard O'Neill**, Justice of the Peace, PATERSON, N.J.

Of **Johanna Tyrell**, a native of PHILLIPSTOWN, Parish of CAPPAWHITE, County TIPPERARY, Ireland. When last heard of (about two years ago) she lived with her aunt (who was married to one **Andrew Tazlerina**, a native of GENOA, ITALY, in Tolo[s]o Street, NEW ORLEANS, LA. Information concerning her will be thankfully received by her uncle **Lawrence Higgins**, 354 Jersey Avenue, JERSEY CITY, N.J.

Of **Michael O'Halloran**, a native of ATHENRY, County GALWAY, Ireland. When last heard from (about a year ago) he was in NORFOLK, VA. Information of him will be thankfully received by his brother, **John O'Halloran**, 195 MULBERRY STREET, NEW YORK.

October 3, 1868

Of **Mary, Bridget** and **Ellen McLaughlin**, natives of DUBLIN City, Ireland. Their brother, **Edward McLaughlin**, who is in this country for the last 18 years, is very anxious to hear from them. When he left home his sisters were living with their cousin, **Miss Mary Halligan**, in Dublin City. Information of them will be thankfully received at the office of the Irish-American, No. 8 North William Street, New York. Dublin papers, please copy.

Of **James O'Neill**, a native of AUGHRAM, County ROSCOMMON, Ireland, who landed in New York in March, 1867. Information of him will be thankfully received by his brother-in-law, **Michael McDonnough**, SCHENECTADY Post Office, SCHENECTADY County, N.Y., in care of the Schenectady Locomotive Works.

Of **Patrick Swiney**, a baker, a native of the Town of FERMOY, County CORK, Ireland, who landed in New York on the 19th of August and left thence for BOSTON, MASS.

Information of him will be thankfully received by his brother, **Wm. Swiney**, 368 Court Street, BROOKLYN, N.Y.

Of **John Keogh**, a carpenter, a native of the Parish of CLONEGALL, County WICKLOW, Ireland, who left there about 21 years ago. When last heard of he was in NEW YORK CITY. Also, of his brother, **James Keogh**, who came here five years later. Information of them will be thankfully received by their sister, **Mary Somers** 934 Broadway, ST. LOUIS, MO. New York papers, generally, please copy.

Of **Catherine McMahon**, daughter of **James McMahon** and **Nancy McCabe**, a native of BALLYBAY, County MONAGHAN, Ireland. When last heard of she was in NEW YORK. Information of her will be thankfully received by her brother **John McMahon**, BALLYBAY, County MONAGHAN, Ireland, or by addressing her cousin, **Margaret McCabe**, 69 Broad Street, NEWARK, N.J.

October 10, 1868

Of **John Flin**, who left LEEDS, ENGLAND, about 13 years ago. When last heard from he was at DWIGHT, LIVINGSTON County, ILL. Information of him will be thankfully received by his sister **Bridget**. Address **Thomas Rowland**, foot of 110th STREET, East River, NEW YORK. Western papers, please copy.

Of **Patrick Shannahan**, of CHARLEVILLE, County CORK, Ireland. When last heard from he was in the State of NEW YORK. Information of him will be thankfully received by his sister, **Catherine Shannahan**, 824 Washington Avenue, PHILADELPHIA, PA.

Of **Nicholas Burke**, a native of the Parish of KILLROSSINTEE, County WATERFORD, Ireland, who came to this country about ten years ago, and is about 35 or 40 years of age. When last seen (about six or seven years since) he was in WORCESTER, MASS., on his way to NEW YORK CITY. Information of him will be thankfully received by his sister **Bridget**, by addressing **John Crotty**, 5 South Irving Street, WORCESTER, MASS.

Of **Joseph Brown**, a native of the Parish of KELLS, County MEATH, Ireland, who, when last heard of, was in NEW YORK CITY, about June or July, 1867. Information of him will be thankfully received by his brother, **William Brown**, 116 Cambridge Street, BOSTON, MASS.

Of **Bridget Makin**, of BRAGINSTOWN, Parish of STABANAN, County LOUTH, Ireland, who came to NEW YORK 14 years ago, and got married there. Also, of **Patrick** and **Michael Henry**, of DUNDALK, her cousins. Information of them will be thankfully received by Bridget's brother, **Thomas Makin**, CONSHOHOKEN Post Office, MONTGOMERY County, PA.

October 17, 1868

Of **William Gavin**, of CARNBAWN, County MEATH, Ireland. Information of him will be thankfully received by his cousin, **Joseph Gavin**, Dean Street and Vanderbilt Avenue, BROOKLYN, Long Island, N.Y.

Of **Thomas Smith**, a native of DOWESTOWN, Parish of JOHNSTOWN, County MEATH, Ireland. When last heard of (about 24 years ago) he was in the employ of **William Plummerfelt**, as a carpenter, in MARKHAM or TORONTO, CANADA. Information of him will be thankfully received by his brother, **Wm. Smith**, at Brewster & Baldwin's, 786 BROADWAY, NEW YORK. Canada papers, please copy.

October 24, 1868

Of **Thomas Doyle**, of CARROW, CLONEGAL, County WEXFORD, Ireland. Passenger per steamer *Caledonia*, June, 1865. When last heard from he was in OHIO. Information of him will be thankfully received by his sister, **Mary Ann Doyle**, Box 3,509, NEW YORK Post Office. Ohio papers, please copy.

Of **William Feeney**, of DROMORE WEST, County SLIGO, Ireland, who came to this country over four years ago, on board the steanship *Etna*. When last heard from he was in PLAINFIELD, N.J. Information of him will be thankfully received by his wife, **Mary Feeney**, Hall Street, 6th house south of Fulton Avenue, BROOKLYN, N.Y. Western papers, please copy. [Appeared Dec. 26, 1868 with some different information.]

Of **Mrs. Honora Farrelly**, a native of the County WESTMEATH, Ireland. When last heard of (about four years ago) she lived in JERSEY CITY, N.J. Intelligence of her will be thankfully received by her brother, **Christopher Foley**, at 169 Newark Avenue, JERSEY CITY, N.J., in care of **John Carrigan**.

Of **Timothy Donohue**, a native of the Parish of KANTURK, County CORK, Ireland, who left home about 22 years ago; he is about 45 years of age. When last seen by his sister **Honora**, he was in NEW YORK CITY, after leaving the Army, about ten years ago. Information of his whereabouts will be thankfully received by addressing his brother, **Daniel Donohue**, 25 MARION STREET, NEW YORK.

Of **Mary Murphy** (widow), a native of BUTTEVANT, County CORK, Ireland. When last heard of she was living in Green-lane, BROOKLYN, Long Island, N.Y. Information concerning her will be most thankfully received by her daughter, **Mrs. Mary Walsh**, 14 North Tenth Street, ST. LOUIS, MO.

Of **Michael Shiels**, a native of GARRYOWEN, LIMERICK, Ireland. When last heard of he was in Dexter's Hotel, QUEBEC, CANADA. Information of him will be thankfully received by his brother, **Patrick J. Shiels**, 1635 Latona Street, PHILADELPHIA, PA. Montreal and Boston Pilot, papers, please copy.

October 31, 1868

Of **William Gilshenan**, of POTTLE, County CAVAN, Ireland. Four years ago he was in VIRGINIA, CONN. His aunt **Kate** is in WATERBURY, CONN. He can have some money that was left by his mother, now deceased, by applying to his uncle, **James Gilshenan**, POTTLE, BALLYHALSE, County CAVAN, Ireland, or to **William Gilshenan**, 143 East Street, MANAYUNK, PA.

Of **James Connell**, a native of the Parish of KILLMEEN, County CORK, Ireland. When last heard of (3 years ago) he worked in SCHUYLKILL County, PA. Information of him will be thankfully received by his brother, **John Connell**, 35 Stockton Alley, BALTIMORE, MD.

November 7, 1868

Of **Peter Nugent**, a native of DROGHEDA, County LOUTH, Ireland, who landed in New York in October, 1854; he worked on the Illinois Rail Road and is supposed to have gone either to IOWA or TEXAS. Information of him will be thankfully received by his brother, **Patrick Nugent**, 335 EAST 28th STREET, NEW YORK. Western papers, please copy.

Of **Martin White**, a native of BORRISOKANE, County TIPPERARY, Ireland. Information of him will be thankfully received by his brother, **James White**, by writing to him in care of **Gannon Clyne**, HELENA, MONTANA TERRITORY. Boston Pilot, please copy.

Of **Patrick Carrigg**, of KILRUSH, Co. CLARE, Ireland. Any person knowing his whereabouts will confer a favor by writing to **George Chambers**, ELIZABETHPORT, UNION County, N.J. Western papers, please copy.

Of **Thomas Finn**, a native of the Parish of CLOYNE, County CORK, Ireland. When last heard of he was in RICHMOND Iron Works, MASS. Intelligence of him will be thankfully received by his brother, **William Finn**, PORTLAND, CONN.

November 14, 1868

Of **J. B. McDonough**, or otherwise **Bernard McDonough**, who resided in CALIFORNIA since 1846, and when last heard from (14 years ago) lived in MARYVILLE, in that State. Information of him will be thankfully received by his brother-in-law, **Thomas Collins**, 1,180 South Eleventh Street, PHILADELPHIA, PA. California papers, please copy.

Of **Bernard Cunningham**, who left LYONS, CLINTON County, IOWA, about 18 months ago. He is supposed to have gone to ST. LOUIS. Information of him will be thankfully received by addressing **M. Cunningham**, SING SING, N.Y.

Of **James Daniel**, who left **Mr. Greams**, of DONADEA, County KILDARE, about 18 years ago. He was seen in the City of NEW YORK in 1865. Information of him will be gratefully received by his brother, **John Daniel**, CLANE, County KILDARE, Ireland.

Of **Daniel O'Shea**, a native of County KERRY, Ireland, who came to this country about 14 years ago, and went to live with **Father Rooney**, in PLATSBURG, NEW YORK; about five or six years ago he was learning either the trade of a blacksmith or baker. It is supposed he is in ALBANY, N.Y. Information of him will be thankfully received by his sisters, **Mary, Alice** and **Julia O'Shea**, by addressing either, in care of **John Flynn**, KENSINGTON, CONN.

November 21, 1868

Of **William Henderson**, of DUBLIN, boot and shoe maker, who left MANCHESTER, ENGLAND, in 1856; was in BOSTON, MASS., in 1858. Information of him, dead or alive, will be thankfully received by his disconsolate wife, care of **D. A. Brosnan**, WASHINGTON, D.C., for **Ann Morrissey**.

Of **Mary McLaughlin**, of the Townland of TAMLAGHT, Parish of DRUNRAUGH, County TYRONE, Ireland. She sailed in the ship *Fanny*, from Londonderry, on the 20th of March, 1849. Information of her whereabouts will be thankfully received by her brother, **Patrick McLaughlin**, 394 High Street, NEWARK, N.J.

Of **Margaret Harden**, (maiden name **Margaret Fitzgerald**), who, with four of her children, left the Parish of DOONE, County LIMERICK, Ireland, and came to BROOKLYN, NEW YORK, one year ago last March. Information of her will be thankfully received by addressing either **John, Catharine**, or **Margaret Harden**, City of LINCOLN, LOGAN County, ILL.

Of **Mrs. Ellen Kelly**, and of her sons, **Richard, James** and **Edward**, also of her daughter **Margaret**, who came to this country from GLENAGAD, near NEW INN, County TIPPERARY, Ireland. When last heard from they were out west. Information of them will be thankfully received by her daughter, **Bridget Morrissey**, by addressing her in care of **Wm. Fitzpatrick**, NEW HAVEN, CONN.

December 5, 1868

Of **Ellen Meehan**, daughter of **John Meehan** and **Mary Keraun**, a native of the Town of GRAUN, BALLYHAVEN, County MAYO, Ireland, who left home about 20 years ago. She came to the State of NEW YORK, and is supposed to have gone to BALTIMORE, MD. Information of her will be thankfully received by her sister, **Winnifred Meehan**, Post Office, COHOES, ALBANY County, N.Y.

Of **James Walker**, a native of the County DONEGAL, Ireland. He has light brown hair, and blue eyes. He left CHICAGO last August. When last heard from he was in MISSOURI VALLEY, HARRISON County, IOWA. Information of him, dead or alive, will be thankfully received by his mother, **Mrs. Ann Walker**, KANSAS CITY, MO.

Of **Bernard Fitzpatrick**, of the Parish of OUGHTROUG, County LEITRIM, Ireland, who left ALBANY, N.Y., four years ago, for CALIFORNIA. Information of him will be thankfully received by his brother, **Patrick Fitzpatrick**, VALATIE, COLUMBIA Co., N.Y. California papers, please copy.

Of **Mary Padden**, from near STROKESTOWN, County ROSCOMMON, Ireland, who landed here from the ship *Isaac Webb*, in June last, and wrote from Castle Garden to her friends; since when she has not been heard from. Any intelligence of her will be thankfuly received by **Patrick Padden**, 24 Neighbor St., BALTIMORE, MD.

December 12, 1868

Of **Thomas Newberry**, who is supposed to have left MASSACHUSETTS, where he lived nine years with **Luther Ranney**, of SHEFFIELD. Any person giving intelligence of him, whether living or dead, will confer a favor on his mother, **Jane Newberry**. Address, **Patrick Short**, FALL RIVER, MASS.

Of **Mrs. Mary Williams**, from STAFFORDSHIRE Potteries, ENGLAND. Information of her will be thankfully received by **Thomas Casey**, PENLLYN Post Office, MONTGOMERY County, PA. [Appeared Sept. 12, 1868 with different information.]

Of **Martin, John** and **Dennis Mullin**, natives of MOYLOUGH, County GALWAY, Ireland. When last heard of, about 2 years ago, they were in MADISON, IND. Any intelligence of them will be thankfully received by their cousin, **Francis Monaghan**, at 267 Wayne St., JERSEY CITY, N.J. Indiana papers, please copy.

Of **John Breheny**, from BOYLE, County ROSCOMMON, Ireland. Information of him will be thankfully received by his wife, **Margaret**, now at Castle Garden.

December 19, 1868

Of **Ellen Murphy**, a native of the County DUBLIN, Ireland. When last heard from she was in No. 26 Bishop Street, City of DUBLIN. Intelligence of her will be thankfully received by her brother, **Edward Murphy**, Co. F, 13th U.S. Infantry, FORT ELLIS, MONTANA TERRITORY. Dublin papers, please copy.

Of **Richard Dowling**, a native of KNOCTOPHER, County KILKENNY, Ireland, who sailed from New Ross, County Wexford, Ireland, in March, 1849, for New York, where he arrived the following month of April. Information as to his whereabouts will be thankfully received by his brother, **William Dowling**. Address care of **Laffan**, Box 558 Post Office, NEW YORK.

Of **John Gilooley**, son of **Michael Gilooley**, who lived near STROKESTOWN, County ROSCOMMON, Ireland, who came to America about nine years ago. When last heard from he was living near JERSEY CITY. Information of him will be thankfully received by his brother, **Michael Gilooley**, who is dangerously ill since the 15th of November, 1868. Inquire at the Delaware Iron Works, PHILLIPSBURG, N.J.

December 26, 1868

Of **William Feeney**, of DRONOR WEST, County SLIGO, Ireland, who sailed on the steamship *Etna*, April, 1864. Information concerning him will be thankfully received by his wife, **Mary Feeney**, 6th house south of Fulton-av., Hall St., BROOKLYN. Western papers, please copy. [Appeared Oct. 24, 1868 with some different information; appeared

Jan. 9, 1869 with the place of origin changed to DROMORE WEST, County SLIGO, Ireland.]

Of **Hanora Guiry**, Parish of CROOM, County LIMERICK, Ireland. When last heard from she was in EAST TROY, N.Y. Supposed she went south. Information of her will be thankfully received by her brother, **Patrick Guiry**, AFTON, CHENANGO County, N.Y.

Of **Michael Huband**, of LABANE, Co. GALWAY, and subsequently of LISCANNOR, Co. CLARE, Ireland. When last heard from (in May last) he wrote home from MAXVILLE, WASHINGTON County, KY. Information of him will be gratefully received by his anxious wife **Louisa** care of H. D. Glynn, Castle Garden, New York.

January 2, 1869

Of **John Ferguson**, of NEW KILLMANEAR], brother of **Ann Griffith**, and of **William Leary**, of ISLAND BRIDGE, Ireland. When last heard from they were in NEW YORK CITY. Any information leading to their whereabouts will be most thankfully received by their nephew, son of Ann Griffith. **Samuel Griffith**, FORT MCKAVETT, TEXAS. [Appeared under County DUBLIN

Of **James Toole**, of NEWTONMOUNTKENNEDY. Emigrated to NEW YORK in 1853. Address to his brother HAROLD'S CROSS, DUBLIN. [Appeared under County WICKLOW]

Of **John** and **Patrick Moran**, of ANAUGBEG, Parish of KILBECONTY, Co. GALWAY, Ireland, was two years ago in NEW HAVEN, went out west when last heard from. John was in MINNESOTA and Patrick in ST. LOUIS. Any information of them will be thankfully received by their brother, **Patrick Moran**, who landed in New Haven in June last. Direct 25 Locust St., NEW HAVEN, CONN.

Of **Andrew Rogers**, son of **Michael Rogers**, who was born in the Parish of TOMGRANEY, County CLARE, Ireland. When last heard from he was in NORWICH, CONN. Any information of him will be thankfully received by his brother, **John Rogers**, LEXINGTON, MCLEAN Co., ILL.

Of **Nicholas Barnett**, a native of DONORE, Co. MEATH, Ireland. When last heard of he was living at **Isaac Smith's** CENTRE ISLAND, OYSTER BAY, L.I. Any intelligence of him will be thankfully received by **John Barnett**, TUCKAHOE, WESTCHESTER Co., N.Y.

Of **Thomas Phillips**, a native of BALLYSHANNON, Co. DONEGAL, Ireland. Left home in June, 1864. When last heard from he was in VIRGINIA, and was in the U.S. Navy; discharged in April, 1868. Any information of him will be thankfully received by his cousin, **Michael McGowan**, at 13 3rd AVENUE, N.Y. CITY. Western papers, please copy.

January 16, 1869

Of **Laurence McAuliffe**, son of **Michael McAuliffe**, native of BROADFOR, County of LIMERICK, Ireland. He lived in PENNSYLVANIA, about twelve years ago. Information concerning him will be thankfully received by his brother **Maurice McAuliffe**, No. 14 Laurence-place, BROOKLYN, N.Y. Western and Southern papers please copy.

Of **John Kelly**, a native of the City of LIMERICK, Ireland, late sergeant in the 1st battalion of the 16th Regiment of Foot, British army, who was discharged on the 14th of October, 1866, while his regiment was stationed in UPPER CANADA. It is supposed that he went to the United States. Any information of the above-named person will be thankfully received by his sister, **Mrs. Mary Anne Marksman** (late **Miss Mary Anne Kelly**), 114 Long Millgate, MANCHESTER, ENGLAND. Canadian and Australian papers, please copy.

Of **Patrick** and **Mary Flynn**, who left Ireland about fifteen years ago, formerly of KILMEUM, Parish of KILA, County WATERFORD, Ireland. When last heard from, about five years ago, they were in TORONTO, UPPER CANADA. Address **John Flynn**, 5 South Irving Street, WORCESTER, MASS.

Of **Catherine** and **Mary Davis**, natives of FAIRFIELD, AHASERAGH, County of GALWAY, Ireland. When last heard of, about 17 years ago, they were living in ROXBURY, BOSTON, MASS. Mary was married at that time to **Mary** [sic] **Craffy**, native of County ROSCOMMON, Ireland. Any information of them will be thankfully received by their brother **William Davis**. Address **Patrick O'Connell**, southwest corner of 1st AVENUE and 59th-ST., N.Y., for William Davis. Boston and South Carolina papers please copy.

Of **John Hussey** and his nephew, **Robert Delany**, of KILTULLA, County ROSCOMMON, Ireland. They reside in some part of MARYLAND. Any information of their whereabouts will be thankfully received by their cousin, **Martin Reaney**, at **Francis Stokes,** Esq., Armat Street, GERMANTOWN, PHILADELPHIA, PA.

Any person knowing the whereabouts of **James O'Connor**, silk peddler, a native of the County CLARE, Ireland, who emigrated to DENVER City, COLORADO, about 2 years ago, will please communicate with Walls & Leahy, 69 Duane Street, NEW YORK CITY. California and Western papers, please copy.

Of **Patrick Sullivan**, who departed from Ireland, County CORK, Parish of KILNOON, ploughland of GUINIEVS, on the 1st of May, 1868. When last heard from, after landing, he was in NEW YORK. Any information of him will be thankfully received by his mother, **Ally Sullivan**, 168 Front Street, BALTIMORE, MD.

January 23, 1869

Of **Michael** and **James Shanahan**, natives of CARRICK-ON-SUIR, County TIPPERARY, Ireland. When last heard from, they were in SANDUSKY, LEE County, IOWA. Information of them will be thankfully received by their sister, **Ellen Shanahan**, 31 Amity St., SOUTH BROOKLYN. California and Iowa papers, please copy.

Of **Hugh King**, son of **Hugh King**, who was born in the Town of ROSSLEA, County FERMANAGH, Ireland. He came to this country about twenty years ago. He was last heard from (about twelve years ago,) through **James McDermot**, of the DEERPARK. Any intelligence of him will be thankfully received by his brother, **James King**, at 33 Baun St., CINCINNATI, OHIO.

January 30, 1869

Of **Patrick Colman**, boot and shoemaker, son of **Michael Colman**, boot and shoemaker, of Flemings place, Baggot Street Bridge, DUBLIN, formerly of DONNYBROOK. He sailed from the North Wall, Dublin, for New York, in the ship *Ashland*, about nineteen years ago. Any information of him will be thankfully received by his sister, **Mary Ann Colman**, by writing to **John McKeon**, 136 South Market Street, NEWARK, N.J.

Of **Bernard** and **Patrick McAneny**, from TULLYRONE, County ARMAGH, Ireland. They have been in this country about fifteen years. When last heard from they were in CANADA. Any information of their whereabouts will be thankfully received by their nephew, **John McAneny**, 121 Barre St., BALTIMORE, MD.

Of **Mr. Terance** and **Mary Malone** (maiden name **Fowler**) natives of KILMOON, County MEATH, Ireland. When last heard from (about 12 years ago) they were in MARYLAND. Any information of them will be thankfully received by her nephew, **Patrick Henchey**, at PITTSTOWN CORNERS, RENSSELAER County, N.Y.

Of **Ellen** and **Honorah McCarthy**, **James Healy**, and **John McCarthy**, natives of the County CORK, Ireland. They formerly lived at BARNA, Parish of CAHARAGH. They were supposed to be either in CONNECTICUT or NEW YORK when last heard of. Since then some of them were said to be in WISCONSIN. Any intelligence of them will be thankfully received by their nephew, **John McCarthy**, GEORGETOWN Post Office, D. C.New York, Connecticut and Wisconsin papers, please copy.

Of **James Raftery**, a native of the County of ROSCOMMON, Ireland. Was in the City of NEW YORK November last. Any information will be thankfully received by his brother, **Patrick Raftery**, at 195 MULBERRY ST., NEW YORK CITY.

Of **John Delahunty**, a native of KILMASPIG, County KILKENNY, Ireland. Was last heard from, in June, 1866, he was living in the City of LEAVENWORTH, KANSAS. Information as to his whereabouts will be thankfully received by his brother, **Thomas Delahunty**, United States Hotel, PORTLAND, ME. California papers please copy.

Of **Henry Torpy**, of BALLYNACALLY, near ENNIS, County CLARE, Ireland. When last heard from (two years ago) he was in TACONY, PHILADELPHIA County, PA. Any information of him will be thankfully received by his brother, **Michael Torpy**, North Adams Woolen Mills, DEWYVILLE, near NORTH ADAMS, MASS.

February 6, 1869

Of **Bridget Fox**, a native of GLYSRAVYMAN, County WICKLOW, Ireland, who sailed for New York in May, 1853. When last heard from she was in BUFFALO, N.Y. Any information of her will be thankfully received by her friend, **Eliza Finley**, at 516 Lombard Street, PHILADELPHIA, PA.

Of **John Roach**, a native of KILFINEN, County LIMERICK, who left home for MALLOW, County CORK, Ireland, about 22 years ago, being then five years of age. Any information of him will be thankfully received by **Wm. Roach**, at 52 Newark Avenue, JERSEY CITY, N.J. Cork and Limerick, Ireland, papers, please copy.

Of **John Ryan**, a native of the County of LIMERICK, Ireland, or of his children, **John** and **Ellen**, or any other member of his family. When last heard from (in 1865) he lived in 1430 Bedford Street, PHILADELPHIA. Any intelligence of them will be thankfully received, and will be to their advantage, by addressing **John Hickey**, 205 SPRING STREET, NEW YORK. Southern and Western papers, please copy.

Of **Patrick** and **Thomas Cotter**, natives of the Townland of COOLNAKILE, Parish of RATHCORMICK, County CORK, Ireland. - When last heard from (about eighteen years ago), Patrick was in PORTLAND, CONN., and Thomas was in SPRINGFIELD, MASS. They will hear of something to their advantage by writing to their sister **Mary**, now **Mrs. John Aheren**, FERMOY; or to their cousin, **Honora Spillane**, now **Mrs. Jeremiah O'Connors**, HARTFORD Post Office, WASHINGTON County, WIS.

February 13, 1869

Of **Joseph Dempsey**, by his mother, at 16 BEEKMAN STREET, NEW YORK CITY, where he last did business. Left or lost. Supposed to have gone to BOSTON or BALTIMORE or PHILADELPHIA. Boston papers, please copy.

Of **James** and **Patrick Fitzpatrick**, natives of CASTLEBLANEY, County MONAGHAN, Ireland. When last heard from, in 1850, they resided with their mother and sisters in GALENA, ILLINOIS. Any information concerning them will be thankfully received by their nephew, son of their brother **Daniel**. Address **Patrick Fitzpatrick**, 28 SPRING STREET, NEW YORK CITY. Western papers, please copy.

Of **Owen, William** and **Daniel Prendergast**, who left BALTINGLAS, County WICKLOW, about twelve or fifteen years ago, by their nephew, **Mark J. McEnroe**, YONKERS, NEW YORK.

February 20, 1869

Of **John McCullough**. He would oblige by calling on or addressing **L. G. Goulding**, Publisher, No. 10 SPRUCE STREET, NEW-YORK.

Of **James Whealan**, aged 60 years, and of his son, **Michael Whealan**, aged 24 years. When last heard from (six months ago) they were in ALEXANDRIA, VA. Any one knowing of their whereabouts will confer a favor on **James Whealan**, by addressing him in care of **John O'Toohill**, 2005 Market Street, PHILADELPHIA, PA.

Of **Michael McInerney**, a native of the City of LIMERICK, Ireland, late Color-Sergeant in the 1st Battalion of the 16th Regiment of Foot, British Army, who left HAMILTON, CANADA WEST, on the 5th of January, 1867. When last heard from (in August, 1867), he was in SPRINGFIELD, MASS. It is supposed that he went to CALIFORNIA. Any person knowing of his whereabouts will confer an everlasting obligation on his friends by addressing J. G. D., 874 Delaware Street, BUFFALO, N.Y. California and Western papers, please copy.

February 27, 1869

Of **Patrick Gallagher**, who left the City of GLASGOW, SCOTLAND, about fifteen years ago for NEW YORK, and enlisted in the 8th Regiment, Company F, of U.S. Infantry, and was discharged in '62 or '63, in FORT MONROE, VIRGINIA. Any information of him will be thankfully received by his brother, **Frank Gallagher**, at J. Ulmans & Sons, WILLIAMSPORT, PA., P.O. box 2683.

Of **James** and **Sarah Yourt** (maiden name **Smith**), natives of ARMAGH, Ireland. Twenty years ago they left their native country for NEW YORK, U.S. Any information concerning them will be thankfully received by her sister **Rachel Smith**. Please direct any communication for her to **George McGinness**, ELIZABETH, NEW JERSEY.

Of **John Carroll**, a son of **Arthur Carroll**, also a son of **Andrew Carroll**, a native of BALLINACLOUGH, PALACE GREEN, County LIMERICK, Ireland. Andrew's son was in CHICAGO, ILL., two years ago. Any information of them will be thankfully received by their cousin, **Matthew Carroll**, NORTHAMPTON, MASS. Southern and Western papers, please copy

Of **Thomas Hehir**, of BALLYREEN, near ENNISTYMON, County CLARE, Ireland. - When last heard from, in 1868, he was in NEW YORK CITY. Any information of him will be thankfully received by his brother-in-law, **Patt Hellery**, DUNKIRK, CHAUTAUQUA County, N.Y.

Of **Bartholomew Higgins**, a native of CALLOW, near FRENCHPARK, County ROSCOMMON, Ireland, who is supposed to have left Queenstown on the 20th of January, 1869, on the steamer *Queen*, and landed in New York on the 9th of February. Any information of him wil be thankfully received by his brother, **Patrick Higgins**, by writing to him, to DERBY, NEW HAVEN County, CONN. Brooklyn and Jersey papers, please copy.

Of **Margaret Daly** (maiden name), a daughter of **Patrick Daly** and **Hanorah Mulchekey**, a native of the Parish of CASTLEISLAND, County KERRY, Ireland, who landed in New York about eight years ago. When last heard from was living with **Joseph Cronen**, 251 South 2nd Street, JERSEY CITY, N.J. Any information of her will be thankfully received by her brother, **Denis Daly**, 4 Centre St., MANCHESTER, N.H.

Of **Margaret Conroy**, of ROSENALLIS, QUEEN'S County, Ireland, who came to America in March, 1866. Any information of her will be gratefully received by her son, **Michael Conroy**, Co. L, 1st Regt. Cavalry, DRUM BARRACKS, CAL.

Of **Mary** and **John Doughen**, who left CLOCH, QUEEN'S County, Ireland, about fifteen or sixteen years ago. Any information concerning them will be thankfully received by their friend, **Thomas Delaney**, ELIZABETH CITY, N.J. Southern and Western papers, please copy.

Of **Anthony Early**, a native of BALLYGLASS, ERRIS, County MAYO. He is a blacksmith by trade, and twelve years in the country. When last heard of (about four or five years ago), he was said to have been in OHIO. Any intelligence of him will be thankfully received by his nephew, **John Barrett**. Address John Barrett, care of the Irish-American, P.O. Box 3,025. Western papers, please copy.

March 6, 1869

Of **John Hogan**, son of **Michael Hogan** and **Ellen Wheelihan**, a native of BALLYWILLIAM, Parish of CLOYNE, County of CORK, Ireland, who left ALBANY, N.Y., about thirteen years ago, and went to CHICAGO, ILL. - Any information concerning him will be thankfully received by addressing his cousin, **Catherine Battersbee** - maiden name, **Catherine Higgins** - as he will hear something to his advantage. Address **John Battersbee**, WEST MERRIDEN, CONN. Western papers, please copy.

Of **Michael McNamara**, a native of RUAN, County CLARE, Ireland. When last heard from, four years ago, he was living in DETROIT, MICHIGAN. Any information of him will be thankfully received by his cousin, **John O'Brien**, 1134 2nd AVENUE, between 59th and 60th Streets, NEW YORK CITY.

March 13, 1869

Of **Thomas Wm. Mathews**, an orphan boy, about eight years of age, who is supposed to be somewhere in the City of NEW YORK. His father, **George Mathews**, a painter by trade, lost his life in 1867 or 1868, in the City of New York, by falling from a ladder while working at his trade. At the time of his death he lived at 325 EAST 31st STREET. He was a native of the County MONAGHAN, Ireland. Any information of the boy will be gratefully received by his aunt, **Margaret Drope** (maiden name, **Mathews**). Address **Neal Mines**, MANITOWOC, WIS.

March 20, 1869

Of **Dennis Enright**, who was supposed to have been in PENNSYLVANIA about two or three years ago. The wife of Dennis Enright landed in this country about a year ago, and is very anxious to hear of his whereabouts. Any intelligence of him will be thankfully received by his friend, **John Enright**, at No. 18 State Street, BROOKLYN, L.I.

Of **Mary O'Connor**, (Ridge,) late of LIMERICK, Ireland. She landed at New York, by steamer *Tarifa*, about Nov. 4, 1868. Address **Patrick Fitzgerald**, MEDFORD, MASS.

Of **David, John** and **Thomas Sheehy**, natives of BALLINGARRY, County LIMERICK, Ireland, by their sister Honora. When last heard from they were living in ORANGE County, N.Y. Address **Honora Sheehy**, care of **Mr. Peter Doremus**, 81 Bridge Street, PATERSON, N.J.

Of **John, Mary** and **Margaret Curran**, who left COURELA, Parish of CARRIGALLEN, County LEITRIM, Ireland. When last heard from they were in PROVIDENCE, R.I. Heard that John joined the U.S. Army in 1862. Information of them will be thankfully received by their cousin. Address **James McGovern**, care of the Irish-American, Box 3025, New-York. Rhode Island, Ohio and Pennsylvania papers, please copy.

March 27, 1869

Of **Anthony Corrigan**. When last seen, about six months since, was in PATERSON, N.J. Any one knowing his whereabouts would confer a favor on his father, **Patrick Corrigan**, by sending a line to that effect to **Bernard O'Neill**, Justice of the Peace, 81 Congress Street, N.J.

Of **Daniel Donovan**, a native of KINSALE, County CORK, Ireland, who came to this country sixteen years ago, landing in Boston; went from there to LAWRENCE, where he worked one year for **William Sullivan**, contractor, and is now in CALIFORNIA. - Any information respecting him will be thankfully received by his sister, **Mrs. Mary O'Donnell** (maiden name, **Mary Donovan**). - Please address Mrs. Mary O'Donnell, 274 Elm Street, LAWRENCE, MASS. California papers, please copy.

Of **James Tyrrel**, and **Daniel Scully**, of the Parish of FUHANY, County GALWAY, Ireland. When last heard from, they were in JERSEY CITY. Any information of them will be thankfully received by **Geo. Bellas**, ROUND VALLEY, PLUMAS Co., CAL.

Of **James Murphy**, a native of the Parish of CHLOER, County KERRY, Ireland, who left ENGLAND in June, 1857. When last heard from, he was in MIDDLE GRAMMEL, State of NEW YORK. Any information concerning him will be thankfully received by his sister, **Johanna Murphy**, 32 WEST 15th STREET, NEW YORK CITY.

April 3, 1869

Of **Thomas Dwyer** and family, natives of CARRICK, near TOMAVARRA, County TIPPERARY, Ireland, who are now supposed to reside at or near POUGHKEEPSIE, N.Y. Intelligence of them will be thankfully received by **Anne Dwyer**, at the Intelligence Office of John McKlune, 376 Pla[ ]e Street, NEWARK, N.J.

Of **Mary O'Neill**, daughter of **John O'Neill**, who left CAPPOQUIN, County WATERFORD, Ireland, in the year 1849, and when last heard from (in 1852) she was living in NEW YORK CITY. Any information of her will be thankfully received by her brother, **William O'Neill**, WASHINGTON GULCH, DEER LODGE County, MONTANA TERRITORY.

Of **Michael** and **Thomas Dillon**, natives of BALLAGHADEREEN, County MAYO, Ireland. They left their native country about twenty-three years ago. When last heard from they were near ROLLA, in PHELPS County, MISSOURI. Any information of them will be thankfully received by their cousin, **Bridget Corcoran**, BLACKINTON, BERKSHIRE County, MASS.

April 10, 1869

Of **Michael Hardy**, a boy 18 years of age. Landed in New York 29th June last on the steamer "*Manhattan*" and strayed away. He has a broad face, brown hair, and dressed in a grey suit of clothes. Any person knowing anything about him will please direct him to **Michael Hardy**, PORT RICHMOND, Vanpelt's Avenue, STATEN ISLAND.

Of **Patrick** and **Mathew McCabe**, natives of the County CAVAN, Parish of KILMORE, Ireland. When last heard of, about eighteen years ago, they were in PENNSYLVANIA. Information of them will be thankfully received by their brother, **James McCabe**, by addressing him at BRIDGEPORT P.O., State of CONNECTICUT, care of **Mr. Harrel William**.

Of **Hester Bradley**, by her sister, **Kate Bradley**; a native of BALLYBAY, County MONAGHAN, Ireland, who left NEW YORK CITY in April, 1867, for CHICAGO, ILL. She will please write to her sister Kate. Address care of Irish-American, Box 3025, New York. Chicago papers, please copy.

Of **James Reidy**, BURNCHURCH, Parish of KILLENAULE, County TIPPERARY, Ireland, who came to America in 1850, and was in LASELLE, ILLINOIS, in 1852. When last heard from indirect, was in SIBLEY or SHIPLEY LANDING on the borders of the Missouri River and married. Any information of him (whether living or dead) or his family would be thankfully received by his aged and sorrowed Father, or his only brother and sisters. Address **John Reidy**, 21 SPRUCE ST., N.Y.

April 17, 1869

Of **Patrick Phillips**, a native of DROGHEDA, County LOUTH, Ireland. Came to this country about twenty-eight years ago. His brother **Thomas** then lived in Townsend Street, DUBLIN. When last heard from (about ten years ago) he was in NEW ORLEANS, LA. Any intelligence of him will be thankfully received by his nephew, **Joseph P. Phillips**. Address care of the Irish-American P.O. Box 3,025. California, Western, and New Orleans papers, please copy.

Of **Patrick Rourke**, a native of the Parish of NEWBAWN, County WEXFORD, Ireland. When last heard from (about two years ago) he was in NEW ORLEANS. Any intelligence of him will be thankfully received by his sister, **Mrs. Shannon** (maiden name **Ellen Rourke**) at 537 THIRD AVENUE, NEW YORK. New Orleans papers, please copy.

Of **Margaret Winn**, daughter of **Owen Winn** and **Mary Kearney**, a native of the Townland of MULLAGHBAWN, Parish of KILMORE, County ROSCOMMON, Ireland. She came to this country with her aunt **Margaret**. When last heard from she was living in WILLETT STREET, NEW-YORK, and left there, about 23 years ago, with a man named **Benjamin B. Coite**, for PITTSFIELD, MASS. She was then about ten years of age. Any information of her will be thankfully received by her sisters, **Bridget** and **Mary Winn**. Address **John Gilroy**, NEW BRITAIN, CONN.

Of **James O'Connor**, 244 DIVISION STREET, NEW-YORK, brother to **Teresa M. O'Shaughnessy**, of BALLINASLOE, County GALWAY, Ireland, who is desirous to hear from him. He has not been heard from for two years. Address **P. W. Dunn**, PEORIA, ILL.

April 24, 1869

Of **Patrick Lillis**, a native of KILDERRY, Parish of FEDAMORE, County LIMERICK, Ireland. When last heard from he was in CLEARFIELD, CENTRE County, PA. Information of him will be thankfully received by his brother, **James Lillis**, No. 1121 Broadway, CAMDEN, N.J. Pennsylvania papers, please copy.

Of **Maurice Brown**, a native of the County CLARE, Ireland. He was last seen about two months ago. Any information of him, dead or alive, will be thankfully received by his sister, **Anne Brown**, 32 WEST 15th STREET, NEW YORK.

Of **Bernard McKeon**, a native of SMITHSTOWN, County MEATH, Ireland, who came to America in 1851, and left GALVA, HENRY County, ILL., in 1862. When last heard from (five years ago) he was in NEVADA TERRITORY, and was about to start for SAN FRANCISCO. Any information of him whether living or dead, will be thankfully received by his sister, **Mrs. Ann McFadden**, GALVA, HENRY County, ILL. California papers, please copy.

Of **Patrick Doyle**, a native of the Parish of DUNHILL, County WATERFORD, Ireland, who left home in the year 1860 for America. Any information of him will be thankfully received by his brother, **John Doyle**, of POUGHKEEPSIE, State of NEW YORK, by addressing a few lines to the **Rev. M. Riordan**.

May 1, 1869

Of **Michael Hearen**, who left PHILADELPHIA, PA., in May, 1868. He is a moulder by trade. His aunt, **Margaret Hearen**, wishes to hear from him by addressing her at **Michael Nary's**, No. 3 Glances Place, 15th Street, between Browne and Parish, PHILADELPHIA, PA.

Of **Thomas Coughlin**, a native of the Parish of GILLAN, KING'S County, Ireland, who parted from his brother **Patrick** on the 10th of April, 1868, since which time he has not been heard from. Information of him will be thankfully received by his mother. Address **Patrick Killan**, No. 77 Spruce Street, HARTFORD, CONN.

Of **Robert O'Neal**, a native of RATHKEALE, County LIMERICK, Ireland, who landed in New York 19 years ago. When last heard from, he was in ST. LOUIS, MO. Any information of him will be thankfully received by his brother, **Patrick O'Neal**, No. 29 CATHARINE STREET, NEW YORK. St. Louis, Mo., papers, please copy.

May 8, 1869

Of **Maria Ford**, a native of the County SLIGO, Ireland. She left NEW YORK about 14 years ago, and went to LIMA, PERU, SOUTH AMERICA. She wrote about 10 years ago, and mentioned that she intended to go to WASHINGTON [ROUTH]. Any intelligence of her will be thankfully received by her brother, **Michael Ford**, NYACK, ROCKLAND Co., N.Y.

Of **Thomas Maher**, who left Ireland about 18 years ago, from the Parish of LITHER, KING'S County, Ireland. When last heard from (15 years ago), he was in CINCINNATI OHIO. Any information of him will be thankfully received by his sister, **Bridget Maher**, at her residence in JERSEY CITY, No. 56 Warren St., NEW JERSEY. Ohio papers please copy.

Of **Widow Burke** (maiden name **Margaret Dwyer**) and of her children **Richard**, **Patrick, Catharine, Mary, Bridget, Anna** and **Margaret** natives of the Parish of DRUMBAN, Townsland of DRUMDIHA, County TIPPERARY, Ireland, who came to this country in 1849 or 1850, Catharine with her husband, **William Bryan**, and her sister Margaret came a year sooner. Any information as to their whereabouts will be thankfully received by her son **John Burke**. Address **John Ryan**, 633 State Street, CHICAGO, ILL., or to **John Dwyer**, RAWLING SPRINGS, WYOMING TERRITORY.

Of **Mary Kavanagh**, daughter of **John Kavanagh**, and sister of **Ellen** and **Annie**, who resided in NEW YORK in 1862, from which place she moved west. Any information of the above person will be most thankfully received by her afflicted father, John Kavanagh, 91 North Second St., WILLIAMSBURGH, Long Island, N.Y. Western papers please copy.

Of **Daniel Brown**, aged about 23. Born in AIRDRIE, SCOTLAND, late of DURHAM, ENGLAND, who came to America, a few years ago; said to have enlisted in an artillery regiment. Address, P.B., Box 115, SYRACUSE, N.Y.

Of **Patrick Delahunty**, a native of KELLS, County KILKENNY, Ireland. When last heard of he was discharged from Co. E, 1st U.S. Infantry, at ST. LOUIS, about Oct. 31, 1864. Any persons having information in regard to his present whereabouts, if living, or such as will help trace him, or knowledge of his death, will please address the same to **Major Joe Kelly**, Box 473 NEW YORK CITY P.O.

May 15, 1869

Of **Ellen Fitzgerald**, a native of the City of CORK, Ireland. She landed in New York about 15 months ago. Any intelligence of her will be thankfully received by her brother,

Patrick Fitzgerald, at 393 WEST WASHINGTON MARKET, NEW YORK CITY, care of **Mr. Andrew Curry.**

Of **Patrick, Jas. Tom** and **Ned Stack**, natives of BALLYDUFF, County KERRY, Ireland. When last heard of (about eleven years ago), they were in WISCONSIN. Intelligence of them will be thankfully received by **Thomas Stack**, son of Patrick Stack, at BRONXVILLE P.O., NEW YORK.

May 22, 1869

Of **Kate Stack**, 28 years of age, tall, dark complexion, a scar on right cheek, light muslin dress, with blue spots, black silk basque, and hat trimmed with green. She left her place in WEST HOBOKEN, on Friday, April 23 at 1 ½ O'clock, P.M. Supposed to be partially deranged. Address her brother, **Morris Stack**, Greenpoint Avenue, GREENPOINT, Long Island.

Of **Miss Kate Ford**, sister of the late **James Ford**, of MERIDEN, CONN. When last heard from she was living in PORT RICHMOND, STATEN ISLAND, N.Y. Any information of her will be thankfully received by **P. B. Ford**, WEST MERIDEN, CONN.

May 29, 1869

Of **Anne McGuiness**, daughter of **Simon McGuiness**, of ARTLUMNY, near NAVAN, County MEATH, Ireland, who left Ireland in 1851; supposed to be married in MUSCATINE, IOWA. Also of her sister **Catherine**, who arrived in this country in 1855. Information of them will be thankfully received by their cousin, **Thomas McNally**, 801 Racine Street, MILWAUKEE, WISCONSIN.

Of **Mary Kearns**, who emigrated from the County DONEGAL, Ireland, about two months ago. Intelligence of her will be thankfully received by her aunt, **Mary Kearns**, by addressing her at 1452 North 12th Street, PHILADELPHIA, PA. Other papers, please copy.

Of **Bridget Hallahan**, of BONMAHON, County WATERFORD, Ireland, who emigrated to NEW YORK about three years ago. Information of her will be thankfully received by her aunt, **Bridget Whelan**, 1542 Fawn Street, PHILADELPHIA, PA. Other papers, please copy.

June 5, 1869

Of **Cornelius Dunn**. When last heard of had shipped in a ship called the *"Washington,"* April 8th, 1867, bound for California. Any information of him will be thankfully received by his mother **Johanna Dunne**, CROMWELL, State of CONN.

Of **Bernard McMahon**, a native of the County MONAGHAN, Ireland. He is by trade a blacksmith, and his last place of employment at home was at DUMEANY, County LOUTH. When last heard from, a year ago, he was about NEW YORK or BROOKLYN. Any information of him will be thankfully received by his sister's sons, **John** and **Patrick Callan**. Address Patrick Callan, CAPE ISLAND Post Office, CAPE MAY County, NEW JERSEY.

June 12, 1869

Of **Thomas Partlin**, County SLIGO, Ireland. When last heard from he lived near SUSPENSION BRIDGE, NEW YORK State. Information will be thankfully received by his mother, **Mrs. Partlin**, rear of 115 Elfreth Street, PHILADELPHIA, PA.

June 19, 1869

Of **Mark Bean**, a native of KILTORMER, BALLINASLOE, County GALWAY, Ireland. He was in NEW YORK 8 years ago. Any intelligence of him will be thankfully received by his brother, **Thomas Bean**, by addressing the Irish-American Office, New York, or to 105 York Street, JERSEY CITY, N.J.

Of **Mary Smyth**, daughter of **Michael Smyth**, of Academy Street, NAVAN, County MEATH, Ireland, who left Ireland about 18 years ago. When last heard from she was in NEW YORK. Information of her will be thankfully received by her brother, **John Smyth**, at 75 Butler Street, BROOKLYN, N.Y.

Of **Ellen** and **Mary Smith**, formerly of DOWESDOWN, Parish of JOHNSTOWN, Co. MEATH, Ireland. When last heard of (about 4 or 5 years ago) they were in PHILADELPHIA, PA. Any intelligence of them will be thankfully received by their brother, **William F. Smith**, at **Theodore Baldwin's**, 786 BROADWAY, NEW YORK CITY.

Of **Godfrey Ryan**, a native of MULLINGAR, County WESTMEATH, Ireland; his mother's maiden name is **Delaney**; he has a brother named **William F.** He had done business some years ago in **Cyrus Fields'** paper store, in CLIFF STREET, NEW YORK, and boarded in PEARL STREET, and afterwards in BATAVIA STREET. Any information of him, dead or alive, will be thankfully received by calling on or addressing **James Madden**, Book and Stationary Store, 268 FIRST AVENUE, NEW YORK, where something very much to his advantage may be learned.

June 26, 1869

Of **T. R. O'Connor**, book and picture dealer. Any information respecting him will be thankfully received by his sister **Mary**, or his brother, **James F. O'Connor**, No. 11 Cherry Street, WORCESTER, MASS.

Of **Cornelius** and **Denis Credden**, natives of CORK HILL, Parish of MILLSTREET, County CORK, Ireland. When last heard from they were in ROUGHWAY, State of NEW JERSEY. Information of their whereabouts will be thankfully received by their sister, **Johannah Credden**, by addressing a letter to **Jeremiah Murphy**, 320 EAST 11th STREET, NEW YORK. New Jersey papers, please copy.

Of **Jerry McCarthy**, son of **Daniel McCarthy** and **Ellen Sullivan**, of DROUMAGURTEEN, Parish of BURNAN, KENMARE, County KERRY, Ireland. When last heard from he was in TOLEDO, OHIO. Information of him will be thankfully received by his sisters, **Mary** and **Ann McCarthy**, at No. 20 NEW BOWERY, NEW YORK.

Of **Patrick Gerraty**, who emigrated from County SLIGO, Ireland in 1847; also of his sister, **Bridget** and **Mary**. When last heard from they were living in WHEELING, VA., in 1854. Any information of them will be thankfully received by their brother **Michael Gerraty**, now residing in PIONEER CITY, BOISE County, IDAHO TERRITORY.

Of **Henry McGurgan**, otherwise **Gordon**, grandson of **Bernard McGurgan**, of Bridge-lane, OMAGH; he was a native of the Parish of DRUMRAH, County TYRONE, Ireland. When last heard from he resided either in NEW YORK or BROOKLYN. If he is alive, by calling personally or communicating by letter with **Patrick McBride**, No. 244 Columbia Avenue, PHILADELPHIA, PA., he will hear of something of importance and which concerns him very much. Other papers, please copy.

July 3, 1869

Of **Michael Conner**, of BROGUE or BALLINAKILL near MARBLEHILL, who came to this country in 1851. When last heard from in 1864, he was in COLUMBUS, OHIO, boarding with **Mr. O'Brien**. He will hear of something to his advantage by addressing his brother **Martin**, care of **Thos. Bagly**, No. 8 Leed Avenue, Broad and Vine, PHILADELPHIA, PA. [Appeared under County GALWAY]

Of **John McCoy**, who was in LIMERICK, Ireland, in 1852. Was born in CHARLEVILLE, County CORK. A boot-maker by trade, and worked for the Constabulary in Limerick. Any information of his present whereabouts will be thankfully received by his brother, **James McCoy**, directed to the Irish-American Office, No. 8 North William St.

Of **Wm.** and **John Keogh**, natives of the County of KILKENNY, Ireland. They are supposed to be in WESTchester County, N.Y. Any intelligence of them will be thankfully received by **Michael Cahill**, at Crossman, Brothers, WOODBRIDGE, N.J.

Of **Johanna Neill**, a native of KILKENNY, Ireland. Twelve months ago she was in NEW YORK. Any intelligence of her will be thankfully received by **Michael Cahill**, at Crossman, Bros., WOODBRIDGE, N.J.

July 10, 1869

Of **John Tuohig**, a native of MACROOM, County CORK, Ireland. When last heard from, he lived in NULTOWN, FAITY Co., INDIANA, U.S. Any information of him will be thankfully received by his sister, **Bridget Tuohig**, at **Mrs. Hanity's**, 109 CLINTON PLACE, NEW YORK. Indiana papers, please copy.

July 17, 1869

Of **John Meridat**, of NEW ORLEANS, and also of **John** and **Thomas Downs**, of OHIO. If they will communicate with **Mary Hogan**, S.E. Corner of German and Tremont Streets, BALTIMORE, MD., they will hear of something to their advantage.

Of **Barney Duffy**, who left PHILADELPHIA in the year 1856, for the west. Information of him will be thankfully received by his brothers, **Michael** and **James Duffey**. Address **James Duffy**, LYCURGUS Post Office, ALLAMAKEE County, IOWA in care of **Michael Dougherty**.

Of **Patrick Madden**, a native of TULLAMORE, KING'S County, Ireland, who sailed from Glasgow, November 20, 1868. When last heard from he was in MERCIL County, WEST MIDDLESEX, State of PENNSYLVANIA. Any information of him will be thankfully received by his mother and brothers, Address **Laurence Madden**, Box 96 MAHONOY CITY, PENNSYLVANIA, SCHUYLKILL, County.

Of **Mary Reynolds**, who left LOUGHREA, County GALWAY, Ireland, between 1848 and 1850 for the United States. When last heard from (about 5 years ago), she was in MALDON, MASSACHUSETTS; is married to **John Carey**, a currier, and a native of the County CORK, Ireland. Also of her brother **Joseph**, who has served in the late Southern Rebellion. Joseph left CAVAN in the year 1856. Their brother **Philip Reynolds** is anxious to hear from them; his address is 187 Concord Street, BROOKLYN, L.I. Care of **Peter Martin**. Boston *Pilot*, please copy.

July 24, 1869

Of **Patrick Doyle**, a carpenter, and **James Doyle**, a bricklayer; and also of **Margaret** and **Eliza Doyle**, who left BAGNALSTOWN, County CARLOW, Ireland, twenty years ago. When last heard of they were in CINCINNATI. Any information of them will be thankfully received by their niece and nephew, **Helena** and **Edward Doyle**, at No. 343 EAST 47th STREET, NEW YORK. Cincinnati and California papers, please copy.

Of **Timothy** and **James Spillane**, (sons of **John Spillane**), who left GURRANEDUFF, Parish of MILLSTREET, County CORK, Ireland, about twenty years ago. Any information as to their whereabouts will be thankfully received by **John T. J. O'Riordan**, BRENHAM, WASHINGTON County, TEXAS.

July 31, 1869

Of **William Keating**, who left ENGLAND four years ago. When last heard of he was in INDIANA. Any information of him will be thankfully received by his mother, **Ann Keating**, and brother, **James Keating**, No. 223 EAST 22nd STREET, 3rd Avenue, NEW YORK.

Of **Frederick Shaw**, who left DUBLIN twelve months ago, and has not been heard from since. His father formerly was book-keeper in the Custom House, Dublin. Should this meet his eye, by calling on or addressing a few lines to **Robert Dixon**, 524 EAST 16th-street, NEW YORK, he will hear from his mother **Elizabeth Shaw**, who is anxiously waiting to hear from him. Dublin and Canada papers please copy.

Of **Hugh Morgan**, a native of ROSSTREVOR, County DOWN, Ireland, who left Ireland in December, 1860. Any information respecting his whereabouts will be gladly received, or by calling in person upon **Edward Lowry**, No. 5 ELDRIDGE STREET. He will hear of something to his advantage.

August 7, 1869

Of **Joseph Wilson**, who lived in NEW YORK with his brother, **Robert Wilson**, where he left for PHILADELPHIA about nine or ten years ago. He is supposed to have enlisted in the Army. Also, of his daughter, **Eliza Wilson**, who is now supposed to be in some part of the State of PENNSYLVANIA. Her uncle, Robert Wilson, is very anxious to hear of her whereabouts. Any intelligence of them will be thankfully received by **Robert Wilson**, at 78 MONROE STREET or 15 ½ CATHARINE STREET, NEW YORK CITY, or by his brother-in-law, **Michael Gill**, FORT RICHMOND, STATEN ISLAND, N.Y. [Appeared Aug. 14, 1869 with Joseph's name changed to **James Wilson** and with additional information.]

Of **Michael Lang**, who left his home at PITTSBURGH last August, since which time he has not been heard from. Should this meet his eye, or any person acquainted with him, they will confer a favor on his mother by addressing a few lines to **Mrs. Sarah Lang**, 319 Manor-street, BIRMINGHAM, ALLEGHENY County, PA.

Of **John English**, a mason by trade, and a resident of HACKERSTOWN, NEW JERSEY, light complexion, reddish moustache, stooped in the shoulders, light hair - a little grey - aged fifty years. When last heard of was in KALAMAZOO, MICHIGAN. Any information of him will be thankfully received by his wife **Mary English**, at the Post-office Buildings, NORTH ORANGE, N.J., or to **Mrs. Donoghoe**, 69 GREENWICH-street, N.Y., or to **Mary White**, HACKERSTOWN, N.J. Western papers please copy. [Appeared Aug. 14, 1869 with John's surname changed to **England**, and Mrs. Donoghoe's address changed to 64 Greenwich-street.]

Of **Edward** and **Margaret Carter**, who left Ireland in the year 1847. They were from the Parish of WICKLOW, CLONMENNON, County WICKLOW, Ireland. When last heard from they were in WINDSOR, CANADA WEST. Any information of them will be thankfully received by their son **Edward Carter**, BRIDGEPORT, CONN.

Of **Peter Duffy**, by trade a shoemaker, of the Parish of ANNAMULLIN, County MONAGHAN, Ireland, who left this City in January last. Any information of him will be thankfully received by his disconsolate wife, **Mary Duffy**, No. 162 WEST 34th STREET, NEW YORK.

Of **William McGee**, of MULLAGHLUST, County FERMANAGH, Ireland. Intelligence of him will be thankfully received by his wife, **Margaret McGee**, at Castle Garden, New York City.

Of **Julia Farley**, of the Parish of MULLAGH, County CAVAN, Ireland. When last heard from (six weeks ago) she was in CINCINNATI, OHIO. Any information of her present whereabouts will be thankfully received by her sister, **Ann Farley**, at 54 Main Street, BROOKLYN, Long Island, N.Y. Cincinnati papers, please copy.

Of **Thomas O'Keefe**, from the City of CORK, Ireland. Intelligence of him will be thankfully received by his wife, **Margaret O'Keefe**, at Castle Garden, New York, City.

Of **Patrick Gorman**, of EASTERFIELD, Parish of BALLINAKILL, County GALWAY, Ireland. Any information of him will be thankfully received by his sister, **Bridget Gorman**, care of **Mr. William Breen**, *Eagle* Office, BROOKLYN, N.Y.

August 14, 1869

Of **James Wilson**, a veteran soldier in the Mexican war, under **Gen. Scott**, (was at the battle of BUENAVISTA, PUEBLA, CHERABUSKO [CHURUBUSCO]. When last heard of he was in CARLISLE BARRACKS, PA., some ten years ago; at that time he had one daughter named **Eliza Wilson**, who is supposed to be in some part of PENNSYLVANIA. Any information or their whereabouts will be thankfully received by his brother, **Robert Wilson**, at 78 MONROE STREET, or 50 ½ CATHARINE STREET, NEW YORK; or at **Mr. Michael Gill's**, FORT RICHMOND, STATEN ISLAND, N.Y.; or at **John Gallagher's**, HUDSON CITY, N.J. [Appeared Aug. 7, 1869 as Joseph Wilson and without as much information.]

Of **Henry Martin**, by his sister, **Norah Martin**. She has forgotten his address. He will please call at No. 19 Nevins Street, BROOKLYN. [Appeared Dec. 25, 1869 with additional information.]

Of **James P. Kelly**, late of the 27th Regiment, United States Infantry, when last heard from was in DAKOTA TERRITORY. Any information of him living or dead will be thankfully received by his distressed parents. Address **Mr. Francis Kelly**, No. 251 7th AVENUE, between 24th and 25th Streets. All Western papers please copy.

Of **John Dunne**, who left DUBLIN about November, 1867. When last heard from he was in ST. LOUIS, MO. Information of him will be thankfully received by his brother, **Sylvester Dunne**, at 29 South King Street, DUBLIN, Ireland. Western papers, please copy.

Of **Mary** and **Eliza McEvoy**, natives of the County WICKLOW, Ireland. When last heard of (about 8 years ago) they were in BUFFALO. Also of **James McEvoy**, who went to VIRGINIA CITY about 3 years ago. Any intelligence of them will be thankfully received by their brother, **Andrew McEvoy**, at 851 Atlantic Avenue, BROOKLYN, L.I.

Of **Mrs. Catherine Grimes**, (maiden name, **Reynolds**), a native of the Parish of KILLOE, Townland of GUIGUE, County LONGFORD, Ireland, who came to this country about 28 years ago, and lived in ROUNDOUT, but is supposed to have gone west. Information of her or of any of her children will be thankfully received at 221 WEST 27th ST., NEW YORK, by her nephew, **Francis Reynolds**. Western papers, please copy.

Of **Bridget Wilson**, a native of THOMONDGATE, LIMERICK, Ireland. She is daughter of **Michael Wilson**, weaver, is married to **Patrick Murphy**, of ROSCOMMON, Ireland, and late of MANCHESTER, ENGLAND. Intelligence of her will be thankfully received by her sister, **Mrs. James McCoy**. Direct to the Irish-American Office, No. 8 North William Street, New York. Manchester papers, please copy.

Of **Patrick Henry Smith**, Attorney-at-law. When last heard from was in SAN FRANCISCO, CALIFORNIA. Also of his brothers **James** and **Thomas** - the former last known of at MERIDEN, CONN., and the latter a machinist of CHICAGO, ILLINOIS. All formerly of BALLUSKEY, County TIPPERARY, Ireland. Information will be thankfully received by their mother, **Mrs. Ellen Smith**, COAL VALLEY, ROCK ISLAND Co., ILL.

Of **Michael Veile**, who left DUNGARVAN, County WATERFORD, in 1863. When last heard from, he was in NEWBURGH, N.Y. - Any information of him would be thankfully received by his niece, **Miss Mary Moran**, No. 108 McCullough Street, BALTIMORE, MD.

Of **Florence Cunningham**, aged 42 years, who was born in the County of CORK, Ireland, within two and a half miles of BANDON. When last heard from, was in the City of BOSTON, MASS. Any information of him will be thankfully received by his brother **Denis Cunningham**. Please direct in care of **Patrick O'Connell**, 1st AVE., corner 59th STREET, NEW YORK. Boston *Pilot* please copy.

August 21, 1869

Of **Michael Keating**, who left NEILSTON, SCOTLAND, for this country, in the summer of 1859. When last heard of was in CHICAGO, ILLINOIS. Any information of his whereabouts will be thankfully received by his brother, **John Keating**, 190 Remsen Street, WILLIAMSBURGH. Western papers please copy.

Of **Julia, Margaret**, and **Patrick Ward**, of KILTEVIN, County ROSCOMMON, Ireland. When last heard from they were in ELIZABETH, NEW JERSEY. This was about six years ago. Their mother was drowned on her passage to America. Any information of them will be thankfully received by **John Ward**, their brother, at 33 Lafayette-street, BROOKLYN, N.Y. Boston *Pilot*, please copy.

Of **James Crowe**, a mason by trade, and a native of DROMLINE, County CLARE, Ireland. When last heard from he was in CLIFTON FORGE, ALLEGHANY County, VA. Any information of him will be thankfully received by his brother, **Thomas Crowe**, at 444 WEST 31st STREET, between 9th and 10th Avenues, NEW YORK. Southern papers, please copy.

Of **Thomas Prendergast**, and **Bridget Prendergast**, ACRES, Parish of MAYO, County of MAYO, Ireland, who came to this country about 16 years ago. Any information of them will be thankfully received by their cousin **Edmond Quinn**. Address HAVERSTRAW Post-office, ROCKLAND, N.Y.

Of **Patrick McCardle**, of the Townland of AHALAUGH, five miles from BALLYBAY, Parish of AHABOG, County MONAGHAN, Ireland. He resided in PRESTON, LANCASHIRE, ENGLAND, for four years prior to 1853. He came to New York in the ship *"Sheridan."* When last heard from, which was in October, 1853, when he sailed from London, England, on either the ship *"CONNECTICUT"* or *"Louisa."* Any information of him will be thankfully received by his brother **Philip McCardle**, 102 Gurley-st., CHICAGO, ILLS.

Of **John Keane**, from KILMURRY, County LIMERICK, Ireland, who came to this country about 10 years since. When last heard from he was in the City of MOBILE, ALABAMA. Any intelligence of him will be thankfully received by **James Hayes**, at this office.

Of **Patrick J. Callinan**, of the City of LIMERICK, who left NEW YORK for SAN FRANCISCO, CAL., about nine years ago, with his sister **Ann Nolan**, wife of **Edward Nolan**, now both deceased. Also of **Cornelius** and **Maurice D'arcy**, of KNOCKLONG, County LIMERICK, brothers-in-law of the undersigned; the former, when last heard from, was in BOWLING GREEN, KY. Address **M. J. Callinan** (GARRYOWEN), Irish-American Office, No. 8 North William-st., New York.

Of **Patrick Lane**, SOUTH KILMURRY, County CORK, who landed in Quebec, in 1845, and the last heard of him was in SYRACUSE, N.Y., in 1854, where he then lived. Any information of him will be thankfully received by his sister **Bridget Singleton**, (maiden name **Bridget Lane**,) WEST STOCKBRIDGE, BERKSHIRE Co., MASS.

[Issue for AUGUST 28, 1869 unavailable.]

September 4, 1869

Of **Samuel Cassidy**, who, when last heard of (about the year 1866), was in MUD SPRINGS, EL DORADO County, CALIFORNIA. Any information of him will be thankfully received by his sister, **Mary Cassidy**, No. 72 Middle Street, NEW BEDFORD, MASS. [Appeared Sept. 18, 1869 with the year 1866 changed to 1861, and "California papers please copy" added.]

Of **James Cavanagh**, a native of the City of DUBLIN, who left home in the year 1863. Any information of his whereabouts will be thankfully received by his cousin, **Ellen O'Brien**. Address **John Cullen**, READING Post Office, BERKS County, PA. Western and California papers, please copy.

Of **Mr. Thomas Tracy**, who left COYLE, County MEATH, Ireland, about 32 years ago. Also, of **Messrs. James, John** and **Peter Morgan**, who left DUNLEER, County LOUTH, Ireland, about the same time. Information of them will be thankfully received by his nephew, **Mr. Andrew Harlin**, No. 33 Kent Avenue, between Myrtle and Park Avenues, BROOKLYN, Long Island, N.Y. [Appeared Sept. 11, 1869 with some different information.]

Of **Michael Masterson**, of the Parish of KELLO, County LONGFORD, Ireland. When last heard from (two years last June), he was in KNOX County, INDIANA. Address his cousins, **Mary A.** or **Bridget Masterson**, care of **Peter Martyn**, 187 Concord Street, BROOKLYN, N.Y.

Of **Hugh Reilly**, who left the Town of BALLYCONNEL, County CAVAN, Ireland, 18 or 20 years ago. When last heard from he was in MEMPHIS, TENN. Information of him will be thankfully received by his sister, **Ellen Fitzpatrick**, at No. 355 3rd AVENUE, NEW YORK CITY.

Of **Cornelius, William** and **John Hayes**, of BALLYBOY, Parish of UPPER CHURCH, County TIPPERARY, Ireland, who came to this country, about sixteen years ago. Any information of them will be thankfully received by their sister, **Mary Hayes**. Also, of **Ned** and **Thomas Corbett**, of CARNAHALO, Parish of DOON, County TIPPERARY, Ireland. Address **John D. O'Leary**, corner of Fifth and Welch Streets, CHESTER, PA.

Of **Ellen O'Brien**, a native of BARRGONE WELL, County LIMERICK, Ireland. She is a daughter of **Patrick O'Brien**, a blacksmith; is married to **Patrick Hourgan**, of KERRY ISLAND. Intelligence of her will be thankfully received by her sister, **Mrs. John Culhane**. Address **John Culhane**, OXFORD Post Office, CHENANGO County, N.Y.

Of **Mary Draddy**, a native of LOUGHADERRY, Parish of MIDDLETON, County CORK, Ireland, who emigrated to America about 15 years ago. When last heard of she was in NEW YORK. Information of her will be thankfully received by her brother, **John Draddy**, at **Wm. O'Leary's**, 318 EAST 11th STREET, NEW YORK. Western papers, please copy.

Of **Margaret Cullinane**, of the commons of CLOYNE, County CORK, Ireland, who came to this country April 21, 1854, from Queenstown. When last heard from she was in BROOKLYN, N.Y., about 11 years ago. Any information of her, dead or alive, will be thankfully received by her sister, **Hanora Cullinane** (who came to this country 4 years ago), in care of **Patrick Curtis**, DEDHAM, MASS.

Of **Maurice Spillane**, who left the Parish of DUNAMORE, County CORK, Ireland, 32 years ago. When last seen by his brother he was in BUCHANAN, VA. Any intelligence of him will be thankfully received by his brother, **John Spillane**, UTICA, LA SALLE County, ILL.

Of **Thomas Pinkman**, and his Sisters, **Bridget** and **Alice Pinkman**, who emigrated from BALLINAMORE, County LEITRIM, Ireland. The two sisters were married in JERSEY CITY, N.J. Bridget's husband's name is **John Guin**. Any information of them will be thankfully received by their brother, **Francis Pinkman**, 505 South 10th Street, READING CITY, PA.

September 11, 1869

Of **Michael Slattery**, who left his home in MANCHESTER, N.H., on or about the 17th of July, 1869, on an Excursion train to THORNTON FERRY, since which time nothing has been seen or heard of him. Any information of him will be thankfully received by his wife **Mrs. Margaret Slattery**, whom he has left with two helpless children, now residing at MALONE, FRANKLIN County, N.Y. Irish-American papers please copy.

Of **Mr. Thomas Tracy**, who left COLPE, County MEATH, Ireland, about 32 years ago. Also, of **Messrs. James, John** and **Peter Morgan**, who left DUNLEER, County LOUTH, Ireland. Information of them will be thankfully received by Thomas Tracy's nephew, **Mr. Andrew Harlin**, at No. 33 Kent Avenue, between Myrtle and Park Avenues, BROOKLYN, Long Island, N.Y. California papers, please copy. [Appeared Sept. 4, 1869 with some different information]

Of **Edward O'Brien**, brother of **Michael O'Brien**, Parish of BALLINGARRY, Co. LIMERICK, Ireland. He left home about 11 years ago, since which time he has not been heard from. Any information of him will be thankfully received by his sister, **Mary O'Brien**, care of **Thomas Roche**, NEW BRIGHTON, (WEST) STATEN ISLAND, FACTORYVILLE, N.Y. [Appeared Sept. 18, 1869 with the name Edward O'Brien changed to **Edmond O'Brien**.]

Of **Nicholas Williams**, a native of the Parish of RATHKEALE, County LIMERICK, Ireland. Served three years in 69th Regt., Irish Brigade. When last heard from (Dec. 25th, 1867,) was employed in Government Stables, WASHINGTON, D. C. Any information respecting him will be thankfully received by his anxious brother, **James Williams**, 209 ½ WOOSTER-street, N.Y. Washington papers please copy.

Of **John** and **Myles McHale**, natives of WESTPORT, County MAYO, Ireland. John is a coach builder by trade, and when last heard from (about 14 years ago) he was in MONTREAL, CANADA. Myles left LOUISBURGH, County MAYO, Ireland, 14 years ago, and has not been heard from since. Any intelligence of them will be thankfully received by their brother **James McHale**, at No. 10 Doughty-street, BROOKLYN, L.I. Canadian papers please copy.

Of **Maria Mullen**, native of CASHEL, Parish of KILLTOLEOUGH, County ROSCOMMON, Ireland. Any information of her will be thankfully received by her only sister, **Eliza Mullen**. When last heard from, she was in the City of TROY, 14 years ago. Please address Eliza Mullen, MULLICA HILL, GLOUCESTER County, N.J. Boston *Pilot* please copy.

Of **Timothy Kavanagh**, County KILDARE, Ireland. When last heard from was in MITCHELL County, INDIANA. Any information of him will be thankfully received by his brother **Mark**, No. 4504 Miller-street, GERMANTOWN, PA. Western papers please copy.

September 18, 1869

Of **Dr. Richard Daily**, who, some nine years ago, left BOSTON, MASS., for parts unknown to the writer hereof. If he be still living he will hear of something to his advantage by communicating with R.V., Editor of the PROVIDENCE *Herald*, R.I. His relatives would do well by attending to this notice.

Of **James Riely**When last heard from was in ESSEX, N.Y. A stone-cutter by trade. Any information of his whereabouts will be thankfully received by his mother, **Margaret O'Riely**. Address **Martin Sally**, OSWEGO, N.Y.

Of **Catherine Mener**, formerly of GURTEEN, QUEEN's County, Ireland. When last heard of (a year ago) was in SPRING VALLEY, ROCKLAND County, N.Y. Any information respecting her will be thankfully received by her niece **Honorah Drennen**, Maltby House, 23 GREAT JONES STREET, N.Y. Rockland papers please copy.

Of **Morris Scollard**, of County KERRY, Ireland, who left SOUTH WALES April, 1866. When last heard from was in CONNECTICUT. Any information concerning him, will be thankfully received by **Bridget Scollard**, Union County Hotel, ELIZABETH PORT, NEW JERSEY.

Of **James Mulhearn**, a native of the County of TYRONE, Ireland. Left home about five years ago and came to NEW YORK, from which place he went to PENNSYLVANIA, returning again to New York. When last heard from he was on the Rocky Mountain Railroad. His mother's name was **Ann Boyler**. Any information concerning him will be thankfully received by his sister, **Anne Mulhearn**, 49 BLEECKER STREET, N.Y. California papers please copy.

Of **Patrick Shiels**, a native of the Town of DROGHEDA, County LOUTH, Ireland. Was discharged by purchase from the 15th regiment, British infantry, at CEYLON, INDIA, November 30th, 1853. He is a printer by trade, and formerly worked on the Drogheda *Argus*. When last heard of was in ROME, ITALY, about 14 years ago. Any information of him will be thankfully received by his brother, **James Sheils**, 133 2nd Street, BROOKLYN, N.Y. Rome papers, Dublin *Irishman*, and Drogheda *Argus* please copy.

Of **James Brandon** and his wife **Maria Brandon**, (maiden name **Dawson**), natives of TRIM, County MEATH, Ireland. When last heard of they were in the State of INDIANA. Any intelligence of them will be thankfully received by **Patrick Martin**, YORKVILLE Post office, N.Y.

Of **Thomas Smith**, of the Parish MYLOUGH, County MEATH, Ireland. He came to America, in 1866. When last heard from he was in NEW YORK. Any information from him, will be thankfully received by his brother, **Patrick Smith**, PONTIAC, LIVINGSTON County, ILLINOIS.

Of **Mary Ann Conlan**, (maiden name **McLaughlin**). A native of the Parish of WATTEN GRANGE, County KILDARE, Ireland. Any intelligence of her whereabouts will be thankfully received by her sister **Margaret McLaughlin**, NEVERSINK Post Office, MONMOUTH County, N.J. Williamsburgh papers please copy.

Of **Mary Robinson**, a native of County TIPPERARY, Ireland; who came to this country about twenty years ago. When last heard from was in BRANDON or BRADFORD, PENN. Any information will be thankfully received by her brother, **John Robinson**, WHIPPANY, MORRIS County, N.J. Pennsylvania and Boston papers please copy.

Of **Michael Henaughin**, son of **Patrick** and **Honor Henaughin**, of BALLINAMORE, Parish of PARTRY, County of MAYO, Ireland. Any information of him will be thankfully received by his brother, **James Henaughin**. Address, No. 3 FULTON STREET, N.Y. Western papers please copy.

September 25, 1869

Of **Thomas McEvilly**, of NEW ROSS, County WEXFORD, who left DUBLIN ten years ago, for this country. If he would call to, or address **Mr. Hogan**, No. 804 SIXTH STREET, NEW YORK, he will learn of something to his advantage. American papers please copy.

Of **James Britton**, a native of the City of KILKENNY, Ireland; arrived in America about 17 years ago. When last heard from, (about 12 years ago), was about leaving MISSISSIPPI for ST. LOUIS. Any information of his whereabouts will be thankfully received by his sister, **Kate Britton**, 82 Common Street, LAWRENCE, MASS.

Of **Timothy Connahan**, a native of KANTURK, County CORK, Ireland. When last heard from (about a year ago), was in NEW YORK. Any information of him will be thankfully received by his wife, **Catharine**, maiden name **Kezie**, at No. 506 WEST 16th STREET, N.Y.

October 2, 1869

Of **James Crowe**, *alias* **James McFarland**, who worked for **Mr. Preston Rudey**, on a farm near PARIS, ILL. He left Mr. Rudey's some seven years ago. Any information of him will be thankfully received by his mother, **Ann McFarland**, 494 GREENWICH STREET, NEW YORK. Western papers, please copy.

Of **William Lennon**, of the Parish of ARMAGH, County ARMAGH, Ireland, who left PHILADELPHIA, PA., October 4, 1854. Any information of him will be thankfully received by his brother and sister, **John** and **Alice Lennon**, 1232 Stiles St., PHILADELPHIA, PA. Boston papers, please copy.

Of **Elizabeth** and **Mary Dunlay**, natives of the Parish of LISGOLD, County of CORK, Ireland, who emigrated to this country about thirty years ago, and lived fifteen years in the Deaf and Dumb Institute, NEW YORK. They are daughters of **Edmund Dunlay** and **Mary Cotter**. Information of them will be thankfully received by their sister, **Ann Dunlay**. Inquire of **Stephen O'Reilly**, 44 ESSEX STREET, NEW YORK.

Of **Michael Ryan**, brother of **William Ryan**, whose first cousin is **Thomas Ryan**, from TEMPLEDERRY, County TIPPERARY, Ireland. He left the above place about two years and a half ago, and came to BALTIMORE, MD. Any information of him will be thankfully received by his brother, **William H. Ryan**, at the office of the Irish-American, New York City. Baltimore papers, please copy.

Of **Bridget Molony**, from CARIGATOGHER, near NENAGH, County TIPPERARY, Ireland, who came to this country about eight years ago. When last heard from she was in the City of TROY, N.Y., in service. Any intelligence of her will be thankfully received by her mother, **Mary Molony**, who arrived on the *City of Washington*, and has lost her daughter's address. Address Irish-American office, or Hubert Glynn, Castle Garden, New York.

October 9, 1869

Of **James McClemments**, of NEWTOWNMOUNTKENNEDY, County WICKLOW, who lived in FONDULAC and SHEBOYGAN, WISCONSIN. Information of him will be kindly received by his sisters **Kate** and **Ellen**, by addressing **James McGinty**, 46 Lafayett Street, ALBANY, N.Y. Fondulac and Sheboygan, Wis., papers, please copy. [Appeared Oct. 16, 1869 with NEWTOWNMOUNTKENNEDY shown as NEWTOWN MOUNT KENNEDY; FONDULAC shown as FOND DU LAC; and McGinty's address as 46 LAFAYETTE STREET, N.Y.; appeared Nov. 6, 1869 with McGinty's address again including the mention of ALBANY, NEW YORK.]

Of **Wm. Kalerher**, who left DANNING, Parish of KILLEAGH, County CORK, Ireland, and came to BOSTON, MASS., with his aunt, **Mary Smiddy**, about 17 years ago, and was not heard from for the last two years. Information of him will be thankfully received by his brothers, **Simon** and **Patrick Kalerher**, PORTLAND, CONN., or by **P. H. Hodnett**, MIDDLETOWN, CONN.

Of **Patrick Cummins**, who left MALLOW, County CORK, Ireland, in 1861 or 1862, or of his wife, **Mary Canty**. When last heard from he was in COLE CARMEL, PUTNAM County, N.Y. Information of them will be thankfully received by their brother, **Timothy Canty**, BRIDESBURG ARSENAL, PA., or **Wm. Roche**, No. 66 MARKET STREET, NEW YORK CITY.

Of **Patrick Bush**, a native of BENNETTSBRIDGE, Parish of TULLOW, County KILKENNY, Ireland. When last heard from (about nine years ago) he was in SOUTHWICK, MASS. Information of him will be thankfully received by his brother, **John Bush**, who has lately arrived in this country. Address John Bush, EAST LONGMEADOW, HAMPDEN County, MASS.

October 16, 1869

Of **Richard Hamilton Moore**, who was last heard of at ST. LOUIS. If this should meet his eye, he will hear of his brother **George** by addressing Post Office, BROOKLYN, N.Y. Western papers please copy.

Of **James Hines**, KILE Parish of FRESHFORD, County KILKENNY, Ireland, by his sister, **Mary**, now **Mrs. Mary Fallon**, MIDDLETOWN, SOUTH FARMS, CONNECTICUT. When last heard from was in REED'S LANDING, MINNESOTA. Western papers please copy.

Of **Thomas Maguire**, native of the County FERMANAGH, Ireland, Parish of NEWTOWN BUTLER, Townland of AUGHADREENAN. When last heard from, in December, 1868, he was in BINGHAMTON, BROOME County, State of NEW YORK. Any information of him will be thankfully received by his sister, **Mary Anne** and his brother, **Patrick Maguire**. Please address 320 South 25th Street, PHILADELPHIA, PA.

Of **Michael Hobins**, a native of the Parish of CLONRISH, County GALWAY, Ireland, who left LIVERPOOL about three years ago. - When last heard from, he was in PHILLIPSBURG, WARREN County, N.J. Any information concerning him will be thankfully received by his brother, **James Hobins**, Taylor Street; or **B. O'Neill**, Justice of the Peace, 61 Congress Street, PATERSON, N.J.

Of **Margaret Rahely**, RASDOUGHAN, in the Parish of TEHILLA, County KERRY, Ireland, who was married to **Daniel Shea**. - When last heard from (about a year ago), was living in YOUNGSTOWN, OHIO. Any information concerning her will be thankfully received by her sister, **Catherine Rahelly**, who is on her dying bed, by addressing a few lines to her in care of **Jeremiah O'Brien**, 33 PARK STREET, NEW YORK.

Of **Anne, Catherine**, and **Elizabeth McKinney**. They left Ireland between the years 1840 and 1845. They belonged to the County LONGFORDdiocese of ARMAGH, and Parish of KILLO,. When last heard from, they were in BOSTON. Anne was married to a man named **Creamer**. Any information respecting them will be thankfully received by their brother, **Patrick McKinney**, 420 WEST 35th STREET, NEW YORK CITY. Western papers, please copy.

Of **John Garrett** and **Robert Garrett**, of the County LIMERICK, Parish of CAPPAMORE, Townland DRUMSALLEY, Ireland, who landed in this country in 1866. Any information of them will be received by **Martin Hogan**, a son to **Catharine Garrett**. Direct to SILVER CREEK, CHAUTAUQUA County, N.Y.

October 23, 1869

Of **Hugh Kilpatrick**, who left PATERSON, N.J., about 17 years ago. When last heard from (about 7 years since) he was in BALTIMORE, MD; he is a blacksmith by trade. Information of him will be thankfully received by his brother, **John Kilpatrick**, or **Bernard O'Neill**, Justice of the Peace, 81 Congress Street, Paterson, N.J.

Of **William Lacy**, a native of WEXFORD, Ireland, who came to this country about 12 years ago. Information of him will be thankfully received by his wife, **Fannie Lacy**. Address, Irish-American Office, New York.

Of **Joseph Ralford**, of the Parish of TAGHMON, County of WEXFORD, Ireland. When last heard from he was in FORT LEE, N.J. Information of him will be thankfully received by his brother, **Mark Ralford**, 185 Bridge Street, BRIDESBURG, PHILADELPHIA, PA.

Of **Edward Carney**, a native of the Parish of TUBBERCLARE, County of WESTMEATH, Ireland. When last heard from he was in NEW ORLEANS, LA. Information of him will be thankfully received by his nephew, **Michael Kearny**, 14 South Prospect Street, HARTFORD, CONN.

Of **Mary Glaney**, of the Parish of GLANFARIN, County LEITRIM, Ireland. When last heard from she was in BROOKLYN, N.Y. Information of her will be thankfully received by her friend, **Thomas Foly**, CONSHOHOCKIN, MONTGOMERY County, PA. Boston papers, please copy.

October 30, 1869

Of **James McCarty**, who left his house in NEW YORK CITY, in the month of August, 1867, and is supposed to have been taken away on a canal boat; he is now 14 years of age, and has dark eyes and dark brown hair. Information concerning him will be thankfully received by his afflicted mother, **Mrs. M. McCarty**, 157 EAST 80th STREET, NEW YORK. Country papers, please copy.

Of **James Began**, a blacksmith, or of his family. They left the County ARMAGH, Ireland, about 20 years ago, and, as believed, went to ILLINOIS. Information of him will be thankfully received by **Patrick Began**, 523 WEST 51st STREET, NEW YORK. Western papers, please copy.

Of **Patrick Carroll**, son of **William Carroll**; also, of his cousin, **Patrick Carroll**, natives of GLENAMADDY, County GALWAY, Ireland, both of whom emigrated from STALEYBRIDGE, ENGLAND, to NEW YORK, in 1863. Information of them will be thankfully received by **Kate, Mary** and **Michael J. Carroll**, brother and sisters of the first, and cousins of the latter. Address Michael J. Carroll, SPRINGFIELD, MASS. Irish-American papers, please copy.

Of **Martin Divney**, a native of the County GALWAY, Ireland. When last heard from he was in LOWELL, MASS. Information respecting him will be thankfully received by his brother, **Edward Divney**, 103 Marshall St., or **B. O'Neill**, 81 Congress Street, PATERSON, N.J.

Of **Margaret Coghlen**, who left NEW VILLAGE, Parish of KILGEVER, County MAYO, Ireland, in 1858. When last heard from she was in WAYNE County, IOWA. Information of her will be thankfully received by her brother, **Denis Coghlen**, LANSINGBURGH, RENSSELAER County, N.Y.

Of **William Quinlavin**, and his wife, **Mary Odell**, natives of ARDAH, County LIMERICK, Ireland, who left the City of LIMERICK, for NEW YORK, about 12 years ago. Information of them will be thankfully received by his brother, **Daniel Quinlavin**, WILMINGTON, N.C.

November 6, 1869

Of **Myles Murphy** and his six brothers, **John, Patrick, Thomas, Morris, Edward** and **Michael**, who left BALLON, County CARLOW, Ireland, about twenty years ago. When last heard from they were in NEW YORK. Any intelligence of them will be thankfully received by their cousin, **Myles Murphy,** PEORIA, ILL.

Of **James McNally**, a baker by trade, and a native of CLOGHER, County TYRONE, Ireland, who landed at Castle Garden, on the 31st of July last, on board the *Europa*. He will receive some interesting intelligence by calling on **Rev. T. Treanor**, 30 MOTT STREET, NEW YORK.

$100 REWARD. The above reward will be given to any person who can tell where **Francis Haynes** or **Hynes**, son to the late **William Haynes,** Esq., of BALLEYHEDA, BALLINHASSIG, near the City of CORK, Ireland, is residing at present. When last heard from, about four years ago, he kept a saloon in ATHENS, ALABAMA, and was employed on the railway there, delivering out and receiving in railway ties. When Francis Haynes left Ireland, several years ago he was accompanied by his cousin, **William Murphy**, of SKEHANNA, who, antecedent to the commencement of the war, is reported to have been engaged in the manufacture of soda water at NASHVILLE, TENNESSEE. The above reward of 100 dollars will be paid for any information leading to the finding of either parties named by **Mr. Nathaniel Craighmire**, dealer in liquors, ATTICA, INDIANA.

Of **William McCarty**, and his wife, who emigrated to this country from the Parish of DRUMCOLLOHER, County of CORK, Ireland, about 21 or 22 years ago. Information of their whereabouts will be thankfully received by his nephew, **Richard Barry**, by addressing him in care of **John Conway**, LOCKHAVEN, CLINTON County, PA.

Of **John Kinsley**, son of **Michael** and **Mary Kinsley**, natives of NOEVOFOOTHA, Parish of GOREY, County WEXFORD, Ireland. He came to this country about seventeen years ago. Any information of him will be thankfully received by his brother, **Patrick Kinsley**, now stopping at **Mr. Henry McGuire's**, 115th STREET, NEW YORK. Boston and Philadelphia papers, please copy.

November 13, 1869

Of **Thomas McDermott**, of BALLINA, County MAYO, Ireland. He is about sixty years of age. He left XENIA, GREENE County, OHIO, about ten years ago, and has not been heard from since. Anybody knowing his whereabouts (dead or alive) will oblige by writing to his son **Michael McDermott** at XENIA, GREENE County, OHIO.

Of **Bernard Canfield**, a native of County MONAGHAN, Ireland, who when last heard from was in HASTINGS, MINNESOTA. Any information concerning him will be thankfully received by his brother **Peter Canfield**, at No. 204 EAST 26th STREET, NEW YORK CITY. St. Paul papers please copy.

November 20, 1869

Of **Owen Riley**, who left STOCKPORT, ENGLAND, about 12 years ago. When last heard of he was in JERSEY CITY. Information of him will be thankfully received by his sister, **Bridget Riley,** No. 18 Little Street, LOWELL, MASS.

Of **William Lynch**, a horse-shoer. He was last heard from in July, 1869. Information of him will be thankfully received by his brother, **John Lynch**, 528 WEST STREET, NEW YORK.

Of **James Higgins**, who, when last heard from, left CHESTERFIEL, ENGLAND, to come to this country, and is now supposed to be in this City. Any information concerning him will be thankfully received by his brother, **Patrick Higgins**, corner of North Fourth and Erie Streets, JERSEY CITY.

$25 REWARD. The above Reward will be paid for the information of **Dennis Sullivan**, son of **William Sullivan** and **Mary Keeffe**, who left WALSHESTOWN, County CORK, Ireland, about 28 or 30 years ago. Address **Michael Sullivan**, shoemaker, BELL ISLE, ONONDAGA County, N.Y.

Of **Thomas Russell**, a native of STONE PARK, CASHEL, County TIPPERARY, Ireland. Also of his sons, **James** and **Thomas**, and of his daughter **Mary**, who came to this country about 21 years ago. Intelligence of them will be thankfully received by his son, **Robert Russell**, in care of **William Kennedy**, WEST MERIDEN, CONN. Boston *Pilot*, please copy.

Edward Smith, formerly of ROSCREA, Co. TIPPERARY, will hear of his mother, brother **Michael** and sister **Margaret** by addressing **Mrs. Monks**, No. 10 PRINCE STREET. Any information will be thankfully received at the above address. Western papers please copy.

November 27, 1869

Of **James Fleming**, from KELLS, Co. KILKENNY, Ireland, who came here about 23 years ago, and was last heard of in NEW ORLEANS. Any intelligence of him will be thankfully received by his brother, **Michael Fleming**, F, Church Street, SOUTH BROOKLYN, L.I. California papers please copy.

Of **William Mangane**, of BALLYCONNERY, County KERRY, Ireland, who left home in 1843. When last heard from (seven years ago) he was in OTAWA, ILL. Information of him will be thankfully received by his sister's children, **Patrick** and **William Purcell**, SPRINGWATER VALLEY, LIVINGSTON County, N.Y. Boston *Pilot*, please copy.

December 4, 1869

Of **Thomas Kelly** and of his sons, **Edward** and **Bryan**, natives of the Parish of MAHERACLOON, County MONAGHAN, Ireland, who emigrated to this country about twenty years ago. When last heard from they resided at WOBURN, MASS., about ten miles from BOSTON. Intelligence of them will be thankfully received by **Mary Winn**, niece of said Thomas Kelly, by addressing **John McKinney**, J.P., 376 Plane St., NEWARK, N.J.

Of **John Kennedy**, aged 40, born in CARRICK-A-NONEY, County TIPPERARY, Ireland, who emigrated to this country from BRADFORD, YORKSHIRE, ENGLAND, four years ago last summer. When last heard from (about three years ago), he was in CLAREFIELD, PA. Information of him will be thankfully received by his brother, **James Kennedy**, 2321 Hamilton Street, PHILADELPHIA, PA.

December 11, 1869

Of **Thomas Mulvaa**, a native of SCHRINA, Parish of KILMANE, County ROSCOMMON, Ireland, who came to this country about four years ago. When last heard from he was in CHICAGO, ILL. Information of him will be thankfully received by **Michael Mulvaa**, 500 WEST STREET, NEW YORK. [Appeared Dec. 18, 1869 with the surname **Mulvaa** changed to **Mulvee**; SCHRINA changed to SKRINE; and "Chicago papers please copy" added.]

Of the **Widow Newman**, maiden name **Anne Masterson**, formerly of the Parish of DUDERRY, County MEATH, Ireland. When last heard from lived in North Fourth Street, WILLIAMSBURGH, Long Island; or, **John Newman** or family, who lived in PRINCE STREET, NEW YORK. Any information of them will be thankfully received by their cousin, **Michael Newman**, son of **James Newman**, OTTAWA Post-Office, CASSELLE County, State of ILLINOIS. Williamsburgh and New York papers please copy.

December 18, 1869

Of **William Finlan**, who left HARA on the 19th of March last, for BARABOO, WIS.; was a constant workman at jack spinning in a woolen factory. He left that place and nothing has been heard of him since. Any information of him, dead or alive, will be thankfully received by his wife, **Mrs. Mary Ann Finlan**, at WEST EATON, MADISON Co., N.Y. Eastern and Western papers please copy.

Of **Michael Cain**, who left WALSAL, STAFFORDSHIRE, ENGLAND, on the 1st of May, 1865. Was in DEPOSIT two years ago, last May; and when last heard from was in BOSTON, MASS. Any information of him will be thankfully received by his father, **Hugh Cain**, and his brother, **John Cain**, at 32 Marshal Street, PATERSON, NEW JERSEY. Boston papers please copy.

Of **John, Hugh**, and **Cecilia Morgan**, natives of the Parish of KILCOO, Co. DOWN Ireland, who immigrated to this country upwards of twenty years ago. When last heard from they were in the Town of CHINA, WYOMING Co., N.Y. Any information respecting them will be thankfully received by their nephew, **Francis Morgan**, residing at STAMFORD, CONN.

Of **Patrick Cosgrath**, of the Parish of CLONFERT, County GALWAY Ireland. The last letter was received from him when he was in MOUNT SAVAGE, MARYLAND. Any information concerning him will be thankfully received by **Michael Quirk**, JOHNSTOWN, CAMBRIA County, PA. Iowa papers please copy.

Of **Bridget Mulcahy**, who left CASHEL, County of TIPPERARY, Ireland, about twenty years ago. When last heard from she was married to **James Skeahan**, and residing in SPRINGFIELD, MASS. Any information respecting her, dead or alive, will be thankfully received by her mother, **Catherine Glashine**, now resident in BLOOMINGTON, ILLINOIS. Please address **William Hackett**, Bloomington, Ill.

December 25, 1869

Of **Henry Martin**. When last seen was at 19 Nevin Street, BROOKLYN, N.Y., last June. Any information of him will be thankfully received by his sister **Norah Martin**, 154 Front Street, HARTFORD, CONN. [Appeared Aug. 14, 1869 with different wording]

Michael Casey will be much obliged to any person who can give any information of his sister **Delia Casey**, native of County GALWAY, born in the Parish of CLARRON, near HEADFORD, who sailed from Ireland about two years ago for this country. When last heard of was living in BROOKLYN. Her father was agent for **Captain Carter**, of DUBLIN. All communications will please be addressed to this office.

January 1, 1870

Of **Patrick, John** and **Arthur Marlan**, of the Parish of DONAGHMAN, Co. TYRONE, Ireland. Information of them will be thankfully received by their brother, **Edward Marlan**, 584 Michigan Avenue, CHICAGO, ILL.

Of **James McBride**, late of 104 West Taylor Street, CHICAGO, ILL., by his nephew, **John Martin**, of TEMPLESHANNON, ENNISCORTHY, County WEXFORD, Ireland. Address John Martin, care of **Daniel Smith**, corner 35th STREET and 11th AVENUE, NEW YORK.

Of **Hugh Kelly**, of the County of MAYO, Ireland. When last heard from, about three and a half years ago, he was in WILKESBARRE, PA. Any information concerning him will be thankfully received by his sister, **Mary A. Sheridan**, at 229 Gold Street, BROOKLYN, N.Y.

January 8, 1870

Of **Michael Fox**. When last heard from (twelve months ago) he was in SHARON, PA. Information of him will be thankfully received by his sister, **Mary Fox**, by writing to her in care of **Patrick McKenna**, No. 227 Independence Street, CLEVELAND, OHIO.

Of **Maurice O'Connell**, from BALLYMACJORDAN, Parish of DUAGH, County KERRY, Ireland, who left home about 20 years ago. Information of him will be thankfully received by his nephew, **Patrick O'Connell**, 121 First Street, NEWBURGH, N.Y.

Of **Florence Keenan**, who, when last heard from, was in MONTREAL, CANADA. Any information of him will be thankfully received by **M. O'Hare**, cor. 37th STREET and EIGHTH AVENUE, NEW YORK. Canada papers, please copy. [Appeared under QUEEN'S County]

Of **John Dwyer**, who left KNOCKAHORNA BORRISOLEIGH, County TIPPERARY, Ireland, three years last July; when last heard from was in HARLEM, NEW YORK State. Any information of him will be thankfully received by his sister, **Mary Dwyer**, 548 South Jefferson Street, CHICAGO, ILL.

January 15, 1870

Of **William Lynch**, a horse-shoer. He was last heard from in July, 18[ ]. Information of him will be thankfully received by his brother, **John Lynch**, 528 WEST STREET, NEW YORK.

Of **Patrick Dougherty** aged about 22 years, of FINTNEY, County TYRONE, Ireland. When last heard from he was with **Bryan Curlin**, in FINTNEY, County TYRONE, Ireland. Any information concerning him will be thankfully received by his sister, **Susan Dougherty**, by addressing her in care of **Daniel Gallagher**, 203 GRAND STREET, NEW YORK.

Of the **Widow Newman**, maiden name **Anne Masterson**, formerly of the Parish of DUDERRY, County MEATH, Ireland. When last heard from lived in North Fourth Street, WILLIAMSBURGH, Long Island; or, **John Newman** or family, who lived in PRINCE STREET, NEW YORK. Any information of them will be thankfully received by their cousin, **Michael Newman**, son of **James Newman**, OTTAWA Post-Office, CASSELLE County, State of ILLINOIS.

January 22, 1870

Of **George Sersfield**, shoemaker, who left BELFAST, Ireland; when last heard from was in KINGSTON, UPPER CANADA. Information to his advantage can be had by calling on or writing to **Mary Ann Crabb**, No. 36 South Main Street, FALL RIVER, MASS. [Appeared under ANTRIM County]

Of **James** and **Sarah Yourt**, (maiden name **Smith**), natives of ARMAGH, Ireland. Twenty years ago they left their native country for NEW YORK, U.S. Any information concerning them will be thankfully received by their sister, **Rachael Smith**. Please direct any communication for her to **George McGinness**, ELIZABETH, NEW JERSEY.

Of **William Lacy**, a native of WEXFORD, Ireland, who came to this country about 12 years ago. Information of him will be thankfully received by his wife, **Fannie Lacy**. Address Irish-American Office, New York.

Of **Bernard Conlon**, boot and shoe maker by trade, and a native of the Parish of CURREN, County MONAGHAN, Ireland, who came to this country about 25 years ago. When last heard from he was in some part of ILLINOIS. Information of him will be thankfully received by his brother, **James Conlon**, MIDDLEBURY, VERMONT. Western papers, please copy.

January 29, 1870

Of **Patrick Morris**, a native of the Parish of KILDAVIN, County WEXFORD, Ireland, who left BALTIMORE, MD., November, 1866, for parts unknown to the writer. Any information of him will be thankfully received by his brother, **Peter Morris**, No. 26 Lemmon Street, BALTIMORE, MD. Boston *Pilot* and Western papers please copy.

Of **Matthew Sullivan**, of MEAR'S COURT, Barony of RATHCONDRA, County of WESTMEATH, Ireland. Any information of him will be thankfully received by his brother, **Charles Sullivan**, MOTT HAVEN Post Office, WESTCHESTER County, N.Y.

Of **John Toban**, a native of TIPPERARY, Ireland, who left CHURCH, LANCASHIRE, ENGLAND, in August, 1857. When last heard of he was on his way to CHICAGO, ILL. Information of him will be thankfully received by **George Filoon**, LABORATORY HILL, FALLS of SCHUYLKILL, PA. Boston *Pilot*, please copy.

February 5, 1870

Of **Miss Maryann Fitzgerald**, who left MALAHIDE, County DUBLIN, about ten years ago. Intelligence of her will be thankfully received by **Bernard Ferry**, at No. 335 New Market Street, PHILADELPHIA, PA.

Of **Charles Miley**, of the Parish of DUNLAVEN, County WICKLOW, Ireland. When last heard from (about eighteen months ago), he was around COLUMBUS, OHIO. Information of him will be thankfully received by his brother **John** and his sister **Jane**, who came to this country last June. Address **James Lacey**, MOUNT GILEAD, MORROW County, OHIO.

Of **James Durkan**, son of **James** and **Sally Durkan**, of BANADA, Parish of KILMACTIGUE, County SLIGO, Ireland, who left KEIGHLEY, YORKSHIRE, ENGLAND, in March 1864. When last heard from he was in CORNING, STEUBEN County, N.Y. Information of him will be thankfully received by his brother, **Phillip Durkan**, HYDE PARK, LUZERNE County, PA. Boston *Pilot*, please copy.

Of **Patrick** (or **Charles Patrick**) **O'Flanagan**, hatter, of CORK, Ireland, who came to America about 8 years ago. When last heard of he resided in Quarry Street, NEWARK, N.J. By addressing **S. Bolger**, 238 HENRY STREET, NEW YORK, something to his advantage may be heard. Newark papers, please copy.

Of **James Dunn**, from the Parish of DRANGAN, County TIPPERARY, Ireland, supposed to be in WILLIAMSBURGH, L.I. By corresponding with his sister, **Mrs. Cahill**, DRANGAN, Ireland; or **James Johnson**, 420 Columbia Street, BROOKLYN, N.Y., he will learn something to his advantage.

Of **Margaret Comeford**, of ENNISBAR, County WATERFORD, Ireland, who came to this country in 1867. When last heard from, she was in FREDERICK County, MARYLAND living with her step-sister, **Mrs. Marooney**. Any information concerning her will be thankfully received by her father and brother, **Richard** and **Thomas Comeford**, at No. 611 WEST 46th ST., N.Y. CITY. [Appeared Feb. 19, 1870 with Ennisbar changed to INSPRW.]

February 12, 1870

Of **Martha Halverson**, who left LE ROY, N.Y. State, about ten years ago. When last heard from, she was in MARSHALL, MICHIGAN. Any information of her will be thankfully received by **Griffith Halverson**, FORT BASCOM, NEW MEXICO.

Of **Patrick Devine**, a native of the Parish of CRESHALAUGH, Townland of DRUMSCRIGAN, County CAVAN, Ireland. When last heard from, about sixteen years ago, he was in SPRINGFIELD, OHIO. Any information concerning him will be thankfully received by his brother **Thomas Devine**, at 143 North 6th-street, WILLIAMSBURGH, N.Y. Ohio and Western papers please copy.

Of **James Hannigan**, a native of FINTONA, County TYRONE, Ireland, who left NEW YORK about five years ago. Any information concerning him will be thankfully received by his wife, **Mary Hannigan**, at No. 512 WEST 25th-street, N.Y. CITY. Canada papers please copy.

Of **Dennis Magehy**, son of **James Magehy**, LOUGHASH, County TYRONE, Ireland. Left Ireland in 1848 for NEW YORK. Any information concerning him will be thankfully received by **Catherine Devine**, FORT HAMILTON, N.Y. Philadelphia papers please copy.

Of **Patrick** and **James McDevitt**, from the Town of STRABANE, County TYRONE, Ireland, who left home about eighteen years ago. When last heard from they were living in 79 Pydress Street, NEW ORLEANS, LA. Information of them will be thankfully received by their sister, **Annie McDevitt**, by addressing her in care of **James Williams**, 2002 Wooster Street, NEWARK, N.J. New Orleans papers, please copy. [Appeared Feb. 19, 1870 with the address 2002 Wooster Street changed to 109 ½ Wooster Street.]

$25 REWARD. The above Reward will be paid for the information of **John** and **Daniel Ryan**, natives of the Parish of BIRDHILL, County TIPPERARY, Ireland. When last heard of they were enlisted in the English army. Intelligence of them will be received by their brother, **Martin Ryan**, NORTHAMPTON, MASS. English papers, please copy.

Any person knowing the whereabouts of **Patrick Lenahan**, a native of the Town of SLIGO, Ireland, who left his home, No. 48 PRINCE STREET, NEW YORK, on 25th of May, 1866, will confer a favor by calling on or addressing **Mary A. Lenahan**, 586 BROADWAY, NEW YORK.

February 19, 1870

Of **Edward Mahon**, who left MONTREAL, CANADA EAST, on the 21st June, 1869. When last heard from he was in BROOKLYN, N.Y. Any information of him will be thankfully received by his father, **James Mahon**, 67 King Street, OGDENSBURGH, N.Y. Boston *Pilot*, please copy.

Of **Kate Garahan**, who left CLOGHERHEAD, Parish of HACKETTSCROSS, County LOUTH, Ireland, about 13 years ago. Information concerning her will be thankfully received by her nephew, **Thomas Garahan**, at **Mrs. Welch's**, 88th STREET, between Third and Fourth Avenues.

Of **Bernard Reilly**, a native of the Town of CAVAN, Ireland. When last heard of (about 12 years ago) he was in NEW YORK CITY. Information of him will be thankfully received by his mother, **Bridget Reilly**, MYSTIC, CONN.

Of **Peter McCann**, who left TULAVIN, County CAVAN, Ireland, about four years ago. Intelligence of him will thankfully be received by his sister, **Catherine Cavanagh**, now in NEW YORK. Address **Mr. P. M. Smith**, No. 8 BROADWAY, NEW YORK.

February 26, 1870

Of **James, Michael** and **Bridget Gagen**, formerly of ATHLONE, County WESTMEATH, Ireland, by their sister **Elizabeth**. James is supposed to be in Florida or MISSISSIPPI, and has been in the United States eighteen years; and Michael and Bridget respectively sixteen and fourteen years. Address H. D. Glynn, Office of Commissioners of Emigration, Castle Garden, New York.

Of **James Hurley**, a native of the Parish of KILBEGNET, County GALWAY, Ireland. When last heard of he was at SANDY HOOK, NEW YORK HARBOR. Information of him will be thankfully received by his brother, **Daniel Hurley**, FARMINGDALE, MONMOUTH County, N.J.

March 5, 1870

Of **Francis Collins**. When last heard of two years ago, he was a working baker in NEW ORLEANS; tall, rather stout, fair hair, and effeminate countenance, rather stooped in the shoulder, age about 34. Any information will be most gratefully received by **Mrs. Cunningham**, 24 Foyle Street, DERRY, Ireland, or by **Mrs. Collins**, TORRANCE, CAMPSIE, by GLASGOW.

Of **Johanna Griffin**, of BALLEYGENANE, Parish of BALLYHEIGUE, County KERRY, Ireland, who left home 14 years ago; landed at Toronto, Canada West; a daughter of **John Griffin**. Any account of her, dead or alive, will be thankfully received by **Jeremiah Coridan**, WESTFIELD, HAMILTON County, INDIANA.

Of **Thomas** and **Michael Burke**, of the County MAYO, Ireland. When last heard of, were in COOK County, ILLINOIS. Any information of the above will be thankfully received by **Elizabeth Burke**, their mother, No. 16 Eleventh Street, FALL RIVER, MASS. Western papers please copy.

Of **Michael** and **James McDonnell**, of Parish BALLYBAY, County MONAGHAN, Ireland. When last heard of, Michael was in BOSTON, at the expiration of the late American war, after serving 3 ½ years in the United States Navy; and James was in NEW YORK. Any information of either will be thankfully received by their brother, **Terence McDonnell**, Cove Mills, STAMFORD, CONN. Boston *Pilot* please copy.

Of **Denis** and **John Holohan**, of TIPPERARY Town. Denis left CORK for America in 1852, and John, a painter by trade, left LONDON in 1860. Any information of them will be thankfully received by their brother, **James Holohan**, care of **P. Hagan**, 413 Fourth Street, TROY, N.Y.

Of **John McCaslin**, a native of County DERRY and formerly a soldier in the 26th Regt. British Army; came to this country in 1861, and visited his brother, **Noble McCaslin**, at PRINCESS ANNE, SOMERSET County, MARYLAND. Any information of him will be thankfully received by addressing Noble McCaslin, PRINCESS ANNE, SOMERSET County, MARYLAND.

March 12, 1870

Of **Thomas Biggy**, a native of the Parish of NOBER, County MEATH, Ireland, who emigrated to America about 18 years ago. When last heard from he was living in MEXICO. Any information of him will be thankfully received by his daughter, **Mary Biggy**, at YONKERS, WESTCHESTER County, N.Y. New Orleans papers, please copy.

Of **Hanorah** and **Bess Dugan**, natives of the Parish of BALLYHOOLEY, County CORK, Ireland. When last heard from they were living in NEW YORK CITY. By writing to **Bernard Hughes**, No. 33 Mulberry Street, ALBANY, N.Y., they will hear of something to their advantage. [Appeared March 19, 1870 with some different information.]

Of **Henry O'Neill**, a native of the Parish of KILGLASS, County ROSCOMMON, Ireland, who left MANCHESTER, ENGLAND, in May, 1854. When last heard from, in connection with his friend, **Wm. McKeirnan**, he was in the neighborhood of NEW YORK. Information of him will be thankfully received by **Edward A. Boyd**, 79 MURRAY ST., NEW YORK CITY.

Of **Andrew, John, Ellen** and **Bridget Keating**, of the Parish of GRAIGNAMANAGH, County KILKENNY, Ireland. When last heard of Andrew was in ST. JOHN, NEW BRUNSWICK, CANADA. Any information of them will be thankfully received by their brother, **Patrick Keating**, 510 North 24th Street, PHILADELPHIA, PA. Boston *Pilot* and Canada papers, please copy.

Of **Mary McCloskey**, wife of **Bernard McCloskey**, stonecutter, of the City of LONDONDERRY, Ireland. Information of her will be thankfully received by her brother, **Patrick Moore**, No. 8 Shoemaker Street, off 8th Street, below Market Street, PHILADELPHIA, PA.

March 19, 1870

Of **Alexander Scariff**, a native of DUBLIN, Ireland, who sailed from Liverpool in the ship *Great Western*, under the name of **Arthur Shaw**; arrived at Castle Garden on the 5th of November, 1862; was then 19 years of age; has not since been heard of by his friends or parents; is supposed to have joined the U.S. Army. Any information of him will be thankfully received by his aunt, **Mrs. J. D. Clinton**, BATH-NORTH, GREENBUSH, RENSSELAER County, N.Y.

Of **Hugh Kehoe**, who emigrated from DUBLIN in 1866. Should this meet his eye, he is earnestly requested to communicate with his cousin, **Annie Cavanagh**, or her husband, **Mr. Charles O'Connor**, now residing at 142 Monroe Street, CHICAGO, in the State of ILLINOIS, America.

Of **John Smith**, harness-maker, a native of NAVAN, County MEATH, Ireland. Any information of his whereabouts will be thankfully received by his sister, **Mary Smith**. Address care of **Wm. S. Toole**, Esq., 195 FULTON STREET, NEW YORK.

Of **Hanora, Hannah**, and **Bess Dugan**, natives of the Parish of BALLYHOOLEY, County CORK, Ireland. When last heard from they were living in NEW YORK CITY. By writing to **Mrs. Barry**, No. 33 Mully Street, ALBANY, N.Y., they will hear of something to their advantage. [Appeared March 12, 1870 with different contact person and address.]

Of **Hanorah Burke**, now **Mrs. Kelly**, who left CROSSMOLINA, near the Townland of NOCKLASS, in the County of MAYO, Ireland, about 23 or 24 years ago. She is supposed to live in OHIO. Information of her will be thankfully received by her niece, **Hanora Cawley**. Address **Michael Preston**, 623 Guilford Street, PHILADELPHIA, PA.

March 26, 1870

Of **John Lee**, of LIVERPOOL. When last heard from he was in BOSTON. Any information of his whereabouts will be gratefully received by his afflicted wife and daughter, as he is not aware of their arrival in this country. Please direct to **Mrs. Lee**, 60 Endicott Street, BOSTON.

Of **Michael Shiels**, a native of GARRYOWEN, LIMERICK, Ireland. When last heard from, he was in Dexter's hotel, QUEBEC, CANADA, and now supposed to be in MONTREAL. If this meet the eye of **Mr. John Murray**, also a native of LIMERICK, he would confer a favor on his brother, **Patrick Shiels**, by giving any information of him, which would be thankfully received at 1,635 Salonia Street, below Federal Street, PHILADELPHIA, PENNSYLVANIA. Montreal papers please copy.

Of **Catherine Kielly**, who left the Parish of CANROSS, Co. MEATH, Ireland, about nineteen years ago. When last heard from she was married to **Thomas Noolen**, in BALTIMORE. Any information of her will be thankfully received by her sister, **Anna Lynch**, 443 FIRST AVENUE, between Twenty-fifth and Twenty-sixth Street, NEW YORK.

Baltimore papers please copy. [Appeared April 2, 1870 with the surname **Kielly** changed to **Rielly**, and Anna Lynch's address shown as 433 FIRST AVENUE.]

Of **James Prior**, a native of AUGHRIM, County CAVAN, Ireland. When last heard from, about four years ago, he was in BLOSSBURG, PENNSYLVANIA. Any information concerning him will be thankfully received by his brother and sister, **Patrick** and **Helen Donoghue**, at 325 EAST 29th STREET, NEW YORK CITY.

Of **Edward Hogg**, who left BALLYMORE-EUSTACE, County KILDARE, Ireland, in 1853. When last heard of he was in PROVIDENCE, RHODE ISLAND. Any information of him will be thankfully received by his sister, **Celia Hogg**. Address **James Lee**, No. 45 MOTT STREET, NEW YORK. Rhode Island papers please copy.

Of **Mathew Welsh**, of the Townsland of WESTMORELAND, Parish of HUGGINSTOWN, County KILKENNY, Ireland, who emigrated to this country about thirty years ago. When last heard from, fifteen years ago, he was in the PHILADELPHIA Navy Yard. He fought under **General Scott** in the Mexican war. Any person giving the necessary information of his whereabouts will receive a reward of forty dollars from his son, **James Welsh**, 578 10th AVENUE, NEW YORK CITY. Boston *Pilot*, please copy.

April 2, 1870

Of **Allen McKenna**, of Company L, Seventh New York Heavy Artillery, who was wounded at the battle of COAL HARBOR. Any person who can prove the same will be handsomely rewarded by giving information at this office, or by writing to **James H. Driscol**, TOMS RIVER, N.J.

Of **Thomas** and **Rechel Killien**, his sister, natives of RATHDRUM, County WICKLOW. Thomas emigrated about 17 years ago and landed in Quebec, Canada, and his sister, about 13 years old, landed in the same place with a family by the name of **Gleeson**. Any information of them will be thankfully received by their cousin, **John Killien**, BRIDGEPORT, CONN., in care of **Mr. Michael Ready**, P.O. box 518.

Of **James Cooney**, native of the Parish of ACHRAN, County ROSCOMMON, Ireland. He went to ENGLAND, from which place he emigrated to this country in 1868; when last heard from he was going to PITTSBURGH, PA. Any information concerning him will be thankfully received by his sister, **Catherine Cooney**, at No. 8 EAST 43rd STREET, N.Y. CITY.

Of **Mary Connelly**, a native of CLIFDEN, County GALWAY, Ireland, who left Ireland about 18 years ago; when last heard of about 8 years ago, she was in LOCKPORT, N.Y.; she was then married to **John Garret**, County LONGFORD, Ireland, any information of her will be thankfully received by her brother and sister, **Peter Connelly**, and **Bridget Connelly**, address Peter Connelly, AMBOY, LEE County, ILLINOIS. Eastern papers please copy.

April 9, 1870

Of **John Griffin**, a basket maker, a native of YOUGHAL, County CORK, Ireland. Any information of him will be thankfully received by his first cousin, **Johanna Griffin**, daughter of **James Griffin**, by writing to her husband, **Martin Hurley**, WAVERLY HEIGHTS Post Office, MONTGOMERY County, PA.

Of **Marianne Maguire**, daughter of **Hugh** and **Catherine Maguire**, of SALMON, Parish of BALROTHERY, BALBRIGGAN, County DUBLIN, Ireland. She left Ireland for America in the year 1837. When last heard of (in 1849) she was married to a man named **Peter Nicholson**, from MULLINGAR, County WESTMEATH, and was then living in SALINA, near

SYRACUSE, N.Y. Information of her will be thankfully received by her sister, **Eliza Maguire**, at No. 7 Mann Street, DUBLIN, Ireland.

Of **James O'Malley**, a native of the City of DUBLIN, Ireland, who served 3 years and 3 months in the 8th Royal Irish Hussars, British Army; got his discharge, and enlisted in the East India Company's Service. When last heard from he was in MADRASS, EAST INDIES. Information of him will be thankfully received by his brother, **Robert O'Malley**, PIEDMONT, MINERAL County, WEST VIRGINIA.

Of **Thomas Clarke**, a native of KILLIMOR, County GALWAY, Ireland, who left home on the 12th of March, 1863. His friends in Ireland heard he joined the Federal Army shortly after landing in New York. Any account of him is requested; and the expense of such will be paid. Please address **Mrs. Clarke**, Campfield House, MOATE, County WESTMEATH, Ireland. Washington, Philadelphia and New York papers, please copy.

Of **Patrick Hurley**, a native of the Parish of KILL, County WATERFORD, Ireland. Information of him will be thankfully received by his brothers, **John, Michael, James** and **Martin Hurley**, now living in MONTGOMERY County, PA. Address Martin Hurley, WAVERLY HEIGHTS Post Office, MONTGOMERY County, PA. Rhode Island papers, please copy.

Of **John** and **Thos. McGinnis**, natives of SHANTHAMUN, County CAVAN, Ireland. Information of them will be thankfully received by their cousin, **Ellen Riely**, by letter or otherwise, at South-east Corner 57th STREET and 3rd AVENUE, N.Y.

April 16, 1870

Of **Godfrey Ryan**, formerly of the County WESTMEATH, Ireland, and lately in the employment of Cyrus Field & Co., of NEW YORK. If he can be found it will be to his advantage. Address Rice, Wilson & Stitt, attorneys, No. 10 Pine St., NEW YORK.

Of **Edward Fleming**, a coachman, a native of the County WEXFORD, Ireland. When last heard from, 17 years ago, he was in NEW YORK CITY. Information of him will be thankfully received by his brother, **William Fleming**, RARITAN Post Office, SOMERSET County, N.J. California papers, please copy.

Of **Patrick Melvin**, son of **Patrick** and **Anne Melvin**, a native of BALLINLOUGH, near LOUGHCREW, County MEATH, Ireland. When last heard from he was employed at the Continental Hotel, INDIANAPOLIS, INDIANA. Information of him will be thankfully received by his father and mother. Address MANHATTANVILLE Post Office, NEW YORK.

April 23, 1870

Of **Michael Galavan**, *alias* **Isaac Gilbert**, coal digger, who left MERTHYR TYDVILLE, GLAMORGANSHIRE, SOUTH WALES, ENGLAND, in 1868. When last heard from (in November, 1868) he was working at a coal bank in HUBBARD, OHIO. He is not aware of his wife and child being in this country. Also, of **Patrick Bourke**, who left the same place two years ago. When last heard from he was in CHICAGO, ILL. Any information of them will be thankfully received by the wife of Michael Galavan. Address **Bridget Galavan**, HUBBARD, Post Office, TRUMBULL County, OHIO. Irish-American papers, please copy.

Of **Susan Weeks**, a native of BRETTIS, SLUDMORE, County DUBLIN, Ireland, who left home about 18 years ago. When last heard of (about nine years ago), she was then married to **Thomas Shehan**, and lived in SAUNDERSVILLE, TENNESSEE. Any information of her will be thankfully received by her sister, **Mrs. Bridget Barry**, No. 155 WEST 31st STREET, NEW YORK. Southern and Western papers, please copy.

April 30, 1870

Of **James Elliott**, a currier by trade, who, when last heard from, was in MILWAUKEE, WIS., in the employ of **Mr. Coen**. Any information of him will be thankfully received by his mother. Address **Hugh Smith**, 76 Market Street, NEWARK, N.J.

Of **Michael** and **Martin Larkin**, bricklayers by trade. When last heard from (in 1863) they were living on the corner of 27th STREET and FIRST AVENUE. Information of them will be thankfully received by their sister, **Julia Caden**, PIONEERVILLE, IDAHO Territory.

Of **Arthur McKowen**, a native of DUNDALK, County LOUTH, Ireland who came to this country in the Summer of 1868. Also of his sister, **Mrs. John Rowe**, who, when last heard of, resided in ST. LOUIS. Any information of them will be thankfully received by their sister, **Ellen McKowen**, Lock Box 227, BUCHANAN, P.O., BIRMINGHAM County, PA. Boston *Pilot*, please copy.

Of **Mrs. Rose Gafny**, from the Parish of BALLINTEMPLE, County CAVAN, Ireland. When last heard from she was married to a man named **Patrick Riley**, of the County LONGFORD. Information of her will be thankfully received by her sister, **Mary Magran**, 212 Levant Street, PHILADELPHIA, PA.

Of **Edmund White,** who formerly lived in the Parish of GRANGE, County TIPPERARY, Ireland, and who came to this country in 1861. Should this meet his eye he will hear of something to his interest by addressing **James B. Lafford**, 530 EAST 12th STREET, NEW YORK.

May 7, 1870

Of **John, Philip** and **Ann Doyle**, from near NEW ROSS, County WEXFORD, Ireland. When last heard from (three years ago), they were supposed to be living in BROOKLYN, N.Y. Address **Patrick Doyle**, at this office.

Of **Michael Moroney**, from the Town of ENNIS, County CLARE, Ireland. He has lately been discharged from the British Service in CANADA, after serving 10 years, and is now supposed to be in some part of the United States. Information of him will be thankfully received by his Brother, **Lawrence Moroney**, NEW BRITAIN, CONN.

Of **Patrick Dinneen**, who left ST. PATRICK's Parish, Townland of SINGLAND, Co. LIMERICK, Ireland, 13 years ago. When last heard from (2 years since) he was in MONROE CORNERS, FRANKLIN County, N.J. Information concerning him will be thankfully received by his sister's son, **Michael Dwyer**, NEWPORT, SULLIVAN County NEW HAMPSHIRE.

May 14, 1870

Of **Thomas Sheahan**, a native of LIMERICK, Ireland. When last seen (about 15 years ago), he was in BUCKS County. Any information concerning him will be thankfully received by his brother, **Patk. Sheahan,** at 309, NINTH AVENUE, N.Y. CITY. Western papers please copy. [Appeared May 21, 1870, showing Thomas as a native of RATHKEALE, Co. LIMERICK; last seen at BUCKS County, PA.; and with **Patk.** changed to **Patrick.**]

Of **Lawrence Egan**, a native of SELBRIDGE, County KILDARE, Ireland, a laborer by occupation, who left PATERSON, N.J., in July, 1869. Any information of him will be thankfully received by his brother, **Patrick Eagan**, No. 166 Marshall Street, or at **B. O'Neill's**, 81 Congress Street, PATERSON, NEW JERSEY. [Also see Sept. 16, 1871]

May 21, 1870

Of **James McCann**, a bootmaker, who, it is supposed, left DUBLIN, Ireland, for the State of ILLINOIS, about fifteen months ago. Any information of him will be thankfully received by his brother, **Philip McCann**, HAMSBURG Post Office, PA.

Of **Michael Fitzgerald**, a native of LIMERICK, Ireland, son of **John Fitzgerald**, of PENNSYLVANIA, who sent for and brought him to this country about 19 years ago. When last heard from (in 18[64]) his address was Sergeant Michael Fitzgerald, Company K, 97th Regiment, N.Y.S.V., WASHINGTON, D.C. Information of him will be thankfully received by his brother, **James Fitzgerald**, No.44 Canal Street, NEW HAVEN, CONN.

May 28, 1870

Of **Michael Timon**, who worked for **Mr. Cunningham** on sewers on the 5th AVENUE, in December last, since which time nothing has been heard of him. He lived in 90th STREET, between 3rd and 4th Avenues, with his wife and child. Any information of his present whereabouts will be thankfully received by his wife **Ann Timon**, No. 4 Third Avenue, between 14th and 15th Streets, SOUTH BROOKLYN. [Appeared June 11, 1870, adding that **Michael Timon** was a native of the Parish of ELPHIN, Co. ROSCOMMON.]

Of **Henry Gavagan**, of GLENAGEARY, County DUBLIN, Ireland. If this should meet his eye by calling on **Mr. Geo. Riggs**, 130 CHURCH STREET, NEW YORK, he will hear of something to his advantage.

Of **Martin Keervin**, late of WICKLOW, Ireland, formerly dancing-master in HILLBROOK, Ireland, and who about twenty years since emigrated to America. His address is wanted by his brother **Denny Keervin**, 9 Ford Street, LIVERPOOL.

Of **John Harnett**, a native of CASTLEMARTYR, County CORK, Ireland, who left NEW YORK for ALTON, ILL, in 1850; or of his wife **Anastacia Ryan**. Any information concerning them will be thankfully received by **Mrs. Mary Hynes**, No 310 E. 49th STREET, NEW YORK CITY. Alton, Ill., papers please copy.

Of **William Jackel** or **Jacie**, shoemaker, a native of NEW ROSS, County WEXFORD, Ireland, who came to this country about 20 years ago; when last heard from was in PHILADELPHIA, PA. Any information concerning him will be thankfully received by **Perry Murphy**, YONKERS, NEW YORK.

Of **Mr. John Charles Tully**, a native of GORT, County GALWAY, Ireland; when last heard from was in the employment of **Mr. J. C. Scott**, Notary Public, ST. LOUIS, MISSOURI. If this should meet his eye he is requested to write at once to his aunt, who is grieved to the heart at not learing from him. St. Louis and all Western papers please copy.

June 4, 1870

Of **Mr. Peter Jennings**, who left his home in ST. LOUIS, MO., Feb. 1st, 1869. When last heard from he was in ENGLAND, intending to return to America. Any information of him will be thankfully received by his daughter, **Mary E. Jennings**, ST. LOUIS, MO.

Of **Michael McDonald**, a native of the Parish of KILLGLASS, County SLIGO, Ireland. Also of **Patrick Duffy**, a native of the Parish of EASKEY, same County. Both emigrated to this country 22 years ago. Any information of them will be thankfully received by a brother's son of McDonald and a sister's son of Duffy, by addressing **James McDonald**, 72 Canal Street, NEW HAVEN, CT. Boston *Pilot*, please copy.

Of **Michael Cox**, brother of **Elizabeth** and **James Cox**, Parish of BOYLE, Townland of GRANGE, County of ROSCOMMON, Ireland; supposed to be in NEW JERSEY. Any information of him will be thankfully received by his sister, Elizabeth and children, 25 MADISON STREET, NEW YORK, rear building, room No. 6.

June 11, 1870

Of **Alice Martin**, who arrived at Castle Garden, per steamship *England*, on the 23rd of April, 1870, and went to BOSTON. Any information of her will be thankfully received by **Mrs. William Gilsenan**, 143 East Street, MANAYUNK, PHILADELPHIA, PA.

Of **John Coyle**, late of GLASGOW, SCOTLAND. When last heard of he was working at Ludlow's Iron Foundry. He will learn of something to his advantage by applying at No. 30 First Place, SOUTH BROOKLYN, N.Y.

Of **Douglas Westman**, a native of MOUNTMELLICK, QUEEN'S County, Ireland, now supposed to be residing in GRANTOWN, CANADA WEST, from which place he was last heard from. Any information concerning him will be thankfully received by **Mr. Michael Whelan**, No. 260 John Street, BROOKLYN, NEW YORK.

June 18, 1870

Of **Thomas** and **John Gibbons**, who left GLASGOW, SCOTLAND, in 1866, for CALIFORNIA; supposed to be in MINNESOTA or CANADA WEST. Any information of them will be gratefully received by their sister, **Catherine Corscaden**, 351 WEST 43rd STREET, or by **Austin Gibbons**, 327 same street, NEW YORK CITY.

Of **William Hennessy**, of KILRUSH, County CLARE, Ireland, aged about fourteen years. Any information of him will be thankfully received by his brother, **Simon Hennessy**, No. 13 ROSE STREET, NEW YORK CITY. Albany papers, please copy. [Appeared Aug. 27, 1870 with additional information.]

June 25, 1870

Of **William O'Brien**, a native of the Parish of BARN DARRIG, County WICKLOW, who came to this country in 1854; shipped as a sailor from BOSTON to CALIFORNIA; when last heard from was in RABBIT GREEK. Any information respecting him will be thankfully received by his uncle **Patrick**, TROY, BRIDGEPORT, CONN. California papers please copy.

Of **Richard Healy** and his sons, **John** and **Richard**, who left PASSAGE WEST, CORK, Ireland, one year ago last May, and came to PEABODY, MASS; left last September for NEW YORK, and have not been heard of since. Information of them would be thankfully received by his sister, **Jane Healy**, Woollen Mill, MERIDEN, MASS. [Appeared July 9, 1870 with MERIDEN changed to METHUEN, and with "Boston *Pilot*, please copy" added.]

Of **Patrick Culleny**, of DROMERONORAH, County CLARE, Ireland, who came to this country a year last May; was formerly stewart to **Sir Colman O'Loghlen**. Any information of him will be thankfully received by his two sisters who arrived in New York three weeks ago. Please address **Anne McNamara**, 260 4th AVENUE, NEW YORK CITY. Western papers please copy.

July 2, 1870

Of **Peter A. Kavanagh**, a boy 13 years old, who left home on March 3rd last; supposed to have gone in the country with a farmer, as he was seen a few days after leaving on a farmer's wagon. Any person who knows anything of him will confer a great favor by letting his mother, **Mrs. Rosanna Kavanagh**, 624, 2nd AVENUE, NEW YORK CITY, know his whereabouts.

Of **Rose Gaffeney**, Parish of BELLENTAMPLE, County CAVAN, Ireland, who sailed from Ireland 21 years ago for CINCINNATI; was married to a man by the name of **Patrick Reilly**; her brother, **Stephen Gaffeney** also resided there. Any information from her will be thankfully received by her sister, **Mary McGrann**, 212 Cevant Street, PHILADELPHIA. Cincinnati papers please copy.

July 9, 1870

Of **Bryan Coyne**, of BALLADUFF, Parish of ST. JOHNS, County ROSCOMMON, Ireland. He is supposed to have come to this country in 1864. Any information of him will be thankfully received by his brother, **John Coyne**, by addressing him in care of **John Doran**, WASHINGTON, WASHINGTON County, TEXAS.

23 July 1870

Of **Mr. Andrew Rourke**, of MAYNOOTH County KILDARE, Ireland. If this should meet his eye he will please write to **Mrs. J. Synnott**, PORTLAND, CONN.

Of **Patrick Johnson**, a native of the County ARMAGH, Ireland, a bricklayer by trade. When last heard from he was in NEWARK, about five years ago; he is supposed to be in BOSTON at present. Any information concerning him will be thankfully received by **William Meddleton**, Foster Home, NEWARK, N.J. [Appeared July 30, 1870 with "five years ago" changed to "five months ago;" appeared Aug. 6, 1870 with "Boston *Pilot*, please copy" added.]

Of **Mary Vallay**, a native of the County of ARMAGH, Ireland, who arrived at Castle Garden, in July, 1869. Any information of her will be thankfully received by **Frank Taggart**, AKRON, SUMMIT County, OHIO. Boston *Pilot*, please copy.

July 30, 1870

Of **John Bennett**, who sailed from London to New York, last Fall, and left thence for KANSAS. Any information concerning him will be thankfully received by his brother, **Thomas Bennett**, SCHENECTADY, NEW YORK.

Of **Margaret Hickie**, who, when last heard of (during the war), was in MEMPHIS, TENN.; also, of **Patrick McNamara**, who, prior to the war, was in the State of VIRGINIA; and also of **John Sheridan** and family, supposed to be in the State of NEW YORK; all from near TOMGRANY, County CLARE, Ireland. Address, **Maurice Sheridan**, American Iron Works, ORNSBY Post Office, BROWNSTOWN, via PITTSBURGH, PA.

August 13, 1870

Of **Edward Poland**, of Co. F, 21st N.Y. (Griswold's) Cavalry. When last heard from he was *en route* from WASHINGTON, D.C., to FORT LEAVENWORTH, KANSAS, with his Regiment, in June, 1865. Any information of him (whether dead or alive) will be thankfully received and liberally rewarded by **T. Poland**, GRAND RAPIDS, MICHIGAN. Please address as above, care of **Wm. Hovey**. Troy, N.Y., papers, please copy.

Of **John McLaughlin**, a carpenter by trade, and a native of the County MAYO, Ireland. When last heard from (about 22 years ago) he was in Argyle Street, HOBERTS TOWN, VANDIEMANS LAND. Any information of him will be thankfully received by his sister-in-law, **Hannagh Ford**, 598 NINTH AVENUE, between 42nd and 43rd Streets, NEW YORK CITY.

August 20, 1870

Of **John, Michael**, and **Margaret Lonergan**. When last heard of, John was in MOUND CITY, ILLINOIS, and Michael was in TORONTO, CANADA WEST. Any information of them will be thankfully received by their brother **Nicholas Lonergan**, GARRISON'S, PUTNAM County, NEW YORK.

Of **Joseph O'Brien**, a native of LOUGH-NA-GEER, County WEXFORD, Ireland. Since he left home in 1864, has been to AUSTRALIA, NEW ZEALAND, and CALIFORNIA. When last heard from, was in NEW YORK CITY, whither he had come from California. Address his sister, **Johanna O'Brien**, 10 Pearl Street, FALL RIVER, MASS. City papers please copy.

Of **Peggy Dwyer**, from FERMOYLE, QUEEN'S County, Ireland, who emigrated to this country some sixteen years ago. When last heard from she was living in ALBANY, N.Y., married to a man named **Dermody**, from LISDOWNEY. Any information of her will be thankfully received by her afflicted mother, **Ellen Dwyer**, care of **Mr. Bernard Loughlan**, 1[ ]3 HESTER STREET, NEW YORK.

August 27, 1870

Of **Thomas Early**, who landed in New York on the 26th of April, 1870, per steamship *Nebraska*. Any information of him will be thankfully received at No. 192 CHERRY STREET, NEW YORK.

Of **William Dooling**, a native of ROSCREA, County TIPPERARY, Ireland. When last heard from he was in COVINGTON, KY. Information of him will be thankfully received by his wife and family. Address **Mary Dooling**, 95 Gold Street, BROOKLYN, N.Y. Boston *Pilot*, please copy.

Of **Rosa** and **Elizabeth McAleer**, who landed in New York about 18 years ago from the Parish of KILLMORE, County MONAGHAN, Ireland. They were daughters of **Patrick McAleer** and **Mary Hughes**. Address **Margaret McAleer** (now **Mrs. Mack**), NORTH-EAST, ERIE County, PA.

Of **Patrick Burk**, a native of AUGHMORE County MAYO, Ireland, who left BRADFORD, ENGLAND, about 17 years ago, for AUSTRALIA; also of his brother, **John Burk**, and wife, who left the same place about 12 or 13 years ago for America. Information of them will be thankfully received by their nephews, **Nicholas** and **Michael Neary**, at 478 PEARL STREET, NEW YORK. American and Australian papers, please copy.

Of **William Hennessy**, a native of KILRUSH, County CLARE, Ireland, who is about 17 years of age. He came to this country in the steamship *Columbia* in 1868, and went to his uncle's residence at OTTUMWA, IOWA. Any information concerning him will be thankfully received by his brother, **Simon Hennessy**, at 13 ROSE STREET, NEW YORK CITY. [Appeared June 18, 1870 with less information]

September 3, 1870

Of **Mary Anne McAlevy**, a native of the United States, who went to Ireland, and left the County MONAGHAN about sixteen years ago. Any account of her will be thankfully received by her brother, **Michael McAlevy**, SIDNEY Post-Office, VENANGO County, PA.

Of **Patrick Honan**, son of **Thomas Honan**, shoemaker, formerly of MILLTOWN MALBAY, County CLARE, Ireland. When last heard from, December 1863, he was working in BROOKLYN, N.Y.; supposed he joined the Army or Navy. Any information of him will be thankfully received by his father. Address **Thomas Honan**, MATAWAN, MONMOUTH County, N.J. [Appeared Jan. 14, 1871 with some different information.]

September 10, 1870

Of **James, William**, or **Patt Mullins**, who left LIMERICK City some eight or nine years ago. When heard from, last year, James was in CHICAGO, ILL. William was in ASHLAND, SCHUYLKILL County, PENNSYLVANIA, three years ago. Any information of them will be thankfully received by their brother, **Thomas Mullins**, at **Mrs. McDonnell's**, 325 Van Brunt Street, SOUTH BROOKLYN, N.Y.

Of **John** or **Mary Foley**, natives of KILLABEHAGH, County MAYO, Ireland, who came to this country about eighteen or nineteen years ago. Any information of them will be thankfully received by their niece, **Mary Faven**, by addressing her in care of **Mr. Thomas Gallagher**, corner of Centre and Wilson Streets, GERMANTOWN, PHILADELPHIA, PA.

September 17, 1870

Of **John O'Grady**, who left LONDON, ENGLAND, in May, 18[6]1. When last heard from he was in the United States Navy. Information of him will be thankfully received by his brother, **Cornelius O'Grady**, No. 936 South 10th Street, PHILADELPHIA, PA.

Of **James Regan**, of ST. JOHN'S, NEWFOUNDLAND, who left HALIFAX, NOVA SCOTIA, in March last, bound for NEW YORK. If this should meet his eye, he is requested to write at once to his brother, **Cornelius Regan**, 139 ½ Spring Street, NEWPORT, R.I.

Of **James Muldoon**, who left KILLCLARE, County LEITRIM, Ireland, about 25 years ago. He is supposed now to be in BOSTON. Any information of him will be thakfully received by his brother, **Bernard Muldoon**, TREMONT, WESTCHESTER County, N.Y.

Of **Johannah Sliney**, now **Mrs. Con. Connors**, who left the Parish of AGLISH, County WATERFORD, Ireland, ten years ago, last May. Any information of her will be thankfully received by her sister, **Catharine Sliney**, 32 CHERRY STREET, NEW YORK.

Of **William Mulcahy**, wine and spirit merchant, formerly of RATHKEALE, Co. LIMERICK, Ireland, now supposed to be in the United States; also, of **Patrick Power**, cooper, and his sisters **Margaret** and **Mary**, of the same place; and also, of **William Darcy**, of KNOCKADERRA. These persons will hear of something to their advantage by writing to **Edward Power**, 68 Murray Street, MONTREAL, CANADA EAST. If either of these persons are dead, any of their friends or acquaintances who may be aware of it, would confer a favor by writing a line to the above address.

Of **Lotty McNamara**, formerly of BUNRATTY, County CLARE, Ireland. When last heard of he was in NEW YORK about Dec. 1866. Any information of him will be gladly received by his cousin, **Michael Halloran**, at 118 WEST 12th STREET, NEW YORK.

September 24, 1870

Of **Peter Connelly**, a native of DARVER, County LOUTH, Ireland. When last heard from (two years ago), he was in VISHINA, POTTOMO County, IOWA. Information of him will be thankfully received by his sister, **Margaret Connelly**, 71 Edward Street, HARTFORD, CONN. Western papers, please copy.

Of **Michael Bernard** and **James Narey**, natives of STROKESTOWN, County ROSCOMMON, Ireland. They are supposed to be in NORTH CUMBERLAND, north of ENGLAND. Information of them will be thankfully received by their sister, **Bridget Narey** ASBURY, WARREN County, N.J. Dublin papers, please copy.

Of **Mary Ann Tucker**, a native of CASTLECONNELL, County LIMERICK, Ireland, who came to this country about seven or eight years ago. When last heard from he was in NEW JERSEY. Any information of her will be thankfully received by her brother, **Edward Tucker**, 327 South Twentieth Street, PHILADELPHIA, PA. New Jersey papers, please copy.

October 1, 1870

Of **John Donnelly**, a native of LISTOWEL, County KERRY, Ireland; son of **Daniel** and **Johanna Donnelly**. He landed in New York in 1863. When last heard from he was in CRACOW, CARBON County, PA. Information of him will be thankfully received by his sister, **Kate Donnelly**, 514 Christian Street, PHILADELPHIA, PA.

Of **Patrick** and **Bridget Smith**. Patrick emigrated from DROGHEDA, County LOUTH, Ireland, in 1848. When last heard from he resided at 156 Levee St., NEW ORLEANS, in Dec. 1868. Bridget arrived in 1856, and remained in NEW YORK up to 1867, when she started for TEXAS. They will hear of something to their advantage by writing to **Mr. P. Courtney**, 115 West St., DROGHEDA, County LOUTH, Ireland, or to **J. Connolly**, 737 Plover Street, PHILADELPHIA, PA. New Orleans papers, please copy.

October 8, 1870

John McCullough will much oblige, by addressing or calling on **L. G. Goulding**, Publisher, 132 NASSAU STREET, NEW YORK. [Appeared June 10, 1871 and June 17, 1871 with some additional information.]

Of **Thomas Lynch**, from BALNAHEE, Parish of KILLUCAN, County WESTMEATH, Ireland. When last heard from was at MILESGROVE, PA. Any information of him will be thankfully received by his brother, **Bernard Lynch**, 73 MULBERRY STREET, NEW YORK.

Of **Mary Gorman**, native of Ireland, KING'S County, Parish of RAHAN, left home 24 years ago. When last heard from she was in BOSTON. Any information of her will be thankfully received by her sister, **Ellen Gorman**, at No. 83 Pearl Street, HARTFORD, CONN.

Of **Ellen** and **Nancy Lyons**, natives of FARRAHY, Parish of KILDOURAGHY, County CORK, Ireland. When last heard of, some 14 years ago, Ellen (**Mrs. Thomas O'Connor**) was in KILBUCK, CATTARAUGUS County, NEW YORK, and Nancy in the State of OHIO. Any information of them will be thankfully received by their brother, **Thomas Lyons**, ANSONIA, CONN.

Of **James Nolan**, of the Parish of DULANE, near KELLS, County MEATH, Ireland. He left home about 23 years ago; he followed the sea; he has not been heard from for 20 years; and he is now supposed to be in SAN FRANCISCO, CAL. Any information of him will be thankfully received by his brother, **Thomas Nolan**, No. 6 Diamond St., BALTIMORE, MD. California papers, please copy.

October 15, 1870

Of **Dan. Keller**, who left the Army in KANSAS, April 25, 1870. When last heard from he was staying at the Dawes House in ST. LOUIS, MO. Also of **Pat Keller**, his brother, who left CORK in February, 1860; when last heard from was in POPE County, ARKANSAS. Any information of them will be thankfully received by their sisters, **Hannah Keller** and **Kate Burke**, 515 EAST 14th-street, N.Y.

Of **Thomas, Michael** and **Catherine Mulheaney**, and also of **Catherine McKinerney**, natives of MYMORE, Parish of TULLA, County CLARE, Ireland, who came to this country about 22 years ago. When last heard of they were in PENNSYLVANIA. Any information of them will be thankfully received by their niece, **Mary McKinerney**, 329 WEST 15th STREET, NEW YORK. Pennsylvania paper, please copy.

October 22, 1870

Of **William Coffe**, who, when last heard of, was in CARLS County, ILLINOIS. Intelligence of him will be thankfully received by his sister, **Delia Coffe**. Please address **Edward Dunn**, STAPLETON Post Office, STATEN ISLAND, N.Y. New Orleans papers, please copy.

Of **Daniel Callen**, a native of the County ARMAGH, Ireland, who came to this country about four years ago, and when last heard of was in PHILADELPHIA, PA. Any information of him will be thankfully received by his friend, **Elizabeth Quinn**, at No. 77 Kent Avenue, BROOKLYN, Long Island, N.Y. Philadelphia papers, please copy.

October 29, 1870

Of **Nicholas Culligan**, who, when last heard from, was in COLD SPRING Foundery, N.Y. Any information of him will be thankfully received by his wife **Mary** (maiden name **Mary Devin**,) formerly of BLAKESTOWN, ARDEE, County LOUTH, Ireland. Address 216 WEST 31ˢᵗ STREET, NEW YORK. Boston *Pilot*, please copy.

Of **Patrick Paton**, a native of the County DONEGAL, Ireland, when last heard from, six years ago, was in NEWTON, DELAWARE County, PENNSYLVANIA; by occupation a laborer. Any information concerning him will be thankfully received by his wife, **Margaret Paton**, PASSAIC VILLAGE, N.J., or **B. O'Neill**, 81 Market Street, PATERSON, N.J.

Of **Michael Brown**, of BRUREE, County LIMERICK, who left BALLINNOW, near BALLINGARRY, 25 years ago, when last heard of was in PHILADELPHIA. Any information of him will be thankfully received by his sister, **Mary Price**, care **Mr. Samuel Colgate**, NORTH ORANGE, NEW JERSEY. Philadelphia papers please copy.

November 5, 1870

Of **Timothy Counihan**, boot and shoe maker, a native of KANTURK, Co. CORK, Ireland, who left home about two years and a half ago. Any information of him will be thankfully received by his wife and son, at No. 163 WEST 27ᵗʰ STREET, NEW YORK. San Francisco, Cal. and Golden City, Colorado, papers, please copy.

November 12, 1870

Of **Michael Murphy**, a native of County WEXFORD, Ireland, who left home in 1861. When last heard from was in CHATHAM, ILL. Any information of him will be thankfully received by his brother, **John Murphy**, care of **Michael Murphy**, 145 Morgan Street, JERSEY CITY, N.J.

November 19, 1870

Of **John Mellen**, a tailor by trade, and of his sisters, **Harriet, Eliza**, and **Jane Mellen**, natives of LIFFORD, County DONEGAL, Ireland. Information of them will be thankfully received by their sister, **ANNE MELLEN**, DEXTER, State of MAINE.

Of **John, Cornelius**, and **Wm. Margey**, from the Parish of BOVEVEGH, Co. DERRY, Ireland. When last heard from, about ten years ago, they were in NEW YORK CITY. Any intelligence of them will be thankfully received by their youngest brother, **Paul Margey**. Direct to care of **Wm. McLaughlin**, 57 Newark Street, NEWARK, N.J. California papers please copy.

Of **Robert Butler**, a native of Co. WATERFORD, Ireland, who came to this country about five months ago, and is now supposed to be in CHICAGO. Any information concerning him will be thankfully received by **Maria Foley**, care of **Mr. Snedecor**, BLOOMFIELD, N.J.

Of **Bridget Roach**, a native of Co. KERRY, Ireland, who came to this country about four years ago, and, up to June was living at No. 18 HAMILTON ST., in this City. Any information concerning her will be thankfully received by her brother, **Patrick Roach**, at HOMEDALE P.O., MONMOUTH Co., N.J.

Of **Maria Long** and **John Tracy**, who left BROOKLYN for OHIO two years ago. Any information of them will be kindly received by **MARY HANORAH LONG**, ELIZABETH P.O., NEW JERSEY, Box 612. Western papers please copy. [Appeared under County LIMERICK]

Of **Michael Carter**, by his niece, **Bridget Carter**, daughter of **Thomas Carter**, of the Parish of COLLUMBKILLE, County LONGFORD, Ireland. Information of him will be thankfully received by addressing No. 348 EAST 33rd STREET, NEW YORK CITY.

November 26, 1870

Of **Jerry Collins**, hatter, who lived some time ago at No. 58 Adams Street, BROOKLYN; also of **John Hegarty**, Sawyer, who worked in Bell & Brown's Ship Yard some years ago; also of the wife of **Charles Collins**. Inquire at this Office.

Of **Patrick Lynch**, a stonecutter, aged about 36 years; height five feet six inches, sharp features, light complexion, blue eyes; he left STAMFORD, CONN., on Sept. 9th, 1869. Any information concerning his whereabouts will be thankfully received by his wife, **Mary Lynch**, STAMFORD, P.O., CONN., care of **Mrs. Pomeroy**. Stonecutters knowing of his whereabouts will please communicate any information to his distressed wife.

Of **Daniel Leahy**, bricklayer, a native of the City of DUBLIN, formerly in **Captain Hugh D. Smith's** Company, 69th New York Regiment. Any information concerning him will be thankfully received by his brother-in-law, **Patrick S. Griffith**, 206 Race Street, PHILADELPHIA, PA.

Of **Mrs. Bridget Callaghan**, (now **Mrs. Egan**); also of her son, **Michael Callaghan**. When last heard of, they were in BOSTON, MASS. Also of her daughters, **Ellen, Mary**, and **Bridget Callaghan**. When last heard from, they were in TROY, N.Y. They are natives of County SLIGO, Ireland. They will confer a favor by addressing **Michael Callaghan**, 67 Underhill Avenue, corner of Bergen Street, BROOKLYN, N.Y. Boston and Troy papers, please copy.

December 3, 1870

Of **Patrick Tierney**, who left ASHTON-UNDER-LYNE, LANCASHIRE, ENGLAND, in February, 1862. When last heard from he was in CRUISO, MEXICO. Any information of him will be thankfully received by his mother, **Mary Tierney**, OLNEYVILLE. Post Office, MERINOVILLE, R.I. Mexico and California papers, please copy.

Of **Dan Grace**, of NORTH STRAND, LIMERICK, Ireland, who emigrated to NEW YORK in 1848, with a young man named **Jack Swinburn**. When last heard from he was in STATEN ISLAND Hospital but was discharged in July, 1850. Any information of him will be thankfully received by his cousin, **J. J. Molony**, 151 ELIZABETH STREET, NEW YORK.

Of **Patrick Shallow**, a native of the City of WATERFORD, Ireland, son of **Philip** and **Elizabeth Shallow**, of said City, both deceased. He arrived in New York, from Liverpool, in the ship *Star of the West*, in the Summer of 1852, and was last heard of about 14 years ago. Any information of him, dead or living, will be thankfully received by **Edward S. Kenney**, *The News* office, WATERFORD, Ireland. Irish-American papers, please copy.

December 10, 1870

Of **Patrick Earley**, who arrived in Melbourne sixteen years ago. When last heard from, in the year 1858, he was night watchman in the mail coach stables, about thirty miles from MELBOURNE, and was formerly employed to break in horses by a well-known horse-dealer named **Richard Nugent**, of that City. He had a friend on the police department there, named **Peter Malloy**. There is a lady residing at ST. JOHN'S, RAPUNDA, ADELAIDE, about 600 miles from Melbourne, named **Eliza Rogers**, who keeps a hotel, and it is likely she could give some information concerning him; all of which will be thankfully received by addressing his brother, **John Early**, 221 ELIZABETH STREET, NEW YORK CITY, U.S. Australian papers, please copy.

Of **Peter Reilly**, who came to this country in 1863, son of **Terence** and **Nabbey Reilly**, and a native of the County LEITRIM, Ireland. He left BALTIMORE 6 months ago, and has not been heard from since. Information of him, dead or alive, will be thankfully received by his three brothers, **John, James** and **Patrick Reilly**. Address Patrick Reilly, St. Nicholas Hotel, BALTIMORE, MD. New York, Philadelphia and Baltimore papers, please copy.

December 17, 1870

Of **Michael Pollard**, a slater by trade, who emigrated from BALLINGARRY, County TIPPERARY, Ireland, about 16 years ago. When last heard from he was in VICTORIA, SANDRIGE near MELBOURNE, AUSTRALIA. Information of him will be thankfully received by his nephew, **Michael Pollard**, COHOES, ALBANY County, N.Y.

Of **John Downs**, native of the Parish of MOULOUGH, County CLARE, Ireland, who left NEW YORK CITY with his sister **Bridget** and sister-in-law and baby, about seventeen years ago, for CHICAGO. If they will write to **John Hurley**, DES MOINES, IOWA, they will hear of something to their advantage. Western papers please copy.

Of **Thomas Rooney**, of VENTRY, Co. KERRY, Ireland. When last heard from was in BUFFALO, NEW YORK. Any information of him will be thankfully received by his brother **Patrick Rooney**, residing in MIDDLETOWN, CT.

Of **Thomas, William** and **Michael Heffernan**, (brothers,) and natives of the Parish of CARRICKBEG, in the County WATERFORD, who came to America some twenty years ago. When last heard of, one year ago, they were living in ORANGE County, NEW YORK. Any information respecting their present location will be thankfully received by their brother **Patrick Heffernan**. Please address to No. [ ]8 Anowan-street, FALL RIVER, MASS., for Patrick Heffernan.

[Issues for December 24, 1870 and December 31, 1870 unavailable.]

January 7, 1871

Of **Martin O'Neill**, by his sister **Catherine**, when last heard from was working on the railway in GREENVILLE, PENNSYLVANIA. Any information of him will be thankfully received, by addressing **Mrs. Nelson**, No. 26 CANAL STREET, NEW YORK CITY.

Of **Christopher Brown**, a native of DUBLIN, Ireland, by trade a Paper-maker; when last heard from, six years ago, he was in BALTIMORE. Any information concerning him will be thankfully received by his sister, **Susan Kearney**, MANAYUNK Post Office, PHILADELPHIA, PA. Baltimore papers please copy.

Of **Eliza Ferguson** (maiden name), who married **Hugh McGuorian**, a brick-layer by trade, and left BELFAST about 20 years since. Information of her will be thankfully received by her cousin, **Frank Ferguson**, 14 Weybosset Street, PROVIDENCE, R.I., (upstairs).

Of **Dan Colombo**, a native of the County ARMAGH, by his cousin, **Eliza Quinn**. When last heard of was in PHILADELPHIA, about four years ago. Please write to 161 WEST THIRTY-THIRD STREET, NEW YORK CITY. Philadelphia papers please copy.

Of **John Baker** who came to this country from County MONAGHAN, some 28 years ago, in company with his father and mother and two sisters. Any information of him and his two sisters will be thankfully received by **John Keenan**, Second-street, between 9th and 10th Streets, WILLIAMSBURGH. Philadelphia papers please copy.

Of **James, Robert, Mary** and **Julia Thompson**, of KILLARNEY, Co. KERRY, Ireland. Mary married **Michael Keogh**, about 13 years ago, they were then in HOMER, CORTLAND County, N.Y. Their sister, **Ellen**, who married **Patrick Brennan**, wishes to hear from them. Address Mrs. P. Brennan, care of **Rev. Father Walters**, CRAWFORDSVILLE, INDIANA.

Of **Michael Smyth**, of MOORETOWN, Parish of FORE, County WESTMEATH, Ireland, who emigrated to NEW YORK 15 years ago. When last heard from was in the State of MISSOURI. Any information of him will be thankfully received by his brother, **Thomas Smyth**. Direct in care **Simon Glennan**, No. 136 Ferry Street, NEWARK, N.J. Missouri papers please copy.

Of **Patrick Kennedy**, of PALLISKENRY, Parish of CHAPELRUSSELL, County LIMERICK, Ireland; was in NEW YORK, in August last. His mother, **Mrs. Margaret Kennedy** is anxious to hear from him. Address her at **Michael Lynch's**, 333 Fourth av., TROY, N.Y.

Of **Margaret Madden**, who came to NEW YORK to her husband, **Thomas Madden**, in 1841, from ROSCREA, County TIPPERARY, Ireland; or of her daughters, **Mary, Jane, Margaret, Hanora**, and **Eliza Madden**; also of her sister, **Bridget**. Information of them will be thankfully received by their brother, **John Brennan**. Address No. 6 Cedar Street, PROVIDENCE, R.I.

January 14, 1871

Of **Patrick Dooley**, KAHAN, QUEEN'S County, Ireland, who emigrated to this County 20 years ago; when last heard from was in ST. LOUIS, MO. Any information of him will be thankfully received by his cousin, **Johanna Dooley**. Direct your letter in care of **Mr. Patrick Smith**, 37th St., West, No. 524 NEW ORLEANS. New Orleans papers please copy. [Appeared Jan. 28, 1871 with Kahan changed to SRABAN.]

Of **Patrick Honan**, son of **Thomas Honan**, Shoemaker, MILLTOWN MALBAY; when last heard from, December, 1863, he was living in BROOKLYN, N.Y. Information concerning him will be thankfully received by his father. Address **Thos. Honan**, MATAWA, MONMOUTH County, NEW JERSEY. [Appeared under County CLARE] [Appeared Sept. 3, 1870, with some different information]

Of **Thomas Clarke**, formerly of MAGHERACLOONE, County MONAGHAN, or of his brother **James**, or sister, **Margaret**. When last heard from, Thomas had a farm in ALLEGHANY, and he is supposed to be living there or in PITTSBURGH now; had his letters addressed in care of **Patrick Martin**, Pittsburgh Bank. Any communication addressed to **Philip V. Manning**, composing-room, NEW YORK *Sun* office, will be thankfully received. Pittsburgh *Chronicle* and other papers please copy. [Appeared Jan. 28, 1871 with Pittsburgh *Chronicle* changed to Pittsburgh *Commercial*.]

Of **Patrick Cantwell**, late of the City of LIMERICK, brother-in-law of **John Walker** and **Tom Casey**; arrived in Boston two months ago with wife and sister-in-law. Pat and wife left 113 Porter St., E. BOSTON, 23rd inst., for N.Y., Stonnington line, forgetting to pay the subscriber the $10 borrowed under false pretences, 24th inst. Limerick men will be cautious. **Joseph Casey**, Asst. Supt. City Temp. Home. [Appeared Jan. 21, 1871 with the surname Cantwell changed to **Hartnett**.]

January 21, 1871

Of **John Wilson**, by his family. He came to America with his eldest daughter, in May, 1863; he was formerly a cattle-dealer in DUBLIN, and was trading in cattle in 1866, between ALBANY and NEW YORK, and lived with his family in NEW YORK for three years. Any information of him will be kindly received by his son. Address, **Judge Wilson**, CALVERT, TEXAS.

Of **Thomas Grimmes**, native of the Parish of CONG, County MAYO, Ireland, or his wife **Sarah**, or her cousin, **Michael O'Donnell**, who emigrated to Iowa in 1861 or 1862; when last heard from were near DUBUQUE, IOWA. Any information of them will be thankfully received by his brother, **PatrickGRIMMES**, No. 26 PRINCE STREET, NEW YORK, or his sister, **ElizabethGRIMMES**, at No. 91 BAXTER STREET. Dubuque, Iowa, papers please copy.

Of **Patrick Hiderman**, a native of DONOUGHMORE, LIMERICK; when last heard of, about 20 years ago, he was working in a foundry in TROY. Any information of him will be thankfully received by his brother, **Timothy Hiderman**, 102 MOTT STREET, NEW YORK. Troy papers please copy.

January 28, 1871

Of **Patrick O'Brien**, from Parish of FEDAMORE, BALLINGARDE, County LIMERICK, Ireland, who came to this country in May, 1867. When last heard of, he was in LANSING, WYOMING County, N.Y., working on a railroad. By sending his address to the Irish-American Office he will hear of something to his advantage.

February 4, 1871

Of **James Davey**, who left BALTIMORE in March, 1869; Destination, IOWA. When last heard of, was in ST. LOUIS. Any tidings concerning him can be sent to **F. Cassidy**, north-west corner Greenmount Avenue and Monument Street, BALTIMORE, MD.

Of **Dr. John Barrett**, who is supposed to be in NEW YORK. He will hear of the whereabouts of **Mrs. Widow Blackwood**, by sending his address to **George Jackson**, *Morning Chronicle* Office, QUEBEC City.

Of **Jeremiah Driscoll**, a tailor by trade, and a native of BANTRY, County CORK, Ireland, who came to this country about three years ago. When last heard of he was in CONNECTICUT, from which place he intended to go to VIRGINIA. Any information concerning him will be thankfully received by his father, **Daniel Driscoll**, at 573 Fulton Avenue, BROOKLYN, Long Island. Southern papers please copy.

Of **Brian Drum**, who, when last heard from, was in DUTCHESS County, N.Y. Also, of his sister **Bridget** and **Ellen Brine**. When last heard from, Bridget was in JERSEY CITY, and Ellen was supposed to be in LONG ISLAND, N.Y. They are natives of the County WESTMEATH, Ireland; it is sixteen years since they have been heard from. Information of them will be thankfully received by writing to their sister **Mary**, in care of **Hugh Reid**, DURANT, CEDAR County, IOWA.

Of **Nicholas Taff**, a native of DROGHEDA, Co. LOUTH, Ireland; he came to this country five years ago; when last heard from, about a year ago, was in CHICAGO, ILL. Any information concerning him will be thankfully received by his sister, **Bridget Taff**, at No. 11 WEST 48th STREET, NEW YORK CITY.

Of **Thomas Carroll**, of LOUTH; married to **Mary Boyle**, of LOUTH; lived 16 years at FLETCHER'S, VERMONT, afterwards in WISCONSIN. Address **Rev. J. Pentony**, DUNDALK, County LOUTH, Ireland.

Of **Mrs. Michael Glantzy** (maiden name **Anna Cannon**), of MAYO, Ireland; came to this country April, 1865. Any information concerning her will be thankfully received by **Patrick Cannon**, PHILLIPSBURGH, NEW JERSEY.

February 11, 1871

Of **Daniel Moughan**, 35 years of age, a native of BALLINAKILL, County GALWAY, Ireland. In July, 1865, he was working in JERSEY CITY, at boiler-making; was last heard from at CINCINNATI, OHIO, in January, 1866. Any intelligence of him will be thankfully received by his brother, **John Moughan**, at No. 436 GREENWICH STREET, corner of Vesey Street, NEW YORK.

The attention of the County ROSCOMMON people is specially invited to the following: - In 1847 or 1848, **Patrick O'Connor**, with his wife **Mary** (maiden name unknown), and their son **John**, then a boy of about four years of age, came to CANADA, settling near NIAGARA, where he obtained work, and saved what could be fairly spared of his earnings, with the view of sending for his two daughters, who were left in charge of their uncle and his brother - supposed to be named **William O'Connor**. This money, saved for the children's passage, was the ruin of both father and mother; for, to possess it, they were both cruelly murdered by a brutal assassin. The little boy, only, by God's providence, miraculously escaped sharing the same barbarous fate. This boy, arrived at manhood, now resides in this City, and wishes most earnestly to obtain such information as will enable him to find or communicate with his sisters, whose Christian names, he thinks, are **Margaret** and **Bridget**, or **Elizabeth**. His father lived on **Major Mahon's** estate. Any such information may be sent in care of **E. P. McDermott**, No. 368 THIRD AVENUE, NEW YORK. Roscommon papers, please copy.

Of **William Gady**, and wife, who is a daughter of **James Mulden**, of the Parish of NEWPORT, County TIPPERARY, Ireland. They came to this country about 23 or 24 years ago from ENGLAND. Information of them will be thankfully received by their sister, **Ellen Mulden**, by writing to her in care of **Samuel Colgate**, NORTH ORANGE, N.J.

Of **William Brophy**, who emigrated to this country, about 10 years ago, from RATHWISE, County WESTMEATH, Ireland, with his family. When last heard from he was living at 84 VESEY STREET, NEW YORK. By sending his address to the office of this paper he will hear of something to his advantage.

February 18, 1871

Of **John** and **James Tobin**, of BOLTON, LANCASHIRE, ENGLAND. They are plasterers by trade, and came to America five years ago. Information of them will be thankfully received by their sister, **Julia Tobin**, at 69 Bedford Avenue, WILLIAMSBURGH, Long Island, N.Y.

Of **Michael Doyle**, who was discharged from the English Army, 4th Battallion, 60th Rifles, at ST. JOHN, NEW BRUNSWICK; a native of the Parish of DUNLAVEN, County WICKLOW, Ireland. Information of him will be thankfully received by his brother, **Henry Doyle**, at No. 96 Anawan St., FALL RIVER, MASS. Canadian papers, please copy.

Of **Phillip McCann**, who left the Parish of KILL, County CAVAN, Ireland, 14 years ago, for America. He is supposed to be at HAMBURGH, BERKS County, PA. Information of him will be thankfully received by his brother, **James McCann**, No. 329 South Halsted Street, CHICAGO, ILL.

Of **Edmond** and **Thomas Cummins**, natives of THOMASTOWN, County TIPPERARY, Ireland. Edmond, when last heard of, was in CALIFORNIA, and Thomas, when last heard of, was in ST. LOUIS. Information of them will be thankfully received by their brother, **Martin Cummins**, ANDOVER, MASS. Boston *Pilot*, please copy.

February 25, 1871

Of **Anne Russell**, of the Parish of TULLOW, County CLARE; when last seen by her brother was in HOBOKEN, NEW JERSEY; went from there to NEW YORK; moved west with family. Any information of her will be thankfully received by her brother, **Patrick Russell**, ASHBURY, WARREN County, N.J. New Jersey and Western papers please copy.

Of **Michael McLaughlin**, who left the County LONGFORD (adjoining SCRADY BRIDGE), Ireland, between 35 and 40 years ago; when last heard of, about 25 years ago, was living in OHIO. Any information will be thankfully received by his daughter, **Anne McLaughlin**, marriage name **Anne Norton**, NEW BRUNSWICK, NEW JERSEY. Ohio papers please copy.

March 4, 1871

Of **Michael Burke**, a native of GORT, County GALWAY, Ireland; he is 60 years of age, and has been in this country a number of years; he is married to **Daniel Kelaghorn's** daughter. Any information of him will be thankfully received by his sister, **Mary Hopkins**, at No. 14 FRANKLIN STREET, NEW YORK. Boston papers, please copy.

Of **Alice** and **Bridget Austin**, natives of the County TIPPERARY, Ireland, who came to this Count[r]y in 1867, and, when last heard from, were in NEW YORK CITY. Information of them will be thankfully received by addressing their brother, **Edmund Austin**, GREENWICH, CONN.

Of **Robert Miller**, a butcher by trade, and a native of QUEENSTOWN, County CORK, Ireland. Information of him will be thankfully received by his daughter **Catharine**. Address **Mrs. McCloskey**, 180 Lorimor Street, WILLIAMSBURGH, Long Island, N.Y.

Of **Bernard Loughren**, aged about 19 years, a native of ENISHBRACK, COOKSTOWN, County TYRONE, Ireland. He left HARTFORD, CONN., in November, 1869. When last heard from he was in NEW YORK CITY. Any person knowing of his whereabouts will confer a favor by addressing **William Mahon**, 75 Windsor Street, HARTFORD, CONN.

March 11, 1871

Of **Alice Conroy** (maiden name **Little**), her son, and husband, who is a Miller by trade. They formerly resided in DUBLIN and DROGHEDA, and are now supposed to be in BOSTON, MASS. Her sister, **Mary Osborne** (maiden name **Little**), of WEST FARMS, WESTCHESTER County, N.Y., wishes to hear from her. Boston papers, please copy.

Of **Richard** and **Peter Power**, natives of KILLARDCLOGH, County KILDARE, Ireland, who left home 20 years ago, sons of **Peter Power**, of said place. When last heard from Peter was in BOSTON, MASS., and Richard was in BROOKLYN, N.Y. Also of **Michael Buggle**, their cousin, of CELBRIDGE, County KILDARE, who left ENGLAND, last May, for NEW YORK, and has not been heard of since. Any information of them will be thankfully received by their brother, **Patrick Power**. Address **Daniel Higgins**, WESTPORT, CONN.

Of **John Croker**, a native of the Parish of FEDAMORE, County LIMERICK, Ireland. When last heard from he was in SOUTH OTTOWA, LOSLEY County, ILL., about 13 or 14 years ago. Also, of **Bridget** and **Mary Normile**; when last heard from, about 13 or 14 years ago, they lived in MONTREAL, CANADA. Bridget was married to **Lawrence Sullivan**, and lived with **Mr. Pandlesgreave**, type founder, Montreal; also, of their sister, **Honora Normile**, who, when last heard from, lived with her uncle, **John O'Brien**, WAIR VILLAGE, MASS., and was married to a man named **Kennedy**. Information of them will be thankfully received by addressing **Thomas Croker**, WESTPORT, FAIRFIELD County, CONN.

Of **Mary Donnelly**, daughter of **John** and **Mary Donnelly** (mother's maiden name **Casey**), of PORTUMNA, County GALWAY, Ireland. The father died about 28 years ago, and when last heard of, in 1848, Mary and her mother were in BALLINASLOE. If this should meet her eye, or that of any friend who knows her present whereabouts, she will learn something greatly to her advantage by sending her address to the office of the Irish-American, New York. Dublin *Nation*, *Irishman* and Galway papers, please copy.

March 18, 1871

Of **Michael** and **Catharine Gannan**, from the Town of FORAGLISH, Parish of CLUNA, who emigrated to this country 25 or 30 years ago. When last heard from they were in MCGREGOR, IOWA. Any information of them will be thankfully received by their sister, **Elizabeth Gannon**, SAND PATCH, PA. Iowa and California papers, please copy.

Of **Peter Duffy**, a shoemaker by trade, and a native of the Parish of ANNAMULLEN, County MONAGHAN, Ireland. When last seen he lived in 241 EAST 28th STREET, in this City, in January, 1869. He will hear of something to his advantage by sending his address to the office of the Irish-American.

Of **Bridget, Mary, Michael** and **James Geoghegan**, natives of ATHLONE, County ROSCOMMON, Ireland. James, when last heard from (about nine years ago), was in the State of MISSISSIPPI. There has been some property in Ireland left to the above family, and it will be greatly to their advantage of either of them to send their address to **Mrs. Anne Moore**, at 320 WEST 40th STREET, NEW YORK CITY.

Of **John Scullion**, a native of BROAGH, County DERRY, Ireland. When last heard from he was in NEW YORK CITY. Any information concerning him will be thankfully received by his brother, **Henry Scullion**, No. 2,325, Biddle Street, PHILADELPHIA, PA.

Of **Mary Kanny**, who came to this country from SCARIFF, County CLARE, Ireland, about the year 1845, having care of the grandchildren of **Dr. Morris**, viz.:— **Willie, Henry**, and **Ann O'Connor**. Should this meet the eye of the above Mary Kanny, or of any of her heirs, they will hear of something to their advantage by calling on **Margaret Smith** (sister of Mary Kanny), No. 4,408 Main Street, FRANKFORD, PHILADELPHIA, PA.

March 25, 1871

Of **Catherine Heffernan**. If any one knowing her whereabouts will call her attention to this notice, or send her address to the undersigned, they will confer a great favor on her husband, **James Heffernan**, No. [1]120 Myrtle Street, ST. LOUIS, MO.

Of **Daniel J. O'Brien**, and of **Ellen O'Brien**, his niece; the former a native of Co. DONEGAL, Ireland. Ellen was born in SPRINGFIELD, MASS. When last heard from (about a year ago) she lived in No. 253 EAST 40th STREET, NEW YORK CITY. Information of them will be thankfully received by Ellen's father, who is in a dying condition. Address **Edward O'Brien**, care of **Mrs. McCann**, Water Street, SPRINGFIELD, MASS. or P. J. Ryan, Emigration Agent.

Of **Judith Hanratty**, maiden name **Judith McConnin**, a native of CARRICKMACROSS, County MONAGHAN, Ireland. When last heard from, in July, 1865 resided in EAST 11th STREET, between Avenue B and C; also of her sister **Mary**. Any information leading to the above parties will be thankfully received by **John Hanratty**, Co. G., 11th Infantry, FORT GRIFFIN, TEXAS.

April 1, 1871

Of **Edward Barry**, who, when last heard from, was living in HAVERSTRAW, N.Y. Information of him or of his sister-in-law, **Anny McCormick**, will be thankfully received by their sister, **Bridget McCormick,** by addressing a letter to **Thomas Sexton,** EAST ORANGE, N.J. Chicago papers, please copy.

Of **Lawrence Joseph Clooney,** aged about 15 years, and of **Margaret Ann Clooney,** aged about 13 years. Both were born at CORNING, STEUBEN County, N.Y. Also of **Mary Clooney,** aged about 11 years, born in PHILADELPHIA, PA. Any particulars of their whereabouts will be thankfully received. Address to **John Smutz,** CORRY, ERIE County, PA., for **Lawrence Clooney.** Canada papers, please copy.

Of **Patrick** and **Mary Finland,** natives of the Parish of POWERPASTY, County WEXFORD, Ireland. When last heard from they were in NEW YORK. Patrick is a shoemaker by trade. Any information of them will be thankfully received by their sister, **Margaret Finland,** Post Office Box 285, CORRY, ERIE County, PA. Philadelphia papers, please copy.

Of **Mary Anne, Bridget,** and **Daniel Howard,** son and daughters of **Michael Howard,** of KILLASKEAHAN, Parish of DRUM, County TIPPERARY, Ireland. Any information of them will be thankfully received by their brother, **Michael Howard,** 51 GREENWICH STREET, NEW YORK.

Of **Michael Kearny,** a native of INNOSHANNON, County CORK, Ireland. When last heard of he was with his brother, **Wm. Kearny,** of DOUGLASTOWN, MIRAMICHI, N.B., CANADA. Any information concerning him will be thankfully received by his cousin, **John Callanan,** No. 3,260 Lancaster Street, WEST PHILADELPHIA, PA. Boston papers, please copy.

April 8, 1871

Of **James Hawksworth,** who, when last heard of, was working on the Alliance Railway, STARKE County, OHIO, as a laborer. Any information of him will be gladly received by his cousin, **Edward Howell,** 1621 American Street, between Oxford and Columbia Streets, PHILADELPHIA, PA.

Of **Mary Anne, Bridget,** and **Daniel Howard,** son and daughters of **Michael Howard,** of KILLASKEAHAN, Parish of DRUM, County TIPPERARY, Ireland. Any information of them will be thankfully received by their brother, **Michael Howard,** 51 GREENWICH STREET, NEW YORK. [Originally run April 1, 1871. Reprinted here for clarity. See next ad.]

Michael Howard, who advertises for information of the above parties, will find his brother **Daniel** and his sister **Anne,** at No. 78 Court Street, ELIZABETHPORT, NEW JERSEY. He is understood to be now in FLATBUSH, Long Island.

April 15, 1871

If **Owen** and **John Farley,** County of LONGFORD, Parish of GRANARD, Town of BUNLAEHY, Ireland, or their children, will communicate their whereabouts to **Thomas Morrison,** Department of State, WASHINGTON, D. C., they will learn something of advantage to them. **Ellen Farley.**

Of **Bridget** or **Bessy Brannan,** from TUBBERCURRY, County SLIGO, Ireland, who sailed from Liverpool on the 20th of April, 1870, bound for New York. Any account of them will be rewarded by sending it to No. 116 Wood Street, PHILADELPHIA.

April 22, 1871

Of **Andrew Kavanagh,** a native of the Parish of BALLINBAY, County MONAGHAN, Ireland, who came to this country about 17 years ago. When last heard from he was in the State of MISSOURI, and is now supposed to be in SAN FRANCISCO, CAL. Any information of him will be thankfully received by **James Kavanagh**, at No. 519 WEST 43rd STREET, NEW YORK CITY.

Of **Ellen Byrne**, a native of the County LIMERICK, Ireland, who came to this country about 20 years ago, and has not been heard from since. Any information of her will be thankfully received by her brother, **Rodger Byrne**, at **Joseph Kelly's**, FORT HAMILTON, NEW YORK HARBOR.

April 29, 1871

Of **Hanora Moran**, a native of CAHIRCIVEEN, Co. KERRY, Ireland, who came to this country about 15 years ago. When last heard from (nine years ago) she was in AKRON, SUMMIT County, OHIO. Any information of her will be thankfully received by **Mrs. Connor**, at No. 44 OLIVER STREET, NEW YORK CITY.

Of **Patrick** and **Anthony Frain**, natives of the Parish of KILMOVEE, Townland of AGOOL, County MAYO, Ireland, sons of **John** and **Bridget Frain**. When last heard of they were in SAGINAW CITY, MICHIGAN. Intelligence of them will be thankfully received by their brothers, **Martin** and **James Frain**. Please address **James Towey**, HOBOKEN CITY P.O., NEW JERSEY. Michigan and Illinois papers, please copy.

Of **Patrick O'Donovan**, a native of TIPPERARY, Ireland, a carpenter by trade, who left BROOKLYN in October last. When last heard from (on the 24th of December) he was in PHILADELPHIA. Any information of him will be thankfully received by his wife and child. Address **Mrs. Bridget Donovan**, 5 Amity Street, BROOKLYN, N.Y. Philadelphia papers, please copy.

Of **Thomas, Daniel**, and **Catherine McCarty**, natives of the Parish of MURROE, Co. LIMERICK, Ireland. Thomas came to this country about 19 years ago, and Daniel and Catherine, about four years ago. Daniel, when last heard from, about four months since, was in STAMFORD, CONN. Any information of them will be received by their sister, **Mary McCarty**, at CAPPAMORE, County LIMERICK, Ireland, or by their brother, **John McCarty**, at the office of the Irish-American.

May 6, 1871

Of **Mary Anne, Bridget**, and **Daniel Howard,** son and daughters of **Michael Howard**, of KILLASKEAHAN, Parish of DRUM, County TIPPERARY, Ireland. Any information of them will be thankfully received by their brother, **Michael Howard**, 51 GREENWICH STREET, NEW YORK.

May 13, 1871

Of **Michael Keogh**, a native of AHASCRAGH, County GALWAY, Ireland, who landed in this country about two years ago. He is a carpenter by trade, and worked at HUDSON CITY, N.J. He was on a visit to his aunt at Christmas, 1869, since which time nothing has been heard of him. Information of him will be thankfully received by his aunt, **Hessie Leonard**, NISKAYUNA, SCHENECTADY County, N.Y. New Jersey papers please copy.

Of **Catherine Roork**, of the Townland of THOMASTOWN and Parish of CARRAUGH, County KILDARE, Ireland. If this should meet her eye, or any of her friends, she will hear of something of interest to her. Call at 404 Baltic Street, BROOKLYN, and the desired information can be obtained of **Mrs. Weekes**. Philadelphia papers please copy.

Of **Mary Williams**, maiden name **Mary Cahill**, from ROSCREA, County TIPPERARY, Ireland, who left LEEDS, ENGLAND about five years ago; when last heard from she was in PATERSON, N.J. Address, her brother-in-law, **James Molloy**, 643 Alaska Street, PHILADELPHIA, PA.

May 20, 1871

Of **James Callan**, son of **Richard Callan**, from near DUNLEER, County LOUTH, Ireland, who came to this country about 30 or 40 years ago. When last heard from he was in NEW YORK State. Any information of him will be thankfully received by his brother, **Thomas Callan**, at No. 1216 Heath Street, PHILADELPHIA, PA.

Of **Richard Madden**, a native of CLARE ISLAND, near WESTPORT, County MAYO, Ireland, who left BLACKBURN, LANCASHIRE, ENGLAND, seven years ago next June, and wrote a letter to his family on the following June, dated at WASHINGTON, D.C. Any information of him will be thankfully received by his sister, **Bridget Madden**, No. 608 Penn Street, PHILADELPHIA, PA. Western papers, please copy.

May 27, 1871

Of **James, Michael** and **Patrick Turner**, natives of County DUBLIN, Ireland. James came to this country about 17 years ago; Michael about 13 years, and Patrick about 8 years. James, when heard from last (about 10 years ago), was in the State of PENNSYLVANIA. Any information concerning him will be thankfully received by their brother, **Andrew Turner**, at No. 7 Grand Street, JERSEY CITY, N.J.

Of **Thomas Neville**, native of the Parish of NEWMARKET-ON-FERGUS, County CLARE, Ireland, who came to this country about 18 years ago; when last heard from he was in NEW YORK CITY. Any information of him will be thankfully received by his brother's son, **Daniel Neville**, FITCHBURG, MASS.

Of **Daniel Lyons**, a native of the Parish of LISELTON, County KERRY, Ireland, who left WALES and came to this country four years ago. When last heard from (two years ago) he was working for the Union Pacific Railroad Company. Any information of him will be thankfully received by his wife, **Johanna Lyons**, at ELIZABETHPORT, N.J.

Of **Maurice Brosnahan**, a native of the Parish of CURRINS, County KERRY, Ireland. When last heard from he was in INDIANAPOLIS, INDIANA. Any information of him will be thankfully received by his nephew, **Philip Luney**, PLANTSVILLE, CT.

Of **Peter Killcash**, a native of the Parish of FORD, County WESTMEATH, Ireland. When last heard from he was in ROCHESTER, N.Y. His sister Bridget lost his address, so she could not write; she is very anxious to hear from him. Any person knowing of his whereabouts will confer a favor by addressing **Bridget Killcash**, care of **J. P. Colgan**, Catholic Bookseller, 532 South 3rd Street, PHILADELPHIA, PA.

Of **Thomas N. Browne**, formerly of BALLINROBE, County MAYO, Ireland, late of NEW YORK. Please to communicate to **Mr. James Larner**, No. 300 34th STREET, corner of Second Avenue, NEW YORK CITY.

Of **Bridet McGinty**, of TUBERCURRY, County SLIGO, Ireland, who left NEW YORK about four years ago. When last heard from she was in CLINTON, MASS. Any information of her will be thankfully received by her brother, **John McGinty**, 52 CLARKSON STREET, NEW YORK. Boston *Pilot*, please copy.

June 3, 1871

Of **Catharine Keelan**, daughter of **Bernard Keelan**, of BALLIGTROW, County MEATH, Ireland. She sailed from Glasgow on April 28, on board ship *Angleo*, and arrived in New York on May 11, and has not been heard from since. Any information of her whereabouts will be thankfully received by her friend, **Thomas Hodgins**, at No. 215 1st AVENUE, NEW YORK.

June 10, 1871

Of **John McCullough**, formerly of NEW YORK. He may hear of something to his advantage by calling on or addressing **L. G. Goulding**, Publisher, 132 NASSAU STREET, NEW YORK. [Appeared June 17, 1871 under the heading for County ROSCOMMON.]

Of **Rev. James Ryan**, a native of the Diocese of LIMERICK, Ireland, who came to this country about 17 years ago. When last heard from (about 12 years since) he was in ILLINOIS, supposed to be near CHICAGO. Any intelligence of him will be thankfully received by his niece, **Mary Anne Ryan** (daughter of his brother **John**), who has lately arrived in America. Direct to office of the Irish-American.

Of **Michael** and **John O'Brien**, sons of **Michael O'Brien** and **Ann Ready**, of MOLOUGH, County CLARE, Ireland. Any information of them will be thankfully received by their anxious mother, **Ann O'Brien**, and their only sister **Maria**, at 545 PEARL STREET, NEW YORK, in the rear. Pennsylvania papers, please copy. [Appeared June 17, 1871 with the following sentence added: "Michael was in TEXAS some ten years ago, and James was in MANYUNK, PA., some three years since."]

June 17, 1871

Of **William Craigh**, aged 19 years, fair complexion, about 5 feet 7 ½ inches in height, who left the Victoria Dock, London, April 27th, 1869, in the steamer "*Paraguay*," bound for New York. Is a laborer and a native of Ireland; but, before he left LONDON, he was working for Mr. Wheen & Son, soap manufacturers, DAPTFORD, KENT County. When last heard from was staying with his cousin **John Flahire**, STATEN ISLAND. He afterwards went to Patterson Avenue, JERSEY CITY. Any information of him will be gladly received by his uncle, **Wm. Shea**, Revere House, BOSTON, whether alive or dead.

Of **Thomas** and **James Humphreys**, and their parents, natives of the Co. WICKLOW, Ireland, who sailed from Dublin to Quebec about 22 years ago. When last heard from they were in COLBURN, IND. Any information respecting them will be thankfully received by their brother, **Geo. Humphreys**, 172 Smith Street, BROOKLYN, L.I. Boston papers please copy. [Appeared Sept. 30, 1871 with additional information.]

Of **James Ryan** son of **Thomas Ryan** and **Bridget Hanley**, otherwise **Gore**, who resided at WOODFORT in the County of LEITRIM, Ireland, and some years since came to NEW YORK, and thence went to CINCINNATI; he will hear of a matter to his advantage by addressing, WILSON & NOLAN, Attorneys-at-Law, No. 10 Pine Street, NEW YORK.

Of the whereabouts of **Mary Cullen**, and of her son **Patrick Cullen**, who arrived in New York about fifteen months ago. Information of them will be thankfully received by **Eliza Ryan** (daughter of Mary Cullen), at Third Avenue, between 15th and 16th Streets, SOUTH BROOKLYN, N.Y. Irish papers, please copy. [Appeared under County ROSCOMMON]

June 24, 1871

Of **Mary Fryer**, daughter of **Martin Fryer** and **Hanora Daly**, of the Parish of KILMACTRANY, County SLIGO, Ireland. She is now supposed to be in this country. Previous to her arrival here, she was employed at BALLYFARNAN, County ROSCOMMON, Ireland. Any information of her will be thankfully received by her cousin, **J. Daly**, at 214 EAST 6th STREET, N.Y. CITY.

Of **George Moriarty**, son of **Michael** and **Catherine Moriarty**; born in KILLARNEY, County of KERRY, Ireland, aged about thirty-five years. When last heard of was in Killarney, about twenty-five years ago. Any one that can give any information in regard to him would confer a favor by writing to **Michael Moriarty**, LOGANSPORT, IND.

July 1, 1871

Of **Joshua Doyle**. When last heard of, in 1865, his address was LENNIA, or LENNEAVILLE, DELAWARE County, PA. Any information of him or of any of his family will be thankfully received by his nephew, by addressing **John T. O'Hanlon**, NORTH ADAMS, MASS.

Of **John Walsh**, a native of TULLA, County CLARE, Ireland. Any information of him will be thankfully received by his brother, **James C. Walsh**, DENVER, COLORADO, in care of **George C. Arnott**.

Of **Peter Kilkelly**, a native of MUNNA, County CLARE, Ireland, who came to this country about 18 years ago, and, when last heard from, was in DEEP RIVER, CONN. Any information of him will be thankfully received by his brother, **Patrick Kilkelly**, STAMFORD, CONN.

Of **Bridget** and **Conner Saxton**, of the County CAVAN, Ireland, who left for America about thirty-five years ago; when last heard of was in BALTIMORE about seventeen years ago. Any information of them will be thankfully received by their son, **Thomas Saxton**, Vineyard Avenue, YONKERS, N.Y. Baltimore papers please copy.

Of **Mary Sharkey**, a native of the Parish of ANNAGH, County ROSCOMMON, Ireland, who left HAWICK, SCOTLAND, for America, on the 15th September, 1850; when last heard from, seventeen years ago, was in the employment of a **Mr.** and **Mrs. Divine** either in BROOKLYN or NEW YORK CITY. Any information of her will be thankfuly received by her brother, **Peter Sharkey**, or her sister, by addressing, **Mrs. Daniel Luby**, 4 Teviot Crescent, HAWICK, ROXBURGHSHIRE, SCOTLAND, or any information sent to **George Deans**, COHOES, N.Y., will be duly forwarded to her brother and sisters.

July 8, 1871

Of **James McInerny**, a native of NEWMARKET-ON-FERGUS, Co. CLARE, Ireland, who came to this country about 13 years ago; when last heard from, about 7 years ago, he was serving in the 96th Regiment, N.Y. Volunteers. Any information of him will be thankfully received by **Michael McInerny**, No. 422 East Baltic Street, BROOKLYN, L.I. Exchange papers please copy.

Of **Peter Dougherty**, from the neighborhood of OMAGH, County TYRONE, Ireland, about thirty-five years in this country. Supposed to be in PHILADELPHIA, PA. Any information of him will be thankfully received by his brother John's son, **John Dougherty**, 35 WILLETT STREET, NEW YORK CITY. Philadelphia papers please copy.

O'Donovan - Information wanted by **Ann O'Donovan**, from or near BANTRY, Co. CORK, Ireland; of the residence of her uncle, **Henry**,or of her sister, **Bridget (Honora,)** who came to America; the former 20, and the latter 10 years ago. Address Dr. Sterling, Castle Garden, N.Y.

July 15, 1871

Of **John, James** and **Bernard Smith**, natives of the Parish of KILLDALLEN, County CLARE, Ireland, who came to this country about 23 years ago. Any information of them will be thankfully received by their brother **Patrick Smith**, at No. 108 NINTH AVENUE, NEW YORK CITY.

Of **Patrick Millmo**, a Carpenter, and a native of SLIGO, Ireland. Any information will be thankfully received by **Susanna Delehoyde**, care *Lowell Courier*, LOWELL, MASS.

Of **Christopher Horan**, native of CLONFERT, County GALWAY, Ireland, who came to this country about 25 years ago; and when last heard from, 16 years ago, was in

BUFFALO, State of NEW YORK. Any information concerning him will be thankfully received by his mother, **Mary Horan**. Address to **Kyron Ney**, WATERBURY, State of CONNECTICUT. Western papers please copy.

Of **James, Philip**, and **Barney Maguire**, Parish of KI[L]BLON, Townland of ESKER, County LONGFORD. Direct to **James Maguire**, No. 744 Bainbridge Street, PHILADELPHIA, PA.

July 22, 1871

Of **Patrick McMahon**, a native of ENNIS, County CLARE, Ireland, who left his friends in NEW BRITAIN, CT., about six years ago. When last heard from he was in DELAWARE. He is about twenty-six years of age. Information of him will be thankfully received by his sister, **Bridget McMahon**, NEW BRITAIN, CT.

Of **Patrick Cagney**, a native of NEWCASTLE WEST, County LIMERICK, Ireland. When last heard from he was in ROCHESTER, N.Y., with his brother, who had subsequently enlisted. Intelligence of him will be thankfully received by his wife and sister, who have lately arrived in this country. Address **Mrs. Julia O'Keeffe**, 198 SOUTH ST., NEW YORK.

Of **John** and **William Clarke**, of ISLELANDEADY, County MAYO, Ireland. When last heard from (in March, 1863,) John was in CINCINNATI, OHIO. Information of them will be thankfully received by their brother, **Richard Clarke**, 16 ½ DOWNING ST., NEW YORK CITY. Boston *Pilot*, and Ohio and Illinois papers, please copy.

Of **Patrick Macnamara**, from the Town of GRANWORTH, County of LONGFORD, Ireland. He will hear of something to his advantage by sending his address to his sister, **Bridget Macnamara**, 138 York St., TORONTO, ONT. If this should meet the eye of **Mrs. McCabe**, his daughter, she will confer a great favor by writing as soon as possible to the above address.

July 29, 1871

Of **Patrick Donnelly**, aged 20, who left MONTREAL in the Spring of 1869. Any information concerning him will be thankfully received by his brother, **Daniel Donnelly**, 85 Murray Street, MONTREAL, CANADA WEST.

Of **Michael Joseph Callaghan**, seaman, of THOMONGATE, LIMERICK, Ireland, son of **Lawrence** and **Catherine Cullinan**, when last heard from, was in RUSSIA. Any information of him will be thankfully received by his sisters **Bridget** and **Mary**, the former married to **Frederick Kraft**. Address Frederick Kraft, PORT CHESTER, WESTCHESTER County, NEW YORK.

Of **Patrick O'Loughlin**, a native of ENNISTYMON, County CLARE, Ireland. Intelligence of him will be thankfully received by his brother **Andrew O'Loughlin**, who resides at **Patrick Carley's**, 161 Degrau Street, BROOKLYN, N.Y.

Of **Patrick Slymon**, and **Mrs. Samuel Davies** (maiden name **Ann Slymon**, natives of the County GALWAY, Ireland. When last heard from they were in NEW ORLEANS, LOUISIANA, but are supposed to be in the State of ILLINOIS. Any information of them will be thankfully received by their sister, **Mary Slymon**, at No. 10 Exchange Place, JERSEY CITY, N.J.

August 5, 1871

Of **Ann Fallon**, daughter of **Patrick Fallon**, born near the chapel of COLLEEN, County ROSCOMMON, Ireland, who came to this country about 29 years ago; landed in New York, and is supposed to be in BROOKLYN or N.Y. CITY. Her sisters, **Margaret, Anne,** and **Catherine**, are very anxious to learn her address. Address Margaret Fallon, Methuen Jute Mills, METHUEN, MASS.

Of **Patrick McBrinne,** age 31, a native of DRUMLANE, County CAVAN, Ireland; came to this country in 1862; when last heard from was in LAWRENCE, MASS. Any information of him will be thankfully received by his brother, **Philip M'Brinne**, at 232 EAST FIFTY-NINTH STREET, NEW YORK.

Of **James Maxwell,** a native of MOUNTGRANVILLE, Parish of DULEEK, County MEATH, Ireland, who came to this country July 3, 1871. Any information of him will be thankfully received by his sister, **Catherine McNabb**, BRICKSBURGH, OCEAN County, N.J. New Jersey papers please copy.

Of **Michael Murtagh**, a native of the County MAYO, Ireland, who left ENGLAND about 5 years ago, and came to NEW YORK, and when last heard from, was on his way to SAN FRANCISCO, CALIFORNIA. Any information of him will be thankfully received by his brother, **D. Murtagh**, LEEDS, ENGLAND, or **P. Ruane**, at No. 3 NORTH STREET, NEW YORK CITY. California papers please copy.

Of **John Fagan**, by his sister **Catherine**, formerly of the Parish of CARIGADMEN ABSHRUEL, County LONGFORD, Ireland. Information of him will be thankfully received by addressing **D. J. Byrne**, corner of Glasson and Greene Avenues, BROOKLYN, N.Y. St. Louis and New Orleans papers, please copy.

August 19, 1871

Of **Mrs. Mary Kinsley**, (maiden name **Miss Mary Hogan**), of CHICAGO, ILL. When last heard from, she was living at No. 433 North Clark Street, CHICAGO, ILL. Any information of her will be thankfully received by her brother, **Robert Hogan**, in care of **Patrick Hogan**, No. 10[0] Hawley St., SYRACUSE, N.Y.

Of **Martin Tracy**, who left MIDDLETOWN, CONN., for NEW YORK, fourteen of fifteen years ago. Information of him will be thankfully received by **Rev. M. Hart**, NEW HAVEN, CONN.

Of **Mrs. Ann Hogan**. When last heard from she was living in BROOME STREET, NEW YORK. Information of her will be thankfully received by her son, **Charles Hogan**, PRINCETON, WIS.

Of **Thomas Nicholson**, who left his home, in BROOKLYN, N.Y., last November. When last heard of he was in BALTIMORE, MD. Information of him will be thankfully received by his father, **Lawrence Nicholson**, Henry Street, corner of Fourth Place, BROOKLYN.

Of **Mathew Keeley**, a native of DUBLIN, Ireland; was not heard from since 1853; at that time he lived in NORTH BRIDGEWATER, ONEIDA County, N.Y. If he or any of his family will apply to **Patrick Merrigan**, 372 CANAL STREET, they will hear of something to their advantage. American papers, please copy.

Of **Michael McQuirk**, a native of WATERFORD, Ireland, and a telegraph Operator by trade; he left ENGLAND for America in 1860 or 1861. Information of his whereabouts will be thankfully received by his widowed mother, **Mrs. McQuirk**, No. 1 Redmond Hill, DUBLIN, Ireland. American papers, please copy.

Of **John Downs, Daniel Denehan** and **Thomas Kennedy**, from the Parish of BALLYLONGFORD, County KERRY, Ireland; supposed to be in NEW ORLEANS. Address **Mary Hogan**, formerly **Barron**, corner of German and Fremont Streets, BALTIMORE, MD.

Of **James Keon**, son of the late **Dr. Keon**, of MOHILL, County LEITRIM, Ireland. By addressing his uncle, **Mr. Myles Keon**, TULLY, CARRIGALLIN, County LEITRIM, Ireland, he will hear of something to his advantage.

Of **Michael Sheridan**, a native of BELLGILL, Parish of NAVAN, County MEATH, Ireland, who came to this country in the year 1852. When last heard of he was in WISCONSIN. Information of him will be thankfully received by his sister, **Mary Fagan** (maiden name, **Mary Sheridan**), PORT RICHMOND, STATEN ISLAND, N.Y. Wisconsin papers, please copy.

September 2, 1871

Of **James Monahan**, of HERTFORD, County GALWAY, Ireland; was in the police force 25 or 30 years ago; first stationed in depot, at BALLINROBE, under **Major Priestly**; sent from there to BALLINGARRY, County TIPPERARY; last heard from was serving at NENAGH about 16 or 17 years ago. Intelligence of him will be thankfully received by his brother, **Patrick Monaghan**Lock Box 513, P.O., OMAHA, NEBRASKA.

September 9, 1871

Of **Edward Shannon**, of HUMPHREYS TOWN, County WICKLOW, Ireland, who came to America many years ago, and left NEW YORK CITY about three years ago. His mother, **Bridget Shannon**, would like to see or hear from him. Address **John Doyle**, 416 CHERRY STREET, NEW YORK CITY.

Of **Dennis Kinsella**, a native of the Townland of SCARAHA, County WICKLOW, Ireland. When last heard from, about 18 years ago, he was in NEW YORK. Intelligence of him or of any of his family will be thankfully received by his brother, **John Leary**, at 518 Christian Street, PHILADELPHIA, PA. Philadelphia, New York, and Boston papers, please copy.

September 16, 1871

Of **Robert Bowen**, who left CHESTER, ENGLAND, two years ago, with his stepfather, **Patrick Greely**. When last heard of he was in AUGUSTA, ME., where he was under the doctor's care, with a wound from an axe in his leg. Information of him will be thankfully received by his mother, who left home in search of him. Address **Elizabeth Greely**, 204 Caster Street, PHILADELPHIA, PA. Augusta, Me., papers, please copy.

Of **Lawrence Egan**, a native of CELBRIDGE, County KILDARE, Ireland. When last heard from, which was last Christmas, he was boarding with **Mrs. Mary Connor**, at DRIPTWOOD, PENN. Any information concerning him will be thankfully received by his brother, **Patrick Egan**, 222 Slater St., or by **B. O'Neill**, stationer, 81 Market Street, PATERSON, N.J. Pennsylvania papers, please copy. [Also see May 14, 1870]

September 23, 1871

Mary Ann Hammond, of MENDON and BELLINGHAM, MASS., in the years 1853 and '54; afterwards married and lived in CHICAGO, ILL., about the year 1864, may hear of something to her advantage by sending her present address to A.B.C., Office of the Irish-American.

Of **Edward Reilly**, a native of DUBLIN, who came to this country about three years ago, and was furnished with work on a railroad by **Mr. James Lamb**, of NEW YORK CITY. Any information of him will be thankfully received by his mother, **Mrs. Margaret Reilly**, 104 C Street, Island, between 1st and 2nd Avenues, WASHINGTON, D. C.

Of **Catherine O'Rourke**, or her brother or sister, **Eliza**. They belong to the Parish of CLARA, Townland of THOMASTOWN, County KILDARE, Ireland. Any information of them will be thankfully received by **Jas. Fox**, now living in LINCOLN, PLACER County, CALIFORNIA.

September 30, 1871

Of **Michael Carroll**, son of **John Carroll**, who left WASHINGTON, three years ago. When last heard from he was in EGG POINT, Mississippi R.R. Information of him will be thankfully received by his father, John Carroll, No. 108 G Street, between 1st and 2nd Streets, N., WASHINGTON, D. C. Mississippi and Washington papers, please copy.

Of **Charles Blaney**, coach-builder, a native of ATHLONE, County WESTMEATH, Ireland. When last heard from he was in NEW YORK CITY. Any information of him will be thankfully received by his niece, **Ellen Blaney**, STONINGTON, CONN.

Of **Thomas** and **James Humphreys**, who sailed to Quebec about 23 years ago, with their parents, **George** and **Catherine Humphreys**. The father is a harness-maker by trade; they are natives of DONNAS, County WICKLOW, Ireland. Information respecting them will be thankfully received by their brother, **George Humphreys**, at 72 Smith Street, BROOKLYN. Boston, Ohio and Chicago papers, please copy. [Appeared June 17, 1871 with less information.]

October 7, 1871

Of **Hiram Moneypenny**. Please address **Mr. Gordon**, No. 225 EAST 35th STREET, NEW YORK (rear building). [Appeared Oct. 14, 1871 with the following added about Moneypenny: "When last seen he was in NEW BEDFORD, MASS., about three years ago."]

Of **John McHugh**, who formerly lived with **Dr. Donohue**, in CARRYGALLON, County LEITRIM, Ireland. He sailed from England for New York about eight or ten years ago. Also, of his sister, **Mary McHugh**, who is now supposed to be living in BOSTON, MASS. Any information of them will be received at the office of the Irish-American. Boston papers, please copy.

Of **Thomas Walsh**, a native of the Townland of DUNMORE EAST, Parish of KILMACOMB, County WATERFORD, Ireland. When last heard from he was in AUCKLAND, NEW ZEALAND. Any information of him will be thankfully received by his brother, **T. Walsh**, in care of **Mr. R. G. Morris**, NEW ROCHELLE, N.Y., United States. New Zealand papers, please copy.

October 21, 1871

Of **Sarah Houraghan**, who lived with her grandfather, **John Hines**, in the Parish of THOMONDGATE, City of LIMERICK; left in April, 1855, for NEW YORK at the age of eighteen years. It is supposed that she might go under the name of **Hines**, owing to her being brought up by her grandfather. High complexion, black hair, and black eyes. Information of her whereabouts will be thankfully received by her mother, **Mrs. J. Anderson**, 99 Portland Crescent, LEEDS, YORKSHIRE, ENGLAND; or, by **Mr. William Morley**, HACKENSACK, BERGEN County, N.J. Quebec papers please copy. [Appeared Oct. 28, 1871 with the surname Hines changed to **Lines**.]

Of **George Knox Robinson**, and his sister, **Eliza Robinson**, from LASSAGH, KEADY, County of ARMAGH, Ireland; left there about 26 or 27 years ago; when last heard from were living in NEW YORK CITY. Their sister, **Mary Anne Dobson**, wishes to find them out. Direct to Mary Anne Dobson, APALACHICOLA, FLORIDA.

October 28, 1871

Of **John O'Dea**, of CAPPAMORE, County LIMERICK, Ireland, who came to this country in 1863; when last heard from he was out West. Any information will be thankfully received by his brother, **Patrick O'Dea**, 59 EAST EIGHTY-SIXTH STREET, NEW YORK CITY. Boston *Pilot* and Western papers please copy.

Of **Andrew Rouhen**, or his wife, **Mary**, (maiden name, **Mary Hayes**) of KILMALLOCK, County LIMERICK, Ireland, who went to CHICAGO about five years ago. Information of them will be thankfully received by their cousin, **Ellen Gorman**, 234 EAST FORTY-FIRST STREET, NEW YORK CITY.

Indexes

Personal Names

Michael, 284
Thomas, 284
HORAN
Bridget, 164
Christopher, 378
James, 262
John, 164, 272
Kieran, 272
Mary, 379
Matthew, 164
Michael, 142
Patrick, 272
Rosanna, 272
Thomas, 164
HORE
Maurice, 277
Patrick, 277
HORGAN
Catherine, 221
John, 146, 221
HORN
Richard, 213
Thomas, 213
Winefred, 213
HORRIGAN
Jeremiah, 26
HOULAHAN
Daniel, 243
John, 77
HOULIHAN
Catherine, 269
Honor, 269
Mary, 269
Simon, 269
Thomas, 269
HOUNS
Edward, 295
HOURAGHAN
Sarah, 382
HOURGAN
Ellen, 343
Patrick, 343
HOURIGAN
Catherine, 282
Ellen, 282
Hanorah, 282
Johanna, 282
John, 282
Margaret, 282
Mary, 282
HOVENDEN
John, 97
HOVEY
Wm., 362
HOWARD
Anne, 374
Bridget, 374, 375
Daniel, 374, 375
Hannah Anna Maria,
159
Jane, 195
John, 159, 195

John C., 215
Martha, 195
Mary, 142
Mary Anne, 374, 375
Michael, 374, 375
William, 195
HOWELL
Alfred, 169
Edward, 374
HOY
Daniel, 119
John, 295
Joseph, 295
Thomas, 56
HOYE
James, 296
HOYT
Gould, 38
HUBAND
Louisa, 329
Michael, 329
HUBBARD
William, 153
HUBBELL
G., 178
G. B., 174
HUDSON
Jas., 292
Mary, 292
HUFFINAN
Catherine, 47
John, 47
HUGGARD
John, 260
Samuel, 260
HUGHES
—, (Mr.), 10
Bernard, 355
Bernard William, 300
Bridget, 137, 300
Esther, 195
Frank, 194
James, 190, 246
John, 190, 246
Joseph, 195, 246
Julia, 274
Margaret, 100
Mary, 59, 137, 246,
300, 308, 363
Michael, 58
Patrick, 137
Peter, 110
Richard, 246
Sarah Jane, 194
Thomas, 143, 246
William, 91
HUMMEL
Louis, 238
HUMPHREYS
Catherine, 382
Geo., 377
George, 382

James, 377, 382
Thomas, 377, 382
HUNT
Bridget, 319
Catherine, 245
Charles, 206
Ellen, 319
James, 227
Johannah, 227
John, 132
Laurence, 227
Rodger, 250
William, 132, 245
HUNTING
James M., (Rev.), 228
HUREL
Henry, 127
Teresa, 127
HURLEY
Daniel, 355
Eliza, 36
Ellen, 190
Hannoria, 254
James, 355, 358
Johanna, 357
John, 36, 254, 306,
358, 368
Julia, 254
Margaret, 190
Martin, 357, 358
Mary, 68, 190
Michael, 358
Patrick, 358
HURLL
Henry, 292
Teresa, 292
HURLY
Joseph, 112
Margaret, 155
HURST
—, (Miss), 45
Charles, 45
HUSEY
Mary, 199
HUSSEY
George, 250
John, 330
Lackey, 278
Mary, 278
Michael, 250
HUTCHINSON
Robert, 7
HUTTON
William, 256
HYAR
John, 324
HYLAND
Ann, 61
Catherine, 61, 116
James, 191
John, 116, 191
John, (Mrs.), 36

Julia, 36, 116
Patrick, 191
HYNES
Catherine, 11, 20,
102
Daniel, 20
Francis, 349
Hanora, 215, 216
Mary, 183, 216, 360
IGO
Patrick, 67
ILLIDGE
Richard, 270
Thomas, 270
William, 270
INGHAM
Bridget, 224
William, 224
IRELAND
J., (Rev.), 225
JACIE
William, 360
JACKEL
William, 360
JACKMAN
Mary, 253
JACKSON
—, (Mr.), 190
Edward, 14
George, 14, 370
Margaret, 36
Patrick, 14
JECKS
Sarah, 42
JENNINGS
Mary E., 360
Peter, 360
Thomas. J., 308
JESSY
—, (Mr.), 34
JOHNSON
Catharine, 35
Elizabeth, 218
Ellen, 5
James, 353
John, 35, 218, 287
Patrick, 362
R. P., 320
JOHNSTON
Eliza, 183
Hugh O., 310
James, 242
JONES
—, 245
—, (Mr.), 291
—, (Mrs.), 204
Bridget, 105
D., (Mrs.), 275
Henry, 114, 286
J. M., 86
Jeseph M., 172
Mary, 105

James, 40, 133
John, 10, 84, 113,
  133
Julia, 28
Laurence, 71
Lawrence, 57
Margaret, 24, 203
Mary, 24, 185, 203
Michael, 40
Owen, 84
Patk. T., 71
Patrick, 185, 207
Richard, 71
Thomas, 138
McCARTNY
John, 218
McCARTY
—, (Mrs.), 24
Catherine, 375
Daniel, 375
Eleanor, 50
John, 375
Mary, 375
Patrick, 50
Thomas, 375
Tim, 94
McCASHIN
Daniel, 168
Denis, 168
McCASLIN
John, 355
Noble, 355
McCAUL
Thomas, 117
McCAULEY
Dennis, 156
James, 131, 156
McCLAIN
Bridget, 103
Hannah, 103
McCLEAN
James, 283
McCLELLAND
Thomas, 91
William, 91
McCLEMMENTS
Ellen, 346
James, 346
Kate, 346
McCLOSKEY
—, (Mrs.), 372
Bernard, 356
Mary, 356
McCLOUD
John, 134, 198
McCLUSKEY
Alice, 160
Anne, 160
Barney, 43
Mary, 43
McCOAY
Margaret, 58

McCOMBS
John, 154
Thos., 154
McCONNELL
Patrick, 11
McCONNIN
Judith, 373
Mary, 373
McCOOK
Patrick, 85
Peter, 85
McCOOL
John, 101, 185
Michael, 101
McCORICK
John, 315
Maria, 316
Martin, 315
Michael, 316
Patrick, 315
Walter, 315
McCORMACK
Bridget, 64
John, 113, 171, 215
Patrick, 113
Peter, 64
McCORMICK
Anny, 373
Bridget, 374
Dennis, 169
Isabella, 148
John, 168, 212
Margaret, 168
Mary, 15
Michael, 114, 212
Peter, 212
Sarah, 212
Thomas, 25
McCOSKER
Charles, (Dr.), 202
John, 202
Thomas, 202
McCOUGHY
Rose, 69
McCOY
Margaret, 4
McCRATE
Eliza, 85
McCRAY
Mary, 270
McCREADY
William, 87
McCREAITH
Jeremiah, 149
Patrick, 149
McCREATH
John, 30
Margaret, 30
Mary, 30
McCROSSON
—, (Mrs.), 93

McCRUDDEN
James, 162
Thomas, 162
McCUDDEN
—, (Miss), 126
Alice, 130
Arthur, 43
John, 43
McCUE
Catherine, 102
Martin, 102
Mary, 46
Patrick, 155
Patt, 102
Rose, 155
McCULLAGH
Jane, 264
Peter, 264
McCULLOCH
James, 55
McCULLOUGH
George, 201
John, 365, 377
McCUREEY
Hannah, 151
McCURLEY
Edward, 281
McDERMOT
Charles B., 296, 297
James, 330
McDERMOTT
Alexander, 143
Ann, 157
Biddy, 14
Bridget, 136
Catherine, 171
Daniel, 143
E. P., 371
Edward, 143
Elizabeth, 179
Francis, 161
James, 14, 143, 161
John, 4, 12, 128
Kate, 157
M, 12
Margaret, 126, 136
Mary, 66, 136
Mary Ann, 157
Michael, 19, 66
Patrick, 217
Peter, 136
Thomas, 19, 143
McDEVITT
Annie, 354
James, 52, 354
Patrick, 354
McDONAGH
Anne, 220
Mary, 220
Patrick, 220
McDONALD
Hugh, 49

James, 360
John, 96
Joseph, 74
Mark, 93
Mary, 96
Michael, 360
Thomas, 97
Thomas J., 141
McDONNELL
—, (Mrs.), 363
Alice, 70
Ann, 177
Charles, 20
Edward, 70, 98
James, 70, 81, 355
John, 81
Kate, 173
Mary Anne, 177
Michael, 355
Owen, 177
Sarah, 98
Susan, 142
Terence, 355
Thomas, 142, 173
Tully, 119
McDONNOUGH
Michael, 324
McDONOGH
Albert Irvin, 120
Jane, 120
McDONOUGH
Bernard, 129
Hugh, 178
J., 112
Thomas, 178
McDOWELL
Ann, 311
Charles (Mrs.), 311
McE[?]LY
John, 58
McELLIGOTT
Catherine, 212
Edward, 85
James, 131
John, 85
Michael, 212
McELLISTRIM
John, 167
Patrick, 167
McELROY
John, 35
Patrick, 35
McELWEE
James, 307
Samuel, 307
McENEANY
Mary, 236
Patrick, 236
McENEMY
Catharine, 185
McENROE
Anne E., 172

TORPY
Henry, 331
Hugh, 66
Michael, 244, 331
Patrick, 244
TOUHY
John, 43
TOWELL
J. F., 256
TOWEY
James, 375
TRACEY
Martin, 322
TRACY
Ann, 313
Bridget, 44
Catherine, 44
Denis, 44
Eliza, 87, 321
James, 140
Johanna, 87
John, 138, 366
Joseph, 107
Margaret, 313
Martin, 380
Mary, 44
Patrick, 44
Peter, 44
Richard, 321
Thomas, 343, 344
Timothy, 89
William, 106
TRAINOR
Ann, 8, 202
Anne, 68
Bridget, 202
James, 202
John, 68
Mary, 202
Patrick, 8
Thomas, 202
William, 68
TRAPP
Ann, 173
John, 173
Maria, 173
TRAVERS
Thomas, 272, 288
TREACY
Michael, 32
TREANOR
Catherine, 84
T., (Rev.), 349
Thomas, 84
TREASEY
John, 269
TROY
Bridget, 13
Eliza, 321
James, 80
Mary, 205
Mathew, 13

Richard, 321
William, 80
TRUSTNAN
Bartley, 275
TUCKER
—, (Mr.), 182
Catherine, 80
Edward, 364
James, 130
John, 130
Mary Ann, 364
Michael, 130
Thomas, 80
TULLY
Bridget, 239
Charles, 277
J. B., 116
John Charles, 360
Mathew, 120
Michael, 120
Patrick, 239
Peter, 277
Thomas, 207
TULTE
—, (Mrs.), 169
TUMILTY
James, 248, 280
William, 248, 280
TUNNEY
Bridget, 282
TUNNY
James, 219
TUOHEY
Bessy, 133
Jerry, 293
Mary, 293
TUOHIG
Bridget, 339
John, 339
TUOHILL
Anne, 42
Catherine, 42
Ellen, 42
Mary, 42
Michael, 42
TUOHY
Thomas Patrick, 156
TUOMEY
John, 108
TUOMY
Edmond, 63
Laurence, 208
TURNBULL
Elizabeth, 294
John, 294
Maria, 294
TURNER
Alice, 267
Andrew, 376
James, 267, 376
Jane, 267
Lebecca, 267

Margaret, 267
Michael, 376
Patrick, 376
William, 131
TWOHIG
Michael, 304
TWOMEY
Cornelius, 96
Jeremiah, 199
John, 199
Laurence, 96
TWOMY
Johannah, 199
Timothy, 199
TYNAN
Timothy, 102
Wm., 102
TYRELL
Bridget, 40
Elizabeth, 40
Jane, 40
Johanna, 324
TYRREL
James, 334
John, 87
Thomas, 26
William, 26
UNLACK
Patrick, 109
URELL
Thos., 28
USHER
—, (Mr.), 190
VALLAY
Mary, 362
VAN BUREN
Henry, 82
VAN ESTE
P. W., 25
VAN NOSTRAND
Abraham, 126
VAN WAGENEN
E., 296, 297
VAN WINKLES
Henry, 280
VARDEN
—, (Rev.), 110
VAUGHAN
Ann, 114
Edward, 32
Ellen, 32
Michael, 117
VAUGHEY
John, 96
VEILE
Michael, 342
VERMULA
J. D., (Rev.), 115
VINCENT
F. Z., Jr., 205
WADE
William, 176

WAFER
John, 104
Sarah, 104
WAITER
—, (Mr.), 183
WALDRON
John, 182
Mary, 257
WALKER
Alfred, 60
Ann, 328
James, 328
John, 369
Kate, 239
Thomas, 239
WALL
Catherine, 196
Ellen, 228
Michael, 196
Nicholas, 226
Simon, 180
Thomas, 140
WALLACE
—, (Mrs.), 251
Ann, 268
David, 265
Ellen, 265
James, 16, 111, 147
John, 16
Stephen, 16
William, 16
WALLAS
John, 260
WALSH
—, (Mrs.), 32
Ann, 276
Anthony, 237
Bridget, 139
Catharine, 46
Catherine, 60, 227,
299
Charles, 113
David, 15, 112, 227,
263
Edward, 89, 159
Ellen, 80, 155, 171,
299
Hannah, 80
James, 12, 53, 93,
184, 203, 221,
319
James (Widow of),
299
James C., 378
Jane, 132
Jeremiah, 96
Johanna, 189
John, 51, 53, 171,
190, 259, 263,
285, 378
John Joseph, 299
John P., 309

WISE
John, 252
WISEMAN
—, (Mrs.), 193
Esther, 193
Johm, 193
Robert, 193
WOLF
—, (Mrs.), 21
WOLFE
John, 52
WOLTEN
Henry, 179
WOOD
B., 64

James F., (Rev.), 118
WOODBURN
John, 188
WOODLAND
William, 151
WOODS
—, (Mr.), 318
Anne, 199
Denis, 238
James, 28, 238
John, 211
Julia, 211
Mary, 28, 109
Michael, 109
Thomas, 238

WORESKEY
Mary, 253
WORRESKEY
Francis, 253
WREN
Joseph, 174
Julia, 174
Mary Anne, 174
WRIGHT
—, (Mr.), 98
WYANT
—, (Mr.), 93
WYKOFF
Joseph, 49

YORK
Eliza, 55
Patrick, 55
YORKSTON
—, (Mrs.), 170
YOUNG
Esther, 152
Henrietta, 120
James Selden, 120
Joseph, 274
Mary Anne, 174
YOURT
James, 332, 352
Sarah, 332, 352

Places in Ireland

Places in the United States

Places Other Than Ireland and the U.S.

Streets in New York City